HANDBOOK ON CITIES AND COMPLEXITY

RESEARCH HANDBOOKS IN URBAN STUDIES

In this urban century the need for innovative and rigorous research on the challenges and opportunities facing our cities has never been so pressing. This timely series brings together critical and thought-provoking contributions on key topics and issues in urban research from a range of social science perspectives. Comprising specially commissioned chapters from leading academics these comprehensive *Research Handbooks* feature cutting-edge research and are written with a global readership in mind. Equally useful as reference tools or high-level introductions to specific topics, issues, methods and debates, these *Research Handbooks* will be an essential resource for academic researchers and postgraduate students.

Titles in the series include:

Handbook of Urban Segregation
Edited by Sako Musterd

Handbook of Megacities and Megacity-regions
Edited by Danielle Labbé and André Sorensen

Handbook on City and Regional Leadership
Edited by Markku Sotarauta and Andrew Beer

Handbook of Cities and Networks
Edited by Zachary P. Neal and Céline Rozenblat

Handbook on Cities and Complexity
Edited by Juval Portugali

Handbook on Cities and Complexity

Edited by

Juval Portugali

Professor of Human Geography, Department of Geography and the Human Environment and Head of the City Center-Tel Aviv University Research Center for Cities and Urbanism, Tel Aviv University, Israel

RESEARCH HANDBOOKS IN URBAN STUDIES

 Edward Elgar
PUBLISHING

Cheltenham, UK • Northampton, MA, USA

Cover image: Pieter Bruegel the Elder, *The Fight Between Carnival and Lent*, 1559, oil on oak wood, 118 × 164 cm. Kunsthistorisches Museum, Vienna, Austria. Source: Wikimedia Commons – public domain.

Published by
Edward Elgar Publishing Limited
The Lypiatts
15 Lansdown Road
Cheltenham
Glos GL50 2JA
UK

Edward Elgar Publishing, Inc.
William Pratt House
9 Dewey Court
Northampton
Massachusetts 01060
USA

Paperback edition 2023

A catalogue record for this book
is available from the British Library

Library of Congress Control Number: 2021943595

This book is available electronically in the **Elgar**online
Geography, Planning and Tourism subject collection
http://dx.doi.org/10.4337/9781789900125

ISBN 978 1 78990 011 8 (cased)
ISBN 978 1 78990 012 5 (eBook)
ISBN 978 1 0353 2525 2 (paperback)

Typeset by Cheshire Typesetting Ltd, Cuddington, Cheshire

Printed and bound by CPI Group (UK) Ltd, Croydon, CR0 4YY

Contents

Contributors

Christopher Alexander, Professor Emeritus of Architecture at the University of California, Berkeley, USA.

Peter M. Allen, Professor Emeritus, School of Management, Cranfield University, UK.

Koen Bandsma, PhD student, Faculty of Spatial Sciences, University of Groningen, the Netherlands.

Marc Barthelemy, Institut de Physique Théorique, Université Paris Saclay, CEA, CNRS, Gif-sur-Yvette and Centre d'Analyse et de Mathématique Sociales (CNRS/ EHESS), Paris, France.

Michael Batty, Centre for Advanced Spatial Analysis (CASA), University College London, UK.

Itzhak Benenson, Department of Geography and the Human Environment, Tel Aviv University, Israel.

Efrat Blumenfeld Lieberthal, The David Azrieli School of Architecture, Yolanda and David Katz Faculty of the Art, Tel Aviv University, Israel.

Yanguang Chen, Department of Geography, College of Urban and Environmental Sciences, Peking University, Beijing, People's Republic of China.

Daniele Chiffi, Politecnico di Milano, Italy.

Sara Encarnação, Interdisciplinary Centre of Social Sciences – CICS.NOVA – FCSH/ UNL, Lisbon and ATP-group, Porto Salvo, Portugal.

Pierre Frankhauser, Thema Research Institute, University of Bourgogn – Franche-Comté and LVMT (University Gustave Eiffel and Ecole des Ponts-ParisTech), France.

Nir Fulman, PhD student, Department of Geography and the Human Environment, Tel Aviv University, Israel.

Carlos Gershenson, Instituto de Investigaciones en Matemáticas Aplicadas y en Sistemas, Universidad Nacional Autónoma de México, Mexico.

Nick Green, Chartered Town Planner and Senior Tutor in the School of the Environment, Education and Development, University of Manchester, Manchester, UK.

Hermann Haken, Institute for Theoretical Physics, Center of Synergetics, Stuttgart University, Germany.

Shlomo Havlin, Professor of Physics, Department of Physics, Bar-Ilan University, Israel.

Orr Levy, PhD, Department of Physics, Bar-Ilan University, Israel.

Stephen Marshall, Professor of Urban Morphology and Urban Design, Bartlett School of Planning, University College London, London, UK.

Stefano Moroni, Professor of Urbanism, Politenico di Milano, Italy.

Jorge M. Pacheco, Centro de Biologia Molecular e Ambiental and Departamento de Matemática e Aplicações, Universidade do Minho, Braga, Portugal and ATP-group, Porto Salvo, Portugal.

Alan Penn, Professor of Architectural and Urban Computing at The Bartlett School of Architecture, University College London and Chief Scientific Adviser, Ministry of Housing, Communities and Local Government, UK.

Margarida Pereira, Interdisciplinary Centre of Social Sciences – CICS.NOVA – FCSH/UNL, Lisbon, Portugal.

Juval Portugali, Department of Geography and the Human Environment, Tel Aviv University, Israel.

Denise Pumain, Professor of Geography at University Paris I Pantheon Sorbonne, France.

Carlo Ratti, SENSEable City Laboratory, Massachusetts Institute of Technology, USA.

Ward Rauws, Assistant Professor of Spatial Planning, Department of Planning, Faculty of Spatial Sciences, University of Groningen, the Netherlands.

Gert de Roo, Professor of Spatial Planning, Department of Planning, Faculty of Spatial Sciences, University of Groningen, the Netherlands.

Paolo Santi, SENSEable City Laboratory, Massachusetts Institute of Technology, USA and Istituto di Informatica e Telematica, CNR, Italy.

Fernando P. Santos, Informatics Institute, University of Amsterdam, the Netherlands, Department of Ecology and Evolutionary Biology, Princeton University, Princeton, USA and ATP-group, Porto Salvo, Portugal.

Francisco C. Santos, INESC-ID and Instituto Superior Técnico, Universidade de Lisboa, IST-Taguspark, Porto Salvo and ATP-group, Porto Salvo, Portugal.

Nimrod Serok, The David Azrieli School of Architecture, Yolanda and David Katz Faculty of the Art, Tel Aviv University, Israel.

Vincent Verbavatz, Institut de Physique Théorique, Université Paris Saclay, CEA, CNRS, Gif-sur-Yvette, France.

Acknowledgements

I would like to thank the authors of this *Handbook* – friends and colleagues who agreed to participate in this project and to contribute their insightful views on the multiple facets of Cities and Complexity. Special thanks to © 'Christopher Alexander/Center for Environmental Structure Archive' for giving me the permission to re-publish Christopher Alexander's paper from 2003 (as Chapter 11 in this volume); specifically to Mrs Maggie Moore Alexander and to my good friend Dr Artemis Anninou who made the link to Mrs Moore Alexander. Many thanks to Senior Supervising Editor Alexandra O'Connell from Edward Elgar Publishing, who first invited me to start this project and helped along the way, and to the Elgar team for their excellent work in the production of this book.

Introduction to the *Handbook on Cities and Complexity*
Juval Portugali

Past decades have witnessed two interrelated developments: the emergence of general theories of complex self-organized systems; and the consequent emergence of complexity theories of cities (CTC), a domain of research that applies the various complexity theories to the study of cities. From a small stream of studies that started at end of 1970, CTC evolved to its current position as a dominant approach to urban dynamics, planning and design. The five parts of *Handbook on Cities and Complexity* comprising 19 chapters, on the one hand, follow this development while, on the other, provide a snapshot of the state of the art of CTC at the beginning of 2021. The list of contributors to this volume includes Hermann Haken, who is one of the founders of general complexity theory, founders of the domain of CTC, as well as the younger generations of scholars of cities as complex systems. The structure of the handbook commences with foundations (Part I), continues with reviews of the leading CTC (Part II), and the links between complexity, languages and cities (Part III), to modelling approaches (Part IV) and, finally, to urban planning and design (Part V). The book concludes with an Epilogue on 'Cities and complexity in the time of COVID-19', a topic that was always 'in the air' while the various contributions to this handbook were written, yet was not explicitly discussed in the various chapters. Ten of the authors volunteered to write short notes about this issue, related to their specific topics and personal experiences.

PART I: FOUNDATIONS

Part I starts with my overview, in Chapter 1, of the evolving perception of the general notions of a complex system and complex adaptive systems (CAS), and the ways they were applied to the domain of CTC. As detailed by Hermann Haken in Chapter 2, the founding complexity theories originated in the material sciences from scientists who revealed that in particular situations (for example, Bénard focuses on instability and the phenomenon of laser) inanimate matter exhibits properties commonly attributed to the domains of life such as history, evolution, unpredictability, irreversibility, nonlinearity, uncertainty and so on (Portugali 1985). At a later stage, as theories of complexity and self-organization were explicitly applied to several domains of life, a new property entered the vocabulary of complexity: adaptation – cities as complex systems were now perceived as CAS – complex adaptive systems. The 'beyond' in the title of Chapter 1 ('Cities, complexity and beyond'), indicates, first, that cities as complex systems have their own uniqueness: beyond being CAS, they are hybrid complex systems composed of artifacts, which are simple systems, and urban agents, which are complex systems. Secondly, in order to understand the behavior of the urban agents, a link should be made to the cognitive sciences.

Thirdly, the application of complexity theories to the study of cities entailed two potentials: (1) to reformulate a 'new science of cities' on the basis of the plethora of quantitative methods and modelling approaches offered by the theories of complexity – this potential was fully realized; and (2) to bridge the century-old gap between the quantitative and the hermeneutic traditions in the study of cities – this potential has yet to be realized.

Chapter 2, by Hermann Haken, provides an insider's first-hand view on 'The emergence of complexity theories: an outline'. Haken is the founder of the theory of synergetics, one of the cornerstones of the general theory of complexity. The notion of 'emergence' entails the impression of a sudden appearance. However, in this chapter, Haken shows how complexity, self-organization, fractals, phase transition, and other notions and properties of complexity theory evolved as a logical consequence of the long history of ongoing discourse in the domain of physics.

For Haken (as for many others) physics functions also as a paradigm for science at large owing to its ability to link 'the abstract world of ideas including mathematics and the concrete world in the form of matter'. As he demonstrates, it was specifically thermodynamics (the branch of physics that deals with heat, work and temperature, and their relationship to energy, radiation and the physical properties of matter) that has played a crucial role in the development of complexity theories. In particular, the notions of free energy and entropy were dominant in the early formulations of complexity theory. Collective phenomena in physics (for example, ice into water, ferromagnetism and superconductivity) have paved the way for notions such as phase transition and steady state, and the relationship between part-whole in complex systems, while the chaos theory of complexity has its origin in the studies of Henri Poincaré (1854–1912) on the problem of the stability of the solar system. Also, for Prigogine, the prototypical example for his dissipative structures was the Bénard instability (Bénard 1900).

Haken then describes, in some detail, synergetics – his theory of complexity; its emergence in connection with the laser device, that is, the laser paradigm that forms synergetics' canonical experiment (based on the process of stimulated emission first introduced by Einstein in 1917). Then Haken discusses synergetics' first foundation as a bottom-up microscopic approach and, later, the second foundation of synergetics as a top-down approach related to information theory. Finally, the notions of Friston's (2010) free energy principle and game theory and their relationship to synergetics are discussed.

Similarly to the general theories of complexity, the current view of cities as complex systems has deep historical roots. As shown in Chapter 3 by Michael Batty, one of the founders of the domain of CTC, the current view has its origin in what Bertallanffy (1968) formulated as general system theory. To this I would add that the view of cities as systems was implicit in the writings of some early twentieth-century studies (for example, Auerbach 1913; Christaller 1933 [1966]) and explicit in works such as Mcloughlin's (1969) *Urban and Regional Planning: A System Approach* or Chadwick's (1978) *A System View of Planning*. Batty mentions the, now classic, studies of Alexander's (1965) 'A city is not a tree' and Jacob's (1961) *The Death and Life of Great American Cities* as forerunners of CTC, which indeed they were (compare Chapter 11 in this volume).

Adopting Weaver's (1948) terminology in 'Science of complexity', Batty refers to the past 60 years of evolving ideas about cities as increasing realization that 'our city systems are complex': first, cities were perceived as simple systems, then as systems of disorganized complexity and, currently, as systems of organized complexity. From this perspective he returns to some of the classic properties of cities identified since the early twentieth century: the rank size rule, central places hierarchies and gravity-interaction models. By re-interpreting these in relation to current urban scaling, allometry and fractals, he shows them to be aspects of the general property of cities as complex systems, conceptually as well as mathematically. As systems of organized complexity, cities are characterized by unpredictability; thus, suggests Batty, although we cannot predict the future, we can still invent it. 'What all this means', he concludes, 'is that in thinking about how our cities function and evolve, we face a barrier of predictability that suggests that our theories can only ever be used to inform our understanding, never to be able to predict the future, only to explore it.'

Similarly to many concepts in science (for example, chaos, catastrophe and energy), the notion of complexity is used in ordinary language to convey a meaning that is not necessarily identical with its usage in the context of science. Chapter 4, by Stephen Marshall and Nick Green, looks at complexity from an ordinary language usage of the term, and thus from the way it was used and understood over time and in the study of cities prior to the emergence of complexity theory and CTC – an approach that takes in a broad sweep of history, ending in the 1990s, when complexity studies of cities started to take off. Borrowing John Maynard Smith's notion of 'major transitions' (Smith and Szathmary 1997), Marshall and Green propose six major transitions that paved the way for the penetration of complexity into the discourse on cities and to its current position in the discourse on cities, planning and design.

The first two transitions are grand transformations of world view: Newton's clockwork universe and Darwin's evolution with a world view that 'all living things are related to each other' (Chapter 4 in this volume), which influenced cities through the work of Patrick Geddes (1915). For Geddes, cities and their planning were perceived as part of the evolution of *Homo sapiens* in its increasingly artificial environment. The remaining four transformations are all in the realm of cities. The third transformation is Jacobs's (1961) 'The kind of problem a city is', which was based on Weaver's (1948) notion of organized complexity and Alexander's (1965) 'A city is not a tree', suggesting a deep, complex and functional order beneath the seemingly chaotic appearance of cities. The fourth transition brought to the fore social life, namely, beneath the seemingly chaotic appearance of poorer areas there exists a deep, complex and functional social order. The fifth transition followed recognition that the story of cities and planning is told and implemented from a very specific perspective, that of the Western male culture and point of view. Finally, the sixth transition brings us on to the path towards CTC; following recognition of the wicked nature of urban reality, the humanistic and structuralist-Marxist criticisms, approaches such as collaborative planning eventually paved the way for CTC.

PART II: COMPLEXITY THEORIES OF CITIES

All theories of complexity were applied to the study of cities giving rise to the domain of CTC. Similarly to the general complexity theories, each CTC sheds light on specific aspect of cities as complex systems. Part II describes some of the leading CTC applications, from their start in the 1970s to their state at end of 2020. Of special influence on the study of cities were/are two leading schools of complexity theory, one led by Ilya

Prigogine whose starting point was chemical kinetics with special emphasis on the notion of time, the other led by physicist and mathematician Herman Haken who, as we have seen in respect of Chapter 2 and see again in relation to Chapter 6, started with the phenomenon of laser.

In Chapter 5, Peter M. Allen opens his discussion on the evolution of cities with Prigogine's notion of dissipative structures and his theoretical model, the Brusselator, which enables the study of phenomena of symmetry breaking and self-organization (Nicolis and Progogine 1977). From this vantage point, Allen explores different types of environmental and urban simulation models, and the way they treat the relationships between bottom-up and top-down processes that typify the dynamics of cities. Allen shows that model building is 'an unending process' since models as interpretive frameworks are always imperfect and so is our understanding of cities as complex systems: 'There is no perfect ultimate "solution" to which we are tending! Life will always possess multiple pathways into the future.'

Next, in Chapter 6, Juval Portugali and Hermann Haken develop the notion of 'Synergetic cities', which started by applying the various aspects of synergetics (compare Chapter 2 in this volume) to cities and continued by elaborating new conceptual and theoretical frameworks that reflect, and are a consequence of, the specific properties of cities, namely, that they are hybrid complex systems (Haken and Portugali 2021). Accordingly, the first part of this chapter introduces synergetics, and its basic paradigms and the way they were applied to cities, while the second part introduces the notions of synergetic inter-representation networks (SIRN), information adaptation (IA) and their conjunction, SIRNIA, as the theoretical foundation for the study of cities as hybrid complex systems. This theoretical discussion is followed and illustrated by three case studies. Finally, the notions of steady state, phase transition and slaving are introduced, and their role in cities is elaborated theoretically and empirically.

'I choose to enter through an object – system of cities – and a discipline – geography' writes Denise Pumain in her abstract to Chapter 7 in a very personal account of cities and complexity. Two interrelated principles stand at the core of her discussion. The first, the title of her chapter 'Co-evolution as the secret of urban complexity', comes to solve the paradox that, despite the changes that cities undergo, 'we observe a very large persistency in the relative positions of cities in the hierarchy of sizes over long time periods'. The second is the spiral construction of knowledge (Pumain 2009), showing that our current knowledge of cities as complex systems has its roots in past conceptions of cities, for example, in the writing of 'Saint-Simonian engineer Jean Reynaud describes as early as 1841' (Reynaud 1841) and decades later in studies such as Auerbach's (1913) rank size rule and Christaller's (1933 [1966]) central place theory.

Of all theories of complexity, fractal geometry is visually the most beautiful. In Chapter 8, Pierre Frankhauser introduces step by step the fractal approaches to cities. He starts by demonstrating the fractal properties that can be observed in the morphology of cities, and continues by employing the Sierpinski carpets class of fractals as a means to model and generate morphologies identical to urban morphologies. He then explores the potential and usefulness of the multifractal approach to deal with the irregularities of urban patterns. These explorations led Frankhauser to develop a software package, Fractalopolis, a planning tool capable of supporting the design of a multifractal plan for an urban region and assessment of the suitability of developing each part of the region.

Chapter 9, by Yanguang Chen, provides a discussion about the inherent relationships between the theories of scaling, fractals and the complexity of cities, with special emphasis on their spatiality. While each of the three theories have already been referred to in previous chapters, here the focus is on their integration as aspect, properties and methodologies of cities as complex systems. Based on mathematical reasoning and empirical findings, the chapter first introduces scaling and its applications to or implications for cities, then it introduces fractals and multifractals in general and in the context of cities, and finally focuses on complexity and the way to explore the spatial complexity of cities in relation to fractals, multifractals and scaling.

Cybernetics; or, Control and Communication in the Animal and the Machine by Norbert Wiener (1948) can be regarded as one of the earliest theories of systems and complexity. Yet, in Chapter 10, Carlos Gershenson, Paolo Santi and Carlo Ratti reiterate the old concept in the context of the current futuristic discussions regarding cities; that is, building 'cybernetic cities' in which advanced information and communication technologies (ICT) will replace humans' urban control loop (composed of information, algorithms and agents). The chapter then discusses the new smart technologies of information, algorithms and agents. The big questions that these smart cybernetic cities pose are, 'If we manage to develop [technologically smart] information, algorithms and agents, and integrate them to solve an urban problem, what would be the outcome? What is the benefit of having cybernetic urban systems?' Interestingly, there are no smart devices that can answer these questions.

PART III: COMPLEXITY, LANGUAGE AND CITIES

The dyad of language–city has a long history in the study of cities, usually when using language or lexical elements metaphorically in order to describe and understand cities, or vice versa, when inferring from cities to languages. 'Our languages' wrote Wittgenstein (1953) 'can be seen as an ancient city: a maze of little streets and squares, of old and new houses' (compare Chapter 19 in this volume). Another example is Lynch's (1960, p. 2) notion of legibility as 'the apparent clarity . . . of the cityscape'. The scientific projects of Christopher Alexander with the centrality of his *A Pattern Language* (Alexander et al. 1977) and of Bill Hillier's (1996) space syntax, suggest moving beyond the metaphoric relations, namely, that there is literally a language of cities with its specific syntax, semantics, pragmatics and the rest. As shown in Chapter 19 of this volume, Alexander explicitly compares his pattern language with natural spoken language.

The triad of complexity–language–city follows on from the synergetic cities view (Chapters 1, 2 and 6 in this volume). One of Haken's central ways to convey the notions of an order parameter and the slaving principle that stands at the core of his theory of synergetics, is by reference to language. Languages emerge out of the interaction between the parts (people) as order parameters, but once they come into being they describe and prescribe (enslave) the behavior of the parts, and so on in circular causality. A similar process takes place in cities. They come into being out of the interaction between the parts – the urban agents – but once they come into being they describe and prescribe (enslave) the behavior of the urban agents, and so on in circular causality.

As noted previously, Alexander's 'A city is not a tree', written at an early stage of his career, is considered a forerunner to the complexity view on cities. For some reason the rest of his life-work has little or no echo in CTC discourse and writing, not even his 2003 paper with its long and informative title that explicitly addresses the relationships between the four volumes of his *The Nature of Order* (Alexander 2002–04) and complexity: 'New concepts in complexity theory arising from studies in the field of architecture: an overview of the four books of the nature of order with emphasis on the scientific problems which are raised'. Chapter 11 by Christopher Alexander puts this forgotten paper squarely in the context of our cities and complexity.

As we have seen from the chapters in Parts I and II, the various complexity theories originated in the hard sciences, such as physics and chemistry, with close association to thermodynamics, then at a later stage were applied to, that is informed, the domain of cities, giving rise to CTC. Alexander suggests a view that diametrically opposes this path, namely, that the study of architecture as he developed it in his four volumes, *The Nature of Order*, should instead inform the sciences in general and thus the science of complexity including CTC. Properties such as value, aesthetics, beauty and wholeness, which throughout most of the twentieth century were expelled from science on the grounds that they are subjective, form according to Alexander, the core of the practice of architecture and should also form the bases of the current science of complexity; in general and in connection with architecture, cities' urban planning and design. In Chapter 11 he develops this view step by step, starting with the notions of 'wholeness and value as a necessary part of any complex system', through recursive processes, measures of coherence, the links to cognition, aspects of subjectivity, symmetries and sub-symmetries, adaptations, structure preserving transformations and concluding with the role of beauty in the science of complexity. At the core of Alexander's view on complexity are 15 properties associated with 15 transformations. 'I believe', he summarizes, 'the fifteen transformations I have discovered will turn out to be naturally occurring, and necessarily occurring in all complex systems.'

Bill Hillier started to develop his space syntax in the 1970s with no explicit links to CTC which started to emerge at the same time. These links were explicated later out of the recognition that language and complexity are interwoven (for example, Hillier 2009). In that paper (Hillier 2009), he notes the absence of formal language that differentiates between one form of complexity and another with the required rigor and consistency. He continues by writing that space syntax research about cities is seeking to redress the balance. When I started to work on this handbook, he and I were corresponding. He suggested writing a chapter to extend the arguments proposed in his 2009 paper 'The city as a socio-technical system'. Sadly, Bill Hillier passed away on the 5 November 2019. Alan Penn, who was working closely with Hillier for many years, agreed to write the chapter in his stead.

Chapter 12, by Alan Penn, is thus in part a memorial to Bill Hillier and his space syntax theory, and in part Penn's specific perspective on space syntax, complexity and the city. Penn first introduces space syntax theory in itself and in connection with complexity science and CTC. Next, he adds his own perspective, which centers around the notion of empathy (among other things) as it entailed the evolving relationship between the architectural construction of pre-urban and urban settlements. He emphasizes that 'while space syntax bears a relationship to complexity, its prime motivation was not to understand complexity per se but to develop a theoretical understanding of the phenomena at hand; of human society, the environments it designs and builds and the interplay between the two'.

PART IV: MODELLING COMPLEX CITIES

Modelling in general, and urban simulation modelling in relation to cities, is a common way to study complex systems cities. The various complexity theories discussed in Part II include their own modelling approaches. The difference is that Part II formulates a general theory of urban dynamics and then shows how it can be applied to specific case studies, while in Part IV, we start from an urban problem to which an appropriate theory and modelling approaches are then applied. Thus, Chapter 13 by Vincent Verbavatz and Marc Barthelemy commence from an urgent problem: 'traffic congestion is becoming an ever-larger problem'; the challenge is how to mitigate car traffic. To solve this problem, we need an appropriate theory and a modelling approach. They start by critically reviewing studies that have become a paradigm of spatial economics and urban planning, and show that these are empirically based, lacking a theoretical basis. They then develop their own theoretical approach that aims 'to capture the essence of the urban mobility phenomenon'. From this new theoretical vantage point they demonstrate that 'car traffic is governed by three main factors: (1) access to MRT [that is, mass rapid transit], (2) congestion effects, and (3) urban sprawl'. Based on this model, they suggest that in order to reduce car traffic it is necessary to increase access to public transport.

Following the founding studies of Barabási (2002), Watts (2004) and others, the 'new' science of networks that suggests viewing complex systems as networks, was enthusiastically embraced by students of CTC. Cities and systems of cities are essentially complex networks, and so are their sub-systems, such as roads networks. In this context of network analysis and theory, percolation methodology is employed as means to evaluate the structural robustness of networks. In Chapter 14, Nimrod Serok, Orr Levy, Shlomo Havlin and Efrat Blumenfeld Lieberthal start by presenting the specific percolation-based approach they have developed, and then apply it to data on the city centers of London and Tel Aviv in two time frames. Based on the recent availability of big data, they study the interplay between the static road network and the dynamics of the traffic flow on the network. This big data, they suggest, makes it possible to follow in real time the state of traffic in cities and thus to equip planners with an efficient tool to monitor and control that traffic. As a planning tool, their suggested approach 'will bridge the gap between static long-term urban planning and the flexible and dynamic urban rhythm, and will enable planners to keep their role in the formation of better cities'.

Data availability also provides the motivation for Itzhak Benenson and Nir Fulman, in Chapter 15, to apply the knowledge accumulated on the complexity of cities to control specific urban phenomena and problems; in this instance, parking in cities. They show that while the problem of parking is only loosely related to traffic, it is nevertheless typified by some of the main attributes of a complex system, such as non-linearity, emergence and path dependence. However, as the title of their chapter indicates, they suggest that parking is a typical example of 'simple-complex' urban phenomena, namely, cases in which the behavior of the urban agents can be considered simple in that, for example, they are routinized and therefore predictable. Thus, in the context of cities as complex unpredictable systems, we can still identify predictable phenomena – evidently an advantage from the viewpoint of the rational comprehensive planning approach, which is based on predictability. Two notes: first, cities are characterized by long periods of steady state interrupted by short-phase transition events. Thus, at least in retrospect, during their steady state cities are predicted. Second, as noted in several cases (Portugali 2011), it is possible to temporarily close a complex system – for example, a city – and treat it as a simple system (compare also Chapter 16 in this volume).

PART V: COMPLEXITY, PLANNING AND DESIGN

The emergence of CTC and the realization that cities are complex, self-organized systems entailed a whole set of questions, dilemmas and challenges to the domains of urban planning and design. Of specific importance are the issues of uncertainty and steering, which are discussed in the first two chapters of Part V. Furthermore, the emergence of CTC coincided with significant changes that took place in past decades in the society, politics and planning of democratic societies around the world. The latter entailed the transition from government to governance. The third chapter of Part V deals with this issue.

Planning and design, as they have evolved throughout the twentieth century, were built on the conviction that science and technology are capable of predicting the future, and if there are difficulties in this task, they are technical matters that will be solved as science and technology progresses. Complexity theories of cities, with their new insight that complexity implies inherent unpredictability and thus uncertainty, created a problem: how to plan toward an unknown future? Chapter 16, by Stefano Moroni and Daniele Chiffi, deals with the relationships between complexity and uncertainty, and the implications thereof to planning. They start by considering a spectrum of certainty, risk, parametric uncertainty and fundamental uncertainty, and concentrate on the latter two forms of uncertainty. They then examine those two forms in two planning situations: first, when the planner has to decide about a given artifact, for example, building a bridge, and second, when the planner has to decide about a regulatory planning policy. Finally, and based on the above, they suggest methodologies to 'cope with different forms of uncertainty by first taking seriously the differences between different decision situations'.

Planning and design, as they have evolved throughout the twentieth century, were also based on the view that their main function is to impose order and organization on the otherwise chaotic urban reality. Complexity theories of cities, with their view that cities are typified by self-organization, entailed a dilemma: if cities self-organize, what is the role of planning and design? Should urban planning strive to steer the self-organized and organizing urban system? If so, how? Chapter 17, by Koen Bandsma, Ward Rauws, and Gert de Roo, suggests the methodology of nudging as a planning instrument capable of influencing the self-organized behavioral pattern of urban agents 'by exploiting the cognitive biases, heuristics and social norms underlying their decision-making'. They start by introducing the general theory of nudging, consider its effectivity in stable-routine versus unstable behavioral pattern in cities' public space, and discuss ethical considerations that should guide governmental planners in their use of this methodology.

As previously noted, the emergence of CTC coincided with significant changes that took place in the past decades in the society, politics and planning of democratic societies around the world. These changes included processes of privatization that entailed the weakening of the welfare state and the emergence of a third sector of non-governmental organizations (NGOs), also named civil society (a term that has roots in Aristotle's *Politics*, Hegel, Marx and others). These structural changes show up in the transition from government to governance, that is, the transition of social discourse, politics and planning from a two-sector game (public and private) into a three-sector game (public, private and civil). What are the dynamics of this new urban reality? How are they associated with the dynamics of cities as complex systems, and with urban planning?

Chapter 18, by Sara Encarnação, Fernando P. Santos, Francisco C. Santos, Margarida Pereira, Jorge M. Pacheco and Juval Portugali, employs evolutionary game theory (EGT) as means to respond to this new reality and the questions it entails. The approach is innovative in several respects: it is the first application of EGT to urban planning; it is based on several recent studies that applied EGT to urban dynamics; and, in the context of EGT, it develops a three-sector (populations) game instead of the more common two-sector population game. The chapter briefly introduces EGT, its recent applications to the study of cities as complex self-organized systems, and elaborates in some detail its usefulness and potential as a planning tool.

Part V closes with Chapter 19 in which I examine the roots of planning and design through the lens of three aspects of humanity subsumed under three notions: *Homo sapience*, referring humans' ability to think and act rationally; Henry Bergson's *Homo faber*, whose core property 'is the faculty of manufacturing artificial objects' (Bergson 1911 [1998], p. 139) and Johan Huizinga's (1949) *Homo Ludens* (*Man the Player*). It is shown that the complementarity between these three homos is at the core of human agency – urban agents' capability to manipulate the environment, as well as of chronesthesia (mental time travel) that forms the cognitive basis of planning and design. Agency and chronesthesia are studied from the theoretical perspectives of SIRN, IA and their conjunction SIRNIA, and their role in the dynamics of cities as hybrid complex systems.

EPILOGUE: CITIES AND COMPLEXITY IN THE TIME OF COVID-19

The various contributions to this handbook were written during the period of COVID-19, a pandemic that came into being and evolved as a typical complex system, exhibiting properties such as abrupt change, non-linearity, unpredictability and uncertainty. Furthermore, the pandemic and cities and urban life coexist in a type of circular causality: on the one hand, cities and urban life had and have important effects on the space–time diffusion of the pandemic, its ups and downs and other properties; on the other, the pandemic affects the dynamics of cities, the opening and closing of businesses, public and private transportation, and urban life in general. In light of the above, and in coordination with Edward Elgar Publishing, each of the contributors was asked (if they had the will and the time) to write a short statement about the pandemic from their chapter topic's viewpoint, as well as from their personal perspective and experience. The authors of ten of the chapters of this handbook agreed to participate and the Epilogue, comprising their short statements, represents views and experiences about cities and complexity in the age of COVID-19 at end of November 2020.

The ten short statements appear in the same order as their source chapters, thus representing the five parts of the handbook. What is specifically interesting is that the pandemic is associated with all the topics discussed by the various chapters: with the notions of the property of unpredictability of cities as complex systems (Batty), the major transitions (Marshall and Green), the order parameter, slaving principle, fluctuations and chaos of the synergetic cities (Portugali and Haken), the evolution of cities and their internal structure (Allen), with complexity and fractal cities (Frankhauser), the absence of cybernetic systems in cities (Gershenson, Santi and Ratti), the logical and emotional dimensions of human responses (Penn), the effects on mobility in cities (Verbavatz and Barthelemy), on risk and uncertainty in urban planning (Moroni and Chiffi) and the use of nudging as a planning tool that affects citizens behavior (Bandsma, Rauws and De Roo).

REFERENCES

Alexander, C. (1965), 'A city is not a tree', *Architectural Forum*, **122**, pt 1 (1), 58–62, pt 2 (2), 58–62.
Alexander, C. (2002–4), *The Nature of Order*, 4 vols, Berkeley, CA: Center for Environmental Structure.
Alexander, C., S. Ishikawa and M. Silvestein (1977), *A Pattern Language*, New York: Oxford University Press.
Auerbach, F. (1913), 'Das Gesetz der Bevölkerungskonzentration', *Petermanns Geographische Mitteilungun*, **59**, 74–6.
Barabási, A.-L. (2002), *Linked: How Everything Is Connected to Everything Else*, New York: Plume.
Bénard, H. (1900), 'Les tourbillons cellulaires dans une nappe liquid', *Révue Générale des Sciences Pures et appliquées*, **11**, 1261–71, 1309–28.
Bergeson, H. (1911), *Creative Evolution*, 1998 trans. A. Mitchell, New York: Dover.
Bertallanffy, L. von (1968), *General System Theory: Foundations, Development, Applications*, New York: George Braziller.
Chadwick, G. (1971), *A System View of Planning*, Oxford: Pergamon Press.
Christaller, W. (1933), *Central Places in Southern Germany*, repr. 1966, Englewood Cliffs, NJ: Prentice Hall.
Einstein, A. (1917), 'Zur Quantentheorie der Strahlung', *Physikalische Zeitschrift*, **18**, 121–8.
Friston, K. (2010), 'The free-energy principle: a unified brain theory?', *Nature Reviews Neuroscience*, **11** (2), 127–38.
Geddes, P. (1915), *Cities in Evolution: An Introduction to the Town Planning Movement and to the Study of Civics*, London: Williams.
Haken, H. and J. Portugali (2021), *Synergetic Cities: Information, Steady State and Phase Transition. Implications to Urban Scaling, Smart Cities and Planning*, Berlin, Heidelberg and New York: Springer Nature.
Hillier, B. (1996), *Space is the Machine: A Configurational Theory of Architecture*, Cambridge: Cambridge University Press.
Hillier, B. (2009), 'The city as a socio-technical system: a spatial reformulation in the light of the levels problem and the parallel problem', in S. Müller Arisona, G. Aschwanden, J. Halatsch and P. Wonka (eds), *Digital Urban Modelling and Simulation*, Berlin: Springer, pp. 24–48.
Huizinga, J. (1949), *Homo Ludens: A Study of the Play-Element of Culture*, London, Boston, MA, and Henley: Routledge & Kegan Paul.
Jacobs, J. (1961), *The Death and Life of Great American Cities*, New York: Random House.
Lynch, K. (1960), *The Image of the City*, Cambridge, MA: MIT Press.
McLoughlin, J.B. (1969) *Urban and Regional Planning: A System Approach*, London: Faber and Faber.
Nicolis, G. and I. Prigogine (1977), *Self-organization in Nonequilibrium Systems*, New York: Wiley.
Portugali, J. (1985), 'Parallel currents in the natural and social sciences', in J. Portugali (ed.), *Links Between Natural and Social Sciences*, special issue of *Geoforum*, **16** (2), 227–38.
Portugali, J. (2011), *Complexity, Cognition and the City*, Berlin, Heidelberg and New York: Springer.
Pumain, D. (2009), 'L'espace, médium d'une construction spiralaire de la géographie, entre société et environnement', in B. Walliser (ed.), *La cumulativité des connaissances en sciences sociales*, Paris: EHESS, pp. 163–97.

Reynaud, J. (1841), 'Villes', *Encyclopédie nouvelle*, vol. 7, Paris: Gosselin, pp. 670–87.
Smith, J.M. and E. Szathmary (1997), *The Major Transitions in Evolution*, Oxford: Oxford University Press.
Watts, D.J. (2004), 'The "new" science of networks', *Annual Review of Sociology*, **30** (August), 243–70.
Weaver, W. (1948), 'Science of complexity', *American Scientist*, **36** (4), 536–44.
Wiener, N. (1948), *Cybernetics; or, Control and Communication in the Animal and the Machine*, New York: Wiley and Sons.
Wittgenstein, L. (1953), *Philosophical Investigations*, trans. G.E.M. Anscombe, Oxford: Blackwell.

PART I

FOUNDATIONS

1. Cities, complexity and beyond
Juval Portugali

1.1 CITIES AS COMPLEX SYSTEMS

Two notions form the title of this handbook – cities and complexity. The first, cities, refers to a form of settlement and way of life that emerged some 5500 years ago and since then has proved to be among the most stable institutions created by humans. Cultures, empires, states and political regimes rose and fell while cities adapted to all transformations and continued to exist. The twenty-first century is to a large extent the Age of Cities: cities have become the most dominant form of human settlement and way of life as more than half the world's population live in cities. The study of cities can be traced back to antiquity, for example, to first-century BC Vitruvius and his ten books on architecture – *De architectura*. However, a starting point of the modern study and science of cities can be seen in Johann Heinrich von Thünen's (1826 [1966]) *The Isolated State* that opens with 'Imagine a very large town at the centre of a fertile plain'.

Similarly to cities, notions of complexity can be traced back to antiquity, to ancient philosophy – 'no man ever steps in the same river twice, for it's not the same river and he's not the same man', wrote sixth-century BC philosopher Heraclitus of Ephesus and with this sentence preceded a basic property of complexity – 'far from equilibrium', namely, that complex systems are always changing, never at rest. However, the complexity we are dealing with here is much younger, referring to a set of theories that started to appear in the 1960s in order to study open and complex systems that exhibit phenomena of selforganization, chaos, and so on. With the exception of Humberto Maturana's *Autopoiesis* theory (Maturana and Varela 1973), these founding complexity theories were first developed in the material sciences (physics, chemistry, and so on) closely linked to thermodynamics: Prigogine's dissipative structures (Prigogine and Stengers 1985) which started from the notion of entropy with close association to fluid dynamics (for example, Bénard's convection), Haken's (1983) synergetics that commenced from the phenomenon of light amplification by stimulated emission of radiation (LASER), chaos theory of Lorenz (1972) and Feigenbaum (1983), Mandelbrot (1983) who expanded the Cantor (1883) set from the nineteenth century into the fractal theory of today, and more. For further details see Chapter 2 in this volume.

In association with the appearance of the above founding complexity theories a link was made with the study of cities. First as a metaphor to convey the distinction between a complex system that is open to its environment and a classical material system that is closed to it. 'The classical formulation [of entropy] due to Clausius refers to isolated systems exchanging neither energy nor matter with the outside world', said Nobel Laureate Prigogine (1977) in his Nobel lecture; and then he asked and answered: 'Are most types of "organizations" around us of this nature?', [that is, characterized by thermodynamic equilibrium?]. '[T]he answer is negative. Obviously in a town, in a living system, we have a quite different type of functional order.' This link to 'a town' did not come out of the blue: during the 1970s, Herman and Prigogine (1979) put forward a 'Two-fluid approach to town traffic' that represents traffic flows in a town, city or metropolitan area.

As far as I am aware, the first to transform the city from a metaphor to a material dissipative structure to a city as a complex system, and thus to trigger the emergence of complexity theories of cities (CTC), were Peter Allen and M. Sanglier in a paper suggesting a 'dynamical model of a central place system . . . derived from the concepts underlying dissipative structures, takes into account the self-organizing aspects of urban evolution, and shows the importance both of chance and of determinism in such systems' (Allen and Sanglier 1981, abstract). This early association between a complexity theory and the dynamics of cities was rather 'smooth' since several of the early classical theories of cities, specifically from the German tradition, were theories about latent complex systems – forerunners to some of the basic properties of complexity. Thus, von Thünen (1826 [1966]) studied the interaction between a town and its agricultural environment, Auerbach's (1913) (rank-size) 'law of population concentration' created the ground for the current power law and urban allometry/scaling studies, while the urban landscapes of the central place theories of Christaller (1933 [1966]) and Lösch (1954) had all the properties of a system approach and of fractal cities, decades before the appearance of Bertalanffy's (1969 [2003]) *General System Theory*, Mandelbrot's (1983) fractal theory and Batty and Longley's (1994) *Fractal Cities*. Denise Pumain (2009; Chapter 7 in this volume) has termed these processes a 'spiral cumulativeness of knowledge' that characterizes social sciences, implying that 'new interpretations are never entirely new' (Chapter 7 in this volume).

1.2   CITIES AS COMPLEX ADAPTIVE SYSTEMS

Parallel to the emergence and development of CTC in the 1980s, while students of cities were busy applying the founding theories of complexity to cities, a new view on complexity came to the fore: the complex adaptive system (CAS) (Gell-Mann 1994a). It followed, and was the creation of, the formation in New Mexico, USA, of the Santa Fe Institute in the mid-1980s. The new property added to the complexity discourse was adaptation, a concept associated with living systems ranging from biology through brain dynamics, cognition, society, culture and politics to artificial intelligence (AI) and A-life. As a consequence of this multiple association,

> the term CAS has different meanings for different researchers . . . Some of us speak of 'artificial life' or 'artificial social life' or 'artificial worlds,' while others, of whom I am one, prefer to consider natural CAS and computer-based systems together. The latter include methods for adaptive computation as well as models and simulations of natural CAS

wrote Murray Gell-Mann (1994b, p. 17), Nobel Laureate in physics 1969, one of the founders of the Santa-Fe Institute and the person who added 'adaptation' to the language of complexity.

Complex adaptive systems entered all levels of CTC: at the local level, each urban agent was now perceived as a CAS whose behavior and action is a particular form of adaptation to the socio-economic and/or morphology of the urban environment; both in real urban situations and in urban simulations, for example, in agent-based urban simulation models. At the mezzo urban scale, the city itself became a CAS that has to adapt to its global environment – the metropolis and the urban system. Urban planning and design became forms and tools for/of adaptation again at the local (Chapter 17 in this volume) and global (Chapter 16 in this volume) scales. Complex adaptive systems also play a central role in studies about urban resilience (for example, Meerow et al. 2016): a city's resilience depends on its adaptation capabilities, to changing environmental conditions, shocks and extreme events.

1.3   CITIES AS HYBRID COMPLEX SYSTEMS

Unlike the general tendency in complexity studies to start with analogies, CASs started by looking at, and searching for, a difference: what is the difference between a material and organic complex system? The answer, as noted in the previous section, was adaptation. Adaptation is a basic property of all organic systems and in order to include organic entities under the umbrella of complexity theory, one has to extend the theory's boundaries.

Complexity theories of cities have successfully applied the material as well as the organic/CAS versions of complexity theories to cities as noted previously and, as is evident from the chapters in this handbook, the study of cities has greatly benefited from these applications. However, can complexity theory benefit from the study of cities in the way that it benefited from the study of organic systems that are characterized by adaptation? Can the study of cities contribute to, and enrich, the general theory of complexity in the manner that CASs did? To do so we have once again to search for the difference: is there an ontological difference between natural – material and organic – complex systems and a city as a complex system? My answer is (Portugali 2011, 2016): natural complex systems – material and organic – are composed of natural parts; cities are composed of natural and artificial parts – they are thus hybrid complex systems.

Artifacts are 'facts of art' – products of human intention, imagination and action; whether they are artistic entities, socio-cultural organizations or machines. Modern science started with 'the world as a clockwork' – the machine as a metaphor for the natural universe at large (compare Marshal and Green's Chapter 4 in this volume). The generality of this mechanistic world view that dominated science for more than 200 years was falsified at the beginning of the twentieth century following Einstein's relativity, quantum theory and, more recently, complexity theory. What was falsified was not the existence of a mechanistic domain, but its generality, namely, the view that its basic properties apply to nature, society and culture. Despite the differences between the theories of relativity, quantum and complexity, they share a common property that differentiates them from mechanistic world views: non-causality: With machines, once you have all the 'ifs', you can, in principle, know all the 'thens'; with complex systems this is not so. Some say that this is because technical limitations in that complex systems have so many parts (for example, a human brain) that identifying all 'ifs' is technically not possible. However, in principle, if it was possible, then determining the 'thens' would be possible. Some (myself included) say that this is ontologically so – there is no limited number of 'ifs' and 'thens'; complex systems are inexhaustible.

1.4   CITIES, COMPLEXITY AND COGNITION

1.4.1   Bounded Rationality

Perceiving urban agents as CASs and cities as hybrid complex systems, compels us to explicitly consider the agents' cognition, motivation, behavior and action. A common approach is to follow classical economics and regard each urban agent as a perfectly rational, self-interested, utility and/or profit maximizer, *homo economicus* that possesses complete information. In an attempt to soften the perfect rationality of the *homo economicus*, Herbert Simon introduced the notion of bounded rationality that replaces the 'global rationality of economic man with the kind of rational behavior that is compatible with the access to information and the computational capacities that are actually possessed by organisms, including man, in the kinds of environments in which such organisms exist' (Simon 1955, p. 99). From this perspective, in the context of urban simulation models, the urban agents as utility or profit maximizers are now replaced by utility or profit satisfiers urban agents (Manson 2006; Hatna and Benenson 2007). Alternatively, in the context of urban design: 'more often than not design deals with *ill-defined* requirements and wicked problems (Buchanan, 1992; Rittel and Webber, 1973). As a consequence, the designer acts under conditions of *bounded rationality* . . . and thus has to accept nonoptimal *satisficing* solutions' (Portugali and Stolk 2014, p. 832, original emphases).

1.4.2   Heuristics

Simon's bounded rationality was formulated in relation to decision making in the context of economics and public administration, yet it contains psychological and cognitive elements. Indeed, at a later stage these elements were fully extended by cognitive psychologists Amos Tversky and Daniel Kahneman's (1974, 1981) studies on the role of heuristics as regards human behavior and decision making under uncertainty. In 2002, Kahneman received the Nobel Prize in Economics for his work with Tversky (who died in 1996), for integrating economic analysis with fundamental insights from cognitive psychology, thus laying the foundation for a new field of research. According to Tversky and Kahneman, when facing complex decision situations with a high degree of uncertainty (that is, ill-defined planning situations), people tend to rely on a limited number of heuristic principles (rules of thumb) that usually work well yet often entail distortions. They have identified five of these heuristics: representativeness, availability, anchoring, similarity and decision frame.

As *The End of Certainty* – the title of Prigogine with Stengers' (1997) book – indicates, uncertainty, which is at the core of Tversky–Kahneman heuristics, is also a fundamental property of complex systems. Also, in several previous studies (Portugali 2000, 2011), a link was made between Tversky–Kahneman heuristics, complexity theory and urban agents' decision making in the context of cities and planning, as well as to the notion of SIRN that is discussed in section 1.5 in this chapter (compare Chapter 6, this volume).

1.4.3 Cognitive Maps

The straightforward approach to explicitly take a position on agents' cognition, behavior and motivation in the context of cities is to consult the cognitive science – *The Mind's New Science* (Gardner 1987) that emerged in the mid-1950s out of a collaboration between several disciplinary domains including psychology, philosophy and AI. Tversky–Kahneman heuristics is only one example of the insight gained by adding to CTC a cognitive dimension. Other examples concern, first, the role of Tolman's (1948) cognitive maps in urban agents' decision behavior and action in cities. Adding cognitive maps to cities and complexity, we realize that 'the map is not the territory' (Korzybski 1933), namely, that there is a gap between the city, the city perceived and the city imagined, and that human behavior in cities is determined much less by the city compared with the perceived and imagined cities. As regards the city perceived, studies on 'distortions in cognitive maps' (Tversky 1992; Portugali 2011, 2018) indicate systematic gaps between the measured cartographic maps and the perceived cognitive maps. They further indicate, that human behavior in cities is determined by cognitive maps (which is part of complexity).

1.4.4 Chronesthesia

Another example of the insight gained by adding a cognitive dimension to CTC is the cognitive property of *Chronesthesia*, also termed mental time travel (MTT). Originally hypothesized by Tulving (1983) with respect to episodic memory, it refers to the brain's ability to think about – that is, to 'mentally travel' to – the past, present, and future. Furthermore, not only do humans have the capability to mentally travel in time, but they cannot avoid it: 'unlike other animals,' write Killingsworth and Gilbert (2010), humans spend about half of their waking hours 'thinking about what is not going on around them, contemplating events that happened in the past, might happen in the future, or will never happen at all.' Studies indicate (Raichle et al. 2001; Buckner et al. 2008) that stimulus-independent thought or mind wandering is the brain's default mode of operation.

The implications for cities, their planning and their design are far reaching (Portugali 2016, 2020). First, each urban agent is a planner at a particular scale with the implication that urban dynamics is an interaction between multiplicity of planners, some of which are regular urban agents (each with its specific plans and designs) while others are professional urban planners with their formal plans and designs. Second is the notion of planning or design behavior, namely, that urban agents are behaving and acting in the city in response to a plan or design, that is, in response to a reality that does not yet exist and might never exist.

1.5 CITIES, COGNITION AND ARTIFACTS

While the linked complexity, cognition and city added new insights to our understanding of cities as complex systems, they also exposed a lacuna: cognitive science ignores and excludes artifacts, and consciously so. According to Chomsky, one of the founders of the cognitive science:

> The notion of E-language has no place in this picture. There is no issue of correctness with regard to E-languages, however characterized, because E-languages are *mere artifacts* . . . the concept appears to play no role in the theory of language . . . The technical concept of E-language is a dubious one in at least two respects. In the first place . . . languages in this sense are not real-world objects but are *artificial*, somewhat arbitrary, and perhaps not very interesting constructs. In contrast . . . statements about I-language . . . are true or false statements about something real and definite, about actual states of the mind/brain and their components . . . (Chomsky 1986, pp. 26–7, emphases added)

Chomsky here makes a distinction between external and internal languages (E- versus I-languages, respectively). E-languages are the spoken languages (Hebrew, English, French, Chinese, and so on), while I-language is the innate universal language with which, according to Chomsky, every human being comes to the world, and by means of which he or she acquires specific E-languages. This view of Chomsky is in line with the general tendency in science: 'the term "artificial" has a pejorative air about it', writes Herbert Simon (1969 [1996], p. 3) in his *The Sciences of the Artificial*.

The outcome is a paradoxical situation: On the one hand, cognitive science tells us (according to Nobel Laureate Kandel 2012, p. 284), about vision, that 'we live in two worlds at once, and our ongoing . . . experience is a dialogue between the two: the outside world . . . and the internal world of the brain's perceptual, cognitive and emotional models'. On the other hand, cognitive science tells us (according to Chomsky 1986, pp. 26–7) that the external world, that is, the world of artifacts, is 'somewhat arbitrary, and perhaps not very interesting'. This anti-artifacts tendency had an effect also on studies related to cognition and the city. For example, Lynch's (1960) main interest in *The Image of the City* was the city itself – its morphology and urban landscape. However, in the context of behavioral and cognitive geography the interest shifted from the city to behavior in space and then to spatial cognition. The city itself became just a passive environment by means of, and within, which behavior and cognition can be studied; in line with the role of the external environment in cognitive science in general. In the latter, the focus of interest was and still is one-sidedly on the details of the inner world, even in the context of the ecological-embodied-extended mind approaches. As elaborated (in Chapter 19 in this volume), in his study about the emergence of human agency in a human infant (compare Figure 19.1), Scott Kelso (2016, p. 494) observed that while the baby's action and behavior were intensively studied, not a single study has recorded the dynamics and reaction of the external environment, 'thereby obviating the possibility of obtaining any information about its relation to the baby's movements'. (See further discussion in Chapter 19 in this volume.)

Chomsky is thus right is saying that E-languages are artifacts, but he is not right in saying that they are not interesting and have no room in the cognitive science – the study of 'mind/brain and their components'. Similarly to cities, E-languages are hybrid complex systems that come into being out of the interaction between the parts – the human agents. Similarly to cities, they are composed of artifacts – the lexical components (the buildings, roads and so on) of each specific E-language, and human agents that speak the E-language. Furthermore, as implied by Kelso's (2016) study, the property 'human agency' (urban agents included) emerges out of an interaction between the human baby as a complex system and the artifact mobile which is a simple system; the artifact is needed for the cognitive property 'human agency' to emerge. That is, artifacts are integral part of cognition. Yet, as noted by Kelso, there is no such theory.

The notions of synergetic inter-representation networks (SIRN), IA and their conjunction SIRNIA were developed as components of a cognitive theory in which artifacts are integral parts of cognition. They are described in some detail by Portugali and Haken (Chapter 4, this volume), including empirical illustrations of several case studies. I present the basic principles of these components.

- SIRN: an artifact is an external representation – externalization in the world of an internal representation – an idea, wish or emotion that originates in the mind-brain. Internal and external representations are 'the two worlds' in which (according to Kandel 2012, p. 284, cited previously) we at once live; and as he further notes, 'our ongoing . . . experience is a dialogue between the two: the outside world' – the world of externally represented artifacts, and the internally represented world – the 'internal world of the brain's perceptual, cognitive and emotional models'. This ongoing dialogue/interaction has been termed inter-representation (IRN) (Portugali 1996). The addition of S that makes it SIRN, came to indicate that the process as a whole evolves in line with the principles of synergetics – Haken's theory of complex self-organizing systems (Haken and Portugali 1996).
- IA: the notion IA complements the SIRN process by elaborating on the dialogue/interaction between the two worlds. It suggests (Haken and Portugali 2015) that this dialogue between the internal and external worlds evolves by the exchange of information; the information constructed in and by the mind-brain, and the data conveyed/transmitted by the external world of artifacts, that the mind-brain transforms into syntactic information. Three forms of information are involved in the dialogue: quantitative-syntactic information that conforms to Shannonian information (SHI), that is, information as defined by Shannon (Shannon 1948; Shannon and Weaver 1949) and two forms of qualitative forms of information: *semantic information* (SI) referring to meaning per se, and pragmatic information (PI) referring to the action possibilities afforded by the environment and objects and artifacts in it – in line with Gibson's (1979) notions of embodied cognition and affordances. For details and the conjunction SIRNIA, Chapter 6 in this volume.

1.6 CITIES, COMPLEXITY AND THE BIG DATA GOLOM

'The medium is the message' is the famous phrase coined by Marshall McLuhan (1964) in his book *Understanding Media: The Extensions of Man*. In the current reality, suggested McLuhan in the 1960s, the media in no longer a tool to convey a particular content, but is the content itself. A view that reminds us of the legendary Golom of Prague that was created by the Rabbi Löw of Prague (known as the Maharal) and at a certain stage ceased being a tool that obeys, and implements, the Rabbi's orders, but started to be the message itself (Dekel and Gurley 2013).

One of the attractions of cities to physicists and mathematicians was, and still is, data or, more specifically, the possibility to apply and test theories and models on urban data. This is probably why, at the turn of the twentieth century, physicist Auerbach (1913) undertook his study on 'the law of population concentration', and this explains why so many physicists and mathematicians are active participants in the domain of CTC. Currently, with the advance of information communication technologies (ICT), AI, the availability of big data and data-mining techniques, this is even more so. According to physicist S. Koonin, director of the new New York University's Center for Urban Science and Progress (CUSP): 'Physics is an attitude as well as a subject. The kind of skills physicists bring to thinking through complicated situations, data driven and so on, are not all that common in urban science and technology at this point. Physicists have a lot to bring to the table here.' This statement appeared in an interview, 'Smart cities will need big data', published in *Physics Today* (Koonin 2013) that defines itself as 'the flag-ship publication of the American Institute of Physics, is the most influential and closely followed physics magazine in the world.'

Information communication technologies and big data represent what Gregory (1978) has termed physicalism – a physicist view of cities. Yet, Koonin, as well as his interviewer, are wrong in implying that it is only now that physicists step into the study of cities. We have mentioned previously Auerbach's 1913 study and at later stages there were several physicalist waves in the study of cities; the previous wave, known as the 'quantitative revolution' in human geography and the study of cities and planning, was during the 1950s and 1960s. It started with great enthusiasm and ended with major frus-tration. An example is David Harvey, a leading theoretician of the quantitative urban-ism of the 1960s, who in the early 1970s wrote that the positivist/physicalist approach is 'incapable of saying anything of depth and profundity' about cities, their dynamics and planning (Harvey 1973, p. 129).

The enthusiasm for big data is not unique to cities but applies to all research domains; for many, as suggested by Chris Anderson (2008), we are witnessing 'The end of theory', since 'the data deluge makes the scientific method obsolete'. Whether CTC practitioners accept this view or not, current CTC studies on urban dynamics are strongly dominated by the 'the data deluge'. The consequence is that ICT, AI and urban data availability are becoming forces that direct research and topics of interest. The medium (data-Golem) to study cities, has become the message. The recently flourishing domain of smart cities, is an example.

1.7   CITIES, COMPLEXITY AND SMALL DATA, OR, SMALL DATA IS BEAUTIFUL

How to study cities as complex systems? The fashionable answer as we have just seen, is big data: the new ICT with data-mining and visual analytic techniques make it possible for the first time to make use of the huge amount of data that is accumulating on the Internet and other networks. Yet, there is an alternative, or at least an addition, to the big data approach; that is, 'Small data is beautiful' (Portugali 2013; Haken and Portugali 2021, ch. 2), a name that rephrases the title of Schumacher's (1973) book *Small is Beautiful: A Study of Economics as if People Mattered*. This book was a critique of the mid-twentieth-century's economic gigantism in the form of mass production, mass media, fast economic growth and urbaniza-tion that, according to Schumacher, entailed the de-humanization of people and their cultures. The subtitle of this section should thus imply, a study of cities as if people mattered.

While most attention in the domain of CTC is directed to big data, there is another type of data that bears directly on human behavior in cities: originating from the cognitive and brain sciences, these data shed light on the innate drivers of human cognition and behavior and as such have the potential to better understand and model urban agents' cognition, behavior and action in cities. An example is the recent wave of studies about urban scaling and allometry, triggered mainly by Bettencourt et al.'s (2007) study on 'Growth, innovation, scaling and the pace of life in cities'. Based on big data, this and subsequent studies observed super-linear relations between city size and the pace of life in cities as it shows up in several urban indicators that concern economic activities, creativity, crime and pedestrian walking speed. That is, the citizens of big cities behave differently from the inhabitants of smaller cities in respect of these indicators. Bettencourt et al.'s (2007) paper entailed studies that criticized and challenged the generality of these findings (for example, Arcaute et al. 2015; Cottineau et al. 2015), others that supported them, and the discussion still goes on (Chapter 9 in this volume). What is common to all is that they refer to, or rely on, big data; the controversies are not on the use of big data but on its quality, for example, 'Does a given data set genuinely represents the size of cities?' What is also common is that generally the question 'Why do people in small and large cities behave differently?' is not asked, and for good reason: big data has no answer; we can speculate, based on assumptions about human behavior (Bettencourt 2013), but these answers are not based on data.

To explain why people behave differently in small and big cities, we have to start, data wise, from the bottom up, that is, from data about the individual urban agent and the forces that motivate its action and behavior in cities of various sizes. An attempt in this direction was suggested by Ross and Portugali (2018) and further elaborated by Haken and Portugali (2019, 2021). This attempt is based on three theoretical foundations. The first foundation is psychologist Higgins's (1997, 1998) regulatory focus theory in respect of humans' innate motivational system, showing empirically that individuals' goal-directed behavior is regulated by a configuration of two distinct motivational systems – promotion and prevention. In order to achieve their goals, promotion-orientated individuals tend to focus on winning and risk taking, whereas prevention-orientated individuals tend to focus on not losing and risk avoidance. The second foundation is the finding of a collective regulatory focus, namely, that a person's promotion or prevention tendencies depend also on his or her personal regulatory focus, and on the atmosphere of the group he or she belongs to (Faddegon et al. 2008). The third foundation is urban regulatory focus (Ross and Portugali 2018), demonstrating empirically that a city's pace of life affects the promotion or prevention tendencies of its inhabitants and users. Finally, the decisive link to cities as complex systems and to urban scaling was made by Haken and Portugali (2019, 2021).

What these studies show is that small and big data complement each other, that is, the proper way to study urban scaling (and urban dynamics in general) is by a circularly causal process in which small data-based studies show how, by means of their interaction, urban agents give rise to the global structure of cities, while big data-based studies show how the global structure of cities, top down, affects the behavior and actions of urban agents, and so on.

This is but one illustration; other potential examples that have yet to be developed concern, for instance, cognitive maps, the way they affect agents' behavior and movement in cities and thus the evolving structure of cities. Another potential example is chronesthesia – the way human ability (or inability) to avoid mental time travel to the past and future, and the implied planning and design behavior noted previously, affect urban agents' behavior and action in the city, and more (Portugali and Haken 2018; compare Portugali, Chapter 19, this volume).

1.8   CITIES, COMPLEXITY AND BEYOND

Complexity Theories of Cities Have Come of Age is the title of our 2012 book that has focused on the implications for planning (Portugali 2012; Portugali et al. 2012). It could just as well be the title of this collection of chapters that can be seen as the state of the art in the domain of CTC at the end of 2020. Such a title is characterized by a Janus face: one face looks backward at what has been achieved and another forward at what has yet to be achieved. As regards the first of these faces, this collection partly follows the evolution of CTC from a narrow stream of studies – written mainly by physicists applying theories from physics – to an established interdisciplinary research domain engaging urbanists, geographers, planners, urban designers, regional scientists, mathematicians and physicists, among others. The second face, as noted, looks forward at what has yet to be achieved. The discussions in sections 1.3–1.7 look forward by suggesting issues that have yet to be fully developed. To the latter I suggest adding a discussion that starts by looking at the potentials of the links between complexity theory and the general study of cities.

Two potentials can be identified, the first being: born in the hard sciences, CTC offered to students of cities an arsenal of sophisticated mathematical tools. This potential was fully realized. As a consequence we now have a single theory – a conceptual framework with mathematical formalism – to several urban phenomena hitherto explained by several theories independent of each other: central place theory, urban scaling, urban land use, spatial segregation, and so on. This is an advantage from the perspective of William of Ockham's (1285–1347/9) (Baker 2010) famous scientific principle: '*pluralitas non est ponenda sine necessitate*' ('plurality should not be posited without necessity'). Known as Occam's razor, this principle gives precedence to simplicity in scientific explanation. The second potential was the possibility to create a link between the two cultures of cities.

As elaborated in detail in the past (Portugali 2006, 2011), since the early twentieth century, the study of cities evolved as a pendulum between two cultures of cities reminiscent of Snow's (1964) two cultures of science: a soft, hermeneutic study of cities inspired by the humanities and social sciences, versus a quantitative-analytical approach inspired by the hard, quantitative disciplines, specifically economics. As suggested in previous studies, CTC created a potential to act as a link between space and place (Portugali 2006, 2011), that is, to bridge the two cultures of cities. This is based on two grounds: first, on Jacobs's (1961) and Alexander's (1965) studies and, secondly, on resemblances between CTC and the social theory-orientated urban studies – in particular the structuralist-Marxist and humanistic (SMH) approaches to cities that dominated the field from the 1970s onwards (Portugali 2006, 2011).

The first ground is Jacobs (1961) in her *The Death and Life of Great American Cities* and Alexander (1965) in his 'A city is not a tree', who strongly criticized the quantitative approach to cities and, specifically, its rational comprehensive planning, from a theoretical position reminiscent of complexity; so much so, that currently, in retrospect, they are considered forerunners of CTC. Mike Batty (2008, pp. 769–71) wrote of the achievements of CTC:

> In the past 25 years, our understanding of cities has slowly begun to reflect Jacobs's message. Cities are no longer regarded as being disordered systems. Beneath the apparent chaos and diversity of physical form, there is strong order and a pattern that emerges from the myriad of decisions and processes required for a city to develop and expand physically.

However, most CTC practitioners never followed Jacobs's and Alexander's criticism of the quantitative-scientific-rational-comprehensive approach. This criticism came, as is well recorded, from the soft hermeneutic culture of cities, specifically from social theory-orientated SMH perspectives on the study of cities (Portugali 2011). For most CTC practitioners the arsenal of sophisticated mathematical tools associated with complexity theories was an opportunity to rebuild the quantitative approach to cities on a new and more advanced mathematical foundation.

The second ground, as observed by Portugali (1985), is that complexity theories have found properties in matter hitherto assigned to the organic and human domains, including history, evolution, irreversibility and nonlinearity. As a consequence, and as illustrated in Figure 1.1, there are resemblances between the conceptual frameworks and languages of CTC and social theory: The notion of revolution in social theories resembles 'bifurcation and phase transition' in the parlance of complexity; mode of production in (Marxist) social theory resembles steady state and (synergetics') order parameter; processes of social and spatial reproduction resemble circular causality, while social theory view reality as ever-changing and transforming resembles complexity notions such as far from equilibrium, chaos, butterfly effect, and so on.

Given the latter potential with its two facets, CTC was, and still is, at a perfect vantage point for addressing the problematics of twenty-first-century urban society that is marked by a whole set of socio-economic and cultural transformations, including globalization, the rise of civil society, intensive processes of privatization that led to the decline of the national welfare state and, more recently, the crisis of democracy. As is evident by studies such as *The People vs Democracy* (Mounk 2018), *How Democracies Die* (Levitsky and Ziblatt 2018), *La France périphérique* (Guilluy 2014) and *Freedom: An Unruly History* (de Dijn 2020), Western democracies are currently torn between non-liberal democracy and non-democratic liberalism.

Also, the twenty-first century is the age of cities. Cities and urban society capture the core of each of the above transformations and crises, a not very surprising situation in a reality where, for the first time in human history, more than 50 percent of the world's population lives in cities, when several cities around the world turned into megacities with populations of over 20 million, the economy and sphere of influence of many world or global cities extend beyond the boundaries of their nation states and, yet, parallel to and within this trend we see a countertrend toward localization or 'glocalization'. As noted by Guilluy's (2014) book, the crisis of democracy is associated with a growing

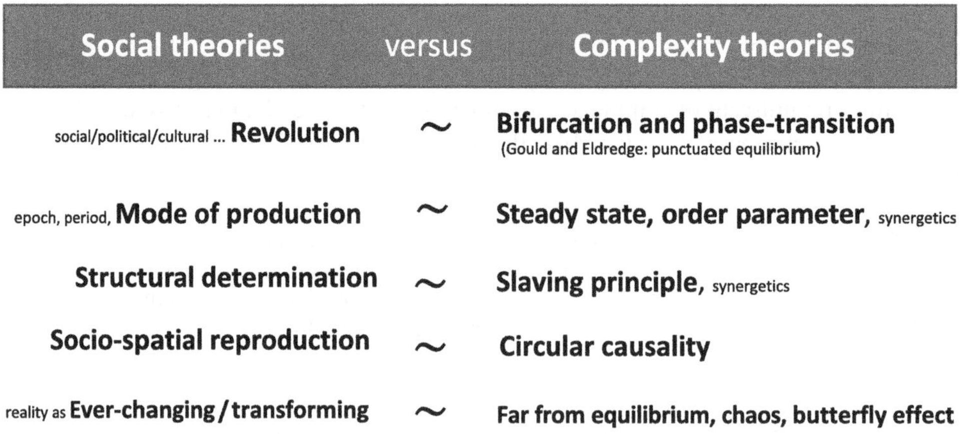

Social theories	versus	Complexity theories
social/political/cultural ... **Revolution**	~	**Bifurcation and phase-transition** (Gould and Eldredge: punctuated equilibrium)
epoch, period, **Mode of production**	~	**Steady state, order parameter,** synergetics
Structural determination	~	**Slaving principle,** synergetics
Socio-spatial reproduction	~	**Circular causality**
reality as **Ever-changing / transforming**	~	**Far from equilibrium, chaos, butterfly effect**

Figure 1.1   Resemblances between the conceptual frameworks and languages of CTC and social theory-oriented urban studies

gap and tension between urban society in the big global cities, with their 'creative class' (Florida 2002), and urban society in peripheral towns and cities. To this might be added that some of the basic aspects of twenty-first century society and cities are often described in the language of complexity theories and CTC; for example, Castells's (1996) *The Rise of the Network Society* and his notions of space, flow and the information city.

Potentially, CTC should have a lot to say about the twenty-first-century city and yet, with few exceptions, it does not. Most researchers in the domain of CTC preferred, and still prefer, to focus on traditional, conservative and anachronistic urban issues, such as central place theory, land use, rank-size distributions of cities, traffic and national systems of cities, which were dominant in the 1950s and 1960s, plus, technical issues, for example, smart machines, cities, and so on. The reason, as noted previously, is the availability of data and thus quantification. The outcome is an ironic situation by which the study of cities is characterized by a division of labor between two cultures of cities: a new complexity-derived scientific approach to cities that deals mainly with old-fashioned urban issues that lent themselves to quantification (plus studies on the role of new ICT) versus an 'old' hermeneutic study of cities that deals with the new urban reality and problematics of the twenty-first century, that does not enable quantification. That is, while for a few of its practitioners CTC was seen as an opportunity to bridge the gap between the two cultures of cities (for example, Portugali 2000, 2011), for the majority it was seen as an opportunity to revive the quantitative approach to cities on the sounder bases of complexity theory.

The exception is urban planning. Here we observe the merging of two streams. The first, communicative planning (Healey 2007; Innes and Booher 2010), attempts to adapt the traditional planning discourse and approach (the rational comprehensive planning) to the changing realities of the twenty-first century, namely (Portugali 2011), to the weakening of the welfare state, the resultant rise of the third sector of civil society as an active planning actor and (as specified in Chapter 18 in this volume) the transition of planning from a two-sector game (public and private) to a three-sector game (public, private and civil). The intensive use of the notion of governance comes to reflect these changes. The other stream attempts to look at planning theory and practice from the perspective and insight of CTC. (Compare the activities of the AESOP's thematic group on planning and complexity.) Unlike mainstream CTC that has a strong analytical and quantitative orientation, here the main approach is hermeneutics. For further bibliography see Roo et al.'s (2020) *Handbook on Planning and Complexity*.

The notions of dual and hybrid complex systems, SIRN and AI were attempts to go beyond CTC mainstream, to materialize the previously noted second potential and pave the way for a deeper involvement of CTC in twenty-first century urban problematics. A more recent attempt is Haken and Portugali's (2021) study that explores steady state and phase transition – two notions that are central to complex systems generally, and which are specific to the synergetics' approach to complexity – slaving principle and circular causality. All four have not as yet been studied in relation to cities and urbanism and, as can be seen in Figure 1.1, all four have commonalities with concepts in a social theory-orientated urban dynamics. It is hoped that these and similar attempts will enable CTC to materialize their full potentials and be directly involved and active in twenty-first-century urban problematics.

REFERENCES

Alexander, C. (1965), 'A city is not a tree', *Architectural Forum*, **122** (1), 58–62.

Allen, P. and M. Sanglier (1981), 'Urban evolution, self-organization, and decisionmaking', *Environment and Planning A*, **13** (2), 167–83.

Anderson, C. (2008), 'The end of theory: the data deluge makes the scientific method obsolete', *Wired*, 23 June, accessed 2 June 2021 at https://www.wired.com/2008/06/pb-theory/.

Arcaute, E., E. Hatna, P. Ferguson, H. Youn, A. Johansson and M. Batty (2015), 'Constructing cities, deconstructing scaling laws', *Journal of the Royal Society Interface*, **1** (102), 20140745, doi:10.1098/rsif.2014.0745.

Auerbach, F. (1913), 'Das Gesetz der Bevoelkerungskonzentration', *Petermanns Geographische Mitteilungen*, **59**, 74–6.

Baker, A. (2010), 'Simplicity', in E.N. Zalta (ed.), *The Stanford Encyclopedia of Philosophy*, Palo Alto, CA: Stanford University.

Batty, M. (2008), 'The size, scale, and shape of cities', *Science*, **319** (5864), 769–71.

Batty, M. and P. Longley (1994), *Fractal Cities*, London: Academic Press.

Bertalanffy, L. von (1969), *General System Theory – Foundations, Development, Applications*, repr. 2003, New York: George Braziller.

Bettencourt, L.M.A. (2013), 'The origins of scaling in cities', *Science*, **340** (June), 1438–41.

Bettencourt, L.M.A., J. Lobo, D. Helbing, C. Kühnert and G.B. West (2007), 'Growth, innovation, scaling, and the pace of life in cities', *Proceedings of the National Academy of Sciences of the United States of America*, **104** (17), 7301–6, doi:0.1073/pnas.0610172104.

Buchanan, R. (1992), 'Wicked problems in design thinking', *Design Issues*, **8** (2), 5–21.

Buckner, R., J. Andrews-Hanna and D. Schacter (2008), 'The brain's default network: anatomy, function and relevance to disease', *Annals of the New York Academy of Sciences*, **1124** (March), 1–38.

Cantor, G. (1883), 'On infinite, linear point-manifolds (sets), part 5' (in German), *Mathematische Annalen*, **21**, 545–91.

Castells, M. (1996), *The Rise of the Network Society*, Oxford: Wiley-Blackwell.

Chomsky, N. (1986), *Knowledge of Language*, New York: Praeger.

Christaller, W. (1933 [1966]), *Central Places in Southern Germany*, Englewood Cliffs, NJ: Prentice Hall.

Cottineau, C., E. Hatna, E. Arcaute and M. Batty (2015), 'Paradoxical interpretations of urban scaling laws', July, *ArXiv*, 1507.07878.

De Dijn, A. (2020), *Freedom: An Unruly History*, Cambridge, MA: Harvard University Press.

Dekel, E. and D.G. Gurley (2013), 'How the Golem came to Prague', *Jewish Quarterly Review*, **103** (2), 241–58.

Faddegon, K., D. Scheepers and N. Ellemers (2008), 'If we have the will, there will be a way: regulatory focus as a group identity', *European Journal of Social Psychology*, **38** (5), 880–95, doi:10.1002/ejsp.483.

Feigenbaum, M.J. (1983), 'Universal behavior in nonlinear systems', *Physica*, **7D** (1–3), 16–39.

Florida, R. (2002), *The Rise of the Creative Class: And How It's Transforming Work, Leisure, Community and Everyday Life*, New York: Perseus Book Group.

Gardner, H. (1987), *The Mind's New Science*, New York: Basic Books.

Gell-Mann, M. (1994a), *The Quark and the Jaguar: Adventures in the Simple and the Complex*, New York: Freeman.

Gell-Mann, M. (1994b), 'Complex adaptive systems', in G. Cowan, D. Pines and D. Meltzer (eds), *Complexity: Metaphors, Models, and Reality*, Reading, MA: Addison-Wesley, pp. 17–45.

Gibson, J.J. (1979), *The Ecological Approach to Visual Perception*, Boston, MA: Houghton-Mifflin.

Gregory, D. (1978), *Ideology, Science and Human Geography*, London: Hutchinson.

Guilluy, C. (2014), *La France périphérique: Comment on a sacrifié les classes populaires*, Paris: Groupe Flammarion.

Haken, H. (1983), *Advanced Synergetics*, Berlin, Heidelberg and New York: Springer.

Haken, H. and J. Portugali (1996), 'Synergetics, inter-representation networks and cognitive maps', in J. Portugali (ed.), *The Construction of Cognitive Maps*, Dordrecht: Kluwer Academic, pp. 45–67.

Haken, H. and J. Portugali (2015), *Information Adaptation: The Interplay between Shannon and Semantic Information in Cognition*, Berlin and Heidelberg: Springer.

Haken, H. and J. Portugali (2019), 'A synergetic perspective on urban scaling, urban regulatory focus and their interrelations', *Royal Society Open Science*, **6**, 191087, doi:10.1098/rsos.191087.

Haken, H. and J. Portugali (2021), *Synergetic Cities: Information, Steady State and Phase Transition. Implications to Urban Scaling, Smart Cities and Planning*, Cham: Springer.

Harvey, D. (1973), *Social Justice and the City*, London: Edward Arnold.

Hatna, E. and I. Benenson (2007), 'Building a city in vitro: the experiment and the simulation model', *Environment and Planning B: Planning and Design*, **34** (4), pp. 687–707.

Healey, P. (2007), *Urban Complexity and Spatial Strategies: Towards a Relational Planning for Our Times*, London: Routledge.

Herman, R. and I. Prigogine (1979), 'Two-fluid approach to town traffic', *Science*, **204** (4389), 148–51.

Higgins, E.T. (1997), 'Beyond pleasure and pain', *American Psychologist*, **52** (12), 1280–300.

Higgins, E.T. (1998), 'Promotion and prevention: regulatory focus as a motivational principle', in M.P. Zanna (ed.), *Advances in Experimental Social Psychology*, New York: Academic Press, pp. 1–46.

Innes, J.E. and D.E. Booher (2010), *Planning with Complexity: An Introduction to Collaborative Rationality for Public Policy*, London: Routledge.

Jacobs, J. (1961), *The Death and Life of Great American Cities*, London: Penguin Books.

Kandel, E. (2012), *The Age of Insight: The Quest to Understand the Unconscious in Art, Mind, and Brain, from Vienna 1900 to the Present*, New York: Random House.

Kelso, S.J.A. (2016), 'On the self-organizing origins of agency', *Trends in Cognitive Sciences*, **20** (7), 490–99.

Killingsworth, M.A. and D.T. Gilbert (2010), 'A wandering mind is an unhappy mind', *Science*, **330** (6006), 932, doi:10.1126/science.1192439.

Koonin, S. (2013), 'Smart cities will need big data', *Physics Today*, **66** (9), 19.

Korzybski, A.H.S. (1933), *Science and Sanity: An Introduction to Non-Aristotelian Systems and General Semantics*, Englewood, NJ: International Non-Aristotelian Library, pp. 747–61.

Levitsky, S. and D. Ziblatt (2018), *How Democracies Die*, New York: Crown.

Lorenz, E.N. (1972), 'Predictability: does the flap of a butterfly's wings in Brazil set off a tornado in Texas?', paper presented at the 139th meeting of the American Association for the Advancement of Sciences, Washington, DC, 29 December.

Lösch, A. (1954), *The Economics of Location*, New Haven, CT: Yale University Press.

Lynch, K. (1960), *The Image of the City*, Cambridge, MA: MIT Press.

Mandelbrot, B.B. (1983), *The Fractal Geometry of Nature*, San Francisco, CA: Freeman.

Manson, S.M. (2006), 'Bounded rationality in agent-based models: experiments with evolutionary programs', *International Journal of Geographical Information Science*, **20** (9), 991–1012.

Maturana, H. and F. Varela (1973), 'Autopoiesis: the organization of the living', repr. 1980 in H. Maturana and F. Varela, *Autopoiesis and Cognition*, Heidelberg: Springer, pp. 63–134.

McLuhan, M. (1964), *Understanding Media: The Extensions of Man*, New York: Signet Books.

Meerow, S., J.P. Newell and M. Stults (2016), 'Defining urban resilience: a review', *Landscape and Urban Planning*, **147** (October), 38–49.

Mounk, Y. (2018), *The People vs Democracy: Why Our Freedom Is in Danger and How to Save It*, Cambridge, MA: Harvard University Press.

Portugali, J. (1985), 'Parallel currents in the natural and social sciences', *Geoforum*, **16** (2), special issue, 227–38.

Portugali, J. (1996), 'Inter-representation networks and cognitive maps', in J. Portugali (ed.), *The Construction of Cognitive Maps*, Dordrecht: Kluwer Academic, pp. 11–43.

Portugali, J. (2000), *Self-Organization and the City*, Berlin, Heidelberg and New York: Springer.

Portugali, J. (2006), 'Complexity theory as a link between space and place', *Environment and Planning A*, **38** (April), 647–64.

Portugali, J. (2011), *Complexity, Cognition and the City*, Berlin, Heidelberg and New York: Springer.

Portugali, J. (2012), 'Complexity theories of cities: achievements, criticism and potentials', in J. Portugali, H. Meyer, E. Stolk and E. Tan (eds), *Complexity Theories of Cities Have Come of Age*, Heidelberg and Berlin: Springer, pp. 47–62.

Portugali, J. (2013), 'Small data is beautiful', Ninth International Space Syntax Symposium, Seoul, 1 November.

Portugali, J. (2016), 'What makes cities complex?', in J. Portugali and E. Stolk (eds), *Complexity, Cognition, Urban Planning and Design*, Berlin, Heidelberg and New York: Springer, pp. 3–19.

Portugali, J. (2020), 'Information adaptation as the link between cognitive planning and professional planning', in G. de Roo, C. Yamu and C. Zuidema (eds), *Handbook on Planning and Complexity*, Cheltenham, UK and Northampton, MA, USA: Edward Elgar, pp. 203–19.

Portugali, J. and H. Haken (2018), 'Movement, cognition and the city', *Built Environment*, **44** (2), special issue, 136–61.

Portugali, J. and E. Stolk (2014), 'A SIRN view on design thinking – an urban design perspective', *Environment and Planning B: Planning and Design*, **41** (October), 829–46.

Portugali, J., H. Meyer, E. Stolk and E. Tan (eds) (2012), *Complexity Theories of Cities Have Come of Age*, Heidelberg and Berlin: Springer.

Prigogine, I. (1977), 'Time, structure and fluctuations', Nobel Lecture, 8 December, accessed 3 June at https://www.nobelprize.org/prizes/chemistry/1977/prigogine/lecture/.

Prigogine, I. and I. Stengers (1985), *Order Out of Chaos*, New York: Bantam.

Prigogine, I. and I. Stengers (1997), *The End of Certainty: Time, Chaos and the New Laws of Nature*, New York: Free Press.

Pumain, D. (2009), 'L'espace, médium d'une construction spiralaire de la géographie, entre société et environnement', in B. Walliser (ed.), *La cumulativité des connaissances en sciences sociales*, Paris: EHESS, pp. 163–97.

Raichle, M.E., A.M. MacLeod, A.Z. Snyder, W.J. Powers, D.A. Gusnard and G.L. Shulman (2001), 'A default mode of brain function', *Proceedings of the National Academy of Sciences of the USA*, **98** (2), 676–82.

Rittel, H.W.J. and M.M. Webber (1973), 'Dilemmas in a general theory of planning', *Policy Sciences*, **4** (June), 155–69.

Roo, G. de, C. Yamu and C. Zuidema (eds) (2020), *Handbook on Planning and Complexity – a Synthesis*, Cheltenham, UK and Northampton, MA, USA: Edward Elgar.

Ross, G.M. and J. Portugali (2018), 'Urban regulatory focus: a new concept linking city size to human behavior', *Royal Society Open Science*, **5**, 171478, doi:10.1098/rsos.171478.

Schumacher, E.F. (1973), *Small Is Beautiful: A Study of Economics as if People Mattered*, London: Blond & Briggs.

Shannon, C.E. (1948), 'A mathematical theory of communication', *Bell System Technical Journal*, **27** (July), 379–423, (October), 623–56.

Shannon, C.E. and W. Weaver (1949), *The Mathematical Theory of Communication*, Urbana, IL: University of Illinois Press.

Simon, H.A. (1955), 'A behavioral model of rational choice', *Quarterly Journal of Economics*, **69** (1), 99–118, doi:10.2307/1884852.

Simon, H.A. (1969), *The Sciences of the Artificial*, repr. 1996, Cambridge, MA: MIT Press.

Snow, C.P. (1964), *The Two Cultures and a Second Look*, Cambridge: Cambridge University Press.

Thünen, J.H. von (1826), *The Isolated State*, English trans. 1966, P. Hall (ed.), Oxford: Pergamon.

Tolman, E. (1948), 'Cognitive maps in rats and men', *Psychological Review*, **55** (4), 189–208.

Tulving, E. (1983), *Elements of Episodic Memory*, New York: Oxford University Press.

Tversky, A. and D. Kahneman (1974), 'Judgment under uncertainty: heuristics and biases', *Science*, **185** (4157), 1124–31.

Tversky, A. and D. Kahneman (1981), 'The framing of decision and psychology of choice', *Science*, **211** (4481), 453–8.

Tversky, B. (1992), 'Distortions in cognitive maps', *Geoforum*, **23** (2), 131–8.

2. The emergence of complexity theories: an outline
Hermann Haken

1. PROLEGOMENON

Since I have worked in the field of complexity theories for such long time, my contribution surely has a strong personal bias. I am also aware that I can present only a small part of the fascinating network of ideas that underlie the emergence of complexity theories.

2. WHAT IS COMPLEXITY (C)?

There is no generally agreed upon definition of C, as it is witnessed by Carlos Gershenson's (1977) collection of articles on this topic (Gershenson 2008). So, I introduce my own definition, which hopefully captures the most relevant aspects of C.

Complexity may refer to a property of the (1) immaterial or (2) material world. Examples are (1) theories, formalisms, algorithms and philosophical constructs, and (2) objects composed of individual parts that form spatial or temporal, or spatio-temporal arrangements (patterns). Their description requires many data, at least in general. However, there are exceptions.

Consider a square lattice. The only datum needed is the distance between vertices. This example hints at one possible approach to define C and at attempts to quantify it (compare the following). A system/patterns is complex if it is difficult, impossible or undecidable (*sensu* Gödel 1931) to find a description using only few data. The problem has been cast into a mathematical form by Solomonoff (1960, 1964a, 1964b), Kolmogorov (1963) and Chaitin (1969) who related it to the concept of the Turing machine (Turing 1937). This machine allows us (in principle) to generate data by means of a program installed on that machine.

The question was, is there a shortest program that allows us to calculate the needed (observed) data? The answer is that there is no general algorithm that allows us to find such a program. This entails that it is impossible to develop a general complexity scale. Nevertheless, it remains an important task for C-theories to develop concepts and algorithms that allow them to compress many, even big data, to few relevant data (compare next section).

3. DIFFERENT GOALS

My above definition of complex(ity) may suggest that C-reduction is the goal of C-theories. I elaborate the corresponding history in the following chapters. Yet, there has been a direction of research that goes in the opposite direction, namely, the generation of (seemingly) complex structures by simple rules. The most prominent

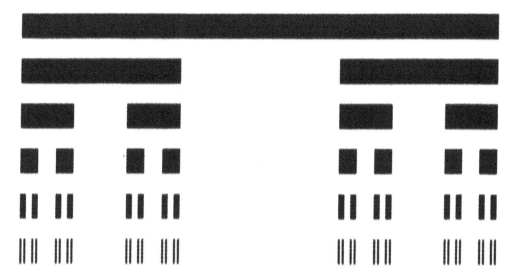

Note: At each step from above to below, the middle third of each bar is removed.

Figure 2.1   Example of construction of a fractal

example is fractal geometry (the term 'fractal' was coined by Benoit Mandelbrot 1983). This type of geometry was found by Georg Cantor (Dauben 1979). An example of a fractal is shown in Figure 2.1. This fractal has the property of self-similarity. When a pattern, originally at a specific degree of resolution, is enlarged (as seen under magnifying glass) the same pattern is observed, but at a finer scale. This self-similarity entails a scaling law.

Cantor's approach is but one method to generate a fractal structure. Another approach that gained much public attention was performed by Mandelbrot, who calculated sets of points in the plane by iteration of two simple equations giving rise to complicated patterns. Especially when colored, these patterns are aesthetically very appealing, but more importantly, they showed the property of self-similarity (including scaling laws). Thus, an interplay between C-generation (iteration procedure) and C-reduction (scaling laws) was established. Fractal structures appear in nature (though only over a limited range of magnification) and in artifacts. Examples are river deltas and blood vessels, but also city structures, communication and supply networks.

In conclusion, we may state that C-theories aim at unearthing general principles underlying the structure and behavior of complex systems.

4.   PHYSICS AS PARADIGM OF A SCIENCE

Physics seems to be an ideal meeting place between the abstract world of ideas including mathematics and the concrete world in the form of matter. Historically, an eminent example is Archimedes' law on the loss of weight of bodies in water. This law holds irrespective of the nature of the body, be it iron, wood or marble, and irrespective of its shape. It subsumes a plethora of phenomena under a simple relationship between volume and loss of weight, or, in our present context, a reduction of many data to just two. This type of reduction has become a hallmark of physical research, as witnessed by Galileo Galilei's studies on falling bodies.

The study of the motion of bodies – again, irrespective of their physical nature – has become the object of mechanics, in particular celestial mechanics. Central to this field is Isaac Newton's second law of motion: temporal change in momentum of a body equals the force acting on it. Historically, the concept of force is that of Robert Hooke (1678), who introduced it in the context of the elongation or compression of a spring.

Newton's law insinuates the interpretation 'a force is the *cause* of an *effect*, i.e. acceleration of a body' (Newton 1687 [1725/26]). The generalization of Newton's second law in conjunction with his third law (reaction equals action) to the mathematical apparatus dealing with the motion of several or many bodies ended in the formulation of classical mechanics. Concerning C-theories, the credo, for a long time, was the concept of one of the leading scientists in this field, Pierre-Simon Laplace. If a 'spirit of the world' knows at some initial time the positions and velocities of all bodies, he can calculate or predict their positions and velocities for all times. This is a very strong statement on predictability that was later shaken by quantum theory and chaos theory.

The equations of classical mechanics, in particular in their form of differential equation, are prototypical for evolution equations formulated and used in many disciplines. The temporal change of a set of quantities at a time t is determined by the size of these quantities at the same time. These equations describe a (continuous) Markov process. Dynamic systems theory deals with the properties of the solutions of evolution equations. A number of C-theories use the results of dynamic systems theory.

In addition to mechanics, thermodynamics has turned out to be crucial for the development of some C-theories. Thermodynamics is a strange mix of everybody's or every day's experience and deep insights. One of its cornerstones is the law of the conservation of energy, discovered by the medical doctor, Julius Robert Meyer (1842), surely a deep insight. Then there are anthropomorphic elements: the concepts of temperature (humans have a type of temperature sense) and, related to it, heat. Also simple observations; when we bring two bodies with two different temperatures in contact, heat flows from the hot body to the cold body, but never in the opposite direction. Heat is dissipated by an irreversible process.

Rudolf Julius Emanuel Clausius (1850, 1865) formulated the first law of thermodynamics (conservation of energy) in the form of

$$dU = dQ + dW \tag{2.1}$$

where the d indicates change of

U: inner energy
Q: heat
W: work.

Clausius recognized that heat is a form of energy. Studying the working of steam engines, Carnot (1824) recognized that heat cannot be completely transformed into work. Each heat engine process requires two heat reservoirs from or to which heat is transported. Under idealized, that is, reversible, conditions the ratio

$$dQ_1/T_1 \qquad (2.2)$$

must equal the ratio

$$dQ_2/T_2 \qquad (2.3)$$

where we have defined dQ previously and T is the absolute temperature.

The larger the difference between (2.3) and (2.2) the less useful work can be gained. That is, the change of the quantity

$$dQ/T \qquad (2.4)$$

is a measure for the quality of a process.

Clausius introduced the concept of entropy

$$S = dQ/T. \qquad (2.5)$$

By its use, the relation (2.1) can be cast into the form

$$dW = dU - TS. \qquad (2.6)$$

The second law of thermodynamics can be formulated as: in a closed system, energy transformations never occur from a state of low quality to one of high quality: entropy always increases.

Hermann Ludwig Ferdinand Helmholtz (1882) reinterpreted the second law by his concept of the free energy (F) (that is, useful energy)

$$F = U - TS. \qquad (2.7)$$

This relation entails that the free energy (in an isolated system) is always smaller than the inner energy.

According to the second law, a closed system acquires an equilibrium state that has – its inner energy given – the highest entropy. The first and second laws (jointly with the third law, which states that entropy is zero at $T = 0$) form the basis of thermodynamics, which is extremely general in that it applies to all forms of matter, with all its states of aggregation and all kinds of energy.

Is it the C-theory we are looking for?

At any rate, thermodynamics is a phenomenological macroscopic theory, because matter is composed of parts, for example, atoms. So, the challenge to physicists has been to interpret concepts and relations of thermodynamics in terms of the physical properties

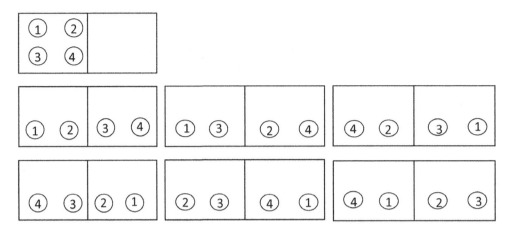

Note: There is only one possibility to put four balls (atoms) in one of two boxes, but there are six realizations to distribute them evenly over the two boxes. This example shows how to calculate *W* in Boltzmann's formula.

Figure 2.2   Visualization of Boltzmann's law

of the parts, especially of atoms and molecules. Here, the central question is, how is entropy *S* related to microscopic states of matter?

By consideration based on combinatorics (compare Figure 2.2) and probability theory, Ludwig Boltzmann (1877) arrived at the conclusion that the transition from an initial state that is out of equilibrium (think of the contact hot/cold body) to the final state of thermal equilibrium (both bodies have the same temperature) means a transition from an improbable state to the most probable one. When Boltzmann applied this reasoning to the second law, he could relate that quantity, which in thermodynamics is denoted 'entropy', to a 'thermodynamic probability *W*'.

Max Planck (1858–1947) cast Boltzmann's result into the formula

$$S = k \ln W \tag{2.8}$$

where k is Boltzmann's constant and W the number of microscopic realizations (Planck 1920) (compare Figure 2.2).

By his work, Boltzmann founded statistical mechanics jointly with Clerk Maxwell (1860) (Maxwell's distribution, gas theory) and Josiah Willard Gibbs (Langley and van Name 1928 [1957]) (Gibbs's potential and so on). In this field, the notion of probability is crucial.

One important problem remained: according to the law of mechanics, all its processes are reversible, whereas those of thermodynamics are irreversible. I shall not dwell on the numerous attempts to solve this deep puzzle. Instead we proceed pragmatically: systems out of thermal equilibrium relax at specific speeds to equilibrium.

5.   COLLECTIVE PHENOMENA IN PHYSICS

Matter appears in different states (phases) of aggregation: solid (ice), fluid (water), gas (water vapor) and plasma (ionized gases). Although, for example, in water the constituents, H_2O molecules, remain the same, both the macroscopic properties (for example, mechanical) and the microscopic configurations of these phases are different: strictly ordered crystals, molecules moving but remaining close to each other, and molecules freely flying and colliding with each other. Transitions between phases occur at specific temperature T_c, for example, melting of ice or evaporation of water (under otherwise constant conditions).

Dramatic qualitative changes of macroscopic properties are observed in ferromagnetism (compare Figure 2.3): vanishing of magnetization or in superconductivity (vanishing of electrical resistivity).

The study of ferromagnetism, more precisely of its Ising model (Ising 1935), has become central to the theory of phase transitions (PTs). It culminated in Kenneth Wilson's (1983) 'renormalization group' theory.

The Ising model represents a ferromagnet as periodically arranged elementary magnets (denoted as 'spins') each of which can point only up or down. When two neighboring spins point in the same direction, their total energy is lowered. Thus, the energetically lowest state is reached when all spins point in the same direction, which is occurs at absolute zero of temperature.

When temperature is increased, thermal agitation leads to spin-flips so that the magnetization decreases, until a critical temperature T_c (Curie-temperature; Pierre Curie 1859–1906) is reached, where M vanishes (Figure 2.3). The approach from $M > 0$ to $M = 0$ close to $T = T_c$ is described by a scaling law

$$M = M_{max} (T_c - T)^\beta \tag{2.9}$$

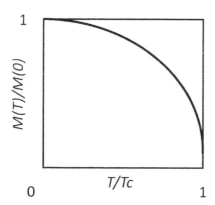

Source: After Kittel (1956).

Figure 2.3   *Plot (graph) of M(T)/M(0) versus T/T$_c$: the vanishing of magnetization M with increasing temperature (in normalizes units)*

with the critical exponent, β. The calculation of *β* had become a central problem. An intermediate result was obtained by Landau's (1908–1968) theory of PTs (compare Landau and Lifshitz 1980). He coined the concept of order parameter (OP) and derived a formula for the probability distribution of an OP based on thermodynamics/statistical physics by expressing the free energy by powers of the OP. The thus predicted value of β disagreed, however, with the experimentally measured β.

Following work by Kadanoff (1937–2015) (1966) and others, Wilson (1983) developed his theory yielding the correct value of β. His work is highly technical, however.

6.   CHAOS THEORY

To reveal the roots of chaos theory, we consider a simple experiment (Figure 2.4). We let a small steel ball fall on a vertical razor blade. The direction of the evolving trajectories sensitively depends on the initial position of the ball in relation to the blade's edge. Thus, this effect is named sensitivity against initial conditions. It entails that the future trajectories cannot be predicted if there is a limit on the realizable precision of the initial conditions, maybe in the real world, or in computing on a digital computer with unavoidable rounding.

This effect was found by E.N. Lorenz (1963) when he treated a model of atmospheric/fluid dynamics, based on three variables. He coined the term 'butterfly effect' (the beat of the wing of a butterfly in Brazil may let arise a tornado in Texas). His discovery was in contrast to Laplace's view on the predictability of the motion of bodies, and aroused considerable attention both in science and in the public.

The trajectories Lorenz studied were, however, not those of a steel ball as in our simple visualization, but belonged to an abstract three-dimensioned phase space. Since the trajectories stay in a limited region, that is, they seem to be attracted to some center, the resulting structure is named 'chaotic attractor' or 'Lorenz attractor' (Figure 2.5, left).

To visualize its structure more closely, think of a ball of wool through which, coming from various directions, a very fine thread is pulled through, time and again. This simple analogy may insinuate that chaotic attractors are intimately related to fractal geometry (discussed previously).

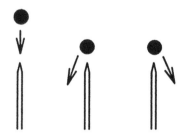

Note: Note the different directions of the evolving trajectories.

Figure 2.4   Steel ball hitting a razor blade

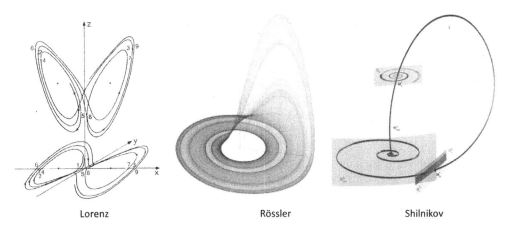

Figure 2.5   *Chaotic attractors: left-hand side – trajectories of the Lorenz attractor,*
projected on the y–x plane (below) and z–x plane (above); middle – Rössler
attractor in three-dimensional phase space; and right-hand side – typical
trajectory of a Shilnikov attractor

The birth of chaos theory is attributed to Henri Poincaré, who won a prize for his approach to solve the problem of the stability of the solar system (Chambers 1997). His approach could be realized by means of computers in the middle of the twentieth century.

In addition to the Lorenz attractor, other types of chaotic attractors have been found, such as the Rössler and Shilnikov attractors (Figure 2.5) (Rössler 1976; Shilnikov 1965). All mathematical approaches are based on nonlinear differential or difference equations (discrete mathematics).

The solutions to these equations critically depend on parameter values, such as the amount of energy input. Various routes to chaos have been discovered, theoretically and/or experimentally. In sophisticated experiments (a small cell filled with a fluid that is heated from below and cooled from above) the route found is as follows: steady-state pattern in the form of a roll, oscillation at one frequency, oscillations at two frequencies, chaos. Other routes are by intermittency and period doubling of oscillations.

7.   THE PUZZLE OF LIFE: SCHRÖDINGER'S IDEA AND PRIGOGINE'S DISSIPATIVE STRUCTURES

Thermodynamics, statistical mechanics and, more generally, statistical physics, provide us with a very general approach to deal with fundamental problems of physics and chemistry, both at the macroscopic phenomenological level (heat and entropy) and the microscopic level (order/disorder).

However, there remained a big puzzle: according to the second law of thermodynamics, in a closed system entropy cannot decrease or, in Boltzmann's atomic view, disorder cannot decrease. That is, order cannot spontaneously be formed. However, the animal world abounds with highly ordered structures that come into existence without external manipulation, that is, without a sculptor.

In his frequently quoted book of 1944, Erwin Schrödinger, one of the fathers of quantum mechanics, suggested that life processes are possible owing to an import of negative entropy (for example, by means of food). A decrease of entropy means an increase of order, for example, a formation of structures. Lowering entropy just amounts to cooling down – surely a deadly process. Juval Portugali found a note by Schrödinger (1944) that he had meant free energy instead of negative entropy, but that for reasons of broader understandability, he used the term 'negative entropy'. However, it seems Schrödinger's insight remained largely unnoticed by the majority of the science community.

In his fundamental and comprehensive work, Ilya Prigogine recognized the important role of energy dissipation in the formation of structures by selforganization in nonequilibrium systems. Hence, his concept of dissipated structures (Prigogine 1945, 1977). As a prototypical example he invoked the Bénard instability (Bénard 1900). Here a thin layer of oil in a pan is heated from below and cooled from above. Beyond a critical temperature difference between the two surfaces, spontaneously a hexagonal pattern of fluid cells emerges (Figure 2.6).

Prigogine also drew attention to the fundamental work by Belousov and Zhabotinsky on specific chemical reactions that showed oscillations (for example, an alternating change of colors red/blue) and spatial patterns.

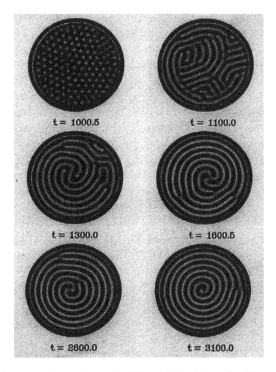

Note: Upper left-hand corner: pattern observed by Bénard. When the walls of the pan are also heated, a spiral pattern evolves (Bestehorn et al. 1993).

Figure 2.6   Pattern formation in a fluid heated from below

Belousov's early work (1959) was difficult to get published in chemical journals because, according to their editors or referees, his results contradicted the second law of thermodynamics, whereas papers that were submitted by Zhabotinsky to biochemical journals were accepted – the responsible scientists were familiar with these phenomena in organisms (Niclas Manz, personal communication 2020). At that time, an understanding of further essential mechanism(s) underlying structure formation was lacking. This changed when Alan Turing (also father of the Turing machine) proposed a model (Turing 1952) in which he considered two diffusion-coupled cells, each initially occupied by the same type of two molecules, where roughly, one type could multiply at the expense of the other.

Turing showed that if initially there is a surplus of the growing type of molecules in one of the cells, eventually it will be present only in that cell. This phenomenon has been termed 'symmetry breaking' and plays a fundamental role in pattern formation in chemical and biological systems (for example, stripes on zebras). There is an aspect that is generally ignored, but quite fundamental: where does the initial surplus comes from? We return to this question later.

Turing's reaction-diffusion model was considerably generalized by Prigogine and Nicolis (1967) and by Prigogine and Lefever (1968; compare also Lefever 1968), who formulated the Brusselator model: reaction diffusion equations with a specific chemical reaction scheme. The solutions of the equations could exhibit oscillations and spatial patterns. Subsequently, a number of authors formulated similar equations, for example, to explain pattern formation on furs, sea-slugs, segmentation of insects, and so on, or more generally, morphogenesis.

For me, the Prigogine, Nicolis and Lefever papers mark the turning point of the research by Prigogine and his school away from thermodynamics, to kinetic equations (compare Prigogine and Nicolis 1967). Thermodynamics rests on the precondition of (at least local) thermal equilibrium that implies that energy is equally distributed over all degrees of freedom. By contrast, in nonequilibrium systems that form ordered structures (such as the Bénard cells), only one or few degrees are highly excited (my personal comment). This view is strongly supported by the laser paradigm where one light wave is strongly enhanced.

8.   THE LASER PARADIGM

The light-source laser is a technical device. Nevertheless, its study has provided us with deep insights into the mechanism of the spontaneous formation of ordered structures in complex systems. Technical devices can be of great help in unearthing general principles, for example, of physics. A famous example is thermodynamics that has its roots in the study of the efficiency of steam engines.

The word 'laser' is an acronym for light emission by stimulated emission of radiation. The process of stimulated emission was introduced by Einstein (1917), when he derived Planck's (1900) famous law of black body radiation. The laser was proposed by Schawlow and Townes (1958) and Basov and Prochorov (1954, 1955) as an extension of the MASER (microwave amplification by stimulated emission of radiation) device into the optical region. This extension presented a highly demanding task both concerning the physical/technical realization and an appropriate theory. Although the laser is an open quantum system, here we leave aside the quantum aspects, as far as possible.

A typical example of a laser device is a glass tube filled with gas atoms that are excited by an electrical current sent through the tube. After each excitation, an atom emits a light-wave. When this wave hits another excited atom, the wave stimulates it to re-enforce this specific wave. Two mirrors at the tube's end-faces reflect the wave a number of times (until it escapes through a mirror that is semi-transparent) so that the stimulation process can be repeated, giving rise to a light avalanche. However, there is a problem; namely, the emitted waves may oscillate at different frequencies. However, the intended task of the laser is the emission of only one single frequency wave of high intensity.

As was shown by Haken and Sauermann (1963) as well as by Tang et al. (1963), under specific conditions (ring laser) the winner-takes-it-all principle can be realized. The various waves compete for the use of the energy resource of the excited atoms. The wave that converts this energy fastest, wins the competition (the approaches were based on nonlinear rate equations for photon numbers that, according to quantum theory, represent the strength of the light-waves). The approaches showed a serious deficiency, however: below laser threshold there should be no light generation at all – in contrast to what happens, naturally, in all light sources. This was owing to the spontaneous emission of light-waves/photons – a quantum mechanical and thus chance effect – being ignored.

Haken (1964) closed this gap by deriving a laser equation that included a fluctuating force and a nonlinearity. By solving it below and above threshold, he showed that the statistical properties of light below and above threshold differ dramatically. Risken (1965) converted Haken's equation into a Fokker–Planck equation for the wave amplitude (or equivalently, photon number). This allowed him to calculate the time independent and dependent photon statistics including the threshold region. Subsequently, Lax (1966), Hempstead and Lax (1967), and Scully and Lamb (1966) achieved equivalent results.

The laser is a highly complex dynamical system: It is composed of many parts, for example, 10^{16} atoms/molecules or more, that produce and interact with many types of light-waves in a nonlinear manner. The laser is coupled to external energy sources and sinks, and thus an open system that is subject to random fluctuations. The formulation of its equations drew on results in many fields. For an early survey, compare Haken (1970).

The complex equations could be stepwise reduced to a single equation (Haken 1964), where the method of adiabatic approximation was essential. The used method is related to the Born–Oppenheimer approximation used in molecular physics (Born and Oppenheimer 1927), where the fast-moving electrons almost instantaneously follow the slow motion of the nuclei. The whole procedure is, among other aspects (compare next section), an example of complexity reduction.

9.   SYNERGETICS: MOTIVATION

The early stages of synergetics are described by Bernd Kröger in his 2013 book. Since I originated this interdisciplinary field of research, some personal remarks on the motivation underlying the general concept may be of interest. At the end of the 1960s, there was a coincidence of favorable circumstances that I just list up. In theoretical physics, there was a great interest to develop a theory of PTs (in thermal equilibrium). My student Robert Graham and I (Graham and Haken 1968, 1970) showed that the transition from disordered to ordered laser light showed the features of a (conventional) PT as described by the Landau theory of PTs (see section 5 in this chapter). In this context, we identified the winning laser wave as 'order parameter', *sensu* Landau, and the fluctuations close to laser threshold as 'critical fluctuations' (Landau and Lifshitz 1980).

Herbert Fröhlich invited me to conferences (1967, 1969 and more) at Versailles that upon his proposal ran under the title 'From theoretical physics to biology', which led me to the question: 'What can our laser theory contribute to the understanding of biological processes?'

An eminent problem is 'selforganization' (see section 7 on Schrödinger). The laser case showed in great detail that selforganization also occurs in the inanimate world and how it functions. The last impetus to formulate the basic question of S – 'Are there general principles underlying selforganization irrespective of the individual parts of a system?' – stems from fields other than physics: that is, (1) molecular biology and (2) sociology.

1. Manfred Eigen published a theory on the evolution of biomolecules that showed Darwin's selection principle 'survival of the fittest' (Eigen 1971). As I observed, Eigen's equations and that of Haken and Sauermann (1963) were identical. This was a strong hint for me that there must be general principles of selforganization.
2. Wolfgang Weidlich translated the Ising model of ferromagnetism (see above) into a model of the formation of public opinion (Weidlich 1971). In analogy of the two spin directions up or down, he considered only two different opinions. At this moment a typical difficulty appears when we try to formalize problems of sociology; in our example, how to denote the different opinions? Up/down, red/green, left/right? Note the problem of connotation. However, leaving this problem aside, Weidlich's model showed, depending on some social temperature that there are two states: demo-cratic, where opinions can freely flip, and dictatorship, which forces citizens' opinion into that of the majority (Rousseau's 'dictatorship of the majority'; see Noelle-Neumann 1980 [2001]). Weidlich developed his theory further to a comprehensive 'socio-dynamics' where he used master equations as a mathematical tool (Weidlich 2002).

Let us summarize. The examples laser, biomolecules and social opinions were a strong argument for me that

1. There are general principles for selforganization.
2. They become particularly visible when we study their PTs.

Therefore, it suggests itself to search for further examples and underlying principles, so that we can draw analogies between different systems, which may be composed of dif-ferent parts.

Ludwig von Bertalanffy, in his 1969 book *General System Theory*, had formulated the same question, but sought the answer on the level of atoms and molecules.

My answer is that these analogies appear on the level of OPs. So, the goal of S is to develop methods by which we can identify OPs and derive their equation. I formulated the term S and this goal in lectures in 1969 that I gave jointly with Robert Graham at the University of Stuttgart.

10.   SYNERGETICS I: MICROSCOPIC APPROACH

This approach (Haken 1977 [1983]) starts from differential equations (evolution equations) for the temporal evolution of parts, components and individuals that interact with each other, and are subject to fixed external conditions (quantified by control parameters) and to internal or external chance events represented by fluctuating forces. The properties of the parts or densities of whole ensembles (for example, molecules in a fluid) are quantified by variables $q_j(t)$. The equations may be derived from first principles where the interaction of the system with its environment is taken into account (leading to damping and fluctuations), or they may be formulated phenomenologically, for example, as in population dynamics including agent-based models in urbanism.

The general approach starts from a structureless state (fluctuations neglected) that is realized for a specific control parameter. When this parameter is increased, that state may become unstable and one (or several) configuration(s) of the parts grow. Their amplitudes are (essentially) the OPs that interact in a nonlinear fashion limiting the further growth of the OPs. In a first version (Haken 1977), the nongrowing configurations (enslaved parts) are eliminated by means of adiabatic approximation based on time-scale separation: the enslaved parts quickly adapt to the slowly varying OPs.

In the 1983 version, based on work by Wunderlin and Haken (1981), the fast variables can be eliminated by an explicit iteration procedure to any desired degree of accuracy, taking fluctuations into account. A special case is known in mathematics as central manifold theorem, of which originally there was only a proof of existence. The Wunderlin–Haken version, the slaving principle, lies at the heart of C-reduction. The resulting OP equations can be discussed or solved by use of methods of dynamic systems theory (compare, for example, Guckenheimer and Holmes 2013) if fluctuations can be neglected. Otherwise, the evolution equations can be interpreted as generalized Langevin equations in which the time-evolution of the variables q_j is determined by a sum of a deterministic force and a stochastic force. This type of equation can be converted into a Fokker–Planck equation for the time-dependent probability distribution.

For the sake of completeness, we also mention that a third type of equations, the master equation, is discussed (compare in particular by Weidlich 2002).

11.   SYNERGETICS II: 2ND FOUNDATION

This approach (Haken 1988) starts from Jaynes's maximum entropy principle (Jaynes 1957a, 1957b). For reasons I explain below, I call it the maximum information entropy

Figure 2.7   Examples of the configurations of three spins

principle (MIEP). To visualize what Jaynes's method means, let us consider the Ising model (see section 5). In the spirit of Boltzmann's probability interpretation, we assign a probability $P(q)$ to each individual spin configuration (compare Figure 2.7). We can enumerate the configurations by $= 1, 2, \ldots$.

We may show that Boltzmann's entropy

$$S = k \ln W \tag{2.10}$$

(k: Boltzmann's constant) can be cast into the form

$$S = -k \sum_q p(q) \ln p(q) \tag{2.11}$$

which is, apart from the factor k and a numerical factor that transforms the natural logarithm ln into log_2, identical with Shannon information

$$S = -\sum_q p(q) \log_2 p(q). \tag{2.12}$$

Jaynes's MIEP requires the maximization of (2.12) under the constraint of a fixed mean energy $\langle E \rangle$ which can be expressed by

$$\langle E \rangle = \sum_q p(q) \, H(q) \tag{2.13}$$

where H is the microscopic expression of the energy of a specific spin configuration. The problem of maximizing S under the constraints (2.13) can be solved by Lagrange multipliers and yields

$$p(q) = \exp(\Lambda_0 - \Lambda_1 E(q)) \tag{2.14}$$

which is just the Maxwell–Boltzmann distribution, where $\Lambda_1 = 1/(kT)$ and T absolute temperature. By inserting (2.13) in (2.12) and rearranging terms, we find a fundamental relation of thermodynamics:

$$\text{free energy } F = \text{mean energy } \langle E \rangle - TS. \tag{2.15}$$

Also, the other fundamental relations of thermodynamics can be derived in a very elegant way. The fundamental question was, can we apply MIEP to nonequilibrium processes, in particular nonequilibrium PTs? Guided by our laser paradigm we found, that we needed entirely different constraints, namely moments/correlation functions of measurable macroscopic quantities/variables up to fourth order. Thus, the simplest example of a probability distribution reads

$$p(q) = \exp(\Lambda_0 + \Lambda_1 q^2 - \Lambda_2 q^4) \tag{2.16}$$

which is just the laser probability distribution. More complicated cases were treated in the context of pattern recognition (Haken and Portugali 2016).

In Haken (1988), MIEP was applied to time-dependent processes. Under the assumption of a Markov process (where a state q at a time t depends only on q at the last preceding time-step) and time-dependent correlations as constraints, a master equation can be derived that, in the limit of time-intervals $dt \rightarrow 0$, becomes a Fokker–Planck equation for the time-evolution of a probability distribution.

To summarize, both in the time-independent and the time-dependent examples, the approach by synergetics' second foundation allows us to deal with complex systems in two ways:

1. Based on sparse data, we may either make guesses on probability distributions or on their evolution equations.
2. With big data, we may compress the inherent information to comparatively simple probability distributions or their evolution equations.

Both goals are aimed at by Friston's free energy principle, see next section.

12.   FREE ENERGY PRINCIPLES

The impetus to develop the free energy principle stems from statistical physics. To see this, we recall Jaynes's approach to thermodynamics/statistical physics. When we insert (2.14) into the normalization condition

$$\Sigma_q\, p(q) = 1 \tag{2.17}$$

and rearrange terms, we arrive at

$$\exp(-\Lambda_0) = \Sigma_q \exp(-E(q)/kT). \tag{2.18}$$

The right-hand side, termed partition function, Z, plays a fundamental role because all mean values, for example, energy, can be calculated by it. However, the calculation of Z is extremely difficult. Based on (2.18), we can show that Λ_0 is just the free energy (up to a factor of $1/kT$).

Richard Feynman (1972) suggested approximating F by a calculable function F_a with free variational parameters where

$$F \leq F_a. \tag{2.19}$$

The details are of no relevance in this context because here we are dealing with open nonequilibrium systems. We may interpret

$$\exp(-\Lambda_0) = \exp(-F/kT) \tag{2.20}$$

as a probability distribution whose exponent F is approximated by a suitable free energy function so that experimentally measured values are optimally approximated. This leads us to Friston's free energy principle (Friston 2010). Note that in this case, F no longer has the meaning of an energy but refers to different quantities.

Friston's approach can best be explained by his prototypical example from neuroscience. A sensory neuron S (with activation strength S) receives signals of strength φ from an external source and is bidirectionally (with strength β) coupled to an action neuron q (with activation strength q). Friston assumes steady state conditions to determine the probability distribution p of s and q under the impact of φ by stepwise measurements of s and q. Writing p in the form $p = \exp(-F)$, the task is to determine the 'free energy F'. Based on a fundamental inequality (Kullback–Leibler divergence; compare Kullback 1951), Friston derives an expression for the approximate F_a so that the exact value of $F < F_a$.

For sake of completeness I mention that Friston's approach implies the method of Bayesian inference; this in an iteration procedure where based on past experience a prediction is made on a further measurement of s and q, compared with the result of the next measurement, and the measurement error is increasingly minimized.

A comparison between Friston's approach and Haken's approach, shows that Friston's approach allows us to follow up the improvement of F_a step by step, whereas Haken's approach assumes that sufficient measurements are already performed (Haken and Portugali 2021).

13. GAME THEORY

When discussing complexity theories, we have to consider game theory (GT), which has become a wide field of research with many ties to other disciplines, such as sociology, economy, politics, behavioral sciences and biology.

Game theory is a mathematical theory that deals with agents that make rational decisions to maximize their benefits either as an individual or as a group. The modern form of GT is due to John von Neumann (1928). Game theory was further developed by von Neumann and Oskar Morgenstern (1944).

During the 1950s, GT boomed, and its impact on economy is witnessed by a number of Nobel prizes. Later, John Maynard Smith applied GT to biology in his fundamental paper (Maynard Smith 1974). In 1980 Robert Axelrod developed computer programs to check different strategies. He found that, in many instances, tit for tat is the best strategy. See also Axelrod (1997).

In conclusion, a hint at two widely recognized topics:

- the prisoner's dilemma as formulated by Merrill Flood and Melvin Dresher in 1950 (cited, for example, by Axelrod 1980 and De Dardt 2003), and

● the concept of the Nash equilibrium where players find the mutually best answers (Nash 1950).

An important aspect of game theory is that it takes into account chance events, whether they are in human encounter by taking initiatives, or in biology/evolution, mutations. This makes game theory attractive to the theory of evolution. In contrast to dynamic systems theory (including bifurcation theory), game theory is a strongly probabilistic theory largely based on the master equation that relies on the Markov assumption.

In general, GT deals with the behavior of two partners, players or species, though occasionally, as stressed by Portugali in the context of city dynamics (Portugali, private communication) three players must be taken into account. (Compare Chapter 18 in this volume.)

In more recent years, the GT assumption of rational behavior has been questioned. An eminent example is the work by Tversky and Kahneman (1974, 1981).

14.   A BROADER VIEW

Since this chapter is a contribution to a handbook on cities, or urbanism, the question arises of how far a history of the emergence of complexity theories may contribute to the development of urbanism. First, the significance of complexity theories for urbanism has been clearly recognized in the comprehensive work by Juval Portugali, who presented important examples of their application to the city as a complex system (Portugali 2011).

My chapter (over-)emphasizes the role of mathematics. Indeed, mathematics covers only some part (or no part at all) of a fundamental theory. In my view, such a theory should provide us with an essential contribution to our world view, giving us deeper insights into and/or a broader view on relations. In each epoch, scientists work under specific collective beliefs, often even prejudices. In Thomas Kuhn's 1962 book, they are termed paradigms. Kuhn shows how they work and how the wrong paradigms are overcome by increasing numbers of counter-examples. In contradiction to the belief that all forms of matter, dead or alive, must have been created (by an agent, similar to a sculptor) is the concept of selforganization. It can be traced back to the antique (compare Paslack 1991), was discussed by philosophers such as Kant and Schelling, and reappeared as a serious scientific question, I believe, following Schrödinger's famous book in 1944.

A typical example is the international Symposium on Self-Organizing Systems in 1959 in Chicago. While it seemed clear that the interaction of the system per se and its environment are essential, the genuine mechanism remained obscure. It was eventually clarified by the laser paradigm that also showed how the emergence of new qualities could be quantified.

However, I stress how important it was that a ground for the new insights had been prepared by previous discussions and suggestions. In this respect, Murray Gell-Mann's (1994) notion of adaptive complex systems is important because it indicates the role of learning in the animate world.

An aspect mostly left aside by complexity theories is the way in which we learn to deal with complex systems. One way is to generalize; another is to draw analogies. In that respect, I highly appreciate the comprehensive work by Douglas Hofstadter (1985,

1996). There is a third way, namely, to perform computer experiments (the concept of modern computers can be traced back to Babbage (1832 [2010]), Turing (1937, 1952), von Neumann (1928) and Zuse. In 1941, Zuse developed the Z3, the first functioning computer. While computers allow us to process big data, the fundamental question remains: how are we to interpret the numerical results in relation to concepts, new or old?

ACKNOWLEDGEMENT

I thank Professor Juval Portugali for a highly fruitful collaboration over four decades and his help to prepare my above contribution.

REFERENCES

Axelrod, R. (1980), 'Effective choice in the prisoner's dilemma', *Journal of Conflict Resolution*, **24** (1), 3–25.
Axelrod, R. (1997), *The Complexity of Cooperation*, Princeton, NJ: Princeton University Press.
Babbage, C. (1832), 'Difference engine', in C. Babbage, *On the Economy of Machinery and Manufactures*, repr. 2010, Cambridge: Cambridge University Press.
Basov, N.G. and A.M. Prochorov (1954), 'Application of molecular beams for radiospectroscopic study of molecular rotational spectra', *Journal of Experimental and Theoretical Physics*, **27** (4), 431–8.
Basov, N.G. and A.M. Prochorov (1955), 'On the possible methods for obtaining active molecules for a molecular generator', *Journal of Experimental and Theoretical Physics*, **28** (2), 249–50.
Belousov, B. (1959), 'Periodicheski deistvuyushchaya reaktsia i ee mekhanism' ('Periodically acting reaction and its mechanism'), *Sbornik referatov po radiotsionnoi meditsine, 1958 (Collection of Abstracts on Radiation Medicine, 1958)*, Moscow: Medgiz, pp. 145–7.
Bénard, H. (1900), 'Les tourbillons cellulaires dans une nappe liquid', *Révue Générale des Sciences Pures et appliquées*, **11**, 1261–71 and 1309–28.
Bestehorn, M., M. Fantz, R. Friedrich and H. Haken (1993), 'Hexagonal and spiral patterns in thermal convection', *Physics Letters A*, **174** (March), 48–52.
Boltzmann, L. (1877), 'Über die Beziehung zwischen dem Zweiten Hauptsatze der mechanischen Wärmetheorie und der Wahrscheinlichkeitsrechnung resp. den Sätzen über das Wärmegleichgewicht, Sitzungsber', *Denkschriften der Kaiserlichen Akademie der Wissenschaften/Mathematisch-Naturwissenschaftliche Classe*, **76**, 373–435.
Born, M. and R. Oppenheimer (1927), 'Zur Quantentheorie der Molekeln', *Annalen der Physik*, **389** (20), 457–84.
Carnot, S. (1824), *Réflexions sur la puissance motrice du feu*, Paris: Bachelier.
Chaitin, G.J. (1969), 'On the simplicity and speed of programs for computing infinite sets of natural numbers', *Journal of the ACM*, **16** (3), 407–22.
Chambers, L.G. (1997), 'Review of *Poincaré and the Three-Body Problem*', *Mathematical Reviews*, MR 1415387.
Clausius, R. (1850), 'Ueber die bewegende Kraft der Wärme und die Gesetze, welche sich daraus für die Wärmelehre selbst ableiten lassen', *Poggendorffs Annalen*, **79**, 368–79, 500–524.
Clausius, R. (1865), 'Ueber verschiedene für die Anwendung bequeme Formen der Hauptgleichungen der mechanischen Wärmetheorie', *Annalen der Physik*, **201** (7), 353–400.
Dauben, J.W. (1979), *Georg Cantor: His Mathematics and Philosophy*, Princeton, NJ: Princeton University Press.
De Dardt, T. (2003), 'Cooperation and fairness: the Flood–Dresher experiment revisited', *Review of Social Economy*, **61** (2), 183–210.
Eigen, M. (1971), 'Selforganization of matter and the evolution of biological macro-molecules', *Naturwissenschaften*, **58** (October), 465–523.
Einstein, A. (1917), 'On the quantum theory of radiation', *Physikalische Zeitschrift*, **18** (121), 167–83.
Feynman, R.A. (1972), *Statistical Mechanics*, Reading, MA: W.A. Benjamin.
Friston, K. (2010), 'The free-energy principle: a unified brain theory?', *National Review of Neuroscience*, **11** (January), 127–38.

Gell-Mann, M. (1994), *The Quark and the Jaguar: Adventures in the Simple and the Complex*, New York: Freeman.

Gershenson, C. (2008), *Complexity: 5 Questions*, Copenhagen: Automatic Press/VIP.

Gödel, K.F. (1931), 'Über formal unentscheidbare Sätze der Principia Mathematica und verwandter Systeme I', *Monatshefte für Mathematik und Physik*, **38** (December), 173–98.

Graham, R. and H. Haken (1968), 'Quantum theory of light propagation in a fluctuating laser-active medium', *Zeitschrift für Physik*, **213** (October), 420–50.

Graham, R. and H. Haken (1970), 'Laserlight – first example of a second-order transition far away from thermal equilibrium', *Zeitschrift für Physik*, **273**, 31–46.

Guckenheimer, J. and P. Holms (2013), *Nonlinear Oscillations, Dynamical Systems and Bifurcations of Vector Fields*, Berlin, Heidelberg, New York and Tokyo: Springer Science & Business Media.

Haken, H. (1964), 'A nonlinear theory of laser light and coherence', *Zeitschrift Physik*, **181** (February), 96.

Haken, H. (1970), 'Laser theory', in S. Flugge (ed.), *Encyclopedia of Physics*, vol. 25/c, Berlin, Heidelberg and New York: Springer.

Haken, H. (1977), *Synergetics: An Introduction*, 1983 3rd edn, Berlin, Heidelberg and New York: Springer.

Haken, H. (1988), *Information and Self-Organization: A Macroscopic Approach to Complex Systems*, Berlin, Heidelberg and New York: Springer.

Haken, H. and J. Portugali (2021), *Synergetic Cities: Information, Steady State and Phase Transition: Implications to Urban Scaling, Smart Cities and Planning*, Berlin, Heidelberg and New York: Springer Nature.

Haken, H. and H. Sauermann (1963), 'Nonlinear intersection of laser models', *Zeitschrift für Physik A Hadrons and nuclei*, **173** (June), 261–75.

Helmholtz, H. von (1882), *Physical Memoirs, Selected and Translated from Foreign Sources. Parts 1–2*, London: Physical Society (GB).

Hempstead, R.D. and M. Lax (1967), 'Classical noise. VI. Noise in self-sustained oscillators near threshold', *Physical Review*, **161** (September), 350–66.

Hofstadter, D. (1985), *Analogies and Roles in Human and Machine Thinking*, New York: Bantham Books.

Hofstadter, D. (1996), *Fluid Concept and Creative Analogies: Computer Models of the Fundamental Mechanisms of Thought*, New York: Basic Books.

Hooke, R. (1678), *De Potentia Restitutiva, or of Spring. Explaining the Power of Springing Bodies*, London: John Martyn, Printer to the Royal Society.

Ising, E. (1925), 'Beitrag zur Theorie des Ferromagnetism', *Zeitschrift für Physik*, **31** (February), 253–8.

Jaynes, E.T. (1957a), 'Information theory and statistical mechanics', *Physical Review*, **106** (4), 620–30.

Jaynes, E.T. (1957b), 'Information theory and statistical mechanics, II', *Physical Review*, **108** (May), 171–90.

Kadanoff, L. (1966), 'Scaling laws for Ising model near Tc', *Physics Physique Fizika*, **2** (June), 263–72.

Kittel, C. (1956), *Introduction to Solid State Physics*, New York: Wiley.

Kolmogorov, A. (1963), 'On tables of random numbers', *Sankhyā*, ser. A, **25**, 369–75.

Kröger B., (2013), *Hermann Haken und die Anfangsjahre der Synergetik*, Berlin: Logos Verlag.

Kuhn, T.S. (1962), *The Structure of Scientific Revolutions*, Chicago, IL: University of Chicago Press.

Kullback, S. (1951), *Information Theory and Statistics*, New York: Wiley.

Landau, D. and E.M. Lifshitz (1980), *Statistical Physics*, 3rd edn, Oxford: Pergamon Press.

Lax, M. (1966), 'Quantum noise. IV. Quantum theory of noise sources', *Physical Review*, **145** (May), 110–29.

Lefever, R. (1968), 'Dissipative structures in chemical systems', *Journal of Chemical Physics*, **49** (11), 4972–8.

Longley, W.R. and R.G. van Name (eds) (1928), *The Collected Works of J.W. Gibbs*, repr. 1957, New Haven, CT: Yale University Press.

Lorenz, E.N. (1963), 'Deterministic nonperiodic flow', *Journal of the Atmospheric Sciences*, **20** (2), 130–41.

Mandelbrot, B.B. (1983), *The Fractal Geometry of Nature*, New York: W.H. Freeman.

Maxwell, J.C. (1860), 'Illustrations of the dynamical theory of gases', *Phylosophical Magazine*, **19**, 19–32, **20**, 21–37.

Maynard Smith, J. (1974), 'The theory of games and the evolution of animal conflicts', *Journal of Theoretical Biology*, **47** (1), 209–21.

Meyer, J.R. (1842), 'Bemerkungen über die Kräfte der unbelebten Natur', *Annalen der Chemie und Pharmacie*, **42** (2), 233–40.

Nash, J.F. (1950), 'Non-cooperative games', PhD thesis, Princeton University, Princeton, NJ.

Newton, I. (1687), *Philosophiae Naturalis Principie Mathematica*, 3rd edn, 1725/6, London: G. and J. Innys, Regiae Societatis typographos.

Noelle-Neumann, E. (1980/2001), *Die Schweigespirale. Öffentliche Meinung – unsere soziale Haut*, Zürich and Munich: Piper.

Paslack, R. (1991), *Urgeschichte der Selbstorganisation*, Heidelberg: Springer Vieweg.

Planck, M. (1900), 'Zur Theorie des Gesetzes der Energieverteilung im Normalspectrum', *Verhandlungen der Deutschen Physikal Gesellschaft*, **2**, 237–45.

Planck, M. (1920), 'The genesis and present state of development of the quantum theory', Nobel Lecture, 2 June, accessed 24 May 2021 at https://www.nobelprize.org/prizes/physics/1918/planck/lecture/.

Portugali, J. (2011), *Complexity, Cognition and the City*, Berlin, Heidelberg and New York: Springer.

Prigogine, I. (1945), 'Modération et transformation irréversible des systèmes ouverts', *Bulletin de la Classe des sciences, Académie royale de Belgique*, **31**, 600–606.

Prigogine, I. (1977), 'Time, structure and fluctuations', Nobel lecture, Oslo, 8 December.

Prigogine, I. and R. Lefever (1968), 'Symmetry breaking instabilities in dissipative systems', *Journal of Chemical Physics*, **48** (4), 1695–700.

Prigogine, I. and G. Nicolis (1967), 'On symmetry breaking instabilities in dissipative systems', *Journal of Chemical Physics*, **46** (9), 3542–50.

Risken, H. (1965), 'Distribution – and correlation – functions for a laser amplitude', *Zeitschrift für Physik*, **186** (February), 85–98.

Rössler, O.E. (1976), 'An equation for continuous chaos', *Physics Letters*, **57** (5), 397–8.

Schawlow, A.L. and C.H. Townes (1958), 'Infrared and optical masers', *Physical Review*, **112** (December), 1940–49.

Schrödinger, E., (1944), *What is Life?*, Cambridge: Cambridge University Press.

Scully, M.O. and W.E. Lamb Jr (1966), 'Quantum theory of an optical maser', *Physical Review Letters*, **16** (19), 853–5.

Shilnikov, L.P. (1965), 'A case of the existence of denumerable set of periodic motions', *Soviet Mathematics: Doklady*, **6** 163–6.

Solomonoff, R. (1960), 'A preliminary report on a general theory of inductive inference', Technical Report V-131, Zator Co. and Air Force Office of Scientific Research, Cambridge, MA.

Solomonoff, R. (1964a), 'A formal theory of inductive inference. Part I', *Information and Control*, **7** (1), 1–22.

Solomonoff, R. (1964b), 'A formal theory of inductive inference. Part II', *Information and Control*, **7** (1), 224–56.

Tang, C.L., M. Statz and G.A. de Mars (1963), 'Spectral output and spiking behavior of solid-state lasers', *Journal of Applied Physics*, **34** (8), 2289–95.

Turing, A.M. (1937), 'On computable numbers, with an application to the Entscheidungs problem', *Proceedings of the London Mathematical Society*, **42** (November), 230–65.

Turing, A.M. (1952), 'The chemical basis of morphogenesis', *Philosophical Transactions of the Royal Society of London*, **237** (641), 37–72.

Tversky, A. and D. Kahneman (1974), 'Judgment under uncertainty: heuristics and biases', *Science*, **185** (4157), 1124–31.

Tversky, A. and D. Kahneman (1981), 'The framing of decision and psychology of choice', *Science*, **211** (4481), 453–8.

von Bertalanffy, L. (1969), *General System Theory – Foundations, Development, Applications*, New York: George Braziller.

von Neumann, J. (1928), 'Zur Theorie der Gesellschaftsspiele', *Mathematische Annalen*, **100** (1), 259–320.

von Neumann, J. and O. Morgenstern (1944), *Theory of Games and Economic Behavior*, Princeton, NJ: Princeton University Press.

Weidlich, W. (1971), 'The statistical description of polarization phenomena in society', *British Journal of Mathematical and Statistical Psychology*, **24** (2), 251–66.

Weidlich W. (2002), *Sociodynamics: A Systematic Approach to Mathematical Modelling in the Social Sciences*, London: Taylor & Francis.

Wilson, K. (1983), 'The renormalization group and critical phenomena', *Review of Modern Physics*, **55** (3), 583–600.

Wunderlin, A. and H. Haken (1981), 'Generalized Ginzburg-Landau equations, slaving principle and center manifold theorem', *Zeitschrift für Physik B*, **44** (March), 135–41.

3.   City systems and complexity
Michael Batty

For a thousand years after the passing of the ancient world, the west turned in on itself, and the knowledge that had been acquired through the inspired thinking of the Greeks and the Romans was largely lost, despite a small flame being kept alight in the religious centres, the monasteries of the emerging dark ages. However, slowly but surely over several centuries, the classical theories of Greece and Rome were resurrected. The Renaissance that began in the fifteenth century in Europe heralded a period during the seventeenth and eighteenth centuries when a new physical science came to be formed around an Enlightenment that rapidly led to the scientific and technological revolutions that began in western Europe in the middle of the eighteenth century. In the east, where civilisations, particularly the Chinese, were rapidly developing in parallel, there was also a retreat into isolationism and it was not until the industrial revolution began that a new world order based largely on western science came to be established (Harari 2016). It was this science that led to the first ideas that cities in their wider societies could be articulated, explained and even manipulated as part of this order.

The seeds of this movement were nurtured throughout the nineteenth century, and by the early years of the twentieth century, the idea that the science of machines – mechanics – could be used to think about how such diverse systems as cities, economies, biologies, psychologies, polities and related artefacts functioned, came to establish itself. Out of this milieu came the systems approach to explaining the way ill-defined artefacts, such as cities, were organised. This is the starting point in this chapter, and we begin by sketching the origins of this systems approach, first by showing how it came to be established and then how it evolved into a much deeper and wider philosophy which has come to be referred to as complexity, complexity theory or complexity science. We detail this history and then define different varieties of unpredictability that characterise these approaches. We also examine different forms of system with different equilibria, and this leads us to examine the properties of complex systems, in particular questions of size, scale and shape that pertain directly to city systems.

To an extent, cities represent the best exemplars we have of the complexity approach in many fields. To impress this, we also introduce the idea of information as a measure of complexity and then illustrate how cities evolve, focusing on the ever-increasing complexity of these human systems, always throwing into doubt the efficacy and relevance of the theory we have at any one time which best explains our systems of interest. We conclude by arguing that complexity represents the obvious approach to inventing future human systems in that this approach embraces the way our knowledge of city systems develops in parallel to the way our systems of interest also develop. Our theory and science is intimately part of the systems that we seek to explain, predict and invent. Thus, our theories are intrinsically linked to the systems to which they apply, and both develop synergistically.

THE SYSTEMS APPROACH AND THE ORIGINS OF COMPLEXITY THEORY

A system can be defined as a set of components or elements that interact with one another. This definition is sufficiently general in that it can be applied to many different levels, sectors or scales, thus enabling a hierarchy of subsystems to be generated. These systems subdivide into subsystems, either distinct or overlapping, which in turn decompose into sub-subsystems and so on, down to their basic components of interaction. The components might be considered individual elements, or even 'atoms' in the general sense of the word, and they usually have well-defined sharp boundaries separating the system or its subsystems from their wider environment. The system's environment is thus defined so that the interactions between components and the environment at this level are minimal. As regards a system which can be conceived as processing energy or information, the environment represents the area where there is least transmission of these flows to and from the system in question. A good example is a city whose components represent households clustered into neighbourhoods whose social interactions with adjacent and more distant neighbourhoods decline in strength. Those same social interactions at the higher level of the city itself are also minimal with respect to other cities that exist within its wider environment.

We can conceive of these systems at different levels of a nested hierarchy where the branches splay out similar to an inverted tree, often being distinct and separate but sometimes following a lattice-like structure akin to a set of overlapping subsystems at different scales. Almost 60 years ago, the architect Christopher Alexander wrote a famous paper, entitled 'A city is not a tree' (Alexander 1965), in which he argued that human systems, particularly cities, were composed of overlapping districts and neighbourhoods manifesting sets of entangled hierarchies, which suggested how the type of diversity and interactions that we see in social interactions in cities play out in real contexts. We can picture the way this type of diversity can be abstracted, also linking Alexander's image of a city system to Jane Jacobs's (1961) conception of the way rich and socially integrated cities produce overlapping neighbourhoods where many different varieties of social and ethnic group are able to interact. One of the limitations of this model of a system is that, at all levels, the components and subsystems that we see in the real world are much less clear than the abstract conceptions that such a theory of systems articulates. Systems theory focuses on ideal types where the power of the theory is to provide structure to our understanding of how systems function through organised processes of interaction. In real systems, there is so much noise that often the structure is hard to disentangle, but this is so for any theory of the type that attempts to formalise and abstract from the messy reality of everyday life.

In his ground-breaking book, *Decision and Control*, the systems theorist Stafford Beer (1966), in talking of systems composed of interactions, posed the essential dilemma when he paraphrased the German philosopher Gottfried Hegel who implied that everything is related to everything else. This is often qualified in a spatial context as, everything is related to everything else, but near things are more related than distant things. This is sometimes referred to as the first law of geography (or Tobler's law) after Waldo Tobler (1970) who first coined it. It is the foundation of how we represent, measure and simulate ways in which cities hang together as regards their physical, social and information networks. It relates to how we might organise our systems of interest which cannot be completely separated from their environment. In a global world, although human groups from households through to cities do appear as clusters at different scales, their separation is never complete and, increasingly, any line between them is blurred. Again in relation to cities, this means that it is increasingly difficult to separate one city from another and this is getting ever more problematic as the world moves towards systems where urban development is continuous, and where interactions take place across any and every spatial scale.

Despite being able to generalise a system into a hierarchy of interconnected, interacting subsystems, the way we articulate their study can differ dramatically. The idea that we can think of any human or social system as a physical system akin to a machine first emerged as the dominant approach to systems thinking during the early twentieth century. This emphasised the idea of a system based on interacting components that could be represented as a hierarchical structure built from the top down. These systems are usually well defined in that they generate deterministic outcomes. The notion of these systems or their components interacting probabilistically is absent from these structures, and to all intents and purposes they are analogues to machines where the concept of the mechanism completely determines ultimate outcomes. From one perspective, cities do appear to function mechanistically, with interactions occurring routinely and with energy being passed around the system in well-defined, tractable ways. However, seen in a wider context, this image of a system is found wanting, although it did dominate our thinking about cities in the mid-twentieth century. Indeed, it lies at the foundation of the systems approach which rapidly developed in analogy to biological and electrical systems through ideas about cybernetics, which Norbert Wiener (1948, p. 2) defined as 'the scientific study of control and communication in the animal and the machine'. This systems approach and its focus on cybernetics was also pursued in an analogy with biological systems from the 1920s onwards by Ludwig von Bertalanffy (1970), among others.

A second representation of a system is where probability or uncertainty dominates the system outcomes. The outputs of these systems can often only be computed in relation to probabilities of occurrence and the systems are much closer to stochastic machines whose outcomes can only be judged within a range of possibilities. These systems often involve the laws of statistical mechanics, which had come to dominate our thinking about how human systems behaved by the mid- to late-twentieth century. This approach has continued to be widely applied to simulating flows such as road traffic where the equilibrium solution is still well-defined, albeit probabilistically and the system is stationary. However, outcomes are highly sensitive to system inputs, ranging from noise to interventions in the system structure. The third approach, which we develop here, is more fundamental in that the dynamics of change in the system are much richer. As regards the first two types of system, change is relatively well-defined, with those systems being characterised by negative feedback. In the third approach, the analogy is no longer with machines but with organisms, a system that evolves in which the dynamics of change are able to admit not only probabilistic outputs, but also outcomes that are innovative and uncertain, sometimes chaotic or catastrophic but admitting states or solutions that are unpredictable. Whereas in the first two types of systems, physics is the generic model for the way those systems function and change, in the third, it is biology, or rather evolution, that characterises their functioning.

THREE VARIETIES OF PREDICTABILITY

The distinction between these three different types of system was first articulated by Warren Weaver (1948) at about the time when he jointly published that other great milestone on information theory with Claude Shannon (Shannon and Weaver 1948). Weaver classified these three approaches to systems with respect to simplicity and complexity. The first approach, he argued, was the oldest and most common, based on deterministic systems conceived of as problems of simplicity. The second approach led to stochastic systems of disorganised complexity, while the third, and by far the most significant according to Weaver, was based on problems of organised complexity. The essential distinction in this characterisation pertained to the richness of the processes defining the system, with dynamics being key. Problems of simplicity involved a simple dynamics in which the ultimate outcomes focused on stable solutions while problems of disorganised complexity were built around statistical uncertainty whose solutions, although stable, could only be simulated probabilistically. The third and final set of systems were problems of organised complexity where purposeful processes akin to decision-making, invention and innovation, as well as the rudiments of evolution, characterised the way the systems functioned. It is this latter type of problem, arguably the closest to any reality that we have to deal with in cities, that defines the core of complexity theory.

These three types of system admit three varieties of predictability, which we might label 'predictable', 'non-predictable' and 'unpredictable'. We deal with each of these in turn but, before we do so, we say a little more about complexity. There are many properties of complex systems that we introduce in the context of cities in the next section, but here we need to define complexity in more detail than merely implying that complex systems are organised. To an extent, all systems depend on their dynamics, but complex systems portray a dynamics that does not lead directly to any form of stable state that we usually define as an equilibrium. The first system, which is classed as simple, usually produces a deterministic equilibrium and its dynamics tends to be straightforward. These systems generate trajectories of change that lead to predictable solutions, at least in terms of their theory. Good examples are systems that handle changes in their inputs in ways that lead to deterministic solutions which are unchanging in their steady state. Many of our system models of land use and transport fall into this category, which makes them mechanistic in that they deal with interactions in a way that restores any equilibrium that is disturbed. That is, there are no mechanisms in these models that change the long-term equilibrium in relation to structure.

The second system does not generate deterministic predictions owing to two features: first these models can activate a positive feedback which changes the trajectory of the models and, second, random perturbations can be introduced as noise or as unexpected changes in inputs, destroying any long-term equilibrium that can only exist if there is no change in inputs. Some models of cities attempt to look at such predictable outcomes but most are only of theoretical value. These systems tend to be in disequilibrium at any one time and the difficulties of handling any prediction as being a stable and certain as regards their predictions limits the extent to which they can be used to help in answering 'what if' questions about the future system The third class, those based on organised complexity, introduce processes that enable the system to innovate – to determine new states that are not implicit in the model's processes in any way. Usually these outcomes can only emerge if the functions in the model are diverse and rich enough so that some form of learning can take place which then changes the structure of the system itself. The implication is that these complex systems never generate traditional forms of equilibrium and are often classed as being 'far-from-equilibrium'.

A key question from this discussion is whether or not the ability to reach an equilibrium defines the degree of predictability. This depends on the extent to which not the theory but the reality to which it is applied is predictable. There is no doubt that some very routinised functions in the city – the peak hour traffic flow, however it is measured – can be highly predictable but every function in the city is subject to extraneous events that can destroy any type of equilibrium that is associated with forecasting. That is, it is hard to envisage any system in the city at any level at which we are studying them which is not subject to extraneous events. However, these models might still be used to inform the predictive process, to engage the debate and to structure the dialogue.

In essence then, complex systems tend to be unpredictable, almost by definition, but with enough uncertainty in our comprehension of them to not ever be able to provide any certainty about their form, functions and dynamics. The move from simple to complex, as our ideas about cities have evolved over the last 60 years, has been spurred on by our realisation that increasingly our city systems are complex. We examine the properties of complex systems in the next section but there are two features of complexity and prediction that we need to note before we do so. First, cities are becoming more complex over time. As we invent increasingly more new technologies and as these technologies become ever more decentralised, individuals have an increasing number of opportunities to change and manipulate their environments. This increases the level of complexity in cities, and thus our theory always tends to lag behind. We need to run to stand still. Second, as we have learnt more about cities, it is increasingly clear that, although we cannot predict the future, we always have the ability to invent it, even if this is rarely possible in practice. This is the issue; we can always control our own destinies at least in theory. Although we can invent the future, we cannot predict what we might invent and thus this unpredictability often limits our collective invention and control (Batty 2018). In thinking about how our cities function and evolve, we face a barrier of predictability that suggests our theories can only ever be used to inform our understanding, never to be able to predict the future, only to explore it.

THE PROPERTIES OF COMPLEX SYSTEMS: SIZE, SCALE AND SHAPE

We have already noted that cities can be described as a hierarchy of subsystems, from the entire system, however it is bounded by its environment, all the way down to its basic components which we assume to be indivisible. The levels defined by these hierarchies usually imply different scales which, in turn, might relate to their size or shape. We put size and shape on one side for the moment, as our first property relates to the nature of the hierarchy itself – the way its levels relate to one another. In this context, there is a general property that we refer to as 'scaling' which suggests that there can be a degree of uniformity or similarity between the different levels that integrates them in an elementary way. West, in his book *Scale*, provides a general definition when he writes that: '*Scaling* simply refers, in its most elemental form, to how a system responds when its size changes' (West 2017, p. 15). It is important in this context to ensure that our definition of scale is completely generic, in that it can apply to any distribution of system elements that show similarity across different levels. Thus we assume that, as we move from one level to another, we either aggregate or disaggregate the system elements. Typically, at the top of the hierarchy – at the first order of scale – this is the most aggregate level, while at the level of the system components, at the bottom of the hierarchy, we are dealing with the most disaggregate level.

These levels can pertain to cities at different spatial scales, to sectors or activities which describe how the city is organised economically with firms being grouped in industries and so on, to households and various social groupings which may be based on social interactions, and even to temporal scales which pertain to the way the city and its components and subsystems change over different time horizons. The principle behind the logic of aggregation or disaggregation is referred to as scaling, and scaling is the mechanism which enables us to move from one scale to another thus revealing the extent to which one scale is similar to another. Different levels of scale which can be derived from other scales by simple arithmetic operations, such as multiplication, reveal pure scaling based on self-similarity, whereas if there is some noise introduced into the scaling, then very often this is referred to as statistical self-similarity. In the latter context, each level of scale is similar to another but only with respect to its statistics. To give all this some substance, we need to introduce examples. This inevitably introduces measures of size, as most change across the obvious spatial hierarchies that define cities and their component parts is related to numbers of activities, populations, and so on.

When we look at different sizes of city, from the smallest hamlet or village to the largest metropolis, we see functions and activities repeating themselves at different spatial scales. Indeed, bigger cities at one level are simply a replication of population elements from lower levels owing to the accumulation of populations through growth and through time. However, as cities change in size, some functions change at different rates. That is, there is qualitative change as cities grow or decline and we can measure this change at different spatial scales. One of the most well-known forms of qualitative change involves what Alfred Marshall, the nineteenth-century British economist, termed 'economies of agglomeration' (Marshall 1890, p. 377), also known as economies of scale. As places grow bigger, they accrue more than proportionate economic advantages owing to the division of labour and the clustering of talent of various types. A standard relationship relating to, say, income and population size can be written as a power law where income varies as a function of city size. The most general and simplest function follows the following nonlinear relation

$$Y_i = kP_i^{\alpha}, \tag{3.1}$$

where Y_i is the income of city i, P_i is the population of city i, k is a normalising constant and α is a scaling constant that controls the process whereby a certain amount of population generates a specific amount of income. There may also be diseconomies of agglomeration so that the scaling coefficient generates less than proportionate increases in income, however, the relationship is completely generic and is referred to as the scaling equation.

It is easy to see the qualitative meaning of equation (3.1) if we form the ratio of the relative change in income to the relative change in population. This equals the scaling coefficient α and if this coefficient is greater than 1, then income grows more than proportionately with city size. This ratio is the elasticity and we can form it by first taking the derivative of equation (3.1) and manipulating the result as

$$\left.\begin{array}{c} \dfrac{dY}{dP} = k\alpha P_i^{\alpha-1} = \alpha\dfrac{Y}{P} \\[2mm] \dfrac{dY}{Y} \Big/ \dfrac{dP}{P} = \alpha \end{array}\right\}. \tag{3.2}$$

In the biological sciences, these relationships define allometric growth, which primarily represents ways in which physiological attributes, such as body mass, metabolic rates and so on, scale relative to one another. These relationships also change qualitatively and there are several physiological constants, such as length of life multiplied by heart rate, which are constant over many different animal species. The best example is that the heart rate of a mouse multiplied by its expected lifetime is the same as that of a human, the consequences of which appear in the surface-mass ratios that govern the shape of both life forms. West (2017) has generalised this theory of scale and size across many human systems, including cities, drawing widely and deeply from the biological sciences and from the study of allometry (Huxley 1932). There are also several explorations of this type of morphological scaling in our own field of cities, particularly with respect to buildings, streets and land parcels (Batty et al. 2008). Buildings, similarly to animals, also change quantitatively with respect to their size and scale, with higher buildings having to use increasingly less floor space as their levels get increasingly higher.

There are many allometric relationships that occur in the physical and human world, and these usually involve defining relationships across scale where the size of the artefacts in question vary systematically. There have been many applications of the economic scaling relationship in equation (3.1) to different systems of cities worldwide since the pioneering paper of Bettencourt et al. (2007) which first demonstrated that, in the US urban system, the scaling coefficient with respect to income and population was greater than 1 (at around 1.14). There is some dispute about the claim that this is a universal relationship, for much depends on what we define as a city and this is complicated by many questions of definition. Moreover, in a global world there is some doubt that the city is necessarily the best unit for which to validate and test for these relationships. There is another relationship between city sizes at different levels of the hierarchy which define how one size of city relates to another, and this is even more basic. This is a power law, the rank-size rule. We first state the rule, which is sometimes termed the rank-size law, or the law of city sizes which is almost nihilistic in its conception. In its purest form, if we were to rank the objects in some distribution by their size, then the relationship between size and rank is assumed to follow a power law. Define as before population size by P_i and we rank the cities from $P_1 > P_2 > P_3 > \ldots > P_n$ where we now consider i is the rank and the lowest ranked city is n which is the size of the smallest city. Then the power law relationship is

$$P_i = P_1/i = P_1^{-i}, \tag{3.3}$$

and we can describe this in a very simple way: the size P_i of any particular city i is equal to the population of the largest city P_1 divided by the rank i of that city. Note that there is a more general relationship, also a power law, but there is now an exponent β on the rank, and this equation (3.1) generalises to

$$P_i = P_1 / i^\beta = P_1 i^{-\beta}. \tag{3.4}$$

If we wish to estimate rank-size relationships from data, then we need to estimate the value of the exponent β and this would give us the value of the largest city, which would also be an estimate. This could come from a log-linear regression on equation (3.4) defined as $ln(P_i) = ln(P_1) - \beta\, ln(i)$, although there are a variety of methods to estimate this equation.

To an extent, this is a very strange relationship, and that it fits many different sets of data for different systems of cities around the world is one of those remarkable observations that is hard to explain. At one level, for complex systems that are capacitated, as one component gets larger, the changes in the remaining components getting equally large reduce. That is, there is only so much resource to go round and thus we end up with a very small number of very large cities and a very large number of small cities. It was Zipf (1949) who first popularised this relationship for city sizes, as well as word frequencies, and the relationship was soon applied to many other systems, such as income distributions and sizes of firms. It is widely referred to as Zipf's law as well as the rank-size rule. There are many stochastic interpretations that enable these distributions to be generated, and there are location models emanating from the economics of central place theory that are consistent with these relationships. However one key use of such models is to enable us to bound the systems of interest, to define the relevant systems of cities by size so that we can assess how actual city size distributions diverge from these ideal types as in equation (3.3) (Cristelli et al. 2012). A summary of the state of the art is provided by Batty (2021), where he demonstrates a variety of rank-size relationships for different types of city system as well as building distributions.

The two relationships we have defined so far – based on allometric scaling and rank size – both define different but related signatures of complex systems, and are sufficiently general in their scope to provide robust indicators that the systems to which they apply meet all the requirements for defining a complex system. That is, it is evident they emerge from different processes that act in similar ways to sorting and structuring the elements of these systems so that they might evolve and learn. These relationships do not, however, reflect the geometry of these systems, which is important for cities, and thus we need to say a little about this before we move on to defining other processes that enable cities to grow and change. To an extent this engages us in thinking about both city systems – what goes on inside cities, which we term intraurban – and systems of cities – what goes on between cities, which we term interurban. Both approaches define key elements that determine the shape of cities.

As we change the size of a city, we can construct a regular hierarchy of places that consumes a decreasing area or hinterland of population as the size of the city decreases. We might begin with a hinterland containing a total population $P(l - 1)$, successively subdividing this population into a fixed number φ of smaller but regular hinterlands each containing $P_k(l)$ population where at any lower level of the hierarchy $l - 1$, the total population $P(l - 1) = \sum_{k=1}^{\varphi} P_k(l)$. At the beginning of this process of cascading, there is a single hinterland for the biggest city which has $P(1)$ population. The process of continued subdivision is a simply multiplicative division which we can write as

$$P_k(l) = \frac{1}{\varphi} P_k(l - 1), \tag{3.5}$$

where the cascade can be written for the next level of hierarchy as

$$P_k(l + 1) = \frac{1}{\varphi} P_k(l) = \left(\frac{1}{\varphi}\right)^2 P_k(l - 1). \tag{3.6}$$

By recursion on equations (3.5) and (3.6), at any level of the hierarchy $l + n$, we can write the progression as

$$P_k(l + n) = \frac{1}{\varphi} P_k(l + n - 1) = \left(\frac{1}{\varphi}\right)^{n+1} P_k(l), \tag{3.7}$$

and it is easy to see from equation (3.7) when we start with the population $P(1) = P$ that

$$P_k(n) = \left(\frac{1}{\varphi}\right)^{n+1} P. \tag{3.8}$$

Each population $P_k(l)$ at the relevant level occupies the same space. If we use an efficient packing of space, such as an hexagonal subdivision at level l of a larger hexagon at the lower level $l - 1$, we subdivide the space at the lower level by 6, that is, we use the ratio $1/\varphi$ at each level. The number of spaces (hexagons) generated as we start from the largest $l = 1$ follows the progression 1, 6, 36, 216, 1296, 7776, . . ., while if we assume we start with a population of $P = 1$ million, this population subdivides into 16 6667, 27 778, 4630, 772, 129, and so on until we generate individual settlements with no meaningful values. Using these numbers, the total number of cities down to units of three persons sums to 335 923 which are all contained in the total population of 1 million, the average city size being 2.9 persons.

We have adopted a hexagon for our idealisation of shape at different levels of the hierarchy as this is the most efficient packing of the plane. It was used as the template for a hinterland in the theory of city size and shape, known as central place theory. This was developed by Walter Christaller (1933 [1966]) and it has since become the default shape for study of urban hinterlands, with many variants based on overlapping market areas using the hexagonal model. Useful examples are found in Isard (1956). If we consider the total population we begin with not as the population of the hinterland, but as the population of the largest city, and that the populations then generated are of increasingly smaller cities in the hierarchy, the progression that we generate is of cities of different sizes that do not sum to a total population of 1 million. We start with a population of 1 million and the next cities generated are of size 166 667, then 27 778 and so on until we reach our lower thresholds of persons which is about three. In this progression, we generate a million persons per hierarchical level, and with eight levels, our system contains 8 million persons. In this process, the ultimate population in the system is always a function of the total number of persons we start with.

We can develop other variants of this process that are not quite so stylised and which allow more diversity in city size but, surprisingly, there has been very little work on this model following these lines. Central place theory remains an ideal type; it is an exemplar of how to think about how a city system might be organised spatially rather than a model of how a real system is organised, and it represents a way of linking hierarchy, size and shape. There are two extensions that are worth noting in relation to our previous discussion. First, we can adopt other methods of tiling the plane – other tessellations – that generate similar hierarchies, for example, by using triangular embedding or even using a regular grid where we can have different numbers of subdivisions. For example we could begin with a square hinterland and divide this into nine regular square subdivisions and as long as we stick with this kind of regularity and symmetry, we can generate tractable hierarchies. If we depart from these constraints, the patterns and scaling we are able to generate become more idiosyncratic. This process also generates a progression of city sizes from a small number of large cities to a large number of small cities. This follows some type of regular relationship similar to a power law, and in the sequence we generated above starting with 1 million persons and subdividing this into a regular number of cities at each level, the sequence follows an inverse rank relationship. It is easy to show that this sequence follows an exponential decay of the form $ln(P(l)) = \phi - \lambda l$ where ϕ is the intercept or normalising constant, λ is the rank-size parameter and l is the rank. The exponential is $P(l) = exp(\phi)exp(-\lambda l)$ and the parameters of this are $\phi = 15.607$ and $\lambda = 1.792$. We might think of this as an inverse exponential rank-size relationship in contrast to an inverse power law.

At the intraurban scale, we can also detect clusters of activities, particularly employment and retailing that follow distinct hierarchies. However, once we begin to deal with spatial extent in contrast to simply focusing on the numbers of cities (or locations) and the mass of population, we invoke the first law of geography (Tobler 1970), which we noted at the start of this chapter, pertaining to the influence of one location on any other. This law introduces our fourth principle of complex urban systems involving the declining influence of a city at one place on places at increasing distance away from the place in question. This too follows an inverse power law, but this time it is not with respect to size or number but with respect to the influence of distance (or any other measure of deterrence, such as travel cost or travel time). We can write this relationship as a power law of the form

$$T_{ij} = G \frac{P_i P_j}{d_{ij}^{\gamma}}, \tag{3.9}$$

where T_{ij} is a flow of activity between city or location i and location j, P_i, P_j are the populations of their respective cities as defined earlier, d_{ij} is the distance between the two cities, γ is a friction of distance parameter and G is a normalising constant. In many instances this equation is formulated as a negative exponential of distance instead of a power law since it is argued that action at a distance is not infinite at the origin while in its traditional form in gravitation theory, G is the gravitational constant and $\gamma = 2$. This is the inverse square law of gravitational attraction.

There are many variants of this type of model and we introduce it merely to demonstrate that size, scale and shape can be synthesised in a generic way. To impress this, it is possible to take the general spatial interaction model in equation (3.9) and apply it to two cities i and j at some distance d_{ij} between them, so that their relationship to the wider hierarchy can be defined. We assume that we can define the trade area or hinterland boundary between i and j at some distance d_{ik} from i and distance d_{jk} from j where $d_{ij} = d_{ik} + d_{jk}$. Then at this breakpoint k we assume that the trips from i to k and from j to k are balanced and equal, that is $T_{ik} = T_{jk}$ or alternatively their ratio is unity: $T_{ik}/T_{jk} = 1$. We can compute the breakpoint which defines the hinterland boundary at that level of hierarchy by substituting equation (3.9) into one of these balance relationships cancelling the common terms. Then

$$\frac{T_{ik}}{T_{jk}} = \frac{P_i d_{ik}^{-\gamma}}{P_j d_{jk}^{-\gamma}} = 1, \tag{3.10}$$

and we can rearrange this as

$$\left(\frac{P_j}{P_i}\right)^{\gamma} = \frac{d_{ik}}{d_{jk}} = \frac{d_{ij} - d_{ik}}{d_{ik}}. \tag{3.11}$$

The breakpoint can be computed from equation (3.11) as

$$d_{ik} = d_{ij} \bigg/ \left\{1 + \left(\frac{P_j}{P_i}\right)^{\gamma}\right\}. \tag{3.12}$$

It is easy to work out the meaning of equation (3.12) if we note that as the population of the city j increases, then the distance from the other city i to the breakpoint decreases, and vice versa. This is for only one level of hierarchy, and the algorithm implied in equation (3.12) has not, to the author's knowledge, been applied systematically either to systems of cities or city systems. It was introduced by Reilly in 1930 (for which see Batty 1978) and named by him as the 'law of retail gravitation'. Spatial interaction models that are largely generalised gravity models enable hierarchical systems with overlapping hinterlands to be simulated directly and, by the time retail forecasting became significant in the mid-twentieth century onwards, Reilly's law was regarded as a historical curiosity and therefore was never widely applied.

We have identified several signatures that define the properties of city systems that we argue are key to the definition of the city as a complex system. Scaling of city size through allometric relationships and through rank-size relationships reveal ever-present power laws that also apply to interactions and flows across space at different levels of hierarchy and at different city sizes. What we have not done, but we need to note it in passing, is propose that there is a coherent theory that ties many of these ideas together through the notion of hierarchies of objects that have the same structure. This is the theory of fractals. Hierarchy is central to fractals in that fractal objects exist at different scales and their form is dominated by the way its elements repeat themselves in a similar fashion over many scales. This self-similarity is their hallmark and, as we have seen previously, cities themselves are composed of objects that get bigger or smaller at different scales, and change in their function qualitatively but remain of similar shape in such a way that we can detect common processes at work across different scales. This modularity is key to the way cities evolve from the bottom up, again one of the hallmarks of complexity theory that suggests to us that in managing and planning cities, we need to pay much more attention to the way in which we intervene in the quest for more sustainable, efficient and equitable urban environments.

A great deal of this rudimentary theory might be tied together to form an integrated theory of cities as complex systems, but this has not emerged yet. Various contributions are beginning to attempt a synthesis, for example, Batty (2013), Barthelemy (2016) and, more recently, Bettencourt (2021), but two features make this difficult. First, there are so many different perspectives on complex systems that a unified and coherent theory, or even framework relating them all, is almost impossible to define. There are many qualitative features of city systems that cannot be embraced in the types of formal structures that are introduced here. The second feature relates to questions of dynamics. A large amount of our current thinking about complexity has found it hard to grapple with the dynamics of change, and there appear to be as many approaches to dynamics as there are theories about the city. Empirical evidence in relation to dynamics is lacking, particularly over longer time horizons, and more recent developments with the real-time streaming of data over very short time horizons has almost led to a parallel theory of cities as complex systems which is based on much more routinised decision-making. Many of the chapters in this book allude to these difficulties, notwithstanding the hard-won advances that the focus on complexity is bringing to our understanding and planning of cities.

INFORMATION AND ENTROPY

The formula which Claude Shannon introduced in 1948, as portrayed in his book with Warren Weaver (Shannon and Weaver 1948), is a measure of system structure that is yet another signature of a complex system. This is the measure of information that can also be articulated as a measure of uncertainty, and as a measure of complexity. It is also termed entropy as it plays a crucial role in the evolution of any system. In statistical physics, entropy is a measure of disorder in the system, which is intrinsic in that as a system uses energy, it reduces the energy left to pursue useful work and this remaining unavailable energy is named entropy. A consequence of the very long-term history of the universe is that its overall entropy is always increasing and, ultimately, the universal system will no longer be able to function as all its energy will have been used up. It will become completely disorganised. In this chapter we do not dwell on this type of evolution, although it is fundamental to complexity. Instead, we focus on how ideas about entropy can be used to define the constituents of any city as a complex systems, with respect to their parts which are its populations and their distribution. In this way we tie all these ideas about entropy back to our earlier signatures relating to size, scale and shape.

We define again a city of n locations with a volume of activity such as population P_i in each. We will assume that the probability of this volume of population in location i is proportional to population and is defined as p_i, so that $p_i = P_i / \sum_i P_i$. With this, the probabilities of location sum to 1, that is, $\sum_i p_i = 1$. Shannon defined the information H or the entropy of a distribution of probabilities $\{p_i\}$ as the sum of the inverse of the log of each probability, weighted by the probability itself

$$H = -\sum_i p_i \ ln \ p_i \,. \tag{3.13}$$

This measure varies between 0 when all the locations but one have zero probability, that is, $p_i = 0$, *all i ≠ k* and $p_k = 1$, and $H = ln \ n$ when all the probabilities are uniform, that is, $p_i = 1/n$. If we reflect on this measure as one of disorder, then when everything is uniform, that is, when entropy is maximised, the system is completely disordered and all the activity is spread evenly. The system is homogeneous and all locations are equally probable. When the entropy or disorder is at a minimum, there is only one location where the activity is located and then the system is entirely organised.

Without anticipating the probability distribution associated with the entropy, we can maximise it in equation (3.13) subject to a constraint on probabilities. Using standard methods, we form a Lagrangian as

$$L = -\sum_i p_i \ ln \ p_i - \vartheta \left(\sum_i p_i - 1\right) = H - \vartheta \left(\sum_i p_i - 1\right) \tag{3.14}$$

and find the maximum derivatives with respect to the probabilities p_i. It is easy to show that the predicted probability is $p_i = exp(1 + \vartheta)$, which is a uniform distribution. This process holds the key to illustrating how the various models introduced in the previous section might be generated. What this process does is suggest that any system left to its own internal logic, would use energy which would continuously reduce the available energy, thus raising entropy to a maximum, subject to its own constraints. In a city system where traffic was generated between locations and whose flows were subject to Tobler's law, then at any point in time there would be a total distance travelled which would use energy. Now we can define the probabilities of interaction between every pair of locations as $p_{ij} = T_{ij}/\sum_i\sum_j T_{ij}$. The constraint that the system has to meet is on the mean amount of travel $D = \sum_i\sum_j p_{ij} d_{ij}$. If we now maximise entropy subject to this constraint, we first form the appropriate Lagrangian as

$$L = -\sum_i\sum_j p_{ij} \ ln \ p_{ij} - \vartheta \left(\sum_i\sum_j p_{ij} - 1\right) - \gamma\left(\sum_i\sum_j p_{ij} d_{ij} - D\right), \tag{3.15}$$

and we then differentiate this and set the result to zero, and by rearranging and taking exponentials, we attain the probability model which maximises entropy:

$$p_{ij} = exp(1 + \vartheta)exp(-\gamma d_{ij})\,. \tag{3.16}$$

Equation (3.15) does not look anything like the gravitational model in equation (3.9) but, through a change of variables and a different version of the entropy formula, this model can easily be derived.

First let us introduce a new information formula which defines what we term a prior probability distribution q_{ij} which we suggest is based on population values P_i and P_j. We formulate this prior as $q_{ij} = \mu P_i P_j = P_i P_j/(\sum_i P_i \sum_j P_j)$. The information formula can now be written as a comparison between priors and posteriors as

$$I = -\sum_i\sum_j p_{ij} \ ln \ \frac{p_{ij}}{q_{ij}}\,, \tag{3.17}$$

and, if we change the constraint on average distance travelled to $\bar{D} = \sum_i \sum_j p_{ij} \log d_{ij}$, we can then form the associated Lagrangian and maximise it as follows:

$$L = -\sum_i \sum_j p_{ij} \ln \frac{p_{ij}}{q_{ij}} - \vartheta \left(\sum_i \sum_j p_{ij} - 1 \right) - \gamma \left(\sum_i \sum_j p_{ij} \log d_{ij} - \bar{D} \right). \quad (3.18)$$

The resultant model can be written as

$$p_{ij} = q_{ij} \exp(1 + \vartheta) \exp(-\gamma \log d_{ij}), \quad (3.19)$$

which can be simplified by collecting various constants together as

$$p_{ij} \propto GP_i P_j d_{ij}^{-\gamma}. \quad (3.20)$$

The machinery for entropy-maximising has been very widely developed in the study of city systems, particularly by Wilson (2010). The tools of derivation and accounting which are fundamental to the technique can be used to provide many kinds of system model. To an extent, these tools are more appropriate to the second type of system identified by Weaver as problems of disorganised complexity, reflecting the definition of entropy as being involved with systems that are intrinsically disorganised. Many of the tools of systems and complexity theory can be used for measuring and modelling elements associated with the three different types of system. Even the different principles and signatures of complexity were defined well before complexity theory came on the scene as a specific approach. Looking at the times when allometry, rank size, hierarchy theory, gravitational models, and so on, were first introduced, it is evident that these were as much part and parcel of the move from simple systems to problems of organised complexity, as much as methods that were developed once this perspective came to be accepted.

What has not been very obvious in thinking of cities as complex systems has been the measurement of complexity per se, through formula such as entropy. Indeed, entropy has been used much more to derive models than to develop substantive interpretations of how energy and entropy change as city systems evolve. However, it is easy to link both types of interpretation to the development of complex system structures. More generally, this will require a much deeper synthesis of these ideas, and significantly more focus on temporal dynamics which we briefly address in the next, and final, section.

THE CHALLENGE UNDERSTANDING THE EVOLUTION OF CITIES

As we have implied, the key distinction between the systems approach and complexity science resides in the way they both treat dynamics and equilibrium. In deterministic systems, equilibrium is always assured and the dynamics of convergence to such a state tend to be well defined, based on negative feedback. That is, a system which is disturbed returns to a similar equilibrium as the disturbance works itself out. Some of the interaction models noted previously fall into this class. If, for example, we change the input variables in the gravitational model in equation (3.9), the model assumes that the new outputs will define a new equilibrium. Sometimes the movement to equilibrium is simulated explicitly but the dynamics are tractable. These models do not change the structure of the system in any way and do not explain innovation or structural change. Complex systems, however, have a very different approach to dynamics, which does admit innovation and changes in structure, and are much richer in relation to the way a new state of the system occurs. Unlike more simple systems, there may be many equilibria, so many that sometimes these systems are said to be far from equilibrium. This complexity is often manifested in bifur-cating paths that suggest that these systems can take on any solution that lies within a solu-tion space that can be reached from any point. By this means, new structures can emerge.

Complex systems evolve and their trajectories tend to be convoluted. This is particu-larly the case where these systems can lead to chaos or catastrophe. Usually, complex systems evolve from the bottom up; that is, their fundamental components interact in diverse ways to produce a hierarchy of subsystems that are forever changing. In con-trast, simple systems almost appear as though they are manufactured from the top down instead than growing and developing from the bottom up. An excellent example of how a systems grows from the bottom up was described by Herbert Simon (1962) in a path-breaking paper, 'The architecture of complexity', where he introduced the example of a system built of many identical components. He showed that in a noisy environment where extraneous change was continually occurring, the only way a stable system could emerge was by building it in parts, assembling a small set of components into a subsys-tem, then the subsystems into higher-order subsystems, continuing in this fashion until the entire assembly had been produced. As the system was built hierarchically, each subassembly was stable relative to the whole, and Simon argued eloquently that this method of construction – evolution perhaps – was the only method that could result in a working system. If the parts were assembled all at once, the system could never be fin-ished because the incomplete system would always be unstable and thence the assembly would always fall apart in a noisy environment.

The hierarchies that we illustrated previously are consistent with this notion of con-struction. In relation to the rank-size rule for cities, cities grow from small to large anyway and it is not possible to build a big city without being a small city first. The small cities in the hierarchy are subassemblies. However, the distribution and growth of cities is more complex than this in that the hierarchy is forever been renewed with births and deaths of cities leading to a continual refreshment of the process. Complex systems do not evolve entirely from the bottom up. A more considered process is where the individual components, people and groups in a city, act to develop the city at any scale but, whether working in bottom up or top down fashion, it is individuals who are the prime motivators for an evolving city. Most cities, in relation to their form, appear to be the product of many bottom-up decisions. Sometimes it is possible to detect exam-ples of practical planning where an individual or collective has imposed some plan on the pattern of development but, in general, cities contain so many diverse systems and individuals that it is impossible for any top-down activity to impose its organisation on the entire city. Moreover, cities grow and fuse into one another and as the world becomes entirely urbanised, evidence of any central planning becomes subsumed into a wider sea of bottom-up decision-making.

In this chapter, we have condensed the elements of complexity theory in terms of the generic properties of different systems as they apply to cities. This is still very much a work in progress and, as we have been at pains to point out, it is probably impossible to expect that there will ever be a well worked out theory that integrates not only the many perspectives which have developed to understand the city, but also the many different approaches which espouse complexity, for example, those that are presented in this book. However, what is evident is that our understanding of systems in general and city systems in particular is maturing, and is being enriched by embracing the knowledge that the world is complex, that the future is unpredictable and that our approaches to designing better cities need to be intimately informed by this new science.

REFERENCES

Alexander, C. (1965), 'A city is not a tree', *Architectural Forum*, **122** (1), 58–62.

Barthelemy, M. (2016), *The Structure and Dynamics of Cities: Urban Data Analysis and Theoretical Modeling*, Cambridge: Cambridge University Press.

Batty, M. (1978), 'Reilly's challenge: new laws of retail gravitation which define systems of central places', *Environment and Planning A*, **10** (2), 185–219.

Batty, M. (2013), *The New Science of Cities*, Cambridge, MA: MIT Press.

Batty, M. (2018), *Inventing Future Cities*, Cambridge, MA: MIT Press.

Batty, M. (2021), 'The size of cities', in E. Glaeser, K. Kourtit and P. Nijkamp (eds), *Urban Empires: Cities as Global Rulers in the New Urban World*, London: Routledge, pp. 210–28.

Batty, M., R. Carvalho, A. Hudson-Smith, R. Milton, D. Smith and P. Steadman (2008), 'Scaling and allometry in the building geometries of Greater London', *European Physical Journal B*, **63** (3), 303–18.

Beer, S. (1966), *Decision and Control: The Meaning of Operational Research and Management Cybernetics*, Chichester: John Wiley and Sons.

Bertalanffy, L. von (1968), *General System Theory: Foundations, Development, Applications*, New York: George Braziller.

Bettencourt, L.M.A. (2021), *Introduction to Urban Science: Evidence and Theory of Cities as Complex Systems*, Cambridge, MA: MIT Press.

Bettencourt, L.M.A., J. Lobo, D. Helbing, C. Kühnert and G.B. West (2007), 'Growth, innovation, scaling, and the pace of life in cities', *Proceedings of the National Academy of Sciences (PNAS)*, **104** (17), 7301–6.

Christaller, W. (1933, 1966), *Die Zentralen Orte in Suddeutschland*, Gustav Fischer, Jena, 1966 trans. (in part) C.W. Baskin, *Central Places in Southern Germany*, Englewood Cliffs, NJ: Prentice Hall.

Cristelli, M., M. Batty and L. Pietronero (2012), 'There is more than a power law in Zipf', *Scientific Reports*, **2**, art. 812, doi:10.1038/srep00812.

Harari, Y. (2016), *Homo Deus: A Brief History of Tomorrow*, London: Vintage Books.

Huxley, J. S. (1932), *Problems of Relative Growth*, London: Methuen.

Isard, W. (1956), *Location and Space Economy: General Theory Relating to Industrial Location, Market Areas, Land Use, Trade and Urban Structure*, Cambridge, MA: MIT Press.

Jacobs, J. (1961), *The Death and Life of Great American Cities*, New York: Random House.

Marshall, A. (1890), *Principles of Economics*, London: Macmillan.

Shannon, C.E. and C. Weaver (1948), *The Mathematical Theory of Communication*, Urbana, IL: University of Illinois Press.

Simon, H.A. (1962), 'The architecture of complexity', *Proceedings of the American Philosophical Society*, **106** (6), 467–82.

Tobler, W. (1970), 'A computer movie simulating urban growth in the Detroit region', *Economic Geography*, **46** (suppl.), 234–40.

Weaver, W. (1948), 'Science and complexity', *American Scientist*, **36** (4), 536–44.

West, G. (2017), *Scale: The Universal Laws of Growth, Innovation, Sustainability, and the Pace of Life in Organisms, Cities, Economies, and Companies*, London: Penguin Press.

Wiener, N. (1948), *Cybernetics: Or Control and Communication in the Animal and the Machine*, Cambridge, MA: MIT Press.

Wilson, A.G. (2010), 'Entropy in urban and regional modelling: retrospect and prospect', *Geographical Analysis*, **42** (4), 364–94.

Zipf, G.K. (1949), *Human Behavior and the Principle of Least Effort*, Cambridge, MA Addison-Wesley.

4. Major transitions in the story of urban complexity
Stephen Marshall and Nick Green

Seeking the roots of understanding the complexity of cities is challenging because while cities are routinely assumed to be complex, the nature of their complexity is not often articulated explicitly. Whole books could be written about cities without necessarily mentioning their complexity. Indeed, cities are so complex that just understanding any one of their various sub-systems – material, social, political, technological, and so on – would of itself be a complex task; and faithfully articulating the complexity of the city as a whole may seem dauntingly beyond our grasp. Yet, the compellingly complex nature of the city – that 'mangle of machines, infrastructures, humans, nonhumans, institutions, networks, metabolisms, matter and nature' (Amin and Thrift 2017, p. 9) – drives us to look again for what insights we can glean through the long lens of history.

Our understanding of complexity can be seen as a piecemeal accumulation over time; but seen over the long perspective of the history of thought, it can also be arranged for simplicity in a series of 'major transitions', to borrow John Maynard Smith's term. Smith and Szathmary's major transitions in biological evolution can be seen as successive changes in the history of life that can be identified with increased complexity and capability in organisms – from replicating molecules to cellular organisms, from single-celled to multicellular organisms, from solitary individuals to societies, and so on (Smith and Szathmary 1997). We do not suggest any direct analogues with the specific transitions, except the sense of there being successive manifestations of increasing complexity.[1] However, for a concise introduction to the history of urban complexity, it will serve us to focus on a series of specific transitions over history.

We propose six major transitions in understanding, each relating to recognition of a new perspective: of living beings as complex things; of *Homo sapiens* as just another species; of organised complexity as a 'good thing'; of the necessary social dimension of urban complexity; of diversity as a necessary dimension of social complexity; and, finally, the wicked nature of intervention in complexity.

Some of these transitions are more a case of successive crystallisations of thought over many years at different places and times, while others are more easily pinned on the inspiration of particular individuals. Our story, as it turns out, is not linear, and perhaps inevitably a simplification – in which we use the term 'complexity' and all other words in their simplest, standard dictionary definitions[2] – but we hope it will provide a convenient structure from which to grasp the more complex whole.

THE FIRST TRANSITION: LIVING BEINGS AS COMPLEX THINGS

In the beginning, according to both mainstream science and some major religions, the world was originally composed of non-living matter, and living beings only came later. The distinction between lifeless worlds of dust and rock and gas and fluid, and the Earth teeming with life is still one of the most fundamental distinctions in science and nature. The English language routinely distinguishes living beings from inanimate things. The idea that life is a privileged state seems almost hard-wired.

Our first transition in understanding of complexity, we contend, involves erasing this age-old distinction, and the realisation that living things could be, after all, just things too. The seeds were sown long before 1828 when Friedrich Wöhler synthesised urea; the first time an organic compound had been created from an inorganic compound. This demonstrated that living things were not made of some special vitalistic matter, separate from non-living matter, but were made up of the same chemicals as everything else: the common dust of the Earth, after all. This transition represents the snuffing out of vitalism – the idea that living things possess some sort of life force, or *élan vital*, not possessed by non-living things – which lingered at least into the twentieth century.

Instead, the contention is that there is a spectrum of things, from the simplest atoms and molecules to longer chain molecules, proteins and, eventually, the chemistry of living bodies; the idea that while these have distinct qualities and functional consequences, they may be related by differences in degree of complexity. Thus complexity enters the frame: living things are just things, after all – albeit the most complex types of thing.

At first, the potential connection between organisms and their otherwise inert constituent matter was perhaps just symbolic or metaphorical: humans being made out of dust. However, with increasingly complex technologies, the hitherto unimaginable gap could start to be narrowed and eventually intellectually bridged.

The historical advance of technology led to the increasing complexity of artefacts and machines. The ancient Greeks had created complex mechanisms such as the Antikythera (Figure 4.1), likened to an analogue computer, but this did not mean that they conceived of the universe as some sort of clockwork mechanism (Bolter 1993). Plato's *Timaeus* invoked technology to explain the universal order; 'nature was a vast living organism' but 'not mechanistic in the modern sense' (Bolter 1993, pp. 22–3).

However, Aristotle's dissection helped reveal the 'craftsmanship of nature' (Lloyd 1970, pp. 104–5). This understanding of the functional complexity of living creatures would eventually pave the way to the idea that an organism could even come to be regarded as an intricate organic machine.

These two tendencies were destined to come together sooner or later, but for a while were tantalisingly intertwined, not least in Leonardo da Vinci's (1452–1519) brilliant conjunction of biological understanding of human and animal bodies, and of complex functional contraptions (Nicholl 2005; Suh 2005). The juxtaposition of da Vinci's detailed drawings of sinews and internal organs, on the one hand, and of hydraulic and flying machines, on the other, looks now to be evidently suggestive of a continuum of technological possibility, even if it was only later that this was consciously expressed. What is significant to our story is the idea that animal bodies and human-built machines could be said to possess a functional complexity, separated by degree, rather than being quintessentially different in kind.

Nicole Oresme (1320–1382) has been hailed as the first to be inspired by the idea of the clock as a miniature universe – implying a precise and ordered cosmos (Bolter 1993, p. 27). Subsequently, the clockwork universe became a mainstream idea, often associated with Isaac Newton or, more precisely, with Newton's descriptions of how the universe

Note: The Antikythera mechanism is the most intricately complex, artificial mechanism known to have existed before medieval cathedral clocks. It was used to calculate and display information about astronomical phenomena.

Source: Accessed 15 May 2021 at https://en.wikipedia.org/wiki/File:NAMA_Machine_d%27Anticythère_1. jpg. Author: Marsyas (original in colour).

Figure 4.1   The Antikythera mechanism

works. In the seventeenth century the telescope and the microscope provided eyes into new worlds of the very small and the very large or far away; as captured in Hooke's *Micrographia* (Hooke 1665 [2019]) teeming with microbes, or astronomical observations, from hitherto unseen stars to details of craters on the Moon. The clock metaphor was applied to both the macrocosm of the world and the microcosm of animals and their bodies; Thomas Hobbes suggested automata had an artificial life (Hobbes 1651; Dyson 2012). See Figure 4.2.

In the development of mechanical automata, perhaps the most celebrated was Vaucanson's 'Canard Digérateur' ('Digesting Duck') (1739), a flapping, defecating duck: an elaborate, authentic-looking facsimile of a real bird in some of its most basic

Note: A clockwork universe, or solar system, is a descendant of the Antikythera mechanism.

Source: Accessed 26 April 2021 at https://www.flickr.com/photo_zoom.gne?id=127601212&size=m.

Figure 4.2   An orrery, showing the Sun and inner planets of our solar system

bodily functions, said to contain over 400 moving parts in each wing alone (Figure 4.3). This could be seen as a model of complexity: more than an ingenious toy, but a concrete manifestation of the idea that the natural world behaved mechanically, making tangible the ideas of Descartes, Huygens or Newton (Bolter 1993, p. 208).

Nineteenth-century thinkers likened the universe to a gigantic heat engine; the living organism was also conceived as a heat engine 'burning glucose or glycogen or starch, fats and proteins into carbon dioxide, water and urea' (Bolter 1993, pp. 31, 32).

What is significant to our story was not so much these marvellous mechanical break-throughs on their own, nor the emerging dexterity of anatomists, but the intellectual breakthrough that their conjunction precipitated: the dangerous idea that man may well be a human machine (Julien Offray de La Mettrie, *circa* 1745 [1748]). Quite apart from the theological or metaphysical consequences of seeing organisms as machines – or machines as organisms – this breakthrough places human designs within the same broad sweep of functional complexity as nature's ultimate designs. This allows complexity to be seen, perhaps for the first time, as a positive, perhaps essential, attribute of good design, as opposed to being simply a neutral, or potentially complicating, by-product of it.

Note: 'The Flute Player' and the 'Tambourine Player' flanking the 'Digesting Duck' which, with its apparent ability to consume food and defecate, outshone its pseudo-human companions.

Source: Accessed 25 May 2021 at https://en.wikipedia.org/wiki/Jacques_de_Vaucanson#/media/ File:Vaucanson_Automata.jpg.

Figure 4.3   Three automata by Jaques de Vaucanson (1709–82)

This mechanistic view of seeing organisms as complex machines could be contrasted with the natural theological view, such as espoused by William Paley, who saw organisms as wonderfully executed products of God's design (Paley 1802). However, both of these ultimately recognised the possibility of living things being complex designs (Figure 4.4).

This first transition – from seeing organisms as fundamentally different types of things from immaterial objects, to seeing them taking their place within the general compass of complexity – was not yet taking place in the realm of urban thought. While Leonardo's notebooks show his sketches for utopian town plans, we cannot yet discern an explicit connection between the urbanism, the mechanism and the organisms. At this stage it seems there was limited linkage between cities and any other analogues. While we can find the occasional anthropomorphic depiction of cities as human bodies, the actual planned cities of the day were more wilfully geometric – not trying to be anthropomorphic or organic in any other way. It was only much later that this first intellectual transition was finally realised in theories of cities; before then, there were other transitions to take place.

THE SECOND TRANSITION: *HOMO SAPIENS* AS URBAN SPECIES

> From these things therefore it is clear that the city-state is a natural growth, and that man is by nature a political animal. (Aristotle, *Politics, circa* 330 BC [1991], s. 1253a)

Note: The fern is an ancient vascular plant of a type dating as far back as the Carboniferous period (359 million years ago).

Source: Photograph by Treasa Creavin.

Figure 4.4   The fern: a fractal structure that also demonstrates the complex order of nature

Distinctions between humans and nature, and between nature and artifice, are deeply ingrained in many societies. Yet, when Aristotle said that 'man is . . . a political animal' he can be seen simultaneously distinguishing *Homo sapiens* from other animals while implicitly including humans in the larger animal grouping. In the same sentence, he claimed that 'the city-state is a natural growth'. This intriguingly both posits the city-state as the environment of humanity, and as artifice, that is, it is a product of human thought and action; but on top of all that, calling it a 'natural growth' implies that it is as natural as the constructed niches of other species – be it the bee in its hive or the bird in its nest (Figure 4.5).

Recognition of humans as just another type of animal is, we suggest, the second transition in intellectual thought in the history of urban complexity. If the potential equivalence of organisms and machines helps bridge between nature and artifice through the recognition or lens of their complexity, the next breakthrough can be seen as one

Source: Photograph by Treasa Creavin.

Figure 4.5   Wasps nest: the complex order of nature in a different form, this one created by living things

bridging between humans and nature in another way, which finally brings in the complexity of the built environment. This takes place, as it were, off-stage, in the realm of biology: Darwin's and Wallace's discovery of the mechanism of descent with modification by natural selection. For evolution provides a common mechanism by which all living things are related to each other in a single biome, thereby erasing the traditional, anthropocentric distinction between humans and all other species. Echoing Aristotle, 'man' must be considered just another animal, after all; this had profound consequences for science and society, and humans' place in the order of things.

As with human versus natural designs, complexity could again be seen as a quintessential distinguishing feature, this time the humans being regarded as the ultimate, most complex of beings, at least in terms of their intellectual capacity and diverse works from tools to cities. Again, this places complexity, from a human point of view, as a positive attribute.

Darwinism had an impact in many walks of life, and not least on that of urban planning. The linkage here can be seen to be simultaneously direct and complex, through the person of Patrick Geddes.

Geddes, whose studies in his youth in Scotland ranged over many topics, eventually trained in biology, but always had a wider interest in the phenomenon of life, including human life and culture, and his later career turned increasingly to sociology and town planning (Welter 2002; Meller 2005).

Geddes readily took for granted the implication of evolution that *Homo sapiens* was related to all other life forms, and that life was an ever-evolving continuum. Human settlements were equivalent to, albeit more complex than, the constructed niches of other species; cities were analogous to bees' hives or beavers' dams; London could be considered a 'man-reef' (Figure 4.6).

Whereas Darwin's theory emphasised selective pressures and competition, Geddes emphasised the power of co-operation, from unicellular to multicellular life, to social organisms coming together in communities, and ultimately cities and conurbations, anticipating major transition theory (Smith and Szathmary 1997).

For Geddes, evolution need not be associated with divisive competitive struggle or social Darwinism, but ever-increasing collaboration, and a positive tendency of

Note: Simple structures created by humans are very different from the complex physical structures created by the hives' occupants.

Source: Photograph by Treasa Creavin.

Figure 4.6   Beehives

populations to evolve (as he saw it, from within themselves, instead of, as with selection, from external pressures) in conjunction with the environment, including the built environment. Cities and conurbations were not just biotic by-products but the fulfilment of organic evolution (Batty and Marshall 2009, 2017; Marshall 2009).

For Geddes, then, town planning was not simply an orderly way of laying out urban development, but could be seen as no less than part of the evolution of *Homo sapiens* in its (increasingly artificial) environment. Town planning must be seen as part of a complex interactive process, between humans (and other species) and our environment, played out over time, and not simply as an architectural project, the small matter of laying out buildings and streets in an ordered plan (Marshall 2009).

This was explicitly recognised at the time by Patrick Abercrombie, one of the foremost town planning academics and practitioners of the emerging profession of the twentieth century:

> It is perhaps safe to say that the modern practice of town-planning in this country would have been a much simpler thing if it had not been for Geddes. There was a time when it seemed only necessary to shake up into a bottle the German town-extension plan, the Parisian boulevard, the English garden village, the American civic centre and park system, in order to produce a mechanical mixture which might be applied indiscriminately and beneficially to every town and village in this country, in the hope that is would be 'town planned' according to the most up-to-date notions. Pleasing dream! First shattered by Geddes, emerging from his Outlook Tower, . . . to produce that nightmare of complexity, the Edinburgh Room at the great Town-Planning Exhibition of 1910. (Defries 1927, pp. 322–3)

This saw the city of Edinburgh, or any city or town, inextricably bound to its hinterland, with layers of interpretive complexity over space and time. Perhaps for the first time, urbanism was seen in its full complexity as we now see it, being not only about bricks and mortar, but seamlessly fusing humanity and all other life forms, and social, economic and cultural concerns, considered holistically in a single ecosystem.

In the simplest terms, Geddes can be seen as a biologist turned town-planner, bridging from Darwin to Mumford, Abercrombie and the emerging twentieth-century profession of town planning; but he also had a subtler, more complex influence. Geddes was not simply using organic analogies to support what could otherwise be conventional town planning. Instead, he was – together with Camillo Sitte – one of the first to appreciate the complexity of traditional urbanism in a positive light, not merely for its material urban properties, but in effect understanding the complex order of the web of human life – instead of seeing the disorder and chaos of unplanned development – and so saw value in existing areas that were considered slums in their day, and the value in regenerating them, through 'conservative surgery' and so on (Defries 1927, pp. 322–3).

As Abercrombie implied, Geddes was ahead of his time in seeing town planning as intervening in a complex system (as we would now have it), rather than simply as an act of creation, or imposition of a new, artificial order (Defries 1927, pp. 322–3). While the early twentieth-century pioneers of town planning attempted to treat urbanism in a more complex, holistic way (that is, by considering the wider demographics and geographical hinterland), it was only in the second half of the century that the understanding of the city itself as a complex system was fully realised.

THE THIRD TRANSITION: ORGANISED COMPLEXITY AS A 'GOOD THING'

In *The Death and Life of Great American Cities*, Jacobs (1962) exposed the problems of top-down planning; its creation of sterile, dysfunctional places, as opposed to the vibrancy of traditional streets and neighbourhoods – including slum neighbourhoods – which Jacobs believed to possess a vitality lacking in the modern planned developments that were often replacing them. In effect, the traditional streets and neighbourhoods had a complex social and economic life inextricable from the buildings and land uses that planners were more directly concerned with.

Jacobs's (1962) argument that complexity both could and should be part of the solution, marked a fundamental change in the way in which urban planners understand cities, and its origins deserve a closer look. Jacobs drew explicitly on scientific notions of complexity as an explanation of 'The kind of problem a city is', as she called her closing chapter.

The chapter title is significant in its own right, for it comes straight to the point of the entire book. Her blunt declaration that a city could not and should not be seen as some sort of linear system that could be controlled through the simple application of statistical approaches was a forthright attack not only on how cities were being planned at the time, but on how they were thought about. A city should be understood, and could only be understood as a thing of 'organised complexity', a phrase she borrowed from Warren Weaver, the Vice-President of the Natural and Medical Sciences at the Rockefeller Foundation. Jacobs quotes Weaver extensively in the book's closing pages, for she had been strongly influenced by his essay for the Rockefeller Foundation's 1958 Annual Report. In his essay, Weaver set out a brief history of scientific thought which could, crudely, be divided into three stages: first, the ability to deal with problems of simplicity; second, the ability to deal with problems of disorganised complexity; and third, the ability to deal with problems of organised complexity (Jacobs 1962, pp. 442–3).

The simple and the disorganised are relatively easy to understand, that is, they are tractable in mathematical terms. Simple problems lend themselves to simple mathematical analysis in relation to one variable being dependent on a second, independent, variable, such as the relationship between mass and volume of a particular material, or between electrical resistance and current flow. The problems of disorganised complexity lend themselves to statistical analysis, which can predict the aggregate behaviour of large numbers of randomly distributed particles, such as gas molecules, but not the movements of any particular particle.

Problems of organised complexity, argued Weaver, fall in a 'middle region' between these two outer regions. Weaver continued:

> The importance of this middle region, moreover, does not depend primarily on the fact that the number of variables involved is moderate – large compared to two, but small compared to the number of atoms in a pinch of salt . . . much more important than the mere number of variables is the fact that these variables are all interrelated . . . These problems, as contrasted with the disorganised situations with which statistics can cope, show the essential feature of organisation. We will therefore refer to this group of problems as those of organised complexity.
>
> What makes an evening primrose open when it does? Why does salt water fail to satisfy thirst? . . . What is the description of ageing in biochemical terms? . . . What is a gene, and how

does the original genetic constitution of a living organism express itself in the developed characteristics of the adult? . . .

All these are certainly complex problems. But they are not problems of disorganised complexity, to which statistical methods hold the key. They are problems which involve dealing simultaneously with a sizeable number of factors which are interrelated into an organic whole. (Warren Weaver, cited in Jacobs 1962, p. 447)

Since cities 'happen to be problems in organised complexity' (Jacobs 1962, p. 448), they can and should be analysed in relation to their many variables 'interrelated into an organic whole' (Jacobs 1962, p. 447).

In drawing these threads together, Jacobs was perhaps the first to bring to bear upon urban theory what we would now consider to be a modern scientific understanding of complexity. Geddes had specifically invoked complexity; he seemed to use it in such a general, all-encompassing way, as to be almost a truism: that humans are part of a complex evolving web of living things and their constructions. The significance of Jacobs's contribution was in more deliberately associating cities with an organic type of complexity, which seemed to have dynamic, vital qualities that conventionally planned urban development lacked; and she more vigorously attacked that lack. It may seem obvious now, and perhaps always was to the majority who understood the city as a lived experience rather than a technical problem, but in the first half of the 1960s, urban planning was seen as a fundamentally technical-aesthetic discipline that required above all else clarity of vision. The messiness of a city was seen almost as a flaw rather than as an inherent quality of the city itself (Figure 4.7).

Three years after Jane Jacobs published *Death and Life*, Christopher Alexander published the first in a long line of works of relevance to cities and complexity. In *A City is Not a Tree* (Alexander 1965), he articulated an argument even more succinctly, contrasting what he saw as the functional complexity of traditional urbanism versus the dysfunctional simplicity of modern planned developments. This he did with reference to explicit mathematical structures (sets and graph theory), which helped encourage urbanists to conceive of urban structure in a scientifically tractable way.

Specifically, Alexander argued that traditional cities were not structured like a mathematical tree – with neatly nested hierarchies of elements wholly contained within a higher-level element – but more similar to a semi-lattice, where a diversity of elements could belong to overlapping higher-order sets. For example, a typical, natural urban neighbourhood would run into or overlap with its neighbours, perhaps sharing facilities – or joined by a high street as a seam – rather than being hermetically distinct cellular units divided by highways, as often occurred in modern planned settlements. One of the most influential essays of its time, and a gateway to all those that followed, *A City is Not a Tree* (Alexander 1965) still resonates today, perhaps partly because the challenges it poses to generating complex designs remain unfulfilled (Marshall 2009; Alexander 2015).

Taken together, Jacobs and Alexander brought to the fore the radical idea – buried in Geddes's complex mass of literary arguments – that traditional urbanism need not be seen as disordered and dysfunctional, but could be seen to have a complex order, that was functional (Figure 4.7). This, the third transition, was the idea that something could be functional because of, not despite, being inscrutably complex; and conversely, that modern planned developments were in danger of being dysfunctionally simplistic.

Note: The value of the complex order of traditional urbanism was finally recognised in the latter half of the twentieth century.

Source: Photograph by Treasa Creavin.

Figure 4.7   Provençal hill town, France: the complex order of traditional urbanism

Whereas the history of town planning had tended to replace complex urbanism with the simple order of planned development, perhaps for the first time it was recognised that more complex order might be positive. Whereas Geddes had attained limited impact in the application of his theorising, it took the reality of the failure of (some) post-war planning and mass-produced, top-down development to convince professionals and public alike of the nature of the problem, and the value of the functional complexity of traditional urbanism: that complexity could and should be part of the solution.

THE FOURTH TRANSITION: THE COMPLEXITY OF PEOPLE'S LIVES FINALLY RECOGNISED

Alexander's and Jacobs's abstract arguments gave intellectual underpinning to a practical suspicion, already growing among urban sociologists such as William F. Whyte in the

United States and Michael Young and Peter Willmott in the United Kingdom, that the technocratic, comprehensive approach to planning created almost as many problems as it set out to solve (Whyte 1943; Young and Willmott 1956).

It was a suspicion that had lingered in the background since the 1940s for Whyte, and then for Young and Willmott, who had explored the ways in which what we would now term 'urban regeneration' had disrupted the complex social networks and structures that knitted a community together.

In the early 1940s, Whyte had looked at the district of North Boston, home to a poor but tightly knit Italian community, and found that whereas the prevailing technocratic view characterised the area as a slum that needed pulling down, the reality was that the fragile, dilapidated physical structures housed complex and long-established social structures that would be destroyed by redevelopment. His resulting book, *Street Corner Society: The Social Structure of an Italian Slum* (Whyte 1943) was a landmark in sociology, and it was followed 13 years later by an equally important work, this time on life in east London.

Young and Willmott's 1956 study, *Family and Kinship in East London* (Young and Willmott 1956) looked at how the lives of people living in Bethnal Green, an inner London district of poor-quality terraced housing, were overturned when they were moved out to new developments of much higher physical quality on London's periphery. The key finding from both studies was that the intricate social networks which had evolved organically over time were easily destroyed. Although for those in London the material living conditions in the newer developments were greatly improved, the social networks were not easily replicated in the newer developments. Often they were not replicated at all, and the improvement in living conditions was often accompanied by an increase in loneliness (Young and Willmott 1956), a classic example of a technically good solution creating new and perhaps unexpected problems of its own.

This is what Jacobs means when she writes of an organic whole; one part cannot be changed in isolation from the rest. In the parlance of complexity theory, the social networks of Bethnal Green were an emergent property of that particular environment, easy to destroy, hard to understand, and harder still to replicate or re-create anew (Figure 4.8).

These were major studies and hugely influential in the field of sociology, valuable lessons in how cities and urban planning might be theorised. Yet these views and lessons from Whyte, Young and Willmott, Jacobs and Alexander were eclipsed by the growing use of computers and the development in the late 1960s of a systems theory of planning. However, Jacobs's insight as regards a city being a problem in organised complexity would eventually embed the general idea of complexity in planning theory from the 1970s onwards, even if it was rarely referred to explicitly in planning texts. The idea, however, stuck, and we return to it shortly.

The fourth transition therefore brought urban sociology to the fore. This is not especially surprising, given that sociologists spend a great deal of their time talking to people about their day-to-day experiences, and only theorising about them later. However, the issue here is that it not only kept the concept of a city as a problem in organised complexity alive in the 1970s and 1980s, but also marked the integration of this concept into the broader discourse on urban planning, which straddles fields from architecture to transport engineering to ecology to sociology, and much else besides.

Note: As with traditional urbanism, the social dimension of urban complexity was also recognised in the second half of the twentieth century.

Source: Photograph by Nick Green.

Figure 4.8   Taxco, Mexico

These ideas continued to be developed, and in 1970, almost three decades after the publication of Whyte's *Street Corner Society*, the American sociologist Richard Sennett published *The Uses of Disorder*. To an extent it prefigured early twenty-first century discussions of diversity, since it was a sophisticated (if sometimes naive) manifesto for rethinking cities as places where disorder can flourish, the better to allow people to coexist in mutual acceptance of one another's differences (Sennett 1970). He argued: 'In extricating the city from preplanned control, men will become more in control of themselves and more aware of each other' (Sennett 1970, p. 198). Again, this book attempts to persuade the reader that a city is not a simple thing that can be understood through systems thinking (the dominant planning theory at the time), but a messy, almost inchoate, thing that had to be accepted on those terms if society were to flourish.

Four years later, Jonathan Raban published *Soft City* (Raban 1974 [1998]), a paean to London in all its chaos. Again, this was an argument for understanding the city in a way almost completely different from how the planner of the time would have seen it. The 'soft city' is the version of a city that each of us creates for ourselves, a city with particular focal points, axes, boundaries, comfort zones and no-go areas that is entirely personal. It is a city of social networks, of changing relationships, of many of those things that the contemporary (and current) models of cities could not possibly capture, but all of which were and remain a part of the organised complexity that makes London, or any city, what it is at any given moment in time.

THE FIFTH TRANSITION: DIVERSITY AS A NECESSARY DIMENSION OF SOCIAL COMPLEXITY

Looking back, we could be forgiven for thinking there was a single, almost linear, unfolding trajectory of complexity gradually being revealed. Not surprisingly, the narrative has reflected the literature and practice of science, urban studies and planning, but until the 1990s that has been largely western and mostly male. As Leonie Sandercock has argued, for much of planning's history, the key decision-makers were drawn from a narrow spectrum of the population, so their perspective was necessarily limited in scope (Sandercock and Forsyth 1992; Sandercock 2000, 2004). The urban reality is more complex than this, as we have different gendered perspectives, from different cultures, and this additional dimension of diversity throws open a kaleidoscopic of perspectives. It was always there, but in the background, and now it needs to be brought into the mix as part of the complexity.

We see this in Elizabeth Wilson's (1991) *The Sphinx in the City* which opened up female perspectives on cities and urbanism, and the consequences for urban solutions. The mid-twentieth century suburban solution to the problem of how to plan cities was often low-density, car-orientated housing estates which suited the classic nuclear family where one parent (usually the man) drove to work, while the other parent (usually the woman) was left to do the shopping and look after the children, but without a car. Predicated on each household owning one car, it was better suited to the man than the woman, who found herself stuck at home in relative isolation, a topic covered in *Family and Kinship* (Young and Willmott 1956) and referred to above.

If we look beyond the western world, we find new areas of complexity unfolding too. Nezar Al Sayyad (1991), for example, challenges western stereotypes of Islamic cities, so that we can learn to appreciate the intricate pragmatic order, as opposed to western perceptions of romantic disorder, of Arab Muslin urbanism. This paved the way for revealing further perspectives on urban informality and an appreciation of the urbanism of the Global South (Al Sayyad and Roy 2003).

These perspectives serve to undermine easy assumptions that solutions developed in one culture can simply be applied in another. This is seen not least in town planning experiments outside the western hemisphere, in places such as Chandigarh and

Colombo, Sri Lanka, where it was noted that town planning was a western import and often blind to the realities of these places (Perera 2002, 2004, 2008).

We can recall that Patrick Geddes may be seen from a western point of view as pioneering a sensitive, bottom-up approach to urbanism locally, but seen through the lens of diversity, his planning work in south Asia can equally be understood as continuing the wider colonial project, framing the town planning problem from the viewpoint of the outsider, rather than the local. As Perera (2008, p. 66) argues, 'planning was seen as a "science" of making particular decisions, and (Western) science is considered culturally neutral, contextless, abstract, and can, therefore, be generalized'. See Figure 4.9.

Even without the colonial dimension, diversity prompts questions regarding the principle of international consultants imposing generic ideas on localities, and assumptions about the 'scientism' of any particular solution. In a foreshadowing of current discourse on diversity, Perera laid out a de facto case that the full diversity of human experience and culture needed to be taken into account if a city was to be properly analysed. Without understanding the full complexity of a place, including distinctions between different social groups and political interests, there would be little hope of solving whatever problems it may have. Ultimately, consideration of diversity teaches us that there is no single way of understanding the problem of the city, nor a single solution likely to fit all needs. This brings us to the final issue, that of intervention.

THE SIXTH TRANSITION: THE 'WICKED' NATURE OF INTERVENTION

For most of the history of city planning, it was assumed that city planning was the solution. However, following the setbacks of the 1960s and 1970s – dysfunctional modernist housing, failed regeneration and blight – it dawned that planning could be part of the problem. Accordingly, the professional planning world produced the very occasional suggestion that whole-hearted acceptance of the messy reality of the city was not merely realistic, but in some instances desirable. The best-known of these came in the form of an article published in the now defunct *New Society* journal, written jointly by Reyner Banham, an architectural historian, Paul Barker, the journal's editor, Peter Hall, a planning academic, and the architect Cedric Price. Hall gives a brief account of it in his book *Cities of Tomorrow* (Hall 1988, p. 260), and it is quoted at length here. The article argued that the solution to the problem of planning could be a 'Non-Plan':

> The whole concept of planning (the town-and-country kind at least) has gone cockeyed . . . Somehow, everything must be watched; nothing must be allowed simply 'to happen'. No house can be allowed to be commonplace in the way that things just are commonplace: each project must be weighed, and planned, and approved, and only then built, and only after that discovered to be commonplace after all. (Banham et al. 1969, cited in Hall 1988, p. 260)

So the group proposed

> a precise and carefully controlled experiment in non-planning to seize on a few appropriate zones of the country, which are subject to a characteristic range of pressures, and use them as launchpads for Non-Plan. At the least, one would find out what people want; at the most, one

Note: Diversity of cultures and religions has been accepted as a necessary dimension of social complexity since the 1970s.

Source: Photograph by Stephen Marshall.

Figure 4.9   Moscow, Russia

might discover the hidden style of mid-20th century Britain. (Banham et al., 1969, cited in Hall 1988 p. 260)

The eventual consequence of these ideas in the UK – the Enterprise Zones of the 1980s – drew criticism, since once again it appeared that even without any form 'planning', local communities were still ignored, over-ridden and generally assumed to be unimportant, except as things to plan for, rather than people to plan with (Brownill 1990). Yet it is the people who not only build the city in a strictly physical sense, but who also make the city what it is, in its being an exercise in organised complexity.

By the mid-1970s, local community activists across Europe were beginning to engage with urban planning and fight back against what they saw as the technocratic and undemocratic approach of the city planners. They felt they were being bulldozed, both literally and metaphorically, and had decided to do something about it, most often by enrolling, whether knowingly or not, the arguments that Jane Jacobs had made well over a decade earlier: cities and neighbourhoods needed to be understood as problems of organised complexity; they were not problems that could be solved with a theodolite, a bulldozer and a trowel.

The Urban Question by Manuel Castells (1979), and *Social Justice and City* by David Harvey (1973), both of which adopted a strong Marxist line of interpretation of urban problems, served to further underline the extent to which a city was much more than just the sum of its physical parts, and in the early 1980s, riots in several major English cities forced the planning profession (among many others) into a period of close self-examination.

The clearest response came from academic planning theory. Patsy Healey argued in a series of papers and then a book that the planning system needed to be more responsive to the needs of the communities it claimed to serve. Thus came about the collaborative planning theory, which argued that planning needed to be much more collaborative, and considerably less technocratic. Only then would it be able to deal effectively with the complex and messy realities of villages, towns and cities, and their constituent neighbourhoods; and only then would the claim be taken seriously that planning really was a democratic endeavour for the betterment of society (Healey et al. 1995; Healey 1997). Hence, Healey brought the concept of complexity directly into the discourse of planning theory, where it has flourished ever since, at least as an essential conceptual dimension, whatever its practical impact.

Ultimately, the problem of urban intervention came to be seen as a 'wicked' problem: where the act of solving a problem in a complex situation creates new problems of its own (Figure 4.10). This can be seen, with hindsight, across much of the planning history of the past century, including the dysfunctional modernist housing and highways decried by Jacobs and Alexander, to the 'prairie planning' of new towns, where the solution of auto-orientated housing layouts created new problems of isolation for many of the inhabitants (Young and Willmott 1956; Wilson 1991). See Figure 4.10.

This, then, is a sixth transition. Here, we finally see the acceptance at both theoretical and practical levels, that the city is a messy, complex, multifaceted, multidimensional thing, whose many problems are frequently 'wicked' in nature, and whose solutions are therefore likely to give rise to still more problems, which will also turn out to be 'wicked'. And it is perhaps the acceptance of this, the understanding of complexity as a means of

Note: Timber is a renewable resource and, when growing, a carbon sink and home to many creatures and its own ecosystem. Harvesting destroys all of that. The commercial timber stand is simultaneously solution and problem, and at the core of a 'wicked' problem.

Source: Photograph by Nick Green.

Figure 4.10   Cleared timber stand, Northumbria

both understanding and doing, and therefore of the arguments made by Jane Jacobs over half a century ago, that has made it possible for complexity theory to be taken seriously as a technical, analytical tool through which we can conceptualise both cities and sometimes their individual neighbourhoods or constituents (for example, Batty 2005), with a view to the eventual creation of practical policies, which may result in small but real improvements.

This final transition meant the time was ripe for urban theory to embrace what had become known explicitly as complexity theory. Notions of complexity theory or complexity science, and their associated techniques as a technical endeavour, were originally pioneered in the post-war decades by individuals such as Ilya Prigogine and Herman Haken, and in the 1980s by organisations such as the Santa Fe Institute. These had, by the 1990s, developed into a mature inter-disciplinary science, led primarily by physicists and biologists, who developed concepts such as self-organisation, phase transitions, emergence and fitness landscapes, with links to chaos theory, fractals and artificial life, and applications via cellular automata; that were now applied to problems in the urban domain (see, for example, Batty and Longley 1994; Batty and Xie 1994; Portugali 1997; Green 1999).

And so, from roughly the 1990s, what became known as complexity theories of cities came to be developed (Portugali 2011; Portugali et al. 2012), fruitfully exploiting insights originally from physics and biology, applied to a realm more traditionally associated with social sciences and built environment disciplines. These theories finally incorporate into urbanism our first identified transition between the non-living and living – and so fulfil the glib but handy trope of chemistry arguably being complex physics, and biology being complex chemistry, and social science being an extended, more complex version of biology. As for urbanism, that became a yet more complex, applied extension of social science which set the stage for complexity theories of cities to come of age.

NOTES

1. Readers may also see parallels with notions from complexity theory of phase transitions, but our concern here is not so much to do with the type of complexity manifested in the physical, biological nature of the transitions in evolutionary history, as to do with how our general understanding of the notion of complexity has changed over time.
2. Unless otherwise qualified, all terms are used in their standard dictionary definitions, instead of in any technical sense. So, references to chaos, complexity, gradual, transition, crystallisation, and so on, which can carry specific technical meanings in particular contexts, should be read in their standard, non-technical meanings, not as technical terms, unless otherwise qualified.

REFERENCES

Al Sayyad, N. (1991), *Cities and Caliphs: On the Genesis of Arab Muslim Urbanism*, Westport, CT: Greenwood Press.
Al Sayyad, N. and A. Roy (eds) (2003), *Urban Informality: Transnational Perspectives from the Middle East, Latin America, and South Asia*, Oxford: Lexington Books.
Alexander, C. (2015), *A City is Not a Tree*, 50th anniversary edn, M.W. Mehaffy (ed.), Portland, OR: Sustasis Press.
Amin, A. and N. Thrift (2017), *Seeing Like a City*, Cambridge: Polity Press.
Aristotle (*c.* 330 BC) *Politics*, in R.A. Allen (ed.) (1991), *Greek Philosophy: Thales to Aristotle*, 3rd edn, New York: Free Press.
Banham, R., C. Price, P. Barker and P. Hall (1969), 'Non-plan: an experiment in freedom', *New Society,* **13** (338), 435–43.
Batty, M. (2005), *Cities and Complexity*, Cambridge, MA: MIT Press.
Batty, M. and P.A. Longley (1994), *Fractal Cities: A Geometry of Form and Function*, London: Academic Press.
Batty, M. and S. Marshall (2009), 'Centenary paper: the evolution of cities: Geddes, Abercrombie and the new physicalism', *Town Planning Review*, **80** (6), 551–74.
Batty, M. and S. Marshall (2017), 'Thinking organic, acting civic: the paradox of planning for cities in evolution', *Landscape and Urban Planning*, **166**, 4–14.

Batty, M. and Y. Xie (1994), 'From cells to cities', *Environment and Planning B: Planning and Design*, **21** (7), S31–S48.
Bolter, J.D. (1993), *Turing's Man: Western Culture in the Computer Age*, London: Penguin Books.
Brownill, S. (1990), *Developing London's Docklands – Another Great Planning Disaster?* London: Paul Chapman.
Castells, M. (1979), *The Urban Question*, Cambridge, MA: MIT Press.
De La Mettrie, J.O. (*c.* 1745), *Man a Machine*, 1748 English translation, accessed 14 May 2021 at http://bactra.org/LaMettrie/Machine/.
Defries, A. (1927), *The Interpreter Geddes: The Man and his Gospel*, London: George Routledge and Sons.
Dyson, G.B. (2012), *Darwin among the Machines: The Evolution of Global Intelligence*, New York: Basic Books.
Green, N. (1999), 'Art and complexity in London's East End', *Complexity*, **4** (6), 14–21.
Hall, P. (1988), *Cities of Tomorrow*, Oxford: Blackwell.
Harvey, D. (1973), *Social Justice and the City*, London: Edward Arnold.
Healey, P. (1997), *Collaborative Planning: Shaping Places in Fragmented Societies*, London: Macmillan.
Healey, P., S. Cameron, S. Davoudi, S. Graham and A. Madanipour (1995), *Managing Cities: The New Urban Context*, Chichester: John Wiley and Sons.
Hobbes, T. (1651), *Leviathan*, London: Andrew Crooke.
Hooke, R. (1665), *Micrographia: Some Physiological Descriptions of Minute Bodies Made by Magnifying Glasses with Observations and Inquiries Thereupon*, Kindle edn 2019, Public Domain Book.
Jacobs, J. (1962), *The Death and Life of Great American Cities*, London: Jonathan Cape.
Lloyd, G.E.R. (1970), *Early Greek Science: Thales to Aristotle*, London: Chatto & Windus.
Marshall, S. (2009), *Cities, Design and Evolution*, London: Routledge.
Meller, H. (2005), *Patrick Geddes: Social Evolutionist and City Planner*, London: Routledge.
Nicholl, C. (2005), *Leonardo da Vinci: The Flights of the Mind*, London: Penguin.
Paley, W. (1802), *Natural Theology: or, Evidences of the Existence and Attributes of the Deity, Collected from the Appearances of Nature*, London: J. Faulder.
Perera, N. (2002), 'Indigenising the colonial city: late 19th-century Colombo and its landscape', *Urban Studies*, **39** (9), 1703–21.
Perera, N. (2004), 'Contesting visions: hybridity, liminality and authorship of the Chandigarh plan', *Planning Perspectives*, **19** (2), 175–99.
Perera, N. (2008), 'The planners' city: the construction of a town planning perception of Colombo', *Environment and Planning A: Economy and Space*, **40** (1), 57–73.
Portugali, J. (1997), 'Self-organizing cities', *Futures*, **29** (4–5), 353–80.
Portugali, J. (2011), *Complexity Theory, Cognition and the City*, Heidelberg: Springer-Verlag.
Portugali, J., H. Mayer, E. Stolk and E. Tan (eds) (2012), *Complexity Theories of Cities Have Come of Age*, Heidelberg: Springer-Verlag.
Raban, J. (1974), *Soft City*, repr. 1998, London: Harvill Press.
Sandercock, L. (2000), 'When strangers become neighbours: managing cities of difference', *Planning Theory and Practice*, **1** (1), 13–30.
Sandercock, L. (2004), 'Towards a planning imagination for the 21st century', *Journal of the American Planning Association*, **70** (2), 133–41.
Sandercock, L. and A. Forsyth (1992), 'A gender agenda: new directions for planning theory', *Journal of the American Planning Association*, **58** (1), 49–59.
Sennett, R. (1970), *The Uses of Disorder: Personal Identity and City Life*, London: Alfred A Knopf.
Smith, J.M. and E. Szathmary (1997), *The Major Transitions in Evolution*, Oxford: Oxford University Press.
Suh, H.A. (2005), *Leonardo's Notebooks*, London: Black Dog & Leventhal.
Welter, V.M. (2002), *Biopolis: Patrick Geddes and the City of Life*, Cambridge, MA: MIT Press.
Whyte, W.F. (1943), *Street Corner Society: The Social Structure of an Italian Slum*, Chicago, IL: University of Chicago Press.
Wilson, E. (1991), *The Sphinx in the City: Urban life, the Control of Disorder, and Women*, London: Virago Press.
Young, M. and P. Willmott (1956), *Family and Kinship in East London*, London: Pelican.

PART II

COMPLEXITY THEORIES
OF CITIES

5. Complexity: the evolution and planning of towns and cities
Peter M. Allen

1. INTRODUCTION

Our society has an interesting conundrum at its heart. Some believe that market-based decision-making leads (miraculously perhaps, and conveniently for them) to the common good, while others think that unfettered and unplanned development leads to a bad outcome for the majority and a terrible outcome for some. Which approach leads to the greater public good? Are commercially based market-driven decisions best for society or can an institution set up by local, regional or national government better define what is in the common good? Both views imply that they can anticipate the outcome of any particular intervention, and can give it a good or bad weighting as regards the impacts. De Roo (2000) and De Roo and Silva (2010) have raised the important issue of the clash between self-organization, which is supposedly bottom up, and rational planning, which is more top down and claims to represent the community as a whole.

In many ways this constitutes one of the main political issues that drives and divides modern politics, and it underlies the reasons why we need to recognize that we live in a complex system and, indeed, drive that system and its complexity as we go. The core of this chapter concerns the difficulties and problems that this gives rise to and how we can possibly deal with them.

A totally top-down system, whether run by a (possibly well-meaning) left-wing government or by an appalling despot, simply seems to make innovation very difficult. Instead of a flood of diverse novel innovations and ideas from multiple (free) minds, and a resulting regime that tries out all sorts of things, the top-down regime has a narrow focus and many opportunities for uniformity. The bottom-up market system tries out all sorts of things that no single mind or committee can imagine; although most of these fail, some succeed and drive the system forward.

Most people who start businesses believe that they will be successful in what they undertake, until failure overtakes them. The whole idea of 'creative destruction' (Schumpeter 1942 [1975], p. 84) and the data concerning the life expectancy of firms (Ormerod 2006) tell us that almost all firms eventually fail, and most fail straight away. Yet nobody starts a firm believing that it will fail. That is, people not only have a poor understanding of their own capabilities and of the difficulties they will face, but also of the reality of complexity and how it makes prediction problematic, and that luck is a real fact of life. (This also explains why pay by performance provoked immense discord, as most people believe themselves to be above average.)

The whole edifice of human life is not based on rational calculations but is part of evolutionary and co-evolutionary processes in which individuals, organizations, towns and, even, cities can appear and disappear, whatever is believed about their future, and whatever had been planned for them. Faced with this turbulence, what is the hope of developing mathematical models to underpin the different policy choices and evaluations that are made?

We first look at modelling complex systems, such as towns, cities and regions, containing agency, diversity and learning through the presence and interactions of multiple agents. To what extent can these systems be modelled usefully? Can models tell us with any degree of certainty what will happen in the future under different possible scenarios of policy, intervention or planning? Can they tell us at least what cannot happen? How then should any such models be used? Is it better to have the models than not to have them?

Finally, we show that the problems of planning and complexity in a specific urban context is no different from many other areas of human existence. Fundamentally, we spend our lives revising our interpretive frameworks (models) and the beliefs that inspire and arise from them. These are developed idiosyncratically as a consequence of our own genetic and experiential particularities.

After Popper (1963), we also now know that science is not a set of proven mechanisms and ideas but consists of ideas that have not yet been disproved. We try to find a model that fits the facts as we currently know them and, when these are seen to be inadequate, we are forced to change our beliefs and the structure of our interpretive framework and models. However, there is no scientific or unique way to modify our beliefs when they have failed, and so we are condemned to carry on throughout our lifetimes trying to make sense of what is going on, what it means and what might happen. This is an unending process, but even though the development and use of interpretive frameworks is always going to be imperfect, it is still better to have this framework than to not have it. Acting without any model to test is simply trial and error without any learning.

2.   COMPLEXITY AND SELF-ORGANIZING SYSTEMS

In the 1970s, scientists started to consider how systems might evolve over time and, in particular, how system behaviour might be calculated if it were open to exchanges of matter and/or energy with its environment, instead of being closed. Until this, systems had been modelled using system dynamics, which simply ran the system mechanically forwards in time. Several notable scientists attempted to reflect on the issue of potential structural changes and, over time, two leading schools emerged – one led by Ilya Prigogine and the other by Herman Haken. Both of these are equally valid and provide ways of exploring the behaviour of open systems, one with a starting point of chemical kinetics, and the other coming from the physics and mathematics of lasers. Here, we focus on work arising from Prigogine's approach (Nicolis and Prigogine 1977), arising from self-organizing systems and dissipative structures, simply because this was the author's route to these ideas. Other chapters of this handbook are based on the ideas of Herman Haken (1977) and synergetics. There are also urban models based on the synergetics approach by Juval Portugali (1999).

2.1 The Brusselator: Morphogenesis

Prigogine spent much of his time thinking about time. He wanted to find the laws that governed physical systems when they were out of equilibrium. That is a chemical system with reactions still running, or flowing liquids or gases. The key example was the Belousov–Zhabotinski reaction.

In order to study the problem, Prigogine introduced a simple chemical model in which chemicals A and B are changed into D and F, with the intermediaries of X and since X is a chemical with a red colour, and Y is blue, then the spatial pattern of the reaction could be seen. Without these colours the whole discovery of self-organization would have been delayed (Figure 5.1).

Depending on the initial concentrations of A and B, the system can oscillate between blue and red, like a clock, or for a spatial model can spontaneously form moving or stationary patterns of red and blue. This demonstrates that our simple chemical system can break symmetry and exhibit creativity. Wonderful complex order could be produced by the system provided that its reactions were maintained out of equilibrium.

This showed us that, in general, an open system can spontaneously break symmetry. In a universe of interacting elements, with energy and material flows occurring widely, then self-organization and symmetry-breaking events could and would occur. Creativity and morphogenesis do not require human activity; indeed, we ourselves are the result of an evolutionary morphogenesis that began long before we existed.

Fluctuations can tip the system to some new, seemingly organized, structure. However, it is not organized to some external purpose, but is simply self-organized by

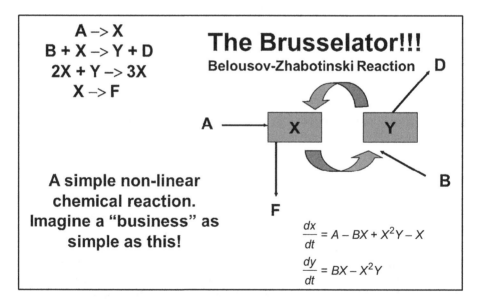

Figure 5.1 *The Brusselator shows us that open systems can create emergent structure and patterns as a result of the feedback interactions between elements (Prigogine was based at Brussels University)*

its own internal nature and its particular historical accidents. The future of the system is no longer given by the dynamics of average behaviour, but also ensues from whatever chance fluctuation happens to occur at the critical time. The average behaviour may be specified by the physical conditions but not the behaviour of individual molecules.

When a system breaks symmetry, then at that moment nobody can say what new behaviour, characteristics and capabilities may emerge. This brings us to the radical conclusion that, despite the enormous power of science, certainty of prediction is impossible for these systems. The best that can be attained might be to say that 'the system, and my predictions about it, will continue forwards as expected, until something new occurs'. Intuitions, non-average thoughts and fluctuations are the imagination and creativity of the system, and do not necessarily express correctly a rational step towards achieving something. It is just that a structure, message or pattern emerges spontaneously from the disequilibrium situation, when non-linear interactions are present.

2.2   The Importance of Creative Diversity

Let us consider a real example related to an attempt in the early 1980s to build a mathematical model of the ecosystem of Chesapeake Bay. A model would then have allowed the prediction of the changing populations, and the impacts of various possible levels of fishing, or of particular pollution or storm events. That is, the mathematical model could be run on the computer and would have provided the basis on which different policies for the management and exploitation of the Chesapeake Bay could be examined and used for decision-making.

Building the model entailed numerous researchers sailing around Chesapeake Bay, collecting and sampling the multitude of biological populations. The samples were duly analysed, the species identified, their biomass measured, and locations and depths noted. It was also possible to identify what ate what and reveal the different food chains making up the ecology. Success! However, when the model was run forward, it collapsed down from hundreds of species to just a few.

The real Chesapeake Bay populations did not do this. Multiple food chains and populations persisted over time, maintaining the great diversity that characterized it initially (Allen and Varga 2007). Why did the model fail to do this? The model failed because it only consisted of populations of average individuals. Over time, the hidden differences between reality and its simplistic average representation really matter. Diversity really matters.

The ecosystem only exists and persists because of the changing diversity of its constituent individuals and species; that is, 'All is flux.' The system persists because it is constantly changing.

If some characteristics make the individual more vulnerable than others, for example, by being in the proximity of a predator or having deficient camouflage for the location, then these more vulnerable individuals will be the first to go. However, over time and as this occurs, the vulnerable individuals disappear and the less vulnerable individuals do not, thus changing the nature of the average fish of that type and the value of the corresponding parameters. This means that for every single population in the diagram (Figure 5.2) on the left, there is a self-restoring capacity that will change the nature and performance of the average in order to improve its ability to recover any loss.

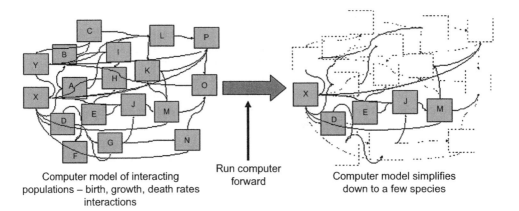

Computer model of interacting
populations – birth, growth, death rates
interactions

Run computer
forward

Computer model simplifies
down to a few species

*Figure 5.2   A mechanistic model of a natural ecosystem fails if run forward; the real
ecosystem does not*

This is all equally true in human systems and, so, any ideas of planning and intervening in socio-political systems need to take on board this issue of complexity.

3.   DEVELOPING URBAN MODELS

In the natural sciences, for many situations we can perform repeatable experiments repeatedly. This enables us to find general laws and patterns, and make predictions about similar situations elsewhere. This has led to the extraordinary bounty of science and technology. We can find robust laws by induction and deduce specific behaviour from deduction. This is hard science.

In social or biological and, especially, human systems, however, repeatable experiments are much more difficult to establish, because the people and organisms that inhabit a situation are in co-evolution with each other and their environment, learning imperfectly from their individual experiences and changing over time. Therefore, it is much harder to use induction to find general rules and patterns that seem to hold, and much more dubious to use these rules or patterns to predict the outcome in any particular case. This is owing to the essence of a repeatable experiment being that you believe the internal constituents and their behaviours and responses are the same in the repeat experiments, and that they are operating in the same environment. However, particular local histories and emergent cultures modify the beliefs and responses of the elements and individuals in any particular social system. Therefore, it can never be totally clear that the knowledge, values and actions will be the same as for any previous experiments. In everyday life we almost certainly learn pragmatically rules that work well enough for us to avoid immediate death, but more benign behaviours may leave trails that are difficult to distinguish in the noise of ordinary life.

We see that the development of complexity science itself already destroys the infallibility of hard science, since open systems of interacting elements can be shown to exhibit multiple possible futures and to defy conclusive prediction. These ideas applied to social

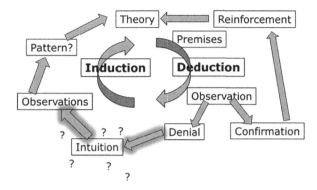

Figure 5.3   *The scientific induction–deduction learning loop; the glowing arrows cannot be defined scientifically*

systems are the central theme of this chapter. Instead of aiming at complete prediction and control, as expected for the old hard science, complex systems models can be built which allow different possible future trajectories and structures to be anticipated. These models may therefore allow us to explore some of the possible outcomes, and future opportunities and difficulties, which are not initially evident. This can enable us to reflect upon possible pathways into the future and consider the advantages and disadvantages that may unfold from different plans of action.

Also, when a plan is chosen and put into action, the model can be used to compare the expected outcome with what actually seems to be happening. Thus, some new situations and issues may be successfully anticipated by our complex models (Figure 5.3). However, we may also notice unanticipated deviations and new phenomena and issues that are occurring, and we can revise our plans and models accordingly, and explore the emerging new range of possible futures.

In social science we seek an understanding and an explanation of a situation involving people. What are the characteristics and elements that make up the structure? Why did it become what it is? Should we act in some way? How might it change and what is a good idea, and for whom? We see that this implies a description of the emergence of the present from the past, and perhaps then an ability to reflect on possible futures. This sounds like a sensible goal if we are to move beyond laissez-faire.

4.   UNDERSTANDING THROUGH SUCCESSIVE ASSUMPTIONS/SIMPLIFICATIONS

Now we can establish the scientific basis for different kinds of model. It will reverse the actual history of urban models and instead of initially supposing that what we observe corresponds to equilibrium and maximum utility for different agents, we examine systematically the basis on which different degrees of understanding arise. We start with no assumptions and gradually adding assumptions that we make in order to reach a useful description.

We exchange uncertainty about the system for uncertainty about the truth of our assumptions. If no assumptions are made then we are in the realm of narrative, where we are limited in our ability to learn or generalize or predict. When we make many assumptions, we appear to have simple, clear predictive models but then are uncertain whether our assumptions are still true. Either way, there is a core of uncertainty that seems to be an irreducible fact.

We move from a full literary impression of a social situation, towards the identification of descriptors, of characteristic variables, and of interactions and mechanisms that make it what it is. We see that literature recounts the different experiences and imaginings of particular individuals in their places, and circumstances can provide potentially millions of different examples and insights into life and its opportunities and dangers. However, we want to derive reduced descriptions – models – that can help us explore how to intervene in a particular urban system. In a fundamental diagram, Figure 5.5 in section 4.2, we identify the vital steps that take us to interpretive frameworks that start off as literary and impressionistic, through an evolutionary tree of changing forms and actions, towards short-term mechanical representations that may move towards possible equilibrium views of reality (Allen et al. 2007).

In Figure 5.4, as we move left to right from reality (the vague cloud on the left), we move from a rich multiplicity of individual stories and details towards successively simpler, more understandable and less detailed representations of that reality. On the right-hand side of Figure 5.4 we deal with the average behaviours of different classes of agents. So, we reduce our view from that of a contemplation of the dazzling complexity of multiple individuals pursuing their different aims and objectives, and move to a more sober representation of how average types are behaving, and how this may enable us to anticipate the dynamics of the city.

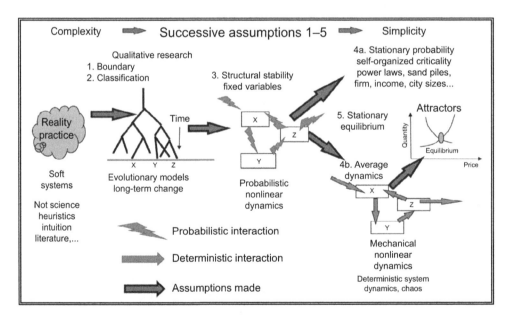

Figure 5.4   Successive assumptions take us from rich, mysterious reality, through evolutionary systems, to probabilistic dynamics, then either to stationary solutions of this, or to average, system dynamics

However, individuals, technology and tastes can change over time as new ideas and discoveries are made and new possibilities emerge. Reality, on the left-hand side of Figure 5.4, can evolve qualitatively over time, adding new ideas, activities, variables and structures, but models on the right-hand side cannot. They are framed in terms of current types or are even assumed to have reached an equilibrium distribution. The models on the right can, at best, only run but not evolve. So, if we monitor reality against our models, then we shall be forced, over time, to create successive modified models – which we shall only be able to do post-hoc. That is, in an evolving world, our representations will always be a picture of the past.

Starting from the left-hand side of Figure 5.4, the following five assumptions are discussed.

4.1   Assumption 1: The Boundary

Our first step (assumption) is to decide on the entity that we wish to study: what is inside? Whose changing behaviour is to be described? What is outside in the environment? We wish to try to understand the behaviour of what is inside in the context of its environment. It may not be clear where exactly the boundary should lie, and so we proceed by choosing an experimental boundary and seeing whether the model that results is useful. The elements within the system will affect each other in the context of the environment, and so this is the core, qualitative specification of what will be studied – the descriptors and variables of the problem.

4.2   Assumption 2: Evolutionary Complex Models – Changing Taxonomy

The contents of an urban system could be different types of people, diverse economic activities, or different types of job within an organization. The functioning of the system will be about the flows of energy, materials, money or products. However, while the constituents of the system might remain the same for some time, there will have been moments when new activities and types appeared and when some older ones disappeared. This is important as it could lead to changes to what is in the system and what things are in the environment. Complex systems can possess emergent behaviours that connect them to new factors in the environment. One of the important properties of a complex system is that it can itself change the boundary of the system. Therefore, the seeker after knowledge must be sufficiently humble to admit that the initial choice of a boundary might need revision at a later date. The issue is that learning is an experiment that seeks a representation that is useful.

Social and economic systems, such as markets, have all evolved and changed over time as innovations, new technologies, new practices and markets have emerged. New types and activities emerge, and others leave. There is a critical question: how do systems get free of the predictable behaviour that the underlying equations of average behaviours and types appear to predict? This is where the work on self-organization of physical systems demonstrated creativity. Prigogine and his team showed that non-equilibrium chemical systems could spontaneously self-organize into patterns and forms. Similarly, Herman Haken working with lasers showed that physical systems, out of equilibrium, could create patterns and forms spontaneously. This is the key idea that led us to

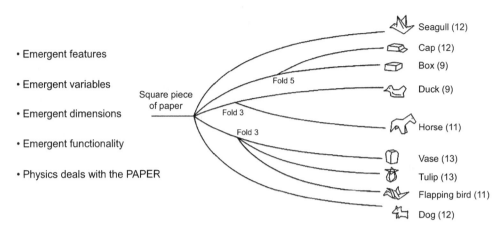

Figure 5.5   Origami illustrates the reality of emergence as symmetry-breaking leads to new dimensions of performance, and variables and selection change qualitatively

understand that systems in general, when far from thermodynamic equilibrium, can spontaneously break symmetries and spontaneously create new forms and functions. The wonderful example of origami shows us how (Figure 5.5). If I have sheet of paper, then by folding it in particular sequences, I can create a range of different objects with emergent characteristics, features and capabilities.

However, the laws of physics and chemistry can only tell us about the colour, elasticity, weight and strength of the paper, and nothing about the emergent characteristics, features and capabilities of the objects that have been created.

By folding the paper, we utilize the freedom of morphological creativity, to escape the boring determinism of the microscopic level. And if there is anything more morphologically creative than a sheet of paper it is a long string with sticky bobbles in it – such as macromolecules like proteins and enzymes – whose creative accidental folding led eventually to living cells, and the many splendours of biology and indeed of humanity. This does not 'bring down' humanity to mere folded molecules but demonstrates that the freedom and creativity that emerges at the levels above that of physics and chemistry is virtually infinite.

The laws of physics and chemistry are always obeyed, but they are channelled by emergent structures that create levels of organization and structure that go well beyond anything imaginable on the basis of the laws of hard science. However, origami and paper-folding show us how new forms, technologies, techniques and practices can lead to entirely new emergent properties and dimensions of performance (Allen 2014).

As the paper is folded, features such as heads, tails and wings emerge, as do functionalities such as flapping wings, ability to hold water, and so on. These features and functionalities allow us to give names to the emergent morphologies, and to potentially make more of those we like. This leads us to an understanding of evolutionary change, whether it is for origami, a biological or a human world.

While at lower levels different folds and changes are occurring, these will be retained or eliminated according to the emergent properties of their morphology. The selection at this upper level of morphology will not be able to suppress experimentation at the lower levels inside individuals or groups. If the ensuing morphology still works as before, then the interior details will be invisible to the outside world. However, this also means that evolution at the lower level cannot be stopped and there will be diversity among individuals, possibility involving several steps before the new morphology, characteristics or capabilities reveal themselves. This can lead to both radical and marginal innovations hidden within populations and enabling both adaptation to changing circumstances and genuine innovations. It is the continuing functionality of an existing morphology that allows experimentation and drift at the lower levels which, in turn, makes qualitative evolution an inevitability. Instead of discussing 'a' or 'the' model of a social system, evolutionary and co-evolutionary changes lead us successively to a series of qualitatively different models – changed behaviours and new ideas.

At the mundane level of trying to understand a social situation, we see that over time new types of individual can emerge, new variables and new levels of organization and structure with emergent functionalities and capabilities. This is the qualitative change that characterizes evolutionary processes. People can adopt new ideas and behaviours that go beyond previous practices and lead to emergent features, capabilities and functionalities at the level above. Any particular mathematical model or representation of a system, developed at a given moment, will be in relation to the pre-existing taxonomy and capabilities. However, reality and the model will diverge over time. Therefore, the assumption of structural stability (systems with a fixed cast of players, or a fixed taxonomy), cannot be taken for granted.

These first two assumptions do not lead to any single clear picture of the system, but instead to an open, diverging series of possible models that correspond to an evolving system with a changing taxonomy. If we think of our assumptions as corresponding to constraints on what the elements in the system can do, then we see that with only these first two assumptions, the elements, and the organizations they are part of, are still free to change. Structural stability is not guaranteed when that much freedom exists in the system. Big changes may well occur after perhaps a long period of protected exploration at the lower, individual level below. This is an absolutely vital issue. Novelties, potential innovations and new ideas need to be nurtured and protected within an organization until they are ready to face the outside world (Allen 1990, 1994).

4.3 Assumption 3: Probabilistic Dynamics of the Current System

Despite the beauty of the ideas in the previous section, the real world tends only to pay for the promise of prediction. This therefore seems to demand further assumptions that take us further to the right of our fundamental diagram (Figure 5.4). The next assumption, therefore, is that our system is structurally stable; the variables, taxonomy, types of individual or agent do not change.

This is about quantitative change, but no longer about qualitative change. Take the variables we currently see in our system and look at how their values change over time. We might be able to make predictions about what will happen or, more interestingly, what will happen with some new action or plan. We then calibrate our model on the situation under study and assume that no new surprise elements or variables can disturb the system. The changing values of the variables derive from the rates of production, sales, growth, declines and movements in and out of the system. We therefore replace the detail that we do not know with probabilities set around the average observed parameter values. We develop a dynamic model of the probabilities of different states for the variables of our system. These types of equations, known as the Master or Chapman–Kolmogorov equations (Allen 1988), govern the changing probability distribution of the different variables. These equations allow for the occurrence of all possible sequences of events, taking into account their relative probability, rather than simply assuming that only the most probable events occur. Instead of considering that only the most probable events occur, this model allows all events to occur, according to their relative probability. Episodes of good and bad luck are thereby included and the models can explore the resilience of the system to possible, but improbable, situations or accidents. These models can be very useful for exploring risks and dangers of various possible catastrophes.

Although, a system that is initially not at the peak of probability will more probably move towards the peak, it can perfectly well move the other way; it just happens to be less probable that it will. It is precisely these fluctuations that probe the stability of the most probable state. Over time, these probabilistic systems can tip spontaneously from one type of solution or attractor to another. It also underlines the very important idea that the average for a system should be calculated from the distribution of its actual possible behaviours – not that the distribution of its behaviour should be calculated by simply adding a Gaussian distribution around the average. The Gaussian is a distribution much loved by economists, which expresses the spread of random shots around a target. The actual distribution is given by the full probabilistic dynamics and can be calculated precisely. However, it will in general have a complicated mathematical form and will be changing over time according to the probabilistic dynamics.

We also need to mention agent-based modelling, which is often used now (Bonabeau 2002; Railsback and Grimm 2011). Instead of choosing classes of agent and developing a model of the dynamics of their average behaviour, we can insert real data into the problem. However, if there are several million agents then, usually, we will take a random sample across the population and use that to test the model. In successive runs, the sampling will give rise to slightly different behaviour and we can explore the spread of behaviours that the system might have. However, we will still be forced to decide on the different classes of agent in the model, and this will also face the problem that, in reality, new types and classes will emerge and the model will cease to represent the system. We discuss this later in the chapter.

4.4   Assumption 4: Either 1 or 2

In order to proceed further with any simple prediction from our model, we have two possible paths forward:

1. Assume the probability is stationary – the assumption that the probability distribution has reached a stationary state leads to the idea of the nonlinear dynamics leading to 'self-organised criticality' and to the power law structure that often characterizes them (Bak 1996).
2. Use the average trajectory, assuming probability remains sharply peaked – system dynamics. Instead of (1) we can look at the average dynamics of the system and

see where this takes the system. The full probabilistic dynamics is a daunting mathematical problem, but this difficulty can be drastically reduced by making the assumption that we can use the average dynamical trajectory. This will exclude the successful description of any bifurcations that may occur, or of any morphogenesis or symmetry-breaking changes.

In some ways this tempting assumption takes away any evolutionary, qualitative change in the variables of our problem. However, it is the difference between a heavy set of probabilistic equations describing the spreading and mixing of possible system trajectories into the future, and a representation in which the system moves cleanly into the future along a single, narrow trajectory. This simple deterministic trajectory appears to provide predictions and the ability for us to carry out 'what if' experiments in support of decision-making or policy-making. It appears to tell us exactly what will happen in the future with or without whatever action we are considering taking. These system dynamic models appear to enable calculation of the expected outcomes of different possible actions or policies and cost–benefit calculations. They can also show the factors to which the real situation is potentially very sensitive or insensitive, and this can provide useful information. However, systems dynamics models are deterministic; they still only allow for one solution or path from a particular starting point. Nevertheless, their predictions enable comparisons with reality and can reveal when the model is failing. Without this, we might not know that the system had changed. Therefore, this provides a basis for a learning experience where the each model is constantly monitored against reality to see when something has changed.

4.5   Assumption 5: Solutions of the Dynamical System

The final assumption that we can make to simplify a problem even further is to consider the possible long-term solutions of the dynamical equations – the attractors of the dynamics. Instead of studying how the system will run, we look at where it might run to. Nonlinear interactions can lead to different possible attractors, such as equilibrium points, permanent cycles or chaotic attractors. This could be useful information, at least for some time.

However, over longer periods, the system will evolve and the equations that worked previously will become untrue, as will the possible attractors. There is a trade-off between the utility and simplicity of predictions, and the strength of the assumptions that are required in order to make them. It is much easier to sell a model that appears to make solid predictions. Owing to this, scientists have often had to underplay the real level of uncertainty and doubt about the possible consequences of interventions, actions, technologies and practices, allowing the seemingly solid business plans and policy consequences to be presented as persuasively as possible. In any event, people usually wish to hear statements that imply knowledge and certainty, and find uncertainty and risk much more disturbing. People will often prefer a lie that comforts them than the uncomfortable truth.

In giving advice it is of critical importance to know how long the assumptions made in the calculations may hold. This is how long the actual complexity and uncertainty of reality can be expected to remain hidden from view. Believers in free markets can get around this problem by stating that whatever occurs is by definition the best possible outcome. However, if we wish to give advice to specific players within the system, then we will need to develop models that can explore possible futures and the risks involved in believing or adopting and responding to any future in particular.

At any given time we would not be able to value different types of micro-diversity, since we would not know which would be important for some future problem. A theory based on the evolutionary emergence of micro-diversity, and the way that evolution itself adjusts its range was developed many years ago (Allen and McGlade 1987), but has not been much commented upon, even by evolutionary economists. Instead of a complex system being successfully described by any fixed set of components and mechanisms, we see that the system of components and mechanisms is not fixed but is itself changing with the events that occur. As the system runs, so it is changed by its running.

5.   SUCCESSIVE URBAN MODELS

5.1   Dynamic, Spatial Urban Models

Since the 1970s, work has been going on that attempted to develop computer models that would take into account the complex interactions of linked responses that lead to a co-evolution of urban structure (patterns of retail, commercial and manufacturing employment, and different qualities of residence) with transportation infrastructure. These models are based on the following characteristics:

- Different types of actor or agent at each zone, with characteristic needs to be fulfilled.
- These characteristic needs are stable, but the behaviour of actors depends on the changing circumstances.
- The spatial distributions of the different types of job and different types of people affect each other as the potential for housing demands, commercial activities and for travel affect and are affected by transportation and land use.

The development of these models has been described in 'Cities and regions as self-organizing systems' (Allen 1997). After an initial phase that developed models suitable for some US and European cities, an example based on Brussels was developed to demonstrate the potential utility of the approach. These models were early agent-based models, but the computing power available could only deal with few spatial zones and agents with average behaviour. Although these simulations are by now very ancient, they nevertheless can help to explain the different steps and stages in the development of complex systems urban models.

The models would also have some random noise added to explore possible bifurcations in the behaviours of the agents. The model represents the interacting behaviours of the actors in the urban system, as they each modify their behaviour as a function of the changing opportunities and pressures, as they each pursue their own goals, for the location and relocation of employment according to the functional requirements, and, as private citizens, as a function of their means and the opportunities. The spatial dynamics can therefore generate and capture the complex effects of housing price dynamics, and the complex effects of planning regulations on commercial and industrial employment, as well as the effects of changes in the transportation systems.

In Figure 5.6 we see the interaction diagram of the different types of actor considered adequate to represent the spatial evolution of a city such as Brussels in the 1980s. It has different possible interaction mechanisms between them, which express the need for flows of goods services and people between different locations, and the pressure of spatial concentration affecting land prices and rents.

These mechanisms, when run under a scenario of overall growth, spontaneously generate self-consistent urban spatial structure for the seven types of actor, as well as the corresponding flows of goods, services and people. A typical evolution is shown in Figure 5.7.

As shown in Figure 5.8, this model, although developed many years ago, can therefore be used to explore the effect of possible urban planning and decisions. This could correspond to plans for new developments, roads, tramways or Metro system. By looking at the changes in structure that follow an intervention, our model could explore the impacts over time of a given intervention, as actors respond to the new situation, and their changed behaviour affects other actors in turn, creating a complex spatial multiplier (Figure 5.9).

This enabled us to examine the complex effects of the cascading interactions under different possible plans for the Metro. What matters are the relative differences between

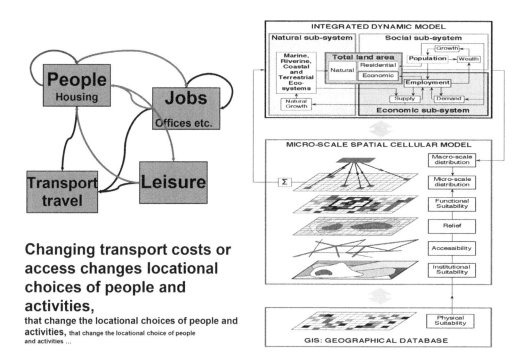

Figure 5.6   *We can view the interacting spatial distributions of people, jobs, leisure facilities and transportation can be studied (White and Engelen 2001)*

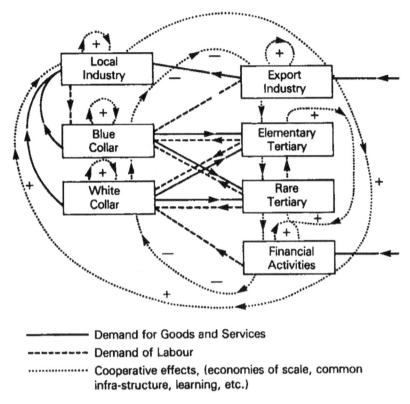

Figure 5.7   Interaction diagram for spatially distributed multiple agents of different types

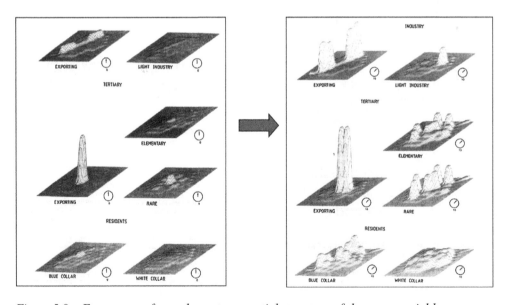

Figure 5.8   Emergence of complementary spatial structure of the seven variables

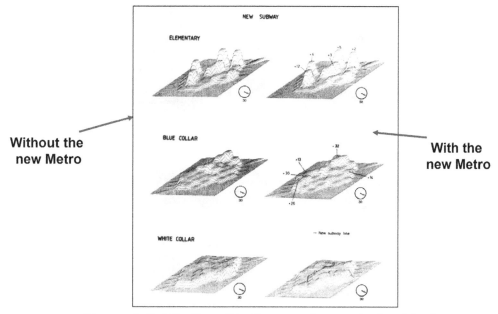

**Changed distribution of tertiary services and of residents
Changed house and land prices, commuting patterns, traffic flows,
congestion and pollution ...**

*Figure 5.9   Distributions of residents and of tertiary activity for simulations with and
without a new Metro system*

simulation outcomes. The model can also show the relative effects of different routes, of more or fewer trains, and so on. Similarly, the model can be used over the longer term to examine strategic issues, such as the effect on decentralization–centralization. This is one of the main questions that affects any city – will this action influence the existing trends and patterns of migration of jobs and people into the periphery? The action of building Metro systems tends to allow people to travel to the central part of the city with some ease. Also, the additional use of park-and-ride car parks at the edge of town Metro systems may even encourage the further out-migration of residents from the city, but anchor employment at its centre.

   Any evaluation of the plans for a Metro system clearly must include not only the projected costs of the system, but also the projected effects on the city. These projected effects cannot be calculated simply from the expected traffic that switches from roads to the Metro, but also needs to encompass the spatial changes brought about to the residential, commercial and employment sectors.

5.2   Regional Models

This type of dynamic modelling can also be used at the regional level as well as for urban planning. In further work (Figure 5.10) we explored the strategic spatial consequences of different possible transport investment plans in West Bengal. This enabled issues such as

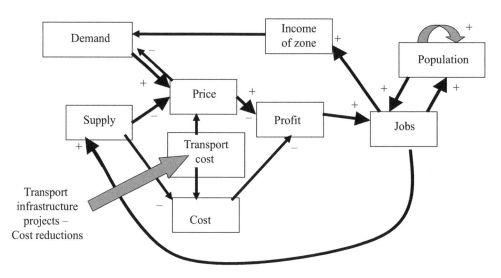

*Figure 5.10   Spatial interactions used in the calculation of economic implications of
reduced transportation costs*

the spatial distributions of the impacts on poverty to be assessed and is something that
has become a necessary precondition for many projects to be sanctioned by international
organizations. The ideas behind the spatial models described previously were adapted
to consider how the gains ensuing from improved transport infrastructure would give
rise to spatial multipliers generating jobs in the different economic sectors. This, in turn,
enabled the calculation of the impact on poverty – where and how much extra employment and wealth would be created.

Thus, the spatial economic and demographic framework of interacting equations can
be used both for practical planning and decision-making, and to look at overarching
political and economic beliefs. The model showed us that the improved transport had the
most beneficial effects on the better off, but it did predict improvements in employment
and in cost reductions.

The model generates the pattern of jobs in agriculture, industry and services created
by the transport infrastructure projects. It also allows an estimation of the pattern of
savings and increased income made by the different socio-economic groups across West
Bengal (Brunner and Allen 2005). The model enables us to see where jobs are gained or
lost, and in which sectors. This then also enables us to see the gains in jobs and income of
the different types and to map the increases in formal employment that will ensue.

This framework was also used to examine the possible economic and demographic
evolution of Nepal in a study funded by the Asian Development Bank. Here the
purpose was to try to capture the impact of an economic investment. These applications
showed the value of the models in order to study and plan possible infrastructure and
development investments.

6. AGENT-BASED MODELS

There is currently a great interest in agent-based models (ABMs) in which, instead of choosing average agents as in system dynamics, people include a large number of agents from the data. They do not focus on any particular representative agents but develop models which include a large part of the distribution. This is because of the arrival of big data, and big computers with big memories, and does avoid the criticism of taking only a few typical agents of different type and using an average dynamic to describe what happens.

Agent-based models capture emergent phenomena. Emergent phenomena ensue from the interactions of individual entities. By definition, they cannot be reduced to the system's parts: the whole is more than the sum of its parts owing to the interactions between the parts. An emergent phenomenon can have properties that are decoupled from the properties of the past. For example, a traffic jam, which arises from the behaviour of and interactions between individual vehicle drivers, may be moving in the direction opposite to the direction of the vehicles that cause it. This characteristic of emergent phenomena makes them difficult to understand and predict: emergent phenomena can be counterintuitive (Bonabeau 2002).

Despite this advance, it still does not get around the fundamental evolutionary problem that, over time, new things occur, attitudes and ideas change, and the world evolves qualitatively. Although ABMs reveal emergent behaviours and forms, this seems to be limited to spatial patterns and does not seem to anticipate the changed internal perspectives, ideas and innovations that agents will experience over time. An ABM that starts today will still not be able to anticipate innovations and changes in behaviour and knowledge (for example, of climate change) which over time may cause agents to change their behaviour.

Looking back some 40 years we see that this is what happened to the Brussels model, which was relevant in the 1980s but is no longer so. The variables we chose such as blue-collar and white-collar workers, of industry, retail and services, were appropriate at the time, but are no longer representative. In the statistics available for building a model in the 1980s, there were simply no categories corresponding to work in computing and information technology. The categories of blue-collar and white-collar workers have changed and quite different socio-economic groups are used in the statistics. Furthermore, the point about these variables for the model was that they were supposed to label different behaviours. Blue-collar workers were supposed to be paid less, travel less far to work and have a different demand function from white-collar workers.

Similarly, there has been a change in the numbers of people employed in industry and manufacturing, and the jobs they undertake, and their socio-economic grouping has become much less well defined. Retail has undergone a change from high streets to supermarkets (and possibly now back again) and there has been a vast increase in services – covering a wide variety of activities. The variables themselves have been overtaken by events, and the issues that a planner might wish to address have changed completely compared with the early 1980s.

While ABMs offer a useful way of getting appropriate data into a model (different types of agent, different activities, different transport choices, and so on) as we can enter samples of the real data, they still cannot anticipate how people's ideas and desires, available technologies, consumption fashions and changing opportunities and threats will evolve over time. That is, initially the agent behaviours will be highly appropriate, but later, as people learn and change and various events occur, the thoughts and actions of the real agents in the world will cease to be those studied in the model.

We therefore need to consider strategic evolutionary models of our evolutionary towns and cities, and their socio-economic systems and permanently bewildered citizens.

7.   THE COMPLEXITY OF STRATEGIC URBAN MODELS

We probably understand and accept that the future is full of significant dangers and potential disasters as well as great opportunities. Hoping for the best will not beat working out the different structures that are possible, which structure seems preferable and trying to achieve it. Without models that can explore the possible future structures and morphologies of the system, then planning and interventions can have no predictable outcomes.

However, models will necessarily be inadequate. The reason for this is that the agents not only change their relationships with each other, and through spatial and transport structures, and so on, but also they change internally as ideas, new perspectives (for example, climate change), new concerns and desires alter their behaviours and responses. Therefore, all models will fail (no matter how large an ABM or how big the data) owing to this internal evolution. The whole idea of big data does not get around this problem.

However, this does not invalidate modelling, since only with models that start to diverge from reality will it be clear that something has changed. Without models we are all in a mess. So modelling, comparing with reality, and reinventing and reimagining will be constantly necessary. The reason for this is that we live in an evolving world, in which we are evolving. Complexity thinking and evolution tell us that although the particular lifestyles and travel modes matter in the short term, the variables relevant to the system will evolve over time and any fixed representation will not only be wrong in the long term, but will be written in terms that are not relevant to the later situation. This does not mean that modelling for planning and intervention purposes is pointless. Instead, it means that without an interpretive framework or model there is nothing to compare an ongoing evolution with its ongoing expected evolution. We will not know that the real world is evolving qualitatively and deviating from our representation of it, unless we can compare the ongoing situation with that predicted by the model. Indeed, it may well turn out that the most useful information that comes out of a model is that it is failing to fit reality and its mechanisms need to be reassessed.

The most important statement we can make about complexity and urban evolution is that even with the sophistication of very large ABMs, the agents themselves will evolve – because, although the model can look at possible spatial links, forms and patterns the agents may adopt, the agents themselves will also change on the inside. Their knowledge, goals, tastes, fears and the technology available to them, in their private and professional lives, will shift and change. However, this does not invalidate our attempts to decide what is the best plan to adopt for any particular zone, activity or population. What we must guard against is the assumption that any current calculations will work for ever. Where possible we need to maintain some flexibility and be ready to revise our plans when we can discern divergence between them and reality, or when conditions that underpinned them have changed.

Let us consider an agent who is inside part of a changing system, with a dotted line separating the agent (or an organization) from the outside world (Figure 5.11). Apart from some aspects of physics where repeated experiments are really possible, we only have beliefs about how the world we inhabit works.

These beliefs, which are our interpretive framework (possibly a model) on which we base our decisions and choices, shape our actions. Every decision and choice, though, is really an experiment that we carry out and which tests whether our beliefs are correct. When our experiences seem to agree with our beliefs, we tend to reinforce our interpretive framework, but when experience does not meet our expectations, we are forced to modify our previous beliefs.

However, there is no scientific or correct way to modify previous beliefs as a result of some inadequacy. Each of us will tend to do that by making some change to our pre-existing interpretive framework. For example, initially, following the financial crisis of 2008, for example, there was little agreement about what was wrong, what might happen and how the failed model should be improved. Over time, though, a social consensus formed around one school or another, or perhaps even several. The reason for this is that our beliefs about what is happening, why it is happening and whether or not it needs intervention of some kind are really all culturally and socially constructed views that arise out of our collective experiences and reading of history.

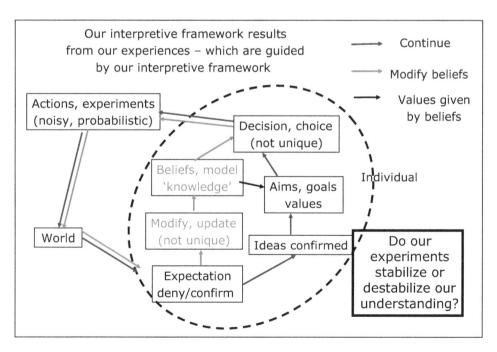

Figure 5.11   Our interpretive frameworks are really permanent works in progress, as our experiences do or do not confirm our beliefs and new issues arise

If Figure 5.11 represents an organization rather than an individual, it will help if different perspectives are brought together to construct its operative beliefs and values, and in this way they can be made explicit rather than hidden. Bringing stakeholders into the development and monitoring of the interpretive framework must be a valuable exercise.

Our beliefs, models and values are just part of the ongoing complex evolutionary processes of the world, and they are not so much true as just part of the system. This offers a fundamentally pragmatic view of our inventions and planning within the highly complex systems that we inhabit. We may learn which actions work, and which do not, by trying things out, but in a changing world we must always be ready for rules that previously worked to fail at a later date. Models are used in order to try to accumulate knowledge about the system, and to guide our experiments as a function of our beliefs. They are also experiments in representation and the interpretation of the multiple facts and issues that surround us, and will serve as a focus for discussion and learning as things evolve.

The fundamental points that have been made concern the scientific basis of, and understanding the limits to, prediction. Understanding, for a time, is achieved in a trade-off between simplicity and realism. The issue is whether or not a simple enough description can be found which is still sufficiently realistic to be useful. In the past, the desire for tractability has led to the use of very strong assumptions, such as that of equilibrium, which is a necessary prerequisite for a normal cost–benefit analysis of a decision. Similarly, the idea that a society with free markets will eventually move to the best possible outcome – maximum utility for consumers and producers – is wrong. The problem lies in defining 'best', since any outcome will be good for some and bad for others. Also, the behaviour of evolutionary complex systems will only ever be predictable for a limited time. They have an internal creativity that after some time will break out from any predictive model.

Planning hopes to explore possible pathways into the future and indicate those that seem to provide a strong basis for a broad success. The history of a successful society within a region is largely a tale of increasing cooperation and complementarity, not competition. Evolution is not about a single type of behaviour winning through its superior performance, but instead increasing diversity and complexity. The models we propose are therefore those that can help us to estimate the overall, integrated effects of the coupled decisions of multiple actors, allowing us better insight into the consequences of possible policies and actions. They also provide the basis from which we shall attempt to deal with previously unanticipated changes and evolution. There is no perfect ultimate solution to which we are leaning. Life will always possess multiple pathways into the future.

REFERENCES

Allen, P.M. (1988), 'Dynamic models of evolving systems', *System Dynamics Review*, **4** (1–2), 109–30.
Allen, P.M. (1990), 'Why the future is not what it was', *Futures*, **22** (July–August), 555–70.
Allen, P.M. (1994), 'Coherence, chaos and evolution in a social context', *Futures*, **26** (6), 583–97.
Allen, P.M. (1997), 'Cities and regions as evolutionary complex systems', *Geographical Systems*, **4** (1), 103–30.
Allen, P.M. (2014), 'Evolution: complexity, uncertainty and innovation', *Journal of Evolutionary Economics*, **24** (2), 265–89, doi:10.1007/s00191-014-0340-1.
Allen, P.M. and J.M. McGlade (1987), 'Evolutionary drive: the effect of microscopic diversity, error making, and noise', *Foundations of Physics*, **17** (7), 723–38.

Allen, P. and L. Varga (2007), 'Complexity: the co-evolution of epistemology, axiology and ontology', *Nonlinear Dynamics, Psychology, and Life Sciences*, **11** (1), 19–50.

Allen, P., M. Strathern and J. Baldwin (2007), 'Complexity and the limits to learning', *Journal of Evolutionary Economics*, **17** (4), 401–31.

Bak, P. (1996), *How Nature Works: The Science of Self-Organised Criticality*, New York: Copernicus Press.

Bonabeau, E. (2002), 'Agent-based modelling: methods and techniques for simulating human systems', *Proceedings of the National Academy of Sciences of the United States of America – PNAS*, **99** (10), 7280–87.

Brunner, H. and P.M. Allen (2005), *Productivity, Competitiveness and Incomes in Asia: An Evolutionary Theory of International Trade*, Cheltenham, UK and Northampton, MA, USA: Edward Elgar.

De Roo, G. (2000), 'Environmental conflicts in compact cities: complexity, decision making and policy approaches', *Environment and Planning B: Planning and Design*, **27** (1), 229–41.

De Roo, G. and E.A. Silva (2010), *A Planner's Encounter with Complexity*, Farnham: Ashgate.

Haken, H. (1977), *Synergetics. An Introduction: Nonequilibrium Phase Transitions and Self-Organization in Physics, Chemistry and Biology*, Berlin: Springer.

Nicolis, G. and I. Prigogine (1977), *Self-organization in Nonequilibrium Systems*, New York: Wiley.

Ormerod, P. (2006), *Why Most Things Fail*, London: Faber and Faber.

Popper, K. (1963), *Conjectures and Refutations: The Growth of Scientific Knowledge*, London: Routledge.

Portugali, J. (1999), *Self-organization and the City*, Heidelberg: Springer.

Railsback, S.F. and V. Grimm (2011), *Agent-Based and Individual-Based Modeling: A Practical Introduction*, Princeton, NJ: Princeton University Press.

Schumpeter, J.A. (1942), *Capitalism, Socialism and Democracy*, repr. 1975, New York: Harper.

White, R. and G. Engelen (2001), 'High-resolution integrated modelling of the spatial dynamics of urban and regional systems', *Computers, Environment and Urban Systems*, **24** (5), 383–400.

6. Synergetic cities
Juval Portugali and Hermann Haken

1. SYNERGETICS, ITS PARADIGMS AND THE CITY

Synergetics is the name assigned by Hermann Haken to his theory of complex, self-organized systems (Haken 1977, 1987, 1988 [2000], 1991 [2004], 1996). As the name synergetics indicates, the theory refers to systems composed of many parts, individuals, subsystems and groups with an emphasis on the synergy, that is, on the interrelations and interactions among the many parts of the system and its overall structure and behavior.

Originating in physics, synergetics is by no means a theory that tries to reduce complex phenomena to the laws of matter. From the start its emphasis was on collective phenomena and properties that typify a variety of material, organic and human domains. This shows up in that many of its basic theoretical notions were revealed and developed in the light of case studies from a variety of disciplines, ranging from physics, through sociology, psychology, cognition and artificial intelligence (AI) to the dynamics of cities and their planning. In applying and developing the theory in the context of the various domains, Haken's (1996, p. 39) central methodological guide was to 'look for qualitative changes at macroscopic scales'. Some of the various applications and case studies, became paradigmatic cases and a convenient way to convey the principles of synergetics. These are the laser paradigm, the pattern formation paradigm, the pattern recognition paradigm and the finger movement paradigm, and are described next.

1.1 The Laser Paradigm

The generic paradigm of synergetics is the process that produces the phenomenon of laser (light amplification by stimulated emission of radiation). A typical example of the instrument laser is of a glass tube, with two mirrors at its ends, filled with a gas of atoms or molecules. The mirrors reflect the light that runs in axial direction causing the light waves to strongly interact with the individual atoms. One of the mirrors is semi-transparent so that the laser light can eventually emerge through it.

The atoms or molecules are excited by an electric current sent through the tube. Unlike a regular lamp in which the excited individual atoms emit individual independent light waves, in the laser, a typical act of self-organization occurs: the individual electrons in the atoms correlate their movements and generate a beautifully ordered coherent light wave (Figure 6.1). Nobody tells the laser system how to behave in such a coherent fashion; it finds its well-ordered behavior by itself.

The interpretation of synergetics commences with Einstein's observation, that when an excited atom emits a light wave, this light wave may cause other excited atoms to deliver their energy to that light wave so that this light wave is enhanced in its intensity.

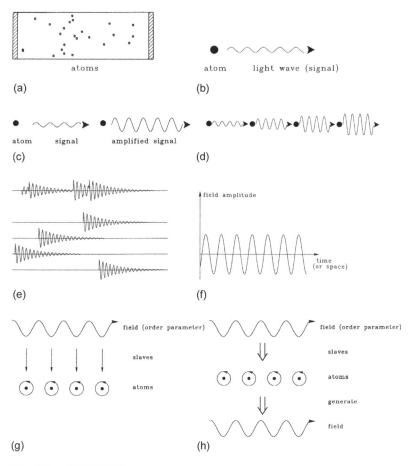

Source: After Haken (1988 [2000]).

Figure 6.1 *The laser paradigm. (a) Typical setup of a gas laser: a glass is filled with gas atoms and two mirrors are mounted at its end faces; the gas atoms are excited by an electric discharge; and, through one of the semi-reflecting mirrors, the laser light is emitted. (b) An excited atom emits light wave (signal). (c) When the light wave hits an excited atom it may cause the atom to amplify the original light wave. (d) A cascade of amplifying processes. (e) The incoherent superposition of amplified light waves produces still irregular light emission (as in a conventional lamp). (f) In the laser, the field amplitude is represented by a sinusoidal wave with practically stable amplitude and only small phase fluctuations: the result is that a highly ordered, that is, coherent, light wave is generated. (g) Illustration of the slaving principle: the field acts as an order parameter and prescribes the motion of the electrons in the atoms; the motion of the electrons is thus 'enslaved' by the field. (h) Illustration of circular causality: on the one hand, the field acting as order parameter enslaves the atoms; on the other, the atoms by their stimulated emission generate the field*

According to synergetics, this process occurs in the laser: initially a number of atoms emit their light waves independently of each other and with different frequencies. Each of these might get support from the other excited atoms. Thus, a type of Darwinian competition among the light waves for the energy resources of the excited atoms begins. This competition is won by that individual light wave which grows fastest. The winning light wave describes and prescribes the order in the laser and it is thus called the order parameter. It dominates the movement of the individual electrons as if by enslaving them and forcing them to move in its own rhythm. In the language of synergetics this is termed the slaving principle.

The transition from the state of a lamp with its microscopically chaotic light field and the state of the laser with its well-ordered light field is abrupt and occurs at a critical strength of the power input by the current into the laser. Thus the change of a single, unspecific, parameter, the power input of the laser, may cause a systemic phase transition. This parameter is termed control parameter.

When the laser wave is perturbed, it adjusts slowly compared with the adjustment time of the individual electrons. This is a general feature: the order parameters are slowly varying quantities compared with the enslaved subsystems. Thus, when excited atoms are shot into the tube, they are enslaved by the order parameter (that is, the light field in that tube) first by delivering their own energy to the order parameter, and then by acquiring its rhythm. This interplay between the rhythms of the system and its subsystems is analogous to many examples in human life: language can be regarded as a slowly moving order parameter. When a baby is born, it is subjected to the language of his or her parents and the other people. The baby learns the language and, in technical terms, is thus enslaved by the language. Yet by doing so, he or she eventually emit their personal energy into the language and in this respect support the language.

1.1.1   The play between the slow and the fast

The above play between the order parameters of a system as slowly moving quantities and their subsystems as fast moving, provided the starting point for Weidlich's and co-workers studies on socio-dynamics as well as on cities and urbanism (Weidlich 1999, 2002); and so he writes: 'If in a system of nonlinear equations of motion for many variables these variables can be separated into slow ones and fast ones, a few of the slow variables . . . are predestined to become "order parameters" dominating the dynamics of the whole system on the macro-scale' (Weidlich 1999, p. 138).

According to this perspective, fast and slow processes are easily identifiable in processes of settlement and urbanism. The fast processes typify the local urban micro level of building sites, streets, subways, and so on, whereas the slow processes typify the macro level of whole regions, which are often described as systems of cities. The relationships between the slow and the fast processes are described by the slaving principle: on the one hand, the regional system 'serves as the environment and the boundary condition under which each local urban microstructure evolves. On the other hand, the . . . regional macrostructure is . . . the global resultant of many local structures' (Weidlich 1999, p. 138).

This circular causality between the local and the global, allows us to study global regional systems by assuming that local processes adapt to the slow regional processes, and to study local urban processes by treating the regional context as given, and to study the complex interplay between the local and the global. In all three instances,

Weidlich (1999) has prescribed a four-stage approach: stage 1 concerns the configuration space of the variables; stage 2, measures the utility of each configuration; stage 3, defines transition rates between configurations which are in fact utility differences; and stage 4 derives stochastic or quasi-deterministic evolution equations for the system under consideration. The central evolution equation is the master equation, which defines the probability that the configuration under examination is realized at a certain time.

The above theoretical procedure has been used to study the role of population pressure in 'fast and slow processes in the evolution of urban and regional settlement structures' (Weidlich 1999), and in urban evolution. Figure 6.2 illustrates some results from these studies, in which the city capacity for building and development is related to population pressure. Figure 6.2(a) shows the evolving city capacity when the urban plain is uniform, and Figure 6.2(b) when it is disturbed in one of its sites.

Evidently, the concept of order parameters and their relationships to the individual parts of the system, a relationship governed by circular causality, applies to a great variety of phenomena in society. On the one hand, the individuals are the parts of a human society and determine its macroscopic manifestations, such as language, religion, form of government, culture, educational system or city structure. On the other, the behavior of the individuals is determined by these macroscopic manifestations or institutions, which play the role of order parameters. Order parameters may compete with each other, or may coexist, or may cooperate. These phenomena are well known in laser physics in respect of the electric field strength acting as order parameters. These phenomena also occur in social life; for example, languages may compete and one language may win the competition as it occurred in the United States, where two main streams were competing with each other, namely, English and German. In other nations, languages may coexist, as in Switzerland and in Israel. Finally, languages may cooperate, for example, when terms originally generated in one language are adopted by another language. This often occurs with technical terms taken from English, for example.

1.2 The Paradigm of Pattern Formation

The case study here is the Bénard instabilities. In this experiment, a thin layer of a liquid (for example, oil) in a pan is heated from below and cooled from above. When the temperature difference between the lower and upper surface is small, heat is transported microscopically and no macroscopic motion of the liquid occurs. If, however, the temperature difference exceeds a critical value, suddenly a macroscopic motion of the liquid becomes visible and hexagonal cells are formed (Figure 6.3, left-hand side). The temperature difference thus controls the macroscopic behavior of the system; in the language of synergetics it is thus termed control parameter.

As the control parameter grows, the liquid starts its motion, rolls are created, their rolling speed increases, and the initial resting state becomes unstable. Instability thus shows up. Slightly above the instability point, the system may undergo different collective motions of role configurations (Figure 6.3, right-hand side). At the beginning, the amplitudes of these role configurations are small and independent of each other. When they grow further, they start to influence each other; in some instances they compete until one configuration suppresses the others, in others, they coexist and even stabilize each other. 'The amplitudes of the growing configurations are called *order parameters*.

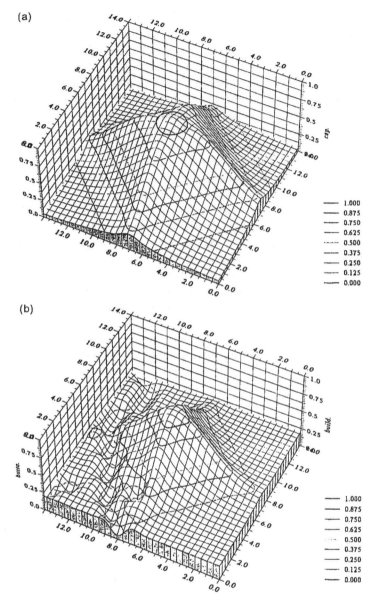

Figure 6.2   Building and development under population pressure (Weidlich 1999). Top: on a uniform urban plain. Bottom: on an urban plain with disturbances

They describe . . . the macroscopic structure of the system' (Haken 1996, p. 39, emphasis added).

The order parameters not only determine the macroscopic structure of the system, but also govern the space–time behavior of its parts. By winning the competition, the order parameters enslave the many parts of the system to their specific space–time motion. This is a basic theorem of synergetics termed, as noted previously, the slaving principle.

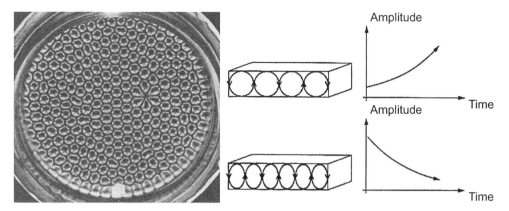

Figure 6.3   Left: top view of a liquid in a circular vessel (from Haken 1996); when the
liquid is heated from below and the temperature gradient exceeds a critical
value, hexagonal cells are formed. Right: two different role configurations in a
fluid, and, the behavior of the amplitudes of these configurations in the course
of time; while in one example the amplitude increases, in the other it decays

In some instances, for example, when the fluid is enclosed in a circular vessel, all directions for roll systems are then possible, each being governed by a specific order parameter. Which pattern will eventually be realized depends on initial conditions. It is as though the system internally stores many patterns. This repertoire of patterns is not stored in a static fashion, but is dynamically generated anew each time. This property is termed multistability.

1.3   The Paradigm of Pattern Recognition

A typical experiment of pattern recognition can start as follows: a test person (or a computer) who has many patterns, of faces, city maps, and so on, stored in memory, is offered a portion of one of the patterns. The task is to recognize the pattern – to decide what face, city map, and so on it is. According to synergetics, what happens is a process analogous to pattern formation, as described previously: at the start, the cognitive system of the person (or computer) is in a state of multistability as it enfolds many patterns, which coexist. When a few features or part of the pattern is offered, several pattern configurations and their order parameters are formed by means of associative memory. The order parameters enter into competition and when a particular order parameter wins the competition and enslaves the cognitive system, the task of recognition is implemented. This analogy, illustrated in Figure 6.4, was first demonstrated by Haken in 1977 and has since become the basis for an intensive study of synergetics of cognition and of brain development and activity (Haken 1977, 1996). Figure 6.5 is a typical implementation in respect of face recognition, by means of the so-named synergetic computer.

As suggested by Portugali and Haken, the above conceptualization offers also an appropriate framework for the study of cognitive maps of cities, regions and large-scale environments (Portugali 1990; Portugali and Haken 1992). The idea is that cities, regions and so on can be regarded as large-scale patterns, which can never be seen in their

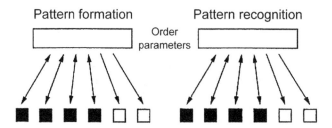

Figure 6.4   Haken's (1979, 1991 [2004]) analogy between pattern formation and pattern recognition. Left: a configuration of some parts of a system gives rise to an order parameter which enslaves the rest of the parts and brings the whole system to an ordered state. Right: a few features of a pattern shown to a person (or a computer) that generate an order parameter which enslaves, and thus complements, the rest of the features, so that the whole pattern is recognized

Figure 6.5   Pattern recognition of faces by means of the synergetic computer. Top: examples of prototype patterns stored in the computer, with family names encoded by letters. Bottom: when part of a face is used as an initial condition for the pattern recognition equations, their solution yields the complete face with the family name

entirety. As a consequence, the cognitive system constructs a whole cognitive map on the basis of only a partial set of features available to it. Thus it can be said that a partial set of environmental features offered to a person triggers a competition between several configurations of features and their emerging order parameters, until one (or a few) wins and enslaves the system so that a cognitive map is established.

1.3.1 Pattern formation and pattern recognition in the city

The analogy between pattern formation and pattern recognition provided the foundation for some of the main advances made in synergetics in connection with issues of cognition and brain functioning (Haken 1996). In light of these studies, Haken and Portugali (1995) suggested that the analogy between pattern formation and pattern recognition is specifically attractive to the study of cities. Cities can be perceived as complex, self-organizing systems, which are both physical and cognitive: individuals' cognitive maps determine their location and actions in the city, and thus the physical structure of the city, and the latter simultaneously affects individuals' cognitive maps of the city. In their preliminary mathematical model, Haken and Portugali construct the city as a hilly landscape which is evolving, changing and moving as a consequence of the movement and actions of individuals (firms and so on). The latter give rise to the order parameters, which compete and enslave the individual parts of the system, and thus determine the structure of the city. The significant and new feature of this exposition is that the order parameters enslave, and thus determine, two patterns: one is the material pattern of the city and the other is the cognitive pattern of the city, that is, its cognitive map(s). This is exemplified diagrammatically in Figure 6.6. The view of cities as 'hybrid complex systems', elaborated in section 2 of this chapter, further extends this view.

One of the more interesting outcomes of the model is the set of attention parameters, which emerge by means of self-organization. Attention parameters can be seen as the order parameters of specific subsystems comprising the pattern. In a state of

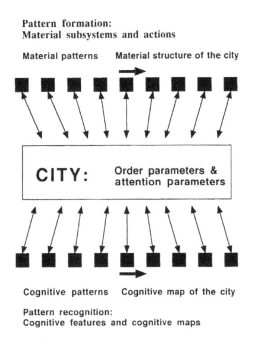

Pattern formation:
Material subsystems and actions

Material patterns   Material structure of the city

CITY: Order parameters &
       attention parameters

Cognitive patterns   Cognitive map of the city

Pattern recognition:
Cognitive features and cognitive maps

Figure 6.6   The city as a self-organizing system that is at the same time both physical and cognitive: its emerging order- and attention-parameters enslave the city's cognitive and material patterns

Figure 6.7   An ambivalent pattern: vase or two faces?

multistability, or in case of an ambivalent pattern (for example, 'vase or two faces?' in Figure 6.7), they determine which aspect of the pattern is seen (that is, attracts attention) first. This is of utmost importance in city dynamics. The city is full of patterns, yet individuals are attentive to only a few of them. The patterns form the cognitive maps of the city and it is according to them that individuals and firms behave, take decisions and act in the city. In the model, we investigate cases were one attention parameter dominates the dynamics and cases where no cross-attention is paid, that is, when two or more urban communities are cognitively not aware of each other. This situation entails the emergence and persistence of an urban cultural or socio-economic mosaic where a few coexisting attention parameters govern the dynamics.

1.4   The Finger Movement Paradigm

The finger movement experiment was first conducted by Kelso (1984) and further modeled by Haken et al. (1985). The physiologist Kelso asked test persons to move their index fingers in parallel to the tempo of a metronome. At the beginning, when the tempo of the metronome and the frequency of the finger movement were small, this behavioral task could be performed well. Gradually the experimenter increased the speed of the metronome and the finger movement. Then suddenly, quite involuntarily, a switch to another type of movement occurred, namely, to a symmetric movement (Figure 6.8). The control parameter here was only the speed of the finger movement. This behavioral phase transition has been treated by means of synergetics in all details, including the critical fluctuations and critical slowing-down.

   This experiment illustrates self-organized behavior of an individual person. Another experiment, conducted by Schmidt et al. (1990), indicates that the same occurs for two persons (Figure 6.9). In the latter, two seated persons were asked to move their lower legs in an anti-parallel fashion and to watch each other closely while doing so. As the speed of the leg movement was increased, an involuntary transition to the in-phase motion

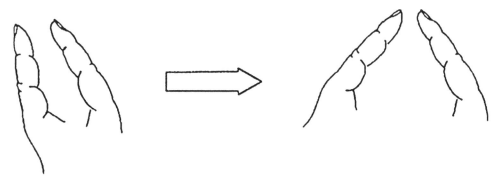

Figure 6.8   Kelso's finger movement experiment: while initially people can move their index fingers in parallel, beyond a critical speed of the finger movements the relative position of the fingers switches involuntarily to the antiparallel, that is, symmetric, position

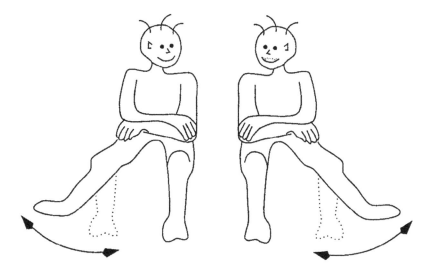

Figure 6.9   The Schmidt et al. (1990) leg movement experiment with results identical to Kelso's experiment

suddenly occurred, in line with the Haken–Kelso–Bunz (HKB) (Haken et al. 1985) phase transition model (Haken 1996, pp. 87–90). This experiment is of special significance because it implies collective behavior – a phenomenon that plays an important role in urban dynamics – an example being pedestrians' walking speed in cities of various sizes.

1.4.1   From finger movement to walking speed

Pedestrian movement is probably the most salient aspect of humans' behavior in cities. In 1976 Marc and Helen Bornstein published a paper showing a correlation between population size of cities and walking speed of pedestrians in these cities (Figure 6.10); this as part of their attempt to study the impact of urbanization on the pace of life.

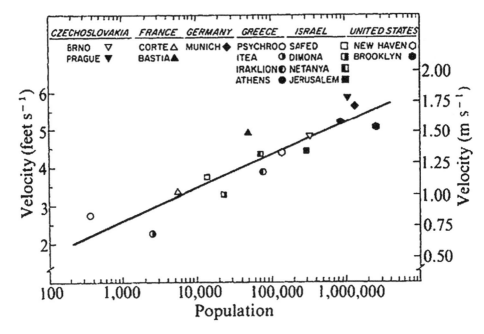

Figure 6.10   *The Bornsteins' correlation between population size of cities and walking speed of pedestrians in these cities*

Subsequent studies have supported and elaborated (Walmsley and Lewis 1989; Levine and Norenzayan 1999). More recently the issue appeared again, this time, however, in the theories of cities as part of an attempt to show that 'many properties of cities from patent production and personal income to electrical cable length' as well as pedestrians' walking speed, 'are shown to be power law functions of population size with scaling exponents, β, that fall into distinct universality classes' (Bettencourt et al. 2007, p. 7301).

Compared with the finger movement (FM) paradigm, the following can be written about the correlation between city size and pedestrians' speed of movement: unlike FM, here there is no explicit, externally determined, task. Instead, the task is a property that emerges out of the overall dynamics. For example, when a newcomer settles in a city, he or she observes the other citizens and makes (hopefully unbiased) guesses as to their behavior. That is, he or she observes the information, and maximizes it under the observed constraints (for example, average velocity). This allows him or her to determine the attractors that instructs him or her on how to behave in accordance with the general behavior.

However, what is the psychological-cognitive origin of this synchronization urge? Why would or should our newcomer synchronize behavior with the other inhabitants, and why do they synchronize their walking speed in the first place? The answer comes from synchronization/coordination dynamics as in the previously mentioned FM and Schmidt et al. (1990) experiments, and the HKB interpretation. As has been well experienced and recorded, people walking together (who know each other) tend to synchronize pace (and their speed). Intuitively, probably the same might occur when many anonymous people in high density areas are walking in the same direction – they will give rise to an order parameter that will enslave their walking speed.

Why the walking speed in large cities is faster? There have been here several suggestions or rather speculations, ranging from the assumption that pedestrians try to avoid social interference (Bornstein and Bornstein 1976) and sensory overload (Milgram 1970) that rises with the size of cities, to suggestions that people try to save time whose economic value is higher the larger the city is (Levine and Norenzayan 1999).

To the latter we can add that behavioral movement in cities might be divided into productive (in workplaces we produce and earn money) and non-productive (movement to workplaces, that is, commuting), which is often considered to be a waste of time. With few exceptions (siestas), the larger the city the longer the non-productive time (journey to work). In small cities where everything is nearby, there is no waste of time, but in large cities it is a problem. In the latter, as part of their attempt to minimize wasted time, pedestrians tend to walk faster.

2.   CITIES AS HYBRID COMPLEX SYSTEMS

Cities are composed of material components and organic or human components. As a set of material components alone, the city is an artifact and therefore a simple system. However, as a set of human components – the urban agents – the city is a complex system. The city is thus a hybrid simple–complex system and it is the urban agents that by means of their interaction – among themselves, with the city's material components and with the environment – that transform the artifact city into the complex artificial system city.

As a complex artificial system, the city emerges out of the interactional activities of its agents that build the artifacts, but once it emerges, it affects (enslaves, in the language of synergetics) the behavior of its agents and so on in circular causality, a process that in the domain of social theory is termed socio-spatial reproduction. That is, the city is a large-scale collective and complex artifact that, on the one hand, owing to its inhabitants and users (the urban agents), interacts with its environment, but on the other, owing to its size, functions as an environment for the large number of people that live and act in cities. The latter effect and property of cities is becoming increasingly more prominent in society as the proportion of people living in cities is growing – as is well recorded (Wimberley et al. 2007). The past century has witnessed the fastest population growth in human history and the fastest urbanization processes, with the consequence that, for the first time, more than 50 percent of the world's population lives in cities. The city in this respect is a complex artificial environment (Portugali 2011, ch. 11).

Artifacts are not just the outcome of human interaction; they are also the media of interaction between the urban agents. Artifacts, such as texts, cities, buildings or roads, are external representations of ideas, intentions, memories and thoughts that originate and reside in the mind/brain of urban agents, that is, internal representations. However, just as as material artifacts (for example, buildings and roads) cannot directly interact among themselves, neither can ideas, thoughts, intentions, plans or other internal representations. They interact by means of the externally represented artifacts, be they utterances, texts, clothes, buildings, neighborhoods or whole cities and metropoles. Urban dynamics thus involves an ongoing interaction between external and internal representations. The notion of synergetic inter-representation networks (SIRN), introduced in section 3 of this chapter, attempts to capture this interaction between internal and external representations.

Furthermore, as discussed at length in *Complexity, Cognition and the City* (*CCCity*) (Portugali 2011), the city as an entity is a (hybrid) complex system and each of its agents is also a complex system. This is not so with material complex systems in which complexity is a property of the global systems but not of the parts. Organic complex systems are different as each of their parts is a complex system too. However, since the parts of organic complex systems (for example, plants or animals) are subject to the slow process of natural Darwinian evolution, the short-term feedback effect of the global system (for example, a flock of birds or shoal of fish) on the parts is negligible and thus the property of duality of these systems can be ignored. The situation is different in respect of the hybrid complex systems cities, as their agents are simultaneously subject to two evolutionary processes: the very slow natural evolution, and the very fast cultural evolution whose effect on the urban agents is instantaneous – urban agents have to adapt to the fast-changing urban environment. How do they adapt to fast cultural changes? By means of their cognitive capabilities. The implication is that we have to engage the cognitive capabilities of the urban agents in the dynamics of cities.

Portugali's *CCCity* (2011) was a first attempt in this direction, with emphasis on the capability of cognitive mapping; namely that, similarly to other animals, the behavior of the complex parts of the city (the urban agents) is mediated, and thus strongly influenced, by their cognitive maps of the city. This is significant, since studies on systematic 'distortions in cognitive maps' of humans (Tversky 1992; Portugali 2011, ch. 6) have shown that 'the map is not the territory', that is, cognitive maps are not one-to-one representations of the environment; instead, they are often systematically distorted in several specific ways.

In a subsequent study, Portugali (2016) directed attention to a second cognitive capability by means of which urban agents adapt to fast cultural changes, namely, their relation to time and, by implication, to planning and design. The urban agents – the parts of the complex system city – are parts of a special kind: they are typified by chronesthesia, that is, the ability to mentally travel in time, back to the past and forward to the future. Unlike cognitive mapping, the cognitive property of chronesthesia seems to be unique to humans (Suddendorf and Corballis 2007). An example of mental time travel (MTT) is prospective memory (Haken and Portugali 2005), referring to human ability to remember to perform an intended or planned action.

A second example is the capability of planning as studied in the research domain of cognitive planning (Miller et al. 1960; Ormerod 2005). Humans are, in this respect, natural planners and designers. However, not only do humans have this ability to mentally travel in time, but they also cannot not mentally travel in time (Portugali 2016); studies show that 'unlike other animals,' human beings spend about half of their waking hours 'thinking about what is not going on around them, contemplating events that happened in the past, might happen in the future, or will never happen at all' (Killingsworth and Gilbert 2010, p. 932). This is so much so, that stimulus-independent thought or mind wandering has been shown to be the brain's default mode of operation (Raichle et al. 2001; Buckner et al. 2008). Therefore, a great deal of urban agents behavior is determined not by response to the present situation in the city, but in response to an urban reality that does not yet exist and might never exist. Now a twofold question arises: how to describe the city as a landscape of potentialities and the way urban agents behave in it? The notions of SIRN, information adaptation (IA) and their conjunction, SIRNIA, were specifically designed to respond to such urban situations. They are introduced next.

3. SIRNIA: SIRN, IA AND THEIR CONJUNCTION

3.1 SIRN

The synergetic notion of order parameter is characterized by a Janus-face property: it initially emerges bottom-up out of the interaction between the parts (urban agents in respect of cities) but, once emerged, it top-down enslaves the parts (that is, the citizens) to its dynamics, and so on in circular causality – a process that in social theory is termed socio-spatial reproduction. The extension of synergetics to the domains of cognition, brain dynamics and artificial intelligence, via its pattern recognition and finger movement paradigms and information theoretic approach (see below), enables a theorization of the global dynamics of cities and the dynamics of the local behavior of the urban agents, under a single theoretical framework; the main product of this approach has been the notion of SIRN – a single theoretical framework that at once captures the dynamics of a single person's behavior, a sequence of people, and the collective behavior and dynamics of an entire city.

The inspiration for SIRN was, first, Bartlett's serial reproduction scenarios, introduced in his book *Remembering* from 1932. Secondly, Stadler and Kruse (1990) demonstration that Bartlett's scenarios evolve in line with synergetics. What we therefore have here is an interaction between internal processes that take place in the mind/brain and external processes that take place in the environment. This interaction takes place in cities between the external domain of urban artifacts (for example, a building, a street, a neighborhood or a city) and the internal-cognitive aspect of cities and their urban agents (for example, cognitive maps). These two aspects of a city were traditionally studied independently of each other. To explore these interrelationships, a simple group dynamics termed city game was devised (Portugali 2011 and further bibliography there). It is a collective serial reproduction scenario in which the players sequentially build a toy city on a floor. The game as it evolves exhibits the interplay between internal representation of a city (cognitive map) constructed in the mind/brain of urban agents, and the externally represented outcome (behavior, action and production), the emergence of a city's order parameter and the way it enslaves the behavior and action of the players; that is, all the ingredients of the SIRN urban process. For further details about the city game, see Figures 19.6–19.8 in Chapter 19 of this volume.

A next step was to build formalism to the city game and, by implication, to urban dynamics as a SIRN process. The starting point was Haken's (1991 [2004]) synergetic computer as a framework from which, in an elegant way, a general SIRN model was derived mathematically and graphically (Figure 6.11). On the left of Figure 6.11 is a graphical exposition of the synergetic computer, described as a three-layer network, with an input layer, an internal layer of order parameters and an output layer. Looking at this network from the side, as indicated by the arrow, we see the net in the center of

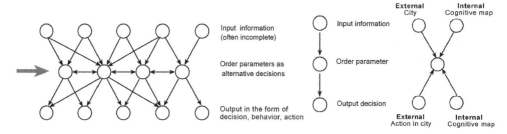

Figure 6.11   The derivation of the basic SIRN model from the synergetic computer

Figure 6.11. Adding to the latter external inputs and outputs, we arrive at our basic SIRN model, shown at the right-hand side of Figure 6.11. Elaborating on this general model, we have further derived three sub-models: An intrapersonal SIRN process, referring to the interaction between internal–external representations of a solitary person painting or writing an article, for instance; an interpersonal sequential SIRN process, as in the Bartlett scenarios; and an interpersonal with a common reservoir SIRN process typifying the previously mentioned city game and the SIRN dynamics of a city. Synergetic inter-representation networks thus became a theory of urban dynamics. (For the mathematical counterpart of this model see Haken and Portugali 1996.)

3.2   Information Adaptation

According to SIRN, a city is an external representation – a collective product of the internal–external interaction of its many urban agents that, once it emerges and comes into being, enslaves its many agents and so on in circular causality. However, what is an external representation and how does it enslave, that is, makes people behave in a certain way? Our answer: because artifacts, including cities, convey information to the observer. Again, what is information? Our first response to these questions was in a study published in 2003 under the title 'The face of the city is its information' (Haken and Portugali 2003). Starting with Shannon's communication theory and its reinterpretation by Haken in his book, *Information and Self-Organization* (Haken 1988 [2000]), we showed that the city as a whole, and elements in it, convey quantities of information that can be measured by means of Shannon's information bits (Figure 6.12). When all buildings in a city are identical, information (I) is low; when they are different from each other, I is high, but often beyond the information processing capability; in these instances, adding a landmark, as in the case of Siena, improves information legibility, but when too many towers are added, as in San Gimignano, there is no effect on the city's information.

As emphasized by Shannon, and as is commonly accepted in information theoretic studies, Shannon's information disregards the meaning of a message; to use Haken's expression, it is information with meaning exorcised. Shannon's information is assumed to be a mathematical quantity without meaning – we showed that the meaning of the information enters in disguise. This is so in all cases where the definition of Shannon information involves human cognition. The reason is simple: to quantify information, some form of categorization is required, and categorization, by definition, implies giving a single meaning to a set of entities.

Figure 6.12   Different configurations and categorizations of buildings convey different quantities of Shannonian information – top, abstract examples, bottom, real examples: when all buildings in a city are identical (top, upper line, bottom, left), information (I) is low; when they are different from each other (top second line, bottom second from the left) I is high, but often beyond the information processing capability; in these cases adding a landmark (top, third line) as in the case of Siena (bottom, third from left) improves information legibility; but when too many towers are added, as in the top, fourth line, and as in San Gimignano (bottom, right), there is no effect on the city's information

Further investigation into Shannonian information revealed that Shannon and Weaver in their collaborative 1949 book, *The Mathematical Theory of Communication*, were fully aware of the semantic aspects of information and Weaver, in his part of the book, described Shannon's information as a basis (Level A) for two forms of information with meaning: Level B as semantic information and Level C as pragmatic information. It was further found, however, that subsequent accounts of information preferred to ignore or dismiss Weaver's conceptualization, with the consequence that the discussions on Shannon information, semantic information and pragmatic information evolved in parallel. What has been found in our exploration was different, namely, that Shannon information and the two forms of information with meaning (semantic and pragmatic) are interrelated in an ongoing process that we have termed information adaptation.

Information Adaptation: The Interplay between Shannon Information and Semantic Information in Cognition, is the title of Haken and Portugali's 2015 book in which it is shown that not only information with meaning (semantic or pragmatic) is required in the definition of Shannon information, but also that Shannon information plays a role in the determination of semantic or pragmatic information. The canonical illustrative example for IA is the process of vision. Following the early findings of Hubel and Wiesel (1962) and recent findings of Livingstone (2002) and others, the IA process evolves as schematically described in Figure 6.13. Data from the world is, first, analyzed by the mind/brain, in a bottom-up manner, into local Shannon information of lines, corners, and so on. This local information triggers a top-down process of synthesis that gives rise to global information, that is, to seeing and recognition. It was further shown, that in vision, information adaptation is implemented by the inflation and/or deflation of Shannon information. In some IA instances, when the data from the world is too little, the mind/brain adds data that does not exist in the row data or information

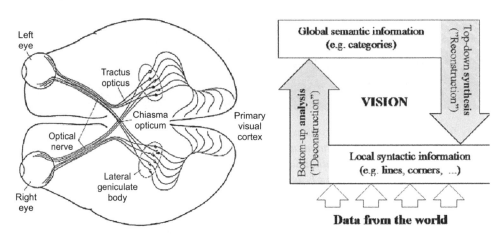

Figure 6.13   The process of vision. Left: the links between the eyes and the brain. Right: a schematic description. The process evolves as follows: data from the world is first analyzed by the brain, in a bottom-up manner; this local information triggers a top-down process of synthesis that gives rise to global information, that is, to seeing and recognition (see Haken and Portugali 2015)

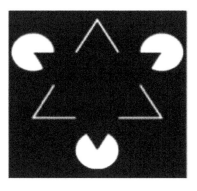

Figure 6.14   Left: the Kaniza triangle illusion. Right: the Olympic rings illusion

Figure 6.15   Stages in doing a puzzle

(Figure 6.14, left-hand side), while in other instances, where the data from the world is superfluous, the brain implements adaptation by the exact opposite, that is, by ignoring data or information that exists in the raw information (Figure 6.14, right-hand side).

To an extent, in relation to IA, vision is similar to doing a puzzle (Figure 6.15): The brain takes a whole picture in the world, deconstructs it into pieces, categorizes them into edge-pieces, color groups, and so on, and then, in a top-down manner, assembles the edge pieces, the different color groups and so on until, eventually, the whole picture is reconstructed. Why does the brain deconstruct and then reconstruct? Because as shown by the synergetics pattern recognition paradigm, the visual data that comes from the environment is very often incomplete, or in some instances superfluous.

The new notion of IA sheds interesting new light on a whole set of cognitive phenomena and urban processes (see next section).

3.3   SIRNIA: The Conjunction between SIRN and IA

The conjunction between SIRN and IA, SIRNIA, suggests that an urban agent is continually subject to two flows (Figure 6.16): a flow of data that comes from the city, and a flow of information that originates in, and comes from, the agent's mind/brain/memory. By means of the latter, and in a bottom-up manner, the agent's brain first transforms the incoming data flow into a quantitative, syntactic, Shannonian information (SHI). This syntactic SHI triggers a top-down process that transforms the quantitative SHI into qualitative semantic or pragmatic forms of information (SI and PI, respectively). This process of IA is implemented by means of information inflation and deflation. The output of this process is SI that refers to the meaning per se (that is, 'this is a chair'), and

SIRNIA: A conjunction between SIRN and IA

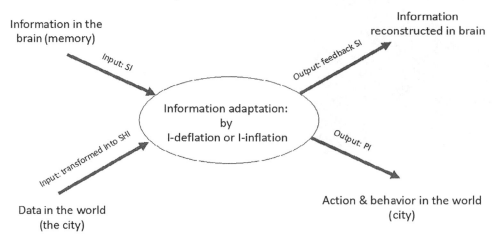

Figure 6.16   The basic SIRNIA model

PI, referring to the action possibilities afforded by an object, similar to Gibson's (1979) notion of affordances (that is, 'this object affords seating'). As can be seen in Figure 6.16, SI feeds back to the agent's mind/brain, whereas PI leads to behavior and action in the city.

3.4   Three Case Studies of SIRN-IA and the City

3.4.1   Lofts

As noted by Weaver in his collaborative book with Shannon (Shannon and Weaver 1949), SHI can be (intuitively) interpreted also as a measure of freedom of choice. Applied to urban reality Portugali (2016) suggested that every urban element can convey objective or syntactic SHI, referring to its legal use. For example, for many years a large number of buildings in New York City were legally defined as a 'warehouse', and since, according to the planning law of New York City, they were to be used in only one way, the SHI of each of them was 0 bits:

$$I = \log_2 1 = 0bits \qquad (6.1)$$

Portugali (2016) has further suggested that every urban element conveys subjective PI, referring to the specific way each urban agent perceives that urban element. For example, in the 1960s, for an unknown New York artist desperately looking for a place to live and to work, motivated by a combination of imagination and pressing needs, the warehouse probably conveyed different meanings (different PI), namely, a potential space for an apartment, a studio or even a shop. For this person the semantically (or pragmatically) determined SHI became about 1.5 bits:

$$I = \log_2 3 \approx 1.5bits \qquad (6.2)$$

This was probably the story of lofts in New York, London and other big cities around the world. As described by Kwartler (1998), in New York City, ad hoc conversion of lofts in SoHo by individuals began in the 1960s, illegally and in contravention of both the New York City Zoning Resolution and Multiple Dwelling Law. Subsequently, this ad hoc activity was legitimized by revisions to both sets of regulations in 1982.

3.4.2 Balconies

A similar scenario unfolded in Tel Aviv (and subsequently across Israel) in what has been described as the 'butterfly effect of Tel Aviv balconies' (Portugali 2011, ch. 15.1.3; see also Portugali and Stolk 2014). Here, in the late 1950s or early 1960s, an anonymous urban agent perceived the future state of his or her open balcony as a half room, planned a set of activities for it, designed the specific form of this half room and implemented the plan and design. Other people were attracted by this solution, closed their balconies too, and before long a process of innovation diffusion started that in a short period of time has transformed the whole of the urban landscape (face of the city) of Israeli towns and cities (Figure 6.17). As in the case of lofts, it took several decades before the planning authorities legitimized closed balconies; in Israel (and by extension Tel Aviv) this occurred very recently, in 2010.

3.4.3 IA at the level of the city as a whole

The above example refers to an IA at the level of a single urban agent. As shown in previous studies (Haken and Portugali 2015), the IA process is often implemented by acting on the city as a whole. To see how, consider Figure 6.18.

If all buildings in the imaginary city of Figure 6.18 (left-hand side), are similar to each other, the (SI determined) SHI conveyed by this city is low; if all buildings in

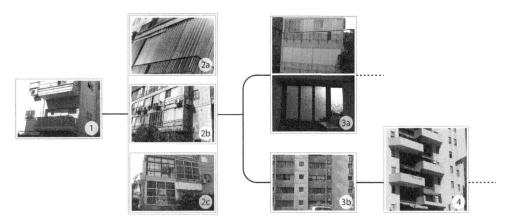

Figure 6.17   *(1) Open balcony. (2a) Closed by asbestos shutters. (2b) Closed by plastic shutters. (2c) Closed by glass windows. (3a) From the outside it looks as a balcony; from the inside part of the living room or a kitchen. (3b) No balconies. (4) Jumping balconies (Portugali 2011; Portugali and Stolk 2014)*

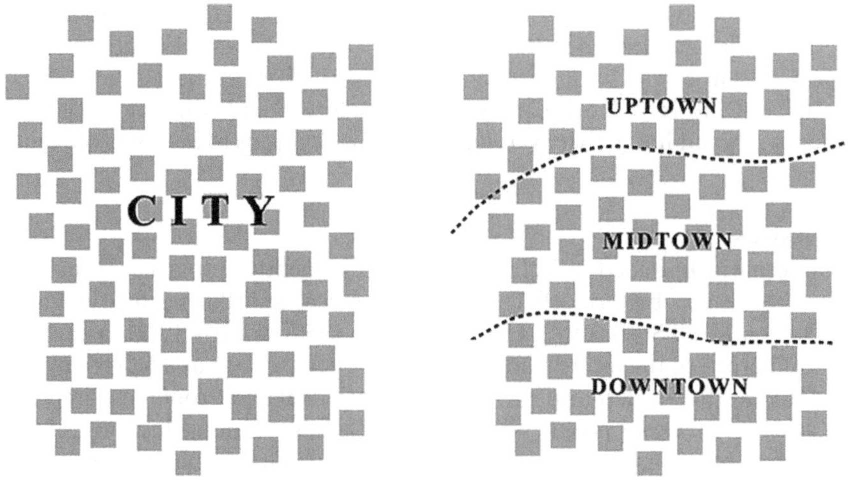

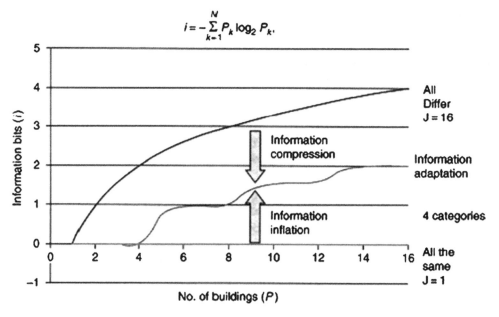

Figure 6.18   IA at the level of a city as a whole

Figure 6.19   The play between information inflation and information deflation (that is, compression) leads to information adaptation

Figure 6.18 (left-hand side), are different, the SHI the city will convey is high. In the first instance, categorization into Uptown, Midtown and Downtown (Figure 6.18, right-hand side) implies information inflation; in the second, information deflation. One of the outcomes of urban dynamics is an IA process (Figure 6.19) that determines the appropriate balance between too much or too little SHI conveyed by a city or the neighborhoods in it. This IA process at the level of a city is usually implemented spontaneously by means of self-organization, but sometimes by means of urban planning and design.

4. STEADY STATE, PHASE TRANSITION AND THE CITY

4.1 On Phased Transitions and Steady States

The canonical scenario of synergetics, is that an order parameter emerges out of the interaction between the parts of a system, but once emerged, it enslaves the parts, and so on in circular causality. Note that in this scenario, the order parameter plays two opposing roles: in the first stage of the process it is an agent of change that brings to an end an old structure with its order parameter and leads to the emergence of a new structure and order parameter, but then, once the new order parameter has emerged, it enslaves the parts to its dynamics, thus becoming an agent of no change. In the language of complexity the first stage of the process is termed phase transition (PT), while the second is steady state (StS). In both PT and StS we are dealing with a far from equilibrium system, that is, with a dynamic system that is never at rest; this leads to the central question of this section: what types of dynamics and movement typify the process of PT and that of StS? This is a general question, but our focus of interest is the city, that is, StS, PT and the city.

As mentioned previously, the central methodological guide of synergetics is to 'look for qualitative changes at macroscopic scales' (Haken 1996, p. 39). When we do so, we can observe that similar to many or most complex systems, cities are characterized, first, by long periods of StS, interrupted by short periods of chaos and instability. The question is, why? To answer this we have to realize that: first, cities are complex adaptive systems (CASs); secondly, StS and PT are two forms of adaptation; and, thirdly, as shown by Haken and Portugali (2021), CASs have an innate tendency (a default adaptive approach) to stay in StS. This is the default adaptive approach; when this approach does not succeed, or fails, adaptation is implemented by PT. The consequence is long periods of StSs interrupted by short PTs.

The city is a CAS and each of its parts is also a CAS, with the implication that what has been written above about complex systems in general, applies to the city as a whole as well as to each of its parts – the urban agents; that is, that StS and PT are two forms of adaptation for the city and for each of its parts. It follows, first, that we must distinguish between StS and PT in the life of an individual urban agent and in the life of a whole group, that is, of the city. Secondly, that we have to identify the interrelationships between StS and PT at individual scale versus whole-city scale.

4.2 Steady State and Phase Transition at Individual and City Scales

A useful illustration of StS and PT at the individual level is Hägerstrand's (1970) time geography, which directs attention to two forms of movement of individuals (Figure 6.20). The first of these, life path, refers, for instance, to a person who in his or her first years lives with their parents, then he or she leaves the parents and lives, say, in

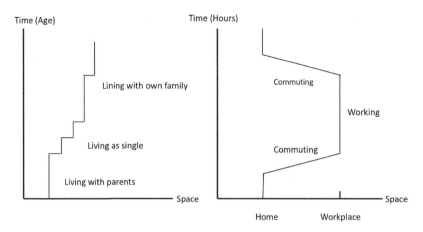

Figure 6.20   Left: typical life path. Right: typical daily path of a person

the city, and then gets married and moves to a suburb. The second form is the daily path, referring to the routinized and repetitive movements that typify the individual's life, for instance, from home to work and back. From the perspective of complexity, the life path is a sequence of PTs in the life of the individual, while the daily path is characteristic of the person's StS periods.

A well-recorded example of PT and StS at a city scale are the intensive suburbanization and urban-sprawl processes that, since the mid-1940s, dominated cities around the world. Following the conjunction between urgent demand for housing, fast development of the automobile industry, the building of highways, and other transportation means, a new order parameter emerged followed by PT: many middle-class families moved to suburbs that were rapidly built on the outskirts of cities. This PT entailed the desertification of city centers and, most importantly, a new StS that is still characteristic of big cities around the world by which millions of people participate in the urban rhythm of commuting.

This StS dominated cities until the early 1970s, when a new order parameter emerged followed by a PT under the title of gentrification: people started to move from the suburbs back to city centers; first yuppies (young, upwardly-mobile professionals) and then all types of middle classes. This PT was associated with major structural and socio-economic transformations in the center of cities including the pushing out of working-class communities or neighborhoods and traditional urban institutions (for example, the food markets of Covent Garden in London and Les Halles in Paris), and transforming them to the new urban middle-class neighborhoods with their cultural-commercial facilities. City centers became the environment of what Richard Florida (2002) has termed the 'creative class'.

From these case studies it can be seen that the links between StS and PT at the individual scale versus that on a whole-city scale is self-evident: the sequence of order parameters in the life paths of individuals determine and are determined by the PTs at the city scale.

4.3   Fluctuations

What is the dynamics by which a new order parameter emerges, brings to an end the old one, takes over and brings the system to a new StS? Part of the answer was given in section 1 of this chapter, in the interplay between order parameters, control parameters and the slaving principle. To complement the picture we have to add to this game a fourth player, fluctuations. According to synergetics, complex systems are typified by random fluctuations caused by the behavior of the individual parts of the system. When they occur during StS periods of the system, they are being enslaved by the system's order parameter and thus do not have an impact on the global system. However, if they take place at time when, owing to the play between control and order parameters, the system is unstable, they often play a major role in driving the system into a PT with a new order parameter and StS.

This is so also with cities, but with one important addition: in cities the main source of fluctuations is the SIRNIA process as described previously. As we have seen in the studies of New York lofts and Tel Aviv balconies (section 3.4), the urban agents that triggered the process acted in contradiction to the prevailing order parameter and StS. Our interpretation was that this is an outcome of the IA component of SIRNIA; that is, owing to IA, for some urban agents the information conveyed by a loft or a balcony contradicted the prevailing order parameter and planning law; but why and how?

Inspired by Higgins's (1997, 1998) regulatory focus theory, several recent studies (Ross and Portugali 2018; Haken and Portugali 2019; Portugali 2020; Chapter 1 in this volume) demonstrated empirically and theoretically that urban agents can be categorized into preventors, who tend to conform with the prevailing order parameter and accept the StS, and promoters, who, in order to achieve their goals, try to interpret it in an innovative way and from time to time even breach the StS and planning law. These innovative breaching acts create fluctuations in the evolving urban system.

4.4   Implications

4.4.1   Urban allometry

Following Bettencourt et al.'s (2007) paper 'Growth, innovation, scaling, and the pace of life in cities', we are witnessing a lively discussion on urban scaling with an emphasis on allometric relationships between city size and a whole set of urban indicators. Based on data from the United States, Germany and China, Bettencourt et al. (2007) showed that the relationships between city size and the various urban indicators can take three universal forms: a sublinear regime, which typifies economies of scale associated with infrastructure and services (for example, road surface area); a linear regime, associated with individual human needs (for example, housing or household electrical consumption); and a superlinear regime, associated with outcomes from social interactions (for example, income and number of patents). Subsequent studies (for example, Arcaute et al. 2015; Cottineau et al. 2015; Batty 2013) were unequivocal about the above findings, while some supported these allometric relationships, others have cast doubts about their generality, demonstrating empirically large variations in scaling estimations.

As regards the issue of urban scaling laws from the conjunctive perspectives of SIRNIA (section 3 in this chapter), Haken and Portugali (2021) demonstrated a link

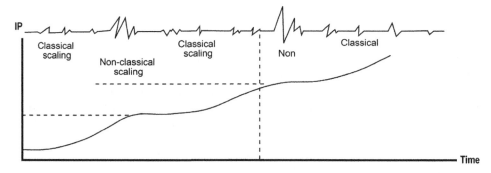

Figure 6.21   The classical scaling law characterizes the city during its steady state; once the city becomes unstable, local fluctuations may give rise to global phase transition and non-classical scaling relations

between the PT and StS of the city, and its urban allometric relationships (Figure 6.21): namely, that the classical scaling law characterizes the system city during its steady state – in this period local fluctuations are enslaved by the city's order parameter(s) and do not affect its global structure. The city at this state is resilient against fluctuations. However, when the global structure of the city becomes unstable for some reason, then local fluctuations have a major effect on the system and may cause or give rise to global change or phase transition.

4.4.2   Urban planning

In the study of cities, the notion of planning commonly refers to professional-institutional planning, which is the main agent in governmental attempts to regulate the dynamic of cities for the citizens' well-being. Yet, as noted by Portugali (2020; Chapter 19 in this volume), there is another type of planning that plays a role in the dynamic of cities, cognitive planning: a domain of research that studies planning as a basic cognitive capability of humans (Miller et al. 1960; Davies 2005; Ormerod 2005; Sela 2016). Portugali (2020) further suggested, that this implies the following. First, each individual urban agent (individual, household, and so on) is also a planner at its specific scale. Secondly, urban dynamics is an ongoing interaction between planners at several scales – cognitive and professional-institutional. Thirdly, a city plan (or its planning law) functions as an order parameter that emerges out of the interaction between cognitive and professional planners but, once emerging, enslaves the parts and leads the city into circular causality and StS.

Fourthly, the promotion-prevention tendencies of urban agents, apply also to urban cognitive planners that participate in the dynamics of cities in the following way: prevention-oriented cognitive planners tend to conform with the prevailing institutional planning order parameter and accept the planning law as it literally is, while promotion-oriented cognitive urban planners, in order to achieve their goals, try to interpret it in an innovative way and, from time to time, even to breach the planning law as order parameter. These promotion-derived innovations and breechings create fluctuations in the evolving urban system with the implications described previously, in section 4.3.

5. CONCLUDING NOTES

Synergetics deals with complex systems, that is, ensembles of mutually interacting parts – urban agents in this chapter. Many of these systems, in the animate or inanimate world, possess the remarkable property of self-organization. They may produce features that are alien to their individual parts (emergence of new qualities). Synergetics tries to elucidate the principles underlying self-organization, by establishing links between the microscopic level (parts) and the macroscopic level (system with new features). This is achieved by concepts (and related mathematical formalism) such as order parameter, slaving principle, circular causality.

When we apply synergetics, with its concepts and/or formalism, to a concrete complex system, we must be aware that synergetics, owing to its generality, cannot be a substitute for disciplines such as psychology, game theory, behavioral science and many others with their special knowledge and tools. Instead, synergetics can serve as a general frame for the formulation of special models in these disciplines. That is, what will be needed is a further intensive dialogue between special knowledge and synergetic insights. This applies also to the study of cities. Similarly to the various complexity theories, synergetics was formulated first, in the context of physics, and at a later stage was applied to complex systems in the life sciences (cognition, psychology, and so on). As specified in section 2 of this chapter, cities differ from both as they are hybrid complex systems, and this should be taken into account.

Furthermore, the study of cities and urbanism to which synergetics and other complexity theories were applied, had a long history of research and practice. When synergetics (as with other complexity theories) was introduced to the domain of cities, the field was torn between two paradigms: the quantitative revolution that started in the early 1950s as an attempt to transform the study of cities into a science; and a second paradigm that started in the early 1970s, which criticized the first and applied social theory (structuralist–Marxist–humanistic) perspectives to the study of cities. Between the two there was, and still is, a gap of dis-communication that is similar to the gap between what Snow (1964) has termed the 'two cultures' of science: the scientists versus the intellectuals.

As elaborated by Portugali in Chapter 1 of this volume, the emergence of complexity theories of cities (CTC) four decades ago created an opportunity to bridge the gap between the two cultures of cities (Portugali 2011). In particular, the theory of synergetics had, on the one hand, rich and sophisticated mathematical formalism that was empirically applied as noted to a whole set of disciplines including cities. On the other hand, as could be observed in the previous discussions, its conceptual framework and theoretical notions resemble some of the basic concepts of social theory. For example, order parameter in synergetics resembles social structure in social theory, phase transition resembles revolution, circular causality resembles social reproduction and StS resembles daily routines. All these concepts have a hard mathematical representation as well as a soft socio-cultural-political representation. It is our view that synergetics has the potential to bridge the gap between the two cultures of cities, and it is our hope that the discussion in this chapter will contribute to the realization of this potential.

REFERENCES

Arcaute, E., E. Hatna, P. Ferguson, H. Youn, A. Johansson and M. Batty (2015), 'Constructing cities, deconstructing scaling laws', *Journal of the Royal Society Interface*, **12** (102), 20140745.

Bartlett, F.C. (1932), *Remembering: A Study in Experimental and Social Psychology*, repr. 1961, Cambridge: Cambridge University Press.

Batty, M. (2013), *The New Science of Cities*, Cambridge, MA: MIT Press.

Bettencourt, L.M.A., J. Lobo, D. Helbing, C. Kuhnert and G.B. West (2007), 'Growth, innovation, scaling, and the pace of life in cities', *Proceedings of the National Academy of Sciences of the USA*, **104** (17), 7301–6.

Bornstein, M.H. and H.G. Bornstein (1976), 'The pace of life', *Nature*, **259** (February), 557–9.

Buckner, R., J. Andrews-Hanna and D. Schacter (2008), 'The brain's default network: anatomy, function and relevance to disease', *Annals of the New York Academy of Sciences*, **1124** (March), 1–38.

Cottineau, C., E. Hatna, E. Arcaute and M. Batty (2015), 'Paradoxical interpretations of urban scaling laws', July, ArXiv:1507.07878.

Davies, S.P. (2005), 'Planning and problem solving in well-defined domains', in R. Morris and G. Ward (eds), *The Cognitive Psychology of Planning*, Hove: Psychology Press, pp. 35–51.

Florida, R. (2002), *The Rise of the Creative Class*, New York: Basic Books.

Gibson, J.J. (1979), *The Ecological Approach to Visual Perception*, Boston, MA: Houghton-Mifflin.

Hägerstrand, T. (1970), 'What about people in regional science?', *Papers of the Regional Science Association*, **24** (December), 7–21.

Haken, H. (1977), *Synergetics – An Introduction*, Berlin, Heidelberg and New York: Springer.

Haken, H. (1979), 'Pattern formation and pattern recognition – an attempt at a synthesis', in H. Haken (ed.), *Pattern Formation by Dynamical Systems and Pattern Recognition*, Berlin, Heidelberg and New York: Springer, pp. 2–13.

Haken, H. (1987), *Advanced Synergetics: An Introduction*, 2nd print, Berlin, Heidelberg and New York: Springer.

Haken, H. (1988), *Information and Self-Organization: A Macroscopic Approach to Complex Systems*, repr. 2000, Berlin, Heidelberg and New York: Springer.

Haken, H. (1991), *Synergetic Computers and Cognition*, repr. 2004, Berlin, Heidelberg and New York: Springer.

Haken, H. (1996), *Principles of Brain Functioning: A Synergetic Approach to Brain Activity, Behavior and Cognition*, Berlin, Heidelberg and New York: Springer.

Haken, H. and J. Portugali (1995), 'A synergetic approach to the self-organization of cities', *Environment and Planning B: Planning and Design*, **22** (1), 35–46.

Haken, H. and J. Portugali (1996), 'Synergetics, inter-representation networks and cognitive maps', in J. Portugali (ed.), *The Construction of Cognitive Maps*, Dordrecht: Kluwer Academic, pp. 45–67.

Haken, H. and J. Portugali (2003), 'The face of the city is its information', *Journal of Environmental Psychology*, **23** (4), 385–408.

Haken, H. and J. Portugali (2005), 'A synergetic interpretation of cue-dependent prospective memory', *Cogn Process*, **6** (2), 87–97.

Haken, H. and J. Portugali (2015), *Information Adaptation: The Interplay between Shannon Information and Semantic Information in Cognition*, Berlin and Heidelberg: Springer.

Haken, H. and J. Portugali (2019), 'A synergetic perspective on urban scaling, urban regulatory focus and their interrelations', *Royal Society Open Science*, **6** (8), 191087, doi:10.1098/rsos.191087.

Haken, H. and J. Portugali (2021), *Synergetic Cities: Information, Steady State and Phase Transition. Implications to Urban Scaling, Smart Cities and Planning*, Berlin, Heidelberg and New York: Springer Nature.

Haken, H., J.A.S. Kelso and H. Bunz (1985), 'A theoretical model of phase transition in human hand movement', *Biological Cybernetics*, **51** (February), 347–56.

Higgins, E.T. (1997), 'Beyond pleasure and pain', *American Psychologist*, **52** (12), 1280–300.

Higgins, E.T. (1998), 'Promotion and prevention: regulatory focus as a motivational principle', in M.P. Zanna (ed.), *Advances in Experimental Social Psychology*, vol. 30, New York: Academic Press, pp. 1–46.

Hubel, D.H. and T.N. Wiesel (1962), 'Receptive fields, binocular interaction and functional architecture in the cat's visual cortex', *Journal of Physiology*, **160** (1), 106–54.

Kelso, J.A.S. (1984), 'Phase transitions and critical behavior in human bimanual coordination', *American Journal of Physiology*, **24** (June), R1000–R1004.

Killingsworth, D.T. and A. Gilbert (2010), 'Wandering mind is an unhappy mind', *Science*, **330** (6006), 932.

Kwartler, M. (1998), 'Regulating the good you can't think of', *Urban Design International*, **3** (1), 13–21.

Levine, R. and A. Norenzayan (1999), 'The pace of life in 31 countries', *Journal of Cross-Cultural Psychology*, **30** (March), 178–205.

Livingstone, M.S. (2002), *Vision and Art: The Biology of Seeing*, New York: Harry N. Abrams.

Milgram, S. (1970), 'The experience of living in cities', *Science*, **167**, 1461–68.

Miller, G.A., E.H. Galanter and K.H. Pribram (1960), *Plans and the Structure of Behavior*, New York: Holt Rinehart & Winston.

Ormerod, T.C. (2005), 'Planning and ill-defined problems', in R. Morris and G. Ward (eds), *The Cognitive Psychology of Planning*, Hove: Psychology Press, pp. 53–70.

Portugali, J. (1990), 'Preliminary notes on social synergetics, cognitive maps and environmental recognition', in H. Haken and M. Stadler (eds), *Synergetics of Cognition*, Berlin, Heidelberg and New York: Springer, pp. 379–92.

Portugali, J. (2011), *Complexity, Cognition and the City*, Berlin, Heidelberg and New York: Springer.

Portugali, J. (2016), 'What makes cities complex?', in J. Portugali and E. Stolk (eds), *Complexity, Cognition, Urban Planning and Design*, Berlin, Heidelberg and New York: Springer, pp. 3–19.

Portugali, J. (2020), 'Information adaptation as the link between cognitive planning and professional planning', in G. De Roo, C. Yamu and C. Zuidema (eds), *Handbook on Planning and Complexity*, Cheltenham, UK and Northampton, MA, USA: Edward Elgar, pp. 203–19.

Portugali, J. and H. Haken (1992), 'Synergetics and cognitive maps', in J. Portugali (ed.), *Geoforum*, **23** (2), special issue, 111–30.

Portugali, J. and E. Stolk (2014), 'A SIRN view on design thinking – an urban design perspective', *Environment and Planning B: Planning and Design*, **41** (5), 829–46.

Raichle, M.E., A.M. MacLeod, A.Z. Snyder, W.J. Powers, D.A. Gusnard and G.L. Shulman (2001), 'A default mode of brain function', *Proceedings of the National Academy of Sciences of the USA*, **98** (2), 676–82.

Ross, G.M. and J. Portugali (2018), 'Urban regulatory focus: a new concept linking city size to human behavior', *Royal Society Open Science*, **5** (25 May), 171478.

Schmidt, R.C., C. Carello and M.T. Turvey (1990), 'Phase transitions and critical fluctuations in the visual coordination of rhythmic movements between people', *Journal of Experimental Psychology: Human Perception and Performance*, **16** (2), 227–47.

Sela, R. (2016), 'Global scale predictions of cities in urban and in cognitive planning', in J. Portugali and E. Stolk (eds), *Complexity, Complexity, Cognition, Urban Planning and Design*, Berlin, Heidelberg and New York: Springer, pp. 181–96.

Shannon, C.E. and W. Weaver (1949), *The Mathematical Theory of Communication*, Champaign, IL: University of Illinois Press.

Snow, C.P. (1964), *The Two Cultures and a Second Look*, Cambridge: Cambridge University Press.

Stadler, M. and P. Kruse (1990), 'The self-organization perspective in cognition research: historical remarks and new experimental approaches', in H. Haken and M. Stadler (eds), *Synergetics of Cognition*, Berlin, Heidelberg and New York: Springer, pp. 32–52.

Suddendorf, T. and M.C. Corballis (2007), 'The evolution of foresight: what is mental time travel, and is it unique to humans?', *Behavioral and Brain Sciences*, **30** (3), 299–313, discussion 313–51.

Tversky, B. (1992), 'Distortions in cognitive maps', *Geoforum*, **23**, 131–8.

Walmsley, D.J. and G.J. Lewis (1989), 'The pace of pedestrian flows in cities', *Environment and Behavior*, **21** (2), 123–50.

Weidlich, W. (1999), 'From fast to slow processes in the evolution of urban and regional settlement structures: the role of population pressure', in J. Portugali (ed.), 'Population, environment and society on the verge of the 21st century', *Discrete Dynamics in Nature and Society*, **3**, special issue, 137–47.

Weidlich, W. (2002), *Sociodynamics: A Systematic Approach to Mathematical Modelling in the Social Sciences*, London: Taylor & Francis.

Wimberley, R., L. Morris and G. Fulkerson (2007), 'Mayday 23: world population becomes more urban than rural', *Rural Sociologist*, **27** (1), 42–3.

7. Co-evolution as the secret of urban complexity
Denise Pumain

1. INTRODUCTION

It is easy for everyone to imagine what a city is, although the recurrent exercises in delineation and the many attempts to harmonize this concept and its measurements across countries show how it may be difficult and even controversial to build a scientific definition (UN 2018). On the contrary, the higher level of spatial organization and differentiation of cities in territories at national or continental scale hardly has any mental representation in the consciousness of the ordinary public. Yet it is at this geographical level that statistical regularities are most frequently observed and most similar in all parts of the world.

These similarities were observed long ago (Pumain and Robic 1996). They justify the early formulation of the concept of a 'general system of cities' (by the Saint-Simonian engineer, Reynaud 1841, discovered by Robic 1982) and its explanatory theories. Since Christaller's famous theory of central places (1933) and the proposal to codify the multiscalar organization of urban territories in the form of nested systems (Berry 1964), cities have become champions of the application of self-organization and complexity theories to the social sciences (Pumain et al. 1989; Portugali 1999; Lane et al. 2009; Portugali et al. 2012). The main achievements of this line of research now appear as building a 'new science of cities' (Batty 2013).

Among the many proposals for complex formalisms applied to cities, we mainly retain here those having contributed to account for the persistence of urban hierarchies, to explain the diversity of cities and to interpret the diversity of urban trajectories among large groups of cities. Zipf's curves, growth models and scaling laws are now integrated into simulation models capable of reconstructing the trajectories of a very large number of cities in all parts of the world (Pumain et al. 2015; Cura et al. 2017). These experiments have helped to validate the principles of an evolutionary theory of city systems (Pumain 1997). That is why I develop here the idea that the co-evolution of cities (Paulus 2004; Raimbault 2020b) is a key concept to investigate for better understanding the generality and diversities of the shape of systems of cities and predicting the future evolution of urbanization.

While briefly retracing here what is a personal experience regarding the emergence of the concept of co-evolution in urban theory, I promote a spiral conception of the cumulativeness of knowledge (Pumain 2009). It is important not to neglect existing theories, which in principle already contain results drawn from a large number of empirical observations, even if their conceptions of society may seem partly out of date or too exclusively rooted in a specific geographical context. It is therefore just as useful and necessary to propose revisions of old theories as to pretend to bring entirely new theories.

2.   FOREKNOWLEDGE OF URBAN CO-EVOLUTION

Using the vocabulary of complex systems sciences, in terms that are meaningful now, we can say that observing the cities' co-evolution leads to the identification of a process of strong emergence. That process brings to light a new geographical object identifiable on a meso- or macro-geographical scale, that of regional, national and, even, continental or global territories, which I name 'system of cities'. The geographical ontology of urban systems characterize three relevant levels for observing urban populations, their activities and artefacts. At the micro level, urban citizens, firms and collective institutions have each specific attributes. The interactions between these diverse stakeholders over time lead to a first strong emergence of the object named 'the city'. A city has collective emerging properties that cannot belong to any individual of the lower level (such as the urban morphology, the centrality, the urban functions or a qualitative ambiance). At a higher geographical level, all types of interactions between cities (either concrete as transfers of goods, persons and investments, or immaterial as exchanges of information between their variety of economic, cultural and political stakeholders) generate, over time, interdependencies in cities' socio-economic evolution. The main emerging properties at that level are the regular hierarchical distribution of city sizes and the functional diversity of cities, as well as their spatial organization. These properties are universal and characterize systems of cities all over the world.

It is evident that this new conception is not a discovery, but an invention, in the social sense, a construction according to the epistemological vocabulary. It is part of a spiral process of construction of knowledge (Pumain 2009) since it revisits many previous concepts. The first mention of a general system of cities appears in the article 'Villes' of a French encyclopedia. In that detailed notice, the Saint-Simonian engineer Jean Reynaud describes as early as 1841 a nested hierarchy of hexagons whose centers are villages of artisans then towns and cities providing rarer services to their surrounding broader and broader region. He estimates that four to five levels of centers can be observed between the smaller artisan villages and the capital of the country. The German geographer Walter Christaller (1933) almost 100 years later formalized that view as a static equilibrium of a nested hierarchy of cities under the headline 'central places theory'. His theory relies on hypotheses about the behavior of consumers and service entrepreneurs according to economic principles at the micro level (charging transportation costs to the consumer, choosing the closest center for each functional level, and services of similar range grouping in the same centers). European and American geographers documented many times the theory in regional monographs for many countries in the world (Berry and Pred 1965). A step further was gained when the American geographer Brian Berry coined the famous phrase 'cities as systems within systems of cities' in 1964. This enabled a shift from the rigid and technical paradigm of a system prevailing at the time of Jean Reynaud, toward the more dynamic representations inspired from living organisms conveyed, for instance, by Bertalanffy's (1968) theory of general systems. Thinking of the temporal dimension of systems of cities, geographers introduced Hägerstrand's theory about the spatial diffusion of innovations to explain urban growth and the hierarchical distribution of urban sizes (for example, Brian Robson 1973 and Alan Pred 1973). After analyzing the historical diffusion of manufacturing and information media among US cities, the latter also scrutinized the evolution of variegated urban interactions in developed countries (Pred 1977). That last mentioned book raised a number of questions about the complexity of processes sustaining the transformation of urban hierarchies over time.

3. A SIMPLE STOCHASTIC MODEL OF URBAN GROWTH AND URBAN HIERARCHY

The concept of co-evolution emerged slowly from a number of surveys and modelling exercises which aimed to solve what can seem a strange paradox. Although the number of cities and their size continue to grow, and this process is accompanied by very significant changes in productive systems and in the living and housing conditions of populations, we observe a very high persistency in the relative positions of cities in the hierarchy of sizes over long periods of time. While innovations appear, with constant renewals in urban societies, referred to as 'creative destruction' by Schumpeter (1942, pp. 82–3), we observe a persistence of functional specialization among urban areas, sometimes for many decades after the time of their creation in particular cities.

A first line of research for answering this issue went through a stage of building databases on the evolution of urban populations and testing simple models. Using the statistical means and calculation tools available during the 1970s, the exercise provided a statistical summary of the shape of the distribution of city sizes and enabled the characterization of the growth process that ensured the cities' evolution. The most abundant literature dealt with models of city size distribution, in particular Zipf's law (Figure 7.1), of which several statistical variants were proposed after the seminal work by Auerbach (1913), but often tested on data that lacked rigor in the definition and delineation of urban entities (see Cottineau 2017 for a review). The diversity of the results obtained led to misunderstandings and badly informed discussions, which I have reported on several occasions in subsequent writings (Pumain 2012).

At that time, few authors had considered the model of settlement size hierarchy proposed by Gibrat (1931), the lognormal distribution, which has the advantage of being testable in its generative process (Robson 1973). The model links the shape of the distribution of city sizes to the process of spatially distributing the growth between cities. Constructing harmonized databases of all the cities (defined as urban agglomerations or urban functional areas) in a national territory, observed at short intervals over a long period of time thanks to census data, therefore made it possible to verify both the degree of adequacy of a theoretical model of urban hierarchies and the plausibility of the growth hypotheses predicted by the model. According to the process of proportional growth as described by Gibrat, it gives rise to a lognormal distribution of city sizes if urban growth rates have equal probabilities whatever the city size and are not correlated with previous rate. Brian Robson (1973) had tested it successfully on the evolution of urban agglomerations in England and Wales during the nineteenth century. He mentioned, however, a few slight deviations between empirical observations and the pure stochastic model, which I also observed when testing it on French data from the nineteenth and twentieth centuries (Pumain 1982).

Although not perfect, the good quality of fit of the model made it a satisfying first approximation for summarizing the urban growth process. The contribution to urban

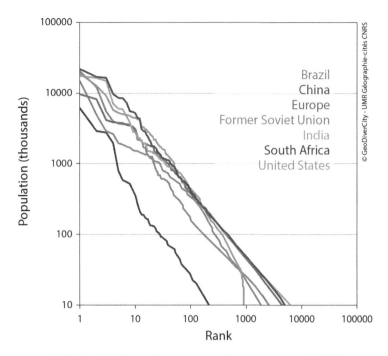

Source: Pumain et al. (2015, p. 706), https://journals.openedition.org/cybergeo/26730?lang=en.

Figure 7.1   Zipf's law for seven systems of cities

theory was thus double: the model provides, first, a statistical explanation of the shape of urban hierarchies and, second, a better understanding of the persistency of their spatial pattern, as cities over time have equal probability of growing according to a process of exponential type. This explanation could be admitted by geographers, but not by specialists of urban economics for whom the rank-size rule remained a 'mystery' (Krugman 1996), mainly because economists wanted to derive it from a process that would be defined at the level of individual firms and persons (see section 6 in this chapter for a more precise discussion on that point).

4.   THE DISCOVERY OF PARALLEL TRAJECTORIES: URBAN HIERARCHY AND THE SPATIAL DIFFUSION OF INNOVATIONS

Looking for a deeper understanding of the urban growth process invites scrutiny of its two demographic components, natural and migratory balances. As natural balance is more homogeneously distributed and highly dependent on previous migratory trends that shaped the population age structure, considering this leads to searching for an explanation by investigating how migrations (that represent the attractiveness of cities) are linked to the jobs cities offer to the population. At particular periods, the fastest growing cities, which are the most attractive, are those where job creating and income-generating activities are developed. Geographers have a long tradition of classifying cities according to their activities and thus defining urban functions, or functional specializations (Alexander 1954; Pumain and Saint-Julien 1976). During the 1970s, multivariate analyses provided a synthetic description of the associations and exclusions of activities in cities (Berry and Smith 1972). Among contemporary cities, and still currently, the most striking difference separates two major families of cities, those with predominantly manufacturing bases and those orientated towards services, with a secondary differentiation playing on the more or less recent character of manufacturing and tertiary specializations. Looking at the relative stability or slow evolution of that fundamental structure over a few decades, for around 200 French cities, we found moreover a surprising parallelism in the relative socio-economic trajectories of individual cities (Figure 7.2). The qualitative and quantitative changes occurring in the social and economic composition of urban populations were almost the same in all cities (Pumain and Saint-Julien 1978). This incremental and distributed process of socio-economic change contributed to a simple homothetic translation of the former hierarchical and functional structure of the urban system.

That observation led to a further discovery. Indeed, each major factor that defined this multivariate structure could be related to subsets of activities and skills that developed at a specific moment in time and had generated waves of marked urban specialization. In the French case, the first factor was a reversal of the inequalities created by the first industrial revolution of the nineteenth century. The less industrialized cities of the nineteenth century acquired higher income levels during the first and second halves of twentieth century; they welcomed more of the new services and had become the most attractive in the second half of twentieth century. Conversely, the flourishing manufacturing cities of the nineteenth century that heavily specialized in steel and textile industries suffered from the competition of global markets and had become the poorest cities. The second factor of multivariate analysis ranked the cities according to their ability in having attracted both industrial and service modern activities that were developing during the second half of the twentieth century (Pumain and Saint-Julien 1978). The significance of the functional differentiation revealed by the axes of multivariate analysis could be related to the innovation waves having boosted the development of subsets of cities at a given period. This interpretation was later confirmed using a further diversity of urban attributes (Paulus 2004) and recognized as providing a good description of the functional disparities of US cities (Paulus and Vacchiani-Marcuzzo 2016) (Figure 7.3) as well as those of emerging countries, such as South Africa (Vacchiani-Marcuzzo 2016) and India (Denis and Zérah 2017), and even in the system of cities governed with central planning, such as China (Swerts 2013).

These results attain several gains in explanation, compared with the simplistic description of urban growth provided by Gibrat's model. First, it is not because they are statistically independent entities (as hypothesized in the stochastic model) that cities grow roughly at the same rate, but because they share the same type of transformation of their economic and social profiles, as being part of a territory under common laws and societal regulations and processes. This is likely to happen owing to the multiple connections between a diversity of stakeholders ensuring a rapid circulation of information between cities (see section 5 in this chapter). Second, Gibrat's model, when completed by including in a simulation model the growth impulses generated through innovation waves and

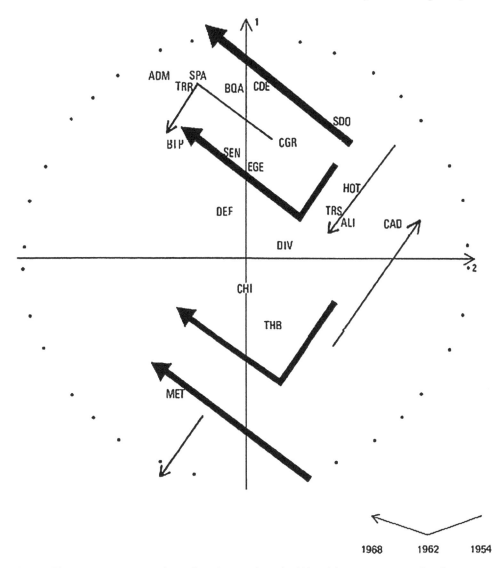

Note: The acronyms represent share of employment in each of 20 activity sectors measured at three census dates (1954, 1962 and 1968) for about 100 urban areas; the thickness of the arrows is proportional to the number of cities following the same trajectory.

Source: Pumain and Saint-Julien (1978).

Figure 7.2 Discovery of urban co-evolution with temporal multivariate analysis

their hierarchical diffusion within the system of cities (Favaro and Pumain 2011), helps to better fit the data of urban population's evolution. In particular, the model better simulates the recurrent deviations that were observed between empirical data on urban growth and Gibrat's stochastic model, that is, a slight positive correlation between growth rates and city size (at the beginning of each innovation wave) and a persistency

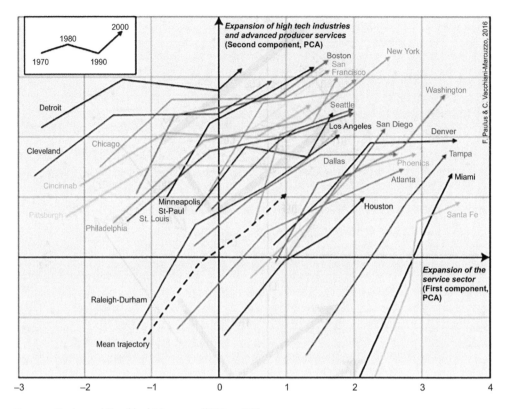

Source: Paulus and Vacchiani-Marcuzzo (2016, p. 165).

Figure 7.3   *Co-evolution 1970–2000 of US metropolitan areas with over 2 million inhabitants*

of high or low growth rates in the same cities over periods of time. This also comforts our conceptual understanding of the bifurcations in the trajectories of individual cities. We can measure the time delays between the inflexions detected in the curves of population growth and the related events marking their major functional specialization, which successively amplify urban growth then urban decline according to the stage they have reached in the corresponding product cycles. Moreover, a sophisticated computing model thus identifies not a single temporal impact of such events, but the diversified array of co-evolution regimes that characterizes the complex urban evolution, as illustrated, for example, in the case of railways infrastructure by Juste Raimbault (2020a).

5.   URBAN SIZE, SPECIALIZATION AND SCALING LAWS

This knowledge enabled the development of an alternative interpretation that is better anchored in geographical urban theory, of the new frame of analysis proposed under the label of 'urban scaling laws' by physicists applying to cities general formalisms of complex systems (Bettencourt et al. 2007). Geographers and other specialists of urban science, including physicists (Pumain 2004; Arcaute et al. 2015; Arcaute and Hatna 2020), challenge both the hypothetical entire novelty of the related findings and the claim about the universality of an urban theory based on pure mathematical and physical principles.[1] The physicists rightly identify the scaling properties of cities as being specific, distinct from those of living organisms, as while metabolic rates of living species are always varying sub-linearly with their size, the urban attributes measuring the urban products may exhibit super-linearity. Thus these authors conceptualize cities as social reactors (places with a high density of interactions linked with close proximity) that generate non-linear relationships between urban attributes and city size. The observed trends are growing returns (that is, super-linear scaling relationships) for income, wages and patents, but also for living costs, pollution and congestion levels, and economies of scale (sub-linear relationships) for urban infrastructure such as length of material networks. They suppose an 'increasing peace of life' for explaining this (Bettencourt 2013, p. 1440). They establish quantitative ratios that could help in predicting the future of cities (Bettencourt and West 2010). However, in the urbanization process they imagine, the largest cities would simply be a replication of smaller cities constrained by universal power laws.[2] That is, they derive longitudinal trajectories (the evolution of one city) from cross-sectional observations (the comparison between cities of different sizes at a given moment).

Conversely, we propose to interpret urban scaling laws from an evolutionary perspective (Pumain 2018). We consider that scaling parameters are not fixed over time nor universal, whatever the level of countries' development. We observe variations in the values of exponents of urban scaling laws that differentiate urban activities and evolve in a regular way. Indeed, these variations depend on the stage of development of the considered urban attributes in the urban system (Pumain et al. 2006). The exponents of non-linear relationships between an urban attribute and city size rise above a value of 1 during the first stage of adoption of innovation in the urban system, as long as they are captured by and concentrated in the largest cities. The exponents decrease then below the value 1 when these activities withdraw in smaller towns of cheaper land rents and wages after their stage of wide diffusion all over the system. This process is still active within countries. It has expanded also across boundaries, with the growing trend in international division of labor enabling multinational firms to exploit wage inequalities between countries and the consequent fragmentation of value chains all over the world. The unequal level of maturity of sectors of economic activity explain, for instance, why manufacturing industries scale below 1 in developed countries while they scale above 1 in emerging economies, such as China or South Africa. We checked that the observed exponent values evolve according to this theory, for a variety of urban attributes, such as employment in economic activities, labor skills or foreign investments, in the systems of cities of countries having very diverse economic and political structures, such as France, the USA, South Africa and China (Paulus 2004; Paulus and Vacchiani-Marcuzzo 2016; Finance and Swerts 2020).

Thus starting from an interpretation of multiple temporal multivariate analyses, we have made a discovery that was later confirmed with a series of different investigations. To summarize that discovery: size inequalities and qualitative socio-economic differences between cities are traces of their co-evolution (which is an interactive adaptation of cities

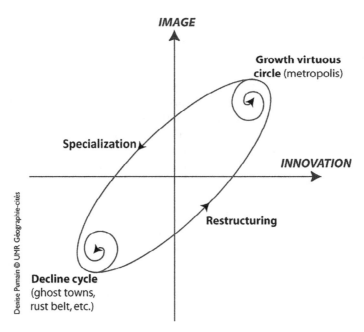

Figure 7.4   Innovation as key factor of adaptive process in systems of cities

with feedbacks to the innovations they create and diffuse between them) (Figure 7.4). Is this a real discovery? Important elements of the theoretical explanation were already there in urban geography. The Swedish geographer Torsten Hägerstrand proposed his theory of hierarchical diffusion of innovations as early as 1952 (Hägerstrand 1967 for an English translation). This is a further illustration of the spiral cumulativeness of knowledge that characterizes social sciences, for which new interpretations are never entirely new (Pumain 2009). Formulating these observations in the language of complex systems enabled us however to develop our investigations and instruments in entirely new directions.

6.   SIMULATION MODELS FOR TESTING AND PROVING COMPLEX CO-EVOLUTION PROCESSES

An important step in developing an evolutionary theory of urban systems occurred through rooting these former insights within the theories of self-organizing complex systems (Pumain 1997). My conception is that urban systems are adaptive complex systems organized for a long time at the meso-geographic scale for sharing information, diffusing innovations, reducing uncertainties of local environments by making benefits from distant complementary resources. Cities and the systems they build through their interactions are socio-economic adapters in a continuous process of territorial competition. I suggested that the common features in the evolution of systems of cities have similarities with the dynamics of other types of systems where an order at a higher level is created through fluctuations at a lower level – as described in the theories of self-organizing systems in natural sciences. These theories, originally in chemistry or physics, enable us to understand under what conditions (open systems far from equilibrium with external source of energy or perturbations) the disorderly, random fluctuations of elementary particles at the micro level can generate observable and persistent structure at the macro level in natural systems. Referring to them was not simply making use of metaphors or rephrasing previous knowledge about urban processes in terms of self-organizing theories. The urban growth and urban socio-economic transformation processes that we observe have the same type of properties. They include an immense number of local fluctuations in the attributes of each city at the micro level (a rapid dynamics that seem random) while their effect at the macro level is a slowly evolving persistent structure. However, this does not mean that the urban stakeholders' actions are irrational or inexplicable, or that their intentions have no direct effect. Indeed, they are so numerous and diverse that they compensate, conflict and imitate, and their consequent combinations produce very small changes in an incremental way at the meso level of each city and at the macro level of the system of cities. It would be impossible to describe these actions in detail, for each element simultaneously, in the whole system defined at the higher observation level. To reconcile the rapid dynamics of the micro level with the slow dynamics of the macro level, the self-organization theories propose mathematical models that we have experimented with. The models were inspired from the theories of dissipative structures developed for chemistry at Brussels by Ilya Prigogine, and transposed towards urban dynamics by Allen and Sanglier (1979), and at Stuttgart by Herman Haken (1983) from the physics of lasers under the name of synergetics. Wolfgang Weidlich and Günter Haag transposed the equations of motions to interregional migrations (Weidlich and Haag 1988). These models represent by non-linear differential equations the temporal evolution of the state variables that define the macroscopic structure of the system, with mathematical functions or parameters representing the microscopic interactions. From this perspective, we lose the notions of uniqueness and non-reproducibility attached to historical objects, but we take into account the irreversibility of their particular trajectory. It is accepted that processes can be formalized, that geographical objects can have a 'banal dynamics' in a historical trend that remains irreversible' (Pumain 1998, p. 364).

We first adopted the models of self-organization to translate the principles of the evolutionary theory of urban systems into dynamic models. The modelling exercise has a first objective to reconstruct the observed past trajectories of cities for testing the relevance of our theoretical explanation through calibration on empirical data. A good fit for the model is a preliminary condition for ensuring the quality of projections estimating future relative positions of cities within inter-urban competition, thus for adjusting intelligent urban policies. Many experiments were attempted at first with mathematical models of systems of non-linear equations. We learned a great deal about a variety of calibration strategies in the presence of non-linear interactions that were often causing too many bifurcations (Pumain et al. 1989). We also discovered that mathematical models with similar formalisms were conceived in very different epistemological perspectives and could not be compared, despite the apparently similar interpretation given to their parameters (Lombardo et al. 1988). The applications of the synergetic model enabled us to estimate more precisely the urban co-evolution, but could do that for only one variable, the population size of cities (Sanders 1992).

The main obstacle to continuing these experiments with mathematical models was their lack of flexibility, especially for representing properly the diversity of spatial interactions that characterize inter-urban dynamics. Multi-agents systems (MASs) are much more flexible than differential equations for simulating spatial and evolving interactions, including quantitative and qualitative effects (Pumain and Sanders 2013). Through the definition of rules at individual level, they can reproduce the circulation of information between cognitive and decision-making agents. They simulate at the upper level the emergence of collective or aggregated structures, which can be tested statistically. The rules can be adapted for varying space and time scales of interaction during the course of history. With the help of computer scientists, we thus designed the SIMPOP series of models that was conceived to explain the hierarchical differentiation of city sizes and their functional geo-diversity. The first MAS model applied to geography was the SIMPOP model (Bura et al. 1996; Sanders et al. 1997), which simulated the emergence of a functionally differentiated system of towns and cities from an initial mainly homogeneous rural settlement system, over a duration of about 2000 years. The computing capacity and the lack of available data at the level of individual urban stakeholders at that time (1990s) led us to implement the model for cities defined as interacting agents. Thus this model differs from most MASs in two respects. First, its agents are immobile, as they represent places in geographical space, even if their interactions are affected by the technical innovations in the communication systems and the increasing level of urban resources that modify the relative situation of elementary cities in the network of their relational space. Second, as SIMPOP is a model of interactions between territories (aggregated geographical objects), the behavior of these agents is not reducible to the behavior of individual persons, for instance, as in models of cognitive economy. The implemented mechanisms between agents (that is, collective agents that represent individual cities) are mainly: a proactive and selective propagation of innovations waves generated by inter-urban competition and emulation; a market exchange between urban functions; a hierarchical selection (top down and bottom up); the appearance of new urban functions (exogenous in first models); an expanding range of inter-urban interaction (as a consequence of space time contraction); and path dependence according to the territorial boundaries that constrain urban interaction. However, compared with the difficulty of representing spatial interactions with parameters such as in mathematical models using systems of differential equations, MAS models enable us to differentiate different types of spatial interactions processes. Within the SIMPOP model, inter-urban interactions for market activities are freely competing but constrained by a distance decay model of gravity type, while administrative functions levy taxes in fixed spatial subdivisions. Specialized activities develop interactions according to specific types of networks that may reach long distances and cross national boundaries. These longer-distance and more freely distributed interactions are linked to the location of resources in respect of manufacturing and to resort amenities in respect of tourism, for instance.

As our knowledge about urban interactions is mainly deduced from the observed changes in state variables at time intervals, and only very partially informed from the direct observation of flows between cities, many unknown parameters have to be estimated while simulating the inter-urban exchanges that are generated according to rules aimed at reproducing the observed modalities of urban changes. Thus, the SIMPOP model represents urban co-evolution as produced through estimated interactions that are generated with random factors. Despite these limitations, our first application of such an MAS led to the following main results: an urban hierarchy cannot emerge if there are no spatial interactions; the emergence of a polycentric hierarchized system of cities can occur under a stochastic process of inter-urban exchanges even if starting from homogeneous initial conditions; but a renewed innovation flow is necessary for maintaining the structural properties of the system of cities over time (Sanders et al. 1997). These first applications were limited by the capacity of computing systems (our first model was restricted to deal with 400 settlements only and calibration was considered as satisfying after around 100 simulations), fortunately the computing speed and capacity have considerably increased since these pioneer times, only 25 years ago.

A second SIMPOP model, built by another computer scientist, Benoît Glisse, enabled us to inform some of the processes that generate the diversity of systems of cities, based on a comparison between Europe and the USA (Bretagnolle and Pumain 2010). A first version of the model was adjusted to the evolution of European cities over four centuries. The version had to undergo significant qualitative changes in order to be able to account for the evolution of American cities over three centuries: a system of New World cities was thus identified in broad outlines, based on the necessary transformation of the rules of the multi-agent model representing the interactions between cities. It forced us, in particular, to introduce the notion of a pioneer front for simulating the colonization of a territory by cities and their dependence on an external demand – that of the metropolis – to ensure the development of the system, in accordance with the dynamics revealed by the calibration on empirical data.

The results of experiments with this model also provided further advances in explaining the evolution of systems of cities, proving the importance of urban networks in generating more urban growth. Until recently, the observed historical main dynamic trend led to increasing size inequalities in the system of cities: they are becoming larger than those that would be predicted with Gibrat's model, contradicting the theories predicting a 'counter-urbanization' process (Berry 1976). We moreover discovered that global cities may have existed since the Middle Ages, as the cities that are at the head of urban hierarchies always expand a significant part of their interactions beyond the boundaries of their own system (Bretagnolle and Pumain 2010). This reflects the main limitation of applying the concept of system to a geographical object, the system of cities, whose boundaries cannot be defined in the same way for all its elements, because the range of urban interactions is increasing with city size and, sometimes, their nature and degree of specialization. Thus, the spatial extension of the subsets of cities that engage in co-evolution is not fixed in space and time, and cannot always be reduced to national boundaries. We have nevertheless verified in further studies made at the scale of single countries, including Europe, the USA and the BRICS countries, that metropolization and simplification from below of urban hierarchies (leading to shrinking cities) are common dynamics trends observed in several systems of cities in the world (Pumain et al. 2015). Thus, harmonized urban data and simulation models proved useful instruments for testing the principles of the evolutionary theory of urban systems.

We could take a qualitatively very important step forward thanks to a much closer and more continuous collaboration between computer scientists and geographers (Pumain and Reuillon 2017). A recurrent criticism against using multi-agent simulations for hypothesis testing is the difficulty in validating their results. The uniqueness of the solutions reached during their calibration, whether based on empirical data or theoretical hypotheses, is difficult to guarantee. We used a new simulation platform, OpenMOLE, which developed sophisticated model validation processes, including genetic algorithms and access to parallel grid computing.[3] We have been able to acquire more certainty in the quality of parameter estimation for a generic model, SimpopLocal (Schmitt 2014), dedicated to the emergence of cities during 4000 years after the Neolithic period with the help of the SimProcess platform developed by Sébastien Rey-Coyrehourcq (2015). Compared with the few hundred simulations that were available when estimating using trial-and-error, by hand, methods in the former experiments with Simpop models, it was possible to develop an almost exhaustive exploration of the space of parameters, through around 500 million replications of the same model (Schmitt et al. 2015). The theoretical hypotheses thus tested and assumed to lead to the emergence of a system of cities based on interactions propagating innovations between population centers are now considered not only as sufficient, but also as necessary to reconstruct an urban hierarchy and the right diversity of urban trajectories – within the context of the chosen model ontology. A new procedure for the rigorous exploration of the behaviors of a model termed 'calibration profile' was developed for that purpose (Reuillon et al. 2015).

This outcome is important for the humanities and social sciences as it opens the door to providing proof when answering questions about complex social processes. Adoption of multi-agent models authorizes more flexible and diverse formulations than mathematical equations to represent part of these processes. However, the number of possible replicas of the simulations often remained too limited and the values estimated by calibration still too uncertain to constitute a sufficient validation of the assumptions introduced into the model. Even if the ambition of these models is never to produce an exact numerical result or a result that would totally optimize only one aspect of the problem, we now have powerful exploration methods that describe all the dynamic behaviors of a model, that produce satisfactory process trade-offs leading to plausible solutions, and that detect whether the contributions of particular processes and parameters to these dynamics are truly effective or not. This new step is important since it advances modelling in the social sciences and humanities towards scientific accuracy and reproducibility.

7.   PATH DEPENDENCE AND CULTURAL VARIATIONS

The research program GeoDiverCity[4] aims to develop simulation models that take into account not only the general urban dynamics for reconstructing common stylized facts, but also the major geographical and historical features that distinguish regions of the world. New methods for building models that included a diversity of geographical environments were developed. The MARIUS model designed by Clementine Cottineau and Paul Chapron, with the help of the OpenMOLE simulation platform, was designed to reconstruct the trajectories of cities within the boundaries of the territorial system of the former USSR (Cottineau 2014). In parallel the authors invented an incremental method of multi-modelling. Before choosing a model, they identified a hierarchy of factors explaining the differential urban growth that was revealed by the statistical analysis of observed trajectories of individual cities. They implemented at first the simplest and more generic model of urban growth (that is, Gibrat's stochastic model without spatial interaction), then introduced more sophisticated mechanisms of constraints on urban growth as well as some specific environmental conditions (Cottineau et al. 2015). At each step, the computed deviation between the observed shape of urban hierarchy and the typology of urban trajectories, and those that were computed, helped to measure the retro-predictive capability of the model. For example, in that case it was important to introduce not only resource location (minerals, oil and so on) for generating functional specialization, but also the political decision of large investments in these urban areas. (National policies developed in the USSR specialized cities more rapidly and to a much larger size than their equivalent in market economies.) Geographical multi-modelling is a new method, which operates at different levels of precision, according to an adjustable focus evaluating the degree of specificity of a particular evolution in a generic dynamic, for a given granularity of description (Cottineau et al. 2015).

The evolution of the social objects is not limited to a universal dynamics because significant differences exist in the parameters that characterize the national or continental urban hierarchies and the interaction rules that have generated those (Pumain et al. 2015; Cura et al. 2017). These differences are widely explained by the path dependency that maintains over very long periods of time (possibly centuries) their distinctive features according to the main historical circumstances that created them. Path dependence is frequently observed in the dynamics of geographical structures (Arthur 1994). The co-evolution processes are constitutive of such a dynamics because the multiple networks conveying persons, goods and information are very often reused for sparing the costs of establishing new infrastructures, designing new learning pathways and acquiring new information in social transactions. The materiality of habitat and the communication networks linking them is another factor contributing to the longevity of urban patterns. Among the main cultural features differentiating the systems of cities in a pervasive way, we identified: (1) the date and type of establishment of settlement systems ('Old' or 'New' World); (2) the type of territorial governance that shaped them (centralized or not); and (3) the steps of their development or the way they became inserted in the colonial empires and phases of globalization (Bretagnolle et al. 2007, 2009). The necessarily limited extent of this chapter does not permit me to elaborate more on the qualitative variations that make the diversity of the urban realm so fascinating worldwide. A recent book published with the help of the Habitat division of the United Nations provides a more detailed and richly informed explanation of that global diversity (Rozenblat et al. 2018).

For a few decades, the current globalization of the economy, society, culture and so on generates ever-growing interdependencies between cities all over the world. This trend amplifies their co-evolution. Multinational firms (Rozenblat 2018; Finance 2016) and especially financial firms (Denis 2020) are major stakeholders in global urban co-evolution. This may represent a new step consolidating the genericity of the concept of system of cities.

8. CONCLUSION

The reader may wonder why I did not start this chapter with a review of the usual definitions and explanations about co-evolution. Even if I borrow that word from biology, the use I make of it has nothing to do with biological processes; there is no analogy and very little metaphor. After reviewing the possible biological connotations, such as referred to in evolutionary economics, Juste Raimbault (2020b, p. 263) provides a useful synthetic and programmatic description: 'the statistical evidence of causal relationships within spatiotemporal niches, for which a practical characterization method uses a weak causality based on lagged correlation'. What I insist on is the multiple sources and evidence of strong interdependence in the evolution of cities, leading us to conceptualize them as parts of systems of cities in all historical times and all regions of the world.

I have traced (in a very simplified manner) one of the intellectual and experimental paths that have led urban geographers to borrow instruments and methods from the complexity sciences (see, for a review, Peris et al. 2018). This path has undertaken several reformulations that have so far led to the theorization of cities and systems of cities as complex adaptive systems. However, this evolutionary theory of urban systems is rooted in the observation of the history of cities and the social processes of the spatial organization of societies on the Earth's interface. It includes among the principles underlying the structuring of cities and systems of cities, a geography and economy of proximity and networks, an anthropology and sociology of innovation and competition that together bring out the properties of hierarchical differentiation, and functional diversity and dynamics common to all city systems. In addition to generic dynamics, in order to understand the variety of current forms of urban organizations and the specificity of their evolution according to the regions of the world, it is also necessary to include in the theory an ecology of planetary resources successively borrowed by technological innovations and a geopolitics of territorial, social and economic domination.

Therefore, the fundamentals of a theory of cities borrow concepts from the entire social sciences. This is in line with my definition of the degree of complexity of a social object, which would be measured by listing the plurality of human and social sciences needed to explain this system, integrating the concepts developed usually separately by each discipline from its own perspective of the complexity.

That is, even if the formalisms stemming from mathematics and by tests using the growing computing power of computers can claim useful generalizations, in my opinion it is not these formalisms that are at the heart of the fundamentals of urban theories, contrary to what is sometimes asserted (Lobo et al. 2020). It is very important to know them in order to distinguish what is trivial and what is specific in an observed evolution; their use gives rise to quantities of measurements and tests that advance knowledge by systematizing comparisons. However, these formal theories alone cannot claim to offer a universal explanation of cities, any more than the very many urban utopias invented by philosophers and based on other formal logics.

What will be the next steps in advancing knowledge and revising and expanding the framework of theories of urban complexity? The research landscape will change rapidly in relation to data availability, especially data about movement's flows (traces of smartphones, GPS trajectories, dedicated sensors, and so on), that reveal connections between people, places and activities. Many rely on these big data, because they produce new information on a micro scale, that of individual practices, and in this they join a methodological individualism that is often claimed to make explanations more acceptable among the social sciences. More research is needed at every scale, and the evolutionary theory of urban systems can thus claim to offer an interdisciplinary scientific basis to inform thinking about the future of cities and their diversity, especially in the current phase of ecological transition.

NOTES

1. This despite the related wave of intellectual enthusiasm leading, for instance, a journalist to entitle his article 'A physicist solves the city' for the *New York Times* (Lehrer 2010).
2. This is not a well-adapted description since systems of cities are not ergodic, see Pumain (2010).
3. View at https://iscpif.fr/projects/openmole/ (accessed 6 May 2021).
4. ERC advanced grant GeoDiverCity 2011–2016 (PI Denise Pumain).

REFERENCES

Alexander, J.W. (1954), 'The basic-nonbasic concept of urban economic functions', *Economic Geography*, **30** (3), 246–61.
Allen, P. and M. Sanglier (1979), 'A dynamic model of growth in a central place system', *Geographical Analysis*, **11** (3), 256–72.
Arcaute, E. and E. Hatna (2020), 'Scaling laws: insights and limitations', in D. Pumain (ed.), *Theories and Models of Urbanization*, Cham: Springer, pp. 45–66.
Arcaute, E., E. Hatna, P. Ferguson, H. Youn, A. Johansson and M. Batty (2015), 'Constructing cities, deconstructing scaling laws', *Journal of The Royal Society Interface*, **12** (102), 20140745.
Arthur, W.B. (1994), *Increasing Returns and Path Dependence in the Economy*, Ann Arbor, MI: University of Michigan Press.
Auerbach, F. (1913), 'Das Gesetz der Bevölkerungskonzentration', *Petermanns Geographische Mitteilungen*, **59** (1), 74–76.
Batty, M. (2013), *The New Science of Cities*, Cambridge, MA: MIT Press.
Berry, B.J.L. (1964), 'Cities as systems within systems of cities', *Papers in Regional Science*, **13** (1), 147–63.
Berry, B.J.L. (1976), *Urbanization and Counter-urbanization*, Beverly Hills, CA: Sage.
Berry, B.J.L. and A. Pred (1965), *Central Place Studies: A Bibliography of Theory and Applications*, Philadelphia, PA: Regional Science Research Institute.
Berry, B.J.L. and K.B. Smith (1972), *City Classification Handbook*, New York: Wiley Interscience.
Bertalanffy, L. von (1968), *General System Theory*, New York: George Brazillier.
Bettencourt, L.M. (2013), 'The origins of scaling in cities', *Science*, **340** (6139), 1438–41.
Bettencourt, L.M. and G. West (2010), 'A unified theory of urban living', *Nature*, **467** (7318), 912–13.
Bettencourt, L.M., J. Lobo, D. Helbing, C. Kühnert and G.B. West (2007), 'Growth, innovation, scaling, and the pace of life in cities', *PNAS – Proceedings of the National Academy of Sciences*, **104** (17), 7301–6.
Bretagnolle, A. and D. Pumain (2010), 'Simulating urban networks through multiscalar space-time dynamics (Europe and United States, 17th–20th centuries)', *Urban Studies*, **47** (13), 2819–39.
Bretagnolle, A., D. Pumain and C. Vacchiani-Marcuzzo (2007), 'Les formes des systèmes de villes dans le monde', in M.-F. Mattéi and D. Pumain (eds), *Données urbaines*, vol. 5, pp. 301–14.
Bretagnolle, A., D. Pumain and C. Vacchiani-Marcuzzo (2009), 'The organization of urban systems', in D. Lane, D. Pumain, S. Van der Leeuw and G. West (eds), *Complexity Perspectives on Innovation and Social Change*, Berlin: Springer, pp. 197–220.
Bura, S., F. Guérin-Pace, H. Mathian, D. Pumain and L. Sanders (1996), 'Multi-agent systems and the dynamics of a settlement system', *Geographical Analysis*, **28** (2), 161–78.
Christaller, W. (1933), *Die Zentralen Orte in Süddeutschland*, Jena: Fischer.
Cottineau, C. (2014), 'L'évolution des villes dans l'espace postsoviétique. Observation et modélisations', PhD thesis, Université Paris 1 Panthéon-Sorbonne, Paris.
Cottineau, C. (2017), 'MetaZipf: A dynamic meta-analysis of city size distributions', *PloS One*, **12** (8), e0183919.
Cottineau, C., P. Chapron and R. Reuillon (2015), 'Growing models from the bottom up. An evaluation-based incremental modelling method (EBIMM) applied to the simulation of systems of cities', *Journal of Artificial Societies and Social Simulation (JASSS)*, **18** (4), 1–9.
Cura, R., C. Cottineau, E. Swerts, C.A. Ignazzi, A. Bretagnolle, C. Vacchiani-Marcuzzo et al. (2017), 'The old and the new: qualifying city systems in the world with old models and new data', *Geographical Analysis*, **49** (4), 363–86.

Denis, E. (2020), 'Population, land, wealth and the global urban sprawl. Drivers of urban built-up expansion across the world from 1990 to 2015', in D. Pumain (ed.), *Theories and Models of Urbanization*, New Delhi: Springer India, pp. 235–58.

Denis, E. and M.H. Zérah (eds) (2017), *Subaltern Urbanisation in India: An Introduction to the Dynamics of Ordinary Towns*, New Delhi: Springer India.

Favaro, J.-M. and D. Pumain (2011), 'Gibrat revisited: an urban growth model including spatial interaction and innovation cycles', *Geographical Analysis*, **43** (3), 261–86.

Finance, O. (2016), 'Les villes françaises investies par les firmes transnationales étrangères: des réseaux d'entreprises aux établissements localisés', PhD thesis, Université Paris 1 Panthéon-Sorbonne, Paris.

Finance, O. and E. Swerts (2020), 'Scaling laws in urban geography: linkages with urban theories, challenges and limitations', in D. Pumain (ed.), *Theories and Models of Urbanisation*, Cham: Springer, pp. 67–96.

Gibrat, R. (1931), *Les inégalités économiques*, Paris: Sirey.

Hägerstrand, T. (1967), *Innovation Diffusion as a Spatial Process*, Chicago, IL: University of Chicago Press.

Haken, H. (1983), *Advanced Synergetics*, Berlin, Heidelberg and New York: Springer.

Krugman, P. (1996), 'Confronting the urban mystery', *Journal of the Japanese and International Economies*, **10**, 399–418.

Lane, D., D. Pumain, S. van der Leeuw and G. West (eds) (2009), *Complexity Perspectives on Innovation and Social Change*, Berlin: Springer.

Lehrer, J. (2010), 'A physicist solves the city', *New York Times*, 17 December.

Lobo, J., M. Alberti, M. Allen-Dumas, E. Arcaute, M. Barthelemy, L.A. Bojorquez Tapia, et al. (2020), 'Urban science: integrated theory from the first cities to sustainable metropolises', *SSRN Electronic Journal*, doi:10.2139/ssrn.3526940.

Lombardo, S., D. Pumain, G. Rabino, T. Saint-Julien and L. Sanders (1988), 'Comparing urban dynamics models: the unexpected differences in two similar models', *Sistemi Urbani*, **9** (2), 213–28.

Paulus, F. (2004), 'Coévolution dans les systèmes de villes: croissance et spécialisation des aires urbaines françaises de 1950 à 2000', PhD thesis, Université Paris 1 Panthéon-Sorbonne, Paris.

Paulus, F. and C. Vacchiani-Marcuzzo (2016), 'Knowledge industry and competitiveness: economic trajectories of French urban areas (1962–2008)', in A. Cusinato and A. Philippopoulos-Mihalopoulos (eds), *Knowledge-creating Milieus in Europe: Firm Cities, Territories*, Cham: Springer, pp. 157–70.

Peris, A., E. Meijers and M. van Ham (2018), 'The evolution of the systems of cities literature since 1995: schools of thought and their interaction', *Networks and Spatial Economics*, **18** (3), 533–54.

Portugali, J. (1999), *Self-organization and the City*, Berlin: Springer.

Portugali, J., H. Meyer, E. Stolk and E. Tan (eds) (2012), *Complexity Theories of Cities Have Come of Age: An Overview With Implications to Urban Planning and Design*, Berlin and Heidelberg: Springer Science & Business Media.

Pred, A. (1973), *Urban Growth and the Circulation of Information: The United States System of Cities, 1790–1840*, Cambridge, MA: Harvard University Press.

Pred, A. (1977), *City Systems in Advanced Societies*, London: Hutchison.

Pumain, D. (1982), *La dynamique des villes*, Paris: Economica.

Pumain, D. (1997), 'Vers une théorie évolutive des villes', *L'Espace Géographique*, **26** (2), 119–34.

Pumain, D. (1998), 'Les modèles d'auto-organisation et le changement urbain', *Cahiers de Géographie de Québec*, **42** (117), 349–66.

Pumain, D. (2004), 'Scaling laws and urban systems', Working Paper No. 04-02-002, Santa Fe Institute, Santa Fe, NM.

Pumain, D. (2009), 'L'espace, médium d'une construction spiralaire de la géographie, entre société et environnement', in B. Walliser (ed.), *La cumulativité des connaissances en sciences sociales*, Paris: EHESS, pp. 163–97.

Pumain, D. (2010), 'Dynamique des entités géographiques et lois d'échelle dans les systèmes complexes: la question de l'ergodicité', *Mathématiques et Sciences Humaines*, **191** (3), 51–63.

Pumain, D. (2012), 'Une théorie géographique pour la loi de Zipf', *Régions et Développement*, **36** (2nd semester), 33–57.

Pumain, D. (2018), 'An evolutionary theory of urban systems', in C. Rozenblat, D. Pumain and E. Velasquez (eds), *International and Transnational Perspectives on Urban Systems*, Singapore: Springer Nature, pp. 3–18.

Pumain, D. and R. Reuillon (2017), *Urban Dynamics and Simulation Models*, Cham: Springer.

Pumain, D. and M.C. Robic (1996), 'Théoriser la ville', in P.H. Derycke, J.M. Huriot and D. Pumain, *Penser la Ville: Théories et modèles*, Paris: Anthropos, pp. 107–61.

Pumain, D. and T. Saint-Julien (1976), 'Fonctions et hiérarchie dans les villes françaises', *Annales de géographie*, **85** (470), 385–439.

Pumain, D. and T. Saint-Julien (1978), *Les dimensions du changement urbain*, Paris: CNRS.

Pumain, D. and L. Sanders (2013), 'Theoretical principles in inter-urban simulation models: a comparison', *Environment and Planning A*, **45** (9), 2243–60.

Pumain, D., T. Saint-Julien and L. Sanders (1989), *Villes et auto-organisation*, Paris: Economica.

Pumain, D., F. Paulus, C. Vacchiani-Marcuzzo and J. Lobo (2006), 'An evolutionary theory for interpreting urban scaling laws', *Cybergeo: European Journal of Geography*, doi:10.4000/cybergeo.2519.

Pumain, D., E. Swerts, C. Cottineau, C. Vacchiani-Marcuzzo, A. Ignazzi, A. Bretagnolle, et al. (2015), 'Multi-level comparison of large urban systems', *Cybergeo, European Journal of Geography*, doi:10.4000/cybergeo.26730.

Raimbault, J. (2020a), 'Indirect evidence of network effects in a system of cities', *Environment and Planning B: Urban Analytics and City Science*, **47** (1), 138–55.

Raimbault, J. (2020b), 'Unveiling co-evolutionary patterns in systems of cities: a systematic exploration of the SimpopNet model', in D. Pumain (ed.), *Theories and Models of Urbanization*, Cham: Springer, pp. 261–78.

Reuillon, R., C. Schmitt, R. De Aldama and J.B. Mouret (2015), 'A new method to evaluate simulation models: the calibration profile (CP) algorithm', *Journal of Artificial Societies and Social Simulation*, **18** (1), 12.

Rey-Coyrehourcq, S. (2015), 'Une plateforme intégrée pour la construction et l'évaluation de modèles de simulation en géographie', PhD dissertation, Paris 1-Panthéon-Sorbonne.

Reynaud, J. (1841), 'Villes', *Encyclopédie nouvelle*, vol. 7, Paris: Gosselin, pp. 670–87.

Robic, M.C. (1982), 'Cent ans avant Christaller . . . une théorie des lieux centraux', *L'Espace géographique*, **11** (1), 5–12.

Robson, B.T., (1973), *Urban Growth: An Approach*, London: Methuen.

Rozenblat, C. (2018), 'Urban systems between national and global: recent reconfiguration through transnational networks', in C. Rozenblat, D. Pumain and E. Velasquez (eds), *International and Transnational Perspectives on Urban Systems*, Singapore: Springer, pp. 19–49.

Rozenblat, C., D. Pumain and E. Velasquez (eds) (2018), *International and Transnational Perspectives on Urban Systems*, Singapore: Springer.

Sanders, L. (1992), *Système de villes et synergétique*, Paris: Anthropos.

Sanders, L., D. Pumain, H. Mathian, F. Guérin-Pace and S. Bura (1997), 'SIMPOP: a multiagent system for the study of urbanism', *Environment and Planning B: Planning and design*, **24** (2), 287–305.

Schmitt, C. (2014), 'Modélisation de la dynamique des systèmes de peuplement: de SimpopLocal à SimpopNet', PhD thesis, Université Paris I-Panthéon-Sorbonne, Paris.

Schmitt, C., S. Rey-Coyrehourcq, R. Reuillon and D. Pumain (2015), 'Half a billion simulations, evolutionary algorithms and distributed computing for calibrating the SimpopLocal geographical model', *Environment and Planning B*, **42** (2), 300–315.

Schumpeter, J.A. (1942), *Capitalism, Socialism and Democracy*, London: Routledge.

Swerts, E. (2013), 'Les Systèmes de villes en Inde et en Chine', PhD thesis, Université Paris 1-Panthéon Sorbonne, Paris.

United Nations (UN) (2018), 'World urbanization prospects, the 2018 revision, methodology', Department of Economic and Social Affairs, Population Division: Working Paper No. ESA/P/WP.252, United Nations, New York.

Vacchiani-Marcuzzo, C. (2016), 'L'Afrique du Sud est-elle un cas à part? Analyse d'une hybridité urbaine', Mémoire d'Habilitation à Diriger des Recherches, Université Paris 1 Panthéon Sorbonne, Paris.

Weidlich, W. and G. Haag (eds) (1988), *Interregional Migrations. Dynamic Theory and Comparative Analysis*, Berlin: Springer Verlag.

8. Fractal geometry for analyzing and modeling urban patterns and planning sustainable cities
Pierre Frankhauser

1. INTRODUCTION

Ever since the industrial revolution, cities have grown constantly and nowadays more than half the world's population lives in urban areas. Many urbanists, planners and ecologists deplore that urban growth seems difficult to control and is the source of an increasing environmental burden. Indeed, urban sprawl fragments natural areas and generates traffic flows between residential outskirts that often have few amenities and city centers or peripheral urban zones where most jobs, commercial outlets and cultural amenities are still concentrated. However, a large number of households in Western countries seek to live in single-family houses with a garden in a quiet green setting. Moreover, social demand is now becoming ever more diversified, and residents must travel to very different locations to satisfy their needs. In making these trips, for which it is often impossible to use public transport, they generate diffuse and complex traffic-flow patterns.

It seems obvious that households that have chosen to live on the outskirts will shun any densification or further urbanization, which would adversely affect their residential environment (Breheny 1997; Gordon and Richardson 1997). As Schwanen et al. (2004) shows, densifying these residential zones may lead households to move to lower-density areas even further away from urban centers.

However, social demand is only one of the driving forces of urban dynamics to which a large number of actors and decision-makers contribute; these include developers, firms seeking an optimal location, all types of pressure groups, such as neighborhood committees, and politicians with their own agendas. So, as has been widely discussed by several authors, we must view agglomerations as self-organizing systems generating macrostructures as the result of complex interactions among different socio-economic actors. We begin by focusing on the shape of the macrostructures of these emerging urban patterns. Despite their apparently irregular shapes, these macrostructures often have some degree of internal ordering that can be described by fractal approaches, as confirmed by numerous investigations (Batty 2005; Batty and Longley 1994; Benguigui et al. 2000; Frankhauser 1994; Goodchild and Mark 1987; Longley and Mesev 2000; Shen 2002; White and Engelen 1993). Indeed, it is well known in complexity theory that, under particular conditions, self-organizing processes can generate patterns exhibiting fractal properties. This holds, for example, for cellular automata and it is not surprising that a small body of research has made use of this approach to explore the dynamics of urban patterns (Batty and Longley 1986; Makse et al. 1995; White and Engelen 1993).

Hence, we can interpret fractal parameters as a type of order parameter in their being synergetic, without claiming that we find fractal order in all urban fabrics at all times. It is instead a type of phase, and in the course of urban growth this order may become unstable and be modified as shown, for example, by the multifractal analysis of Beijing (Chen and Wang 2013).

It seems difficult to identify precisely in what way different socio-economic processes contribute to generating urban fabrics. However, enquiries into residential choice behavior identify a number of arguments liable to contribute to the fractality of urban patterns. Residents' observed preferences prompt us to ask whether it is possible, using specific characteristics of the emerging phase, to devise a sustainable planning concept, taking into account social demand but simultaneously avoiding the adverse impacts of sprawling urban fabrics. This follows the logic of Beaucire et al. (1999) who suggest attempting to channel urban sprawl instead of trying to avoid it at all costs. Hence, we consider to what extent fractal geometry corresponds to optimization criteria as regards both social demand and environmental requirements. This leads us to present the Fractalopolis concept.

1.1 Fractal Geometry and Urban Patterns

We may wonder why applying fractal geometry provides greater insight into the spatial organization of urban fabrics. The fundamental morphological property of fractals is that they are multiscalar, unlike Euclidean objects that belong to a well-defined scale. With fractals, the same type of structure appears across an unlimited number of scales. One striking feature about today's urban fabrics is that they are made up of structural elements belonging to a large range of scales, from individual buildings to entire metropolitan areas. We illustrate this by considering the settlement pattern of the metropolitan area of Basel in Switzerland (Figure 8.1(a)). The simplified map in Figure 8.1(b) reveals that this metropolitan area consists of a certain number of different-sized clusters unevenly distributed in space. Each has an irregular boundary consisting of large and small bulges and bays. Moreover, settlements are concentrated along valleys or the main transportation routes and separated by low-density zones, that is, urbanized areas alternating with more rural areas (Mohajeri et al. 2013). Three key features can be identified in these patterns,

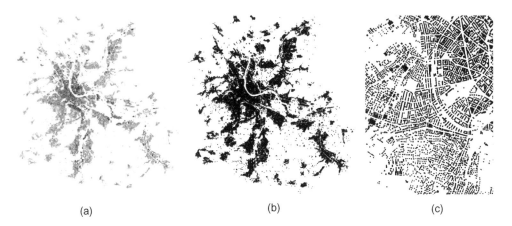

(a)   (b)   (c)

Figure 8.1   (a) Basel metropolitan area; (b) the built-up area after dilation; (c) closing in on an urban district of Basel

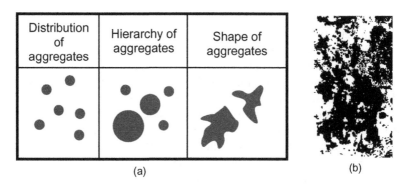

Source: 8.2b: https://render.fineartamerica.com/images/rendered/small/print/images/artworkimages/
square/2/rusty-surface-scratched-numbers-dimitris-kolyris.jpg.

Figure 8.2   *(a) Different features of urban pattern morphology; (b) rust on a surface*

as illustrated in Figure 8.2(a). We find similar features when considering the rusty surface in Figure 8.2(b). However, it is known that such rusty surfaces have fractal properties. As shown in Figure 8.1(c), similar features appear on a local scale where there are few big buildings but an increasing number of smaller buildings. Likewise, the buildings are separated by a few large vacant areas and comparatively many small vacant areas.

Early investigations of the Stuttgart metropolitan area using a coarse-grained map such as that in Figure 8.1(b) revealed that the lengths and the surface areas of urban clusters tend to be proportional. This is contradictory to Euclidean geometry, since the surface areas should be proportional to the square of the edge lengths. However, the result is fully consistent with fractal geometry (Frankhauser and Sadler 1991).

Many investigations confirm that fractal analysis of urban patterns provides a good description of their morphology (Batty 2005; Batty and Longley 1994; Benguigui et al. 2000; Frankhauser 1994; Goodchild and Mark 1987; Longley and Mesev 2000; Shen 2002; White and Engelen 1993).

2.   FRACTAL MODELS FOR URBAN PATTERNS

Bearing in mind the three morphological features in Figure 8.2, we can now illustrate that fractal models describe well the observed specificities of urban patterns. Theoretical fractals can be constructed by iteration. To do this, a generator is defined that step by step transforms the initial figure into the fractal. A defined number of smaller replicates of the initial figure are placed within the area of the initial figure without any overlap. This rule holds for all future steps, vacant areas generated at any one step can never be occupied at subsequent steps. To focus on the morphology of urban patterns, we use a specific class of fractals particularly suited for this purpose and known as Sierpinski carpets. By using only one reduction factor, we obtain a unifractal, whereas combining several factors generates what is termed a multifractal. In unifractals, all elements are the same size at each step, whereas a multifractal generator combines the different reduction factors in the course of iteration to generate a hierarchically organized set of disks of

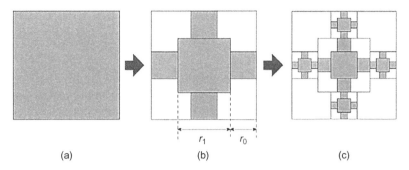

(a)   (b)   (c)

Note: The generator consists of elements reduced by two different factors r_1 and r_0.

Source: Frankhauser (2012).

Figure 8.3   Generating a multifractal Sierpinski carpet

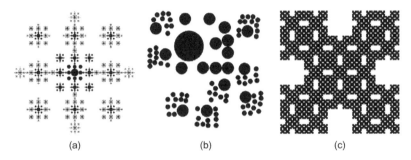

(a)   (b)   (c)

Source: Frankhauser (2015).

Figure 8.4   Different Sierpinski carpets at their third iteration: (a) axial urban growth and a hierarchical structure of centers; (b) randomized Sierpinski carpet also displaying a hierarchy of centers; (c) a unifractal with a tattered boundary and bays of different size

different sizes reminiscent of the hierarchical organization of city systems consisting of a few large centers and a growing number of ever smaller ones. Figure 8.3 shows how to construct a multifractal Sierpinski carpet, based on two reduction factors, by iteration.

Figure 8.4 shows examples of the third iteration step. Figure 8.4(a) illustrates the concentration of elements along dominant axcs with smaller aggregates in peripheral areas. Vacant lanes of different sizes separate the clusters. Here the initial figure was a circle and the generator reduces that circle into smaller circles by using two reduction factors. Figure 8.4(b) uses a similar generator, but the position of the elements was chosen randomly in the course of iteration in strict compliance with the stated fractal rules. In contrast, Figure 8.4(c) shows a unifractal, which illustrates that we can obtain patterns with a tattered boundary with bays of different sizes.

These examples show that we can develop reference models that are closer to the actual morphology of urban patterns than Euclidean figures. We will subsequently use fractal models for producing sustainable urban planning concepts.

3.   MEASURING THE FRACTALITY OF URBAN PATTERNS

3.1   Methodological Aspects

Thus far we have argued in a generally heuristic way. We now summarize some results of fractal analyses of urban patterns. The investigations focus on the spatial distribution of built-up space but also on a more intricate matter, the analysis of urban boundaries. Technically there is no such thing as an urban boundary. Apart from for historical centers, town walls no longer delimit cities. Therefore, the only morphological boundaries to be found are the walls of buildings. However, Figure 8.1(b) shows that 'blowing up' buildings generates in some sense urban boundaries, which we can analyze. This observation shows that the morphological properties change in passing from a local scale, corresponding generally to that of buildings, residential streets and courtyards, to a more aggregated level. This approach has been used for exploring urban boundaries but also for defining a procedure to identify a criterion by which to morphologically delimit metropolitan areas (Tannier et al. 2011).

Remember that fractal analysis refers to the scaling relationship of fractals, which for unifractals is written:

$$N_n(\varepsilon_n) = a \cdot \varepsilon_n^D \tag{8.1}$$

For constructed fractals, $N_n(\varepsilon_n)$ is the number of elements of size ε_n, which is the base length of the element at iteration step n. Both the number $N_n(\varepsilon_n)$ and the base length ε_n follow a geometric progression and the dimension is here directly linked to the parameters of the generator, that is, the number of elements N in the generator, the length of the initial figure L, and the reduction factor r (Mandelbrot 1983):

$$\varepsilon_n = L \cdot r^n \quad N_n(\varepsilon_n) = N^n \tag{8.2}$$

The fractal dimension D describes the extent to which the structure is hierarchized. A value close to $D = 2$ refers to a near-uniform distribution, whereas low values correspond to a strong hierarchy of clusters with high concentrations at each scale. The notion of fractal dimension is consistent with the usual definition. Hence, lines have the dimension one and surfaces the dimension two. For multifractals, the situation is more complex. The previous definition gives rough information about the structure and there exists a series of fractal dimensions.

Fractal dimension is not to be confused with density. A low-density garden city consisting of uniformly distributed individual houses would be of dimension two just as a densely built city would. The prefactor a globalizes the properties of the structure not arising from scaling and is the mass or measure of the object (Thomas et al. 2007).

Often the logarithmic transformation of this relationship is used:

$$\log N_n(\varepsilon_n) = \log a + D \log \varepsilon_n \tag{8.3}$$

This is a linear relationship in which the fractal dimension corresponds to the slope value.

Empirical patterns are interpreted as random fractals for which no generating procedure is known. Hence, there are a couple of methods that count the number of elements $N_n^{emp}(\varepsilon_n)$ corresponding to the sites of the explored structure, for example, urban patterns, corresponding to the variable distance parameter ε_n. We refer here to results obtained by the following methods.

- Box counting: this is the most frequently used method. A mesh of squares of size ε_n covers the pattern and we count the number of grid squares containing an occupied site. We repeat this procedure for different grid square sizes ε_n. However, it should be emphasized that this method does not guarantee that we obtain the minimum number of boxes necessary to cover the structure that is mathematically required. Box counting is often used for multifractal analysis, which turns out to be difficult to perform for perforated fractals, such as Sierpinski carpets.

- Dilation analysis: mathematically, the logic is similar to that of box counting. At each step n, we dilate each built-up site by an amount λ. Hence, in the course of dilation, nearby clusters merge in the first steps and the number of clusters decreases. More remote clusters merge only after a greater number of steps, illustrating the metric of the urban pattern. At each step, we divide the total area of the patches obtained by the area of the reference square with base length $\varepsilon_n = n \cdot \lambda$. Hence, we obtain information about the number of squares $N_n^{emp}(\varepsilon_n)$ of size ε_n we need to cover the structure. Both methods discussed so far provide information about the fractal properties within a previously selected zone. Hence the results generally depend on the window chosen.

- Radial analysis: here we choose a counting center and count the number of occupied sites at different distances ε_n from the center. Since there is a large amount of vacant space at local scales, the empirically obtained curves are usually less regular than those obtained by the other methods. However, the information obtained is different from that obtained by the methods discussed previously, since it provides exact information about the scaling properties around a given site and does not depend on any window.

- Correlation analysis: this is a specific multifractal analysis method and refers to radial analysis. Within a defined window, we perform a radial analysis for each occupied site and compute the mean scaling for each distance ε. This type of analysis is the most stable and reliable.

The empirical values $N_n^{emp}(\varepsilon_n)$ serve to estimate the dimension value and the prefactor, enabling us to compute a theoretical fractal function which we relate to the set of empirical data by correlation. This correlation between the theoretical and empirical tells us how closely the fractal model corresponds to reality.

To further the analysis of the empirical curves, we use the logarithmic version of the fractal relation and represent for each value ε_n the corresponding slope value, which should be constant for a pure fractal. An example is given in Figure 8.5. Deviations inform us about changes in the scaling behavior at particular distances (compare Frankhauser 1998). We term this representation the curve of scaling behavior.

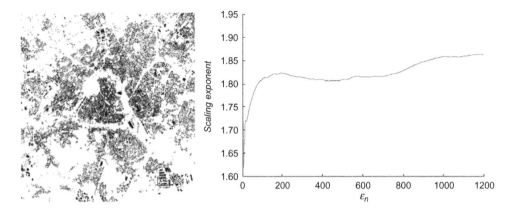

Figure 8.5   The city center of Lille (France) and the curve of scaling behavior for the correlation analysis

3.2   The Scale of Agglomerations

Most of our studies use correlation analysis. The curves of scaling behavior are usually irregular for short distances up to about 20 meters (Figure 8.5). This corresponds to the scale of buildings, residential streets and courtyards. In general, beyond this threshold, urban patterns follow a relatively regular scaling law across a generally wide range of distances with very good fits. It turns out that the historical context of urbanization as well as certain topographical conditions influence the values of the fractal dimension more than the national context does (Frankhauser 2003, 2008). For example, for cities having grown mainly along transport routes or valleys, such as Besançon (France) and Basel (Switzerland), or for coastal cities, such as Helsinki (Finland), dimensions are lower than for cities marked by the industrial revolution such as Charleroi or Liège (Belgium), which are more compact and homogenous. Conurbations incorporating several pre-existing cities, such as Montbéliard, Bayonne-Anglet-Biarritz, Lille-Roubaix-Tourcoing or Cergy-Pontoise (France) also have lower dimensions since they are less compact.

Table 8.1 provides the results for some agglomerations obtained by correlation analysis.

In order to gain greater insight into the morphology of urban patterns, we compare the distribution of built-up areas and urban boundaries extracted by dilation. If urban fabrics were really Sierpinski carpets, the fractal dimension of the built-up surface and boundary would be the same if we take into account the entire boundaries, for example, also that of the inner gaps in the fractal in Figure 8.4(c). In this figure, the outer boundary is fractal, too, but is of a different dimension to the occupied sites and the total boundaries including gaps. Moreover, it should not be expected that, even considering the complete boundaries, the dimension would really be identical.

Hence comparing the dimensions of built-up space, of the outer border of the main cluster and the total border, informs us about the compactness and fragmentation of urban patterns (compare Figure 8.2). Figure 8.6 shows three examples, the city of St Priest close to Lyon (France), the city of Stuttgart (Germany) and the city of Fellbach

Table 8.1   Measured correlation dimension of built-up areas for different agglomerations

Agglomeration	$D^{(surf)}$	Agglomeration	$D^{(surf)}$
Bayonne-Anglet-Biarritz	1.483	Liège	1.914
Bergamo	1.752	Lille-Roubaix-Tourcoing	1.683
Besançon	1.638	Lyon	1.786
Basel	1.723	Montbéliard	1.558
Brussels	1.883	Namur	1.526
Cergy-Pontoise	1.695	Sarrebruck	1.659
Charleroi	1.857	Strasbourg	1.785
Helsinki	1.708		

close to Stuttgart. For all three examples, we determined first the surface area of the built-up area. In a second step, we dilated the pattern by up to a resolution of 16 meters, thus eliminating the local effects discussed and obtaining real clusters with boundaries. We then measured the fractal dimensions of the total boundaries including vacant inner space, such as squares or parks, and the dimension of the main aggregate. Hence, the total boundary dimension should be close to that of built-up areas, whereas the main cluster boundary is a linear structure taking into account just one object while neglecting inner gaps. The values show that for Stuttgart and Fellbach the surface dimensions are high and tend more to uniformity than for St Priest which exhibits inner gaps of various sizes. This is why the total boundary of St Priest has a very high dimension, exceeding the surface area dimension, whereas that of Stuttgart is closer to the surface area dimension. Fellbach has a low total boundary dimension since there are few vacant inner-urban spaces. The outer boundary dimensions of St Priest and Fellbach are higher than those of Stuttgart. Stuttgart's planning policy seeks to round off the urban boundary, which is not so for the other two cities where the boundaries have been less controlled and are therefore more fragmented. Indeed, both these towns are peripheral to large urban centers and are marked by industrial activities that dominate their urban dynamics.

These examples show that this type of analysis provides fresh insight into the spatial organization of urban patterns and can be linked to local history and planning policies. We now present results obtained as part of a cooperation between the ThéMA institute (France) and the CORE institute at Louvain-la-Neuve (Belgium). We analyzed a total of 262 municipalities of the Walloon region in Belgium. For all patterns, we estimated surface area dimensions and boundary dimensions using the same database and the same number of dilation steps, for extruding boundaries. We used a method based on bivariate Gaussian distributions (McLachlan and Peel 2000) to explore whether different morphological classes can be identified (Thomas et al. 2008a). We selected six classes and it turned out that each of these corresponds to a particular historical or geographical situation. Heavy industry marked the cities along the Sambre and Meuse valleys, for which surface area dimensions range between 1.58 and 1.84, whereas boundary dimensions lie between 1.68 and 1.75. Recent outskirts of the Brussels metropolitan area show low surface area dimensions of between 1.39 and 1.57 and high boundary dimensions of 1.76 to 1.87, which is typical for the fragmented patterns of these low-density areas. The rural villages in the Ardennes upland region have very low surface area dimensions ranging

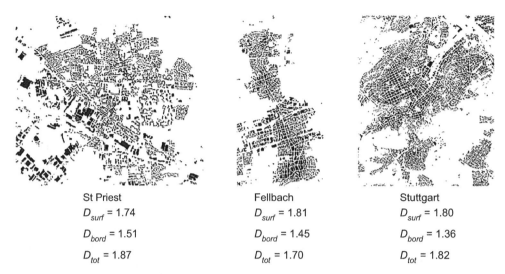

St Priest	Fellbach	Stuttgart
$D_{surf} = 1.74$	$D_{surf} = 1.81$	$D_{surf} = 1.80$
$D_{bord} = 1.51$	$D_{bord} = 1.45$	$D_{bord} = 1.36$
$D_{tot} = 1.87$	$D_{tot} = 1.70$	$D_{tot} = 1.82$

Note: D_{surf} is the surface area dimension; D_{bord} is the border or edge dimension of the main aggregate obtained after four dilation steps; and D_{tot} is the border dimension of all aggregates together.

Figure 8.6   Comparing three urban patterns of different shapes

from 0.54 to 1.00 and the range of the boundary dimensions is very broad, from 1.33 to 1.75. This means that we observe both compact and tattered patterns.

3.3   The Neighborhood Scale

We also examined a set of neighborhoods of different European cities using correlation analysis. A first set consisted of 97 neighborhoods in 18 cities. We used the fractal dimension and the prefactor to distinguish different classes, which were identified by a Ward classification (Thomas et al. 2010). For another set consisting of nine Belgian, French and German cities, we compared the shapes of the curves of scaling behavior by means of the *k*-medoid algorithm (Bishop 2006) that provides more detailed information on their spatial organization and different classes were identified (Thomas et al. 2012):

- For city-center neighborhoods the curves of scaling behavior are regular and fractal dimensions high ($D > 1.7$), hence the trend toward uniformity, that is, gaps are not very clearly hierarchized.
- Zones that are more peripheral are less dense, but also have relatively high dimensions since they often have regular morphology and buildings are aligned along streets. Owing to the numerous small distances between buildings, the curves of scaling behavior show a drop for short distances.
- Another class corresponds to more irregular patterns where dwellings and nonresidential buildings are mixed. In these neighborhoods, often dating from the period 1950 to 1980, dimensions are lower (about $D = 1.67$).
- Two other classes refer to neighborhoods where buildings are unevenly distributed. In one class with $D < 1.75$ we find the new town of Cergy-Pontoise, built

according to a particular planning scheme. The curves of scaling behavior show that these patterns are homogenous for short distances, but more contrasted at the scale of neighborhoods. A similar situation with values between 1.6 and 1.9 occurs for neighborhoods built in line with the specific Corbusian planning concept, consisting of apartment blocks in regular formations named Les Grands Ensembles in France.

- Finally, industrial zones with great distances between large buildings have regular curves of scaling behavior since the size of buildings smooths the drop-down effect for short distances.

Comparing the fractal properties of agglomerations on a European scale reveals that the size of the city does not directly influence the dimension values. Planning policy, geography and history come into play instead, but not strongly so (see, for example, Thomas et al. 2008a, 2008b). Ariza-Villaverde et al. (2013) used multifractal analysis to explore street networks on an intra-urban scale but the differences between the values of the different dimensions observed for two areas are very small, confirming a rather unifractal behavior on this scale.

4. FROM SELF-ORGANIZATION TO FRACTAL-ORIENTATED DEVELOPMENT

4.1 Fractality as a Self-Optimizing Principle

Previously discussed results show that, on the scale of agglomerations, a certain type of spatial organization seems commonplace and is closely related to the scaling property of fractals. We emphasize, however, that this does not mean that all urban fabrics at all times are structured according to a fractal order. Moreover, scaling is not just a simple property that can be brought out by using multifractal analysis. With multifractality, different scaling properties are mixed within the same structure, and this is illustrated by the diversity of scaling properties on the scale of urban districts mentioned previously. Multifractal structures are characterized by a series of dimensions, whereas unifractal structures all have the same value. The wider the range of dimensions, the more complex the structure. Finally, if empirical curves are completely irregular, then there is no scaling at all.

An unpublished analysis of the Besançon agglomeration in which we took into account the intensity of land use, that is, the local population densities, showed that the range of dimensions was small for the historical city center as well as for a highly planned urban district outside the city. However, the range was broader for the peripheral zones surrounding the historical center where different types of architecture are mixed. Detailed investigations of the urban pattern of Beijing by Chen and Wang (2013) show that during periods of upheaval, urban patterns become more irregular, and scaling behavior is less present or even absent. This holds for peripheral growth areas of expanding cities, but also for urban areas undergoing wholesale reconfiguration. Hence we prefer to write of a fractal state of order as a phase that develops often but that may or may not be stable depending on circumstances.

In order to measure whether and how the fractality of a given urban pattern changes over time, we introduced an order parameter (Frankhauser 2000, 2008). We used radial analyses of several agglomerations for which we had maps for different dates. The order parameter refers directly to the curves of scaling behavior which have been processed by Gaussian smoothing to remove local fluctuations. These smoothed curves preserve the structural changes of scaling behavior at particular scales. We then computed the mean of the scaling parameter over the whole distance range under analysis, which was our reference value. Next we computed the mean variance σ_{res} of the original data in respect of the smoothed data over the total variance of the original data in respect of the mean value σ_{tot}. We combined these values in an indicator based on the logic of the correlation ratio η^2 used in statistics (for details, see Frankhauser 2000, 2008). This informs us as to the degree of fluctuation of the curves of scaling behavior. If fluctuations are high, σ_{res} tends to σ_{tot} and η^2 tends to 0. This means that the relationship is weak, and no particular fractal behavior is observed. Conversely, when the original values do not deviate much from the smoothed curve, $\sigma_{res} \to 0$ and η^2 tends to 1, which is so especially if the original values are all equal and thus correspond to a perfect fractal structure. Hence, the parameter fulfills the requirements of an order parameter as defined in physics.

Figure 8.7 shows the change over time of this order parameter for a number of agglomerations.[1] For Berlin, the fractal order increases continuously over time. We observe for Munich a slight decrease for an intermediate period. The fractal order increases first for the small town of Lons-le-Saunier in eastern France, and decreases slightly for the final period. The Montbéliard agglomeration (France) is of particular interest. For the historical center the η^2-value declines during an initial period and increases slightly thereafter while, when choosing the Peugeot factory as the counting center, a substantial increase is observed. Audincourt, forming part of the same conurbation, remains at a constantly low level too. We are confronted with an enslaving phenomenon; the dynamics of the Peugeot company dominates the development of the entire spatial system; the new urban areas are constructed around this factory and not close to the ancient center of

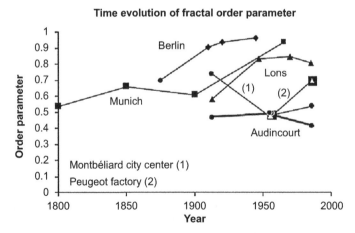

Source: Frankhauser (2000).

Figure 8.7   Evolution over time of the fractal order parameter for different agglomerations

Montbéliard, which has become a peripheral area of the factory. The shape of its curve of scaling behavior resembles that of a peripheral ward.

These examples show that usually fractal order increases during the course of urban development, but the Montbéliard example shows that this is not a trivial effect, and is reminiscent of the observations of Chen and Wang (2013).

We may summarize that scaling seems to be a widespread, emerging, order principle in the morphology of metropolitan areas. This leads us to inquire into the reasons for growth of this type. We know from complexity theory that particular types of interactions may generate fractal structures. This holds, for example, for cellular automata where simple local interaction rules generate fractal structures. Hence it is not surprising that several scholars were quick to focus on the link between self-organization concepts, cellular automata and city growth simulation (Couclelis 1985; Phipps 1989). More explicitly, other authors developed city growth models based on cellular automata (Batty 1991; Batty and Longley 1986; Frankhauser 1994; White and Engelen 1993). Let us emphasize that some of these models start from a morpho-descriptive approach and refer to physical models (Batty 1991; Batty and Longley 1986), whereas others introduce behavioral aspects of different types of actors (White and Engelen 1993).

Urban pattern formation is a consequence of interactions among a great number of agents on a micro-scale, often in compliance, synergetically, with specific competition and selection mechanisms (Haken 1990). Several authors have addressed the issue of the extent to which urban pattern formation may be considered to be a self-organization process (Allen and Sanglier 1981; Batty 2005; Chen 2012; Chen and Zhou 2008; Portugali 2000, 2005, 2011; Pumain et al. 1989; Weidlich and Munz 1990). For social systems, micro-dynamics refers to individual decision-making processes and these processes result from individual experiences and cultural contexts (Frankhauser and Ansel 2016). These correspond to what Portugali (2011) terms dual complex systems. This makes it difficult to explain straightforwardly the emergence of fractal patterns by considering the interactions between all individuals including the role of collective phenomena belonging to a mesoscopic scale, such as that of different types of pressure groups (Figure 8.8), which may belong to outside systems, for example, national or international firms or trusts, or national political decision-making bodies.

We have opted to focus on an aggregate level by referring to the empirical results for the observed criteria involved in residential choice behavior in general in a given socio-cultural context. This is, we refer to the dominant trends influencing urban pattern formation on the aggregated scale of urban fabrics. This view point refers to synergetics and corresponds on this scale to order phenomena from what are something similar to enslaving principles (Haken 1990; Portugali 2011; Weidlich 2000).

This approach is also consistent with the theory of needs based on Maslow's pyramid, which considers human needs from a general anthropological standpoint. Max-Neef (1991), referring to Maslow (1954), supplements this approach by introducing the concept of satisfiers. For example, food is considered as a satisfier of the basic need of subsistence, education becomes a satisfier of the need for understanding, and so on. Depending on its value system, each society sets up and manages the satisfiers and its customs and traditions. Planning should respond to this social demand (Yamu et al. 2016), which may be in part contradictory, as shown by the well-known not-in-my-backyard (nimby) effect. Residents may criticize the construction of a road close to their

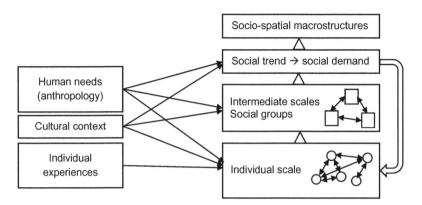

Figure 8.8   From the micro-scale of individuals to the macro-scale of urban pattern formation

home but this does not necessarily mean that they engage in virtuous environmental behavior and do not use cars.

These arguments led us to develop a sustainable planning concept for metropolitan areas, designed to reconcile residents' preferences, which may be self-contradictory, and environmental priorities. Fractal geometry helps optimize the spatial structure of metropolitan areas in relation to this.

4.2   Fractals as an Optimizing Principle for Urban Planning

In Western countries, urban dynamics is largely influenced by residential choice behavior. Hence, since motorization crucially improved mobility, choosing a residence by taking into account different criteria became possible, which was not possible, or at least less so, before. Many households prefer to live in peripheral areas, which ensure better living conditions, than in densely populated centers. These areas offer the possibility of buying a single-family house with a garden, and enjoying peace and quiet and a green environment. However, in reality, while choosing their residence, households also take into account accessibility to a large set of sites they frequent. They consider the distance or the travel time to work (Brun and Fagnani 1994; McDowell 1997), retail centers (Lerman 1976) and leisure areas (Guo and Bhat 2002). However, preferences include the nearby residential environment and individuals prefer natural environments to built-up environments (Lamb and Purcell 1990). This influences lot prices, which fall in general with distance from parks or green areas (Bolitzer and Netusil 2000; Hobden et al. 2004; Luttik 2000). This illustrates the importance households attribute to green spaces close to home (Bolitzer and Netusil 2000).

The negative environmental impacts of urban sprawl have been widely discussed since the investigations of Newman and Kenworthy (1989). Outskirts often lack jobs and shopping amenities even to satisfy everyday needs. Urban sprawl increases the length of daily trips and promotes car use, since transit is crucially lacking in these areas. Moreover, new road construction contributes more to land consumption than does building new single-family houses. For example, Tourneux (2006) shows that during the period 1987–97 on the outskirts of the metropolitan area of Paris, residential and mixed-use constructions consumed only 1.4 percent of space, whereas 50 percent of newly constructed space was used for completing the road network. Roads often intersect with natural areas, which thus become ever more fragmented, and is one of the primary causes of the extinction of species (Linehan et al. 1995). This has prompted various authors to call for landscape connectedness to ensure biodiversity is maintained (Grumbine 1994; Jongman et al. 2004).

Given the level of land consumption, the risks for biodiversity and the exorbitant use of cars, numerous scholars emphasize the need to return to compact cities. However, it seems obvious that households, having chosen to flee density, will not accept a move to a dense urban environment (Von Hoffman and Felkner 2002). Breheny (1997) has noted that coming back to dense centers increases housing costs and traffic congestion, and reduces the accessibility of leisure areas. However, vegetation close to residences has an important impact on health and well-being (Evans 2003; Latkin and Curry 2003). Moreover, owing to climate change, densification becomes highly questionable since intra-urban green spaces reduce the emergence of heat islands. Several scholars go further and state that intra-urban green areas should not be isolated but linked to rural areas, which ties in with the concept of green lanes (Kuttler et al. 1998; Spronken-Smith and Oke 1999). Frey (2000) refers to the Copenhagen finger plan, which defines urban development zones along public transportation network routes separated by green lanes. Several planning blueprints have introduced this logic. The earliest was that proposed by Eberstadt et al. (1910) for the greater Berlin area and Schumacher followed this example with his palm plan for Hamburg (compare Kallmorgen 1969).

However, a crucial criterion for residential choice is accessibility to the different amenities frequented by residents. This is also important from the environmental view point since potentially it generates traffic flows. Hence, two aspects come into play: good accessibility, preferably within walking distance of shops for everyday needs, and good access to public transport in order to reduce car use.

The Copenhagen and Hamburg planning concepts take into account this aspect by concentrating urbanized areas close to public transport routes. The more recent concept of urban villages of Calthorpe (1993) goes further. This concept localizes shops and services for daily needs close to residential areas located around a public transportation node. Moreover, at least two types of urban centers are considered. Daily needs can be satisfied at all centers, whereas more rarely used services are to be found in the higher-order centers. This idea corresponds to central place theory, which introduces a hierarchy of services according to their purchase rate (Christaller 1933 [1980]). Hence, greater distances can be accepted for rarely used services than for daily needs.

We summarize that the real lifestyle leads to complex moving patterns since residents frequent a great diversity of amenities. Uncontrolled urban growth tends to lengthen trips, since important amenities and job offers are localized too far away from residential areas, thus compounding negative environmental impacts. However, plain densification runs contrary to social demand and will not be accepted in the long term. Moreover, it is undesirable from the view point of the urban climate and public health. Some planning concepts suggest solutions based on the articulation of urbanized and green areas, offering good accessibility to satisfiers for basic needs and promoting the use of public transportation.

4.3   The Fractalopolis Concept

On the one hand, we see that the idea of articulating vacant space and urbanized areas is an aspect thought important by several authors in order to provide leisure areas close to residential areas and to concentrate urbanization near public transportation networks. On the other, one of the striking features of emerging urban patterns is that their boundaries are contorted, which is characteristic of fractals. Indeed, while generating Sierpinski carpets by iteration, the borderline is over-proportionally lengthened at each step and tends finally to infinity. In urban patterns this ensures a good articulation between open space and urbanized areas. It can be imagined that the fractal character of urban patterns is linked in some way to this property. Lots situated on the boundary between urbanized areas and parklands are particularly sought after, which holds even for intra-urban green space. Lot prices are usually high in the vicinity of parks and decrease with distance from them (Hobden et al. 2004; Bolitzer and Netusil 2000). This can influence urban dynamics since residents benefiting from this type of situation will try to undermine projects to build in their vicinity, thereby accentuating the complex morphology of settlement boundaries. Moreover, residents on the outskirts will, in general, be hostile to excessive growth of their village and strive to preserve their rural character, a phenomenon we have termed blocking dynamics (Frankhauser 1994). Peeters et al. (2015) have shown analytically that beyond a particular threshold for acceding to open landscape, urbanization will come to a halt and new residents will prefer to settle further away from the center in smaller villages. This is a type of phase transition effect. However, let us underline that, before motorization, axial growth along train lines or suburban tram lines dominated urban expansion, reinforcing the fractal character of agglomerations. Motorization reduces fractality, since villages in interstitial areas between the main transportation routes are made easily accessible by car use. Hence, for example, the fractal dimension of the greater Strasbourg area increased in the period from 1986 to 1996 from $D = 1.80$ to $D = 1.86$, reflecting that space was filled more uniformly.

This raises the issue of the extent to which fractal geometry is optimal in respect of particular criteria. However, even if this is mathematically not easy to prove, we find fractal-like structures in many systems when looking at the world of nature. In these systems different types of spatial systems must be articulated while ensuring a maximum number of interconnections, which applies just as much to trees as to bronchi. Light must penetrate within the crown of trees so that the leaves within can receive light, while bronchi must maximize the number of alveoli interconnecting veins and the air.

This led us to reflect on the issue of whether fractal geometry can be used for designing sustainable urban blueprints by articulating green space and urbanized areas across scales, thereby ensuring good ventilation and good access to leisure areas. The concept should avoid fragmentation for urbanized areas and green areas alike, and should aim to shorten journeys and car use. To support this argument, we explored in two papers the impact of fractal-like urban patterns on household satisfaction (Cavailhès et al. 2004, 2010). This made it obvious that for households, which have preferences for both urban amenities and green amenities and which is to an extent contradictory, such a model provides advantages that we measured by market-induced lot prices.

The Fractalopolis model uses a multifractal reference model similar to that in Figure 8.3 to ensure these goals. The concept also includes the hierarchy of service offers discussed previously.

The model begins with a generator, consisting of one large central square, which we associate with the highest ranked main center of a metropolitan area. This main center is surrounded by four first-order subcenters. The following iterations complete the hierarchy stepwise; each first-order subcenter is surrounded by four second-order subcenters, and so on. However, iteration entails a degree of degeneration, since squares belonging to different orders are the same size. This is a consequence of the multiplicative character of the iteration process. In order to identify each square's position in the hierarchy, we introduce a coding system as illustrated in Figure 8.9. In the generator, we name the main center '1' and the subcenters '0'. In the next step, we add to the right a digit following the same logic. Hence, we see that squares with the same code '10' and '01' are of the same surface area, but their functions are different. However, second-order centers are different in size; the center '10', directly associated with the main center '11', is larger than '00', associated with the secondary center '01'. This is realistic enough, since moving out from the main center, cities providing comparable functions are in general smaller. Let us emphasize that the concept aims to concentrate the development zones along a nested system of public transportation routes, which become the backbone of the system, similar to the branches of a tree illustrated by the upper branch of the first iteration step in Figure 8.9.

Shops and services are hierarchized according to this nested logic. The highest ranked main center offers the entire range of amenities, whereas the first-order subcenters do not offer the highest-ranked amenities, such as operas, universities, central administrations, highly specialized shops and large leisure complexes. Finally, the lowest-ranked centers provide only goods for daily needs. For medium-sized metropolitan areas we reach a local level of urban districts or, even, residential blocks after three or four iteration steps

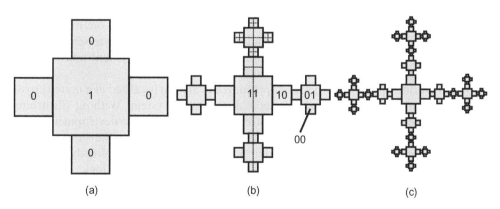

(a)   (b)   (c)

Note: The coding systems distinguish the functions of the center '01' from '10'. In (b) the public transportation routes are indicated for the upper branch by dashed lines.

Source: Frankhauser (2012).

Figure 8.9   Generating the Fractalopolis reference model by iteration

and, so, three or four service levels are distinguished. We use the number of four separate service levels even for large metropolitan areas such as the Grand Paris area where we can use up to seven iteration steps. The service levels correspond to their importance for residents. The area of the squares defines the service levels, which must be present within this area. Hence, in the zones with code '01', the main center of the first-order subcenter area '0', all services attributed to this level and all lower-ranking services should be present, whereas in '00' only the lowest-ranked services should be found. Shops and services for daily needs should be accessible within walking distance, as should small green areas and playgrounds. However, other amenities, for example, general practitioners or pharmacies, should also benefit from good accessibility. This reasoning refers to the theory of needs, which ranks them according to their importance for survival and well-being (Frankhauser 2020; Max-Neef 1991).

It is possible to associate a typical accessibility with each service level. This accessibility links the distance residents accept they will travel to the different types of amenities, with the importance they ascribe to this amenity. We measure this importance by means of the percentage of residents who frequent each type of amenity. For France, these data are available from surveys. Moreover, French population data are available on the scale of a mesh with grid squares with 200-meter sides. Hence, we know for each geo-referenced shop or service the potential number of consumers served within an acceptable distance. We aggregate these evaluation data on the scale of the Fractalopolis zones and so produce synthetic indicators of the quality of services on this scale. The formalization, detailed in Frankhauser (2020), uses a fuzzy logic approach.

The spatial model is supplemented by a population distribution model, which ascribes the percentages of a given population to the different zones according to the underlying multifractal hierarchical logic. Figure 8.10(a) shows an example of a potential population distribution along the main axes of the scheme in Figure 8.9. Note that, unlike mathematical Sierpinski carpets, the non-development zones are not vacant. We distinguish for them, too, different types of zones according to the iteration step at which they were generated (Figure 8.9(b)). We accept a higher population density in non-development zones lying close to main centers and the further away we are from the main center, the larger these zones are and the less populated they should be. The model allows us to parameterize the degrees of concentration for both the development and the non-development zones (Frankhauser 2020; Frankhauser et al. 2018).

For real-world applications, the development zones are not localized in a nested cross-like manner but take into account the actual settlement system. Without disturbing fractal logic, we can freely localize the squares corresponding to the development zones within the development zone from which they are derived in the previous iteration step as shown in Figure 8.10(b). This means that non-development zones already generated cannot be attributed in further steps, thereby preserving the nested logic. Moreover, we can freely choose the number of subcenters in the generator as well as their sizes. However, intersections of zones must be avoided. Let us add that the square-like shape of the development zones can be transformed into polygons for which the same rules as before remain valid when generating further steps. Changing the shape of the elements in this way does not affect the model's fractal character.

Figure 8.11 is an example of an application to the Grand Paris metropolitan area explored in an ongoing project conducted in conjunction with the LVMT research

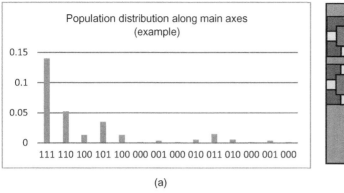

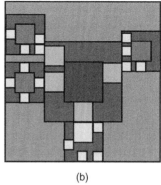

(a)   (b)

Note: The light grey zones are those generated in the first step for which only very slight development will be accepted, the darker grey zones, lying closer to the centers, generated at the second step, can support slightly more population. The shades of grey for the development zones illustrate the degree of population concentration.

Figure 8.10   (a) An example of the concentration/deconcentration of population in the nested urban system (Frankhauser 2020) along the right branch of the main axes in Figure 8.9(c). (b) The squares can be localized freely respecting the basic rules of generation which preserve the hierarchy of the non-development zones

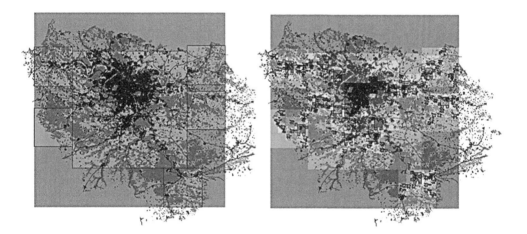

Note: The shades of grey correspond to the hierarchical levels of the non-development zones.

Figure 8.11   The generator and the fourth iteration step for the Grand Paris model

institute (the French institute of science and technology for transport) at Marne-la-Vallée. On the left-hand side of the figure is the chosen generator and on the right-hand side the fourth iteration step. We displayed the nested non-development areas in shades of grey. The development zones are located in already urbanized areas and follow public transportation routes. We have excluded already widely developed zones in northern

Paris from future development. In the south-east we extended the development area outside the development zone to preserve the large Fontainebleau forest area. As part of this research project, we propose to reduce density in a crowded district of eastern Paris and create green corridors by linking existing parks and forest areas.

5.   CONCLUSION

We have seen that the fractal approach provides new insight into the morphology of urban patterns. Urban fabrics exhibit particular scaling characteristics that can be explored and visualized by means of fractal geometry, which does not mean that they are fractal. Future research should further explore the use of the multifractal approach by developing models and improving the measuring methods. Their multiscale irregular aspect and urbanization often generating a fractal-like order incited us to reflect on the potential reasons for the emergence of these forms, and led us finally to the conclusion that the approach can be used for developing a sustainable planning concept that fulfills both social and environmental purposes. The Fractalopolis software package enables us to develop these planning scenarios on the scale of master plans and to evaluate their impact in respect of accessibility to different kinds of amenities. Hence, it is possible to evaluate scenarios by shifting the location of different development zones, densifying and de-densifying certain areas, and adding or removing amenities. Future research will focus on the evaluation of environmental aspects, such as biodiversity and climate.

ACKNOWLEDGMENTS

The research presented has been financed for the most part by the PREDIT research program supported by the French Ministries of transport and of research and other partners including the ADEME (French energy management agency).

NOTE

1. The datasets used for Munich and Berlin are from aggregated maps by the Städtebauliches Institut (University of Stuttgart), whereas the other databases were developed at ThéMA from topographic maps (1:50,000).

REFERENCES

Allen, P.M. and M. Sanglier (1981), 'Urban evolution, self-organization and decision making', *Environment and Planning A*, **13** (2), 167–83.
Ariza-Villaverde, A.B., F.J. Jimenez-Hornero and E.G. De Rave (2013), 'Multifractal analysis of axial maps applied to the study of urban morphology', *Computers, Environment and Urban Systems*, **38** (March), 1–10.
Batty, M. (1991), 'Generating urban forms from diffusive growth', *Environment and Planning A*, **23** (4), 511–44.
Batty, M. (2005), *Cities and Complexity: Understanding Cities with Cellular Automata, Agent-Based Models, and Fractals*, Cambridge, MA: MIT Press.
Batty, M. and P. Longley (1986), 'The fractal simulation of urban structure', *Environment and Planning A*, **18** (9), 1143–79.

Batty, M. and P. Longley (1994), *Fractal Cities: A Geometry of Form and Function*, London and San Diego: Academic Press.

Beaucire, F., S. Rosales-Montano, E. Duflos and I. Turchetti (1999), 'Les outils de planification urbaine au service de la relation urbanisme/transport: approche dans la perspective du développement durable', Synthèse de recherche, Projet DRAST/ PREDIT 98MT115, Fédération Nationale des Agences d'Urbanisme, Paris.

Benguigui, L., D. Czamanski, M. Marinov and Y. Portugali (2000), 'When and where is a city fractal?', *Environment and Planning B*, **27** (4), 507–19.

Bishop, C. (2006), *Pattern Recognition and Machine Learning*, Berlin: Springer.

Bolitzer, B. and R. Netusil (2000), 'The impact of open spaces on property values in Portland, Oregon', *Journal of Environmental Management*, **59** (3), 185–93.

Breheny, M.J. (1997), 'Urban compaction: feasible and acceptable?', *Cities*, **14** (6), 209–17.

Brun, J. and J. Fagnani (1994), 'Lifestyles and locational choices – trade-offs and compromises: a case-study of middle-class couples living in the Ile-de-France Region', *Urban Studies*, **31** (6), 921–34.

Calthorpe, P. (1993), *The Next American Metropolis: Ecology, Community, and the American Dream*, Princeton, NJ: Architectural Press.

Cavailhès, J., P. Frankhauser, D. Peeters and I. Thomas (2004), 'Where Alonso meets Sierpinski: an urban economic model of fractal metropolitan area', *Environment and Planning A*, **36** (8), 1471–98.

Cavailhès, J., P. Frankhauser, D. Peeters and I. Thomas (2010), 'Residential equilibrium in a multifractal metropolitan area', *Annals of Regional Science*, **45** (3), 681–704.

Chen, Y. (2012), 'Fractal dimension evolution and spatial replacement dynamics of urban growth', *Chaos, Solitons & Fractals*, **45** (2), 115–24.

Chen, Y. and J. Wang (2013), 'Multifractal characterization of urban form and growth: the case of Beijing', *Environment and Planning B: Planning and Design*, **40** (5), 884–904.

Chen, Y. and Y. Zhou (2008), 'Scaling laws and indications of self-organized criticality in urban systems', *Chaos, Solitons & Fractals*, **35** (1), 85–98.

Christaller, W. (1933), *Die zentralen Orte in Süddeutschland*, Jena: G. Fischer, re-edited 1980 Darmstadt: Wissenschaftliche Buchgesellschaft.

Couclelis, H. (1985), 'Cellular worlds: a framework for modeling micro-macro dynamics', *Environment and Planning A*, **17** (5), 585–96.

Eberstadt, R., B. Möhring and R. Petersen (1910), *Gross-Berlin. Ein Programm für die Planung der neuzeitlichen Grosstadt*, Berlin: Wasmuth.

Evans, G.W. (2003), 'The built environment and mental health', *Journal of Urban Health*, **80** (4), 536–55.

Frankhauser, P. (1994), *La fractalité des structures urbaines*, Paris: Anthropos.

Frankhauser, P. (1998), 'The fractal approach: a new tool for the spatial analysis of urban agglomerations', *Population: An English Selection*, **10** (1), 205–40.

Frankhauser, P. (2000), 'La fragmentation des espaces urbains et périurbains – une approche fractale', in P.H. Derycke (ed.), *Structures des villes, entreprise et marchés urbains*, Paris: L'Harmattan, pp. 25–54.

Frankhauser, P. (2003), 'Morphologie des villes "émergentes" en Europe à travers les analyses fractales', report, UMR 6049 Théma, Université de Franche-Comté, Besançon.

Frankhauser, P. (2008), 'Fractal geometry for measuring and modeling urban patterns', in *The Dynamics of Complex Urban Systems – An Interdisciplinary Approach*, Heidelberg: Physica-Verlag (Springer), pp. 213–43.

Frankhauser, P. (2012), 'The Fractalopolis model – a sustainable approach for a central place system', working paper, 4 December, accessed 8 June 2021 at https://hal.archives-ouvertes.fr/hal-00758864.

Frankhauser, P. (2015), 'From fractal urban pattern analysis to fractal urban planning concepts', in M. Helbich, J.J. Arsanjani and M. Leitner (eds), *Computational Approaches for Urban Environments*, Geotechnologies and the Environment Vol. 13, Cham: Springer International Publishing Switzerland, pp. 13–48.

Frankhauser, P. (2020), 'FRACTALOPOLIS – a fractal concept for the sustainable development of metropolitan areas', in P. Sajous and C. Bertelle (eds), *Complex Systems, Smart Territories and Mobility*, Cham: Springer, pp. 13–25.

Frankhauser, P. and D. Ansel (eds) (2016), *Deciding Where to Live – an Interdisciplinary Approach of Residential Choice in Social Context*, Berlin: Springer.

Frankhauser, P. and R. Sadler (1991), 'Fractal analysis of agglomerations', in M. Hilliges (ed.), *Natural Structures: Principles, Strategies, and Models in Architecture and Nature*, Stuttgart: University of Stuttgart, pp. 57–65.

Frankhauser, P., C. Tannier, G. Vuidel and H. Houot (2018), 'An integrated multifractal modelling to urban and regional planning', *Computers, Environment and Urban Systems*, **67** (1), 132–46.

Frey, H.W. (2000), 'Not green belts but green wedges: the precarious relationship between city and country', *Urban Design International*, **5** (1), 13–25.

Goodchild, M. and D. Mark (1987), 'The fractal nature of geographic phenomena', *Annals of the Association of American Geographers*, **77** (2), 265–78.

Gordon, P. and H. Richardson (1997), 'Are compact cities a desirable planning goal?', *Journal of the American Planning Association*, **63** (1), 95–106.

Grumbine, R.E. (1994), 'What is ecosystem management?', *Conservation Biology*, **8** (1), 27–38.

Guo, J. and C. Bhat (2002), 'Residential location modeling: accommodating sociodemographic, school quality and accessibility effects', working paper, University of Texas, Austin, TX.

Haken, H. (1990), *Synergetik – Eine Einführung*, Berlin: Springer.

Hobden, D.W., G.E. Laughton and K.E. Morgan (2004), 'Green space borders. A tangible benefit? Evidence from four neighbourhoods in Surrey, British Columbia', *Land Use Policy*, **21** (2), 129–38.

Jongman, R.H., M. Külvik and I. Kristiansen (2004), 'European ecological networks and greenways', *Landscape and Urban Planning*, **68** (2), 305–19.

Kallmorgen, W. (1969), 'Schumacher und Hamburg: eine fachliche Dokumentation zu seinem 100. Geburtstag , zusammengestellt und kommentiert zum 4. November', Deutsche Akademie für Städtebau und Landesplanung, Landesgruppe Hamburg und Schleswig-Holstein.

Kuttler, W., D. Dütemeyer and A.-B. Barlag (1998), 'Influence of regional and local winds on urban ventilation in Cologne, Germany', *Meteorologische Zeitschrift*, **7** (April), 77–87.

Lamb, R.J. and A.T. Purcell (1990), 'Perception of naturalness in landscape and its relationship to vegetation structure', *Landscape and Urban Planning*, **19** (4), 333–52.

Latkin, C.A. and A.D. Curry (2003), 'Stressful neighborhoods and depression: a prospective study of the impact of neighborhood disorder', *Journal of Health and Social Behavior*, **44** (1), 34–44.

Lerman, S.R. (1976), 'Location, housing, automobile ownership, and mode to work: a joint choice model', *Transportation Research Record*, **610** (1), 5–11.

Linehan, J., M. Gross and J. Finn (1995), 'Greenway planning: developing a landscape ecological network approach', *Landscape and Urban Planning*, **33** (1–3), 179–93.

Longley, P. and V. Mesev (2000), 'On the measurement and generalisation of urban form', *Environment and Planning A*, **32** (3), 473–88.

Luttik, J. (2000), 'The value of trees, water and open space as reflected by house prices in the Netherlands', *Landscape and Urban Planning*, **48** (3–4), 161–7.

Makse, H.A., S. Havlin and H.E. Stanley (1995), 'Modelling urban growth patterns', *Nature*, **377** (6550), 608–12.

Mandelbrot, B. (1983), *The Fractal Geometry of Nature*, San Francisco, CA: Freeman.

Maslow, A. (1954), *Motivation and Personality*, New York: Harper & Row.

Max-Neef, M.A. (1991), *Human Scale Development*, New York and London: Apex Press.

McDowell, L.M. (1997), 'The new service class: housing, consumption and lifestyle among London bankers in the 1990s', *Environment and Planning A*, **29** (November), 2061–78.

McLachlan, G. and D. Peel, (2000), *Finite Mixture Models*, New York: Wiley.

Mohajeri, N., J. French and M. Batty (2013), 'Evolution and entropy in the organisation of urban street patterns', *Annals of GIS*, **19** (1), 1–16.

Newman, P.W.G. and J.R. Kenworthy (1989), *Sustainability and Cities: Overcoming Automobile Dependence*, Washington, DC: Island Press.

Peeters, D., G. Caruso, J. Cavailhès, I. Thomas, P. Frankhauser and G. Vuidel (2015), 'Emergence of leapfrogging from residential choice with endogenous green space: analytical results', *Journal of Regional Science*, **55** (3), 491–512.

Phipps, M. (1989), 'Dynamical behaviour of cellular automata under the constraint of neighbourhood coherence', *Geographical Analysis*, **21** (3), 197–215.

Portugali, J. (2000), *Self-Organization and the City*, Berlin, Heidelberg and New York: Springer.

Portugali, J. (2005), 'The scope of complex artificial environments', in J. Portugali (ed.), *Complex Artificial Environments*, Berlin, Heidelberg and New York: Springer, pp. 9–30.

Portugali, J. (2011), *Complexity, Cognition and the City*, Berlin, Heidelberg and New York: Springer.

Pumain, D., T. Saint-Julien and L. Sanders (1989), *Villes et auto-organisation*, Paris: Economica.

Schwanen, T., M. Dijst and F.M. Dieleman (2004), 'Policies for urban form and their impact on travel: the Netherlands experience', *Urban Studies*, **41** (3), 579–603.

Shen, G. (2002), 'Fractal dimension and fractal growth of urbanized areas', *International Journal of Geographical Information Science*, **16** (5), 419–437.

SprONKen-Smith, R.A. and T.R. Oke (1999), 'Scale modelling of nocturnal cooling in urban parks', *Boundary-Layer Meteorology*, **93** (2), 287–312.

Tannier, C., I. Thomas, G. Vuidel and P. Frankhauser (2011), 'A fractal approach to identifying urban boundaries', *Geographical Analysis*, **43** (2), 211–27.

Thomas, I., P. Frankhauser and D. Badariotti (2012), 'Comparing the fractality urban districts: do national processes matter in Europe?', *Journal of Geographical Systems*, **14** (2), 189–208.

Thomas, I., P. Frankhauser and C. Biernacki (2008a), 'The morphology of built-up landscapes in Wallonia (Belgium): a classification using fractal indices', *Landscape and Urban Planning*, **84** (2), 99–115.

Thomas, I., P. Frankhauser and M.-L. De Keersmaeker (2007), 'Fractal dimension versus density of built-up surfaces in the periphery of Brussels', *Papers in Regional Sciences*, **86** (2), 287–308.

Thomas, I., C. Tannier and P. Frankhauser (2008b), 'Is there a link between fractal dimensions and other indicators of the built-up environment at a regional level', *Cybergeo*, **413**, 25 February, accessed 2 May 2021 at http://www.cybergeo.eu/index16283.html.

Thomas, I., P. Frankhauser, B. Frenay and M. Verleysen (2010), 'Clustering patterns of urban built-up areas with curves of fractal scaling behavior', *Environment and Planning B*, **37** (5), 942–54.

Tourneux, F.P. (2006), 'L'évolution de l'occupation du sol dans les franges franciliennes: des artificialisations concentrées plus qu'un étalement urbain?', in A. Larceneux and C. Boi-teux-Orain (eds), *Paris et ses franges: étalement urbain et polycentrisme*, Dijon: Editions universitaires de Dijon, pp. 101–27.

Von Hoffman, A. and J. Felkner (2002), 'The historical origins and causes of urban decentralization in the United States', working paper, Joint Center for Housing Studies, Harvard University, Cambridge, MA.

Weidlich, W. (2000), *Sociodynamics*, New York: Dover.

Weidlich, W. and M. Munz (1990), 'Settlement formation. Part I: a dynamic theory', *Annals of Regional Science*, **24** (2), 83–106.

White, R. and C. Engelen (1993), 'Cellular automata and fractal urban form: a cellular modelling approach to the evolution of urban land-use patterns', *Environment and Planning A*, **25** (8), 1175–99.

Yamu, C., G. de Roo and P. Frankhauser (2016), 'Assuming it is all about conditions. Framing a simulation model for complex, adaptive urban space', *Environment and Planning B: Planning and Design*, **43** (6), 1019–39.

9. Scaling, fractals and the spatial complexity of cities
Yanguang Chen

1. INTRODUCTION

Cities are typical complex spatial systems, and urban research is developing into a science based on spatial complexity. To describe and model a system such as a city, we need to find its characteristic scales. A good mathematical model involves three levels of scales: the large scale of macro level, the small scale of micro level and the characteristic scale of basic level (Hao 1986). Geographical systems such as cities fall into two types: one is those bearing characteristic scales, and the other, is those possessing no characteristic scales. The former can be modeled and analyzed by using conventional mathematical theories and quantitative methods, while the latter cannot be effectively described and measured by the conventional methods of advanced mathematics and statistical analysis. For this we need scaling ideas, fractal theory and complexity science.

There are three major problems in scientific description and modeling, that is, spatial dimension, time lag and interaction. All these problems, especially spatial dimension, are associated with nonlinearity and are unavoidable in urban studies. The traditional urban space can be regarded as distance-based space. However, if we cannot find characteristic scales for distance, the distance-based urban space will not work. As an alternative approach, the new spatial analysis based on fractal dimension can be selected for urban research. This geographical space of cities can be treated as dimension-based space. Fractals involves the concept of scaling, and scaling indicates complexity. Fractal geometry provides a powerful tool for scaling analysis, and scaling analysis provides a novel approach to finding parameter solutions for the models of nonlinear systems. However, the association and differences among scaling, fractals and complexity are not yet clear. This work is thus devoted to discussing three urban problems: first, how to understand scaling in cities based on the concept of characteristic scales; second, how to understand fractal cities based on the concept of scaling; and third, how to understand the spatial complexity of cities by using ideas from both scaling and fractals.

2. SCALING IN CITIES

2.1 Characteristic Length

To explain scaling we must make clear the definition of characteristic length. The characteristic scale is the geometric characteristic quantity reflecting the key properties of an entity. Generally, a characteristic scale is expressed by a one-dimensional measure, so it is often termed characteristic length (Hao 1986; Liu and Liu 1994; Takayasu 1990;

Wang and Li, 1996). Common characteristic lengths include the radius of a circle, the side length of a square, the bottom and height of a triangle, the eigenvalues of a correlation matrix, the mean and standard deviation of a sample, and so on. For a system, as long as the characteristic length is known, other relevant measures of the system can be calculated or predicted. For example, as soon as the radius of a circle is determined, the perimeter and area of the circle can be computed. If the mean and standard deviation of a normal distribution is known, we can make statistical analysis and inference for the corresponding population. For a lake or urban envelope, we can find the radius of its equivalent circle; and for a geographical sampling, we should count its average value and standard deviation. A good model of a geographical system involves three scales, the macro scale reflecting the global level and geographical environment, the micro scale reflecting the local level and geographical element interaction, and in particular, the characteristic scale reflecting the basic level and central structure. The key to mathematical modeling is to search out the characteristic length for geographical analysis.

Theoretically, the characteristic length can be revealed by appropriate mathematical transformation. Generally, a good mathematical model is an eigenfunction under some transformation, and the corresponding eigenvalue is a characteristic length or a function of the characteristic length. A function with invariance under a certain transformation can form a good mathematical model of geographical systems (Chen 2008). The functional equation can be expressed as

$$\mathbf{T}f(x) = \lambda f(x), \tag{9.1}$$

where $f(x)$ denotes the function, which can be used to model an urban phenomenon, x refers to an argument, for example, distance, $\mathbf{T}$ represents a mathematical transformation, and λ is the eigenvalue of the transformation. An eigenvalue is also termed characteristic root. Equation (9.1) suggests that the function $f(x)$ has no essential change under the transformation $\mathbf{T}$. Clark's model of urban density can be employed to explain characteristic scales in urban geography. Based on digital maps, urban population density follows Clark's law, which can be expressed as a negative exponential function (Clark 1951). The standard form of Clark's law is

$$\rho(r) = \rho_0 e^{-r/r_0}, \tag{9.2}$$

where $\rho(r)$ denotes the population density at the distance r from the center of city ($r = 0$). As for the parameters, ρ_0 refers to the urban central density $\rho(0)$, and r_0 to the characteristic radius of the population distribution (Batty and Longley 1994; Chen 2015; Takayasu 1990). Clark's model proved to be an eigenfunction under spatial translational transformation

$$\mathbf{T}f(r) = \rho(r - \gamma) = \rho_0 e^{-(r-\gamma)/r_0} = e^{\gamma/r_0} \rho_0 e^{-r/r_0} = \lambda f(r), \tag{9.3}$$

where $\mathbf{T}$ represents translational transformation, γ denotes the translational scale factor, the eigenvalue $\lambda = \exp(\gamma/r_0)$, and thus $r_0 = \ln(\lambda)/\gamma$ refers to the characteristic length. Translational scale reflects geographical position, which is associated with distance. This indicates that the eigenvalue depends on location, instead of size, of an urban pattern.

Moreover, Clark's model also proved to be an eigenfunction under differential transformation, that is

$$\mathbf{T}f(r) = \frac{d}{dr}\rho(r) = -\frac{1}{r_0}\rho_0 e^{-r/r_0} = \lambda f(r),$$ (9.4)

where $\mathbf{T}$ represents differential transformation, the eigenvalue $\lambda = -1/r_0$, and thus $r_0 = 1/|\lambda|$ refers to the characteristic length. Where the absolute value is concerned, there is a reciprocal relation between the eigenvalue and characteristic radius of a city. It can be seen that the eigenvalues of urban density are related to characteristic radius r_0, but not to central density ρ_0, no matter the translational transformation or differential transformation.

2.2   Scaling and Scaling Analysis of Cities

The mathematical core of scaling is dilation symmetry, which indicates the structural invariance under enlargement and reduction transformation. The dilation symmetry is also termed scaling symmetry, indicating scale invariance of contraction or dilation transformation (Batty 2010; Batty and Longley 1994; Chen 2008; Mandelbrot 1982, 1989). The process of zooming in or out of a geographical map on a scale (size is variable) without changing its projection mode, and thus without changing its structure (shape is invariable), is just a process of scaling. A fractal is a typical scaling phenomenon, and self-similarity is simply a scaling process or pattern. If an urban system bears some type of scaling property, it can be modeled by an eigenfunction of scaling transformation and satisfy the following scaling relationship:

$$\mathbf{T}f(x) = f(\gamma x) = \gamma^a f(x) = \lambda f(x),$$ (9.5)

where $\mathbf{T}$ represents a scaling transformation, $f(x)$ denotes the eigenfunction of the scaling transformation $\mathbf{T}$, x refers to an argument, γ is a scale factor for the scaling transformation, a is a scaling exponent and $\lambda = \gamma^a$ refers to the eigenvalue of the transformation. If $f(x)$ refers to a map of a city, and γ to a scale, then $\mathbf{T}$ represents a process of zooming in and out. In this example, the eigenvalue λ indicates the ratio of a map to be enlarged or reduced in terms of the scale γ. A power law is the most common and basic solution to the functional equation (9.5). Therefore, power law is always associated with scaling law (Batty and Longley 1994; Bettencourt et al. 2007; Chen 2008; Liu and Liu 1994; Mandelbrot 1982; West 2017). If a model of cities satisfies the scaling relation stipulated by equation (9.5), it is treated as scaling law in positive studies.

A simple example can illustrate the eigenfunction of scaling transformation. Traffic network density of a city based on digital maps or remote sensing images can be modeled by Smeed's law (Smeed 1963). The standard form of Smeed's model is usually expressed as an inverse power law

$$\rho(r) = \rho_1 r^{-\alpha} = \rho_1 r^{D-d},$$ (9.6)

where $\rho(r)$ denotes the traffic network density at the distance r from the center of city $(r = 0)$, $d = 2$ is the Euclidean dimension of the embedding space, D is the fractal dimension of traffic networks, ρ_1 refers to traffic network density near city center and $\alpha = d - D$ to the scaling exponent of the urban traffic network (Chen et al. 2019). It is easy to testify that equation (9.6) follows scaling law, that is

$$\mathbf{T}\rho(r) = \rho(\gamma r) = \rho_1(\gamma r)^{D-d} = \gamma^{D-d}\rho_1 r^{D-d} = \lambda\rho(r), \tag{9.7}$$

where $\mathbf{T}$ refers to the scaling transformation, $\rho(r)$ proved to be the eigenfunction of transformation $\mathbf{T}$, and $\lambda = \gamma^{D-d}$ refers to the corresponding eigenvalue. This eigenvalue is the function of fractal dimension D. It is evident that the eigenvalue λ depends on the scale factor γ. Similarly, it is easy to demonstrate that Zipf's law of the rank-size distribution of cities satisfies the scaling relation, equation (9.5), and thus follows the scaling law. In contrast, Clark's model does not follow scaling law. Applying equation (9.5) to equation (9.2) yields

$$\mathbf{T}\rho(r) = \rho(\gamma r) = \rho_0 e^{-\gamma r/r_0} = \rho_0^{1-\gamma}\rho(r)^{\gamma} \neq \lambda\rho(r), \tag{9.8}$$

which shows that Clark model does not have invariance under scaling transformation, no matter what value λ takes except for 1. This means that there is a fundamental difference between the Clark model and the Smeed model: the former represents simple geographical phenomenon with characteristic length, while the latter reflect complex spatial systems without characteristic scales.

For urban density, spatial distribution and probability distribution represent two sides of the same coin. Whether in respect of geographical space or geographical probability, there are two representative types of distributions. One type is the distributions with characteristic lengths, and the other is the distributions without characteristic length. The most typical distribution with characteristic length is Gaussian distribution. This distribution bears effective mean and standard deviation, and is termed normal distribution. In contrast, the typical distribution without characteristic length is Pareto distribution. This distribution is equivalent to Zipf distribution and can be regarded as scale-free distribution (Figure 9.1). For the characteristic scale distribution, we can undertake analyses and make predictions for cities by means of mean values. Alternatively, for the scale-free distribution, we cannot make judgement and inference for cities with the help of mean values. Scale-free distribution suggests scaling property of cities, and scaling indicates fractals and nonlinearity in urban evolution.

Complex systems, such as cities, are nonlinear systems which must be described with nonlinear equations of cities. In this case, numerical solutions often replace analytical solutions. Based on the process of numerical solution, computer simulation analysis of urban evolution can be carried out. In many instances, it is hard to find the solutions to nonlinear equations. However, if a nonlinear equation follows scaling law, we can find the parameter solution instead of the common analytical solution to the nonlinear equation by means of scaling transformation (Liu and Liu 1994; Takayasu 1990). The key parameters are always associated with eigenvalues of scaling transformation. Scaling analysis is very significant for exploring the spatial complexity of cities. At least, we know that power laws are the basic solutions to the general scaling functional equations. Thus, we can employ power laws to describe complex spatial systems including cities. The basic scaling exponent is fractal dimension, which is the characteristic parameter of fractal models.

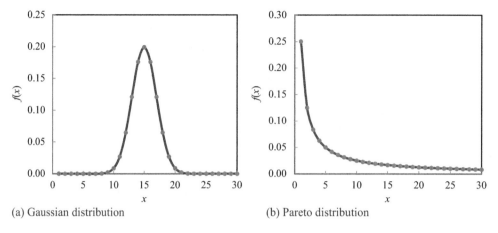

(a) Gaussian distribution　　　　　　　　　　　(b) Pareto distribution

Note: Generally, a distribution with characteristic scale forms a unimodal curve indicative of valid mean, while a scale-free distribution forms a long-tailed curve indicating invalid mean.

Figure 9.1　Two types of probability distributions: Gaussian distribution and Pareto distribution

3.　FRACTALS IN URBAN STUDIES

Fractal geometry provides effective mathematical tools for scaling analysis of complex spatial systems, such as cities and regions. If an urban phenomenon bears characteristic lengths, it can be modeled and quantitatively analyzed by using conventional mathematical methods and statistical theory. Unfortunately, in many aspects, urban form and networks of cities have no characteristic lengths, and thus fractal theory based on scaling notion is often the best selection for urban modeling and quantitative analysis. Fractal geometry can be employed to build models and make quantitative analyses in intraurban geography (individual city as a system), interurban geography (systems of cities) and urbanization. A city can be treated as a fractal phenomenon struggling between chaos and order (Hao 2004; White and Engelen 1994). Fractals bear three properties: fractional dimension, scaling law and entropy conservation.

3.1　Fractal Dimension

Fractal objects such as cities cannot be effectively described with conventional measures such as length, radius, area, volume, density, characteristic roots, means and standard deviation. The basic parameter of fractals is fractal dimension. Common fractals are always thin fractals, which differ from fat fractals. All the thin fractals bear effective fractal dimension. Generally, fractal dimension is a fractional number, which is greater than the topological dimension of the fractal object. The simplest fractal model of cities is a power function as follows:

$$N(r) = N_1 r^{\pm D}, \tag{9.9}$$

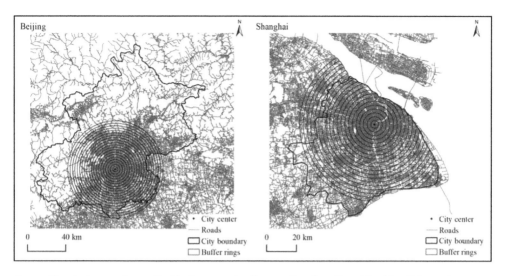

Note: The cluster growing method is also termed radius-area/length scaling. After identifying and determining the center of a city, we can make a set of concentric circles for spatial data extraction. For example, based on the scaling relationships between the variable radius and lengths of traffic networks, we can estimate the radial dimension of cities such as Beijing and Shanghai.

Figure 9.2 Sketch maps of cluster growing method for radial dimension measurement of urban traffic networks

where r denotes a variable measurement scale, $N(r)$ is the corresponding measure based on the variable scale, N_1 is the proportionality coefficient and D is the fractal dimension of city fractals. In theory, $N_1 = 1$ (Huang and Chen 2018). For example, in urban studies based on remote sensing images, r represents the radius to the city center and $N(r)$ represents the number of urban land use pixels or length of traffic lines within this radius (Figure 9.2). In this instance, D is the radial dimension (Frankhauser and Sadler 1991; Jiang and Zhou 2006; White and Engelen 1993). This is a type of local fractal dimension. If we use the box-counting method to measure fractal dimension, then r represents the linear size of boxes and $N(r)$ represents the number of nonempty boxes (Benguigui et al. 2000; Chen and Wang 2013; Feng and Chen 2010; Murcio et al. 2015). In this example, D is the box dimension. In practice, the common box-counting method can be substituted by the functional box-counting method (Figure 9.3), which was employed by Chen (1995) to explore fractal systems of cities and towns.

3.2 Scaling Symmetry

Fractal objects, including city fractals, follow scaling law. Fractal structure indicates scaling symmetry, that is, invariance under contraction or dilation (Mandelbrot 1989). In mathematics, symmetry implies invariance under certain transformation. Equation (9.10) follows the scaling law, that is

$$\mathbf{T}N(r) = N(\gamma r) = N_1(\gamma r)^{\pm D} = \gamma^{\pm D} N_1(r)^{\pm D} = \lambda N(r), \tag{9.10}$$

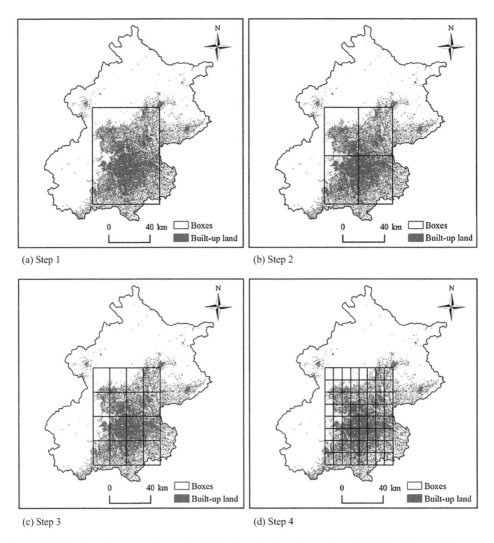

Note: The functional box-counting method is based on the idea of recursive subdivision of space. This method can be utilized to generate multifractal spectrums of Beijing (Chen and Wang 2013; Huang and Chen 2018).

Figure 9.3   *A sketch map of the functional box-counting method for fractal dimension measurement of Beijing city (first four steps)*

where **T** represents the scaling transformation, and fractal dimension D represents a scaling exponent of cities. This suggests that a fractal model of cities is an eigenfunction of scaling transformation, and fractal dimension D is associated with the eigenvalue λ, that is, $\lambda = \gamma^{\pm D}$. Apparently, the eigenvalue λ depends on the scale γ. Therefore, we have

$$D = \pm \frac{\ln \lambda}{\ln \gamma}. \tag{9.11}$$

That is, the fractal dimension is the absolute value of the ratio of the logarithm of the eigenvalue, $\ln\lambda$, to the logarithm of the scale factor, $\ln\gamma$. For the hierarchy of cities with cascade structure, if city size distribution follows pure Zipf's law, then $\gamma = 1/2$ suggests $\lambda = 2$. In this instance, Zipf exponent $q = 1/D = 1$ (Chen 2008, 2012a). Based on the box-counting method, the fractal parameter satisfies the condition $d_T < D < d_E$, where d_T refers to the topological dimension of a fractal object and d_E to the Euclidean dimension of the embedding space in which the fractal object exists. However, the similarity dimension of a fractal system may be greater than the embedding space dimension d_E, owing to the overlap of fractal elements (Chen 2020b).

3.3   Entropy Conservation

All fractal systems follow the law of entropy conservation. Cities as fractals can be described by a transcendental equation:

$$\sum_{i=1}^{N(r)} P_i(r)^q r_i^{(1-q)D_q} = 1, \tag{9.12}$$

where P_i denotes the growth probability of the ith fractal elements, r_i is the linear size of the ith fractal elements, q denotes the order of moment and the exponent D_q represents the generalized correlation dimension, which can also be regarded as generalized information dimension. Three regular growing fractals of central place systems can be utilized to illustrate equation (9.12). For a monofractal, that is, a simple self-similar fractal, say, the mono-scaling Koch snowflake of models of central place systems (Chen 2011), we have $D_q = D_0$ (Figure 9.4); for a self-affine fractal, different directions have different fractal dimension values, but for a given direction, we have $D_q \equiv D_0$. However, for a multifractal system, say, the multi-scaling Koch snowflake of models of central place systems (Chen 2014), this is complex. Different parts of a multifractal system have different characters, and can be described with different fractal dimension values (Figure 9.5).

4.   THE SPATIAL COMPLEXITY OF CITIES

4.1   Understanding the Spatial Complexity of Cities

Fractals and scaling reach the same goal by different routes in the studies on spatial complexity. Cities and regions are complex spatial systems (Allen 1997; Batty 2005; Portugali 2000; Wilson 2000). A regional system includes networks of cities and towns, and their related hinterlands. Complexity is always related to the concepts of scaling, symmetry breaking, nonlinearity, emergence, self-organization and irreducibility. The spatial complexity of cities can thus be understood from four aspects: nonlinearity of spatial relationships, scale dependence of spatial measurements, irreducibility (non-reductionism) of spatial analysis and asymmetry of mathematical laws. Understanding the four properties of complex systems will help us understand the spatial complexity of cities.

First, spatial complexity implies nonlinearity of spatial relations of cities. Cities are nonlinear systems, and nonlinearity suggests complexity. The study of cities encounters

(a) With shadow effect   (b) No shadow effect

Note: The classical models of central place systems are based on two-dimensional space and possess a Euclidean structure despite the fractal texture. By using the idea from intermittency, we can generate two types of Koch snowflake models for central place systems (Chen 2011).

Figure 9.4   Two types of self-similar fractal models for central place networks with intermittency (the fourth step)

three obstacles: spatial dimension, time lag and interaction. Spatial dimension involves dimensional consistency (Lee 1989) that cannot be guaranteed by Euclidean geometry. On the other hand, time lag implies feedback and response delay that always results in nonlinearity. Interaction and nonlinearity represent two different sides of the same coin. Owing to nonlinear processes of urban evolution, cities cannot be effectively described by linear equations, and cannot be effectively predicted by conventional probability structure. Owing to nonlinear relationships, the whole is different from the sum of its parts. For statistical analysis, the mean is based on the valid sum, and variance and covariance are based on valid mean values. Owing to the wholeness of cities as nonlinear systems, the probability structure based on mean, variance and covariance are not always valid in common statistical analysis. The wholeness of urban systems can be measured by spatial autocorrelation indexes such as Moran's index, Geary's coefficient and Getis-Ord's index (Chen 2020a). Nonlinear processes lead to irregular patterns. Owing to the irregularity of spatial distribution, urban form cannot be described with Euclidean geometry and the mathematical tools based on Euclidean geometry such as calculus theory. Alternatively, spatial irregularity suggests spatial heterogeneity, and the core of spatial heterogeneity is spatial nonstationarity. Spatial nonstationarity comes from the difference of probability structure from place to place. Owing to spatial nonstationarity, statistical analysis in urban studies often leads to biased results.

Second, complexity involves scale dependence of spatial measurements of cities. Cities are scale-free systems, which cannot be effectively characterized by common

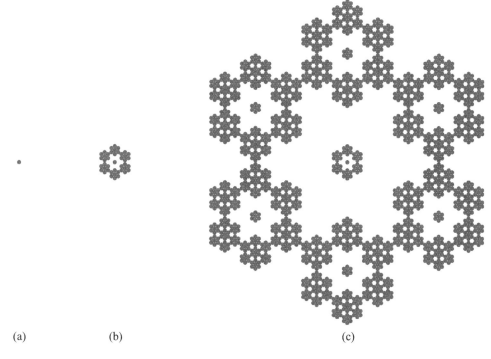

(a)   (b)   (c)

Note: No urban systems in the real world take on monofractals. By the ideas of multifractal scaling and intermittency, we can construct multifractal Koch snowflake models for central place systems (Chen 2014).

Figure 9.5   A regular multifractal growing model of central place systems indicative of spatial diffusion (the first three steps)

mathematical tools. The scale-free property of cities indicates scale dependence of spatial measurement and description. The core of scale dependence of measurements is scaling symmetry, which has been discussed in detail previously. Many difficult problems in urban studies are associated with scale-free properties, including the dimensional problem of gravity models (Haynes 1975), the scaling factor problem of allometric growth law (Lee 1989) and the modifiable areal unit problem (MAUP) (Cressie 1996; Kwan 2012; Openshaw 1983; Unwin 1996). Scaling symmetry is one of the basic characters of spatial complexity.

   Third, spatial complexity indicates irreducibility (non-reductionism) of spatial analysis of cities. As nonlinear systems, cities cannot be effectively researched by reductionist approach. The properties of cities cannot be fully explained by an understanding of its component parts. Irreducibility suggests complexity (Gallagher and Appenzeller 1999; Waldrop 1992). The emergence of Zipf's rank-size distribution of hierarchy of cities cannot be explained by means of interaction of cities and towns, and the emergence of fractal structure of urban form cannot be explained by interaction of various buildings and residents. Zipf's distribution and fractal patterns are the emergence results of the self-organized evolution of cities (Chen 2008). However, we do not know the intrinsic mechanism of city development from chaos to order.

Fourth, spatial complexity suggests asymmetry of scientific laws of cities. The mathematical laws of cities do not satisfy space–time translational symmetry. The translational symmetry in space and time implies universality of scientific laws (for example, the laws in classical physics). Unfortunately, we cannot find universal laws in urban science. For example, the law of universal gravitation in physics is universal, while the gravity law of cities is not. The mathematical structure and parameter values of geographical gravity models are variable, that is, they vary with time and place. Indeed, there are no cast-iron laws in urban geography (Chen 2017). The mathematical rules of cities proved to be laws of evolution rather than laws of existence (Chen 2014). For classical physics, a counterexample is enough to overturn a law. If the observed facts do not agree with the mathematical model, the mathematical law must be wrong. However, an urban geographic system is different from a classical physical system. For a mathematical law on cities, several counterexamples are not enough to overturn it. Geographical laws have two characteristics. One is the nature of evolution, and the other is scaling symmetry. On the one hand, with the self-organization evolution of urban systems, the performance of mathematical laws is getting increasingly better (Benguigui et al. 2000). On the other, the mathematical laws of cities take on invariance of contraction or dilation (Chen 2008).

4.2 Exploring Spatial Complexity by Fractal Geometry

Simple systems bear characteristic scales, and can be modeled by conventional mathematical methods and analyzed by conventional quantitative methods. However, complex spatial systems, such as cities, bear no characteristic scale in many respects and cannot be modeled and analyzed by traditional methods. In this instance, the spatial analyses of cities based on characteristic scales should be substituted with the methods based on scaling. Currently, many mathematics-based theories can be utilized to make scaling analyses for cities. In addition to fractal geometry, the theories related to scaling include allometry theory, network theory and wavelet analysis. All these theories are associated with fractals and fractal dimensions. Allometric growth processes and patterns are related to fractals. An allometric scaling exponent is a ratio of the fractal dimension of one measure to the fractal dimension of another correlated measure. Complex networks include scale-free networks and hierarchical networks. The scaling exponent of a scale-free network is similar to an allometric scaling exponent in mathematical property. The scaling exponent of a hierarchical network is equal to fractal dimension plus one. This suggests that hierarchical networks contain fractal structure. Wavelet analysis can be associated with multifractal analysis and are applied to complex spatial analysis of cities and systems of cities. Based on network science, allometric growth and fractal geometry, an integrated theory of how cities evolve is being slowly developed (Batty 2008, 2013; Chen 2008).

4.3 Multifractal Scaling for Characterization of the Spatial Complexity of Cities

Among various approaches for characterization of the spatial complexity of cities, one of the most effective tools is multifractal spectrums. Simple fractals are usually termed monofractals or unifractals, which represent homogenous self-similar structures with a single scaling process. In contrast, multifractals represent the heterogeneous self-similar structure with multiple scaling processes. In a multifractal system, there are a great many fractal units, each unit bears a scaling exponent, and each scaling exponent corresponds to a fractal dimension. It is impossible to measure and estimate the varied fractal dimension values of different parts of a multifractal city. An advisable method is to substitute fractal parameter sets with fractal dimension spectrums. To simplify the process of spatial measurement, the varied linear scales r_i can be substituted with a unified scale r. If we utilize the box-counting method to measure fractal parameters, the measurement scale r refers to the linear size of boxes. Thus, equation (9.12) can be re-expressed as

$$D_q = -\frac{M_q(r)}{\ln r} = \frac{1}{q-1}\frac{\ln \sum_{i=1}^{N(r)} P_i(r)^q}{\ln r}, \tag{9.13}$$

where M_q denotes Renyi entropy, that is, the generalized information entropy. In the set of generalized correlation dimension, three parameters are significant. If $q = 0$, we have capacity dimension D_0; if $q = 1$, we have information dimension D_1; if $q = 2$, we have correlation dimension D_2 (Grassberger 1983). The Renyi entropy can be expressed as

$$M_q(r) = -\ln C_q(r) = \frac{1}{1-q}\ln \sum_{i=1}^{N(r)} P_i(r)^q = -D_q \ln r, \tag{9.14}$$

in which $C_q(r)$ refers to generalized correlation function. Equation (9.14) suggests that the generalized correlation dimension D_q is just the characteristic value of Renyi entropy based on spatial scale r. The generalized correlation dimension can be transformed into the mass exponent as

$$\tau_q = (q-1)D_q = \frac{(1-q)M_q(r)}{\ln r}, \tag{9.15}$$

where τ_q is termed the mass exponent of a multifractal structure (Feder 1988; Vicsek 1989). Equation (9.15) shows the relationships between the generalized correlation dimension, the mass exponent and Renyi entropy. The generalized correlation dimension D_q and the mass exponent τ_q comprise the set of the global parameters of multifractal models. The two parameters can be converted into local parameters of multifractal subsets by Legendre's transformation

$$\alpha(q) = \frac{d\tau(q)}{dq} = D_q + (q-1)\frac{dD_q}{dq}, \tag{9.16}$$

$$f(\alpha) = q\alpha(q) - \tau(q) = q\alpha(q) - (q-1)D_q, \tag{9.17}$$

where $f(\alpha)$ refers to the fractal dimension of the fractal units of certain sizes, and $\alpha(q)$ is the corresponding singularity exponent (Feder 1988; Stanley and Meakin 1988). The local dimension $f(\alpha)$ and the singularity exponent $\alpha(q)$ combine to form the local parameter set of multifractal analysis. By means of generalized correlation dimension D_q, we can generate a global multifractal dimension spectrum, namely, the D_q-q spectrum. By using the scaling exponent $\alpha(q)$ and fractal dimension $f(\alpha)$, we can produce the local multifractal spectrum, that is, $f(\alpha) - \alpha(q)$ spectrum. The local dimension spectrum is also termed the $f(\alpha)$ curve in literature (Feder 1988). Thus, the parameters of fractal subsets in a multi-scaling fractal system are mapped into the multifractal spectral curves through the order of moment parameter q.

Multifractal theory provided effective approaches for describing spatial heterogeneity of urban form and networks of cities. In urban studies, multifractal scaling can be employed to explore urban form and growth (Ariza-Villaverde et al. 2013; Cavailhès et al. 2010; Chen and Wang 2013; Murcio et al. 2015), central place networks (Chen 2014), city rank-size distribution (Chen 2012b) and the spatial patterns of urbanization (Chen 2016). More recently, the multifractal method has been applied to exploring the spatial complexity of the city of Zhengzhou, the capital of Henan Province, China (Chen and Chen 2020). The measurement object is urban land use patterns from 1986 to 2018, and the study area is defined by two spatial scales: urban agglomeration (based on urbanized area) and metropolitan area (based on administration region).

By means of the multifractal spectrums, we can obtain useful geographical information of Zhengzhou's urban form and growth. First, the spatial patterns of Zhengzhou's urban land use take on multifractal features. The D_q–q spectrum takes on an inverse S-shaped curve (Figure 9.6), while the $f(\alpha)$ – $\alpha(q)$ spectrum takes on a unimodal curve (Figure 9.7). These are typical characters of multifractals. Also, the fractal dimension values of a metropolitan area differ from the corresponding fractal dimension values of urban agglomeration. Fractal dimension values depending on the size of study area suggests the multifractal structure of cities (Chen 2019). Second, the suburbs and the fringe zones of centers at all levels of Zhengzhou bear complicated spatial structures. When the order of moment $q < 0$, the generalized correlation dimension D_q exceeds the Euclidean dimension of embedding space significantly. If $q \rightarrow -\infty$, the D_q values become greater than 3 or, even, 4 (Figure 9.6). This suggests that the zones of low density of land

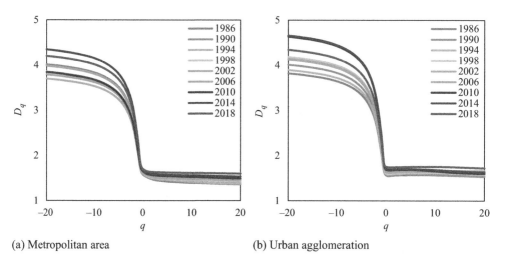

(a) Metropolitan area   (b) Urban agglomeration

Note: Where the global level is concerned, the inverse S-shaped spectral curves of the generalized correlation dimension are typical features of multifractal scaling of cities.

Figure 9.6   The generalized correlation dimension spectrums of urban land use of Zhengzhou (1986–2018)

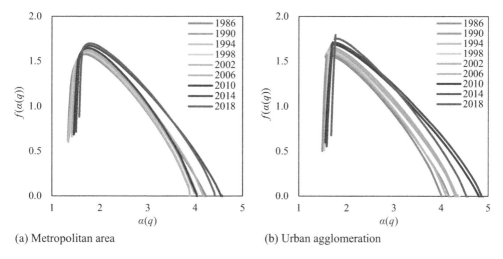

(a) Metropolitan area   (b) Urban agglomeration

Note: Where the local level is concerned, the unimodal spectral curves of fractal dimension based on fractal subsystems are typical features of multifractal scaling of cities.

Figure 9.7   *The local dimension spectrums, that is, f(α) curves, of urban land use of Zhengzhou (1986–2018)*

use bear disordered spatial distribution (Chen 2020b). Third, the land use of Zhengzhou has changed from the stage of centripetal agglomeration to the stage of outward expansion. The $f(\alpha)$ curves take on left-leaning unimodal curves (Figure 9.7). This suggests an outward spread process of urban evolution. If it was an inward aggregation process, the $f(\alpha)$ curves should take on right-leaning unimodal curves (Chen 2014). Also, for the urban agglomeration, the single peak curve showed local kinks (Figure 9.7(b)). This suggests some disordered structure resulting from improper human actions. Scientific city planning should be employed to improve the spatial structure of the city.

Modeling fractal dimension change over time will provide evolutionary information for cities. The fractal dimension increase curves can be described with a logistic function or generalized logistic functions (Chen 2018). Differing from the fractal growth of the cities in European and American countries, Zhengzhou's urban growth cannot be modeled with the usual logistic function, but can be characterized by generalized logistic functions (Figure 9.8). The capacity dimension growth of land use in metropolitan areas can be described by a quadratic logistic function. The model is

$$D(t) = \frac{2}{1 + 0.2612e^{-(0.0194t)^2}}. \tag{9.18}$$

The goodness of fit is about $R^2 = 0.9900$. The capacity dimension growth of land use in urban agglomeration can be modeled by a fractional logistic function. The model is

$$D(t) = \frac{2}{1 + 0.2705e^{-(0.0404t)^{1.72}}}. \tag{9.19}$$

The goodness of fit is around $R^2 = 0.9905$. The latent scaling exponent is about 1.72, which is near 2. Thus equation (9.19) can be approximately treated as a quadratic logistic

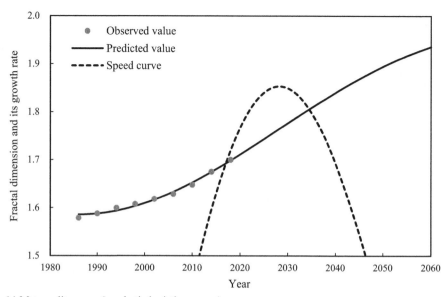

(a) Metropolitan area (quadratic logistic process)

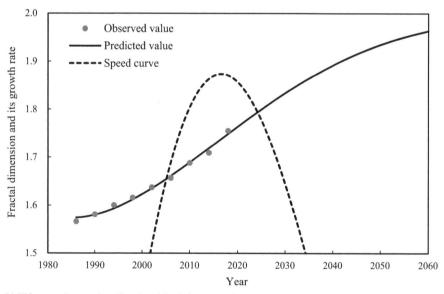

(b) Urban agglomeration (fractional logistic process)

Note: The growth rate was magnified 250–280 times. Otherwise, a growth curve and its corresponding speed curve cannot be displayed in the same plot. For the urban agglomeration of Zhengzhou, the peak of land use has passed; while for the metropolitan area, the peak of land use has not yet arrived.

Figure 9.8   *The generalized logistic curves of the fractal dimension increase of Zhengzhou's urban land use (1986–2018)*

model. The quadratic logistic model and fractional logistic models belong to generalized logistic models. Using these models, we can predict the future growth of Zhengzhou, and make analyses of spatial dynamics for Zhengzhou's evolution. A preliminary judgement is as follows. If the urban growth is a bottom-up evolution process dominated by a self-organized mechanism, the fractal dimension increase curves will satisfy the conventional logistic function. In contrast, if the government-led city development overwhelms the market-driven city development, and the top-down force overwhelms the bottom-up force of urban evolution, the fractal dimension increase curves will meet the quadratic logistic curve.

5.   CONCLUSIONS

Scaling, fractals and spatial complexity are three correlated important concepts in modern geo-spatial analyses of cities. Scaling indicates symmetry of scale transformation, fractals indicate self-similarity, self-organized evolution and scaling symmetry, while spatial complexity indicates nonlinearity, asymmetry, scale dependence and irreducibility. The spatial complexity of cities seems to come between contradictory processes: breaking of space–time translational symmetry and reconstruction of dilation symmetry. The main points of this work can be summarized as follows.

First, scaling is an important space–time property of cities, and the core of scaling is dilation symmetry of city development. The mathematical models of cities bear invariance under contraction or dilation transformation. The basic and common solution to the scaling functional equation is power functions. Therefore, power laws are the main symbol of scaling in cities as systems and systems of cities. Among various power laws in urban geography, the most important are distance decay law (for example, gravity models), rank-size law (for example, Zipf's law) and allometric growth law (for example, urban area–population scaling relationship). Scaling and characteristic scale are sometimes the unity of opposites. In urban systems, there are many phenomena with characteristic scales. A typical urban phenomenon with characteristic scale is urban population density distribution, which follows Clark's law and takes on negative exponential decay. Scaling can be regarded as a feature of complex spatial systems, and there are simple evolution rules behind the spatial complexity of cities.

Second, fractals suggest scaling and order of urban evolution, and fractal geometry provides effective tools for scale-free spatial analysis of cities. The visual characteristic of city fractals is irregularity, while the statistical characteristic of city fractals lies in self-similarity. However, the mathematical basis of fractals lies in scaling symmetry, fractional dimension and entropy conservation. Fractal patterns represent spatial order emerging from urban self-organized evolution. Owing to scaling in cities, an urban system has no characteristic length in many aspects and cannot be effectively described and modeled by using conventional mathematical methods. The common measures, such as length, area, volume and density, are always invalid for describing cities. Fractal theory provides a new way of mathematical modeling and quantitative analysis of urban systems.

Third, the spatial complexity of geographical systems is related to scaling, and the methodology based on scaling analysis, such as fractal geometry, is an important approach to exploring complexity and singularity of cities. The spatial complexity of cities bears four basic properties: (1) nonlinearity – the whole is not equal to the sum of its parts of a city system, thus the average values are invalid; (2) scale-free property – cities have no characteristic scales in many aspects, and cannot be effectively characterized by common mathematical methods; (3) irreducibility – cities cannot be effectively researched by a reductionist approach; and (4) asymmetry of mathematical laws. The mathematical models and parameters do not satisfy space–time translational invariance. The scale-free property indicates scaling. Owing to scaling in cities, characteristic length such as average values cannot reflect the basic characters of urban form, growth, shape and size. Geometric and statistical measures are usually replaced by scaling exponents, including fractal dimension, distance exponent, allometric exponent and rank-size exponent. Fractal geometry is an effective tool for scaling analysis, and therefore fractal theory may be the most important approach for exploring spatial complexity and singularity of cities. City fractals can be treated as a type of emergence behavior of urban self-organized evolution.

ACKNOWLEDGEMENTS

This research was sponsored by the National Natural Science Foundation of China (Grant No. 41671167). The support is gratefully acknowledged. I would like to thank my students: Dr Yuqing Long, who helped me to draw Figures 9.2 and 9.3, and Ms Qing Chen, who provided the essential materials for the case study in Section 4.2.

REFERENCES

Allen, P.M. (1997), *Cities and Regions as Self-Organizing Systems: Models of Complexity*, London and New York: Routledge.
Ariza-Villaverde, A.B., F.J. Jimenez-Hornero and E.G. De Rave (2013), 'Multifractal analysis of axial maps applied to the study of urban morphology', *Computers, Environment and Urban Systems*, **38** (March), 1–10.
Batty, M. (2005), *Cities and Complexity: Understanding Cities with Cellular Automata*, Cambridge, MA: MIT Press.
Batty, M. (2008), 'The size, scale, and shape of cities', *Science*, **319** (5864), 769–71.
Batty, M. (2010), 'Space, scale, and scaling in entropy maximizing', *Geographical Analysis*, **42** (4), 395–421.
Batty, M. (2013), *The New Science of Cities*, Cambridge, MA: MIT Press.
Batty, M. and P.A. Longley (1994), *Fractal Cities: A Geometry of Form and Function*, London: Academic Press.
Benguigui, L., D. Czamanski, M. Marinov and J. Portugali (2000), 'When and where is a city fractal?', *Environment and Planning B: Planning and Design*, **27** (4), 507–19.
Bettencourt, L.M.A., J. Lobo, D. Helbing, C. Kühnert and G.B. West (2007), 'Growth, innovation, scaling, and the pace of life in cities', *PNAS*, **104** (17), 7301–6.
Cavailhès, J., P. Frankhauser, D. Peeters and I. Thomas (2010), 'Residential equilibrium in a multifractal metropolitan area', *Annals of Regional Science*, **45** (3), 681–704.
Chen, Q. and Y.G. Chen (2020), 'Multifractal spectral analysis of urban land use patterns of Zhengzhou city: 1986–2018', *Urban Development Studies*, **27** (3), 46–55 (in Chinese).
Chen, T. (1995), 'Studies on fractal systems of cities and towns in the Central Plains of China', Master's thesis, Department of Geography, Northeast Normal University Changchun (in Chinese).
Chen, Y.G. (2008), *Fractal Urban Systems: Scaling, Symmetry, and Spatial Complexity*, Beijing: Science Press (in Chinese).
Chen, Y.G. (2011), 'Fractal systems of central places based on intermittency of space-filling', *Chaos, Solitons & Fractals*, **44** (8), 619–32.
Chen, Y.G. (2012a), 'Zipf's law, 1/f noise, and fractal hierarchy', *Chaos, Solitons & Fractals*, **45** (1), 63–73.

Chen, Y.G. (2012b), 'The rank-size scaling law and entropy-maximizing principle', *Physica A*, **391** (3), 767–78.

Chen, Y.G. (2014), 'Multifractals of central place systems: models, dimension spectrums, and empirical analysis', *Physica A*, **402** (May), 266–82.

Chen, Y.G. (2015), 'Power-law distributions based on exponential distributions: latent scaling, spurious Zipf's law, and fractal rabbits', *Fractals*, **23** (2), 1550009.

Chen, Y.G. (2016), 'Defining urban and rural regions by multifractal spectrums of urbanization', *Fractals*, **24** (1), 1650004.

Chen, Y.G. (2017), 'Multi-scaling allometric analysis for urban and regional development', *Physica A*, **465** (January), 673–89.

Chen, Y.G. (2018), 'Logistic models of fractal dimension growth of urban morphology', *Fractals*, **26** (3), art. 1850033.

Chen, Y.G. (2019), 'The solutions to uncertainty problem of urban fractal dimension calculation', *Entropy*, **21** (5), art. 453.

Chen, Y.G. (2020a), 'New framework of Getis-Ord's indexes associating spatial autocorrelation with interaction', *PLoS ONE*, **15** (7), e0236765.

Chen, Y.G. (2020b), 'Fractal modeling and fractal dimension description of urban morphology', *Entropy*, **22** (9), art. 961.

Chen, Y.G. and J.J. Wang (2013), 'Multifractal characterization of urban form and growth: the case of Beijing', *Environment and Planning B: Planning and Design*, **40** (5), 884–904.

Chen, Y.G., Y.H. Wang and X.J. Li (2019), 'Fractal dimensions derived from spatial allometric scaling of urban form', *Chaos, Solitons & Fractals*, **126** (September), 122–34.

Clark, C. (1951), 'Urban population densities', *Journal of the Royal Statistical Society*, **114** (4), 490–96.

Cressie, N.A. (1996), 'Change of support and the modifiable areal unit problem', *Geographical Systems*, **3** (2–3), 159–80.

Feder, J. (1988), *Fractals*, New York: Plenum Press.

Feng, J. and Y.G. Chen (2010), 'Spatiotemporal evolution of urban form and land use structure in Hangzhou, China: evidence from fractals', *Environment and Planning B: Planning and Design*, **37** (5), 838–56.

Frankhauser, P. and R. Sadler 1991), 'Fractal analysis of agglomerations', in M. Hilliges (ed.), *Natural Structures: Principles, Strategies, and Models in Architecture and Nature*, Stuttgart: University of Stuttgart, pp. 57–65.

Gallagher, R. and T. Appenzeller (1999), 'Beyond reductionism', *Science*, **284** (5411), 79.

Grassberger, P. (1983), 'Generalized dimensions of strange attractors', *Physics Letters A*, **97** (6), 227–30.

Hao, B.L. (1986), 'Fractals and fractal dimensions', *Science*, **38** (1), 9–17 (in Chinese).

Hao, B.L. (2004), *Chaos and Fractals*, Shanghai: Shanghai Science and Technology Press (in Chinese).

Haynes, A.H. (1975), 'Dimensional analysis: some applications in human geography', *Geographical Analysis*, **7** (1), 51–68.

Huang, L.S. and Y.G. Chen (2018), 'A comparison between two OLS-based approaches to estimating urban multifractal parameters', *Fractals*, **26** (1), 1850019.

Jiang, S.G. and Y.X. Zhou (2006), 'The fractal urban form of Beijing and its practical significance', *Geographical Research*, **25** (2), 204–13 (in Chinese).

Kwan, M.P. (2012), 'The uncertain geographic context problem', *Annals of the Association of American Geographers*, **102** (5), 958–68.

Lee, Y. (1989), 'An allmetric analysis of the US urban system: 1960–80', *Environment and Planning A*, **21** (4), 463–76.

Liu, S.D. and S.K. Liu (1994), *Solitary Wave and Turbulence*, Shanghai: Shanghai Scientific and Technological Education Publishing House (in Chinese).

Mandelbrot, B.B. (1982), *The Fractal Geometry of Nature*, New York: W.H. Freeman.

Mandelbrot, B.B. (1989), 'Fractal geometry: what is it, and what does it do?', *Proceedings of the Royal Society of London A: Mathematical and Physical Sciences*, **423** (1864), 3–16.

Murcio, R., A.P. Masucci, E. Arcaute and M. Batty (2015), 'Multifractal to monofractal evolution of the London street network', *Physical Review E*, **92** (December), 062130.

Openshaw, S. (1983), *The Modifiable Areal Unit Problem*, Norwich: Geo Books.

Portugali, J. (2000), *Self-Organization and the City*, Berlin: Springer.

Smeed, R.J. (1963), 'Road development in urban area', *Journal of the Institution of Highway Engineers*, **10** (1), 5–30.

Stanley, H.E. and P. Meakin (1988), 'Multifractal phenomena in physics and chemistry', *Nature*, **335** (September), 405–9.

Takayasu, H. (1990), *Fractals in the Physical Sciences*, Manchester: Manchester University Press.

Unwin, D.J. (1996), 'GIS, spatial analysis and spatial statistics', *Progress in Human Geography*, **20** (4), 540–51.

Vicsek, T. (1989), *Fractal Growth Phenomena*, Singapore: World Scientific.

Waldrop, M. (1992), *Complexity: The Emerging of Science at the Edge of Order and Chaos*, New York: Simon and Schuster.

Wang, F.Q. and H.Q. Li (1996), *Fractals – the Artistic Structure of Nature*, Jinan: Shandong Education Press (in Chinese).

West, G.B. (2017), *Scale: The Universal Laws of Growth, Innovation, Sustainability, and the Pace of Life in Organisms, Cities, Economies, and Companies*, London: Penguin Press.

White, R. and G. Engelen (1993), 'Cellular automata and fractal urban form: a cellular modeling approach to the evolution of urban land-use patterns', *Environment and Planning A*, **25** (8), 1175–99.

White, R. and G. Engelen (1994), 'Urban systems dynamics and cellular automata: fractal structures between order and chaos', *Chaos, Solitons & Fractals*, **4** (4), 563–83.

Wilson, A.G. (2000), *Complex Spatial Systems: The Modelling Foundations of Urban and Regional Analysis*, Singapore: Pearson Education.

10. Cybernetic cities: designing and controlling adaptive and robust urban systems

Carlos Gershenson, Paolo Santi and Carlo Ratti

1. INTRODUCTION

Cities have become central to our species, with an increasing majority of people living in them (Cohen 2003; Butler 2010) and producing most of the wealth of our globalized society (Dobbs et al. 2011; Sassen 2011). They serve as magnets for migration as they offer several advantages and opportunities over rural areas (Bettencourt et al. 2007; Bettencourt and West 2010; Glaeser 2011). Densification of population is desirable for a sustainable urban development. However, a high population density also generates several problems which we must face, better sooner than later. We can identify urban problems related to mobility (Gakenheimer 1999), pollution (Bulkeley and Betsill 2003), sanitation (Jacobi et al. 2010), segregation (Musterd and Ostendorf 2013), marginalization (Adler de Lomnitz 1975) and crime (Glaeser and Sacerdote 1996), to name just a few.

Even when we are increasingly dependent on urban systems, they are becoming unmanageable with traditional techniques. This is owing to the inherent complexity of cities. The term complexity comes from the Latin *plexus*, which means intertwined. A complex system's elements are difficult to separate. As elements are interdependent, their future depends not only on initial and boundary conditions, but also on the interactions that take place in time and space, generating novel information (Gershenson 2013b). This information, generated by interactions, limits predictability. Since traditional techniques (such as optimization) rely on predictability, they cannot cope with the increasing complexity of our urban systems.

Complexity is increasing as interactions and interdependencies are increasing. A more connected system can have advantages; since information, energy and matter can spread faster through it, it can respond faster to changes (Khanna 2016). However, an increased connectivity also has its drawbacks; with many components affecting each other, this can potentially increase the fragility of a system (Taleb 2012; Helbing 2013).

Given the complex nature of urban systems, they change constantly (Batty 1971), and thus problems change as well, that is, they are non-stationary (Gershenson 2007). Moreover, we humans are complex and changing on our own and as part of cities, making them hybrid complex systems (Portugali 2011, 2016). That is, cities can be seen as cyber-physical and cyber-social systems (Gershenson 2020). This implies that trying to find optimized solutions will be inefficient, as the optimal solution changes with the problem. If traditional techniques cannot cope with the complexity and dynamics of urban systems, how can we regulate them? Adaptation is required to let urban systems change their behavior according to their current situation (Gershenson 2013a; Rauws and De Roo 2016). We have plenty of examples of adaptation in living systems, which can serve as an inspiration for urban solutions (Alexander 2003–04; Gershenson 2013c).

2.   CYBERNETICS

The term cybernetics comes from the Ancient Greek *kybernētēs*, which means steersman or governor. Plato used it to refer to the self-governance of city states. Ampère described *la cybernétique* as the science of governance. Its modern usage as the study of 'control and communication in the animal and the machine' came in mid-twentieth century (Wiener 1948; Ashby 1956; Pask 1961). It was in this movement that the study of adaptivity in systems began. The relevance of cybernetics lies in that it was the first scientific attempt to study phenomena independently from their substrate, focusing more on the function of systems than on their composition (Gershenson et al. 2014). This enabled the cross-fertilization of different scientific fields, for example, electrical engineering and neuroscience, where similar functions are required by systems composed by different components.

One of the most used concepts from cybernetics is that of the control loop (Heylighen and Joslyn 2001). As illustrated in Figure 10.1, a controller perceives inputs from the controlled, and acts with its outputs on the controlled. The controlled has its own dynamics, that is, its variables are changing. This is why the controller must perceive, to detect the changes, make decisions and take actions to keep the variables controller within a desired state. Note that control loops can take place at multiple scales: subunits, units, modules, systems or metasystems.

In general, a controller will try to steer a system (controlled) towards a goal (desired state, configuration or behavior). Note that goals are set by an observer or designer, and different people probably will disagree on what the proper goals of a system should be, or how to prioritize them. Perturbations (internal or external) might deviate the system, so the controller should compensate those perturbations. This can be achieved by buffering, feedback or feedforward mechanisms. As illustrated in Figure 10.2, these mechanisms can be used to counteract the effect of perturbations on the controlled systems. Buffering is passive. It diminishes or nullifies the effect of perturbations. For example, insulation reduces the effect of temperature differences. Feedback mechanisms act after the system has been perturbed, trying to return the variables of the system to their desired state. For example, a thermostat can detect that the temperature is lower than desired and switch on the heating until the desired temperature is reached. Feedforward mechanisms act before the perturbation manages to affect the system to prevent their effect. For example,

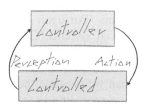

Figure 10.1   An abstract cybernetic control loop

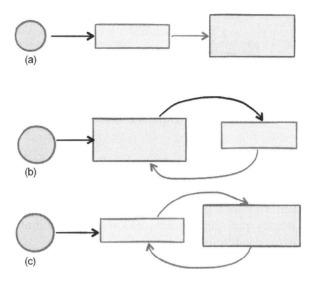

Figure 10.2   *Perturbations (circles) on systems (larger rectangles) can be controlled by (a) buffering, (b) feedback or (c) feedforward mechanisms (smaller rectangles)*

if a smart thermostat knows that the temperature might decrease at night, it might switch on the heating before the temperature decreases, so it never leaves its desired state. Feedback and feedforward mechanisms are active. A system can adapt to perturbations using these mechanisms.

We can define adaptation as 'a change in an agent or system as a response to a state of its environment that will help the agent or system to fulfill its goals' (Gershenson 2007, p. 19). Adaptation can be achieved by reaction (feedback mechanisms) or anticipation (feedforward mechanisms). Feedback can be positive, increasing the effect of the perturbation (sometimes leading to a phase transition), or negative, reducing the effect of the perturbation (for example, using the enslaving principle; Haken 1981). It would be desirable to predict all possible perturbations to a system, so that they could be handled before they can affect the variables of a controlled system using anticipation. However, since predictability is limited owing to complexity (Morin 2007), we can always expect unexpected perturbations. For all the unpredictable perturbations, it is necessary to react *a posteriori* using feedback mechanisms.

To prevent the effect of perturbations, buffering can increase the robustness of systems. A system is robust if it continues to function in the face of perturbations (Wagner 2005). Robustness is desirable to minimize perturbations, but since change is unavoidable, adaptation (active control) is required; on the one hand, because all perturbations cannot be predicted (in order to build a perfect buffer) and, on the other, because too much robustness can limit adaptation (Gershenson et al. 2006). Moreover, adaptation can increase robustness, as adaptive change is made precisely to preserve the function of a system.

These and other cybernetic concepts have permeated into all disciplines. For example, Stafford Beer used cybernetic concepts to achieve adaptive organizations (Beer 1966;

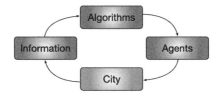

Figure 10.3   Requirements of cybernetic cities: an urban control loop

Gershenson 2008). This was applied at a national scale in Chile in the early 1970s with the Cybersyn project (Medina 2011), which served as a nervous system for the country. Unfortunately, the system was dismantled in 1973 by the dictatorship. Cybernetic ideas also found their way into the built environment with responsive architecture (Negroponte 1975; Beesley et al. 2006), where sensors enable buildings to adapt to their environment and current conditions.

With the propagation of personal computers (Pagels 1989), the scientific study of complex systems (Bar-Yam 1997; Mitchell 2009) continued the cybernetic tradition of studying phenomena in respect of their properties and functions. More recently, network science has provided tools for studying the components of complex systems (represented as nodes) and their interactions (represented as links) (Newman et al. 2006; Newman 2010). This has enabled the application of concepts developed in different disciplines – including cybernetics, complex systems and network science – to the understanding of urban systems (Batty 2005; Portugali et al. 2012; Batty 2013b; Bettencourt 2013). As technology has progressed, there have been several examples of the benefits of adaptivity in urban systems (Gershenson 2013c).

In this chapter, we sketch an urban theory that addresses the requirements to build cybernetic cities, their features and their effects. We divide the requirements into three components: information, algorithms and agents. These loosely correspond to the cybernetic sensors, control and actuators, as illustrated in Figure 10.3. Traditionally, humans have fulfilled the roles of information, algorithms and agents. However, advances in technology are assisting or replacing humans in different aspects of this urban control loop.

In the next sections, we detail information, algorithms and agents, before presenting the implications of building such adaptive cities.

3.   INFORMATION

Information can be understood as anything that an agent can sense, perceive or observe (Sloman 2011; Gershenson 2012). This is in accordance with Shannon's (1948) definition, in that receiving information reduces uncertainty (Prokopenko et al. 2009). Any system requires information about the situation it is facing to make better-than-chance decisions. This is evident in animals but applies to any system. Without relevant information, how could a system make the correct choice from a variety of potential decisions?

In urban systems, there are different sources of information which can be exploited for different purposes, such as measuring pollution or detecting traffic jams. Smart-city initiatives have integrated sensors pervasively (Perera et al. 2014), from parking spaces (Pierce and Shoup 2013) to trash bins (Gea et al. 2013). On the one hand, sensor and information and communication technology (ICT) costs are being reduced. On the other, the number of devices connected to the Internet of things (IoT) (Sarma et al. 2000; Gershenfeld et al. 2004; Atzori et al. 2010) is increasing. This creates the opportunity to obtain big data at a scale, never before possible (Batty 2013a).

Nevertheless, most urban sensors and the information they generate have been the property of private companies. As an alternative, some cities have crowdsourced their information collection. For example, the City of Boston released the application (app) Street Bump (Carrera et al. 2013) to allow drivers to use their smartphones to automatically report potholes. This data-donation approach (Castillo et al. 2014) reduces the cost of sensor deployment, as most citizens carry potential sensors in their pockets (Ratti et al. 2006; Gonzalez et al. 2008) and smartphones are becoming increasingly pervasive. Still, the massive adoption by citizens of the data-donation approach is a main obstacle for cities obtaining relevant information for free. There has been a certain success of crowdsourced information (Lee et al. 2016) with platforms such as Ushahidi (Okolloh 2009; Marsden 2013) or Influenzanet (Paolotti et al. 2014) but, in these report-based initiatives, information has to be entered by a human, thus limiting the amount and speed of information received. Also, simply data-mining big data can be misleading (Lazer et al. 2014). Gamification has also been used to promote user participation, although with limited success (Odobasic et al. 2013).

Another approach for obtaining information is from data citizens voluntarily publish on social networks, such as Twitter (Bollen et al. 2011; Dodds et al. 2011; Bertrand et al. 2013; Piña-Garcia et al. 2016). This research has focused on detecting moods and emotions, but it has the potential to expand to gain insights into further aspects of urban and social life (Axhausen 2008; Cho et al. 2011). This is relevant because many variables in urban systems are subjective, such as social values, solidarity, justice, fashion and popularity, and others related to ethics, public opinion and political inclinations, for example. However, that they are (partially) subjective does not mean that they are not relevant, nor that they can be measured.

An important aspect concerning urban information is that of privacy (Helbing and Balietti 2011; Lane et al. 2014; Enserink and Chin 2015), as it has been shown that, under particular conditions, few data are required to uniquely identify citizens (de Montjoye et al. 2013, 2015). Information is required for adaptive cities, but there are potential risks if specific information becomes public. This creates a tension between efforts which strive for open access to information and individual privacy, which has led to proposals for data anonymization (Ghinita et al. 2007; de Montjoye et al. 2014) and self-regulatory information sharing (Pournaras et al. 2016).

4.   ALGORITHMS

We are having an increasing amount of information at our disposal; but what to do with it (Harford 2014)? That is, what is the best way of extracting meaning out of this information (Haken and Portugali 2015)? One approach would be to use artificial intelligence to process information (Arel et al. 2010). Still, many algorithms have been proposed and it seems that each is useful in a particular context. That is, there is no general detailed recipe for understanding all possible information that sensors could gather. Moreover, there are reasons to believe that there will never be such a recipe (Wolpert and Macready 1995, 1997).

There are deeper limitations that go beyond not having a general recipe for solving problems. Even if we had all relevant information in real time about an urban system, our predictability is limited by their complexity (Gershenson and Heylighen 2005): the components of urban systems are constantly interacting, and these interactions produce novel information which cannot be found in initial or boundary conditions (Gershenson 2013b). Since our predictability is limited, optimization has to be complemented with adaptation (Gershenson 2013a).

We might not have ready-made algorithms to solve every possible problem, but we can have methodologies which will assist their design. One of these methodologies is based on self-organization (Gershenson 2007). An example of self-organization can be seen with collective motion (Vicsek and Zafeiris 2012): elements interact to generate a global pattern. This pattern is not determined by a single individual, nor by an external source, but is the product of the interactions of the elements. The components generate the pattern, but the pattern also regulates the components. A system described as self-organizing is a system in which elements interact in order to dynamically achieve a global function or behavior. Self-organization can help us build adaptive systems, as elements can self-organize when the conditions change, at the same timescale at which changes occur. Thus, with self-organizing algorithms we can face the unpredictability of urban systems inherent in their complexity (Ottino 2004; Frei and Di Marzo Serugendo 2011; Yamu et al. 2015).

Examples of algorithms that use self-organization to regulate urban problems have already been proposed for coordinating traffic lights (Gershenson 2005; Lämmer and Helbing 2008), regulating public transport (Gershenson 2011), logistics (Helbing et al. 2006), managing human organizations (Gershenson 2008) and synchronization in power grids (Rohden et al. 2012), among others. They are promising for building cybernetic cities (Gershenson 2013c; Yamu et al. 2015; Rauws and De Roo 2016), as they use real-time information and self-organizing algorithms to achieve an efficiency close to optimal (Virágh et al. 2014; Zubillaga et al. 2014); or, even, supraoptimal (Gershenson 2011; Tachet et al. 2016), that is, the performance being better than what traditional theories predicted.

Nevertheless, self-organization also has limitations. If all control is based on local information, sometimes the performance will be worse than considering global information. This depends on the precise problem. Finding the right balance between local and global control is one of the challenges of adaptive systems (Forrest and Mitchell 2016) (see law of requisite variety in section 6 of this chapter). However, we know that once this balance is found, the system will adapt in the best possible way.

5. AGENTS

Information processed by algorithms has to impact urban systems through agents, that is, entities that act on their environment. Citizens are certainly agents, as we constantly act on the urban fabric. However, we are embedded in sociotechnical systems which constrain and promote our actions, and can produce actions of their own (Vespignani 2012; Helbing 2015).

Sociotechnical systems are highly complex (Vespignani 2009), and this complexity limits their predictability. Not only do interactions between components of urban systems generate novel information, but agents acting on cities will change the environment for the rest of the agents. Actions are evidently essential but, in many cases, solutions can potentially generate novel problems. This is another reason for requiring adaptation in urban systems: if agents are changing urban problems while trying to solve them, our solutions must adapt to the changes that they themselves induce.

Technology is not only increasing the information we can collect, but also the agency of humans. We are coordinating actions in ways which were not possible only a few years ago (Marsden 2013). This capability has been useful for disaster response and has the potential to improve other urban systems, empowering citizens to act by exploiting information and algorithms.

Artificial agents in cities have been increasing their degree of autonomy for decision-making in recent decades. For example, traditional traffic lights have to be set up by humans. Semi-autonomous systems allow for the adjustment of phases of traffic lights, with supervision and potential override by humans. Fully autonomous systems do not require human intervention to operate, and adapt to changes in their environment (Gershenson 2005).

Perhaps the largest transformation we are witnessing in cities is related to the automation of vehicles. Their potential impact on urban mobility is manifold, as they promise to increase safety and efficiency while reducing emissions and congestion. However, there are many open questions on the precise way in which autonomous vehicles will be introduced into cities. Will they be owned by individuals? Shared by companies? Used as public transport by city governments? Probably all of these, but the most appropriate balance still has to be decided.

Autonomous vehicles are promising not only for the transportation of citizens, but also for logistic and delivery services. Also, they are not restricted to cars, as autonomous boats and drones will probably find their niche as well.

From this perspective of autonomous vehicles, how much of a city can be automatized? Could a city self-regulate most of its systems? To do this, information, algorithms and agents must be integrated properly, as discussed in the next section.

6.   IMPLICATIONS

Traditionally, urban planning has taken care of control in cities. However, the feedback mechanisms are so slow that a single control loop could take decades. Systems that can adapt at the scales at which changes occur can be potentially more efficient than those that do not. A key difference between the cybernetic and the traditional view of a city is adaptation speed. A cybernetic city will strive to adapt as fast as relevant changes occur. It is only recently that we have the technology to achieve this, and the changes can be seen. We have been increasing the adaptation speed of different urban systems.

If we want to build cybernetic urban systems, we must ask ourselves: how will we obtain relevant information? Which algorithms will we use? Which agents will act on the city? If we do not have a clear answer to one of these questions, it will be serendipitous if our system performs as desired. Also, it is not only proper information, algorithms and agents that we need to have. These also must be integrated effectively, that is, the information acquired from the city has to be available to algorithms, algorithms should coordinate agents and agents need to act on the city.

If we manage to develop information, algorithms and agents, and integrate them to solve an urban problem, what would be the outcome? What is the benefit of having cybernetic urban systems?

Imagine we had all relevant information about urban mobility in a whole city: where all citizens and vehicles are and where they are heading. Combining historic and current information, we could develop self-organizing algorithms that can find the best possible route for every citizen, for every vehicle. If these algorithms manage to act on all citizens and vehicles (easier with autonomy), then we could say that such a city would have optimal mobility. This mobility would be optimal not because there would be no waiting times, but because there would be no better option given the current circumstances of demand and infrastructure. This system could also detect where new infrastructure would have the greatest impact for improving urban mobility, or where it might be most fragile. These suggestions could guide cities in building the most efficient and resilient transportation systems possible. Technically, it could be done already. In practice, we do not have access to all relevant information, and it is not obvious that we will ever have it. We can understand why such a system would produce optimal mobility, owing to Ashby's law of requisite variety (Ashby 1956; Bar-Yam 2004; Gershenson 2015): in order to respond to a given variety of states in its environment, a control system must have at least the same variety. That is, a system must be able to distinguish all different possible states which require a different action. Note that variety grows exponentially, so it is not feasible to directly specify the requisite variety of the controller. This is precisely why adaptivity is necessary. Systems with a large variety will often be in states never before visited. An adaptive controller does not require all states to be predefined to react in an efficient way, which is why algorithms are used instead of functions.

Humans have a limited variety, and our control is also limited. Technology is allowing us to leverage some of that variety. In this way, we can expand our control capabilities, by exploiting technology to do some of the controlling. Moreover, technology also can be used for coordination. This can combine the variety of several humans or artificial systems to tackle systems with even more variety.

More variety implies more complexity. This precisely requires an integration of information, algorithms and agents. If a system to regulate urban mobility has at least the same variety as the whole transportation system, that is, all possible combinations, then it will be able to respond to all possible situations. Thus, it will always be optimal, given the circumstances. The same reasoning applies to any urban system: if through the proper integration of information, algorithms and agents we can have at least the same variety as the urban aspect the system is trying to control, then our adaptive urban system will be optimal, that is, performing in the best possible way for the given circumstances. If a controller does not have enough variety (less than the controlled), then we can distribute control using self-organization, increasing effectively the variety across several controllers. The precise scales at which control should be applied will depend on the variety of the controlled at different scales.

Even if we manage to achieve such optimality with cybernetic urban systems, we must be cautious. If we are considering only specific variables for optimization, it does not imply that we are solving a problem completely. For example, even if we achieve maximum efficiency in urban mobility, such a system would not solve social issues which are partly an outcome of the processes which shape a city. Integrating a broader set of variables in the development of cybernetic systems requires communication between all sectors of society. We are still in the exploratory process of finding efficient ways of achieving such communication (Zuckerman 2014) and promoting social participation (Pickard et al. 2011). This would certainly be necessary if we intend to achieve optimal governance or sustainability (Trantopoulos et al. 2011).

Cities have made efforts in recent years to increase their sustainability and resilience (Stumpp 2013). The discourse on resilient cities has focused mainly on hazards (Godschalk 2003) and climate change (Newman et al. 2009; Prasad 2009), which can also benefit from the concepts described here (Pickett et al. 2004).

7.   CONCLUSIONS

Adaptive cities have the potential to increase quality of life for citizens (Ratti and Claudel 2016), but how equitable will this increase of quality of life be? Will all citizens benefit? At what cost? This is relevant, as even when cities accumulate most of the wealth of the planet, they are also the loci of greatest inequality. The answers to these questions will depend on how the cybernetic urban technology is implemented, regulated and managed in each city, and how this technology relates to citizens. This will require the effective interaction of governments, companies, academia and society, as each sector may have different perceptions of the best way of managing cities.

For example, autonomous vehicles have a great potential to improve urban mobility. However, will this technology benefit few private companies, and/or the majority of citizens? The same technology can enslave or emancipate; the difference lies in how we use it. Also, the question is not so much who owns the technology. The key is how much can it interact. For example, initially, the Internet infrastructure was mainly owned by academic and government institutions. Now mainly private companies own the infrastructure. However, their business models allow the Internet to be an open system with standards where new technology and applications can thrive. Dedicated short-range communications (DSRC) have been designed specifically for automotive communication. Yet there are important differences across countries, which limit compatibility as global standards are lacking. If this does not change, it will be difficult for vehicles to communicate among themselves and with infrastructure. Imagine that each website would require a different browser. If interactions are not possible, the potential of urban systems will be limited. For public transportation systems, the General Transit Feed Specification (GTFS) standard has been adopted by most cities, allowing information to be shared and exploited for novel applications (Antrim and Barbeau 2013). The same would occur with standards in other urban systems. The future of urban systems will depend not so much on who owns them, but on how openly can we interact with them.

ACKNOWLEDGEMENTS

We should like to thank Juval Portugali and Anthony Vanky for useful suggestions. C.G. was supported by PASPA program from UNAM's DGAPA and CONACYT projects 212802, 221341, 260021, and SNI membership 47907.

REFERENCES

Adler de Lomnitz, L. (1975), *Cómo sobreviven los marginados*, Mexico: Siglo XXI.

Alexander, C. (2003–04), *The Nature of Order: An Essay on the Art of Building and the Nature of the Universe*, vols 1–4. Berkeley, CA: Center for Environmental Structure.

Antrim, A. and S.J. Barbeau (2013), 'The many uses of GTFS data – opening the door to transit and multimodal applications', technical report, Location-Aware Information Systems Laboratory, University of South Florida, accessed 7 May 2021 at http://tinyurl.com/gv5n77z.

Arel, I., D.C. Rose and T.P. Karnowski (2010), 'Deep machine learning – a new frontier in artificial intelligence research', *IEEE Computational Intelligence Magazine*, **5** (4), 13–18, doi:10.1109/MCI.2010.938364.

Ashby, W.R. (1956), *An Introduction to Cybernetics*, London: Chapman & Hall.

Atzori, L., A. Iera and G. Morabito (2010), 'The internet of things: a survey', *Computer Networks*, **54** (15), 2787–805, doi:10.1016/j.comnet.2010.05.010.

Axhausen, K.W. (2008), 'Social networks, mobility biographies, and travel: survey challenges', *Environment and Planning B: Planning and Design*, **35** (6), 981–96, doi:10.1068/ b3316t.

Bar-Yam, Y. (1997), *Dynamics of Complex Systems*, Boulder, CO: Westview Press.

Bar-Yam, Y. (2004), 'Multiscale variety in complex systems', *Complexity*, **9** (4), 37–45, accessed 7 May 2021 at https://necsi.edu/multiscale-variety-in-complex-systems.

Batty, M. (1971), 'Modelling cities as dynamic systems', *Nature*, **231** (18 June), 425–8, doi:10.1038/231425a0.

Batty, M. (2005), *Cities and Complexity*. Cambridge, MA: MIT Press.

Batty, M. (2013a), 'Big data, smart cities and city planning', *Dialogues in Human Geography*, **3** (3), 274–9, doi:10.1177/ 2043820613513390.

Batty, M. (2013b), *The New Science of Cities*, Cambridge, MA: MIT Press.

Beer, S. (1966), *Decision and Control: The Meaning of Operational Research and Management Cybernetics*, New York: John Wiley and Sons.

Beesley, P., S. Hirosue, J. Ruxton, M. Trankle and C. Turner (2006), *Responsive Architectures: Subtle Technologies*, Cambridge, ON: Riverside Architectural Press.

Bertrand, K., M. Bialik, K. Virdee, A. Gros and Y. Bar-Yam (2013), 'Sentiment in New York City: a high resolution spatial and temporal view', 20 August, accessed 7 May 2021 at http://www.necsi.edu/research/social/newyork.

Bettencourt, L.M.A. (2013), 'The origins of scaling in cities', *Science*, **340** (6139), 1438–41, doi:10.1126/science.1235823.

Bettencourt, L. and G. West (2010), 'A unified theory of urban living', *Nature*, **467** (7318), 912–13, doi:10.1038/467912a.

Bettencourt, L.M.A., J. Lobo, D. Helbing, C. Kühnert and G.B. West (2007), 'Growth, innovation, scaling, and the pace of life in cities', *PNAS*, **104** (17), 7301–6, doi:10.1073/pnas.0610172104.

Bollen, J., A. Pepe and H. Mao (2011), 'Modeling public mood and emotion: Twitter sentiment and socioeconomic phenomena', in *Proceedings of the Fifth International AAAI Conference on Weblogs and Social Media (ICWSM 2011)*, 17–21 July, Barcelona, pp. 450–53, accessed 7 May 2021 at http://arxiv.org/abs/0911.1583.

Bulkeley, H. and M.M. Betsill (2003), *Cities and Climate Change: Urban Sustainability and Global Environmental Governance*, London and New York: Routledge.

Butler, D. (2010), 'Cities: the century of the city', *Nature*, **467** (7318), 900–901, doi:10.1038/467900a.

Carrera, F., S. Guerin and J. Thorp (2013), 'By the people, for the people: the crowdsourcing of "streetbump": an automatic pothole mapping app', in C. Ellul, S. Zlatanova, M. Rumor and R. Laurini (eds), *International Archives of the Photogrammetry, Remote Sensing and Spatial Information Sciences*, vol. XL-4/W1, London: ISPRS, pp. 19–23.

Castillo, J., C. Gershenson and G. Gómez-Mont (2014), 'Living mobilities', Audi Urban Future Award 2014 winners, accessed 7 May 2021 at http://arq911.com/portfolio/aufa-2014-2/.

Cho, E., S.A. Myers and J. Leskovec (2011), 'Friendship and mobility: user movement in location-based social networks', in *Proceedings of the 17th ACM SIGKDD International Conference on Knowledge Discovery and Data Mining, KDD '11*, New York: ACM. pp. 1082–1090, doi:10.1145/2020408.2020579.

Cohen, J.E. (2003), 'Human population: the next half century', *Science*, **302** (5648), 1172–5, doi:10.1126/science.1088665.

De Montjoye, Y.A., C.A. Hidalgo, M. Verleysen and V.D. Blondel (2013), 'Unique in the crowd: the privacy bounds of human mobility', *Scientific Reports*, **3** (1376), 1–5, doi:10.1038/srep01376.

De Montjoye, Y.A., L. Radaelli, V.K. Singh and A.S. Pentland (2015), 'Unique in the shopping mall: on the reidentifiability of credit card metadata', *Science*, **347** (6221), 536–9, accessed 7 May 2021 at http://science.sciencemag.org/content/347/6221/536.abstract.

De Montjoye, Y.A., E. Shmueli, S.S. Wang and A.S. Pentland (2014), 'OpenPDS: protecting the privacy of metadata through safe answers', *PLoS ONE*, **9** (7), 1–9, doi:10.1371/journal.pone.0098790.

Dobbs, R., S. Smit, J. Remes, J. Manyika, C. Roxburgh and A. Restrepo (2011), *Urban World: Mapping the Economic Power of Cities*, Washington, DC: McKinsey Global Institute, accessed 7 May 2021 at https://www.mckinsey.com/featured-insights/urbanization/urban-world-mapping-the-economic-power-of-cities.

Dodds, P.S., K.D. Harris, I.M. Kloumann, C.A. Bliss and C.M. Danforth (2011), 'Temporal patterns of happiness and information in a global social network: hedonometrics and twitter', *PLoS ONE*, **6** (12), e26752, doi:10.1371/journal.pone.0026752.

Enserink, M. and G. Chin (2015), 'The end of privacy', *Science*, **347** (6221), 490–91, doi:10.1126/science.347.6221.490.

Forrest, S. and M. Mitchell (2016), 'Adaptive computation: the multidisciplinary legacy of John J. Holland', *Communicatuons of the ACM*, **59** (8), 58–63, doi:10.1145/2964342.

Frei, R. and G. Di Marzo Serugendo (2011), 'Advances in complexity engineering', *International Journal of Bio-Inspired Computation*, **3** (4), 199–212, accessed 7 May 2021 at http://cui.unige.ch/~dimarzo/papers/AdvancesComplexity.pdf.

Gakenheimer, R. (1999), 'Urban mobility in the developing world', *Transportation Research Part A: Policy and Practice*, **33** (7–8), 671–89, doi:1016/S0965-8564(99)00005-1.

Gea, T., J. Paradells, M. Lamarca and D. Roldán (2013), 'Smart cities as an application of internet of things: Experiences and lessons learnt in Barcelona', in *Innovative Mobile and Internet Services in Ubiquitous Computing (IMIS), 2013 Seventh International Conference on*, pp. 552–7, doi:10.1109/IMIS.2013.158.

Gershenfeld, N., R. Krikorian and D. Cohen (2004), 'The internet of things', *Scientific American*, **291** (4), 76–81, accessed 7 May 2021 at http://www.scientificamerican.com/article/the-internet-of-things/.

Gershenson, C. (2005), 'Self-organizing traffic lights', *Complex Systems*, **16** (1), 29–53, accessed 7 May 2021 at http://www.complex-systems.com/pdf/16-1-2.pdf.

Gershenson, C. (2007), *Design and Control of Self-organizing System*, Mexico City: CopIt Arxives.

Gershenson, C. (2008), 'Towards self-organizing bureaucracies', *International Journal of Public Information Systems*, **4** (1), 1–24, accessed 7 May 2021 at http://www.ijpis.net/ojs/index.php/IJPIS/article/view/51.

Gershenson, C. (2011), 'Self-organization leads to supraoptimal performance in public transportation systems', *PLoS ONE* **6**(6), e21469, doi:10.1371/journal.pone.0021469.

Gershenson, C. (2012), 'The world as evolving information', in A. Minai, D. Braha and Y. Bar-Yam (eds), *Unifying Themes in Complex Systems*, vol. 7, Berlin and Heidelberg: Springer, pp. 100–115.

Gershenson, C. (2013a), 'Facing complexity: prediction vs. adaptation', in A. Massip and A. Bastardas (eds), *Complexity Perspectives on Language, Communication and Society*, Berlin and Heidelberg: Springer, pp. 3–14.

Gershenson, C. (2013b), 'The implications of interactions for science and philosophy', *Foundations of Science*, **18** (4), 781–90, doi:10.1007/s10699-012-9305-8.

Gershenson, C. (2013c), 'Living in living cities', *Artificial Life*, **19** (3 and 4), 401–20, doi:10.1162/ARTL a 00112.

Gershenson, C. (2015), 'Requisite variety, autopoiesis, and self-organization', *Kybernetes*, **44** (6–7), 866–73, accessed 7 May 2021 at https://www.emerald.com/insight/content/doi/10.1108/K-01-2015-0001/full/html.

Gershenson, C. (2020), 'Guiding the self-organization of cyber-physical systems', *Frontiers in Robotics and AI*, **7** (April), 1–13, doi:10.3389/frobt.2020.00041.

Gershenson, C. and F. Heylighen (2005), 'How can we think the complex?', in K. Richardson (ed.), *Managing Organizational Complexity: Philosophy, Theory and Application*, Charlotte, NC: Information Age, pp. 47–61.

Gershenson, C., S.A. Kauffman and I. Shmulevich (2006), 'The role of redundancy in the robustness of random Boolean networks', in L.M. Rocha, L.S. Yaeger, M.A. Bedau, D. Floreano, R.L. Goldstone and A. Vespignani (eds), *Artificial Life X, Proceedings of the Tenth International Conference on the Simulation and Synthesis of Living Systems*, Cambridge, MA: MIT Press, pp. 35–42.

Gershenson, C., P. Csermely, P. Erdi, H. Knyazeva and A. Laszlo (2014), 'The past, present and future of cybernetics and systems research', *Systema: Connecting Matter, Life, Culture and Technology*, **1** (3), 4–13, accessed 7 May 2021 at http://www.systems-journal.eu/article/view/213.

Ghinita, G., P. Karras, P. Kalnis and N. Mamoulis (2007), 'Fast data anonymization with low information loss', in *Proceedings of the 33rd International Conference on Very Large Data Bases, VLDB '07*, Vienna: VLDB Endowment, pp. 758–69.

Glaeser, E. (2011), 'Cities, productivity, and quality of life', *Science*, **333** (6042), 592–4, doi:10.1126/science.1209264.

Glaeser, E.L. and B. Sacerdote (1996), 'Why is there more crime in cities?', Technical Report 5430, National Bureau of Economic Research, Cambridge, MA, accessed 7 May 2021 at http://www.nber.org/papers/w5430.

Godschalk, D. (2003), 'Urban hazard mitigation: creating resilient cities', *Natural Hazards Review*, **4** (3), 136–43, doi:10.1061/ (ASCE)1527-6988(2003)4:3(136).

Gonzalez, M.C., C.A. Hidalgo and A.L. Barabasi (2008), 'Understanding individual human mobility patterns', *Nature*, **453** (7196), 779–82, doi:10.1038/nature06958.

Haken, H. (1981), 'Synergetics and the problem of selforganization', in G. Roth and H. Schwegler (eds), *Self-Organizing Systems: An Interdisciplinary Approach*, New York: Campus Verlag, pp. 9–13.

Haken, H. and J. Portugali (2015), *Information Adaptation: The Interplay between Shannon Information and Semantic Information in Cognition*, vol. 12, Cham, Heidelberg, New York, Dordrecht and London: Springer.

Harford, T. (2014), 'Big data: a big mistake?', *Significance*, **11** (5), 14–19, doi:10.1111/j.1740-9713.2014.00778.x.

Helbing, D. (2013), 'Globally networked risks and how to respond', *Nature*, **497** (7447), 51–9, doi:10.1038/nature12047.

Helbing, D. (2015), *Thinking Ahead-Essays on Big Data, Digital Revolution, and Participatory Market Society*, Cham: Springer.

Helbing, D. and S. Balietti (2011), 'From social data mining to forecasting socio-economic crises', *European Physical Journal Special Topics*, **195** (1), 3–68, doi:10.1140/epjst/ e2011-01401-8.

Helbing, D., T. Seidel, S. Lämmer and K. Peters (2006), 'Self-organization principles in supply networks and production systems', in B.K. Chakrabarti, A. Chakraborti and A. Chatterjee (eds), *Econophysics and Sociophysics*, Weinheim: Wiley, pp. 535–59.

Heylighen, F. and C. Joslyn (2001), 'Cybernetics and second order cybernetics', in R.A. Meyers (ed.), *Encyclopedia of Physical Science and Technology*, vol. 4, 3rd edn, New York: Academic Press, pp. 155–70.

Jacobi, P., M. Kjellen, G. McGranahan, J. Songsore and C. Surjadi (2010), *The Citizens at Risk: From Urban Sanitation to Sustainable Cities*, London and New York: Routledge.

Khanna, P. (2016), *Connectography: Mapping the Future of Global Civilization*, New York: Random House.

Lämmer, S. and D. Helbing (2008), 'Self-control of traffic lights and vehicle flows in urban road networks', *Journal of Statistical Mechanics*, (April), 1–34, doi:10.1088/1742-5468/2008/04/P04019.

Lane, J., V. Stodden, S. Bender and H. Nissenbaum (eds) (2014), *Privacy, Big Data, and the Public Good: Frameworks for Engagement*, New York: Cambridge University Press.

Lazer, D., R. Kennedy, G. King and A. Vespignani (2014), 'The parable of google flu: Traps in big data analysis', *Science*, **343** (6176), 1203–5, doi:10.1126/science. 1248506.

Lee, M., E. Almirall and J. Wareham (2016), 'Open data and civic apps: first-generation failures, second-generation improvements', *Communications of the ACM*, **59** (1), 82–9, doi:10. 1145/2756542.

Marsden, J. (2013), 'Stigmergic self-organization and the improvisation of Ushahidi', *Cognitive Systems Research*, **21** (March), 52–64, doi:10.1016/j.cogsys.2012.06.005.

Medina, E. (2011), *Cybernetic Revolutionaries: Technology and Politics in Allende's Chile*, Cambridge, MA: MIT Press.

Mitchell, M. (2009), *Complexity: A Guided Tour*, Oxford: Oxford University Press.

Morin, E. (2007), 'Restricted complexity, general complexity', in C. Gershenson, D. Aerts and B. Edmonds (eds), *Philosophy and Complexity, Worldviews, Science and Us*, Singapore: World Scientific, pp. 5–29.

Musterd, S. and W. Ostendorf (eds), (2013), *Urban Segregation and the Welfare State: Inequality and Exclusion in Western Cities*, London and New York: Routledge.

Negroponte, N. (1975), *Soft Architecture Machines*, Cambridge, MA: MIT Press.

Newman, M. (2010), *Networks: An Introduction*, Oxford: Oxford University Press.

Newman, M., A.L. Barabási and D.J. Watts (eds) (2006), *The Structure and Dynamics of Networks*, Princeton, NJ: Princeton University Press.

Newman, P., T. Beatley and H. Boyer (2009), *Resilient Cities: Responding to Peak Oil and Climate Change*, Washington, DC: Island Press.

Odobasic, D., D. Medak and M. Miler (2013), 'Gamification of geographic data collection', in T. Jekel, A. Car, J. Strobl and G. Griesebner (eds), *GI Forum 2013*, Vienna: Verlag der Österreichischen Akademie der Wissenschaften, pp. 328–37.

Okolloh, O. (2009), 'Ushahidi, or "testimony": Web 2.0 tools for crowdsourcing crisis information', *Participatory Learning and Action*, **59** (1), 65–70.

Ottino, J.M. (2004), 'Engineering complex systems', *Nature*, **427** (6973), 399, doi:10.1038/427399a.

Pagels, H.R. (1989), *The Dreams of Reason: The Computer and the Rise of the Sciences of Complexity*, New York: Bantam Books.

Paolotti, D., A. Carnahan, V. Colizza, K. Eames, J. Edmunds, G. Gomes, et al. (2014), 'Web-based participatory surveillance of infectious diseases: the influenzanet participatory surveillance experience', *Clinical Microbiology and Infection*, **20** (1), 17–21, doi:10.1111/1469-0691.12477.

Pask, G. (1961), *An Approach to Cybernetics*, New York: Harper.

Perera, C., A. Zaslavsky, P. Christen and D. Georgakopoulos (2014), 'Sensing as a service model for smart cities supported by internet of things', *Transactions on Emerging Telecommunications Technologies*, **25** (1), 81–93, doi:10.1002/ ett.2704.

Piña-García, C.A., C. Gershenson and J.M. Siqueiros-García (2016), 'Towards a standard sampling methodology on online social networks: Collecting global trends on Twitter', *Applied Network Science*, **1**, art. 3, doi:10.1007/s41109-016-0004-1.

Pickard, G., W. Pan, I. Rahwan, M. Cebrian, R. Crane, A. Madan et al. (2011), 'Time-critical social mobilization', *Science*, **334** (6055), 509–12, doi:10.1126/science.1205869.

Pickett, S.T.A., M.L. Cadenasso and J.M. Grove (2004), 'Resilient cities: meaning, models, and metaphor for integrating the ecological, socio-economic, and planning realms', *Landscape and Urban Planning*, **69** (4), 369–84, doi:10.1016/j.landurbplan.2003.10.035.

Pierce, G. and D. Shoup (2013), 'Getting the prices right', *Journal of the American Planning Association*, **79** (1), 67–81, doi:10.1080/01944363.2013.787307.

Portugali, J. (2011), *Complexity, Cognition and the City*, Berlin and Heidelberg: Springer-Verlag.

Portugali, J. (2016), 'What makes cities complex?', in J. Portugali and E. Stolk (eds), *Complexity, Cognition, Urban Planning and Design*, Cham: Springer International, pp. 3–19.

Portugali, J., H. Meyer, E. Stolk and E. Tan (eds), (2012), *Complexity Theories of Cities Have Come of Age: An Overview with Implications to Urban Planning and Design*, Berlin and Heidelberg: Springer-Verlag.

Pournaras, E., J. Nikolic, P. Velásquez, M. Trovati, N. Bessis and D. Helbing (2016), 'Self-regulatory information sharing in participatory social sensing', *EPJ Data Science*, **5**, art. 14, doi:10.1140/epjds/s13688-016-0074-4.

Prasad, N. (2009), *Climate Resilient Cities: A Primer on Reducing Vulnerabilities to Disasters*, Washington, DC: World Bank.

Prokopenko, M., F. Boschetti and A.J. Ryan (2009), 'An information-theoretic primer on complexity, self-organisation and emergence', *Complexity*, **15** (1), 11–28, doi:10.1002/cplx.20249.

Ratti, C. and M. Claudel (2016), *The City of Tomorrow: Sensors, Networks, Hackers, and the Future of Urban Life*, New Haven, CT: Yale University Press.

Ratti, C., R.M. Pulselli, S. Williams and D. Frenchman (2006), 'Mobile landscapes: using location data from cell phones for urban analysis', *Environment and Planning B: Planning and Design*, **33** (5), 727–48, doi:10.1068/b32047.

Rauws, W. and G. De Roo (2016), 'Adaptive planning: generating conditions for urban adaptability. Lessons from Dutch organic development strategies', *Environment and Planning B: Planning and Design*, **43** (6), 1052–74, doi:10.1177/0265813516658886.

Rohden, M., A. Sorge, M. Timme and D. Witthaut (2012), 'Self-organized synchronization in decentralized power grids', *Physics Review Letters*, **109** (6), 1–5, doi:10.1103/PhysRevLett.109.064101.

Sarma, S., D. Brock and K. Ashton (2000), 'The networked physical world, proposals for engineering the next generation of computing, commerce & automatic-identification', technical report, Auto-ID Centre, Massachusetts Institute of Technology, Cambridge, MA.

Sassen, S. (2011), *Cities in a World Economy*, 4th edn, London: Sage.

Shannon, C.E. (1948), 'A mathematical theory of communication', *Bell System Technical Journal*, **27** (3), 379–423, correction (4), 623–56, accessed 7 May 2021 at http://people.math.harvard.edu/~ctm/home/text/others/shannon/entropy/entropy.pdf.

Sloman, A. (2011), 'What's information, for an organism or intelligent machine? How can a machine or organism mean', in G. Dodig-Crnkovic and M. Burgin (eds), *Information and Computation*, Singapore: World Scientific, pp. 393–438.

Stumpp, E.M. (2013), 'New in town? On resilience and "resilient cities"', *Cities*, **32** (June), 164–6, doi:10.1016/j.cities.2013.01.003.

Tachet, R., P. Santi, S. Sobolevsky, L.I Reyes-Castro, E. Frazzoli, D. Helbing et al. (2016), 'Revisiting street intersections using slot-based systems', *PLoS ONE*, **11** (3), 1–9, doi:10.1371/journal.pone.0149607.

Taleb, N.N. (2012), *Antifragile: Things That Gain From Disorder*, New York: Random House.

Trantopoulos, K., M. Schläpfer and D. Helbing (2011), 'Toward sustainability of complex urban systems through techno-social reality mining', *Environmental Science & Technology*, **45** (15), 6231–2, doi:10.1021/es2020988.

Vespignani, A. (2009), 'Predicting the behavior of techno-social systems', *Science*, **325** (5939), 425–8, doi:10.1126/science.1171990.

Vespignani, A. (2012), 'Modelling dynamical processes in complex socio-technical systems', *Nature Physics*, **8** (1), 32–9, doi:10.1038/nphys2160.

Vicsek, T. and A. Zafeiris (2012), 'Collective motion', *Physics Reports*, **517** (3–4), 71–140, doi:10.1016/j.physrep.2012.03.004.

Virágh, C., G. Vásárhelyi, N. Tarcai, T. Szörényi, G. Somorjai, T. Nepusz, et al. (2014), 'Flocking algorithm for autonomous flying robots', *Bioinspiration & Biomimetics*, **9** (2), art. 025012, http://stacks.iop.org/1748-3190/9/i=2/a=025012.
Wagner, A. (2005), *Robustness and Evolvability in Living Systems*, Princeton, NJ: Princeton University Press.
Wiener, N. (1948), *Cybernetics; or, Control and Communication in the Animal and the Machine*, New York: Wiley and Sons.
Wolpert, D.H. and W.G. Macready (1995), 'No free lunch theorems for search', Technical Report SFI-WP-95-02-010, Santa Fe Institute, Santa Fe, NM, accessed 7 May 2021 at https://www.santafe.edu/research/results/working-papers/no-free-lunch-theorems-for-search.
Wolpert, D.H. and W.G. Macready (1997), 'No free lunch theorems for optimization', *IEEE Transactions on Evolutionary Computation*, **1** (1), 67–82.
Yamu, C., G. de Roo and P. Frankhauser (2015), 'Assuming it is all about conditions. framing a simulation model for complex, adaptive urban space', *Environment and Planning B: Planning and Design*, **43** (6), 1019–39, doi:10.1177/0265813515607858.
Zubillaga, D., G. Cruz, I.D. Aguilar, J. Zapotécatl, N. Fernández, J. Aguilar, et al. (2014), 'Measuring the complexity of self-organizing traffic lights', *Entropy*, **16** (5), 2384–407, doi:10.3390/e16052384.
Zuckerman, E. (2014), 'New media, new civics?', *Policy & Internet*, **6** (2), 151–68, doi:10.1002/1944-2866.POI360.

PART III

COMPLEXITY, LANGUAGE AND CITIES

11. New concepts in complexity theory arising from studies in the field of architecture: an overview of the four books of the nature of order with emphasis on the scientific problems which are raised[1]

Christopher Alexander[2, 3]

PREAMBLE

The four books of *The Nature of Order* were written, originally, in order to lay a scientific foundation for the field of architecture. In writing them, over the course of the last twenty-seven years, I found myself forced to confront unexpectedly deep problems, touching not only architecture, but other scientific fields as well. Some of these questions go so deep that they raise questions rarely, if ever, faced in the scientific community.

I therefore found myself trying to give answers to these questions; starting with answers at least adequate for the field of architecture. I was never writing directly from the point of view of physics, or mathematics, or cosmology, or biology, or ecology or cognitive theory. Yet all these fields are likely, in one way or another, to be touched by some of the findings I have made.

We thus have a situation, perhaps new, where architecture, generally, in the past very much the recipient of received wisdom from the natural sciences, is now generating new material, and new ideas of its own, which have direct bearing on the solution of problems now classed as 'complexity theory,' and doing so in ways which, though obviously helpful to anyone concerned with building, have not arisen before in the mother fields of science itself. To understand exactly what I mean, we might compare architecture today, with Grigor Mendel's garden of sweet peas in 1880. Sweet peas, then, were not part of science – merely a part of life potentially containing questions, originally unassuming in their content. Yet they implicitly contained questions and focused our awareness on new questions which became – years later – what we now know as genetics. That is the role that architecture, with its peculiar problems and challenges, might play for science today.

The situation is complicated by the fact that architecture itself (the field where I have most claim to expertise) has been in an atrocious muddle, intellectually. This muddle had to be cleaned up. And that was my main task during the last thirty years as a scientist; and as a builder of buildings and communities. (The huge difficulties in architecture were reflected in the ugliness and soul-destroying chaos of the cities and environments we were building during the 20th century – and in the mixed feelings of dismay caused by these developments at one time or another in nearly every thinking person, indeed – I would guess – in a very large fraction of all people on Earth.)

Trying to come to grips with these difficulties, required construction of new concepts, able to cope with the massive and complex nature of the difficulties, and able to focus a rational searchlight on questions which were, it seemed, largely beyond the reach of methods previously invented in other sciences. These difficulties arose, in part, I gradually discovered, from widespread but wrong-headed assumptions about the very nature of architecture – and, in considerable part, too, from the dry positivist view too typical of technical scientific thinking in the most recent era. But they also required new ways of thinking about issues which had not received much attention in the natural sciences, simply because there was no need for them in such fields as chemistry or biology.

Facing problems of architecture frankly, required conceptual breakthroughs in several areas, because one could not honestly confront the problems of design, without facing fundamental questions of human feeling, spirit, beauty, and above all two areas of content: the nature of configurations themselves, and the genesis of new configurations (i.e. the processes by which buildings are conceived and made). So, whether I wanted to or not, I had to deal with these difficult matters, because they lie at the very root of architecture, and cannot be avoided: even though the scientific world view and establishment had previously not encountered them.

But this is where things get turned on their head – where it is architecture that informs science rather than vice versa. Architecture places a new kind of searchlight on certain new scientific areas of thought fundamental to the study of complex structures – and thus becomes relevant to a large class of problems recently beginning to gain attention in the scientific community itself. We therefore have the almost unprecedented case of architecture raising scientific concepts, questions, and answers, that bear on matters of hard science – but which have not, previously, been entertained.

BACKGROUND ON ARCHITECTURE

What are the essential problems of architecture that require a new focus, as it might be understood by any scientist who applied himself to the questions of architecture.

1. There are issues of value, that cannot be separated from the main task of serving functional needs. Thus, aesthetics – dismissed as subjective in much contemporary science – lies at the core of architecture.
2. There is the issue of context – a building grows out of, and must complement, the place where it appears. Thus there is a concept of healing (or making whole) and building into a context.
3. There is the issue of design and creation – processes capable of generating unity.
4. There is the issue of human feeling: since, of course, no building can be considered if it does not connect, somehow, to human feeling as an objective matter.
5. There is the issue of ecological and sustainable and biological connection to the land.
6. There is the vital issue of social agreement regarding decision making in regards to a complex system: this arises naturally when hundreds of people need to make decisions together – often the case in the human environment.
7. There is the issue of emerging beauty of shape, as the goal and outcome of all processes.

Considered carefully from a scientific viewpoint, these issues lead to certain questions, and to certain conclusions.

Architecture presents a new kind of insight into complexity because it is one of the human endeavors where we most explicitly deal with complexity and have to create it – not typical in physics or biology, at least not yet. Creation of software in computer science, is another such arena; and organization theory is another. In order to succeed in this very difficult task, which poses challenges quite unlike those raised in physics or biology, I have encountered questions, and given solutions to problems, which I believe are not only useful in architecture (where they are demonstrably so); but that in part these solutions and new concepts are almost certainly transferable to help solve problems in physics, biology, and perhaps other fields. Although computer science and organization theory are the fields where this appreciation of complexity has first made itself felt, biology cannot be far behind: and even questions in physics, though apparently more simple, will (I firmly believe) ultimately turn out to depend on the same kinds of issues of complexity.

Let me give some numbers. We may understand by using the concept of mistakes. A typical house contains about 3000 man hours of labor. Studies suggest that in these 3000 man hours (including both design time and construction time) there is a potential for some 5 key decisions of adaptation, per hour. This means, if handled wrongly, there is opportunity for as many as 5–10000 possible mistakes in the house – decision points where an error can be made. Or, on the side, 5–10000 cases where, if handled well, the house can have beautiful and perfect fit among its parts, and to its environment, and to its users' needs.

Of course an embryo contains a far larger potential for mistakes: 2^{50} or 10^{15} – a thousand trillion possible mistakes. But so far in the history of science, people have not actually confronted the necessity of generating mistake-free adaptation; [i.e. they have not had to put theory into practice, beyond observing, what nature itself practices for us].

Architecture, because it is so ordinary, affects billions of people, and covers a huge volume of physical stuff, is, from a study point of view, and from a theoretical point of view, one of the first cases we have encountered collectively, as a civilization, where it really matters whether you do things right or not [with the emphasis on *do* – i.e. this is about practice mattering].

And it is here, for the very same reason, that new theory is forced into existence. The insights into complexity raised in these four books are related, without doubt, to the insights that have occurred in the last decades of biology, meteorology, etc. But they are different in kind. In those fields the scientists are passive as to the issue of creation. In architecture, we are the active proponents. We have more at stake. If we are wrong, we create a mess. And the insights we have gained, so far, though vaguely related to the insights gained in physics, chaos theory, and biology, are unique, more powerful, more practical – and if I may say so, far deeper in content than the insights gained in the passive sciences.

That is why we must start paying attention to architecture, as a major source of insight in the field of complexity. The creation of finetuned, well-adapted complexity – as encountered for example in architecture – must now take shape as a major topic of theoretical science. Our ability, or failure, to master this science, is crucial to our survival.

SOME EMERGING SCIENTIFIC CONCEPTS BEARING ON COMPLEXITY WHICH COME FROM STUDIES IN THE FIELD OF ARCHITECTURE

1.   Wholeness and Value as a Necessary Part of Any Complex System

What can be a measure or criterion of success for a complex system? If a self-respecting scientist was to tackle the problem of giving structure to the world, in the large – and that is essentially the problem of architecture – then regardless of what shibboleths may say, there must be a shared criterion of success. If science, as presently conceived does not have one that is useful for architecture, then regardless, we must, of course, find one. And for it to be shared, we need to find one which is essentially universal, yet capable of being shared by people of different faiths, cultures, and opinions.

The positivistic, value-free idea of art, which came from science, and the desire that science had to create a value-free science, pervaded most 20th-century thought, and finally infected architecture itself – one of the silliest intellectual transfusions of all time – since of course architecture – by its very nature – cannot manage without a common sense shared criterion of good quality.

Indeed, as we may see upon reflection, a variety of other scientific fields would also benefit if value were understood to be a necessary part of the study of complex systems. Biological systems cannot be viewed as value free, ecological systems cannot, land management and erosion control, and hydrological management in the large, also cannot manage without a criterion of what is good. Nor, frankly, can an ordinary activity like gardening. Genetics is plainly in a situation today, where problems of value are beginning to surface. And software design, has run into the very same problem, and software engineers and computer scientists have begun to realize that a sense of value, if objective and careful, is almost the only thing that can get them out of the present mess.

The very first thing any scientist would do, if trying to make a sensible theory of architecture, would be to recognize that there must be, at the bottom of it, a shared notion of quality, of what we are, collectively, aiming for.

If everyone is trying to do something different in a town or community, different in kind, not different in detail of execution, then of course there will be chaos; just, indeed, what we have experienced in modern urbanism.

Yet for the last hundred years or so, there has been a taboo in the scientific community which virtually forbids a scientist (when talking as a scientist) from talking about value or quality as though they really exist. Instead, it has been an article of faith that good science comes only when we make abstract machine-like pictures that do not let our feelings or judgments of goodness get in the way.

This has been a useful article of faith, and has served science well for four hundred years. But it cannot serve us well now. Why? Because, although it is a feature of non-complex systems that they can be studied without focusing on value, it is also a feature of complex systems that they cannot be studied successfully in this way.

Although science (and 20th-century architecture, too) managed to get through the 20th century, by refusing to come to grips with this problem, in fact in the long run we cannot get on without solving it. It MUST be solved in some form. In the spirit of science we shall not expect to solve it all at once. But we must make an effort, make a tentative stab at it . . . and try it out, and then see how we are doing, and improve what we have, until we get something workable.

Of course architecture in the 20th century also contributed to the taboo on talking about quality or goodness as though it really exists. Infected by positivism, by postmodernism, and by deconstructivism, and exhilarated by a phony pluralism of 'anything goes,' architects tried to get by, by saying everyone should do 'their' thing . . . each person is entitled to his view, her opinion, and so on. All true enough as comments on the freedom of human beings. But not a way to do architecture successfully. You cannot throw the baby out with the bathwater in quite this way, and go on to say there is no such real thing as quality in architecture. This attitude destroys truth to such an extent that it cannot make a successful environment.

So, continuing to repeat the mantra that we scientists should not mess with value, is becoming short sighted and silly. The fact that in architecture – if we keep our common senses – we MUST deal with questions of value, does not mean that science cannot benefit from architecture. On the contrary, it means, rather, that the existence of such questions in architecture – if sensible answers are given to them – is likely to be a source of inspiration and encouragement to other sciences which are suffering from the same problem.

But of course, acknowledging that it would be desirable to have a shared criterion of value is only the first step. That, by itself, does not get you to an operational process for establishing shared value, or to a sharable, operational procedure for evaluating a part of the environment, in a way that can get shared results. It seems to me that we would do best if we agree to keep this an open question, and not close off the possibility of it being solvable, merely according to scientific taboos.

2.   An Intuitive Model of Wholeness as a Recursive Structure

If we ask ourselves what kind of criterion of value we might be able to rely on, and especially what kind of criterion we might wish to rely on as a standard for the goodness of a complex system, it would be rather reasonable to say something along the following lines.

In a good system, we would expect to find the following conditions: Any identifiable subsystems, we would hope, would be well – that is to say, in good condition. And we would hope that the larger world outside the complex system is also in good order, and well. Thus, the mark of a good system would be that it helps both the systems around it and those which it contains. And the goodness and helping towards goodness is, in our ideal complex system, also reciprocal. That is, our good system, will turn out to be not only helping other systems to become good, but also, in turn, helped by the goodness of the larger systems around it and by the goodness of the smaller ones which it contains.

Is this a platitude, perhaps too vague to be taken seriously, or worse, tautologous? Not at all. As we know from recursive function theory, surprisingly simple ideas, when applied recursively at a variety of nested levels, can have profound and effective consequences – and, often, surprising ones. Both Ian Stewart and Brian Goodwin acknowledge the importance of recursive ideas, and say that in their view, too, recursiveness of qualities is likely to be a feature of all living structure.

So, although it appears to be circular to use goodness as a concept within the definition of goodness itself, this apparent circularity is only apparent, not real, and a recursive structure of this kind, if followed through, can have remarkable and deep results.

And, as a word of caution to the reader: Is this definition trivial, when applied in practice? Indeed it is not. We have only to imagine a row of houses, in which every house helps the street; and in which every garden helps every house, to see that even this simple description already takes us far beyond present day architecture. Clearly contemporary housing estates or tracts do not achieve this ideal, even according to the most intuitive judgments. So this seemingly obscure yet actually concrete statement is very much about something, not merely a collection of empty words.

Indeed, if the world were marked by systems, large and small, of which this criterion (that each system helps the other systems, in concrete and discernible ways) could be said, the world would obviously be a much better place. Water, food production, vegetation, social conditions, families, education, roads, parks, the rooms in a house even, the very windows too, would all be better. This criterion is a deep one, and it behooves us to find a precise and reliable way of ascertaining what it means (in precise terms), and of applying the criterion to real cases, so that we can judge their successes and deficiencies.

The only problem is that we do not yet have a mathematical representation powerful enough to achieve this, just as we do not yet have a satisfying mathematics of embryonic growth. In *The Nature of Order* I have taken first steps – very tentative ones – towards just exactly such a representation, incomplete though it may still be.

3. A Mathematical Model of Wholeness Identifying Wholeness as a Well-Defined Recursive Structure of a New Type

There is a relatively long-standing tradition of talking about wholeness of spatial configurations and situations in the world.

It has been recognized informally, sometimes more strongly, that wholeness is the key to many naturally occurring events, phenomena, and aspects of system behavior. For example, Bohr's insistence that the key to quantum mechanics lies in the dependence of the movement of electrons on the configuration and behavior of the whole: Bohm's discussion of the wholeness of a quantum experiment as the origin of the behaviors of electrons in the field; Goldstein's discussion of the human organism; Wertheimer's and Köhler's discussions of gestalt phenomena in figure recognition and cognition. The term has also, in recent years, been used in a variety of religious and therapeutic contexts. However those, almost always well intentioned, have rarely, if ever, been clear.

As a result of experiments I conducted at the Center for Cognitive Studics at Harvard in the early 1960s, I became convinced that wholeness, 'the wholeness we see,' is a real, well-defined structure, not merely a cognitive impression. That the thing we recognize as the 'gestalt' of a figure, the pattern of flows in a hydrodynamic field, the 'something' about an individual human face which seems like that person's wholeness, and which we recognize instantly, is – in each case – a describable mathematical structure.

However, there was no then-existing mathematical structure I knew of, which was able to capture this 'something' or which could embody it.

After several years of thought, as to how this structure might be represented, I came to the conclusion that the crucial issue lay in the nested system of wholes that cover the space. By a whole I mean any relatively coherent spatial set, with the understanding that different wholes may have relatively different degrees of coherence. The wholeness, then, of a particular configuration, is an ordering on the different overlapping and nested wholes and systems, according to their degree of coherence – in short the relative coherence of the entire system of sets and subsets in a part of space. I became sure, slowly, that this system of sets with relatively different levels of coherence, was the clue to the kind of structure which would capture 'the' wholeness.

The wholeness is that global structure which pays attention to, and captures, the relative strength of different parts of the system, paying attention both to the way they are nested in one another, and how the pattern of strength varies with the nesting.

4.   Objective Measures of Coherence in Complex Systems, and the Unavoidable Relationship between Structure, Fact, and Beauty

There is a sense in which Philip Ball and I differ profoundly. The substrate of his view of science – at least as it comes across in the interview – seems to be that science is about facts, and therefore it cannot be concerned with aesthetics, because aesthetics is inherently concerned with matters of subjective human judgment, except insofar as aesthetics is considered a matter of cognition. Possibly Ian Stewart, too, shares some such view – at least some of his comments on Jencks suggest that may be so. My view is that aesthetics is a mode of perceiving deep structure, a mode no less profound than other simpler forms of scientific observation and experimentation.

How true is it really that aesthetics is nonfactual? And, I would ask, especially, how true can this be, as our scientific efforts move into the new territory of highly complex structures?

Consider the relatively simple question of coherence. Within complex structures the relative coherence of different parts, different systems, is paramount, and plays a paramount role in their behavior. But there is a very thin line – in fact, I would argue there is no substantial line at all – between the issues of relative coherence of subsystems in a physical-mechanical system, and the more complex distinctions of coherence in an aesthetic entity – the phrasing of a piece of music for example.

We routinely study relative coherence in crystals and economic systems. For example we can analyze the cleavage planes by seeing that some portions of the crystal are relatively more coherent than others, and that fractures will occur between the more coherent parts. We can analyze the subsystems of an economic system by studying inputs and outputs and decomposing the matrix. Such things can be analyzed by a variety of mathematical techniques all depending on numerical analysis of relative degrees of connection within, and between the subsystems.

The relative coherence of more complex entities – the relative beauty of one column in a building, versus another, uglier column – is susceptible to precise observation, and can be made a part of science by new kinds of experiment, using the human observer as a measuring instrument. If we can construct these experiments in such a way that we get agreement among different observers, and thus obtain hardnosed observations of relative coherence in these more complex cases, in what way is it helpful to call these judgments subjective?

I believe it is retrogressive, and will merely close the door on study of more complex phenomena, to state that we should ignore such observations as necessarily subjective. Rather it seems to me that they must be studied, if we are to understand the newly complex systems we aspire to deal with within 21st-century science. At the very least we should leave the possibility open.

Indeed, as I have suggested in the books, wholeness itself is a cousin-like structure to topology – akin to structures in topology where we have a system of nested overlapping sets, some 'open' and others 'closed.' In the case of topology, there is a two-valued measure for the different sets, 1 or 0, open or closed. In the definition of wholeness I have offered, we have systems of nested, overlapping sets which can take an infinite set of coherence-values from 0 to 1 along the continuum of least to maximal coherence. The wholeness, so defined, describes a vast family of structures that comes from differentiated relative coherence, and shows (at least aims to show) how that structure of relative coherence then creates (by recursion) the coherence of the larger structure.

Obviously, this structure cannot be studied – or even thought – without introducing the idea of coherence as an objective concept. It is in this sense – possibly disturbing to scientists unused to the idea of recursion – that the conceptual framework is recursive.

Further, the issue is greatly complicated by the fact that the relative coherence of one set, depends on a recursion of values which are given to its subsets. I am only too aware that we do not yet have a nicely worked out mathematical model for this idea. But, albeit preliminary, it is in any case a mathematical model of a new type – and one suggested by architecture.

Wholeness itself, for example, cannot be discussed without making evaluative statements. So where will science be, if it cannot effectively discuss wholeness. Wolfgang Köhler recognized this problem about seventy years ago . . . but hardly anyone reads Köhler anymore.

Scientists speak constantly as if there is some kind of great divide between fact and aesthetics – the one the province of science; the other the province of subjectivity and art. Yet the whole purpose of my four books, is to demonstrate that we cannot have an adequate world view without a single view of science that embraces both what we now think of as fact, together with what we regard as aesthetic facts and observations.

Where after all, did the idea come from that aesthetic judgments are subjective? The ancient Greeks did not think of them as subjective. Nor did the Romans. Nor did the ancient Chinese. Nor did the great artists of Islam. Indeed the idea that aesthetic judgment is subjective is a relatively recent arrival on the scene of human thought, and one which was recently fueled by the positivist and mechanistic way of thinking less than 100 years ago – which scientists themselves are now rejecting.

There is no need for such arbitrary pronouncements. Indeed, such pronouncements will kill genuine scientific investigation in advanced complexity theory, not help it.

After all what is science? It is the study of what really happens, how the world works. Done in such a way that agreement can be forged by clear thought, and by empirical procedures. That is the picture I have provided. There is clear thought about structure; and there is empirical basis and procedure specified, which allow people to form agreed on shared observations, and thereby to reach – at least tentatively and roughly at first – shared understanding, and reliable results.

5.   Fifteen Geometric Properties as Necessary and Inevitable Geometric Features of Reality in Any Complex System

The possibility, which is set out in *The Nature of Order*, that wholeness is built, essentially, from fifteen features of space, comes very close indeed, to Brian Goodwin's 'science of qualities.' These fifteen features are described at length in chapters 5 and 6 of Book 1, where they are described as they arise in artifacts, and as they arise in natural systems. Goodwin has made a compelling argument that qualitative features are observable, and objective in the sense that they are apprehended by many observers. He implies, but does not exactly say, that these features – macro-features of systems which are not necessarily to be described by numerical parameters – do control vital aspects of behavior, interaction, and dynamics. Thus they are not only important because they are there, but also because they often play a controlling or decisive role in the behavior of the systems where they occur.

This corresponds closely to my own view. In the description of functional behavior given in Books 1, 2 and 3, again and again, it is the fifteen properties which play a decisive role in the way things work. This is, I believe, because the 15 properties describe the way that centers are made more alive. Any interaction, in which one coherence interacts with another, will often circle around the way that centers in mutually interacting systems support one another, or modify one another – often to create a new wholeness. That this should happen when the properties come into play, is only natural, since it is these properties which cause the functional behavior of the aggregate. There is, in my view, a link between the larger, more qualitative aspects of systems, and their functional behavior.

Thus, in the properties described in Book 1, and in the dynamic aspect of these properties (the transformations described in Book 2), we gain insight into the dynamical emergence of new structure and new behavior.

Let me give an example. Boundaries, and especially thick boundaries with substance, can play a role in helping the goodness of a center, or in strengthening a center. This happens because, if two systems are interacting, the boundary condition is often turbulent or a source of possible confusion. When the boundary zone itself has dimension, it can then take on an 'inbetween' structure, which mitigates or smooths out the potential interacting processes in the inner and outer zones. Familiar examples are to be seen in the very thick boundary around a living cell (which contains so much vital functionality), in the edge ecology between a forest and a lake, or in the corona of the sun which mitigates the interactions of the sun's interior and the processes taking place further out in the near vacuum beyond.

The boundary plays a huge role in the effect and behavior of any system made of other systems, since the system will literally be riddled with such boundary layers and boundary zones. Although one cannot say that every center must have a boundary of this kind, it is certainly one of the ways in which a living center gets its stability and strength, and capacity to interact with other systems.

Not surprisingly, then, a transformation which gives a given entity such a boundary zone – not a very difficult kind of transformation to induce mechanically as part of any developmental process – is likely to create a niche for desirable effects. The transformation which preserves and enhances structure, by introducing boundaries, is likely to bring with it a variety of positive effects. Thus evolution, ontogeny, planning, building, and design, are all likely to benefit (at the very least in a heuristic or probabilistic fashion) from such transformations.

The idea that there can only be a limited number of these transformations, and that there is a calculus of these fifteen transformations as the driving force of all emergence, must of course be a matter of enormous interest.

6. A Meeting Point between Cognition and Objective Reality?

Ball especially, and to some extent Stewart too, come again and again to the notion that what I have described is really all about cognition; that is, about the structure which appears in our minds – not the structure which appears in the world. As such it may have something to do with cognitive theory, but sheds little light on the 'hard' sciences as a commentary on how the world is made.

This is a very deep issue, and in some respects it is the central kernel of my claim that *The Nature of Order* is about science and about the nature of the universe, not merely about human cognition or psychology.

Let us begin with the idea that it is in any case indeed *also* about cognition. Here Ball and Stewart would agree with me, I think. The idea of wholeness as a recursive structure made of locally occurring centers, that centers are made of other centers, and the idea that the fifteen properties are the main glue that makes sense have coherence . . . these are all legitimate concepts for cognitive theory. So, too, is the concept that the more coherent a thing is, cognitively, the more it will be seen as a picture of the self, or of the soul – as a subjective experience of the knower.

And indeed much of this material had its beginnings in work I undertook, forty years ago, in the Center for Cognitive Studies at Harvard, where I was then working experimentally on problems of cognition under Jerry Bruner and George Miller, with Bill Huggins, Harris Savin, Susan Carey, and others.

I myself, when I am in my most sober and pessimistic mode find the cognitive interpretation useful, mainly because when we think of the results this way, it is then quite certain that they all make sense within a familiar mechanistic mode of thinking. It is a failsafe way of looking at the theory, because it is unassailable, verifiable, and poses no deep and unpleasantly disturbing problems of ontology.

But that does not mean that it is true, or that it is the most interesting or deepest way to understand the scientific meaning of the facts I have presented. Obviously, if the facts are facts about the universe, they will indeed also show up in cognition, and the cognitive interpretation will hold up. It is, therefore, an entirely safe interpretation.

And of course, one could also have a theory of architecture which is cognitive in origin, and based on cognition for its foundations. This would, however, be rather narrow – even arbitrary. After all, why should we pick a cognitive theory of architecture? Why not an anthropological theory, or an ecological theory, and so on.

More important, the theory sheds practical light on issues which have no connection with cognition. For example, structural design is made easier and better, when viewed from the point of view of this theory. The flow of forces in a complex system of structural members, can hardly be dismissed as a cognitive problem. The forces have real behavior and real existence, outside of ourselves. If this theory of wholeness and unfolding leads to good results, and enables us to find structures which elegantly and cheaply resolve the forces, we have crossed over into questions of physical reality. Yet, it is just so. Accumulated evidence from my laboratory shows, in case after case, that it is so.

Similarly, problems of traffic flow are made more solvable, from within this perspective. Although traffic flow is, remotely, a cognitive issue, this is once again stretching the point. Here again we find the theory giving us useful, sometimes penetrating insights into realistic problems of design in a physical field that is largely independent of human cognition.

The flow of water in an ecologically sensitive landscape, is also helped by concepts from this theory. Once again, this subject, in recent years an object of considerable study in ecology, cannot be considered a cognitive problem. It is a problem about the complex living system which occurs in a hilly terrain on the earth's surface. Yet, again, there is convincing evidence to suggest that the concepts of wholeness, centers, fifteen properties, and structure-preserving transformations, shed useful light on ways to organize water and riparian areas in a terrain.

7.   A New, Experimental Way of Determining Degree of Coherence, Degree of Life, and Relative Value

In *The Nature of Order*, an entirely new empirical procedure, very different from traditional forms of experiment – has been proposed. It has three characteristics:

1.   The procedure asks a person to evaluate, experimentally, through subjective self-examination, the degree to which a certain system, or thing, or event, or act enhances the observer's own wholeness.
2.   It turns out that people are able to carry out this process.
3.   It turns out that there is a very considerable degree of agreement in their findings.

It appears then, that after centuries, there may exist a reliable and profound empirical method for reaching shared judgments about the degree of value inherent in a complex system. For reasons that are discussed extensively in *The Nature of Order*, and especially in Books 1 and 4, there are powerful reasons for thinking that the value which inheres in wholeness reflects on physical reality. It is not like the kind of trivial social agreement we get when a hundred people say, 'Yes we all love Big Macs best,' something we might loosely call merely intersubjective agreement. It is a different kind of agreement, which reflects on real physical systems, and is more akin to the agreement several different cancer specialists might share when they say that a certain person's haggard features suggest the presence of an undetected tumor. This is not at all like the agreement shared by the Big Mac enthusiasts. It is a judgment, not an opinion, and is a judgment about reality which can be tied to the presence of definable underlying structures. Just so with the cases I describe in *The Nature of Order*.

8.   The Science of Complexity Must Make Room for Subjectivity, Not in the Sense of Idiosyncracy [*sic*] of Judgment, but as a Connection to the Human Being

Philip Ball says my 'definition of life' as given in *The Nature of Order* is 'utterly subjective.' What does he mean by this?

To untangle this statement, one must distinguish sharply, between two meanings of 'subjective,' two quite different ways in which the word is used.

1. We can call a judgment subjective, and mean that it is idiosyncratic: that is, it is a product of one person's mind or ideas, and not part of shared canon, or capable of being part of a shared canon. That of course, is a valid criticism of anything purporting to be scientific, since the essence of science is the achievement of judgments that can be shared, and established according to well-defined experiment.
2. We can also call a statement subjective, if it engages, or includes, the personal subjectivity of the observer, the I-ness or consciousness or feeling of an observer. This is fairly commonplace in science. It occurs for example, in Chomsky's famous opening of structural linguistics, when he used his own perceptions of what is grammatical, knowing that others would make roughly the same judgments he made: and that structures perceived therefore had objective standing, even though subjective in the way they were experienced.

Now, it is certainly true that *The Nature of Order* is filled with examples of this second kind, since union of system behavior with the subjective experience of the observer is fundamental to what I have to say, fundamental to the idea of wholeness as something not merely present in an objective material system, but also present in the judgment, feeling, and experience of the observer. In short, cognitive/subjective experience is affirmed by objective reality.

In accusing me, if that is the right word, of subjectivity, Ball implies that some bad science has crept into Book 1 (subjectivity of type 1); when in fact it is only in the second sense that my comments are subjective, but not in the first.

Possibly one of the most important notions in a valid theory of architecture, is that the judgments of fact, about quality, reside in reachable feelings in any human observer. Indeed, the neutral observations we need, in order to reach adequate discussion and comprehension of wholeness, are observations of a type which *can only be obtained when we agree to use the observer's feeling of his or her own wholeness, as a measuring instrument.* Yet, subjective as it sounds to our mechanist ears, this is nonetheless objective. It opens the door to a new standard of observation, and a new methodology of measurement. In architecture, anyway, where my observations have been most careful and extended over several decades, I can say positively that valid and profound results, and findings, cannot be reached without meeting this condition.

I strongly suspect the same will turn out to be true in the other scientific disciplines dealing with complexity.

9. Local Symmetries and Sub-Symmetries

In a coherent structure we are likely to see a well-developed system of local symmetries and sub-symmetries. Thus, complex systems will be marked by a preponderance of local symmetries, usually appearing in a framework of larger asymmetries. I have always been interested in Ian Stewart's discussions of symmetry, symmetries, and symmetry breaking, and have myself spent quite some time making calculations about symmetries, and trying to find out how they appear in complex systems, and how they influence the structure of complex systems. Moving on to mathematics, I will now give an example from symmetry, which shows something of the kind of power, in very exact mathematical terms, which the wholeness structure has potentially within its scope.

A number of years ago, I made a series of carefully controlled experiments to study simple configurations of black and white squares, and to obtain estimates of their relative simplicity and coherence. To do this I used experiments designed to measure ease of perception, ease of giving a name, speed of recognition, ability to remember, and so on – a variety of cognitive measures, each susceptible to precise experiment.

Several findings:

- First, the strong correlation between all these measures, although they are cognitively quite different in character and process.
- Second, very strong overall correlation among subjects: meaning that what different people see as simple or coherent is measurable, and does not vary enormously from person to person.
- Third, that differences of perception disappear altogether when we induce people to see configurations in their wholeness. Experiments show that such a holistic mode of perception is achievable, natural, and that once it is attained it is stable and reliable.

Armed with the results of these experiments, I set out to find a common factor which explained the rank ordering of coherence among the different configurations. It took two years to discover it. Finally, it turned out that when you count the total number of sub-symmetries in the pattern (not the overall symmetry, but the set of all local symmetries in connected sub-regions of the configuration), the most coherent patterns are those that have the largest number of local sub-symmetries within them. This does not mean they are globally symmetrical configurations. It is a totally different kind of quality.

Now, what is interesting about this quality, is that it is plainly a deep structural feature of the configurations – not something about the way they are seen, but something about the way they are.

Further, the presence or absence of this kind of coherence is strongly correlated with appearance of structure in nature, in buildings, in crystals, in fluid flow, in plant colonies and so on. And, indeed, it is not far from that observation to the observation that transforming a structure to increase its density of local symmetries, is one example of the kinds of structure-preserving transformations I have described in Book 2. There is no way this can be dismissed as cognitive.

It is mathematics: and it is mathematics of real physical structures that unfold in three dimensional space. But it departs in an interesting way from present conceptions of mathematics, and once again provides insight into the kinds of developments which may be expected, when one starts working with the model of wholes and wholeness that I have described.

10.   Deep Adaptation as a Central Concept in Complex System Theory and in Architecture

I define deep adaptation as the type of spatial adaptation which occurs between neighboring elements and systems, and which ultimately causes the harmonious appearance and geometrical cohesion we find in all living matter. Deep adaptation is the process whereby the landscape, or a system, or a plant, or a town, proceeds by a series of spatially organized adaptations in which each part is gradually fitted to the parts near it: and is simultaneously fitted by the whole, to its position and performance in the whole. This concept, greatly needing elaboration, is possibly the most fruitful point of contact between the theory of complex systems, and the problem of architecture (it is the subject of a new book, now in preparation). Interestingly, neither biology, nor ecology, nor architecture, nor city planning, so far have a profound or illuminating model of this kind of adaptation: mutual adaptation among the parts *within* a system.

Adaptation, as a general idea, is a vital concept, for example, in John Holland's writing on complex adaptive systems. But sophisticated as Holland's work is, the adaptation he describes is nearly always described as the process by which systems of numerical parameters are brought within certain numerical ranges. Complex adaptation is then described as adaptation for many variables, at once, often interacting. But little of this kind of thinking has yet allowed us to form a good mental picture of what an adapted system really is, *structurally*, when it occurs, nor how we might picture it in detail for ourselves.

What does adaptation among parts typically look like in a landscape? What physical structure does it have, typically, when it has occurred in a system? Well of course, that is what my effort to describe living structure in Books 1 and 2 and 3 of *The Nature of Order* is all about. I have tried to focus on the physical character of a highly adapted or co-adapted system. But this is a first attempt, hardly paralleled at all, by contemporary writing in physics, or biology, or ecology.

As a result, not only is our understanding of adaptation limited: we are naive, almost like infants, when it comes to inventing an adaptive process which creates suitably complex, beautiful, and sophisticated well-adapted structure in almost any real-world system: among others, highly adapted structures in a farmer's field, or in a town, or in a street, or in a room.

In Wolfram's *A New Kind of Science*, for example, fascinating as it is, and ostensibly about complex system theory, there are 1200 pages discussing the richness of step-by-step recursive systems of rules. Yet there is hardly a word (actually, there is not one single word, I believe), on the question of how such rule systems, for all their richness, might be aimed at the production of good structure.

How can we even say that we have a theory of complex systems, when we have so little to say about the most crucial point of all?

11. The Absolute Necessity for Successful Adaptation to be Achieved by Generative Means

Philip Ball remarked in his discussion, that he believes I may be right that the processes of architecture (and construction) would need to be dramatically changed, in order to help create a living world.

I found this comment reassuring when I read it, since it seems to me to illuminate one of the deepest points of contact between architecture and science.

The idea that complex structures can only be made successfully by generative techniques is obvious in biology, but not yet obvious in architecture. Nor is it obvious in organization theory, or in computer science, hardly even in ecology where it has perhaps made some headway. Yet in all these cases generative methods must in the long run be applied if we are to succeed in creating living structure on the surface of the Earth.

I had an extraordinary discussion recently with a consultant in management theory, who was interviewing me. I discussed with him the idea that adaptational complexity – hence the richness and depth of structure needed in a complex organization – can only be achieved by generative means. We were discussing the case of architecture, where it is also something almost hidden from view, and has been replaced with the silly and impossible idea that good design (on the drawing board) can make up for step-by-step adaptation.

My interviewer was enthusiastic. We spoke about human organizations, and I asked if it was commonly understood that a complex organization would only be created step by step, that is to say, generated; and asked how this was working in contemporary American corporations. 'Oh, we only talk about it,' he said. 'Even though it is obvious, almost no one actually does it, or tries to generate a living structure of a human organization by these means.'

I tried to push it. 'Are there not at least theories, ideas how to do it, floating about in the most advanced circles,' I asked. 'No, no one really tries to do anything like that,' he said. 'It is just a theoretical idea.'

So to him it was obvious, necessary, true . . . yet for all that, it has not yet been placed on the agenda of practical action in the business world, a place where innovation is usually rapid and inventive.

Wolfram has done a great service by placing attention on the impact of generative methods, and on the extraordinary richness of generative schemes, and generated structures. I have made similar inroads in a different sphere. In Book 2, I have described a new class of generative sequences for architecture: and have argued, I think truly, that living structure cannot be attained in any sphere, without such generative sequences.

The difference between my generative schemes and Wolfram's is that mine are uniformly based on one target: the target of generating living structure. They are not morally or ethically neutral.

12.   The Effect of Structure-Preserving Transformations on the World and their Role in the Unfolding of Wholeness

In my view, possibly the most significant single scientific idea in *The Nature of Order* is the concept, first presented in Book 2, of a structure-preserving transformation. This concept arises, naturally, from the concept of wholeness. Once we have a concept of wholeness which is not vague mumbo jumbo, but a coherent and in-part mathematically definable structure for any given configuration, we are then able to ask, of any change, or modification of this structure, or for any evolution of that wholeness, whether the new wholeness emerges and continues naturally from the previous state of the structure, or if it is in some sense a violation of its previous structure.

In any case, complexity theory itself certainly has the knowledge and vision about the importance of dynamic approaches to adaptation. Genetic algorithms, annealing algorithms, and the entire theory of computationally derived dynamic structure, all attest to it. Yet, where in complexity theory, is there a straightforward, common sense exposition of the general principles underlying the successful adaptation of a complex structure, in real time, as a real practical matter?

Possibly the most important lesson of the discussions in *The Nature of Order*, lies in the way that the concept of a structure-preserving transformation or wholeness-preserving transformation – fundamental to the proper design or planning or construction of any building which has life – may turn out to be a foundation stone, in the end, of the whole science of complexity theory.

I believe it is clear to us, intuitively, that it is very hard to reach a well-adapted state of any system we are trying to meddle in, or build. It is certainly clear as a topic in theoretical biology where Stuart Kaufmann, for example, has tried to show how this happens in a typical biological system. To my knowledge, the difficulty of finding good configurations in a landscape, or in a street, or in a building – equally difficult problems – have not yet been widely acknowledged by architects. This is mainly because in architecture the 'goodness' of different configurations has not yet been accepted as a matter of *fact*. That makes it impossible, of course, even to ask how hard it is to find the good configurations.

However, in *The Nature of Order* I have established, I believe, that the goodness of an environment is a matter of fact (you would need to read the whole of *Nature of Order* to understand why), not of subjective aesthetic judgment. This has therefore allowed me, perhaps for the first time, to ask concrete questions about the type of process – of design, or of construction, or of planning, or of step-by-step urban renewal – and to ask what kind of processes might enable us to get a higher rate of success in reaching good structures in our surroundings.

Here I have had some considerable success – and, as in other cases mentioned in this paper, it seems to me that the scientific community might learn a great deal about complexity, by focusing on the character and technique of this success.

13. The Hugeness of Configuration Space and the Way the Trajectory of a Complex System Can Reach Adaptation

It is very difficult to find or design, or plan, complex structures of the type of complexity typically encountered in buildings, neighborhoods, gardens, even rooms. There are many possible configurations. Only a few of them work well, and only very few of them show the subtle co-adaptation among the parts which creates true harmony, or truly good functional behavior.

Kaufmann has spoken eloquently about the fitness landscape and the problem of finding the good solutions. This problem exists because the good solutions are so tiny, like specks of dust in the vastness of a configuration space. The relatively rare living structures, viewed as points in configuration space, are so small and so far apart, that the chance of finding them by search, by design, is almost vanishingly small. It is to all intents impossible.

In Book 3, I have given a numerical estimate of the relative number of good (well-adapted) configurations compared with the number of all possible configurations. In one calculation I reached the conclusion that the ratio of successful, well-adapted, configurations to all possible configurations is a staggering 1 in $10^{12,000}$. This is so sparse (remember, there are only 10^{44} molecules in the ocean, and only 10^{80} particles in the known universe) – that one can hardly imagine how a system ever finds these few isolated configurations.

Of course, the way it works in nature is not by *search*. The system does not wander about in configuration space, looking for these tiny and very rarely occurring configurations. Instead, it just goes there. The grain ripens. The corn forms. The stalks are threshed. The flour is milled. The stubble is ploughed back into the soil. One thing follows another, and in a particular way which leads from one good configuration to another, and in such a way that any natural process gradually leads towards and homes in on the good, well-adapted configurations.

Kaufmann has begun an effort to make this process precise by means of autocatalytic sets, and by showing the kind of path such a system takes, and that it leads, more likely than not, to the well-adapted configurations. Of course his work is incomplete, and he leaves us wondering just *how, exactly* does this work.

My own view, based on thirty years of trying to solve this problem with buildings, is that the technique which must be used, is a new technique that focuses on emergence via well-defined structure-preserving transformations. It takes us to the sweet spots in configuration space by a series of transformations based on the fifteen properties identified earlier. These transformations, when calculated properly, and when carried out in a disciplined manner, have the power to reach the very rare and hard-to-find good solutions by stepwise transformations, where a search procedure or a design procedure just simply cannot reach it in a finite amount of time. In other words, design cannot succeed in producing optimal or sub-optimal solutions. Systems of well-oriented transformations performed over time, can work, do work, and are the only tools for creating deeply adapted living structure in towns and buildings.

What this means, in practice, is that as a structure evolves, we guide its evolution by particular sequences of structure preserving transformations: these are the transformations defined by the fifteen properties. In case after case, I have shown that effective adaptation occurs when it is guided by carefully chosen sequences of these fifteen transformations, applied one after another, to the product of the previous transformations.

14. More on Adaptational Success as a Special Kind of Trajectory through Configuration Space

There has been mention of Stu Kaufmann, and his innovative ideas. It may help put the present discussion in context, if I make a few remarks about the nature of his achievement, as I view it, and how it pertains to the scientific problems raised in *The Nature of Order*.

In all complex systems, the key question is: How does the complex system receive its order? It occurs in the growth of an organism, and its trajectory as it becomes fit for its environment; it arises in the breaking of a wave to produce the beautiful configurations captured by Hokusai; it arises in the evolution of organisms, and in the attempt to find a genome which is well adapted; it occurs in architecture, and the attempt to make a building, or a place in a town become well adapted.

What is common to these cases, is the extraordinary numerical problem which every adaptive system faces.

In *The Nature of Order* (Book 3 appendix) I have made a crude estimate comparing the number of possible configurations in a given building design problem, with the number of those possible solutions that are likely to be well adapted – hence to have living structure. The ratio of these two numbers is truly astonishing.

In my estimate there are, in all, $10^{2,000,000,000}$ possible configurations; and of these there are approximately $10^{1,998,000,000}$ good configurations. The absolute number of configurations both in the 'good' pile and in the 'all' pile, are immense – immense beyond imagining. There is therefore no shortage of good solutions to any given problem. But it is the ratio of the two numbers which staggers the imagination. The ratio between the two numbers is, in rough terms, about $10^{12,000}$. Further, although there are huge numbers of possibly good configurations, these good ones are sparsely scattered throughout configuration space, they are certainly not nicely grouped in any one part of configuration space. What this means is that the problem of finding the relatively good configurations is, in principle, a problem of staggering difficulty. It is not merely like finding a needle in a haystack. It is not even like finding a single particle, among all the particles in the known universe; that would merely be a problem of finding one particle among 10^{80}. This problem is inexpressibly large by comparison. The compactness of the written arithmetic expression $10^{12,000}$ belies the true immensity of the actual number.

This task is so huge as to be almost unimaginable. But we may imagine it like this. Consider the number of water molecules in the earth's oceans: about 10^{40}. Suppose then, that we initiated a process which allowed us to find one of a million specially marked molecules, among these 10^{40}. Let us imagine now, that we stand on the surface of that one molecule, and once again, we imagine that one molecule like earth's ocean, with 1040 of its own miniature particles, and again we have to find one particular tiny particle among the 10^{40}, which is a good one. Now we have searched for something with a rarity of 1 in 10^{80}. Let us now jump down again, and again treat this second earth as the real earth, and once again, now find our way to a particular particle which has a rarity of 1 in 10^{120}.

Let us now continue this procedure again and again and again. In order to find a particle with rarity of 1 in $10^{12,000}$, we have to perform this extraordinary jump into as yet smaller universes, no less than three hundred times: we have to perform this jump into a domain as large as the molecules in the earth's ocean, no less than three hundred times, one after the other. Only then do we get near to our objective.

And remember, this search for the needle in this gargantuan haystack is not an extraordinary task. This is, arithmetically, what happens in *all* adaptation. It is a process which happens every time that successful adaptation takes place.

15. Wholeness-Preserving Transformations Are the Primary Ways the Trajectory of a Complex System Is Able to Reach Successful Adaptation

How can a complex system find its way to the good configurations? In a theoretical sense, we may say that the system walks through configuration space, taking this turn and that, and always arriving at a well-adapted configuration.

The huge question, of course, is how this walk is controlled: what are the rules of the walk, that make it lead to good adaptation? Although a few, very preliminary answers have been given to this question, no good ones have yet been given. This is, perhaps, THE scientific question of our present era.

In particular, in architecture, it is essential that we find practical ways of traversing configuration space! What this means, in common sense language, is the following. There are far too many possible configurations for a given design problem. We cannot hope to find good, or well-adapted designs, merely by looking for them. Instead, we must have processes which – when applied to a given starting point for a design problem, or for a planning process – will take us to good answers.

Nature has a way – built into the majority of systems, of finding its way to a well-adapted state for any given complex system – at least for most cases. We do not have a way. For buildings – and indeed for any complex system – this is the most fundamental practical issue of all. And for all the complex systems on our planet, that is the most vast, and most significant problem of our era.

In general we may characterize this task, as a task of walking through configuration space, until we reach good results. The assumption is that there are (indeed, there must be) some kinds of paths through configuration space which can get a system to the good places. When configuration space is smooth like a softly hilly terrain, one can get to the peaks, generally, by walking uphill until you get to the top: if I get to the top of one hill and it is not high enough, I walk to another hill, and go uphill further. These hill-climbing procedures only work on smooth hilly terrain, with not too many hills. Kaufmann argued correctly, that real configuration space is not nicely behaved like this, and so he attempted to give an answer as to how an adaptive system does get to the infinitesimally rare points that represent good adaptation.

Stu Kaufmann has made similar calculations, and published a few years ago, in his monumental work on theoretical biology where he showed that in principle, anyway, certain kinds of movements in the fitness landscape (as he calls configuration space), which may indeed home in on 'good' areas – and has offered a number of in-principle explanations suggesting the emergence of living systems is probable, not improbable, because of constrained movements in configuration space which lead autonomously towards well-adapted systems.

I applaud his work, and have been inspired by it. However, that said, one must also acknowledge that Stu has not yet given specific explanations, which describe, through such and such detailed mechanisms, how any specific features that appear in living organisms actually arise. His explanation is at a very high level of generality, and though convincing, leaves the hard work of figuring out how it really works, to create the geometrical configurations we observe, to others.

This is of particular concern to me. In the world of building one really does face the entire configuration space – since we can nowadays do virtually anything, and natural processes are not steering us towards regions of the configuration space. The fact that we, as creators of buildings, have to find the tiny, nearly invisible needles in the vast configuration haystack, makes our practical task still harder.

I have therefore spent much of the last twenty years, trying to find out what practical methods there are, for helping us traverse configuration space, and for finding genuinely profound and well-adapted buildings. It turns out that the fifteen properties associated with wholeness, described at length in Book 1, provide a substantial part of the answer. In Book 2, I have shown how living structure arises when reached by a series of movements in configuration space which are 'structure-preserving' paths. This involves the use of the fifteen properties as transformations, not merely as geometric properties. When we have a random configuration, and are trying to improve it step by step, we are most likely to reach zones of living structure (the good spots in configuration space), as we apply these transformations successively. The repeated use of these transformations – intensifying centers, emphasizing alternating repetition, increasing density of local symmetries, and so on – have immediate beneficial effects. These are real explanations, which have practical effects in real practical buildings. And what it amounts to, in informal language, is that the transformations represent a coded and precise way that aesthetics – the impulse towards beauty – plays a decisive role in the co-adaptation of complex systems.

If I am right, the consequence of my arguments go further, and would seem to suggest that adaptation – the successful movement around configuration space – cannot succeed unless it uses this technique. Indeed, I believe the structure-preserving transformations are likely to have real practical effect on our understanding of evolution and ontogeny. In these fields, too, I believe it will turn out that these concepts are indispensable, and give answers to presently open questions.

It might be said that these fifteen transformations coupled with the idea of structure-preserving transformations, do in part finally accomplish what Stu Kaufmann has not yet attempted. They give us real (and practically workable) indications of how to reach the tiny 'good' zones in configuration space, by traversing the space, step by step, in an incremental manner.

This might be powerful enough, in principle, to help us act as nature does – to create adaptation and beauty in complex systems, not only efficiency – and to restore to the landscape of Earth what we have been busy, for two centuries, unintentionally taking away.

A Summary: The Role of Beauty in the Science of Complexity

All in all, to wrap up, this might be said: The beauty of naturally occurring patterns and forms has rarely been discussed by scientists as a practical matter, as something needing to be explained, and as part of science itself. Yet the fifteen transformations, if indeed they provide a primary thrust in the engine of evolution, and in the many engines of pattern formation, give us a way of understanding how beauty – aesthetics – plays a concrete role, not an incidental role, in the formation of the universe.

I believe the fifteen transformations I have discovered will turn out to be naturally occurring, and necessarily occurring in all complex systems. The laws leading to their existence, will turn out, I think, to be inevitable or necessary results of the unfolding of wholeness, under the right conditions. And I believe, too, that our 20th-century notion that mechanical effects, without the guiding influence of these fifteen transformations, can create the beautiful structures we encounter in the universe, is simply wrong. In other words, it is the action of wave motion, mitigated by the fifteen transformations, that creates the beauty of the breaking wave; it is the operation of natural selection, mitigated by the action of these fifteen transformations, which generates discernible and coherent forms in the play of genetics and evolution; I believe it is the operation and unfolding of the most ordinary flower or stem of grass, mitigated by the operation of the same fifteen transformations, which generates the beauty of the flower. I believe that it is the same fifteen transformations which mitigate and channel the crumbling and heaving and bending of the geologic strata which generated the beauty of the Himalaya; and these fifteen transformations, too, which mitigate the action and swirling of the vortices on Jupiter, or the rippled piebald configurations we call a mackerel sky.

I know this must seem a fantastic claim, especially since we have learned so much in the last two centuries, by invoking pure mechanism, un-guided and un-channeled. But we should remember that our current claims for the success of contemporary methods, are indeed only claims, not yet proven to be sufficient. Indeed, in the writings of each of the three scientists interviewed – Brian Goodwin, Philip Ball, and Ian Stewart – there is from time to time very frank acknowledgement of certain subtle, unsolved problems, usually residing in the more holistic aspects of the emergence of certain truly complex wholes. All these subtle problems have to do with certain phenomena for which one cannot quite give believable operational rules to explain, or predict their occurrence. Nor can one typically create the truly beautiful new configurations – except when we know already what they are – in which case we can of course always give after-the-fact explanations of how they got there. As an architect, I am particularly aware of this problem, since, by trade, I am always trying to get to new, beautiful configurations, which have not been seen before. And I have learned how to do it successfully.

I am therefore particularly interested in the fifteen transformations (which I have described as the 'glues' of wholeness), as the most powerful heuristics in configuration space that I know of, because it turns out that these transformations do have the power to help reach new, and truly beautiful configurations, and I believe they do also have predictive force in helping to understand how naturally occurring complex adaptive systems find their way to truly beautiful new configurations.

Why do the creationists keep on making their fuss about evolution? I do not think it is only because of religion, but rather because some of them are aware that this problem of emergent beauty is not really solved. Why does Dawkins engage in such intense hand-to-hand combat with the creationists – something one would think hardly worth the ink? Is it not because of his own failure to acknowledge, more frankly, that the larger question of emergence of new, and beautiful configurations in evolution is not yet solved – at least not in the sense that computer simulations, using the algorithms of selection as currently understood, could yet arrive at truly beautiful new configurations and thus demonstrate the truth of the ideas of evolution as we currently understand them? Approximations to beautiful configurations can be simulated, yes – just as in the case of snow crystals. The real thing – just as in the case of snow crystals – not quite yet.

The successful evolution of new biological forms is, in my view, undoubtedly modified by transformations able to move toward structures that are inherently – that is to say, geometrically – coherent. I believe this process accompanies natural selection, and is the crucial missing part of current explanations: a vital component in the gamut of selective pressures. We need more frankly to acknowledge such a possibility, and in my view scientists who aspire to realistic explanations, like Dawkins, should stop dueling with creationists (which is far too easy), and instead try to focus on this geometrical problem at its root (which is much harder). I believe the fifteen transformations I have described go some distance to laying a path toward the solution of these difficulties.

Most scientists, and most lay people, share intuitions (not always acknowledged) which ascribe something great to the action of the universe. Roughly expressed, these intuitions rest on intuitive assessments that some deeper coherent, and more whole-oriented transformations, coupled with the action of the ordinary mechanisms we understand, and strengthening and reinforcing the wholeness which exists, can give birth to new and beautiful configurations from the wholeness which exists. What the arguments in *The Nature of Order* attempt, is to make these intuitions precise, and susceptible to experiment.

And let me underline the point: The fifteen transformations defined in *The Nature of Order* are rooted precisely in the qualities which make things beautiful. That is how I found them. And that is why they work.

Is it not preferable (and more likely) that some relatively straightforward process of the kind I have described, rooted in beauty – yet definable and in principle mathematizable, as these transformations are – is acting to help produce global, whole-oriented structures, rather than ascribing their appearance to creation, or to luck, or to blind chance, or to the action of purely local, over-simplified, equation-driven processes?

CONCLUSION

The richness of these concepts, their associated questions, and the inherent interest of some tentative answers to these questions, do indicate a new source of stimulation for the classical hard sciences – all of which, for the moment, emanates from architecture.

I wonder if it may not be worth making the following comment, on the mental world which scientists inhabit, and on a possible way of extending that world, to the benefit of us all.

I said at the outset of this paper, that scientists only rarely make things, and even the talk about complexity current in the last two decades, chooses very limited forms of complexity, looked at from very limited points of view.

Yet the rich source of scientific concepts and explanation I have sketched, suggests that it is the real adaptational complexity of the everyday world around us, which is potentially a rich source of science: and also a profoundly fitting arena for scientific effort.

If the house, the garden, the street, cities, landscapes, works of art, were to become normal objects of our interest, and that the creation of such things, instead of being split off as 'art' or 'planning' were to be given the deep affection, passion which it deserves – if, in short, the aims of science would move from analysis and hypothesis making, to a larger view, in which making were also to be included – would we not then have a more beautiful science, one which really deals with the world, one which not only helps us understand, but which also goes to a deeper level, and begins to encompass the wisdom of the artist, and begins to take its responsibility in healing the world which unintentionally it has so far created, and which it has, sadly, and unintentionally, so far helped to destroy.

In such a world, scientists would do better, the profound questions of health, wholeness, nature, ecology, and human joy, would be part of a single world view, in which it would be recognized as part of science – scientia – that is to say, knowledge – and in which scientists and artists together, speaking a common language, would take part in this joy, to the benefit of all humankind.

But, of course, this could not be the drystick view of mechanizable questions such as traffic flow, or strength of materials. They would have to embrace the real questions, the hardest questions, of the relationship between human joy and health, and the geometrical organization of the planet, as a source of life, at every scale.

That would, indeed, change science for ever.

Of course there are some who would say that work of this kind is wholly inappropriate for science, and that they prefer a vision of science which is more modest, small in scale, and deals only with potentially and immediately answerable questions. As someone who was myself also nurtured in that English empiricist tradition, I have much affection for that view.

But in any case, even if one takes Philip Ball's sensible, modest and empiricist view, it cannot be denied, I think, that the questions raised in this paper, are important scientific questions by any standard at all, that the means of solving these questions exist, are new but workable, and that, to make progress in existing and now coming fields of scientific enquiry these questions must be answered. Even the tentative, and necessarily partial answers to these questions which I have given, do open new doors, and mark new paths of enquiry and offer empirical solutions to problems in the natural sciences.

NOTES

1. Brought courtesy of © Christopher Alexander/Center for Environmental Structure Archive. This chapter was originally published in 2003 in two places:

    1. In the Nature of order website: http://www.natureoforder.com/library-of-articles.htm.
    2. In Katarxis: http://www.katarxis3.com/SCIENTIFIC%20INTRODUCTION.pdf.

2. In writing this short overview for a scientific audience, it was very helpful to read preliminary comments made by Brian Goodwin, Ian Stewart and Philip Ball who had just read selected pages from proof copies of Book 1. Their comments contained ideas and reactions that other scientific readers might share when first examining the four books of *The Nature of Order*. They were kind enough to draw attention, especially, to certain difficulties a scientific reader might have, in considering the problems introduced, or in making them useful to fields such as biology, ecology, physics, mathematics or computer science, and extending to many matters currently covered by complexity theory. I have written this chapter to make the connection to various scientific fields more clear, and to encourage comment and debate by working scientists.

3. Professor Alexander's education started in the sciences. He was awarded the top open scholarship to Trinity College, Cambridge in 1954, in chemistry and physics, and went on to read mathematics at Cambridge. He took his doctorate in architecture at Harvard (the first PhD in architecture ever awarded at Harvard) and was elected fellow at Harvard University in 1961. During the same period he worked at MIT in transportation theory and in computer science, and worked at Harvard in cognition and cognitive studies of wholeness and value. He became Professor of Architecture at Berkeley in 1963, taught there continuously for 38 years, and is now Professor Emeritus at the University of California. He is widely recognized as the father of the pattern language movement in computer science. He was elected Fellow of the American Academy of Arts and Sciences in 1996 for his contributions to architecture.

12. The dialectic as driver of complexity in urban and social systems
Alan Penn

This chapter was originally to have been written by Bill Hillier who sadly passed away on the 5 November 2019 following a long and progressive illness that attacked his body leaving his mind intact. He was working and writing up until days before his death. I have taken on the task of writing the chapter in his stead but cannot possibly hope to emulate either his intentions for it, as we never discussed these, or his acute and creative intellect which would undoubtedly have given the task an entirely new twist. Instead I precis an argument he first made in a keynote paper to the Conference on Spatial Information Theory (COSIT) in September 2009, and subsequently published in *Digital Urban Modeling and Simulation*, edited by Stefan Müller Arisona, Gideon Aschwanden, Jan Halatsch and Peter Wonka and published by Springer. The subject of that paper, 'Cities as socio-technical systems' (Hillier 2009), is entirely appropriate for this volume, and if you have not read it already, I commend it to you. My precis is inevitably partial and fails to do justice to his full argument.

Instead I build upon this argument and elaborate some key aspects of it that are of direct relevance to this volume. This elaboration is most certainly not what Bill would have written, and although I hope that he would have agreed with the thrust of what I say and would not have disagreed too violently with my interpretation and representation of his ideas, I have little doubt that he would have preferred to take it away, turn it upside down and emerge with a much more eloquent and nuanced version of his own. It was ever thus.

My twin aims are, first, to locate space syntax theory in respect of complexity science and, second, to locate complexity science in respect of architectural and urban phenomena. In writing this I reflect on space syntax as a body of theory and the way that it has developed. In particular, I use the comparison between space syntax and complexity theory to comment on the process through which space syntax theory has developed, and the way this draws on the phenomena of the world we live in, and what this says about Bill Hillier's ways of working and thinking that have led to the unique contribution he has made to science. I have added my own perspective to his key theoretical postulate set out in the COSIT keynote – the objective subject – and I ask whether this can help us resolve two paradoxes: Pareto's paradox in sociology that in spite of people making decisions based on emotion, they seek to justify these in rational terms; and Marx's historical paradox that a materialist history should lead inexorably to an idealist future. In summary, I argue that by combining the objective and the subjective into the two sides of a single dialectic sheet of paper, this may reconcile contradictions while simultaneously demonstrating how complexity arises in social and urban systems. However, the implications go further. By considering subjective experience of place and time as objective events, I build a picture of history and human progress, and develop a sketch of this as a dynamic system.

Part of my argument rests on the art of storytelling, and here I know of no better exposition than that given by Dr Greenslade to Richard Hannay in the introductory chapter of John Buchan's *The Three Hostages*. Dr Greenslade is explaining how to write a thriller:

> 'Quite simple. The author writes the story inductively, and the reader follows it deductively. Do you see what I mean?'
>
> . . .
>
> 'Look here. I want to write a shocker, so I begin by fixing on one or two facts which have no sort of obvious connection.'
>
> . . .
>
> 'Well, imagine anything you like. Let us take three things a long way apart –' He paused for a second to consider – 'say, an old blind woman spinning in the Western Highlands, a barn in a Norwegian *saeter*, and a little curiosity shop in North London kept by a Jew with a dyed beard. Not much connection between the three? You invent a connection – simple enough if you have any imagination, and you weave all three into the yarn. The reader, who knows nothing about the three at the start, is puzzled and intrigued and, if the story is well arranged, finally satisfied. He is pleased with the ingenuity of the solution, for he doesn't realise that the author fixed upon the solution first, and then invented a problem to suit it.' (Buchan 1924, p. 15)

Evidently, academic writing does the opposite. We lay out the problem first, and then present various pieces of evidence before pulling the solution, like a rabbit, out of the hat.

SPACE SYNTAX AND COMPLEXITY SCIENCE

As I write this, I am sitting in the space syntax laboratory alongside Bill's library of books. Among these is a yellow four-volume hardback set of proceedings of the 1968 International Union of Biological Sciences (IUBS) symposium series 'Towards a theoretical biology' edited by C.H. Waddington. The first symposium had just 19 scientific delegates and the proceedings aimed to capture not only the papers given, but something of the discussion in the room and subsequent correspondence during the editorial process. Some papers authored by one of the delegates have a written commentary by others. The first paper in Volume 1 by Waddington, for example, is commented on by Rene Thom, and so on. In addition to those that were already elder statesmen at that time, such as Waddington and Thom, the delegates included a younger generation of biologists and mathematicians; among them, Lewis Wolpert, Stuart Kaufmann and Christopher Zeeman.

While the IUBS hope to develop a theoretical biology as a parallel to theoretical physics may, with hindsight, be seen to have failed by comparison with the amazing successes of empirical and experimental biology, there is no doubt that the attempt was significant in its aim to apply mathematical representations to biological phenomena and processes. It is evident from reading the proceedings that time was devoted to sharing a common understanding of different terminology between fields.

The papers and commentaries are replete with Bill's underlining and marginalia, and give an insight into those aspects of the discussion in biology that Bill found interesting in his parallel and almost contemporaneous programme to develop a theoretical approach to architecture, urban phenomena and society.

Both biological and urban phenomena have offered fertile territory for the development of complexity science. Take, for example, Peter Allen's urban simulations, described in Ilya Prigogine's *Order Out of Chaos* (1993). However, both the biological sciences and the development of space syntax must be seen as largely independent of complexity science, driven as these each were by a desire to understand the lawfulness of their primary phenomena. As regards biology, these include metabolism, heredity and development, and for space syntax it might be seen as the lawfulness of built environments and their relationship to the societies that produce and inhabit them; however, I feel that this is too imprecise. In this chapter I propose to bring more precision to the question by transposing the questions of urban function and urban development into a more directly social form. How do we account for progress in human society over history? How might the ideas on which society is based move from one generation to the next? How do these ideas evolve and change so rapidly on some occasions, and yet remain in apparent stasis over generations on others? How does technological innovation and science fit into this picture?

PARADOXES OF MARX AND PARETO

These questions are not new. Many have written on them, but here I focus on two key thinkers, each of whom raises a paradox that may shed some light on this question. The first relates to the apparent contradiction between Karl Marx's materialist view of history and his apparently idealist view of the inevitability of the end of capitalism. The second was a paradox identified by Vilfredo Pareto, an engineer turned economist and, latterly, sociologist and political scientist. Both thinkers deal with the dynamics of progress in human society, each from very different starting points,[1] but with different points of intersection. Of relevance to this discussion is that both deal in different ways with the Hegelian notion of opposing positions in philosophical debate and the need to synthesise these. For Marx this formed the basis for dialectical materialism, while Pareto took the opposition between what people stated as their reasons for doing something and their underlying beliefs as the starting point for his synthesis.

Marx's belief is that all history is a history of class struggle. There is a clear element of Darwinian 'survival of the fittest' that underlies this position. In this view, human progress is to be accounted for on the basis of competition, or antagonism, between different classes. At this point Marx's economic analysis comes to bear. In the modern capitalist era, he shows that the ruling class maintains its position by extracting surplus value from the labouring class and harnessing new technologies to increase productivity and, so, surplus value. These profits create the capital required to invest in still greater innovation and productivity, thereby generating further profit. Thus the surplus value created by labour is extracted by the bourgeoisie. The cycle is built upon exploitation of labour by capital, and it is this antagonism that Marx holds is destined to see the fall of capitalism to be replaced by socialism, a return to a form of society where each individual is enabled to fulfil their potential.

Here lies the paradox. In spite of his materialist conception of history, Marx – with Engels – adopted an idealist position in respect of individual action. They called for revolution to hasten the inevitable demise of capitalism and to install communism in its place

(Marx and Engels 1848). This tension has perhaps best been summed up by Schumpeter (1942) in his characterisations of Marx the prophet, the sociologist, the economist and the teacher.

Pareto's final treatise was on general sociology (Pareto 1916 [1935]). He came to this late in life, having reviewed historical data on salary and wealth in various societies over history as an economist, and he drew the depressing view that the distribution of wealth in society was always highly skewed with just a few extremely wealthy individuals and the vast majority less well off. His conclusion, that there was always an elite and revolution merely serves to replace one elite with another leaving the majority just as badly off as before, brought him into tension with Marxism and earned him possibly unwelcome support from the Italian far right. It is probably for this reason, more than that his treatise on sociology ran to over a million words and is not the easiest read, that his thesis has not gained the attention it deserves.

In spite of their ideological differences, there is agreement between these two thinkers. Marx's economic analysis provides a mechanism to account for the emergence of an elite in capitalism. Where they may differ is in their projections into the future. Marx's view of an inevitable destiny is based on the idealistic belief that we will progress to fulfil our potential. Pareto's more pessimistic view, having looked back over history, was that not much has ever changed. One ruling elite is replaced by another. He then seeks to account for this by calling on an essentially psychological argument. We behave all too often non-logically, our decisions governed by instinct or sentiment and yet the reasons we give when we speak of why, are couched in rational terms.

Pareto based his social theory on a question which I paraphrase as follows: 'Why is it that in spite of the fact that people make decisions based on instinct and emotion, they seek to justify these in rational terms?' The distinction he draws between emotional and rational, or heart and mind, aligns closely to that between the subjective and objective.

This raises a methodological problem. How should we study non-logical behaviours scientifically? How do we know what is in people's minds if we can only observe their actions or listen to what they say? Usually, he says, we rely on what people say to explain their behaviours. However, there is another factor that is important, and that is what people believe. Sometimes this is formalised as a creed, but often it is not. By studying the relationship between beliefs or creeds, acts or behaviours and what people say (their expressions), we can go some way towards deducing what might be their state of mind (their sentiments). Since each of these factors may in principle affect the others – the way people act may affect what they believe, for example – the challenge is complex. In this way Pareto places an analysis of the dialectic – a key, in the differently defined concept for Marx – centrally in his treatise, although he does not state it as this.

CITIES AS SOCIO-TECHNICAL SYSTEMS

Hillier's view of the relationship between social systems and complexity is characteristically clear. He argues that an essential component of complex systems is that they are characterised by emergence. The emergence we see in cities happens in two primary ways. First, they are built over time by many different builders, each responding to the conditions and existing geography of the city at that time, each building according to the geometric and physical constraints of materials and the affordances of space, and out of this emerges a more or less comprehensible urban structure. Second, they are used by individuals and groups of people who engage in communal social and economic activities. They work, shop and party; they socialise and travel; they rent and invest; and, from time to time, they build. The city is socio-technical in that it arises out of a technical process of construction and a social process of function, and the two are intrinsically related, each causal to the other and each emerging from the other. This form of two-way causality is one of the elements that distinguishes Hillier's thinking from reductionism and determinism, and relates it directly to theories of complexity.

Bill Hillier's 2009 COSIT paper explicitly sets out to discuss how space syntax can be seen in relation to complexity science by developing this discussion. He draws on Jack Cohen and Ian Stewart's dual insights, that although the world is complex, living in the world requires us to see it in terms of its simplicities (Cohen and Stewart 1994), and that complexity arises through the interactions of numerous simple entities at a level below. It is through the interplay of the simple and the complex that urban form and function are related. However, I will suggest it is by extracting the simple from the complex that the whole edifice of Western science has been built, and that this more than any other factor influences the destiny of humans and the planet we live on.

Hillier's argument in the COSIT paper develops in stages. He shows how restrictions on aggregation probabilities can lead to the emergence of patterns of open space. A pattern in relation to this is not merely a visual form of the kind that we might see on wallpaper, but a systematic regularity of a more general kind. He shows how these in turn can be more or less intelligible in that local properties of space can be correlated or uncorrelated with global properties (one type of regularity). If local and global are correlated, then a human subject inhabiting that environment can learn to infer information about their global position from their perception of local context. In effect, they can learn the correlation and so make a prediction and act accordingly. If uncorrelated, then learning to make that inference is certainly more difficult and may be impossible.

Next Hillier demonstrates the lawfulness of spatial configuration. By investigating the effects on distance to all other points, of placing a block to movement or visibility in different locations within a space, he shows that the results of configurational choices are both systematic and quantifiable. Most importantly, local choices have global effects. This lays a basis for his key insight that cities comprise two main systems. First, a vertical system of emergence of form through many discrete actions of those that build them over time. If, for example, each builder places their next building (which acts as a block to visibility and access) in a location selected in order to maximise the total distance between all other locations, a very different global form will emerge than if they place it to minimise total distance. Second, a lateral process of function, exploiting or appropriating the pattern properties of space for socially meaningful action. So, for example, if shop owners choose more accessible locations in preference to more isolated ones, then these will attract shoppers and so amplify the effects of accessibility on occupancy and movement behaviour. Conversely, if they choose less accessible locations, they will need to invest in marketing their wares or in the relative quality of product and service to attract customers.

He concludes that human cognition is centrally related to both vertical and lateral processes, and that, in the generalised form of the objective subject, cognition acts to link these processes together. That is, the objective subject comprises those aspects of cognition and action that are common to multiple individuals – a type of statistical average that characterises a whole population. We might think of the objective subject as that which is learned about the regularities in the environment and which acts to inform individual action or behaviour. Hillier's objective subject resolves a fundamental dualism that has dogged urbanism; that of a divide between the urban environment and the experiencing human subject. He shows, instead, that the mathematical laws of space can be internalised and act to inform behaviour. While behavioural decisions remain subjective, their basis is neither arbitrary nor random, but objective and encoded in the configurational patterns that human society builds and uses.

In this way human cognition is intimately related to both the production of spatial configuration and to the behaviour and patterns of use people make in and of space. By coupling the vertical and lateral processes, he accounts for the way that humans can appropriate found and natural environments as well as the way that they can construct new environments to suit their purposes. He also accounts for an environment constructed by one group or generation being able to function for another, although the way it functions may be distinct since the objective subject of the new generation or group may be different from that of the original builders.

For Hillier the built environment, produced as it is by cognitive agents, but always subject to the mathematical laws that determine possible configurations and their functional consequences, is both objective and subjective at the same time, so resolving the dualism and the paradox. Viewed this way, the apparent divide between the experiencing subject and their environment evaporates to be replaced by a single functional complex. This also applies to the divide between multiple individual subjects who instead, and at the same time, can be seen to compose dynamic social groups that give form to the objective subject.

Cohen and Stewart's proposition is that, instead of to explain complexity, the more rewarding question is to explain the simplicities that seem to characterise the world one level up. They note that science generally explains complex phenomena through simpler theories. They give the example in statistical physics of simple gas laws relating to temperature, pressure and volume arising out of the massively complex interactions among numerous gas molecules. Hillier uses the analogy of our ability to throw a ball of paper to land in a waste basket. It seems that we have learned to compute trajectory, gravity and air resistance just by living in the world. Hillier's objective subject can be thought of in similar terms if we take that to be the commonalities among different individuals' perceptions of, and actions in, their environment that we each learn, and which enable us to predict enough about the reactions of others to our own actions to allow us to behave with intention in a social world. Here is the twist. While the objective subject is based on the similarities exhibited by multiple individuals, it is this that allows each individual to behave with autonomy and intent.

There is an obvious distinction between physical and social phenomena. While gas molecules are inanimate, humans have beliefs, intentions and desires. We have perceptions and memories. We behave purposefully, and appropriate and shape our environments to satisfy our needs and preferences. This requires that a theoretical account of a social phenomenon must be cognitively plausible. Crucially however, we have imagination and can envision different worlds to any that we have yet experienced. We can communicate these plans to others and then we can work together to create them. This gives a dynamic to the historic process that might be described as progress and gives a central place in this to the practice of architecture.

Before I turn to this, however, I describe two ways that space syntax research seems to have approached the issue of identifying simplicities in a cognitively plausible manner. I argue that these illustrate general principles that apply to science as well as to practical intervention in the world.

WHAT IS SIMPLICITY?

Two key features of the pursuit of underlying simplicity have emerged in space syntax research. The first involves identifying the most appropriate representation. The second involves something similar to convolution developed in machine learning in the search for regular or repeated patterns of behaviour among sets of variables. Humans are inveterate pattern-makers in that we continually search the phenomena of experience for pattern and meaning.

Hillier's objective subject places cognition as the central link between urban and social systems, but how exactly might that link work? The type of mechanisms of interest are those that relate human cognition to the configuration of their environment. Here there are two key pieces of evidence. The first passes through the nature of representation in analysis. One of the defining characteristics of space syntax research lies in a (possibly perverse) concern with exactly how best to represent the phenomena of interest – the configuration of space through which people move and in which they are brought into contact or kept apart. Within the discipline there is continual debate over whether one form of representation or another is better. What exactly is meant by 'better' is too often poorly defined, but there is a general consensus that it has to do with the ability to explain or discover hidden regularities in observed human behaviours. Over time, different representations are devised and put to the test. Most often this test is against data on observed aggregate movement through space. Here there is much to be learned from traffic engineering, which builds models to inform the management of traffic in cities.

REPRESENTATION AS A SIMPLIFYING ASSUMPTION

Current engineering practice in modelling movement behaviour in urban systems is based on an economic assumption that rational humans must seek to maximise benefits and minimise costs. In relation to moving around urban space, the view is that they will be attracted by specific destinations and will select routes to these in order to minimise cost. Costs are most often considered in relation to metric distance or time taken. Traffic modelling starts this way. First an origin–destination matrix is constructed to represent the demand for movement from all origins to all destinations – from home to work, for example, on the basis of survey data. Next the minimum distance routes between all origin–destination pairs are calculated and trips assigned to these. In most models there follows a process to take account of congestion in which the capacity of each link is considered and, if the trip demand exceeds the capacity on any link, a new fastest route avoiding that link is calculated and trips are reassigned. In a detailed model, traffic management is considered, such as speed limits on links or traffic-light timings at intersections. It is generally assumed that after a number of iterations the model will converge to an optimal solution.

There are several assumptions behind this type of model:

- The prime mover that drives human movement is the distribution in space of attractor land uses, such as places of work or exchange.
- Time in transit is a cost to be minimised, and time depends on distance and speed.
- People have perfect knowledge not only of the different routes available to them, but also of other users' demands, capacity and, so, of congestion.
- In order to minimise cost, people will change behaviour.
- Ultimately, the model will converge on an optimal solution.

In fields with a strongly held paradigm such as this, assumptions tend to disappear and to insert themselves generally unquestioned into practice. For example, the first assumption that the prime mover in urban systems is the distribution of attractors of movement, leads directly to land use planning as a primary tool. This, in turn, leads to plans characterised by functional zones linked by efficient transport networks. The second assumption, that efficiency is to be measured in transit time, leads to networks whose prime function is to move people from origin to destination.

A transport model of this kind is relatively data and computationally hungry and, although computer power has increased massively, when these methods were first developed this had a significant effect on the development of models. The early models were based on zonal data, for example, on employment and residence in administrative areas, for which census data made possible the construction of the origin–destination matrix, and on skeleton representations of transport networks between these zones. In these it was simplest to represent administrative areas as nodes in a network and the distances and capacities of the network as properties of the links. Thus the detail could be reduced to that which was computationally feasible given the power of computers at the time. A graph created this way is generally planar, and from a mathematical viewpoint this has attractions.

As computational power and more granular geographic data have enabled models to be built at ever finer spatial resolution, this form of representation has been maintained. Ultimately, in models that seek to represent the full urban street grid in detail, metric distance (cost) and street width (capacity) are properties of street segments between intersections, and so these are considered to be links and the intersections between streets as nodes. I suggest that this representation has become another hidden assumption within practice.

The findings of space syntax research have brought the assumptions, and the planning practices based on them, into question. First, it found that a representation of the street network in relation to axial lines considered as nodes, and intersections between lines as links, could explain a high proportion of the variance among observed movement flows on streets in urban areas. An axial line is the longest line of sight and access that can be drawn down a street. In a long, straight street an axial line will pass through many intersections with other cross streets. Since the axial line is represented as a node in the graph, this representation does not include metric distance in a direct manner. Neither does this representation incorporate the density or scale of attractor land uses. That is, it creates a topological representation that when transformed into a graph loses explicit metric information. These graphs are non-planar.

The issue of planarity turns out to be important. In a planar graph, the nodes near the geometric centre of an area will be closer to all other nodes in the network, while those near the edge will be deeper. This makes measures of centrality in a planar graph representation almost entirely dependent upon choice of boundary, something that in most continuous urban areas is arbitrary, while those of the non-planar axial graph are much less sensitive to the choice of boundary and are determined instead by connectivity. A well-connected line is likely to have a high closeness centrality regardless of where it is located relative to the boundary.

The axial representation drew criticism from those closely wedded to the conventional modelling paradigm (Ratti, 2004;[2] Steadman 2004) who noted that the reduction of a long line to a single node in the graph left no scope to account for variation in function along the length of a long street. Neither did it distinguish between a slight angular deviation between lines and a right angle turn or hairpin bend. To address these issues a segment angular representation was developed. This maintained the space syntax approach of considering space as the thing. Each segment of a street between intersections was represented as a node in the graph with the link to other street segments weighted according to angle of intersection. Continuation straight ahead was given a zero weight (thus in effect salvaging the axial line) while a right or left turn was weighted according to the angle in radians; thus a 90-degree turn would be weighted at 1 and a hairpin bend returning on itself would gain a weighting approaching 2.

The segment representation also allowed the incorporation of metric distance between segments by using the metric distance from centre to centre of each segment as a weighting on that link. Bill Hillier and Shinichi Iida (2005) turned this representation to effect by asking a different question. By setting graph measures of the axial, angular and metric representations as the independent variable against four pedestrian and vehicular movement data-sets for areas in London, they asked which best accounted for observed pedestrian and vehicular movement flows. The result, they suggested, would provide circumstantial evidence for the way that individuals must be representing and thinking about the urban environment. If people generally were behaving rationally to minimise metric distance, then metric measures of centrality would be expected to better explain observed movement behaviour than measures of the representations without a metric component.

Their findings were clear. The metric representation had only poor explanatory power, with the segment angular representation providing strong and significant correlations, closely followed by the axial representation. Although nothing in these findings could be described as conclusive, it is notable that there has been considerable doubt in cognitive science that humans depend on a metric understanding of the world (for example, Montello 1991; Tversky 2019). Instead we should entertain the idea that a simpler relational representation of space in the world may underpin cognition. If that is the case, then the question I turn to next is how might this representation 'get into people's heads'?

FROM EGOCENTRIC TO ALLOCENTRIC, OR FROM MULTIPLE INDIVIDUAL TO ONE SOCIAL VIEW

It is a truism that we inhabit and move through space and time linearly, but that, importantly, we experience both as multi-dimensional. Although I may only be here in this place at this precise moment, my experience is informed by my immediate perceptions as well as both my memory of this and other places, and my anticipation and expectations of here and wherever next I plan to go. This equally applies in respect of time, since both memory and anticipation are temporal (Rovelli 2017 [2019]).

This experience is amplified by architecture. Although I may be physically present at just one location in space at any moment, my perceptions extend into the distance ahead and around me, shaped as these are by the architecture of my surroundings and the perceptual fields of sight, sound, touch and smell that this affords. The objects and people in my immediate vicinity are to be made sense of in the context of objects and people in the distance; the music and traffic noise or smells from around the corner or the babble of voices across the square. It is this that converts an apparently linear route through space and in time into a multi-dimensional construct. The choices I make, of which way to turn, where to focus my attention or where to move next, are all part of this sense-making. Space is never one dimensional in the choice it affords for movement – at the very least we can always turn around and return the way we came. My choices of how to move are an active component in this, but so too is the spatial context which affords me these choices. Neither is prior to the other. A peripatetic viewer is not merely a passive observer, but an active agent in constructing a sense of place by synthesising these multiple dimensions.

A possible mechanism for this synthesis is implied by the notion of intelligibility, defined in (Hillier 1989). As I have described above, space syntax research is based on representations of spatial configuration as local spatial entities – for example, the axial line – connected to one another through a relationship of intersection. This enables the construction of a graph representing properties of the whole configuration in consistent terms. Graph properties can be thought of as local, that is, those that we can measure standing where we are without moving, and global, that is, those that require us to explore the whole graph. A local measure is the connectivity of a node in the graph (that is, the number of other axial lines each line intersects with). A global measure might be the closeness centrality of a node in the graph (that is, the average number of other axial lines that must be traversed to visit every axial line in the system, taking simplest, fewest changes of direction, trips). The degree of correlation between a local and a global measure defines the intelligibility of a system. This correlation asks a cognitive question: 'How confidently can I estimate a global measure of the graph from local information?' or 'From what I can see standing here, how well can I infer where I am in the whole system?'

Intelligibility in the axial graph is a property regularly found in urban systems, however, this is by no means a foregone conclusion. It is possible to construct graphs (and their axial maps) which show a positive, a negative or no relationship between local and global, or even where the correlation is degenerate owing to exactly the same conditions being replicated multiple times. The environments we build, regularly show this local–global correlation. There are notable exceptions. Particular cultures produce relatively unintelligible urban forms, and modern social housing projects of the 1960s and 1970s in the UK were often characterised by repetition and, so, were the degenerate type. It may be unsurprising that these were referred to at the time as unintelligible or labyrinthine.

Intelligibility as defined here is the correlation between two variables and so the question of how this might be realised by human experience requires a cognitively plausible mechanism. One possible mechanism for information compression is that offered by Hermann Haken and Juval Portugali as information adaptation (Haken and Portugali 2015). Machine learning offers a different analogy in the form of convolution (LeCun et al. 1989). Convolution is a method for embedding information in a neural network on the way that two functions overlap. By taking a series of windows of different sizes on the data, patterns at different scales can be captured. From this, after training a neural network, given the state of one function, the corresponding state of the other can be retrieved. This method has proven highly effective to derive patterns from graphic data for applications such as face recognition and, from temporal data, for speech processing.

Now consider the peripatetic observer as capturing a window on their environment. As they move, the window shifts. Their memory allows the relative size of the window to vary from an instantaneous snapshot to, say, several minutes. This enables the integration of different observable features of the environment at different scales. Let me describe an example from an imagined walk through London. As I walk along a street, I am aware of its extent and width, the height of its buildings, their architectural style, the kind of land uses – residential, retail, commercial, institutional – the traffic speed and volume, the ambient noise, the pedestrians and their behaviour. In general, these factors are uniform along the length of the street, but when I turn a corner they all change – the street narrows, the buildings reduce in height, the nature of property uses changes perhaps from predominantly commercial to more retail, and the volume and speed of traffic reduces, but relative to that there seem to be greater numbers of pedestrians. The micro-behaviours of the pedestrians change, people walk more slowly and browse the shops, perhaps in couples or groups. There is a smell of cooking from restaurants or street vendors. Turn the corner again and the property use changes from retail to predominantly residential. Pedestrian and car traffic reduce, and the street is lined by parked cars, and so on through the neighbourhood.

Here I am describing a type of urban experience, which will be different in detail in every city, or part of a city, that we might visit around the world. However, I hope that the experience is recognisable and generic; cities vary in the way that different features come together and in the way that these change as we move through space, but they are consistent in that their features do vary together with the physical geometry and network topology of space. It is this co-variation which makes cities learnable with features that can, at least in principle, be extracted by a convolution-like process and then used to make predictions: 'If I do this, then that is likely to follow.' This is the move from an egocentric peripatetic observer to an allocentric compressed description of the spatial and socio-economic function of the urban landscape; a set of internal consistencies that comprise one of Cohen and Stewart's simplicities. If instead of co-variation and some degree of consistency, the features of our environment were randomly distributed in relation to one another, then there would be nothing for it but to map or to learn their disposition in the full detail of their complexity. It is the possibility to derive a compressed description – a simplicity – that not only makes cities intelligible and meaningful to us, but which gives us autonomy and allows us to behave with intention. This is central to providing subjectivity to Hillier's objective subject.

CREATING CONSISTENCIES: FROM THE COGNITIVE TO THE ECONOMIC, AND BACK

How might these consistencies arise? Here I must hypothesise. I suspect that what we are seeing is the outcome of a series of closely coupled processes, and it is this close coupling that produces co-variation and consistency. The first of these is Hillier's vertical process of production of urban form through many individual acts of building. The second is through the processes by which the resulting spaces are appropriated for social and economic purposes – Hillier's lateral process.

I start with an example. Anybody who has ever camped in drifting snow soon learns three things. First, pitch your tent with the door facing into the wind; second, don't pitch it in the lee of another tent; third, don't pitch your tent too close upwind of another tent. The reason for this is all to do with the way that snowdrifts accumulate downwind of an obstacle. You really do not want to wake up in the morning with your door buried in your own drift, having been buried in a neighbour's drift or having caused a drift to bury your neighbour.

The moral is that every act of construction is a response to at least two things: first, an existing environment with an inherent set of constraints and affordances; and, second, a desire on the part of the builder to change these affordances to be more conducive, that is, to create a more comfortable or pleasing setting for life. This might be considered an aesthetic pursuit (Penn and Turner 2018). Close coupling occurs because the first act of building changes the environmental affordances for the next builder, and their reaction takes this into account. The second builder's action, in turn, will change the environment for the first and may require them to adapt. This cycle is close coupled. What emerges through this process are a set of consistencies that reflect both the underlying physics, in this example of wind and snow, and the social obligation not to bury our neighbours. Our driving motivations are to camp comfortably despite the blizzard and to get on with our neighbours. Accomplishing these successfully brings fulfilment, and I would argue this is largely emotional rather than rational in nature.

Harold Hotelling's observation that two ice-cream sellers will tend to gravitate together towards the centre of a beach is an example of a similar type of close coupling (Hotelling 1929). It is also an economic example and calls into play not only the actions of the two ice-cream sellers as stall-builders, but of the whole population of their customers along the length of the beach. Here the phenomenon shifts from Hillier's vertical process of construction to his lateral process of appropriation for a desired socioeconomic outcome. We are no longer only concerned with the inanimate actions of drifting snow or the way the wind blows, but with the purposeful actions of people looking to buy and sell. It turns out that this type of process drives many of the consistencies we observe in cities. Here I argue in contrast, our driving motivations as economic agents are more rational.

In 1993 Bill Hillier published a paper describing a law of 'natural movement' (Hillier et al. 1993). This made what at the time seemed a bold claim: that the prime mover in cities was not the distribution of land uses, but the distribution of pedestrian movement that served to attract those land uses. The claim was based on logic and empirical data. Observations of pedestrian movement in urban areas regularly found that there were greater flows of pedestrian movement on shopping streets than on streets without shops. It was this observation that formed the basis for the prevailing conventional view that people were attracted by retail land use and that land-use distribution was the prime mover in urban systems. This led to land-use and transport models based on an assumed Newtonian distance decay from attractor land uses. However, Hillier showed that using the axial map and measures of closeness centrality ('integration' in Hillier's terminology) both the distribution of shops and of pedestrian movement correlated with the configuration of space. Since the axial model contained no reference to the land-use distribution the implication was clear. The correlation between pedestrians and shops was caused by each being correlated with an intervening variable – the configuration of the street grid. Taking the evidence one step further, Hillier showed that in areas without shops the relationship between integration and pedestrian movement was broadly linear, but in areas that contained retail land uses there was a power or exponential relationship. This suggested that pedestrians moved through the street network according to patterns of accessibility, and that shops located preferentially to take advantage of the passing trade. These shops then attracted additional pedestrian movement, creating a multiplier effect. Figure 12.1 explains the implications.

The close coupling of spatial configuration, pedestrian movement and retail land-use distribution seems to be a primary consistency in urban phenomena. However, this has been found to propagate through other land-use types as a consequence of the market in land and the ability of retail to outbid other land uses for the most accessible sites. Research by Laura Narváez Zertuche (Narváez Zertuche et al. 2013; Narváez Zertuche 2015) has shown that urban bid rent curves postulated by William Alonso (1964) are seldom concentric, as he suggested (Figure 12.2(a)), when looked at in detail, but are defined by the axial configuration of the street network rather than 'as the crow flies'

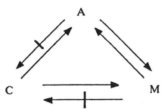

Note: A is attraction, C is configuration, M is movement. Attractors and movement may influence each other, but the two other relations are asymmetric. Configuration may influence the location of attractors, but attractors cannot influence configuration. Likewise, configuration may influence movement, but movement cannot influence configuration. If strong correlations are found between configuration and both movement and attractors, the only logically possible lines of influence are from configuration to both movement and attractors, with the latter two influencing each other.

Source: Hillier et al. (1993).

Figure 12.1   Implications of the axial model

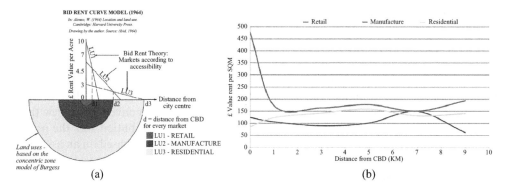

Source: Narváez Zertuche (2015, fig. 4.4).

Figure 12.2   *(a) William Alonso's theoretical bid rent curves; (b) Laura Narváez*
Zertuche's empirical bid rent curves for Cardiff, UK

distance on the map. Figure 12.2(b) shows that retail outbids other land uses throughout the radius of the city, suggesting that axial integration which links edge to centre, better explains retail location.

Here is one explanation for the experience of turning a corner and everything changing as described previously in our imagined walk through London. The peripatetic observer retrieves a set of consistent co-variations of stimuli – as they turn a corner, new things come into view, traffic changes, land uses change and so on – but this is a consequence of an underlying set of economic processes that govern these distributions in the first place. Central to this patterning is that the configuration of the network of space governs both the movement opportunities for the observer and the economic process through which urban functions locate in space. Thus, the observer is in effect retrieving a description of the underlying social and economic processes that gave rise to the city and maintain its function.

If I am correct that the process through which the observer learns these consistencies may operate similarly to convolution, it implies that somewhere in their cognitive capacity exists a compressed description of these same social and economic processes, learned through experience. Let us imagine that the observer is an active agent in the system, say, someone searching for a good meal in an unfamiliar city. In many cities in the world there is a cluster of restaurants catering for the tourist market, often along a single street. The maîtres d' tout for business and show their menus, each competing with their neighbours for your custom. What leads to this cluster if all are competing; surely it would be better to move away from your competitors? This is Hotelling writ large. By clustering together, they all benefit by attracting the tourist trade from across the city. As a consequence, more of the passers-by are looking for a meal than would be so on an average street. More of them no doubt are tourists, and unlikely to return or provide repeat custom. This makes the task of business strategy relatively straightforward. Employ a persuasive maître d', ensure that the menu and the front of house looks attractive, pay a premium rent for the pitch on the restaurant street, but save on the chef and quality of ingredients. Given that the game here is to optimise on a first sale to tourists who will be unlikely to return, this sets the parameters for a dissatisfied customer. The maître d' may be accomplished in fending off complaints by offering a complimentary aperitif, but what the tourist learns is either to take a local with them – not all restaurants on the street operate the same business model, but without local knowledge it is hard to tell them apart – or, failing that, to turn the corner once or twice. Look for a restaurant in a more isolated, lower-rent location but with a thriving clientele. Spatial isolation coupled with good custom is a sure sign of a restaurant that competes on quality and is known locally for that.

Let us imagine instead that the observer is not the customer but someone who wants to set up shop. They walk the streets and from what they see of the local context, they retrieve from their compressed description learned over a lifetime of experience a forecast of the possible implications of any choice they might consider. They use this to inform their actions – whether to bid for premises here or there, how much to pay, what business model to operate – whether to compete, for example, on price or quality. I am not suggesting that the compressed description is a construct that the individual has direct and conscious access to, nor that they explicitly and consciously perform a search in this way. Anecdotally, shop owners (or more likely their agents) searching for new premises walk the streets and count the footfall of passing trade. They look at other shops in the area that may be similar and judge how successful they are. Just as customers looking for a meal, they look at how popular a restaurant appears to be. These all form a part of informing our actions.

INTENTIONAL BEHAVIOUR AND SEARCH

Alasdair Turner and I conducted a series of experiments (Penn and Turner 2004) to investigate the effects of spatial configuration and shop location on the time it took a random search using a sampler/agent with long-distance, forward-facing vision to search an environment and to find something they were looking for. Alasdair's implementation of long-distance vision was cunning (Turner and Penn 2002). He used a visibility graph of an environment in which an arbitrarily fine grid of points are connected if they are inter-visible through open space in an environment. Next, for each point in the graph he constructed a lookup table of the connected points divided into 32 bins according to orientation. This enabled precomputation, and therefore a very rapid, impromptu, search for visible locations within the field of view of a forward-facing sampler at any location and facing in any direction. Additional features of the environment could be stored as variables associated with nodes in the graph and accessed rapidly. Thus, shops could be located at the faces of buildings and the sampler could see them. This simulation was named exosomatic visual architecture (EVAS).

The samplers search an environment by moving through it stochastically. They select a point at random from those in their visual field, turn towards it and move three steps, then repeat the process. The turn and move change the visual field of the sampler at the next iteration. They are in effect doing a random search of a graph, albeit a complex graph involving, as it does, orientation and a forward-facing and long-distance field of view constrained by the placement of blocks to vision in the environment. This search was found to replicate observed pedestrian movement patterns in a range of urban and

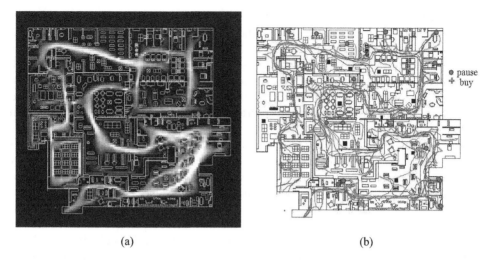

(a)   (b)

Figure 12.3   (a) IKEA showroom floor analysed by EVAS. (b) Observations of shopper movement patterns by Farah Kazim

built environments, including unusual environments such as the showroom in IKEA stores (Penn 2005) which have been designed intentionally to induce in shoppers a disorientating and characteristically sinuous movement pattern (Figure 12.3).

The experiments with search efficiency are described in detail in Penn and Turner (2004), but the significant findings were that: (1) the time it took for an agent to find a first shop depended on how dispersed shops were in the environment; (2) clusters of shops took longer to find, but once found the second, third and so on were already available; and (3) if the agent was searching for a specific flavour of goods, the more shops searched, the more likely they were to find the desired item (Figure 12.4). The conclusion was that dispersion supported convenience, while clustering supported comparison shopping. The restaurant street is attractive to a tourist who wants to compare a number of menus before making a choice, while corner shops are located to be close to a local market catchment.

It is important to note that the samplers in the EVAS simulation are not agents in any conventional sense of social simulation (see, for example, Bratman 1987 [1999]). They hold no internal model of the world, nor beliefs, desires or intentions. They have no processing power or memory. All the intelligence, if any exists, is inscribed exosomatically in the environment and its structure. The search differs from Brownian motion in just two ways. First, interaction is over a long distance; as far as the eye can see, constrained by the built form in any given environment. Second, the interactions are anisotropic. The sampler has an orientation and a forward-facing field of view, and gains information from the environment from one direction at any given moment. In this way the stochastic search of the visibility graph can be thought of as emulating some important characteristics of embodied human visual perception. However, since the EVAS algorithmic simulation is essentially a stochastic search of a graph structure, the process is Markov and therefore deterministic. From this viewpoint, it may be surprising that the EVAS analysis shows any relationship at all to observed human behaviour.

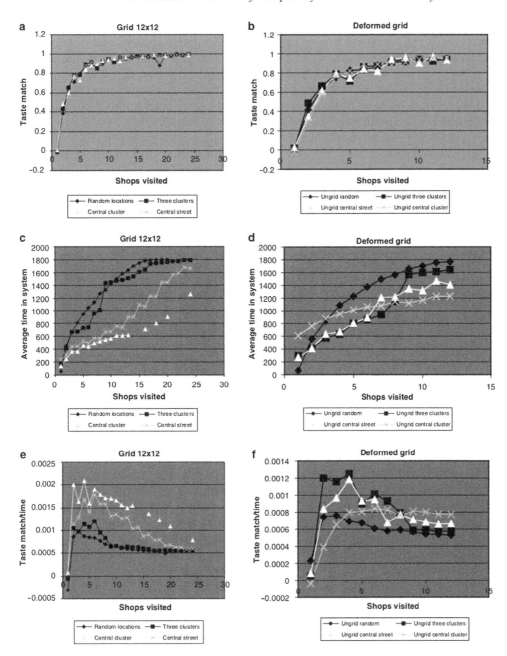

Source: Penn and Turner (2004, fig. 11).

Figure 12.4   Graphs of agent search performance

This illustrates that what may appear as the most intentional of behaviours – when we actively set out to find something specific in our environment to satisfy our wishes – are determined to a significant degree by a set of objective structures in the world, including the way that we have evolved forward-facing vision and how this affects our route choices, the configuration of the built environment that we have constructed and the way that markets in land have allocated functions. How can we balance this with the strong feeling that we are autonomous subjects behaving with intention?

My suggestion is that people engage as active agents in meaning-making, and this is a process that may account for our feelings of subjectivity and intention. We bring our individual experience to bear in interpreting the physical, spatial and social phenomena that we encounter, and then we act to achieve our subjective aims. Against this background however, we face and play out a number of constraints defined by the possibilities inherent in the way that urban form is constructed, the way that functions are located, and the restrictions and affordances that this imposes on its use. These constraints are both lawful and objective in nature.

STORYTELLING AND EMOTIONAL ENGAGEMENT

The process I am suggesting may be analogous to storytelling. On the face of it a story consists of a sequence of episodes or events, the scenes in a play or film or chapters in a book, told or heard over time in a linear sequence. However, according to Marie Laure Ryan (1991), a well told story is not a linear construct transmitted from active storyteller to a passive listener, but it engages the listener actively in meaning-making. The characters of the protagonists are developed, the events and clues in the context described, and the listener forms hypotheses and expectations of the meaning of past events and what will happen next. In doing this we construct causal hypotheses, the 'who done it' of the detective thriller or the 'who will marry prince charming' in a fairy tale.

These are informed by the listener's knowledge of the genre of the story: the types of narrative structure and knowledge of these structures guide the listener in terms of what to expect. However, equally, a well told story keeps the listener guessing and it is this active engagement in meaning-making and revising our guess as new information is revealed, that makes the story more than linear and so 'tellable'. The conversion from a linear sequence into a multi-dimensional network of events and relationships between events, possible events and causal hypotheses, occurs because the listener is not a passive receiver of information but is engaged as an active meaning-maker. The listener imagines possible futures for the story which may or may not transpire in the narrative as it is presented linearly in chapters on the page. It is this that creates anticipation and suspense in the listener, surprise at events, or sympathy and antipathy to the characters. This is how emotion is created, and the way that any underlying moral message hits home.

It will not have escaped you that the active listener's path through a story bears a resemblance to our imagined peripatetic observer's walk through London. I suggest that the process of meaning-making in narrative may also involve a similar convolution-like process to construct emotional engagement.

Here we can return to Pareto since now we have a plausible mechanism through which beliefs, behaviours and what people say – their expressions – may be related to emotion and state of mind. I suggest that it is through the active engagement of the subject in the objective act of meaning-making that emotion and sentiment enter the subject's state of mind. By becoming personally engaged in active interpretation of the phenomena we perceive, we internalise our own place among these phenomena and it becomes part of our own identity. I notice that, when waking from a dream, often the events dreamt make little or no rational sense, but the emotion is palpable. Current theories of dreaming as memory consolidation and reconsolidation (Zhao et al. 2018) suggest that this may form part of the way we have evolved to consolidate our memories of the most important of our daily activities. If Pareto is correct that sentiment and emotion drive people's choices and decisions, then this may be one mechanism underlying both Hiller's objective subject and the dialectic.

THE SPACE OF IDEOLOGY

I have described elsewhere a possible relationship between the architectural construction of spatial configuration and the emotions of empathy (Penn 2018). Empathy – the ability to put oneself in another's place, to see their point of view and to infer how they might act – is a fundamental emotion for both a social species and a predator. We see examples every day, when traffic slows apparently for no better reason than to look at an accident on the other carriageway, or when we see the cook slice their finger and cringe involuntarily, feeling their pain.

To summarise the argument, the act of construction of built form shapes inter-visibility in open space in its immediate surroundings (Figure 12.5). The effects of shelter construction on inter-visibility of points in space, and therefore on human occupancy, is no less lawful than their effect on the way that snowdrifts accumulate. Construction creates the affordances which humans as social animals appropriate and, I argue, among the primary emotions which this serves to structure, are those associated with empathy, especially for strangers. Although we can empathise with people we know well purely through imagination, it is hard to empathise with someone that you do not know unless you can see or hear them.

The same affordance of visibility that allows the social animal to empathise, also allows the predator to watch and to anticipate the likely behaviour of its prey. It allows

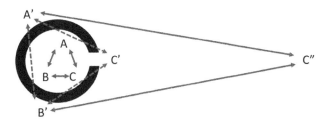

Source: Penn (2018, fig. 1).

Figure 12.5   *An elementary enclosure affects inter-visibility among agents in the landscape*

Jeremy Bentham's panopticon to act as a machine of surveillance and control for a prison or a machine of supervision and care for a hospital. That such similar machinery of the brain and environment can work to accomplish very different ends is what allows it to support both collaborative and competitive forms in social relations.

Both Marx and Pareto saw the evolution of society in essentially Darwinian terms. For both, survival of the fittest entails competition and struggle. Marx held that class struggle explained the history of human development. Pareto also saw that a governing elite maintains its power through a show of strength. It was his apologia for authoritarian government that endeared him to the Italian right in the early decades of the twentieth century. Both thinkers held that human destiny was to some extent inevitable; however, they differed on the nature of that destiny. For Marx, it was inevitable that capitalism would fall through revolution, to be replaced by communism. For Pareto, revolution would merely lead to one elite replacing another, and effectively for the masses there would be no change.

There is another view. Jane Jacobs sees human progress as largely owed to humanity's superior ability to cooperate and to collaborate for a common purpose based on empathy and altruism (Jacobs 1969). Jacobs does not deny that on occasion people have built city walls as defensive structures to protect from aggression, but as often as not she says they were used to define boundaries for the purpose of taxation, and this is about trade and exchange; necessarily cooperative activities. This highlights that the key ideological divide in politics is not between the extremes of right and left, but between those that hold human progress to result from competition, struggle and revolution, and those from the liberal centre that hold the primary driver to have been collaboration.[3] Pareto recognised this distinction, noting that the imperative of the former was largely emotional while that of the liberal was logical and rational. He went further, noting that one problem of liberal rationality was that it lay itself open to being usurped by authoritarian regimes that valued force over legitimacy. It was this that, he held, accounted for a pendulum or cycle in history that swings between authoritarian/emotional and liberal/rational regimes.

In his discussion of complexity, Bill Hillier alighted on Jack Cohen and Ian Stewart's notion that the most interesting aspect of complexity was the simplicities that seem to arise one level up. This mirrored Bill's idea that although emergence of new forms was interesting, the phenomenon that required explanation was the convergence that could be seen into a relatively small number of specific spatial types; for example, streets and the deformed wheel integration core that seem regularly to occur through history. It is these structures that deliver mechanisms to allow controlled access by strangers into the middle of a settlement for the purpose of trade and transaction. In effect, they are mechanisms to enable us to have it both ways, that is, to allow access by strangers for the purpose of collaboration, but to maintain control and safety.

On many occasions and at different levels in this discussion it seems that space syntax provides a unifying structure allowing the reconciliation of apparently opposite tendencies: collaboration/competition; material/ideal; convenience/comparison; and rational/emotional. Hillier's key conceptual tool in achieving this reconciliation is the objective subject, and it is by unpacking potential mechanisms at play in both the human mind and the environments they build that space syntax contributes to our understanding of urban phenomena.

The thrust of my argument is that while space syntax bears a relationship to complexity, its prime motivation was not to understand complexity per se, but to develop a theoretical understanding of the phenomena at hand; of human society, the environments it designs and builds and the interplay between the two. I reflect that the scientific process that Bill and his colleagues pursued during the construction of this body of architectural theory has been characterised by a set of principles of scientific practice that has proven remarkably effective in breaking theoretical new ground. In each case, however, the science is related to architectural practice.

Architectural practice, similar to science, proceeds by testing hypotheses. The hypotheses I am thinking of are the ideas for a building that respond to the client's or community's needs or wishes. These wishes are not generally for the building itself, but for a social or economic outcome that the building helps realise. Here James Gibson's (1966) notion of an affordance is useful. What architects design is an environment together with a set of affordances. It is these affordances, more than the physical object itself, that create value; it is less about what the building is than what it does and what it enables its occupants to do. The following three main principles of science and architectural practice seem to have emerged from space syntax research.

Representation

Representations are active agents in science, and therefore never accept current representations as given but keep inventing new representations. Bill termed this 'creating phenomena', after Ian Hacking (1984). No single representation will capture the full spectrum of any phenomenon, so develop multiple representations and use these to triangulate a problem. Since a representation is active, it must also be subject to critique and design. For example, the choice to represent the space of a street as a node in a graph and the intersection as a link (or the reverse), as I have shown, is not an arbitrary decision.

Architectural practice also makes use of representations. Representations are most often thought of in relation to their role in communicating the idea for a building from the architect's mind to others; that is, other designers, the client and the builder. They allow the act of designing to become social. By externalising onto physical media a representation of the idea for a building currently in one architect's mind, that conception can be shared. Using physical, tactile and graphic representations, these engage with the experiential as well as the rational senses. This opens the concept to analysis and critique by others, and in a design team this enables the creative process to shift from an individual basis to a social basis. Donald Schön described this process as reflective practice (Schön 1983, 1990). This dynamic and emergent process of design can be thought of as a complex system in which ideas for a building and representations of those ideas iterate until a specific design proposition is agreed.

However, representations also play an active role which has received relatively scant attention. They allow architects to detach themselves from the design in their mind's eye and, by distancing themselves, to flip between synthetic and critical analytic roles. Architects sometimes refer to this as holding a conversation with the design. The use of multiple representations and of layering representations in series, are among the tricks of architectural craft. 'Turning the tracing paper over', changing scale of representation, changing media and shifting between plan, section, elevation and perspective, all enable architects to sense the implications of a design configuration that otherwise might elude the mind's eye and at the same time to conceive of new opportunities.

Universality

A valid theory must be universal – it is pointless to have an urban theory that only holds for, say, Western cities but cannot account for the full range of urban phenomena found around the world in the archaeological and anthropological record – therefore do not accept boundaries to the application of a theory. If you discover an anomaly, place it centrally in your research programme as this is the only way that progress can be made. This derives from the principle of universality. Anomalies point towards the boundaries of application of a theory and, in order to be universal, a theory must expand to encompass anomalous phenomena. This pinpoints an important feature in the dynamics of progress in science. Creating phenomena is often a process of developing a representative framework within which new anomalies become apparent. These then become the central driver for new theory to explain all pre-existing phenomena and the new phenomena within a common theoretical model. In this way the explanatory power of the theory, its universe, expands.

In architecture, universality also applies; everything is endogenous and there is no such thing as an exogenous variable. What I mean by this is that a single architectural construction must resolve functional and ideological challenges of all types. We cannot exclude any variable and claim that it lies outside our problem definition. Equally, there is no boundary to a given site; we have to consider the context relevant to our design, however proximate or distant.

Caveat deceptae

Beware of importing theoretical frameworks from one field of science to another (*caveat deceptae* literally translates as beware misconceptions). While there are lessons to be learned, the temptation to make the evidence fit the theory can lead us astray. This has perhaps best been described by Richard Feynman in his famous 'cargo cult' critique of the social sciences (Feynman 1974). Architectural history is also littered with examples of the application of ideas drawn from other fields. Ideas such as the territorial behaviour of birds are adduced in support of designs that segregate neighbourhoods. Newton's theory of gravity is used as a basis for traffic modelling. Too often these imported ideas are found at best to be unhelpful and often to be dangerously misleading.

As with biological systems, space syntax bears a relationship to theories of complexity – it would be surprising if it did not since urban and social systems are highly complex in both structure and function – but the principles outlined above are also architectural in a deep sense that relates to the epistemology of science as an emergent process.

Considered in the dynamic way I describe, the progress of scientific understanding can be seen to emerge from a cycle of phenomena > representation > pattern or anomaly > hypothesis, then (following Karl Popper 1969) further empirical evidence > phenomena . . . and ultimately, new theory. As time passes anomalies arise and new phenomena require new theory, and so the cycle continues. There is no reason to expect an imported theory that has emerged in this way out of the phenomena of one field, to capture the structures involved in a different field. It is for this reason that the use of theoretical frameworks derived in one field to explain another can, at best, be considered as metaphors or thought experiments. There are those who differ with this in a search for underlying mathematical structures that explain phenomena of widely different systems. Complexity theory may be one of these, however, my ambition here is less. I believe that complexity and simplicities arise out of the type of dynamic and virtuous cycle I describe. If this cycle helps describe the process through which science has developed, then I argue there is an equivalent cycle that relates to other aspects of human progress.

THE PROGRESS OF CIVILISATION AS A DYNAMIC SYSTEM

I have proposed elsewhere (Penn 2018) a model for the emergence of organised social structures and institutions around 10 000 BC on the Anatolian plateau. The core of my argument was that the appearance at that time and over the space of just a few millennia of dense proto urban settlement, writing, token currency, specialisation in production, domestication of staple foods, storage and irrigation infrastructure, law and the apparatus of the state, were not coincidental. Nor was it the intentional act of some external agency although it has been suggested that the climatic transition from the Pleistocene to the Holocene brought the stability required for settled agriculture, and therefore settlement (Richerson et al. 2001). I suggest, instead, that the series of innovations were the product of a self-reinforcing cycle of cause and effect, or perhaps a set of coupled cycles as depicted in the Figure 12.6.

The nub of my argument was that the built environments that began to be constructed at that time in history served a very specific role, that of providing a common setting for social action. They provided an objective background for the objective subject. Equally, they were the creation of the objective subject – an externalisation that enabled sharing and collaboration. It was this externalisation of part of our cognitive machinery into the configuration of the environment that served to shift the trajectory of development of the species into the social sphere. Instead of development and innovation passing away within the lifespan of the inventor, the scale and density of settlement increased the chances of innovations being learned and passed on. This, in turn, made possible specialisation and division of labour, but as a consequence required increased transaction between specialised producers – obsidian workers must have traded for food, for example. Transactions, in turn, spawned innovations, including symbolic recording – token currency and, ultimately, writing. Increased transaction will have resulted in dispute and required arbitration and, ultimately, law and the machinery of state.

In Figure 12.6 I use two opposing arrows to indicate 'enables' and 'requires' directions in the cycles, but this is merely a shorthand to indicate a more complex idea. It is central to my argument that these interdependencies are not causal in having a temporal arrow of time, but are strictly two way. The invention of symbolic writing, for example, required learning and divided the population between the literate and illiterate. The

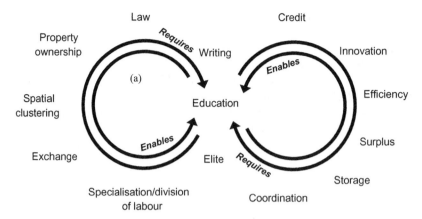

Note: Spatial clustering requires property ownership which requires law. Conversely, law enables ownership which enables clustering. The two cycles are held together through a common dependency on writing, education and the development of an elite.

Source: Penn (2018, fig. 4).

Figure 12.6   Cycles of feedback and reinforcement

former gain access to additional information and power. This creates an elite. However, an elite with power may have time to invest in learning rather than surviving, and so can become literate. This is akin to Marx's dialectic, or to the relationship between objectivity and subjectivity in Hillier's objective subject, or between the logical and non-logical in Pareto's schema.

A similar duality exists between science and technology. It is generally unclear and probably not useful to discuss which predates the other. The steam engine was invented before the laws of thermodynamics for which it was probably a main stimulus. Physics, in turn, has become a primary tool for the engineer. Considered in relation to the progress of scientific understanding described previously, engineering innovation designed to solve practical problems of living in the world has been a main contributor of precisely those anomalies that require new scientific theory to explain them. Thus the duality is another of those two direction cycles.

It is for this reason that instead of searching for some type of family tree in the history of human progress, we may be better off considering a series of bifurcations between different states, triggered by innovations that took hold and propagated if they were found useful, so becoming self-reinforcing. Undoubtedly, dense urban settlement was one of these, as were the division of labour, currency, writing and the apparatus of state formation. So, too, was the emergence of science and technology.

There still exist today, on the verge of extinction, hunter-gatherer groups whose social structures and lifestyles are in all likelihood similar to those of our ancestors before 10 000 BC. It is not useful to think of these as in any way primitive and our own society as modern if by this we imply some kind of temporal dimension. Both they and we are equally a part of humanity in 2021. More than that, it was exactly this type of group that decided to settle and build on the Anatolian plateau, and triggered the explosion of human progress we are still experiencing today.

NOTES

1. Both thinkers were prolific, and for Marx, certainly the amount written about his thinking far exceeds his own voluminous writing. For a concise overview of both bodies of thought I would point to Raymond Aron's *Main Currents in Sociological Thought*, Vol. 1 for Marx and Vol. 2 for Pareto. For a more extensive reading of Pareto short of the full four volume treatise (Pareto 1916 [1935]), I recommend Pareto, V. (1976), *Sociological Writings*, selected and introduced by S.E. Finer and translated by D. Mirfin.
2. It should be noted that the editors published a rebuttal of Ratti's paper in the same issue of the journal (Hillier and Penn 2004), together with Ratti's response to that. As Thomas Kuhn (1962) noted, paradigm shifts often elicit this type of reaction.
3. We might go further to describe the space within which ideology is embedded, instead of as a plane with left and right, as a cylinder in which these two wings come together at the far side (Figure 12.7). It is tempting to go one step further and suggest they might be embedded in a non-Euclidean Mobius strip where left- and right-handedness are themselves undefined.

Figure 12.7   See note 3

REFERENCES

Alonso, W. (1964), *Location and Land Use*, Cambridge, MA: Harvard University Press.
Aron, R. (1965), *Main Currents in Sociological Thought*, vols 1 and 2, Harmondsworth: Pelican Books.
Bratman, M.E. (1987), *Intention, Plans, and Practical Reason*, repr. 1999, Cambridge, MA: Harvard University Press.
Buchan, J. (1924), *The Three Hostages*, London: Hodder and Stoughton.
Cohen, J. and I. Stewart (1994), *The Collapse of Chaos: Discovering Simplicity in a Complex World*, New York: Penguin Books.
Feynman, R. (1974), 'Cargo cult science', Caltech Commencement Address, Pasadena, CA, June.
Gibson, J.J. (1966), *The Senses Considered as Perceptual Systems*, London: Allen and Unwin.
Hacking, I. (1984), 'Creating phenomena', in I. Hacking, *Representing and Intervening*, Cambridge: Cambridge University Press, pp. 220–35.
Haken, H. and J. Portugali (2015), *Information Adaptation: The Interplay between Shannon Information and Semantic Information in Cognition*, Cham: Springer.
Hillier, B. (1989), 'The architecture of the urban object', *Ekistics*, **56** (334–5), 5–21.
Hillier, B. (2009), 'Cities as socio-technical systems', in S. Müller Arisona, G. Aschwanden, J. Halatsch and P. Wonka (eds), *Digital Urban Modelling and Simulation*, Berlin: Springer, pp. 475–90.
Hillier, B. and S. Iida (2005), 'Network and psychological effects in urban movement', in A.G. Cohn and D.M. Mark (eds), *Spatial Information Theory*, Berlin and Heidelberg: Springer, pp. 475–90.
Hillier, B. and A. Penn (2004), 'Rejoinder to Carlo Ratti', *Environment and Planning B: Planning and Design*, **31** (4), 501–11.
Hillier, B., A. Penn, J. Hanson, T. Grajewski and J. Xu (1993) 'Natural movement – or, configuration and attraction in urban pedestrian movement', *Environment and Planning B*, **20** (1), 29–66.
Hotelling, H. (1929), 'Stability in competition', *Economic Journal*, **39** (153), 41–57.
Jacobs, J. (1969), *The Economy of Cities*, New York: Random House.
Kuhn, T. (1962), *The Structure of Scientific Revolutions*, Chicago, IL: University of Chicago Press.
Laure Ryan, M. (1991), *Possible Worlds, Artificial Intelligence, and Narrative Theory*, Bloomington, IN: Indiana University Press.

LeCun, Y., B. Boser, J.S. Denker, D. Henderson, R.E. Howard, W. Hubbard et al. (1989), 'Backpropagation applied to handwritten zip code recognition', *Neural Computation*, **1** (4), 541–51.

Marx, K. and F. Engels (1848), *The Communist Manifesto*, London: Communist League.

Montello, D.R. (1991), 'The measurement of cognitive distance: methods and construct validity', *Journal of Environmental Psychology*, **11** (2), 101–22.

Narváez Zertuche, L. (2015), 'Architecture, economy and space: a study of the socio-economics of urban form in Cardiff', PhD thesis, University College London.

Narváez Zertuche, L., A. Penn and S. Griffiths (2013), 'Spatial configuration and bid rent theory: how urban space shapes the urban economy', in Y.O. Kim, H.T. Park and K.W. Seo (eds), *Proceedings of the Ninth International Space Syntax Symposium*, Seoul: Sejong University, pp. 95.1–95.23.

Pareto, V. (1916), *Trattato Di Sociologia Generale*, English trans. 1935, A. Livingstone (ed.), *The Mind and Society*, 4 vols, New York: Cape.

Pareto, V. (1976), *Sociological Writings*, selected and introduced by S.E. Finer, trans. D. Mirfin, Oxford: Blackwell.

Penn, A. (2005), 'The complexity of the elementary interface: shopping space', in A. van Nes (ed.), *Proceedings of the 5th International Space Syntax Symposium*, Delft: Techne Press, pp. 25–42.

Penn, A. (2018), 'The city is the map: exosomatic memory, shared cognition and a possible mechanism to account for social evolution', *Built Environment*, **44** (2), 162–76.

Penn, A. and A. Turner (2004), 'Movement-generated land-use agglomeration: simulation experiments on the drivers of fine-scale land-use patterning', *Urban Design International*, **9** (2), 81–96.

Penn, A. and J.S. Turner (2018), 'Can we identify general architectural principles that impact the collective behaviour of both human and animal systems?', *Philosophical Transactions of the Royal Society B*, **373** (1753), 20180253, doi:10.1098/rstb.2018.0253.

Popper, K. (1969), *Conjectures and Refutations: The Growth of Scientific Knowledge*, London: Routledge & Kegan Paul.

Prigogine, I. (1993), *Order Out of Chaos: Man's New Dialogue with Nature*, New York: Flamingo.

Ratti, C. (2004), 'Space syntax: some inconsistencies', *Environment and Planning B: Planning and Design*, **31** (4), 487–99.

Richerson, P.J., R. Boyd and R.L. Bettinger (2001), 'Was agriculture impossible during the Pleistocene but mandatory during the Holocene? A climate change hypothesis', *American Antiquity*, **66** (3), 387–411.

Rovelli, C. (2017), *L'ordine del tempo*, English trans E. Segre and S. Carnell, 2019, *The Order of Time*, New York: Penguin Random House and London: Allen Lane.

Schön, D. (1983), *The Reflective Practitioner: How Professionals Think in Action*, New York: Basic Books.

Schön, D. (1990), *Educating the Reflective Practitioner: Toward a New Design for Teaching and Learning in the Professions*, San Francisco, CA: Jossey-Bass.

Schumpeter, J. (1942), *Capitalism, Socialism, and Democracy*, New York: Harper and Brothers.

Steadman, P. (2004), 'Guest editorial: developments in space syntax', *Environment and Planning B: Planning and Design*, **31** (4), 483–6.

Turner, A. and A. Penn (2002), 'Encoding natural movement as an agent-based system: an investigation into human pedestrian behaviour in the built environment', *Environment and Planning B*, **29** (4), 473–90.

Tversky, B. (2019), *Mind in Motion: How Action Shapes Thought*, New York: Basic Books.

Waddington, C.H. (ed.) (1968), *Towards a Theoretical Biology*, Chicago, IL: Aldine.

Zhao, H., D. Li and X. Li (2018), 'Relationship between dreaming and memory reconsolidation', *Brain Science Advances*, **4** (2), 118–30. doi:10.26599/BSA.2018.9050005.

PART IV

MODELLING COMPLEX CITIES

13. Modelling car traffic in cities
Vincent Verbavatz and Marc Barthelemy

1. INTRODUCTION

Understanding and modelling urban traffic has become essential to our societies. Since most humans now live in urban areas and two-thirds of world population will live in cities by 2050 (United Nations 2014), traffic congestion is becoming an ever-larger problem. In cities, both in developed and developing countries, traffic congestion is a usual part of daily commuting and a major issue for policy makers. As city dwellers get stuck in traffic jams – the average American now loses around 100 hours a year sitting in traffic (Buchanan 2019) – traffic is a source of substantial productivity losses and decline in quality of life. It is accountable for the increase of fine particle emissions (Gray and Cass 1998) and the root of deterioration of health conditions. Transport is also accountable for 15 percent of world greenhouse gas emissions (Herzog 2009), and it is now more than urgent to abate car traffic and, in particular, congestion that makes car trips lengthier and more polluting.

The urgency of tackling climate change has made traffic mitigation paramount. While some believe that self-driving cars, smart cities and machine-learning can optimize car routes and naturally reduce congestion, these technologies are arriving a great deal more slowly than enthusiasts expected (Buchanan 2019). Ride-hailing services and carpooling were also supposed to reduce car ownership, but it seems that in cities where they have been introduced, traffic delays have gone up, not down (Erhardt et al. 2019; Henao and Marshall 2019).

Attempts to mitigate traffic in cities have often stemmed from the cities themselves and mainly focused on individual car use. Solutions comprise congestion charging in some, such as London or Singapore, reducing the number of roads or traffic lanes in Paris, dedicated lanes for carpoolers in Los Angeles and, finally, expanding public transport networks. We note that the decision to close an important road in Paris (the *voie sur berge*) showed a lack of ability to predict the subsequent effects and to assess the impact on the traffic and air quality at the city level. This suggests that we crucially lack theoretical grounding and empirical evidence for an in-depth understanding of urban phenomena. Cities are complex systems, mobility patterns are complex phenomena and collective behaviors within these systems are not obviously predictable. Why would someone drive and not use public transport? Who are the drivers and what are their needs? Without answering these questions, it is hard to prove that the aforementioned proposals are efficient and not counterproductive. For instance, reducing the number of roads could be to no avail, if commuters have no alternative to driving. Even worse, if the number of drivers is constant, in the absence of any other transport substitute, such a decision could induce an increase of congestion with more emissions and spreading over secondary roads. Some experts have also been skeptical about the effect of expanding public transport. For example, economists Duranton and Turner (2011) argued that luring some drivers off the roads and onto trains and buses leaves less congested roadways, which then attract other drivers to these same roads. It is equivalent to the act of building more roads does not reduce congestion but just attracts new drivers onto the roads. This is the fundamental law of road congestion in transport economics. However, the empirical evidence for these effects is scarce and relies mainly on econometric arguments. We therefore need a theoretical framework, consistent with empirical observations, in order to understand car traffic and how to mitigate it. Without any prior judgments on how to regulate traffic in the best manner, we review briefly in this chapter past and recent empirical studies and elaborate a simple, yet sound, model of car use in cities.

2. STUDIES OF CAR TRAFFIC

2.1 A Seminal Empirical Result

Understanding urban mobility patterns has become essential for reducing transport-related greenhouse gas emissions and crucial for planning efficient environmental policies (Newman and Kenworthy 1989; Newman 2006; Dodman 2009; Glaeser and Kahn 2010; Oliveira et al. 2014; Creutzig et al. 2015). In a 1989 seminal paper, Newman and Kenworthy correlated transport-related quantities (such as gasoline consumption) with a determinant spatial criterion: urban density. Higher density areas were shown to have reduced gasoline consumption per capita and thus reduced gas emissions. This result was mainly based on empirical evidence, such as that shown in Figure 13.1. Plotting the gasoline consumption per capita (or here the transportation energy use per capita) versus the urban density was used as a demonstration of the importance of urban density. The result had a significant impact on urban theories over past decades and has become a paradigm of spatial economics and urban planning (Pumain 2004).

This study was purely empirical and has no theoretical foundation, which casts some doubts on the importance of density as the sole determinant of car traffic mitigation. The model also predicts that gasoline consumption increases sharply for low-density cities, which is surprising and needs justification. More generally, we have to understand why the energy use (or gasoline consumption) decreases as a simple function of density. Also, this result was not reproduced in other independent works, which cast doubts about its reproducibility. It is thus necessary to understand this result by using theoretical approaches of modelling.

2.2 Theoretical Insights

At a theoretical level, car traffic has been studied at various granularities. Most approaches have focused on the traffic in a single lane, with various tools ranging from agent-based modelling (see, for example, Gonzalez et al. 2008; Bettencourt and West 2010), cellular automata (Batty 2008) or hydrodynamic approaches (see, for example, the review, Barthelemy 2016, on various physics-type approaches). For a network, an important theoretical assumption that led to many mathematical works is that of equilibrium. This idea, proposed by Wardrop (1952), is related to the Nash equilibrium and states that the journey times on all used routes are less than or equal to those that

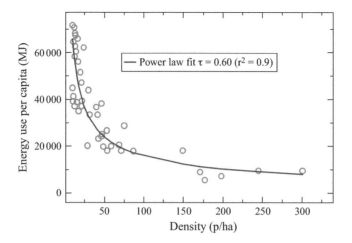

Note: The continuous line is a power law fit (of the form $E \sim \rho^{-\tau}$) as a guide to the eye. The exponent is $\tau \approx 0.60$.

Source: Graph drawn from the data in Newman and Kenworthy (1999).

Figure 13.1 Energy use per capita (for transport) versus population density

would be experienced by a single vehicle on any unused route (user equilibrium). That is, each user chooses the best route for themselves and cannot improve their journey duration by unilaterally choosing another route. The second idea, the system optimum, states that at this equilibrium the average journey time is at a minimum. A famous consequence of these assumptions about car traffic is Braess's (1968) paradox. This paradox states that adding one or more roads to a network can augment congestion and traffic times for all drivers, thus resulting, *inter alia*, in increased greenhouse gas emissions. The situation is mainly equivalent to a multiplayer problem in game theory, such as the prisoner's dilemma. Individually, drivers have no interest in sacrificing for others and the system converges to a Nash equilibrium which is far from the optimal collective solution. Without considering any new driver or car owner, the simple extension of the road network can result in increased traffic and emissions. Braess's paradox thus highlights the importance of taking into account collective behaviors and feedbacks when dealing with traffic modelling.

These ideas are intellectually very attractive and have the advantage of putting car traffic in mathematical terms. However, the empirical validity of the Wardrop assumptions was recently challenged with new data sources such as the Global Positioning System (GPS) (Zhu and Levinson 2015). These studies in particular showed that most people did not choose the shortest path. These results demonstrate again that we need a new theoretical framework validated by empirical observations in order to construct robust route choice models that are integrated into traffic simulations.

2.3 Econometric Studies

Car congestion was also considered from the viewpoint of economics with discussion about its determinants (see, for example, Branston 1976; Fujita and Ogawa 1982; Louf and Barthelemy 2013, 2014). A cornerstone of econometric studies of car traffic is the fundamental law of road congestion, first suggested by Anthony Downs (1962, 1992) and more recently reinvestigated by Duranton and Turner (2011). This law states that increased provision of roads in metropolitan areas is unlikely to relieve congestion of these roads. New roads induce new drivers and, as a corollary, mass transit does not reduce congestion. To assess their statement, Duranton and Turner compared the total length of roads within American metropolitan statistical areas (MSAs) to a measure of traffic: vehicle-kilometers traveled (VKT). Vehicle-kilometers are determined by multiplying the number of vehicles on a given road by the average length of their trips measured in kilometers. Duranton and Turner claimed that VKT is a linear function of the total road length of the urban network and that a change in the road length network results in a proportional increase of the VKT. Hence, they proved that new roads do not relieve old roads, they just attract new drivers and increase total driving distance.

By expanding their reasoning, they attempted to prove that new public transportation networks are to no avail in reducing congestion. Commuters lured off roads onto mass transit networks relieve roads and hence lure new drivers onto roads. Considering large buses in peak service per 10 000 population, showed that the number of buses has no effect in reducing VKT. Duranton and Turner did not consider rapid transit (trains, subways and light rail) in their study, crucially undermining the relevance of their conclusions.

2.4 Applied Methods for Urban Planning

On a more applied note, traffic forecast models such as the four-step model and variants (see, for example, Barthelemy 2016 and references therein) are used for key purposes in transportation policy and planning. The four-step model, ubiquitous in transport forecasting, attempts to link land use with individual behavior, and therefore macrostructures of traffic. The four steps of these models are usually (McNally 2000):

1. Trip generation – for each local zone of the model, the number of incoming or outgoing trips is assessed from local land use as well as from demographic and socioeconomic factors.
2. Trip distribution – origins are matched with destinations, usually resorting to the gravitational model (Erlander and Stewart 1990), which is akin to Newton's gravitational law of attraction. Trips from zone A to zone B are proportional to the offer of trips in A, the demand of trips and B and inversely proportional to the travel distance between A and B.
3. Mode choice – mode of transportation is chosen for each trip, depending on travel time, travel cost and access to mass transit.
4. Route assignment – the best (fastest) route for the chosen mode is calculated on the network. Traffic on each road is back-propagated into trip distribution and mode choice.

These models usually rely on data about a specific area, such as population, employment and actual traffic. They are used to forecast the traffic on a given infrastructure (or a project) and its environmental impact. In all instances, these models are fine-tuned for specific areas and are very likely to over fit.

Hence, we do not have a generic model that is able to predict the value of traffic-related quantities for any city and, from a more fundamental level, to indicate the critical parameters and dominant mechanisms of traffic in urban areas.

3.   NEW SOURCES OF DATA

Newly released sources of data may, however, help in building a new universal framework for understanding urban traffic. New datasets of congestion are now available (see Table 13.1) and make traffic visible and measurable. The INRIX Global Traffic Scorecard (INRIX Global 2018) gives the average number of lost hours in congestion, whereas the TomTom congestion level (TomTom Traffic Index 2018) gives the increase in commuting time owing to congestion in comparison with free flow.

However, national and supranational statistical agencies have generalized the availability of modal share (or modal split) in urban areas. Modal share is the percentage of travelers using a particular type of transportation (de Dios Ortúzar and Willumsen 2011). In addressing the question of the environmental impact of transport, modal shares are crucial to assess the relevance of public policies as well as the forecasting efficiency of transport models.

Finally, a new metric, which we will prove to be essential, albeit not common, in the following is the access to mass rapid transit (MRT). Access to MRT is the availability of a fast transit network within a specific area. Typically, it can be seen as the share of population living close to MRT stations, say within walking distance (15 minutes' walk or 1 kilometer, for instance).

In the following section, we propose a new simple, yet robust, universal model of car traffic in cities that rely on these new datasets and metrics. We follow the main lines of Verbavatz and Barthelemy (2019).

Table 13.1   Urban areas ranked according to the number of hours lost in congestion (per year), and the congestion level

Rank INRIX 2018 (hours lost)	Rank TomTom 2018 (congestion level)
Bogota (272)	Mumbai (65%)
Rome (254)	Bogota (63%)
Dublin (246)	Lima (58%)
Paris (237)	New Delhi (58%)
Rostov (237)	Moscow (56%)
London (227)	Istanbul (53%)
Milan (226)	Jakarta (53%)
Bordeaux (223)	Bangkok (53%)
Mexico City (218)	Mexico City (52%)
Moscow (210)	Recife (49%)

Source: INRIX Global (2018) for congestion, and TomTom Traffic Index (2018) for congestion level.

4. IDENTIFYING CRITICAL INGREDIENTS

In order to understand the physics of the traffic system, we make some simplifying assumptions. All the assumptions we use in this section are approximations to the reality, but we claim that our model captures the substance of the traffic phenomenon in large urban areas. Starting with a model containing all these various parameters would not be tractable and would hide the critical ingredients.

We first assume a monocentric city with a unique central business district (CBD) in which are concentrated most jobs. We also assume that individuals are distributed uniformly over the whole urban area. The existence of a single CBD, the location of homes and the density of MRT are considered as exogenous variables. The important endogenous variable is here the share of car users and the time spent in traffic jams (allowing us to estimate carbon dioxide, CO_2, emissions, for example).

In order to discuss commuting costs, we assume that a proportion p of the population has access (has to walk less than 1 kilometer) to MRT, such as subway or elevated rail (we neglect buses here, which are traffic dependent), whereas a share $1 - p$ of the population has no choice but to commute by car (we assume that all individuals can drive a car if needed). That is, p is the probability of having access to the MRT (see Figure 13.2), but it does not imply that it is the mode chosen: if one agent has access to rapid transit, that agent needs to compare the costs G_{car} and G_{MRT} in order to choose the least costly transportation mode.

The fraction p of individuals that have a choice between car and MRT chooses the transport mode with the lowest generalized cost. Generalized cost takes into account monetary costs and trip duration. For cars, this includes congestion as described by the Bureau of Public Roads function (Branston 1976), and the corresponding generalized cost reads (Louf and Barthelemy 2013, 2014).

$$G_{car}(x) = C_c + \frac{d(x)}{v_c} V \left(1 + \left(\frac{T}{c} \right)^\mu \right), \tag{13.1}$$

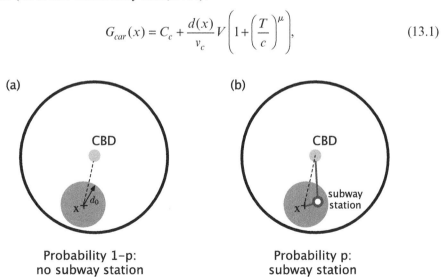

(a)

CBD

d_0

x

Probability 1−p:
no subway station

(b)

CBD

subway
station

x

Probability p:
subway station

Figure 13.2 Schematic description of the model: in order to reach the CBD, individuals have a probability p to have access to an MRT station

while for the MRT the generalized cost reads

$$G_{MRT}(x) = V\left(f + \frac{d(x)}{v_m}\right),$$ (13.2)

where C_c is the daily cost of a car, v_c and v_m are the car and MRT velocities, respectively, c is the road capacity of the city, f the walking plus waiting time for transit, $d(x)$ the distance between home located at x and the CBD, T the total car traffic and μ the exponent that characterizes the sensitivity of the road system to traffic. The quantity V is the value of time defined in transport economics as the amount that a traveler is willing to pay in order to save one hour of time. It is an increasing function of income and is bounded by the hourly wage. We assume here that driving is faster than riding on public transport ($v_c > v_m$) but is more expensive ($C_c > 0$; as in Glaeser et al. 2008, we assume that the cost of MRT is negligible). When an individual has chosen a mode, they stick to it and will not reconsider their choice even if the traffic evolves. That is, individual habits have a longer time scale than traffic dynamics.

Individual mobility is then governed by comparing these costs G_{car} and G_{MRT} and depends on exogenous parameters (such as car and MRT velocities and car costs) and endogenous parameters, such as the commuting distance or the value of time. In the general mode choice theory (see, for example, Ben-Akiva and Lerman 1985), given the values of the costs G_{car} and G_{MRT}, there is a probability $P_C = F(G_{car} - G_{MRT})$ to choose the car. The function F is in general smooth and satisfies $F(-\infty) = 1$ and $F(+\infty) = 0$ and we consider here the simplest case where $F(x > 0) = 0$ and $F(x < 0) = 1$. An individual located at x with access to the MRT will then choose to use the car if $G_{car} < G_{MRT}$, which implies a condition on the value of time of the form: $V < V_m(x)$ where $V_m(x)$ depends on the parameters of the system and on $d(x)$ and reads

$$V_m(x) = \frac{c_c}{f + d(x)\left[\frac{1}{v_m} - \frac{1}{v_c}\left(1 + \left(\frac{T}{c}\right)^\mu\right)\right]}.$$ (13.3)

Also, writing the equality $G_{car} = G_{MRT}$ between generalized costs of car and MRT leads to the definition of a critical distance given by

$$d(V,T) = min\left(L, \frac{\frac{c_c}{V} - f}{\frac{1}{v_m} - \frac{1}{v_c}\left(1 + \left(\frac{T}{c}\right)^\mu\right)}\right),$$ (13.4)

where $L \sim \sqrt{A}$ (A is the area size of the city) is the largest extent of the city. This distance is the maximal extent of MRT relative advantage. Below that commuting distance, the car is too expensive (and not fast enough) to be worth investing in. Beyond that commuting distance, the situation reverses and the car is more advantageous (see Figure 13.3).

This critical distance evolves as traffic increases, translating into driving is less advantageous when the traffic is heavy. This expression also allows us to show that poor individuals are more likely to use public transport, since they are more apt to spend time than

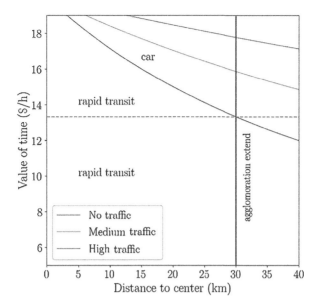

Note: The limit (critical distance) between the two areas evolves with congestion: the larger the traffic (curves from 'No traffic' to 'High traffic') and the larger the area in which rapid transit is beneficial compared to car driving. The solid vertical line corresponds to the size of the urban area and indicates the critical value of time (dashed line) below which rapid transit is advantageous in the whole agglomeration whatever the value of congestion.

Figure 13.3   *The most advantageous mode of transport depends on the value of time of individuals and the distance to the urban center*

money. Distance to the center is hence pivotal in this decision process: too far from the center – further than the critical distance $d(V, T)$ – and individuals favor driving to avoid lengthy journeys, and the richer they are, the shorter this distance. For heavy traffic, this critical distance is greater than the city size $L \sim \sqrt{A}$ (where A is the area size of the city), implying that riding on the MRT is more advantageous for all individuals who have access to it. Thus, writing $d(V, T) \sim L$ gives a critical maximum traffic T^*, above which driving is less beneficial in the whole agglomeration.

When population increases, car traffic has two sources: first, individuals may not have access to the MRT and, second, if they have access to it, they might be too far away and will prefer to take the car. This can be summarized by the following differential equation for the variation of car traffic T when P varies

$$\frac{dT}{dP} = 1 - p + p\left(1 - \eta\left(d\left(V, T\right)\right)\right), \tag{13.5}$$

where the first term of the right-hand side corresponds to the $1 - p$ share of individuals far from MRT stations, and the second term to the fraction η of individuals living further from the center than $d(V, T)$ while having access to MRT (η is a function of density). Assuming that density is constant or decreases with distance to the center, we can show that at the dominant order we have $T < T^* : T \simeq \left(1 - \dfrac{p}{Ab^2}\right)P$, where b is a function of the exogenous parameters. For $P^* = \dfrac{T^*}{\left(1 - \dfrac{p}{Ab^2}\right)}$, the only source of car traffic comes from

individuals who do not have access to the MRT, which leads to

$$T = (1-p)(P - P^*) + T^*. \tag{13.6}$$

Compiling data from 25 megacities in the world, for which we had an estimate of the population having access to the MRT, we computed the critical levels T^* and P^*. For reasonable values of time (Crozet 2005; Numbeo 2018), we have T^* small ($T^* \ll P$) for almost all cities considered here, which means that the MRT is more advantageous than driving in the whole agglomeration, even at low traffic: public transport is so economical that people living near rapid transit stations are highly likely to use them. Traffic does not appear as a determinant parameter in individual mobility choices as it concerns mostly people who have no choice but to drive and who suffer from onerous commuting costs and unavoidable time-consuming trips as traffic increases. Since we have in general T^*, $P^* \ll P$, we obtain the simple prediction:

$$\frac{T}{P} \simeq 1 - p \tag{13.7}$$

Despite the simplicity of this prediction, it is a non-trivial consequence of rapid transit cheapness and individual choices of mobility. We compared the empirical car modal shares $\frac{T}{P}$ of these cities with our prediction in Figure 13.4, and observe a very good agreement and a relevant linear trend highlighting the efficiency of public transportation in reducing traffic. Deviations from the prediction are mostly owing to the existence of other modes of commuting (in European or Asian cities) or lower car ownership rates (for example, in Buenos Aires; Roque and Masoumi 2016).

At this stage, we also note that this result is easily transposed into the polycentric model of cities. Indeed, considering k subcenters with the same behavior would equally lead to the same conclusion for all subcenters and hence the whole city.

Our model also provides a prediction for the transport-related gas emissions and we will focus on the CO_2 case for which we obtained data. As these emissions are (roughly) proportional to the total time spent on roads, we have

$$Q_{CO_2} = \sum_{\text{drivers } i} d(i)\left[1 + \left(\frac{T}{c}\right)^{\mu}\right], \tag{13.8}$$

where $d(i)$ is the distance from the home of driver i to the CBD. On average we then obtain that the CO_2 emitted by car and per capita is given by

$$\frac{Q_{CO_2}}{P} \propto \sqrt{A}(1-p)(1+\tau), \tag{13.9}$$

where $\tau = (T/c)^{\mu}$ is the delay due to congestion and is empirically accessible from the TomTom database (TomTom Traffic Index 2018). We compare our predictions with disaggregated values of urban CO_2 emissions in Figure 13.5 and observe a very good agreement. We observe some outliers, such as Buenos Aires which has a very small car ownership rate and thus lower than expected CO_2 emissions, and areas such as New York which appears to be one of the largest transport CO_2 emitters in the world (OECD 2016).

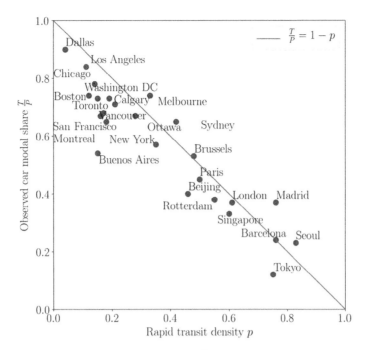

Note: The diagonal line is the prediction of our model ($R^2 = 0.69$). Discrepancies to the predicted value are probably mostly owing to the existence of other modes of transport, such as walking or cycling.

Figure 13.4   Comparison between the observed car modal share and the share of population living near rapid transit stations (less than 1 kilometer) for 25 metropolitan areas in the world

This result illustrates the role played by public transport and traffic in modulating transport-related CO_2 emissions. Most importantly, we identify urban sprawl ($\sqrt{A}$) as a major criterion for transport emissions. We note that if we introduce the average population density $\rho = P/A$, we can rewrite our result as

$$\frac{Q_{CO_2}}{P} \propto \frac{\sqrt{P}}{\sqrt{\rho}}(1-p)(1+\tau), \tag{13.10}$$

that is, $\dfrac{Q_{CO_2}}{P} \propto \rho^{-\frac{1}{2}}$ since $\sqrt{P}$ is a slowly varying function within the scope of large urban areas. We understand how Newman and Kenworthy (1989) could have obtained their result by assuming the density to be the control parameter. However, even if fitting data with this form is possible, our analysis shows that it is qualitatively wrong: the area size A and the public transport density p seem to be the true parameters controlling car-related quantities such as CO_2 emissions. Mitigating the traffic is therefore not obtained by increasing the density but by reducing the area size and improving the public transport density. We note that

$$\partial log Q_{co2} / \partial p = -1 / (1-p) \tag{13.11}$$

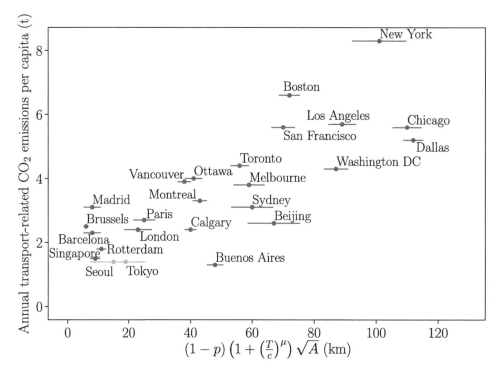

Note: The line by each city is the linear fit of the form $y = ax$ where $a = 0.06$ t/km/hab/year ($R^2 = 0.41$). We had no congestion estimate for Seoul and Tokyo and used an average congestion rate $\tau = 50\%$.

Figure 13.5   *Comparison between the annual transport-related CO_2 emissions per capita and the effects of congestion, area and rapid transit predicted by our model*

can be relatively large, while

$$\partial log Q_{CO_2} / \partial A = -1/2A \qquad (13.12)$$

is generally small and suggests that the increase of transport density is more efficient. We also understand that if MRT is efficient in reducing transport-related greenhouse gas emissions, then reducing road capacity c (to deter individuals from driving) may not be a good remedy, as we identified drivers with individuals with no other solution. Worse, by making their trips longer, diminishing c indirectly contributes to higher emissions and pollution as well as potentially socially segregating situations.

Finally, we can also compute the one-trip commuting time averaged over the population, which will read $\bar{\tau} = p(f + g\sqrt{A} / v_m) + (1 - p)g\sqrt{A} / v_c(1 + \tau)$ where g is a geometrical factor that describes the average commuting distance. Comparison with empirical data is shown in Figure 13.6.

Even if we observe relatively large fluctuations, our analysis seems to have captured the main trend. We also note that we overestimate the commuting time for large metropolitan areas, such as New York, which might be a consequence of polycentrism (Louf

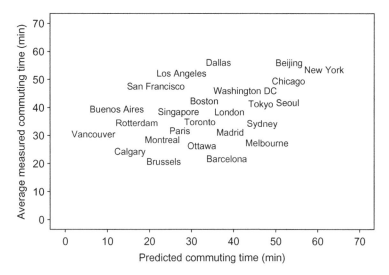

Note: Correlation coefficient = 0.65.

Figure 13.6   Average commuting time measured for different cities versus the predicted value of our model obtained by fitting over the geometrical factor g ≈ 0.203 consistent with a density decreasing from the center

and Barthelemy 2013, 2014), which is neglected in this study but generally limits the typical commuting distance in large metropolitan areas.

5.   DISCUSSION: PERSPECTIVES

We discussed the main approaches for understanding car traffic in large cities. We highlighted some of the problems with standard approaches, in particular their fragility with respect to empirical validation. We presented another type of approach where, in contrast with previous works, it was not assumed that urban density was pivotal. Many parameters, such as other transportation modes (buses, tramways), polycentrism, the transport network structure, fuel price and tax or dynamic road pricing, were not considered here, but our main aim was to fill a gap for understanding traffic in urban areas by proposing a parsimonious model with the smallest number of parameters and the largest number of predictions in agreement with data. Given the simplicity of this model we cannot expect a perfect agreement with data for various and different cities, but it seems that this approach captures correctly all the trends, and identifies correctly the critical factors for car traffic, a basic requirement before adding other factors and increasing the complexity of the model.

Our main goal was to capture the essence of the urban mobility phenomenon while keeping a reasonable number of parameters. Our analysis showed that car traffic is governed by three main factors: (1) access to MRT, (2) congestion effects, and (3) urban sprawl. In order to reduce car traffic, our model suggests an increase in access to public transport. This can be achieved, for example, by increasing the urban density around MRT stations, or to reduce the urban area. This last solution being impossible in most contexts, it advocates for strongly limiting urban sprawl. This model also suggests that increasing car-use cost is unable to lower car traffic in the absence of alternative transportation means. In addition, and in contrast with the Newman–Kenworthy result, increasing blindly the density at fixed area size and MRT access will, in general, increase the car traffic and CO_2 emissions. Bringing easier access to public transit systems would, however, be highly effective. As discussed in Buchanan (2019), some experts envision the emergence of a dense microtransit mesh of public and private shuttles linking transit stations with everyone's doorstep. This proposal is supported by our model and seems to be a sound way to reduce road traffic. It illustrates the importance of this type of modelling and the importance of identifying critical ingredients in mitigating car traffic.

REFERENCES

Barthelemy, M. (2016), *The Structure and Dynamics of Cities*, Cambridge: Cambridge University Press.
Batty, M. (2008), 'The size, scale, and shape of cities', *Science*, **319** (5864), 769–71.
Ben-Akiva, M.E. and S.R. Lerman (1985), *Discrete Choice Analysis: Theory and Application to Travel Demand*, Cambridge, MA: MIT Press.
Bettencourt, L.M.A. and G. West (2010), 'A unified theory of urban living', *Nature*, **467** (7318), 912–13.
Braess, D. (1968), 'Über ein Paradoxon aus der Verkehrsplanung', *Unternehmensforschung*, **12** (1), 258–68.
Branston, D. (1976), 'Link capacity functions: a review', *Transportation Research*, **10** (4), 223–36.
Buchanan, M. (2019), 'The benefits of public transport', *National Physics*, **15** (September), 876.
Creutzig, F., G. Baiocchi, R. Bierkandt, P.P. Pichler and K.C. Seto (2015), 'Global typology of urban energy use and potentials for an urbanization mitigation wedge', *Proceedings of the National Academy of Sciences*, **112** (20), 6283–8.
Crozet, Y. (2005), 'Le temps et les transports de voyageurs', Rapport de la 27eme table ronde d'Economie des Transports, Conférence Européenne des Ministres des Transports (CEMT-ECMT), Paris.
De Dios Ortúzar, J. and L.G. Willumsen (2011), *Modelling Transport*, Hoboken, NJ: John Wiley & Sons.
Dodman, D. (2009), 'Blaming cities for climate change? An analysis of urban greenhouse gas emissions inventories', *Environment and Urbanization*, **21** (1), 185–201.
Downs, A. (1962), 'The law of peak-hour expressway congestion', *Traffic Quarterly*, **16** (3), 393–409.
Downs, A. (1992), *Stuck in Traffic: Coping with Peak-hour Traffic Congestion*, Washington, DC: Brookings Institution Press.
Duranton, G. and M.A. Turner (2011), 'The fundamental law of road congestion: evidence from US cities', *American Economic Review*, **101** (6), 2616–52.
Erhardt, G.D., S. Roy, D. Cooper, B. Sana, M. Chen and J. Castiglione (2019), 'Do transportation network companies decrease or increase congestion?', *Science Advances*, **5** (5), eaau2670.
Erlander, S. and N.F. Stewart (1990), *The Gravity Model in Transportation Analysis: Theory and Extensions*, Utrecht: VSP.
Fujita, M. and H. Ogawa (1982), 'Multiple equilibria and structural transition of non-monocentric urban configurations', *Regional Science and Urban Economics*, **12** (2), 161–96.
Glaeser, E.L. and M.E. Kahn (2010), 'The greenness of cities: carbon dioxide emissions and urban development', *Journal of Urban Economics*, **67** (3), 404–18.
Glaeser, E.L., M.E. Kahn and J. Rappaport (2008), 'Why do the poor live in cities? The role of public transportation', *Journal of Urban Economics*, **63** (1), 1–24.
Gonzalez, M.C., C.A. Hidalgo and A.L. Barabasi (2008), 'Understanding individual human mobility patterns', *Nature*, **453** (7196), 779–82.
Gray, H.A. and G.R. Cass (1998), 'Source contributions to atmospheric fine carbon particle concentrations', *Atmospheric Environment*, **32** (22), 3805–25.
Henao, A. and W.E. Marshall (2019), 'The impact of ride-hailing on vehicle miles traveled', *Transportation*, **46** (6), 2173–94.
Herzog, T. (2009), 'World greenhouse gas emissions in 2005', working paper, World Resources Institute, Washington, DC.

INRIX Global (2018), 'Traffic scorecard ranking', accessed 27 May 2021 at https://inrix.com/scorecard/.

Louf, R. and M. Barthelemy (2013), 'Modeling the polycentric transition of cities', *Physical Review Letters*, **111** (19), 198702.

Louf, R. and M. Barthelemy (2014), 'How congestion shapes cities: from mobility patterns to scaling', *Scientific Reports*, **4** (1), 1–9.

McNally, M.G. (2000), 'The four step model', in D.A. Hensher and K.J. Button (eds), *Handbook of Transport Modelling*, vol. 1, Amsterdam: Pergamon, pp. 35–41.

Newman, P.G. (2006), 'The environmental impact of cities', *Environment and Urbanization*, **18** (2), 275–95.

Newman, P.G. and J.R. Kenworthy (1989), *Cities and Automobile Dependence: An International Sourcebook*, Aldershot: Gower Technical Press.

Newman, P.G. and J.R. Kenworthy (1999), *Sustainability and Cities*, Washington, DC: Island Press.

Numbeo (2018), 'Rankings by city of average monthly net salary (after tax) (salaries and financing)', accessed 27 May 2021 at https://www.numbeo.com/cost-of-living/city_price_rankings?itemId=105.

Oliveira, E.A., J.S. Andrade Jr and H.A. Makse (2014), 'Large cities are less green', *Scientific Reports*, **4** (1), 13–21.

Organisation for Economic Co-operation and Development (OECD) (2016), 'The OECD Metropolitan Areas Database visualized through the Metropolitan eXplorer', accessed 10 May 2021 at https://stats.oecd.org/Index.aspx?DataSetCode=CITIES.

Pumain, D. (2004), 'Scaling laws and urban systems', working paper, Sante Fe Institute, Santa Fe, NM.

Roque, D. and H.E. Masoumi (2016), 'An analysis of car ownership in Latin American cities: a perspective for future research', *Periodica Polytechnica Transportation Engineering*, **44** (1), 5–12.

TomTom Traffic Index (2018), 'TomTom Traffic Index', TomTom International BV, accessed 27 May 2021 at https://www.tomtom.com/en_gb/traffic-index/.

United Nations (2014), 'World Urbanization Prospects: The 2014 Revision, Highlights', Report ST/ESA/SER.A/352, Department of Economic and Social Affairs, Population Division, United Nations, New York.

Verbavatz, V. and M. Barthelemy (2019), 'Critical factors for mitigating car traffic in cities', PLoS ONE, **14** (7), e0219559.

Wardrop, J.G. (1952), 'Some theoretical aspects of road traffic research', *Proceedings of the Institution of Civil Engineers*, **1** (3), 325–62.

Zhu, S. and D. Levinson (2015), 'Do people use the shortest path? An empirical test of Wardrop's first principle', PLoS ONE, **10** (8), e0134322.

14. Studying the dynamics of urban traffic flows using percolation: a new methodology for real-time urban and transportation planning

Nimrod Serok, Orr Levy, Shlomo Havlin and Efrat Blumenfeld Lieberthal

INTRODUCTION

There is an extensive body of work that deals with the interdependencies between urban planning and, in particular, land-use planning for urban traffic (Mitchell and Rapkin 1954; Manheim 1979; Meyer and Miller 2001; Meurs 2002; Giuliano 2004; Hanson and Giuliano 2004; Wegener and Fürst 2004; Banister 2005; te Brömmelstroet and Bertolini 2008). This is not surprising, since the urban street network is being used for movement between different parts of cities and for different urban needs (commuting between different neighborhoods, moving commodities, deliveries, and so on). This results in circular causality where land uses generate a map of origins and destinations for urban movement, which in its turn affects the development of the city (Hillier 1996, 2002), as human mobility patterns affect the level of exposure of different locations, which can be leveraged as a growth generator for businesses and alternative land uses. These interdependencies between urban traffic and urban development are one of the most significant factors in current traffic planning (te Brömmelstroet and Bertolini 2008). Therefore, currently, there is considerable agreement among scholars, planners and politicians that, in order to achieve sustainable and efficient urban mobility patterns, the integration between urban and transportation planning must be improved (Cervero 1998; Meyer and Miller 2001; Massachusetts Institute of Technology and Associates CR 2001; World Business Council for Sustainable Development 2004; Banister 2005).

The traffic availability within and between different areas acts as a major factor in decision-making for different land uses, as well being as an important factor in real estate value variations. This has been tested and proven widely since the early works on urban economy in the nineteenth century (von Thünen 1826) and onwards (Alonso 1964; Mills 1967; Muth 1969; Waddell et al. 2007; Ibeas et al. 2012). Currently, there exists a vast literature regarding the connection between the physical structure of the streets network and the traffic movement on it (Hillier 1996, 2002; Bailenson et al. 2000; Crane 2000; Penn 2003). However, this body of work refers to the urban system as static, while in reality the traffic movement network is dynamic. This is particularly true when referring to different time scales, such as different hours during a day, different days of the week and, even, different months of the year.

Traditionally, planners also used static transportation planning to influence the nature and the characteristics of different areas in the city. For example, highway streets were planned as wide roads with commerce/services land uses, while residential neighborhoods were planned with narrow streets and cul-de-sacs that were designed to hold the volume of transportation of their residents only. This helped drivers navigate in the city as they used the primary network for their navigation as a route choice strategy (Pailhous 1970, 1984; Kuipers 1978; Chase 1983; Timpf et al. 1992; Kuipers et al. 2003). In fact, this method of planning influenced the volume of traffic in different types of streets and therefore worked as a useful planning tool.

New navigation applications (apps) (for example, Waze and Google Directions) have changed the way people use the urban roads network, as they are being directed to residential streets to avoid traffic congestions. These apps do not integrate into their algorithms considerations concerning public well-being or the quality of urban life, as they are mainly motivated by their objective to minimize the duration of the journey. The intensive use of these apps has changed in many instances the nature of quiet residential neighborhoods and disrupted the life of their residents. That is, the penetration of real-time navigation technologies has weakened the relationship between traffic and urban planning, as planners are no longer the leading influencers on the nature of traffic in urban streets. In the past few years, we have witnessed an increase in the percentage of smartphone users (it is assumed that in the USA, the UK and Israel, more than 70 percent of the population owns smartphones). On the one hand, this trend also increases the use of these navigation apps, but on the other, this can be (and is being) used to collect bottom-up data on the spatio-temporal movements of vehicles in cities. The outcome is the availability of big data on urban mobility, which can be used to study urban dynamics and influence urban traffic. We argue that new planning perceptions should integrate real-time data and intervene in urban traffic flows not only in long-term plans but also in real-time interventions. By doing this, planners can join global trends by moving to real-time decision-making methods and regain influence over the nature of urban streets and urban life.

In this chapter, we present a new framework, based on complex networks theory and, in particular, percolation of networks. This interdisciplinary field addresses, among other things, spatially embedded transportation networks that control many aspects of modern urban life and thus affect problems such as traffic jams, urban sprawl and epidemiology (Barthelemy 2011). Many researches analyze public transportation networks, such as airlines (Barrat et al. 2004; Colizza et al. 2006; Daqing et al. 2011), marine lines (Wei-Bing et al. 2009), trains (Sen et al. 2003), buses (Sienkiewicz and Hołyst 2005) and underground trains (Latora and Marchiori 2002). However, in these studies, most of the work focuses on the network topology where the nodes (stations or airports) and the links between them are fixed in time and set top down (for a comprehensive review of this, see Barthelemy 2011). Some studies on traffic networks defined the networks using fixed nodes with dynamics links (that is, the links between the nodes vary and are usually formed as a consequence of bottom-up forces). Examples of these networks can be found in human intra-urban movement where each node represents a building (Chowell et al. 2003), in bicycle-sharing systems where the nodes represent docking stations (Austwick et al. 2013) or, even, in commuting networks where the nodes represent towns (de Montis et al. 2007). The influence of the street-networks topology on traffic volumes has also been studied extensively (Freeman 1977; Girvan and Newman 2002; Costa 2004; Guimerà et al. 2005; Borgatti 2006; Serrano et al. 2009; Ercsey-Ravasz and Toroczkai 2010; Goh et al. 2011; Ercsey-Ravasz et al. 2012; Grady et al. 2012). Yet, here also, most of the work on that subject overlooked the dynamic of the traffic flow and the influence it has on the overall urban system.

Recent work introduced an innovative approach that employs percolation processes to identify urban clusters (Li et al. 2015; Arcaute et al. 2016) and to identify links that act as significant and repetitive temporal bottlenecks in urban traffic networks (Li et al. 2015). The percolation process they used examined relative velocities in street segments, calculated the relative speed on each street segment at a given time, and used a speed threshold to define street clusters that represent functional modules, composed of connected roads with traffic speed higher than the threshold. Li et al. (2015) defined the percolation threshold based on the maximal size of the second-largest component, and then examined the resultant clusters and focused on the links that were identified as bottlenecks. This methodology (which has been tested on real urban data) not only reveals the blocked links, but also presents the ensuing decomposing process of the city as spatio-temporal clusters that correspond to different traffic flows at different time scales (daily and weekly). This is based on a description of the city as a collection of local functional traffic-flow clusters connected by temporal bottlenecks. By examining the temporal speed on each link (road segment) and comparing it with a threshold, the researchers were able to classify the different links as blocked or unblocked at each given time and to follow the dynamics of the percolation process of the road network as discrete clusters.

Despite the significance of the linkages between traffic volumes and the structure of the city (that is, the combination of the built volumes, land uses and the street network), to the best of our knowledge, the correlation between the dynamic percolation process of the traffic loads and the static streets-morphology is still unclear and has yet to be tested. These relationships may lead to meaningful insights and could be used in planning processes and be developed into new planning tools. Thus, we present in this chapter an innovative percolation process that unveils the inter-relationships between the urban streets-network and the dynamics of traffic in it. This can be developed into new, real-time, decision-making tools that can be used by planners.

We use network percolation analysis (which examines the robustness of the traffic-flow network to failure) to identify street clusters that represent functional modules (that is, continuous areas where traffic flow is fluent), composed of connected roads with traffic load lower than a predefined threshold. Unlike Li et al. (2015), we define a fixed threshold for the percolation process (see the methodology section for further elaboration) and focus on the clusters themselves rather than on the links that connect the different clusters. Based on the above, we identify spatially embedded clusters and track their dynamics at different temporal scales, ranging from one hour to a week. By doing this, we present the different patterns of urban mobility, its evolution and dynamics, and highlight areas and times that require the interventions of planers in order to improve urban life quality. These interventions might include traditional planning tools, such as changing land-use mixture, controlling the volumes of the built environment, formulating local business policies, planning public transportation systems or, even, changing infrastructures. However, they should also include real-time prioritizing tools for adaptive and dynamic traffic-light systems.

The rest of this chapter is as follows: first, we present the percolation method we developed to describe the dynamics of urban traffic flows and the datasets we used to test it. Then, we elaborate on the analysis tools we use to evaluate different spatio-temporal processes. Finally, we present the results for our analysis and summarize with discussion and conclusions.

METHODOLOGY

In this section we describe the methodology we developed to follow the spatio-temporal dynamics of traffic flows. We define two types of clusters: the first is temporal clusters that represent the traffic flows at a given time (for example, a snapshot in time and space), and the second type is clusters that represent the change in the traffic flow over time. We analyzed the dynamics of the traffic flows and created spatially embedded, directed networks, where the nodes represent intersections and the directed links represent road segments between two intersections (where motorized traffic is allowed in the examined direction). We set the temporal weight of each link as the momentary relative speed in respect of its maximal measured value (Figure 14.1A). Differently from Li et al. (2015), a link is defined as functional if its relative velocity (defined here as traffic 'availability') is higher than a set threshold $q = 0.5$, which, based on the canonic Greenshields equation (Greenshields et al. 1935), represents a maximal flow, which is the maximal number of vehicles per hour, derived from the speed (kilometers per hour)–density (vehicles per kilometer) relationship (Figure 14.1B). We defined clusters as strongly connected components (Daqing et al. 2011) of streets with availability higher than $q = 0.5$ (that is, a cluster is a collection of streets where one can drive from each point to all other points without facing heavy traffic, in this instance – a relative speed < 0.5).

Clusters with size larger than 100/50 streets were defined as functional temporary clusters (FTCs) (Figure 14.1C). Owing to the size differences between the cities, we set the minimum number of streets as 100 for London and 50 for Tel Aviv.

To follow the dynamics of the traffic flow in specific areas, we develop a method that integrates spatially overlapping FTCs into new clusters: dynamic spatial clusters (DSCs). For that, we defined cores that represent spatial anchors for the FTCs at different times. The core was defined based on the following stages. (1) For each link, we measured the percentage of time it was associated with any of the FTCs (Figure 14.1D). (2) Streets that appeared in 70 percent or more of the examined hours in an FTC were defined as anchor streets (Figure 14.1D). This threshold was chosen as it defines anchor streets that represent different neighborhoods in the examined cities. This threshold can be changed in order to control the number of DSCs; increasing it will result in a decrease in the number of DSCs and decreasing it will enlarge their number (as elaborated next). (3) After a collection of connected anchor streets was defined as the core of a DSC, an FTC is assigned to a DSC if the core of the latter is included (partially or in full) in the former. Consequently, an FTC can be either assigned to a unique DSC or to different DSCs and thus represent the spatial continuity or discontinuity of the traffic flow between the different cores at specific times. A set of FTCs that were assigned to one core defines a DSC. That is, a DSC is a collection of FTCs with a mutual spatial anchor (Figure 14.1E). Finally, after all the DSCs were defined, we identified spatially overlapping DSCs and united them into a single entity. If the percentage of overlapping links crosses the threshold, the two DSCs are merged into one. These thresholds are site specific and based on the characteristics of the examined area, and thus are different for each city. We examined different values of this threshold for each city and chose those that yielded a maximal number of DSCs while merging spatially adjacent cores (that originally were located one street or two streets apart). Thus, the thresholds for London and Tel Aviv were set as 80 percent and 85 percent respectively (which also corresponds

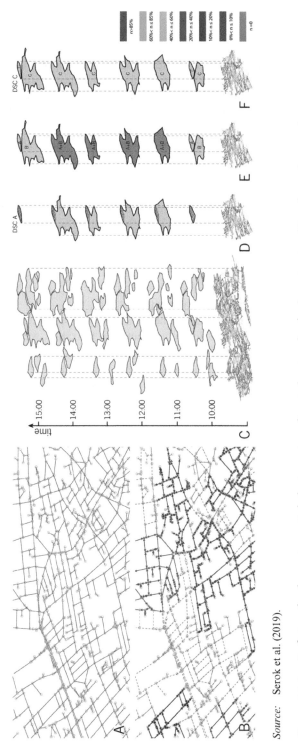

Source: Serok et al. (2019).

Figure 14.1 *Defining the dynamic spatial clusters. A: a directed network of urban streets of London, where nodes represent intersections and links represent street segments. The weight of the links is dynamic and represents their traffic availability (relative velocity) at different times. B: snapshot example of London FTC where traffic availability (relative speed) ≥ 0.5. Different colors represent different clusters. C: a map of functional streets (with traffic speed ≥ 0.5) that represents the superposition of all the FTCs. In dark green: streets that are included in any of the FTCs more than 70 percent of the samples (in this instance, over 51 out of the 60 samples). D: the streets that are in dark green are the cores of potential DSCs, that is, a set of all overlapping FTCs that contained (at different times) the core streets. E: different DSCs with significant overlapping of their streets (80–85 percent) are united into a single DSC, which is used for the analysis in F*

278

to the findings of Gfeller et al. 2005). We continued this process until there were no more DSCs that could be merged (Figure 14.1F).

We performed the above analysis on the data of London and Tel Aviv centers for two time-frames: the first includes 24 hours for a seven-day week; the second includes daytime only (12 hours between 0800 and 2000) for the five working days. The characteristics of traffic flow during night-times and weekends were found to be significantly different from its characteristics during the daytime on weekdays. During the night-time, traffic availability, as expected, was considerably better and more stable in comparison to daytime traffic. The weekend, however, was characterized by less predictable traffic behavior in comparison to weekdays. As we have collected data for only one weekend, we could not compare the behavior of the traffic flows on these days with the weekdays or other weekends. Thus, in this work, we focus on the working days' dataset and present only the results yielded from this dataset.

As for the two examined cities, Tel Aviv and London, we chose these cities as they represent different types of urban systems in respect of their size (the sampled area of the center of London is 2.5 times larger than the area of the center of Tel Aviv) and the transportation system within them. While London has an underground, overground and national railway, in addition to a developed bus system, Tel Aviv has only a bus system and a national railway that operate within its center. In addition, London has a congestion charge (£11.50 daily charge) for driving a vehicle within the charging zones (that are included in the examined area) between 0700 and 1800, Monday to Friday. Tel Aviv has no such restriction, and vehicles move free of charge in the city center throughout the entire week. Yet, London is considered the most congested city in Europe and our results support that it is significantly more congested than Tel Aviv despite the relative advantages in its transportation systems.

We collected the velocities of 8850 road sections in London center and 2950 road sections in Tel Aviv center. The sampling frequency was 15 minutes over a week (data for London was collected between 21 and 27 March 2018 and the data for Tel Aviv center was collected between 12 and 18 February 2017). We used interpolation to calculate the velocities of additional 9200 and 2450 road sections in London and Tel Aviv, respectively.

We used the traffic-flow averages of each road segment to identify the cores of the DSCs and found 20 DSCs for London and nine for Tel Aviv (Figure 14.2). The colors represent the percentage of times each link appeared in the SCT. Dark green represents links that appeared more than 85 percent of the time (that is, at least 51 out of the 60 samples) and include the cores of the DSCs. Grey represents links that were never associated with the SCT, that is, during the examined week – there was no option to move from the core of the SCT to these streets at a relative speed (availability) ≥ 0.5.

The DSCs in the two cities present different characteristics (see the next section). While some of the variances between the cities could be explained by their different scales, others are related to other differences between the cities (for example, the characteristics of the DSCs).

S2 - All Dynamic Spatial Clusters (DSC) : Head/Tail Analysis

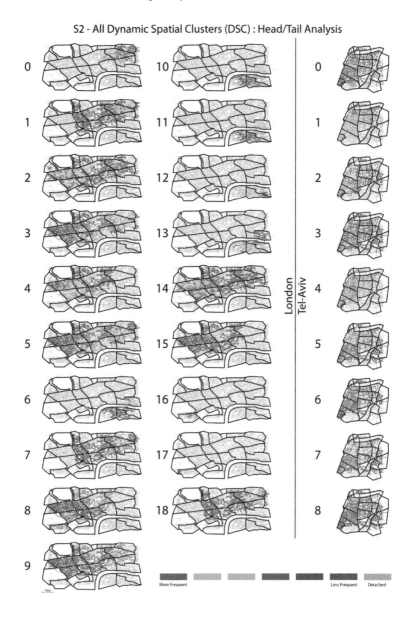

Notes: The DSCs in London are: 0 Shoreditch; 1 Finsbury and Islington; 2 Regent's Park; 3 Holborn; 4 Marylebone; 5 King's Cross; 6 City of London; 7 Barbican; 8 Mayfair; 9 Soho; 10 South Bank East; 11 Southwark – St George; 12 Southwark – London Bridge; 13 Borough Market; 14 Fitzrovia; 15 Somers Town; 16 Belgravia; 17 Knightsbridge; and 18 Ferrington.The DSCs in Tel Aviv are: 0 King George; 1 Bavli-Bney Dan; 2 Kerem HaTeymanim; 3 Ben Gurion; 4 Ben Gurion – Dizengoff; 5 Jabotinsky East; 6 Shikun HaKtsinim; 7 Rokach West; and 8 Reading Terminal.

Source: Serok et al. (2019).

Figure 14.2   Rank-size distribution of all the DSCs in London and Tel Aviv

ANALYSIS AND RESULTS

To explore the spatio-temporal characteristics of the traffic flow we based our analysis on different aspects of the DSCs. In this section, we present the analyses we developed and used, and their significance. We start with the estimation of DSCs' traffic quality, continue with the probability of links to be included in the same DSC at different times, and conclude with the spatio-temporal stability of the DSC. These attributes were chosen as they provide a holistic picture of the dynamics of the traffic and highlight planning issues that need to be addressed (demonstrated through some examples).

Traffic Quality

To evaluate the traffic quality and its dynamics, for different streets and areas we developed an index named Traffic Quality (TQ). We based this index on the assumption that good traffic is represented by a low number of FTCs that cover large areas. That is, good traffic flow allows fluent mobility in large areas and, thus, the best traffic quality is achieved where there is only one FTC that covers the largest area of the surface. The TQ is defined based on equation (14.1):

$$TQ = \sum_1^n \frac{\sum L_i}{R_i},\tag{14.1}$$

where n represents the number of FTCs at the examined time, $\sum L_i$ represents the sum of the lengths of the streets in an FTC ranked i, and R_i represents the rank of the FTCs where $R_1 = 1$ indicates the largest area and $R_i = n$ the smallest area. Therefore, TQ is an indicator of the physical area of the DSCs, which represents the area with good traffic flow.

We analyzed the traffic quality of the DSCs based on their dynamics at different times, as well as on their rank-size distributions. To explore the variation of the area coverage of the TQ in different DSCs, we used their standard deviation (σ). Low σ corresponds to steady area coverage at different times, while high σ indicates large variation in the TQ. While the σ values of the TQ in Tel Aviv are similar for all the DSCs, in London they increase for DSCs with high TQ (Figure 14.3). That is, these results show that the TQ of DSCs in Tel Aviv varies similarly (and significantly) for all sizes, which means that the traffic flow in Tel Aviv is unstable for most of the examined area.

In London, however, DSCs that cover small areas are more likely to remain small at different times, while DSCs that cover large areas are more likely to change their size at different hours and days. This index identifies neighborhoods that are well connected to the rest of the city (at different times) and others that are constrained in their traffic flow. It provides an overall insight on the spatial dynamics of the DSCs at each city and thus, can be used as a decision-making tool for planners. Our results also suggest that the dynamics of the DSCs do not follow a universal law and are location dependent. This strengthens the need to integrate real-time, bottom-up data that emerges from the local setting, in planning processes and tools.

Next, we explored the dynamics of the TQ for each DSC individually. For that, we examined the dynamics of the TQ over time and their rank-size distribution. The rank-size distribution of each DSC describes the lengths of the different FTCs that

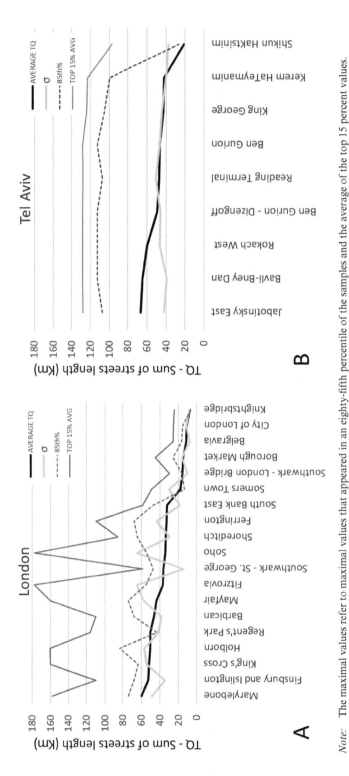

Note: The maximal values refer to maximal values that appeared in an eighty-fifth percentile of the samples and the average of the top 15 percent values.

Source: Serok et al. (2019).

Figure 14.3   Average and maximal TQ values and standard deviation for DSCs in London and Tel Aviv

compounded it during the examined period. The largest FTC is ranked 1, the second-largest FTC is ranked 2, and so on. This analysis disregards the exact time (hour and day) of the FTCs and focuses on the overall behavior of the DSC in its physical area (described here by the TQ), where high values of TQ indicate better traffic flow and accessibility from the core of the DSC to the rest of the city, and vice versa. The decay of the rank-size distribution (examples for several DSCs are presented in Figure 14.4A and B) corresponds to the spatial behavior of the DSCs. Dynamic spatial clusters that have good traffic flow from and to their cores, throughout the day and in the different days, will result in continuous distributions. However, DSCs that are connected to the rest of the city during specific hours only, and are isolated most of the time from their surroundings, in respect of traffic flow, will result in a step-function distribution. These differences are presented in Figure 14.4 where DSCs such as Finsbury and Islington (Figure 14.2, DSC 1 in London), or Marylebone (Figure 14.2, DSC 4 in London) and DSCs such as Bavli-Bney Dan (Figure 14.2, DSC 1 in Tel Aviv) present a continuous decay. These DSCs have a good connection to their surroundings throughout the different days and hours (as can be seen by the appearance of the colors green, light green, yellow and red in Figure 14.2). Dynamic spatial clusters, such as Soho (Figure 14.2, DSC 9 in London) and Shikun HaKtsinim (Figure 14.2, DSC 6 in Tel Aviv) present step-function behavior. This corresponds to the fact that most of the time their connectivity is limited to a small area, and they are connected to larger areas only several times during the examined week (as can be seen by the limited appearance of the colors green, light green, yellow, and red in Figure 14.2).

The dynamics of the TQ over time (Figure 14.4C, D) reveal that the maximal TQ values of the different DSCs ranged from 6365 to 83 185 meters in London and from 26 320 to 112 790 meters in Tel Aviv. Moreover, the two cities show a major difference in the dynamics of their TQ: in London, high TQ is found in the early morning (0800) or late afternoon (after 1700), whereas in Tel Aviv, high values of TQ occur at different hours on different days. This supports our previous findings and suggests that the dynamics of traffic-flow patterns in Tel Aviv are less predictable than those in London.

The TQ of most of the DSCs in London reaches very high peaks at distinct hours and does not follow any continuous trends (see Figure 14.4B). An example of this behavior is found in the Soho DSC. During most hours, it is limited to the west part of Soho and thus has very low values of TQ. However, in the mornings (at 0800 every day) it is connected to most of the other neighborhoods in the north bank of the River Thames, and twice in the examined week, after 1700, it was connected to its adjacent neighborhoods: Mayfair, Marylebone and Covent Garden. Finsbury and Islington DSC (Figure 14.5A) is an example of a different type of behavior. Its core is not constrained to one neighborhood but crosses two nearby ones (Finsbury and Islington). In more than 40 percent of the time, the streets included in it covered most of Shoreditch, Hoxton, Clerkenwell and the eastern part of the Barbican. The rest of the time, it spanned to the surrounding areas of these neighborhoods, and once (on Monday at 1700) it covered most of the streets in the north bank of the River Thames. We found that at this particular time, most of the DSCs presented significantly high values of TQ, but we could not find any event that might have caused this irregularity.

In Tel Aviv, the changes in the TQ of the DSCs are more moderate and smoother, as the TQ of the DSCs varies and reaches high values many times at different hours

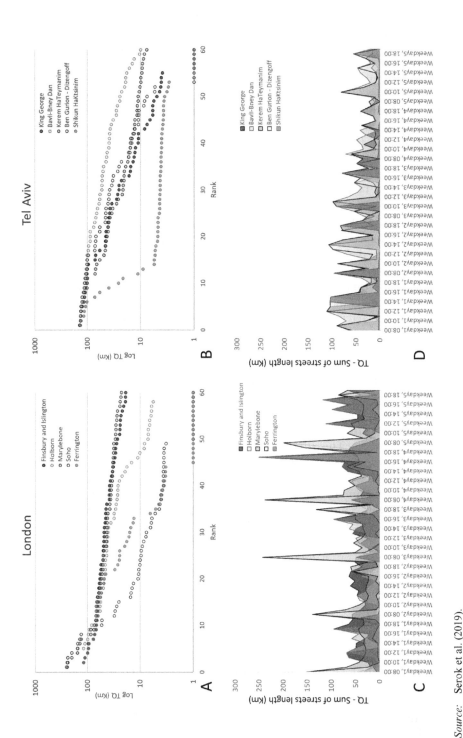

Source: Serok et al. (2019).

Figure 14.4 Rank-size distribution of five typical DSCs in (A) London, and (B) Tel Aviv; and the dynamics of the TQ during five weekdays of these DSCs in (C) London and (D) Tel Aviv

284

More Frequent   Less Frequent   Detached

Note: The colors represent the percentage of time each link was included in the DSC in the entire studied period (12 hours over five weekdays).

Source: Serok et al. (2019).

Figure 14.5   *Examples for DSCs in London and Tel Aviv: (A) Finsbury and Islington, London, (B) The City of London, (C) Bavli-Bney Dan, Tel Aviv, and (D) Kerem HaTeymanim, Tel Aviv*

(Figure 14.4D). We assumed this to occur because the traffic flow in Tel Aviv is not constrained by neighborhoods but is more regional. The Bavli-Bney Dan DSC (Figure 14.5C) is a good example of that, as its core spans from the northeast to the northwest neighborhoods of Tel Aviv. For more than 40 percent of the time, it covered parts of four different neighborhoods in the northern area of the city, while for the rest of the time it covered most of the examined area. This DSC is better described as the northern region of the examined area, rather than just by its core (named after the neighborhood where the core was identified).

An exception is Shikun HaKtsinim, which presents low TQ values for most of the examined period, with several peaks at a few different times (Figure 14.4D). This behavior cannot be explained only by the size of this DSC, as Kerem HaTeymanim (Figure 14.5D) resembles it in relation to the number of links the two DSCs hold (Figure 14.6). An explanation for this might be found in its unique morphology: this clustered area, compounded of mostly cul-de-sacs, is connected to the rest of the city for only 10 percent of the time, and during the rest of the hours, it covers a small area and presents very low values of TQ.

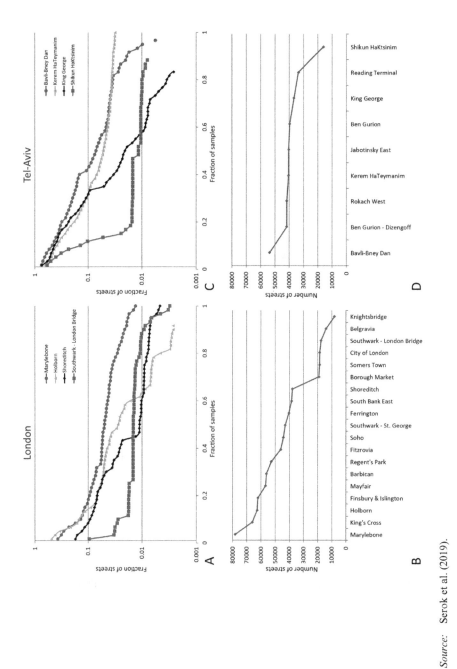

Source: Serok et al. (2019).

Figure 14.6   The probabilities of links (streets) being included repeatedly in different DSCs: (A) London, (C) Tel Aviv and the area-stability values of the DSCs, calculated as the integral of the CDF presented in A and C multiplied by the number of measured streets B London and D Tel Aviv

Area-Stability: The Probability of Links to be Included in a DSC at Different Times

Next, we analyzed the descending cumulative distribution function (CDF) of the DSCs and its integral, in order to evaluate the DSC in respect of their spatial size as well as the stability of the links they hold at different times. The descending CDF shows the probability of any fraction of links to appear at least x fraction of the time in a DSC (see Figure 14.6). The integral of the CDF indicates, for each DSC, both the number of links it contained throughout the entire week as well as their stability. That is, the integral of the descending CDF can be used to evaluate the quality of a DSC in respect of size (represented by the number of streets) and spatio-temporal stability (the appearance of the same links in the DSC at different times). The graph that holds the values of these integrals provides an overall perspective of the urban systems and allows a comparison between different DSCs in a city and between different cities.

Figure 14.6(A, C) presents some examples of the descending CDF of different DSCs in London (6A) and Tel Aviv (6B). The curve of each DSC provides meaningful insights into its characteristics as regards size and stability. Holborn and Marylebone DSCs for example, cover at their maximal size 50 and 37 percent of the measured area, respectively. However, the CDF of Holborn DSC decreases faster than that of Marylebone DSC. Thus, in 90 percent of the samples, Marylebone DSC includes significantly more streets than does Holborn DSC. This indicates that Marylebone DSC has better traffic flow as it has more streets that are included repeatedly in it. Southwark – London Bridge is a small but stable DSC: a fixed number of streets (that represents its core) appears in more than 90 percent of its samples. This number is higher than the number of streets that appeared repeatedly in Holborn DSC (and represent its core) for 40 percent of the time. Figure 14.6(B, D) presents the values of the integrals of each of the DSC curves, multiplied by the total number of the measured streets. This multiplication is used to integrate the different sizes of the DSCs in the stability-area index, that is, the area-stability values of a DSC are represented both by the total number of links that were associated with it at all times and by the probability distributions of links to be included in it at different fractions of times. This index also highlights the differences between the two examined cities: while most of the DSCs in Tel Aviv present similar characteristics in respect of their size and stability, London DSCs can be divided into three groups: DSCs with high, average or low values of size and stability. The DSCs in the first group are similar to the DSCs in Tel Aviv as they span beyond one neighborhood on a regular basis. The DSCs in the second group occupy, most of the time (40 percent or more), the area of one neighborhood, and those in the final group mostly occupy only parts of a single neighborhood. The two DSCs with the lowest values, Knightsbridge and Belgravia, are a good example of the strength of this tool. The area of London's center, as set in this study, does not cover the entire area of these neighborhoods but splits them in the middle. The result is broken traffic-flow patterns, which are revealed in their low values of area stability (Figure 14.6). However, DSCs such as the City of London (the historic business district, presented in Figure 14.6B) or the DSCs in the South Bank present low values of area stability owing to their area coverage. These DSCs cover the entire neighborhood of their cores less than 20 percent of the measured time. During the rest of the time, the DSCs cover only part of these neighborhoods. In this respect, the DSC of the City of London is different from that of the Barbican, its adjacent neighborhood. The DSC with its core in the Barbican area spans north to Clerkenwell and Islington more than 40 percent of the time. Both neighborhoods (City of London and Barbican) are part of the business district of London, but while the first is constrained in respect of traffic flow, the second is better connected to its surroundings. For planners this information can be used to prioritize different planning decisions, such as infrastructure improvements. Another example is the DSCs in the South Bank. In this small area, there are four different DSCs with their cores located in proximity to each other (Figure 14.2). The area includes two major neighborhoods: South Bank and Southwark where the latter has three different DSCs within its boundaries. These DSCs present low area-stability values, which indicates to planners the traffic flow in this area needs improvements.

Stability

Although the descending CDF function provides information regarding the spatio-temporal characteristics of the DSCs, this information is at a high level and does not separate stability from the size of the DSC or indicate stability at different hours. Thus, we developed another index that indicates the level of spatio-temporal stability for each DSC during a given window of time.

For that, we calculated the spatial stability of the DSCs for each hour during weekdays only. We based this decision on the results of a previous analysis (presented in the methodology section) that indicated significant differences between weekdays and weekends in respect of traffic flow. The spatial stability, S, for a specific DSC at a specific time is calculated based on equation (14.2):

$$S = \frac{\sum_1^m l_{FTC}}{m * L_{SCT}}, \tag{14.2}$$

where l_{FCT} represents the number of links (street segments) in each of the FTCs included in the examined DSC at the examined hour, and L_{SCT} represents the total number of links that appeared at least once in the examined DSC at that hour. m represents the number of days used for the calculation, which is five in our example (corresponding to working days only). $S = 1$ is at its maximum, when $\sum_1^n l_{FCT} = m * L_{SCT}$. This indicates that all the FTCs are spatially identical in all the examined days at a specific hour. When $\sum_1^n l_{FCT} = L_{SCT}$ none of the links appears more than once in the DSC, and its stability is at its minimum. For our calculation this minimum = 0.2. To allow a comparison between different calculations we normalized these results to a range between 0 and 1. Unlike other methods (for example, the Jaccard index) our method indicates, in one simple number, not only the overlapping that occurs in all the examined samples (days), but also considers overlapping that occurs only in some of the days. By using this method, we can follow the temporal stability of the spatial behavior of the traffic flows.

The stability index of the DSCs in London and Tel Aviv at different times also presents significant differences (Table 14.1). The average stability for the DSCs in London is 0.41 ± 0.21 in comparison to 0.19 ± 0.12 in Tel Aviv. The stability values of the DSCs in London range from 0 to 0.96 and half of them present average stability values ≥ 0.4. High stability values (0.6 and higher) are observed for different DSCs at different hours throughout the examined period. Thus, generally, most of the DSCs in London are

Table 14.1   Stability values, S (equation 14.2), for the DSCs in London and Tel Aviv at different hours

London	08:00	09:00	10:00	11:00	12:00	13:00	14:00	15:00	16:00	17:00	18:00	19:00	Average
Somers Town	0.05	0.9	0.52	0.88	0.88	0.87	0.85	0.45	0.9	0.88	0.16	0.96	0.69
Southwark - London Bridge	0.56	0.46	0.65	0.76	0.82	0.67	0.61	0.95	0.46	0.16	0.39	0.9	0.62
Regent's Park	0.12	0.67	0.77	0.82	0.82	0.72	0.79	0.65	0.8	0.11	0.27	0.2	0.56
Belgravia	0.68	0.57	0.77	0.5	0.3	0.5	0.55	0.67	0.45	0.65	0.68	0.4	0.56
Knightsbridge	0.68	0.48	0.84	0.69	0.24	0.84	0.23	0.24	0.46	0.68	0.48	0.73	0.55
Marylebone	0.53	0.6	0.5	0.57	0.45	0.6	0.64	0.43	0.54	0.51	0.35	0.28	0.50
Southwark - St George	0.52	0.45	0.5	0.48	0.48	0.49	0.66	0.52	0.58	0.4	0.4	0.29	0.48
South Bank East	0.44	0.15	0.47	0.33	0.37	0.52	0.62	0.54	0.58	0.36	0.32	0.24	0.41
Borough Market	0.52	0.25	0.61	0.41	0.64	0.51	0.52	0.57	0.31	0.16	0.19	0.18	0.41
City of London	0.44	0.29	0.25	0.42	0.53	0.28	0.41	0.51	0.43	0.42	0.61	0.17	0.40
Finsbury and Islington	0.52	0.3	0.32	0.43	0.29	0.43	0.56	0.36	0.27	0.25	0.42	0.46	0.38
King's Cross	0.35	0.62	0.45	0.39	0.23	0.48	0.39	0.35	0.34	0.23	0.29	0.42	0.38
Barbican	0.5	0.24	0.47	0.34	0.22	0.39	0.55	0.33	0.3	0.23	0.29	0.46	0.36
Mayfair	0.5	0.43	0.28	0.41	0.27	0.23	0.58	0.2	0.51	0.54	0.19	0.1	0.35
Holborn	0.34	0.6	0.35	0.31	0.34	0.17	0.31	0.13	0.33	0.2	0.17	0.37	0.30
Soho	0.53	0.29	0.14	0.34	0.42	0.22	0.47	0.16	0.18	0.04	0.14	0.07	0.25
Shoreditch	0.34	0.2	0.24	0.15	0.09	0.22	0.2	0.29	0.23	0.32	0.36	0.22	0.24
Ferrington	0.3	0	0.2	0.09	0.15	0.13	0.39	0.29	0.21	0.18	0.05	0.34	0.19
Fitzrovia	0.53	0.31	0.23	0.16	0.25	0	0	0.17	0.13	0.06	0.19	0.07	0.18
Tel Aviv	**08:00**	**09:00**	**10:00**	**11:00**	**12:00**	**13:00**	**14:00**	**15:00**	**16:00**	**17:00**	**18:00**	**19:00**	**Average**
Kerem HaTeymanim	0.23	0.31	0.24	0.17	0.12	0.63	0.19	0.2	0.3	0.31	0.41	0.32	0.29
Bavli-Bney Dan	0.2	0.32	0.28	0.25	0.26	0.29	0.3	0.33	0.21	0.24	0.26	0.25	0.27
Shikun HaKtsinim	0.04	0.62	0.05	0.58	0.69	0.09	0.03	0.03	0.34	0.05	0.14	0.09	0.23
Rokach West	0.07	0.14	0.18	0.24	0.23	0.22	0.21	0.32	0.21	0.19	0.2	0.03	0.19
Ben Gurion - Dizengoff	0.14	0.16	0.28	0.1	0.06	0.14	0.14	0.33	0.19	0.27	0.14	0.15	0.18
Jabotinsky East	0.09	0.19	0.27	0.16	0.18	0.29	0.24	0.23	0.04	0.09	0.16	0.04	0.17
Ben Gurion	0.18	0.12	0.26	0.13	0.06	0.13	0.15	0.23	0.19	0.27	0.07	0.07	0.16
King George	0.18	0.2	0.23	0.16	0.03	0.03	0.03	0.17	0.19	0.27	0.07	0.14	0.14
Reading Terminal	0.07	0.03	0.03	0.13	0.17	0.22	0.21	0.25	0.2	0.2	0.1	0.06	0.14

stable in respect of their spatial dynamics. Unlike the area-stability values, the stability index presents the stability of the DSCs at specific hours, while the area-stability values refer to the spatio-temporal stability of the DSCs throughout the entire week. Thus, five DSCs, such as Holborn, Soho, Shoreditch, Ferrington and Fitzrovia, present average to high area-stability values (Figure 14.6) but their stability index values are low. Looking at the other end of the scale, the DSCs in the South Bank have low area-stability values and high stability index values. The explanation of these examples is rooted in that the stability-area values consider both factors while the stability index includes the stability of DSCs regardless of their size. Each of these analyses provides different insights regarding the overall traffic flow of the DSCs as well as the entire city. They are needed in order to address different aspects; for example: while the area-stability values can be used to prioritize planning and regulation, the stability index can be used for local modifications in Underground or bus frequencies or traffic-light operation.

In Tel Aviv, most of the DSCs show low stability values that range between 0 and 0.35, with a few exceptions that are related to two DSCs: Shikun HaKtsinim and Kerem HaTeymanim. These DSCs have the lowest average TQ (Figure 14.3) and cover mainly the immediate surroundings of their cores, which are characterized by unique morphologies. Shikun HaKtsinim contains a few parallel cul-de-sac streets that are connected to a perpendicular street, which connects them to the rest of the city. Kerem HaTeymanim, one of the oldest neighborhoods of Tel Aviv, is typified by a dense, orthogonal grid of one-way streets. Thus, it can be assumed that the high stability index of these DSCs is a consequence of the constraints their morphology imposes on their intra- and inter-traffic.

To summarize, we showed that the spatial behavior of the traffic flow in London is more stable (and thus predictable) than that of Tel Aviv in respect of hourly behavior. Tel Aviv, however, presents a more stable overall behavior in respect of the similarity between the area-stability values of its DSCs. We assume that this is because the traffic flow in London is, generally, constrained most of the time to local neighborhoods, while the traffic flow in Tel Aviv is more regional than local. Tel Aviv is a relatively new city, built on a North–South and West–East road network, which can explain the regional traffic flow within it. London, having developed organically for centuries, has a more obvious neighborhood structure and the intra-traffic flow (within the neighborhoods) is different from the inter-traffic flow between different parts of the city.

SUMMARY

Historically, the nature of urban streets and their land uses are in correlation with the volume of the streets' traffic flows. These two parameters are interdependent and together with other urban factors (for example, social and cultural) create urban variety and dynamics. Understanding these interdependencies, may shed light on different urban phenomena and could be developed into new, real-time, decision-making tools that can be useful for planners. We based our work on the perception that was introduced by Hägerstrand (1970), and has been widely tested since, that the city is a dynamic entity in respect of its spatio-temporal behavior. Thus, we developed an innovative method for the identification of functional dynamic areas in the city in relation to their traffic flow. Our method is based on a percolation process where links (representing street segments) are removed if their traffic flow does not meet a threshold of traffic availability equal to or larger than 0.5. This threshold represents fluent traffic flow and thus this percolation process results in two types of spatio-temporal clusters: the first is the FTC, which represents temporal functional clusters that contain connected streets in terms of fluent traffic. These clusters exist at specific times and change over time. The second type is the DSC, which integrates spatially overlapping FTCs into one cluster that represents the change in traffic flows to and from a specific spatial core over time. We employed our methods on two datasets – London and Tel Aviv centers – and analyzed the DSCs based on their spatial size (measured as the sum of the streets' length) and their spatio-temporal stability. Our findings revealed differences between the two cities as well as differences and similarities within each city. The first index we developed is the traffic quality, which integrates both the number and the size of the FTCs in a unique DSC. It reveals that, while the DSCs in Tel Aviv vary significantly for all sizes, those in London are more size dependent and large clusters are more likely to change over time than are small ones. This index also highlighted the dissimilarities between different DSCs in each city: the global and the local in London and the spatially constrained in Tel Aviv. This tool succeeded in singling out areas with unique morphologies that imposed constraints on the traffic flows (for example, Shikun HaKtsinim in Tel Aviv), as well as areas that were well connected to the surroundings over time (for example, Finsbury and Islington in London). We showed that high traffic quality is achieved in London mainly in the early mornings and the late afternoons, while in Tel Aviv some areas presented high traffic quality at different hours and on different days (for example, Bavli-Bney Dan). Based on that, we conclude that good traffic flow is more predictable (although it lasts for shorter periods) in London than in Tel Aviv.

We also analyzed the area-stability values of the DSCs in both cities. These values show for every DSC, the fraction of time it contained a fraction of the same links. This unique value provides information on both the overall size of the DSC over time and its spatio-temporal stability. Thus, very stable but small clusters will have lower values than very stable but large clusters. We found, that most of the clusters in Tel Aviv present similar area-stability values. In London, however, we identified three groups of DSCs based on these values. The DSCs with high values of area stability resembled those in Tel Aviv and frequently extended beyond one neighborhood (for example, Holborn). The DSCs in the second group covered a single neighborhood during most hours (for example, Somers Town), and those in the final group occupied only parts of a neighborhood at all times (for example, the City of London or the DCSs in the South Bank). However, while these values provide insights into the overall spatio-temporal behavior of the DSCs, it does not offer information on the similarity of the DSC at specific hours (that is, how similar the spatial distribution of a DSC is at the same hour on different days).

To complete this information, we also developed the stability index, which ranges between 0 and 1, where 1 indicates that all the FTCs in the DSC are spatially identical at a specific time through all the examined days, and 0 indicates that none of the FTCs appears more than once in the DSC. The stability results showed considerably higher stabilities in London than in Tel Aviv. They also suggest that DSCs with small areas (for example, Southwark in London and Shikun HaKtsinim in Tel Aviv) are often more stable than others that cover larger areas (for example, Soho in London or

Bavli-Bney Dan in Tel Aviv). These results support the understanding that the larger DSCs have a more global behavior while smaller DSCs are usually limited within the boundaries of a neighborhood.

In particular, we demonstrated how our proposed methodology could be used as a comparative tool to study the spatio-temporal behavior of different cities as well as different neighborhoods within a city. The proposed percolation enables the identification (both in real time and over time) of the areas in the city, where traffic flows are fluent, as well as the identification of the boundaries of these areas. This can be useful for developing decision-making support tools for urban and transportation planners in their long-term planning processes (for example, land-use distribution, infrastructure development and alternation, and public transportation routes) as well as for real-time interventions (for example, implementing adaptive traffic-light systems that correspond in real time to traffic jams, or changing public transportation frequencies owing to dynamic demand). In addition, revealing the dynamic boundaries of the DSCs is significant for planners, as these boundaries (and the area they hold) affect pedestrians, bicycle riders, businesses, and others.

Urban and transportation planning is currently being challenged by real-time navigation apps that aim to find the fastest route for their users. The companies that operate these apps are motivated by their goal to minimize travel time and do not integrate consideration of urban life quality or public well-being in their algorithms. Yet, they are being used extensively by drivers and therefore have a major effect on urban life. For example, the navigation app Waze (purchased by Google in 2013) has been facing lawsuits (in many locations around the world) filed by residents of what used to be quiet neighborhoods before the Waze app started to direct large volumes of traffic through their streets. We follow Hillier (2002) who claimed that: 'The relation between micro-economic activity and space, like the relation between culture and space, is largely mediated by movement' and argue that in the era of real data in real time in which we live, in order to be able to intervene and affect the nature of different urban areas, planners must adopt new tools that are based on adaptive and responsive real-time approaches. These will bridge the gap between static long-term urban planning and the flexible and dynamic urban rhythm, and enable planners to keep their role in the formation of better cities.

ACKNOWLEDGEMENT

This work was supported by the PMO Foundation for Innovations in Transportation. Also, we acknowledge partial support from the China-Israel Science Foundation.

REFERENCES

Alonso, W. (1964), *Location and Land Use: Toward a General Theory of Land Rent*, Cambridge, MA: Harvard University Press.

Arcaute, E., C. Molinero, E. Hatna, R. Murcio, C. Vargas-Ruiz, A.P. Masucci, et al. (2016), 'Cities and regions in Britain through hierarchical percolation', *Royal Society Open Science*, 3 (4), 150691.

Austwick, M.Z., O. O'Brien, E. Strano and M. Viana (2013), 'The structure of spatial networks and communities in bicycle sharing systems', *PLoS ONE*, 8 (9), e74685.

Bailenson, J.N., M.S. Shum and D.H. Uttal (2000), 'The initial segment strategy: a heuristic for route selection', *Memory & Cognition*, **28** (2), 306–18.

Banister, D. (2005), *Unsustainable Transport: City Transport in the New Century*, London and New York: Taylor & Francis.

Barrat, A., M. Barthelemy, R. Pastor-Satorra and A. Vespignani (2004), 'The architecture of complex weighted networks', *Proceedings of the National Academy of Sciences of the United States of America*, **101** (11), 3747–52.

Barthelemy, M. (2011), 'Spatial networks', *Physics Reports*, **499** (1–3), 1–101.

Borgatti, S.P. (2006), 'Identifying sets of key players in a social network', *Computational & Mathematical Organization Theory*, **12** (1), 21–34.

Cervero, R. (1998), *The Transit Metropolis: A Global Inquiry*, Washington, DC: Island Press.

Chase, W.G. (1983), 'Spatial representations of taxi drivers', in D. Rogers and J.A. Sloboda (eds), *The Acquisition of Symbolic Skills*, Boston, MA: Springer, pp. 391–405.

Chowell, G., J.M. Hyman, S. Eubank and C. Castillo-Chavez (2003), 'Scaling laws for the movement of people between locations in a large city', *Physical Review E*, **68** (6), 066102.

Colizza, V., A. Barrat, M. Barthelemy and A. Vespignani (2006), 'The role of the airline transportation network in the prediction and predictability of global epidemics', *Proceedings of the National Academy of Sciences of the United States of America*, **103** (7), 2015–20.

Costa, L. da Fontoura (2004), 'The hierarchical backbone of complex networks', *Physical Review Letters*, **93** (9), 098702.

Crane, R. (2000), 'The influence of urban form on travel: an interpretive review', *Journal of Planning Literature*, **15** (1), 3–23.

Daqing, L., K. Kosmidis, A. Bunde and S. Havlin (2011), 'Dimension of spatially embedded networks', *Nature Physics*, **7** (6), 481–4.

De Montis, A., M. Barthelemy, A. Chessa and A. Vespignani (2007), 'The structure of interurban traffic: a weighted network analysis', *Environment and Planning B: Planning and Design*, **34** (5), 905–24.

Ercsey-Ravasz, M. and Z. Toroczkai (2010), 'Centrality scaling in large networks', *Physical Review Letters*, **105** (3), 038701.

Ercsey-Ravasz, M., R.N. Lichtenwalter, N.V. Chawla and Z. Toroczkai (2012), 'Range-limited centrality measures in complex networks', *Physical Review E*, **85** (6), 066103.

Freeman, L.C. (1977), 'A set of measures of centrality based on betweenness', *Sociometry*, **40** (1), 35–41.

Gfeller, D., J.-C. Chappelier and P. De Los Rios (2005), 'Finding instabilities in the community structure of complex networks', *Physical Review E*, **72** (5), 056135.

Girvan, M. and M.E. Newman (2002), 'Community structure in social and biological networks', *Proceedings of the National Academy of Sciences*, **99** (12), 7821–6.

Giuliano, G. (2004), 'Land use impacts of transportation investments', in S. Hanson and G. Giuliano, *The Geography of Urban Transportation*, New York: Guilford Press, pp. 237–73.

Goh, K.-I., B. Kahng and D. Kim (2011), 'Universal behavior of load distribution in scale-free networks', in M. Newman. A.-L. Barabási and D.J. Watts (eds), *The Structure and Dynamics of Networks*, Princeton, NJ: Princeton University Press, pp. 368–71.

Grady, D., C. Thiemann and D. Brockmann (2012), 'Robust classification of salient links in complex networks', *Nature Communications*, **3** (1), art. 864.

Greenshields, B., W. Channing and H. Miller (1935), 'A study of traffic capacity', *Highway Research Board Proceedings*, **14**, pt 1, 447–77.

Guimerà, R., S. Mossa, A. Turtschi, et al. (2005), 'The worldwide air transportation network: anomalous centrality, community structure, and cities' global roles', *Proceedings of the National Academy of Sciences*, **102** (22), 7794–9.

Hägerstrand, T. (1970), 'What about people in regional science?', *Papers of the Regional Science Association*, **24** (1), 6–21.

Hanson, S. and G. Giuliano (2004), *The Geography of Urban Transportation*, New York: Guilford Press.

Hillier, B. (1996), 'Cities as movement economies', *Urban Design International*, **1** (1), 41–60.

Hillier, B. (2002), 'A theory of the city as object: or, how spatial laws mediate the social construction of urban space', *Urban Design International*, **7** (3), 153–79.

Ibeas, Á., R. Cordera, L. dell'Olio, P. Coppola and A. Dominguez (2012), 'Modelling transport and real-estate values interactions in urban systems', *Journal of Transport Geography*, **24**, 370–82.

Kuipers, B. (1978), 'Modeling spatial knowledge', *Cognitive Science*, **2** (2), 129–53.

Kuipers, B., D.G. Tecuci and B.J. Stankiewicz (2003), 'The skeleton in the cognitive map: a computational and empirical exploration', *Environment and Behavior*, **35** (1), 81–106.

Latora, V. and M. Marchiori (2002), 'Is the Boston subway a small-world network?', *Physica A: Statistical Mechanics and its Applications*, **314** (1–4), 109–13.

Li, D., B. Fu, Y. Wang, G. Lu, Y. Berezin, H.E. Stanley and S. Havlin (2015), 'Percolation transition in dynamical traffic network with evolving critical bottlenecks', *Proceedings of the National Academy of Sciences*, **112** (3), 669–72.

Manheim, M.L. (1979), *Fundamentals of Transportation Systems Analysis; Volume 1: Basic Concepts*, Cambridge, MA: Massachusetts Institute of Technology Press.

Massachusetts Institute of Technology and Associates CR (2001), *Mobility 2001: World Mobility at the End of the Twentieth Century and its Sustainability*, Geneva: World Business Council for Sustainable Development.

Meurs, H. (2002), 'Land use and sustainable mobility', *European Journal of Transport and Infrastructure Research*, **3** (2), special issue, doi:10.18757/ejtir.2003.3.2.3682.

Meyer, M.D. and E.J. Miller (2001), *Urban Transportation Planning: A Decision-Oriented Approach*, New York: McGraw Hill.

Mills, E.S. (1967), 'An aggregative model of resource allocation in a metropolitan area', *American Economic Review*, **57** (2), 197–210.

Mitchell, R.B. and C. Rapkin. (1954), *Urban Traffic*, New York: Columbia University Press.

Muth, R.F. (1969), *Cities and Housing*, Chicago, IL: University of Chicago Press.

Pailhous, J. (1970), *La représentation de l'espace urbain: l'exemple du chauffeur de taxi*, Paris: University Press of France.

Pailhous, J. (1984), 'The representation of urban space: its development and its role in the organisation of journeys', in R.M. Farr and S. Moscovici (eds), *Social Representations*, Cambridge: Cambridge University Press, pp. 311–27.

Penn, A. (2003), 'Space syntax and spatial cognition: or why the axial line?', *Environment and Behavior*, **35** (1), 30–65.

Sen, P., S. Dasgupta, A. Chatterjee, P.A. Sreeram, G. Mukherjee and S.S. Manna (2003), 'Small-world properties of the Indian railway network', *Physical Review E*, **67** (3), 036106.

Serok, N., O. Levy, S. Havlin and E. Blumenfeld-Lieberthal (2019), 'Unveiling the inter-relations between the urban streets network and its dynamic traffic flows: planning implication', *Environment and Planning B: Urban Analytics and City Science*, **46** (7), 1362–76.

Serrano, M.Á., M. Boguná and A. Vespignani (2009), 'Extracting the multiscale backbone of complex weighted networks', *Proceedings of the National Academy of Sciences*, **106** (16), 6483–8.

Sienkiewicz, J. and J.A. Hołyst (2005), 'Statistical analysis of 22 public transport networks in Poland', *Physical Review E*, **72** (4), 046127.

Te Brömmelstroet, M. and L. Bertolini (2008), 'Developing land use and transport PSS: meaningful information through a dialogue between modelers and planners', *Transport Policy*, **15** (4), 251–9.

Thünen, J.H. von (1826), 'Der isolierte staat', *Beziehung auf Landwirtschaft und Nationalökonomie*, Hamburg: Wirtschaft & Finan.

Timpf, S., G.S. Volta, D.W. Pollock and M.J. Egenhofer (1992), 'A conceptual model of wayfinding using multiple levels of abstraction', in A.U. Frank, I. Campari and U. Formentini (eds), *Theories and Methods of Spatio-Temporal Reasoning in Geographic Space*, Berlin and Heidelberg: Springer, pp. 348–67.

Waddell, P., G.F. Ulfarsson, J.P. Franklin and J. Lobb (2007), 'Incorporating land use in metropolitan transportation planning', *Transportation Research Part A: Policy and Practice*, **41** (5), 382–410.

Wegener, M. and F. Fürst (2004), 'Land-use transport interaction: state of the art', 1 January, doi:10.2139/ssrn.1434678.

Wei-Bing, D., G. Long, L. Wei and C. Xu (2009), 'Worldwide marine transportation network: efficiency and container throughput', *Chinese Physics Letters*, **26** (11), 118901.

World Business Council for Sustainable Development (2004), *Mobility 2030: Meeting the Challenges to Sustainability*, Geneva: World Business Council for Sustainable Development.

15. The simple complex phenomenon of urban parking

Itzhak Benenson and Nir Fulman

1. SOME URBAN COMPLEX SYSTEMS ARE SIMPLER THAN THE OTHERS

A city is a canonic example of the complex system. The literature is full of descriptions of urban dynamic phenomena that perfectly match classical examples of self-organization, emergence and criticality. Eventually, these examples build on the standard background of non-linear feedbacks, negative and positive, between the aggregate components of urban phenomena at various levels of aggregation (Thurner et al. 2018).

Unlike systems studied by the natural sciences, cities are human-made and human-driven, and the dynamics of urban phenomena are defined by the behavior of humans and human institutions. As each person or institution is a complex system in itself, it is hardly possible to define the laws of urban system dynamics in a physical sense: human-dependent feedback relationships, no matter how likely they are, cannot be considered as strictly causal and cannot be used for extrapolation of the system dynamics for the future.

The phenomenological nature of the urban feedback entails a type of post-modernist trend among students of urban dynamics: The model is considered as a reflection of the researcher's view of the phenomenon and not of the reality itself (Batty 2017). That is, the causality of relationships does not demand comprehensive validation and the model is not intended to become an operational tool for evaluating the future of the urban system. Taken literally, this viewpoint undermines the trust in modeling as a tool for urban management and planning.

Can we go beyond the phenomenological match between physical models, such as power law or self-organized criticality (Thurner et al. 2018) and urban phenomena? Are we able to identify and estimate real urban feedbacks, recognize causal or close to causal dependences between urban parameters and estimate the effect of these dependencies on the complex urban phenomena? Can we exploit this knowledge for establishing urban models for urban planning and management?

We advocate that the positive reply to this epistemological enquiry should be sought among the phenomena for which the behavior of the involved humans can be considered to be simple. The candidate circumstances are those in which:

1. Human behavior and decision making are routine.
2. Human knowledge of the variability of constraints and potential consequences of the possible decisions covers the entire state space of the investigated system.
3. The relationships between the investigated sub-system and other parts of the urban system are loose and can be considered in relation to aggregate parameters and boundary conditions.

In this chapter, we name these system phenomena 'simple complex phenomena'. We claim that for the simple complex urban phenomena we are able to estimate empirically causal urban relationships and then assess the effects of these relationships on the system dynamics. Taking the risk of being tautological, we claim the dynamics of the simple complex urban systems can be predicted.

2.   THE PARKING SEARCH AND PARKING AS A SIMPLE COMPLEX PHENOMENON

The parking search is a basic component of urban traffic in every big city. Parking search time is essentially non-zero when the instantaneous demand is below the instantaneous parking supply. During working hours, supply is below demand in the city's central business district (CBD), while in the residential areas parking is a problem in the evening and overnight.

Parking is a fast phenomenon that satisfies all three suggested criteria of the simple complex systems. (1) Drivers' parking search behavior is a routine procedure performed at the end of every trip, and the vast majority of drivers have adequate knowledge about the state of parking in the vicinity of their destination. This includes on-street parking permissions, on-street and off-street parking prices, fluctuations of parking occupancy at the hour of arrival, the chance of being fined for illegal parking, and so on. (2) Parking patterns emerge and dissolve anew every day and, after very few trials, drivers directly experience or can easily imagine the entire spectrum of conditions at the area of their destinations. (3) Parking phenomenon is only loosely connected to general traffic dynamics, and a driver who has arrived at the destination has no choice but to find parking regardless of the level of traffic congestion around.

Understanding parking dynamics can be directly exploited to establish urban parking policy. This policy is an important example of the inherent controversy that urban management and planning involves. The major incentive of the parking policy, in the short run, is to reduce drivers' parking search time. However, a fast and successful parking search increases the attractiveness of an area for private cars and this contradicts the long-term goal of the parking policy, which is to encourage urban residents and visitors to abandon private cars in favor of public transport. Parking constraints or high parking fees support both goals, but are socially and politically unattractive.

In this chapter, we investigate urban parking as a simple complex phenomenon. We demonstrate that parking exhibits all the main properties of a complex system: that is, non-linear dependency of parking search time on the occupation rate, emergence of the complex patterns in the uniform conditions and path dependence. Yet urban parking can be managed and predicted.

The structure of the chapter is as follows: section 3 introduces parking phenomenon formally; section 4 proposes aggregate and non-spatial models that capture the basic properties of parking dynamics; section 5 proceeds with a spatially explicit model of parking in abstract homogeneous space; section 6 connects the abstract and realistic models of parking dynamics; and section 7 discusses problems of parking management and pricing. We discuss and conclude our research in section 8.

3. BASIC PROPERTIES OF PARKING PHENOMENON

3.1 Parking as a Collective Phenomenon

Parking is a typical collective phenomenon (Benenson et al. 2008). The parking search of a driver c who starts a search at a moment t, is determined by the parking pattern in the vicinity $U(v_c)$ of c's destination v_c. This pattern is an outcome of (1) the parking search of other drivers before t, and (2) cruising conditions during the period of c's search determined by the number, destinations and search behavior of the drivers who search for parking simultaneously with c. Note that the meaning of the destination's vicinity $U(v_c)$ may be different for different drivers and should be further specified in applications.

Let us consider parking in urban area A of the total parking capacity C_A. The collective outcome of the parking search of drivers at a particular time t is a parking pattern $\pi_A(t)$. From the driver's viewpoint, the main parameter of $\pi_A(t)$ is the occupancy $o_A(v_c, t)$ in the vicinity $U(v_c)$ of c's destination v_c that is, the fraction of parking spots that are vacant there. Interchangeably, we can use the value of $1 - o_A(v_c, t)$ representing the fraction of the vacant spots. The second basic parameter is the parking price $p_A(v_c, t)$ within the $U(v_c)$. Note that different drivers can react differently to the same $o_A(v_c, t)$ and $p_A(v_c, t)$ depending on their general willingness to pay or time pressure.

The main aggregate parameters that define the dynamics of the $\pi_A(t)$ are arrivals at and departures from A. The arrival rate $a(t)$ represents a number of drivers who will arrive at A during the time interval $[t, t + 1]$, while the number of drivers $d(t)$ who quit their parking during $[t, t + 1]$ represent the departure rate. Both $a(t)$ and $d(t)$ may depend on the state of $\pi_A(t)$, such as instantaneous or averaged occupancy, or on the pattern of the parking fees in A. In case v_c is close to the A's boundary, $U(v_c)$ can be partially outside A, which is why, in applications, it is convenient to consider parking in a relatively isolated area, bounded, for example, by the main streets (Figure 15.1).

3.2 The Scale of the Parking Phenomenon

As any complex spatial system, the parking phenomenon should be considered in relation to its characteristic spatial and temporal dimensions. As a human-driven phenomenon, parking should be also characterized in relation to drivers' parking behavior (Figure 15.2).

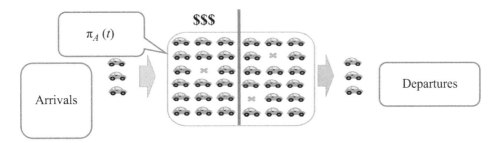

Figure 15.1   Parking as a balance between arrivals, departures and prices

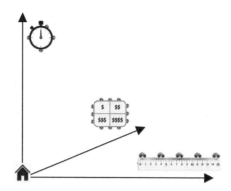

Figure 15.2   The three scales of parking: distance to destination, duration of search and price

1. Spatial scale – close versus distant parking. In this chapter, we consider a parking place as being close to a driver's destination if the walk to the destination takes up to 1–1.5 minutes. For the standard walking speed of *circa* 1 meter per second (3.6 kilometers per hour), a close spot should thus be at a distance of up to 50–100 m to the destination, which is a typical length of the street link in the European cities. We thus consider a parking spot as close to a driver's destination if they are located at the same or at connected street link. A parking place is far if it is beyond the radius of a typical driver's search area of 300–400 meters around the destination (Fulman et al. 2020). The walk from the distant parking place to the destination will take 5–10 minutes.

2. Temporal scale – short versus long parking search time. We consider the parking search to be short when it takes less than 0.5–1.0 minute. Parking search speed is *circa* 3–4 meters per second (10–15 kilometers per hour) (Carrese et al. 2004). Therefore, parking search time is short if a vacant spot is found after traversing three or four street links at most. The parking search is long if the driver has to traverse an essential part of the typical search neighborhood of 300–400 meters around the destination, which would take at least 5–7 minutes.

3. Price scale – cheap versus expensive parking. The meaning of cheap and expensive parking is less universal than that of a close or far spot and a short or long search time. Historically, many cities have established cheap parking lots to encourage citizens and visitors to park there instead of cruising around urban areas. We consider this minimal price as a scaling unit. Typically, the expensive parking near the attractive location in a large city's CBD is ten and more times higher than the minimal parking price.

4.   BASIC MODELS OF PARKING

Until the ubiquitous 5G mobile network and a real-time parking system direct us to the optimal parking spot, a driver c will start the parking search near the destination v_c with very partial information about the state of the parking pattern around the area. Yet a driver has to decide how to search for parking based on previous and instantaneous experience of occupancy and pricing patterns $o_A(v_c, t)$ and $p_A(v_c, t)$, respectively, over the $U(v_c)$ and A as a whole.

Let at each time step $a(t) = a$ that is, a constant number a of vehicles arrive at the area for parking. As regards the departure process, two views are possible:

1. Every parking car has a constant probability δ to leave the spot per a time step. In this instance the average dwell time τ_m in A is $\tau_m = 1/\delta$.
2. Drivers arrive at A for an activity that takes time. Departure process is thus defined by the distribution of dwell time. Let d_i be the probability that the car's dwell time is i, $\sum_i d_i = 1$. The average dwell time in this case is $\tau_m = \sum_i i d_i$.

4.1 Parking as a Balance between Arrivals and Departures: Model 1

Let us start with a non-spatial view of the parking phenomenon, as presented in Figure 15.1. The system is characterized by one aggregate parameter only: the fraction $o_A(t)$ of the occupied parking spots.

4.1.1 Constant probability δ of departure

Let $O_A(t) = o_A(t)C_A$ be the total number of the occupied spots in A. Total departure from the area will be $\delta O_A(t)$ and the dynamics of $O_A(t)$ can be represented by the following simple equation (index A is omitted):

$$O(t+1) = (1-\delta)O(t) + a \cdot \tag{15.1}$$

Model 1 has one equilibrium:

$$O^* = a / \delta \text{ or } O^* = a\tau_m. \tag{15.2}$$

This equilibrium is globally stable: denoting the deviation from it as $\Delta O(t) = O(t) - O^*$, we obtain the equation of the $\Delta O(t)$ dynamics, the solution to which converges to zero for any positive δ:

$$\Delta O(t+1) = (1-\delta)\Delta O(t). \tag{15.3}$$

The hidden problem, however, is that the model does not account for the limited parking capacity C_A of A. The equilibrium (15.2) is indeed meaningful for $O^* \leq C_A$. However, for $O^* \geq C_A$, after some initial period of time, $O(t)$ reaches C_A and some of the newly arriving vehicles would just add to a queue that would grow at a rate $a - \delta C_A = \delta(O^* - C_A) = (O^* - C_A)/\tau_m$ per time unit.

4.1.2 Depart after your dwell time is over

Let us, for simplicity, consider a specific case in which a fraction d_1 of the drivers arrive at A for an activity that takes less than 1 time step and fractions d_2, d_3, d_4 of drivers arrive for the activities that take 2, 3 and 4 time units, respectively, $\sum_{i=1}^{i=4} d_i = 1$. In this case, the state of parking in A can be described by a vector $\overline{O(t)}$ that represents the number of drivers who arrived at A at t, $t-1$, $t-2$ and $t-3$: $\overline{O(t)} = (O_0(t), O_1(t), O_2(t), O_3(t))$, where $O_i(t)$ represent the number of cars that arrived at A and parked at a time $t-i$.

Recalling that a number of vehicles arriving at A per time step is a, the dynamics of a parking system is described by the following system of equations:

$$
\begin{aligned}
O_0(t+1) &= a \\
O_1(t+1) &= (1-d_1)O_0(t) \\
O_2(t+1) &= (1-d_2/(1-d_1))O_1(t) \\
O_3(t+1) &= (1-d_3/(1-d_1-d_2))O_2(t)
\end{aligned}
\tag{15.4}
$$

In a vector form, the system of equations (15.4) can be written as:

$$
\overline{O(t+1)} = \overline{O(t)}M + \overline{a}, \tag{15.5}
$$

where M is a matrix:

$$
M = \begin{pmatrix}
0 & 1-d_1 & 0 & 0 \\
0 & 0 & 1-d_2/(1-d_1) & 0 \\
0 & 0 & 0 & 1-d_3/(1-d_1-d_2) \\
0 & 0 & 0 & 0
\end{pmatrix}, \text{ and } \overline{a} = (a,0,0,0).
$$

It is easy to demonstrate that for any initial vector $\overline{O(0)}$, the solution of (15.4) – (15.6) converges to the steady equilibrium:

$$
\overline{O^*} = (a, (1-d_1)a, (1-d_1-d_2)a, (1-d_1-d_2-d_3)a). \tag{15.6}
$$

Let $O_{tot}(t) = O_0(t) + O_1(t) + O_2(t) + O_3(t)$ represent the total number of occupied spots in A. Evidently, the meaning of the $O_{tot}(t)$ is the same as of the $O(t)$ in case of constant probability to leave in the previous section. Accounting for the condition $\sum_{i=1}^{i=4} d_i = 1$, the equilibrium number of the occupied spots in A is:

$$
O_{tot}^* = (4 - 3d_1 - 2d_2 - d_3)a = (d_1 + 2d_2 + 3d_3 + 4d_4)a = a\tau_m. \tag{15.7}
$$

That is, the equilibrium number of the occupied parking spots in A is the same for both views of the departures and, as long as $O_{total}^*(t)$ exceeds the total parking capacity C_A of A, newly arriving vehicles would just wait in a queue that grows at a rate $(O^* - C_A)/\tau_m$ per time unit. For the arbitrarily distribution of the parking times d_i, $i = 1, \ldots, T$ formula (15.7) has the form:

$$
\overline{O^*} = \left(a, (1-d_1)a, \ldots, \left(1 - \sum_{i=1}^{i=t} d_i\right)a, \ldots, \left(1 - \sum_{i=1}^{i=T-1} d_i\right)a \right). \tag{15.8}
$$

The major difference between the two views of the departure process is in the distribution of the parking cars by their dwell time. Figure 15.3 presents these distributions for $\tau_m = 1$ hour that corresponds, in case of constant probability to leave, to $\delta = 1/60$ per minute, while for the activity-based view, we have chosen uniform distribution of drivers' dwell time on [30, 90] min. Note that given τ_m, these distributions do not depend on a.

To conclude:

- Given a constant arrival rate a and average dwell time τ_m in an area A of a total parking capacity C_A, the number of parked cars there always stabilizes.
- In case $a\tau_m \leq C_A$, the equilibrium number of occupied parking spots in A is $O^*_{total}(t) = a\tau_m$ and the equilibrium occupation rate is $O^*_{total}(t)/C_A$.
- If $O^*_{total}(t) > C_A$, then A is always fully occupied and the queue of cars waiting for parking in A grows at a constant rate of $(O^* - C_A)/\tau_m$.

Note that, in reality, $a = a(t)$ and $\delta = \delta(t)$ and vary by the time of day. The parking occupation rate $o(t)$ is thus always in the process of convergence to an elusive equilibrium.

4.2 The Spatio-Temporal Dynamics of Parking: Model 2

Parking is a spatial phenomenon and it is important for the driver to find a vacant spot close to the destination. Our basic parking model must be thus extended to incorporate spatial dimensions of parking.

Let us consider a driver c who is cruising for parking vicinity $U(v_c)$ of c's destination v_c. If cruising continues, c has to decide whether to search further away from the destination or drive to more expensive parts of $U(v_c)$ that may be avoided by the other drivers. A spatial view of parking makes it possible to make a step from the occupation rate to the most important parameter for a driver – the expected cruising time $\theta_c(v_c)$.

To understand the basic relationship between the occupation rate and the expected cruising time we consider a one-dimensional parking area A as in the Figure 15.4. Each side of the polygon in Figure 15.4 is a two-way street link $l_1, l_2 \ldots l_N$ of 100 meters in length with $c_n = c = 20$ parking spots on the right-hand side. We assume that drivers cruise for parking at a speed 12 kilometers per hour (Carrese et al. 2004).

We use junctions as proxies for drivers' destinations and assume that a driver whose destination is a junction j starts cruising for parking in a counterclockwise direction. If the link is fully occupied, a driver continues driving in the same direction. In this abstract model a driver may make several full loops before parking.

The arrival and departure processes in the spatial case are the same as in the temporal one, but we consider them as stochastic. Let the average number a_j of drivers who arrive for parking near the destination j be the same for each j, $a_j = a$, while the probability of leaving the spot δ is the same for all spots on all links. The average total number of arrivals is thus Na and of the departures $N\delta$, and the non-spatial dynamics of the system is the same as in the model 1: the average occupancy of each link n is equal to $O^*_n = a/\delta$, in case $a/\delta \leq c$, while for $a/\delta > c$, the number of drivers that search for parking grows at a constant rate $N(a/\delta - c)$ per time step.

Spatial model 2 reveals a qualitatively new effect that is the result of the stochastic variations in arrivals and departures. This stochasticity is unimportant when $O^* \ll c$, and every arriving driver easily finds a vacant spot at the link that is adjacent to the driver's destination j. It is also unimportant for $O^* > c$, when the system's capacity is insufficient to accommodate the demand. However, when O^* is below but close to c, the instantaneous number of drivers that want to park at a link can be, by the stochastic reasons, higher than link's capacity despite $O^* < c$. The drivers who fail to park on this link then drive

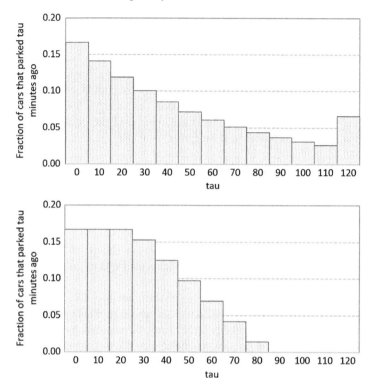

Note: In both (a) and (b), $\tau_m = 1$.

Figure 15.3   Equilibrium distribution of the dwell time for area A with 100 parking spots, and constant probability to leave $\delta = 1/60$ per hour (a), dwell time uniformly distributed on the interval [30, 90] minutes (b)

to the next link, increasing the arrival rate there and the system behaves as if the average number of arrivals to the link is $a + x$, where $x > 0$.

Let the order of traversing links in the one-dimensional parking space in Figure 15.4 be $l_1 \rightarrow l_2 \ldots \rightarrow l_n \ldots \rightarrow l_{N-1} \rightarrow l_N \rightarrow l_1$. Let $a_n(t)$ be exogenous arrivals to a link l_n, $i_n(t)$, the total number of drivers entering l_n, $e_n(t)$ be the number of the vacant spots on l_n, $\delta_n(t)$, the total number of departures from the occupied spots on l_n, and $u_n(t)$ the number of drivers that do not succeed to park on l_n and will continue to search on the link l_{n+1}. Thus, $a_n(t)$ is a Poisson stochastic variable with an average a, while $\delta_n(t)$ is a sum of $c - e_n(t)$ Bernoulli processes, each with the probability δ.

The dynamic of parking can be expressed by the following system of equations that relate from the state of l_n at $t + 1$ to the state of l_n and surrounding links at t:

$$i_n(t+1) = a_n(t) + u_{n-1}(t) \tag{15.9}$$
$$e_n(t+1) = \ \max\ \{e_n(t) + \delta_n(t) - i_n(t+1), 0\}$$
$$u_n(t+1) = \ \max\ \{0, i_n(t+1) - e_n(t+1)\}$$

where $n = 1, 2 \ldots N$, and the drivers from l_N continue to l_1.

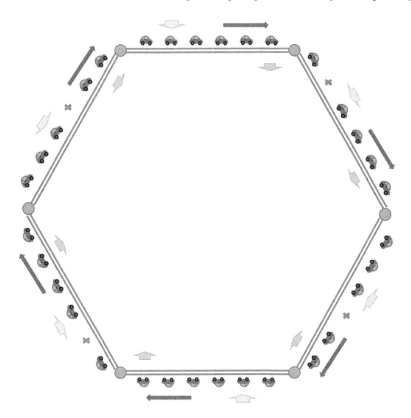

Note: Wide arrows outside the hexagon denote arrivals at the destination located on the link, wide arrows inside the hexagon denote departures from the link, and long arrows denote cars that move to a link after failing to park at the previous link.

Figure 15.4   The one-dimensional parking area considered in the spatial model of parking

Transition of the unsatisfied demand to the adjacent link critically changes the occupation patterns, and Figure 15.5 illustrates this for a case of A consisting of 16 links of the 100-meter length, and drivers cruise at a speed of 12 kilometers per hour. At this speed it takes a driver 30 seconds to traverse a link, which is therefore the model time step. The departure rate δ per these 30 seconds is $\delta = 1/120$, entailing the average parking time of 60 minutes. Let us examine the emerging occupation pattern as dependent on arrival rate a. For the values of $a < 24/hour$, for which $O^* = a\tau_m < 0.8c = 16$, the instantaneous occupation rate of each link l_n always remains far below 1 no matter what the stochastic deviation of arrivals and departures are and that drivers always park at the first link after the destination. With the increase in a and $O^* > 16$, some of the links, owing to stochasticity, become fully occupied at some time steps, and with the further increase in O^*, these fully occupied links merge into fully continuous chains. This phenomenon becomes essential when O^* passes 0.9. The growth of the lengths of the chains with the increase in O^* is non-linear (Figure 15.5). These chains of fully occupied links decrease the chances of finding parking despite the availability of the vacant spot. These spots are just not at

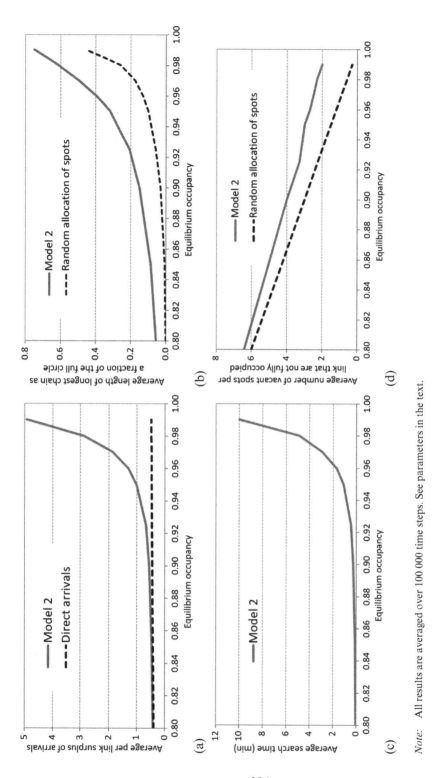

Note: All results are averaged over 100 000 time steps. See parameters in the text.

Figure 15.5 *Average characteristics of the parking patterns that emerge on the 16-links circle as dependent on the equilibrium occupation rate: (a) total arrivals to the link; (b) length of the longest chain of fully occupied links; (c) search time; (d) number of vacant spots on non-fully occupied links*

a link where the drivers look for them and not at the links where the drivers would look for them in the nearest future.

Let us stress that the case when the equilibrium occupation O^* is smaller but close to the link's capacity c is, practically, the most important. Indeed, nobody remembers about parking when the demand is below the supply. The opposite case of $O^* > c$ is, practically, very complicated and cannot be managed with the simple models we investigated previously because drivers and parking managers know of the mismatch in advance. Managers try to resolve the problem by imposing constraints on arrivals and increasing parking prices, while drivers park far away from the area, pay more or just use public transport to reach the area. As a consequence, the system evolves to a user equilibrium (in a broad sense), where $O^*/c \sim 1$ again.

To conclude, the basic characteristics of the spatio-temporal dynamics of parking process in the homogeneous area A of the capacity C_A for the constant arrival and departure rates a and δ:

- If $a/\delta \ll C_A$, the parking pattern stabilizes at the level of $O^*_{tot} = a/\delta$.
- If $a/\delta \geq C_A$, the area will be fully occupied and the queue of cruising drivers will grow linearly at a rate $\delta(O^*_{tot} - C_A)$.
- The most practically important case is when O^*_{tot} is lower than C_A but close to it, $0.9 < O^*_{tot}/C_A < 1$. In this case, parking pattern self-organizes into the long 100 percent occupied chains and gaps between them. The location of these chains cannot be predicted, while the average cruising time of a driver grows, with the increase in O^*_{tot}/C_A, essentially non-linearly.

In the next section we consider several models of parking dynamics that demonstrate these phenomena in more detail. These models differ in their spatio-temporal resolution and level of abstraction. We start from the abstract two-dimensional models and advance to models and algorithms that aim to manage real complex parking systems. Our goal is to preserve a balance between understanding the complexity of parking reality and applying it to the management of real-world parking.

5. BASIC SYSTEM PROPERTIES OF THE PARKING PHENOMENON IN TWO DIMENSIONS

5.1 Analytical Models

The step ahead of the basic model 2 is queue models (Millard-Ball et al. 2014; Dowling et al. 2020). The queue models investigate a two-dimensional street grid network, considering each link l that has n_l parking spots as a server that can serve n_l requests (cars). When all spots are occupied, the server link rejects further requests which are forwarded to the adjacent servers (links), where the adjacency is defined by the network topology. Similar to the one-dimension model 2, a flow of arrivals is a Poisson process with a constant average, while the departure process is represented by the constant probability to be served, that is, to leave the spot.

Queue theory properly reflect the phenomenon of the additional amount of cruising cars (Figure 15.5(a)), but we are not aware of the theoretical studies that analytically prove the emergence of the long continuous chains of fully occupied links in one dimension of continuous patches of fully occupied links in two dimensions (see section 5.2). To the best of our knowledge, the analytical results that relate to the cruising time and the equilibrium occupation rate o^* are not available yet.

5.2   Simulations

To extend the basic one-dimension model 2 into the two-dimension model 2, let us consider a 20 × 20 grid city A of two-way streets of 100-meter length, with $c_l = c = 20$ parking spots on each side of the street (Figure 15.6). To avoid the boundary effects we consider the one-dimension model on the circle. For the same purpose in the two-dimension model, we project the grid on to a torus. As in model 2, each of 400 junctions j serves as a proxy of a destination and is characterized by the hourly demand $a_i = a$, which is the same for all destinations. The overall capacity of a city is thus $C_A = 32\,000$ parking spots and the ratio of the total number of curb parking spots to the number of destinations is equal to 80.

Drivers traverse the city at the speed of 12 kilometers per hour. At the end of each 30-second tick, a driver who fails to park on a link l reaches the junction at the end of it and at the beginning of the next tick decides on the next link to cruise to. Unlike the one-dimension model, drivers do not want to park too far from the destination, and the probability $w_{d(l)}$ of searching for parking at a link l that is at a distance d from the destination decreases as d increases, nullifying at a distance of 500 meters (see Figure 15.9a in the next section), as discovered in a serious game of parking search (Fulman et al. 2020;

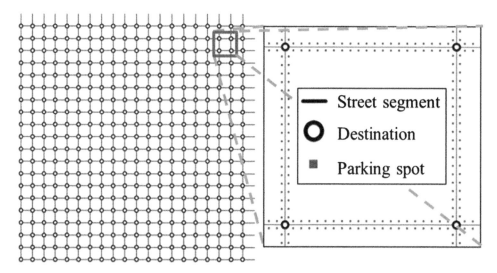

Source: Fulman and Benenson (2021).

Figure 15.6   20 × 20 grid city with zoom to a city block

see also section 6.1 in this chapter). Drivers park for a time that is uniformly distributed on [1,2] hours interval and their average parking time is thus 1.5 hours.

As we demonstrate in Fulman and Benenson (2021), the emergent two-dimension parking occupation pattern in a grid city A is qualitatively similar to the pattern emerging in the one-dimension model 2. With the growth of $o^* = a\tau_m/C_A = 1.5a/80$, the fraction of fully occupied links non-linearly grows and, similar to the emergence of continuous fully occupied chains in one dimension, continuous two-dimension patches of links emerge and their average size increases non-linearly. Importantly, the weighted, by probability $w_{d(l)}$ of visiting, fraction $F_{U(v)}$ of fully occupied links within the search neighborhood $U(v)$ determines the probability of failure for a driver whose destination is v:

$$F_{U(v)}(t) = \sum_{l \in U(v)} \{w_{d(l)} \mid o_l(t) = 1\} \tag{15.10}$$

The patches of full occupancy emerge and dissolve in time, but under realistic turnover rates $F_{U(v)}$ barely changes during the time of the driver's search. That is why we can approximate the probability to cruise longer than τ as:

$$p(\tau, v) = (1 - F_{U(v)}) * F_{U(v)}^{\tau} \tag{15.11}$$

See Fulman and Benenson (2021) for more details.

To conclude, the properties of the two-dimension parking pattern repeat the properties of the one-dimension pattern that we have revealed with model 2: the continuous patches of the fully occupied links are self-organizing and this process intensifies non-linearly when the equilibrium occupation rate is approaching 1. In addition, the use of (15.10) – (15.11) enables the step from the homogeneous grid city to the heterogeneous reality – the fraction of the fully occupied links $F_{U(v)}$ in (15.10) can be estimated in the heterogeneous case in the same way as it is achieved in the homogeneous case. Let us make this step.

6.   BRIDGING THEORY AND REALITY

6.1   The Basic Laws of Drivers' Parking Behavior

To make a step from the basic quantitative view of parking theory to parking reality we have to establish the model of drivers' parking search behavior. This behavior is defined by the parameters of the parking environment, such as prices and occupancy, as well as on the driver's personal characteristics, for example, time stress, willingness to pay, and personal attitude to the on- and off-street parking. All these parameters, apart from one, parking occupancy, are known to the driver when he or she starts the search. The driver may have knowledge of the typical occupancy from the previous parking experience in the area or from observations on the way to the destination, but this knowledge does not help much when cruising becomes longer than expected. Until drivers become totally obedient to the future parking search system, the parking search in highly occupied areas would remain very uncertain.

It is hardly possible to recognize drivers' decision making while searching for parking in the highly occupied area. We thus chose to imitate these circumstances in a serious parking game, PARKGAME (Fulman et al. 2020). The goal of the game is to understand two intertwined parking choices of the driver: *where to cruise* and *when to quit* unsuccessful cruising.

PARKGAME players use the keyboard to search for parking in a virtual urban road network represented by geographical information system (GIS) layers of street links. They start a game 300–400 meters from their destination, and their goal is to be in time for a doctor's appointment at the destination (Figure 15.7).

The players can park either on-street or at the parking lot near the destination. They start each game with a fixed budget out of which the on-street or lot parking costs are deducted based on the eventual parking choice. Parking at a lot is always available but at a double price of on-street parking, which on the other hand is very scarce. Players who search for too long and arrive at the meeting later than anticipated are fined based on a per-minute lateness rate. Thus, as in reality, the goal of the players is to find parking quickly and close to the destination. Players play the game many times and the parameters of the game are set in a way that the optimal player's strategy that maximizes the average gains of the player is to search for on-street parking until the very end of the game.

We examined drivers' decision to quit the on-street search by estimating the time τ from the start of the game to when they gave up on cruising and parked at the lot instead. The hazard rate $h(\tau)$ grows from the start of the game until the meeting time, and then sharply decreases, which clearly shows that players do not search for maximizing (Figure 15.8).

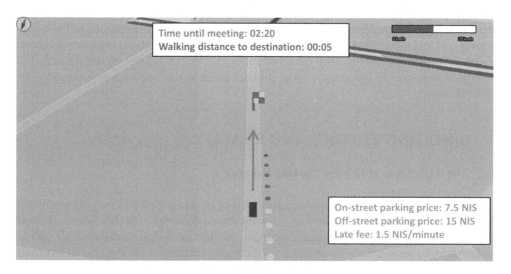

Note: Details important for the driver's decision making are presented on the screen.

Source: Fulman et al. (2020).

Figure 15.7   *Game screenshot: the player is about to reach the destination (chequered flag) and observes a vacancy five parking places ahead (dot nearest to the flag)*

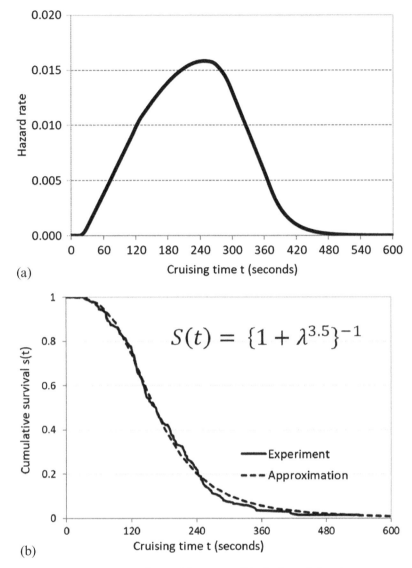

(a)

(b)

Figure 15.8 *(a) Instantaneous hazard function; (b) the best fit log-logistic survival curve, λ is a linear function of the duration of time between the start of the search and the meeting*

Drivers' spatial behavior before they decide to quit is adequately described by the model of biased random walk with memory. That is, (1) players who choose to continue cruising do not want to cruise far away from their destination, and (2) when deciding on whether to approach or recede from the destination and/or parking lot they prefer to repeat their decision from the previous junction – if they drove further away they would probably continue to recede, if they approached, they would probably continue to

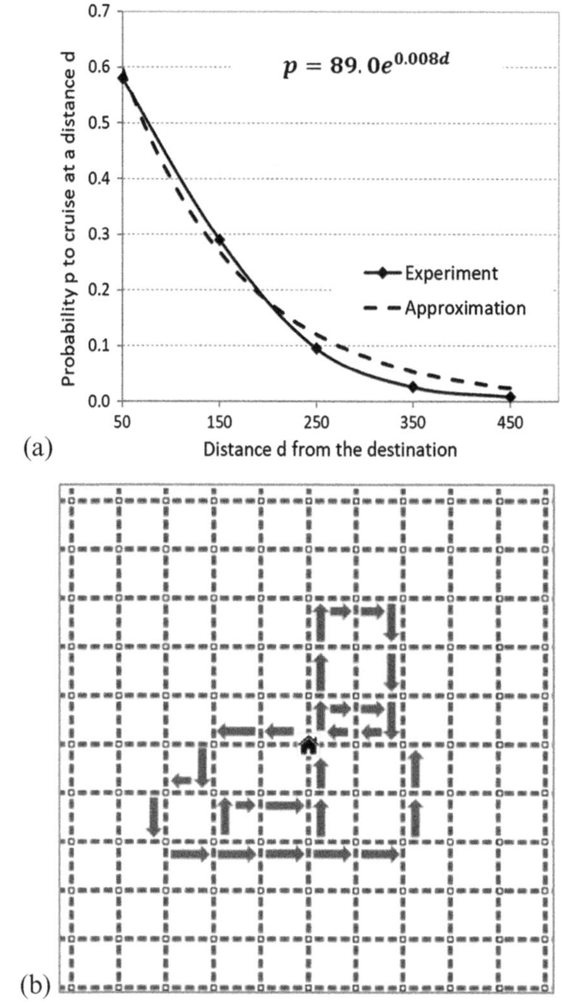

(a)

(b)

Source: Fulman and Benenson (2021).

Figure 15.9   *Probability of visiting the link at distance d from the destination (a), and a typical driver's search trajectory (b) in an abstract city*

approach to the destination. This formal behavior results in typical circling around the axis connecting the destination and the parking lot (Figure 15.9).

6.2   From Drivers' Behavior to Simulation

The rules of drivers' spatio-temporal behavior presented in section 6.1 are sufficient to establish a simulation model of parking dynamics. Drivers' destinations in the model are real buildings each characterized by its demand for parking, while the parking supply is represented by GIS layers of street links with known parking constraints and parking

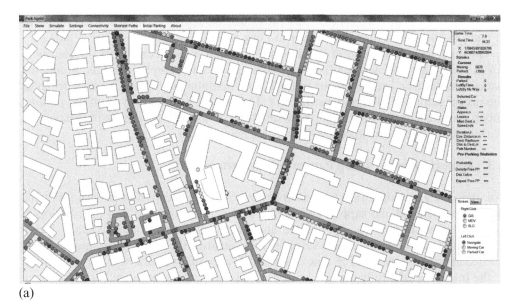

(a)

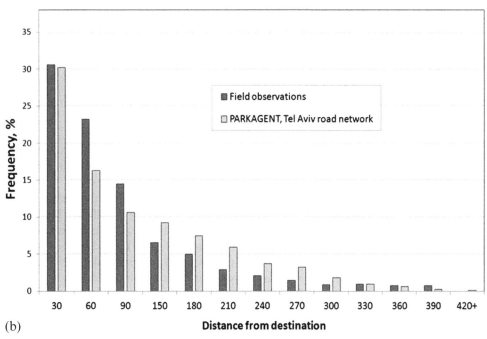

(b)

Source: Figure 15.10(b) – Levy et al. (2013, 2015).

Figure 15.10   *PARKAGENT model interface (a) and the match between the model outcomes and parameters estimated in the field (b), according to Levy et al. 2013, 2015)*

lots with known capacity. The results of simulation repeated the real urban pattern (Figure 15.10) and we direct the reader to Levy et al. (2013, 2015) for more details.

The fundamental problem of the simulation models is their complexity. While useful for modeling heterogeneity and studying dependencies in complex systems, simulating parking in realistic heterogeneous settings is computationally expensive and demands the proper setting of all model parameters. The next step on the way from the parking theory to practice is to suggest the approximate methods for assessing the properties of a parking pattern that are necessary for parking management.

6.3 Approximating a Parking Pattern in Heterogeneous City

An approximating algorithm for constructing a parking occupation pattern given the patterns of demand and supply, arrival rate as dependent on time, and distribution of the dwell time, is proposed by Fulman and Benenson (2019). The Maximally Dense (MD) pattern that they describe is sufficient for estimating the most important parameter needed to estimate the cruising time of the driver who aims to park near the destination v: the fraction of the fully occupied links $F_{U(v)}(t)$ within the search neighborhood $U(v)$. The algorithm of constructing the MD pattern repeats, many times, three major steps:

1. Generate a list G_t of <car, destination> pairs for all drivers who arrive at t and randomly reorder it. G_t defines the order in which the parking requests of these cars will be considered at t.
2. Loop by cars in G_t. For each car, consider the vacant parking spot that is closest to its destination and park there.
3. Release spots that were occupied by cars whose parking time is over at t and consider it as an initial parking pattern for the next repetition.

This algorithm is applied many times and each time it generates a parking pattern that varies depending on the order of the arriving and departing cars. The MD pattern is an average of these pattern and it is accompanied by the necessary statistics.

The MD algorithm reflects two major features of drivers' behavior: the search for a vacant spot over the pattern that emerged following the parking search by the drivers who arrived at the area earlier, and the preference for parking as close as possible to the destination. As we demonstrate in Fulman and Benenson (2021), it adequately reproduces the emerging clusters of fully occupied parking that determine the cruising time curve. Based on the MD pattern, we can address two basic practical problems: estimation of the parking search time and establishing parking prices.

7. MANAGING PARKING

7.1 Estimating Parking Occupation and Search Time

Given the pattern of demand and supply, arrival rate as dependent on time, and distribution of the dwell time one can construct the MD pattern and then, based on equations

(15.10) and (15.11), estimate distribution of the cruising time for a driver who aims to park near a given destination. Figure 15.11 presents the maps of the average cruising time and the maps of the probability of cruising longer than a given time τ in the city of Bat-Yam, a satellite of Tel-Aviv. We direct the reader who is interested in more details to Fulman and Benenson (2021).

7.2 Establishing Parking Prices

Higher than minimal prices are the basic tool of parking management in the city. We can expect that the increase in parking prices over an area will enforce drivers to shorten their dwell time or not to park in the area at all, thus decreasing the demand. If, however, the parking remained underpriced and demand still exceeded supply, the fully occupied patches will continue to emerge and the drivers whose destinations are within or close to these patches would search for parking for a long time. The overpriced parking that results in too low occupation does not make sense either and, thus, establishing the balances prices is critical for the parking management.

Several cities in the world have begun to manage demand for parking via dynamic pricing (LADOT 2019; SDOT 2019; SFMTA 2014). Within these policies, parking occupancy is measured and parking prices are increased locally, when the parking occupancy on the single road link, several connected links or over some predefined area nears the capacity. Some drivers thus park further away from their destinations, and pay less, while others switch to a different mode of transportation. In the cities that employ this policy, parking prices are updated repeatedly until, finally, the occupation rate in every unit converges at the acceptable level. Dynamic pricing policies have proved their effectiveness (Pierce and Shoup 2013) but their adoption is slow. The reason for this is the investment necessary for measuring the parking occupation at the resolution of a single road link at the level of a single spot, which needs to be achieved by means of sensors, and these sensors are still very expensive to deploy and operate.

Understanding the laws of parking pattern dynamics makes it possible to establish dynamic parking prices based on the standard data on demand, supply, arrivals and dwell time, without the direct real-time assessment of the spots' occupation. Fulman and Benenson (2019) present an algorithm for establishing dynamic prices that extends the MD algorithm for assessing the cruising time. The idea is simple: according to the MD algorithm, the driver prefers a parking place closer to the destination. Let the driver react not only to the distance to destination, but also to the price of the spot by combining distance and price within a spot utility function. If the price increases and the driver is sensitive to it, less expensive and more distant spots can become more attractive for him or her. Thus, prices can be adjusted for establishing a parking pattern of the uniform occupation rate that is below 100 percent.

Formally, let $A_{c,p}(d)$ be the attractiveness of a parking spot p at a distance d from the driver's destination c, and f_p be the parking price of p. Fulman and Benenson (2019) establish $A_{c,p}(d)$ to decrease with the increase in d:

$$A_{c,p}(d) \sim 1 / d^{\alpha}, \text{ where } 0 < \alpha < 1, \tag{15.12}$$

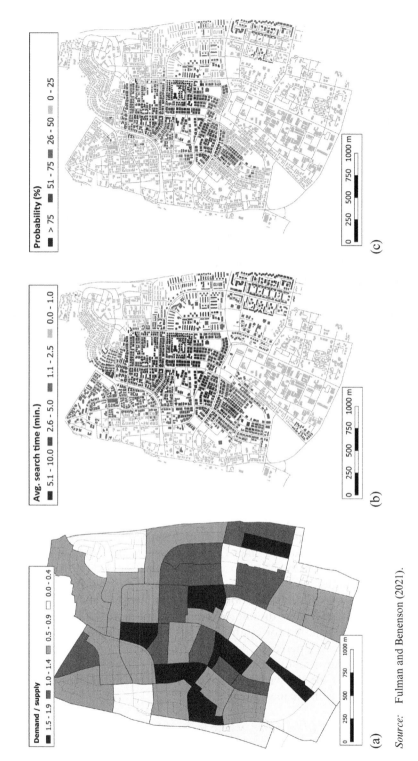

Source: Fulman and Benenson (2021).

Figure 15.11 Cruising time in Bat Yam: (a) demand to supply ratio by the Transportation Analysis Zones (TAZs); (b) average search time; (c) probability of searching for over 5 minutes

Parking price (ILS)
■ > 20   ■ 10.1 - 20   ■ 3.1 - 10   ■ 1 - 3

Parking price (ILS)
■ > 14.9   ■ 10 - 14.9   ■ 3 - 9.9   ▢ 1 - 2.9

0   250   500   750   1000 m

0   250   500   750   1000 m

(a)   (b)

Source: Fulman and Benenson (2020).

*Figure 15.12   Maps of overnight prices for the city of Bat Yam: (a) by street link;
(b) by TAZ*

and assume that c is sensitive to the parking price f_p only when it is above a specific threshold level, $f_p > f_{negligible} > 0$:

$$A_{c,p}(d) = min(1, \ min(1, f_{negligible} \ / \ f_p) \ / \ d^\alpha). \tag{15.13}$$

Drivers who fail to find parking at a distance less than 500 meters from their destination owing to low attractiveness of the available spots, are assumed to park far away and use alternative means of transportation to reach their destinations. Note that the utility functions different from equations (15.12) and (15.13) can be also employed.

The above algorithm can be applied to any partition of the city into the pricing units: Figure 15.12 presents the maps of the overnight prices for the city of Bat Yam for per night $f_{negligible} = ILS1$ and $\alpha = 0.5$, and the desired occupation rate of 0.85 at resolution of street links and TAZ. According to equations (15.10) and (15.11), the occupation rate of 85 percent guarantees a shorter that 2.5 minutes parking search for 99 percent of the cruising drivers.

8.   SYSTEMIC PROPERTIES OF THE PARKING PHENOMENON

The analysis of parking phenomena confirms each of the conditions we advocate for the simple complex system: (1) the parking system is loosely connected to the environment (general traffic); (2) its dynamics are repeated daily, thus enabling drivers to adapt to emerging phenomena and prices; and (3) parking dynamics are robust to the uncertain drivers' behavior owing to the overlap between drivers' search areas. This makes it possible to fully understand the phenomenon and exploit this knowledge to establish real-world parking policies. Let us summarize the system properties of the parking phenomenon.

Order parameter and emergence: as we demonstrated, driver's c parking search time in the vicinity $U(v)$ of the destination v is defined by the arrival rate α and average parking time τ_m of the drivers who include $U(v)$ in their search area while cruising for parking. Given the $U(v)$ capacity C, the product $\alpha\tau_m$ of these two parameters defines the emergence of the fully occupied patches and, thus, the driver's search time there. As far as the value of $\alpha\tau_m/C$ exceeds ~0.9, that is, less than 1 vacant spot per 10 is expected, on average, to be vacant, the fully occupied patches emerge and grow. The larger these patches, the longer the search. All these dependencies can be estimated numerically in the heterogeneous urban space with the dynamic simulation model or with the static MD approximation.

Non-linearity: as long as the average occupancy increases towards 1, drivers' search time grows and this growth is essentially non-linearly. This non-linearity is highly intuitive: an increase in occupancy from 90 percent to 90.5 percent cannot significantly influence parking search time, whereas an increase from 99 percent (1 spot out of 100 is vacant) to 99.5 percent (1 vacant spot out of 200) should increase parking search time at least twice.

Path dependence: the details of the parking pattern dynamics during the day do not depend on its details from the day before, while the within-day dynamics of the parking pattern is defined by the daily history of the emergent spillovers, which become essential when $U(v)$ increases to 0.9 and above, and a patch of fully occupied road links emerges and expands. The drivers whose destination is close to v would be forced to search for parking outside fully occupied patches while still trying to park as close as possible to their destinations. This positive feedback will enforce further growth of fully occupied patches and result in non-uniform distribution of vacant spots, with non-uniformity increasing when there is high occupancy. The stochastic nature of the arrival process does not allow us to predict, even when there is uniform supply and demand, where the patches will emerge and how they will grow, making the dynamics of the parking pattern path dependent.

The complexity of parking phenomenon does not make it unpredictable. Simple and effective algorithms make it possible to construct intertwined high resolution maps of the expected search time and locally defined prices that guarantee that the search time would not exceed the predefined threshold. These maps provide the basis for parking management, for which the goal would always be to keep parking search time within reasonable limits.

REFERENCES

Batty, M. (2017), *The New Science of Cities*, Cambridge, MA: MIT Press.

Benenson, I., K. Martens and S. Birfir (2008), 'PARKAGENT: an agent-based model of parking in the city', *Computers, Environment and Urban Systems*, **32** (6), 431–9.

Carrese, S., E. Negrenti, and B.B. Belles (2004), 'Simulation of the parking phase for urban traffic emission models', paper presented at the TRISTAN V-Triennial Symposium on Transportation Analysis, Guadeloupe, 13–18 June.

Dowling, C.P., L.J. Ratliff and B. Zhang (2020), 'Modeling curbside parking as a network of finite capacity queues', *IEEE Intelligent Transportation Systems Magazine*, **21** (3), 1011–22.

Fulman, N. and I. Benenson (2019), 'Establishing heterogeneous parking prices for uniform parking availability for autonomous and human-driven vehicles', *IEEE Intelligent Transportation Systems Magazine*, **11** (1), 15–28.

Fulman, N. and I. Benenson (2020), 'Spatially-explicit toolset for establishing and assessing heterogeneous parking prices in the smart city', *ISPRS Annals of the Photogrammetry, Remote Sensing and Spatial Information Sciences*, **6** (September), 63–70.

Fulman, N. and I. Benenson (2021), 'Approximation method for estimating search times for on-street parking', *Transportation Science* (in press).

Fulman, N., I. Benenson and E. Ben Elia (2020), 'Modeling parking search behavior in the city center: a game-based approach', *Transportation Research Part C: Emerging Technologies*, **120** (November), 102800.

Levy, N., K. Martens and I. Benenson (2013), 'Exploring cruising using agent-based and analytical models of parking', *Transportmetrica A: Transport Science*, **9** (9), 773–97.

Levy, N., M. Render, and I. Benenson (2015), 'Spatially explicit modeling of parking search as a tool for urban parking facilities and policy assessment', *Transport Policy*, **39** (April), 9–20.

Los Angeles Department of Transportation (LADOT) (2019), 'What is LA Express ParkTM?', accessed 10 December 2020 at http://www.laexpresspark.org/about-la-expresspark.

Millard-Ball, A., R.R. Weinberger and R.C. Hampshire (2014), 'Is the curb 80% full or 20% empty? Assessing the impacts of San Francisco's parking pricing experiment', *Transportation Research Part A: Policy and Practice*, **63** (May), 76–92.

Pierce, G. and D. Shoup (2013), 'Getting the prices right: an evaluation of pricing parking by demand in San Francisco', *Journal of the American Planning Association*, **79** (1), 67–81.

San Francisco Municipal Transportation Agency (SFMTA) (2014), 'SFpark Pilot Project evaluation', accessed 10 December 2020 at http://sfpark.org/about-the-project/.

Seattle Department of Transportation (SDOT) (2019), 'Performance-Based Parking Pricing Program', accessed 10 December 2020 at https://www.sfmta.com/sites/default/files/reports-and-documents/2018/08/sfpark_pilot_project_evaluation.pdf.

Thurner, S., R. Hanel and P. Klimek (2018), *Introduction to the Theory of Complex Systems*, Oxford: Oxford University Press.

PART V

COMPLEXITY, PLANNING AND DESIGN

16. Complexity and uncertainty: implications for urban planning
Stefano Moroni and Daniele Chiffi

1. INTRODUCTION: COMPLEXITY AND UNCERTAINTY

Uncertainty is the core feature of complexity. Complexity is a problem which warrants attention because it is associated with situations of radical, unavoidable uncertainty. As Batty and Marshall (2012, p. 43) write: 'A good analogue to complexity . . . is uncertainty and it could be argued that a complex system is one that we will always be uncertain about'. The same point is stressed by Giezen (2013, p. 724): 'Although complexity is often considered to be a problem, it is the uncertainty built into that complexity that is the true source of worry'. That is, 'Uncertainty and complexity are strongly related to one another, but it seems that . . . uncertainty is key' (Giezen, 2013, p. 725).[1]

In this chapter, we focus on those forms of uncertainty usually encountered in the assessment of, and intervention in, complex urban systems. After some pioneering contributions in the 1980s and 1990s,[2] the issue of uncertainty has more recently gained new traction in urban studies and the planning literature,[3] but, in our opinion, not always in the substantial manner that it requires. There are still difficulties in fully acknowledging the disruptive implications of uncertainty and going beyond a mere and generic adaptive planning approach in response to it. Moreover, the flexibility of public regulations (which is not always desirable[4]), and the flexibility of the social-spatial system under these regulations (which is always desirable), are not always adequately distinguished.

In this regard, this chapter deals with the following three main questions: (1) what exactly is uncertainty in the urban realm? (2) How does it affect (public) planning? (3) How can (public) planning cope with uncertainty?

The chapter is divided into four sections. The first introduces some preliminary specifications on uncertainty. The second section distinguishes two cases in which public decision-makers have to deal with uncertainty in a significant way. The third suggests possible ways to cope with uncertainty in the two cases identified, and the final section concludes by summarizing the main achievements and considering open questions.

2. PRELIMINARY SPECIFICATIONS ON UNCERTAINTY

It is crucial to distinguish here among situations of (1) certainty, (2) risk, (3) parametric uncertainty and (4) fundamental uncertainty.[5]

1. In a situation of certainty, the possible events are listable, and the consequences of choice are clearly known to the decision-maker. Each decision is easily recognized as leading to a specific outcome.

2. In a situation of risk (strictly speaking[6]) the possible events are still listable, and the decision-maker can specify the (objective) probability of the events.
3. In a situation of parametric uncertainty,[7] the possible events are still in some way listable, but the decision-maker lacks 'complete knowledge ex ante about the values that specific variables within a given problem structure will take ex post' (Langlois 1994, p. 118).
4. In a situation of fundamental uncertainty – also known as radical, structural, genuine, deep or severe uncertainty – the decision-maker is even uncertain about what states of affairs will obtain (Wubben 1995; Dequech 2000, 2001). The situation requires action but resists analysis of risk and parametric uncertainty. Fundamental uncertainty implies the unlistability of all the potential outcomes of a decision: the issue is that we are always faced with an uncompletable list of contingencies (O'Driscoll and Rizzo 1985). As regards unlistability in uncertain conditions, 'it is not merely that we do not know which possibility out of a given set will occur, but the set itself is unbounded' (O'Driscoll and Rizzo 1985, p. 4). The concept of fundamental uncertainty involves an open-ended set of possibilities that make it particularly problematic to interpret uncertainty by means of probabilistic tools. Fundamental uncertainty, indeed, refers to a state of uncertainty in which probabilities are not well definable or computable. In particular, it would be difficult to assign initial probabilities in advance to events never previously encountered or conceived.[8]

3. PUBLIC DECISION-MAKING UNDER UNCERTAINTY: TWO MAIN CASES

Uncertainty – especially fundamental uncertainty – is a key issue for planning. It derives from a number of sources including natural hazards, financial shocks and technological innovations, as well as the unpredictable everyday choices of present and future urban actors (Savini 2017). Fundamental uncertainty in planning is usually connected with wicked problems (Rittel and Webber 1973; Hajer et al. 1993), that is, those problems that are difficult to be consistently and concisely stated in advance since their understanding and their resolution are concomitant to one other. The main idea here is that wicked problems always come in a complex form, and they are often ill defined a priori.

While critical reflection on risk (and parametric uncertainty) is a well-established field, analysis of strategies regarding fundamental uncertainty has received less attention, in the planning field as well. Interestingly, however, many of the decisions concerning future events occur under conditions of fundamental uncertainty rather than under conditions of risk or parametric uncertainty.

As Kahneman (2011, p. 270) writes: 'Every significant choice we make in life comes with some uncertainty'. It is worth noting that the notion of decision itself implies that 'the future is not predetermined, different outcomes are possible, and some uncertainty will always be present' (Abbott 2005, p. 238).

In order to delve deeper into how to cope with uncertainty in planning, it is necessary to distinguish more clearly between at least two different decision situations.

The decision-maker considered here is a public subject (for example, the local government), and the decision required is therefore a public decision (for example, a planning decision). Planners, as civil servants and practitioners, cooperate in taking decisions of this kind.[9]

The decision-maker that we are considering, being a public subject, faces additional problems in comparison with (any) private decision-maker. This is not always clearly recognized in orthodox discussions on decision-making under conditions of uncertainty. Some of the research on everyday decisions in conditions of uncertainty, and on heuristics useful in these situations (see Kahneman et al. 1982; Kahneman 2011), is relevant to the public subject as well, but in the latter there are additional and very specific problems (Simon 1983 contains some preliminary, pioneering, insights on this aspect).[10]

On considering local governments, and planning intervention in particular, we distinguish two main cases (case A and case B) in which the public subject usually has to take decisions in cases of uncertainty:

- Case A is a situation in which decision-makers must decide on how to act themselves; for instance, if, where, when and how to build an artefact, such as a bridge, a new metro station or a public hospital, and so on.
- Case B is a situation in which the decision-maker has to decide how to regulate someone else's decision on how to act; for instance, how to design planning rules and building standards that will constrain and channel the decisions of developers, architects, ordinary citizens, and so on in relation to the creation or transformation of artefacts (Needham et al. 2019).[11]

The underlying idea is that the two cases are profoundly different. This conviction is implicit in Portugali (2012b). He writes:

> On the one hand, there are certain planning activities that unless they are fully (or almost fully) controlled they would not be attempted at all. In other words, unless one can create a closed system for them one would not attempt to implement them. For example, one would not build a bridge or a building unless one can 'close the system', at least temporarily. (Portugali 2012b, p. 130)

By contrast, 'in a self-organized . . . system such a requirement doesn't exist, for instance, when making a city plan. In the latter case once the city plan is completed and implemented, the story just begins – it triggers a complex and unpredictable dynamics that no one fully controls' (Portugali 2012b, p. 130; see also Portugali 2012a, p. 230).

In order to define more systematically the differences between the two cases, the main features of both have to be specified in detail. The ten most typical features of case A are the following:

1. The decision (of the public decision-maker) is about an action (or a sequence of actions); for instance, the action of producing an artefact. In this case the alternatives are different actions (or different sequences of actions).
2. The decision-maker and the owner coincide (for instance, a bridge is built on public land, or on land acquired for that purpose).[12]
3. The decision-maker and the actor roughly coincide. Here 'action' means a form of implementation (even when the action to build an artefact is delegated to a private

actor, things do not change greatly; the decision-maker and the actor remain strictly in line, and the actor has to scrupulously implement the publicly stated design and programme). The relationship between decision and action is here horizontal.

4. Possible outcomes are listable; that is, a specific list can be made of them (even if their specific probability is unknown). This is parametric uncertainty, or what is reducible to this kind of uncertainty.

5. Some types of prediction are required (for example, number of people using a bridge in a day). The closed-world assumption (Portugali 2012b) can be adopted, in that almost all the potential scenarios associated with the decision to create the new artefact can be imagined and assessed.

6. Technologies to transform the built environment are pre-defined (for example, technologies for constructing bridges).

7. Space and time – of the possible actions on which the public decision is focused – are pre-determined (for example, the bridge must be built in place Y, within X years, starting from next month).

8. If no one, or very few people, will use the artefact built after the public decision has been taken and implemented (for example, a bridge) this would be a typical and incontestable failure.

9. Financial and economic evaluations as regards the decision to construct the artefact are possible and usually taken into consideration: financial analysis, cost–benefit analysis, and so on (for example, Mohapatra 2017).

10. Resources are directly needed to activate and operationalize the decision (for example, public money to build a bridge).

The typical features of case B are the following (listed in the same order as for case A):

1. The main (public) decision is on how others can decide their own actions (for example, in building artefacts themselves). In this case, the alternatives under decision consist of different sets of rules. Final actors are truly creative (or they can be creative, Moroni 2011; Cozzolino 2019). The relationship between decision and action is here vertical.

2. The decision-maker and the owners of what is subject to rules do not coincide. People will mainly act to transform their own properties (for example, private land and buildings).

3. The decision-maker and the actors (those who directly transform the urban environment) do not coincide (Mazza 2004).

4. The range of possibilities (for example, the ways in which people will use and transform the urban environment) is in this case unlistable in practical terms but also in theoretical terms. This is a case of fundamental uncertainty. An open-world assumption (Portugali 2012b) is unavoidable.[13]

5. Specific predictions are not necessarily required. We do not, for instance, need to know the number of pedestrians who will survive in order to oblige car drivers to stop at pedestrian crossings, or how many people of the same gender will get married in order to make them legally entitled to do so.

6. Technologies to transform the built environment are, for the most part, unspecified and free; that is, they are left to subsequent actions and innovations.

7. Space and time of further (private) possible decisions and actions upon which the main (public) decision is focused are not fully determined.

8. If no one exploits the rule stated by a public subject (for example, the possibility of constructing commercial buildings in zones explicitly devoted to them), this is not in itself a failure. There are rules that have never been used; this notwithstanding, they shape the nomosphere (Delaney 2010) and create possibilities.

9. Financial and economic evaluations of decisions to be taken by the public subject (on rules) are not always possible, since the full consequences are unknown. Moreover, these types of decisions have an independent (deontological) ethical meaning.[14]

10. No resources (for example, public money) are directly needed to (simply) introduce the rules in question.

In conclusion, we maintain that a typical mistake in planning theory and practice in the twentieth century has been to consider case B as identical with, or very similar to, case A. This is one of the reasons why the traditional idea of plan (in an orthodox and correct way mainly employed for sequences of actions that directly transform the built environment, for example, building infrastructure and public spaces, as in our case A), has been extended also to case B (Moroni 2020). Not considering the differences between the two cases, created and still creates serious problems in trying to cope with uncertainty.[15]

4.   METHODOLOGICAL, PRAGMATIC AND PROCEDURAL STRATEGIES FOR COPING WITH UNCERTAINTY IN THE TWO CASES

Recognition of the existence of uncertainty does not imply in itself that we can know nothing or do nothing (Simon 1996). It simply asks for adequate strategies to cope with it. As Babovic et al. (2018, p. 554) write, 'deep uncertainty does not reflect a state of complete ignorance about the future. It is possible to generate plausible states of the world and potentially rank them in order of likelihood. . . . However it is extremely difficult to explore all possible uncertainties and futures'. The complex structure of a city has been considered sometimes as something unknowable. More reasonably, we hold that things such as cities are not unknowable, but fundamentally uncertain in that we can gain particular types of new knowledge about them even if it is likely that we will always face great uncertainty in dealing with them.[16]

Let us now return to our two cases. In case A, two main strategies (methodological and pragmatic) may help in dealing with an uncertain urban world. First, we have methodological strategies; we may, for instance, develop specific forms of scenario building instead of traditional forecasts in order to replace linear predictions with open futures (see, for example, van der Heijden 1996; Xiang and Clarke 2003; Martelli 2014; Zapata and Kaza 2015), for example, by imposing a branching-time structure on the future and planning according to those different potential future scenarios. We have to imagine that each potential future scenario has been materialized and we take decisions in the present that are very likely to be justified retrospectively in (almost) all those future scenarios.[17] The assumption in this context is that events are determined by causes or statistical trends so that they may contribute positively to foreseeing alternative ways in which the future will materialize (Derbyshire and Wright 2014). Thus, scenarios in case A are used in order to understand, on the basis of current trends or previous (causal) knowledge, what a plausible future may look like and how likely it may be.

Second, we have pragmatic strategies: for instance, (1) involve the main stakeholders from the beginning; (2) where possible, prefer small interventions to big interventions (Moroni and Cozzolino 2019);[18] (3) consider incremental development of a project from the outset (Moreau 2004);[19] (4) arrange in advance for possible new needs in the future, for example, by providing space for further enlargement of a highway (Holcombe 2013); (5) increase the resilience of the infrastructure system, that is, its ability to continue functioning in the face of unexpected changes (Bertolini 2007).

In case B (and in addition to adopting a prudent underlying critical evolutionism on the issue of rules[20]), we again have methodological strategies, but also what we term 'procedural strategies'. From a methodological perspective, extreme events that are very unlikely to occur should enter our imagined scenarios when they might entail severe consequences. This requires engaging in a possibility analysis and focusing on imagined scenarios that might seem *prima facie* unlikely to happen but are still conceivable in principle. Possible scenarios usually have an exploratory nature (Börjeson et al. 2006) and should (1) be in conformity with basic physical and (ideally) behavioural principles; (2) show internal consistency; and (3) seem reasonable (Amara 1991). The key feature of this type of scenario is not causality, nor risk, but fundamental uncertainty. This implies an acknowledgement that (the magnitude of) past events may not be always representative of (the magnitude of) events that have not yet happened, as the causal or statistical framework of reference may be extremely complex and unknown (Derbyshire and Wright 2014). Indeed, the scenarios in case B aim at understanding what a merely possible future may look like, trying to reflect, in particular, on its imagined negative aspects.

A complete list of the scenarios involved in case B is impossible to obtain; nonetheless, the main ideas are (1) to reduce bias in the selection of scenarios, (2) to balance positive and negative arguments (for instance, by maintaining an effect fixed and changing the potential causes or maintaining the causes fixed and looking for new potential effects), and (3) to ensure that less tangible effects are considered in a specific scenario (Hansson 2011).

We imagine these merely possible scenarios in order to reduce uncertainty and anticipate strategies to deal properly with complexity. Then, we evaluate these scenarios in accordance with value-based considerations relying on normative constraints shaping desirable future situations or objectives. However, objectives and values justifying our decisions may change (Chiffi and Pietarinen 2017). Hence, scenarios involving decisions that are irreversible and may create interference with large complex systems – widely extended in time and space – should be scrutinized in depth and avoided as much as possible, as they may result in very problematic and unmanageable events (Hansson 2011).

However, beyond methodological strategies, we believe that strategies to deal with fundamental uncertainty need in this case to be mainly procedural. In particular, we should prefer rules that are as abstract and general as possible (that is, referring to typical situations for an indefinable number of subjects), and that are mainly negative (that is, banning particular negative externalities instead of imposing specific behaviours)

(Moroni 2015). Observe that formulating positive obligations (for example, roofs must be built in way X) usually requires more knowledge than is needed to formulate negative rules (for example, avoid externality Z). As Kasper and Streit (1998, p. 97) note: those who want to prescribe the behaviour of actors should be aware of the means at their disposal and of their skills, as well as of the possible consequences of the prescribed behaviours; by contrast, those who merely rule out certain types of action, as in the case of negative rules, only need to know that particular behaviours are undesirable without trying to list all potential different modes in which urban actors (individuals, groups or organizations) may respond to the decision of a public actor; the decision regarding the details of the specific behaviours, and the assessment of their effects, is left to urban actors.

Urban codes provide a good example of an institutional strategy to cope with uncertain urban environments (Alfasi and Portugali 2007; Moroni 2015; Alfasi 2018).

5. CONCLUDING REMARKS

In discussing uncertainty and planning, Zandvoort et al. (2018, p. 97) underscore two main problems: (1) 'where planners only partially understand uncertainty their interventions may be redundant or deficient', and (2) 'if planners act with a poor understanding of uncertainty, decisions and interventions may turn out to be maladaptive'. That is, not being able to understand, and deal with, uncertainty in decision-making processes has significant costs (Abbott 2005, p. 238). Unfortunately, 'decision makers are either unaware of the presence of deep uncertainty or are not familiar with how to manage it' (Babovic et al. 2018, p. 554). In stressing that persistence of policy failures is a recognized but usually not well-understood phenomenon in the policy literature, Howlett et al. (2015) discuss the levels of uncertainty in policy knowledge and practice as one of the crucial explaining factors.

Recognizing this challenge, this chapter has mainly focused on how planning can cope with different forms of uncertainty by first taking seriously the differences between different decision situations (what we termed 'case A' and 'case B'). The chapter is mainly conceptual; therefore, we have not delved deeply into the techniques and methods mentioned. Moreover, we have not dealt directly with how planning can reduce uncertainty for private urban actors. We hope to be able to develop this additional issue in future research (an interesting starting point could be, for instance, the discussion of Sela 2016). The underlying idea here has been that if public planning is able to cope effectively with uncertainty, this will also, in turn, be helpful for urban actors.[21]

In conclusion, uncertainty is indeed crucial in planning and needs to be understood in a manner that can inform viable strategies to address it. Cities are extremely complex entities. Hence, the key is not to forecast their future accurately but to be prepared to embrace their fundamental uncertainty without abandoning (adequate) planning (Rauws 2017).

NOTES

1. On all of this, see also McDaniel and Driebe (2005).
2. See, for example, Goulter et al. (1983), Christensen (1985), Pearman (1985), Kartez and Lindell (1987), Keys (1987), Banai-Kashani (1990) and Haddawy (1994).
3. See, for example, Kato and Ahern (2008), Abbott (2005, 2009), Nyseth (2012), Jabareen (2013), Rauws and De Roo (2016), Spirandelli et al. (2016), Rauws (2017), Savini (2017), Zandvoort et al. (2018), Skrimizea et al. (2019), Stults and Larsen (2020) and Beauregard (2021).
4. To be useful, a rule has to be stable (Moroni 2007).
5. Such demarcations are clearly not always black or white, and some overlaps among them are possible in certain particular circumstances.
6. Observe that sometimes 'risk' covers both what we term 'risk' in the strict sense and what we term 'parametric uncertainty'. In addition, 'risk' is also used in other non-technical senses.
7. For the distinction between parametric and fundamental uncertainty, see mainly, Langlois (1986, 2007), Langlois and Everett (1992) and Harper (1996). See also Tatang et al. (1997) and Kiang et al. (2018).
8. The distinctive features of fundamental uncertainty are due to the irreversibility of certain phenomena. Irreversibility may no longer be considered as something that would disappear if we had complete knowledge. This means that fundamental uncertainty may not be converted easily into complete knowledge owing to the irreversibility and complexity of many dynamic phenomena which have, in a specific system of reference, a very high degree of sensitivity to initial conditions (Prigogine 1997).
9. As Hoekveld and Needham (2013, p. 1639) write:

   A planning agency has the responsibilities and powers granted by public . . . law to make and implement spatial plans. This activity involves using public powers over private persons and organizations (building permits, compulsory purchase, public funding, taxes or subsidies, prohibitions and so on), and decisions to implement them should be made only by those empowered by the law to do so;

   therefore, 'decisions to adopt and execute plans' are made by public authorities, 'not by individual planners' (Hoekveld and Needham 2013, p. 1639).
10. For a critical reading of Kahneman's and Tversky's approach to (everyday) decisions in conditions of uncertainty, see, with a specific focus on urban problems, Portugali (2011, pp. 356–66).
11. Strictly, also the determination by the public subject to regulate someone else's decision to act may be interpreted simpliciter as a type of act (of the public subject). Here, the crux of the matter is the distinction between decisions regarding the construction of an artefact and decisions imposing or banning some actions of other individuals, companies, and so on. Expressed this way, the two cases are clearly different. Finally, we are abstracting here from the multifaceted relationships existing between the decision to build an artefact, say, a new bridge, and the company that will construct the bridge.
12. On this specific point, and on the difference between case A and case B in this regard, see particularly, Slaev (2016).
13. Note that this is not necessarily a form of adaptive behaviour, since it only means that the set of explanatory hypotheses associated with a decision can hardly be conceived as complete given the intricacies of fundamental uncertainty.
14. Observe that this is also a criticism of utilitarianism, especially 'act utilitarianism', as an ethical decision principle (and, therefore, a criticism of attempts at enlarging the scope of cost–benefit analysis to include law issues as well). As Hayek (1982, vol. 2, p. 20) observes, the trouble with the utilitarian perspective

   is that, as a theory professing to account for a phenomenon which consists of a body of rules, it completely eliminates the factor which makes rules necessary, namely our ignorance. It has indeed always amazed me how . . . utilitarians . . . could have failed to take seriously this crucial fact of our necessary ignorance of most of the particular facts, and could have proposed a theory which presupposes a knowledge of the particular effects of our individual actions when in fact the whole existence of the phenomenon they set out to explain, namely of a system of rules of conduct, was due to the impossibility of such knowledge.

   He interestingly concludes: 'Man has developed rules of conduct not because he knows but because he does not know what all the consequences of a particular action will be' (Hayek 1982, vol. II, pp. 20–21). For the critical debate on applying cost–benefit analysis to law, see Driesen (1997, 2006).
15. Similarly, there is sometimes confusion between conditions of probabilistic risk and those of fundamental uncertainty. This confusion has been termed in the literature the Tuxedo fallacy (Hansson 2009). The idea is that we cannot apply traditional probabilistic risk analysis which mimics the probabilistic rules of playing at the casino when facing the fundamental uncertainty of entering a jungle where many scenarios

and hazards are deeply unknown and unexpected. For an abductive approach to the potential anticipation of deeply unknown events, see Chiffi et al. (2020).

16. Cities are extremely complex objects of investigation; nonetheless, some common trends have been acknowledged (see, for example, Batty 2005; Bettencourt and West 2010; Ross and Portugali 2018).

17. Similar methodologies have also been used for ethical retrospective evaluations (Hansson 2007) and for traditional theories of prudence based on future hindsights (Vanden Houten 2002). However, these are heuristic methods that may be defeasible since, for instance, there is no guarantee that the real future scenario is one of the possible branching time paths considered previously, or that the principles and rules guiding our decisions remain fixed when performing hypothetical retrospective evaluations. Still, hypothetical retrospective evaluations may have something to say as regards moderate forms of uncertainty.

18. In a complex, uncertain world,

> large infrastructure projects are more subject to cost estimation errors; they entail greater financial and technical risks and are subject to long, often uncontrollable execution times; and they are inevitably far less adaptable to the areas through which they pass, and hardly exploit existing network economies at all. In contrast, small-scale infrastructure projects are less subject to forecasting errors, entail far smaller financial and technical risks, have shorter and more controllable execution times, and benefit far more from network economies as they are generally, improvements on or additions to already existing action networks. (Moroni and Cozzolino 2019, p. 48)

> For cases in which large infrastructure projects are necessary and unavoidable, see the critical discussion, and suggestions, by Giezen (2013) and Salet et al. (2013).

19. 'In a world where radical uncertainty reigns, where future changes in the environment are mostly uncontrollable, incrementalism turns out to be a non-losing strategy, if not a winning one. If policymakers proceed through a succession of incremental changes, they avoid serious lasting mistakes in several ways' (Moreau 2004, p. 870).

20. The issue (for the public subject) is not to always invent totally new rules but, often, to be able to recognize, operationalize and implement those rules that have (even independently) evolved over time, and have proved to foster beneficial forms of social order (Moroni 2010).

21. This research has been partly supported by the Departmental Excellence Project 'Fragilità Territoriali' (Department of Architecture and Urban Studies, Politecnico di Milano, 2018–2022; Law no. 232 of 2016).

REFERENCES

Abbott, J. (2005), 'Understanding and managing the unknown: the nature of uncertainty in planning', *Journal of Planning Education and Research*, **24** (3), 237–51.

Abbott, J. (2009), 'Planning for complex metropolitan regions: a better future or a more certain one?', *Journal of Planning Education and Research*, **28** (4), 503–17.

Alfasi, N. (2018), 'The coding turn in urban planning', *Planning Theory*, **17** (3), 375–95.

Alfasi, N. and J. Portugali (2007), 'Planning rules for a self-planned city', *Planning Theory*, **6** (2), 164–82.

Amara, R. (1991), 'Views on futures research methodology', *Futures*, **23** (6), 645–9.

Babovic, F., A. Mijic and K. Madani (2018), 'Decision making under deep uncertainty for adapting urban drainage systems to change', *Urban Water Journal*, **15** (6), 552–60.

Banai-Kashani, A.R. (1990), 'Dealing with uncertainty and fuzziness in development planning', *Environment and Planning A*, **22** (9), 1183–203.

Batty, M. (2005), *Cities and Complexity*, Cambridge, MA: MIT Press.

Batty, M. and S. Marshall (2012), 'The origins of complexity theory in cities and planning', in J. Portugali, H. Meyer and E. Stolk (eds), *Complexity Theories of Cities Have Come of Age*, Berlin: Springer, pp. 21–46.

Beauregard, R. (2021), 'The entanglements of uncertainty', *Journal of Planning Education and Research*, **41** (2), 217–25.

Bertolini, L. (2007), 'Evolutionary urban transportation planning: an exploration', *Environment and Planning A: Economy and Space*, **39** (8), 1998–2019.

Bettencourt, L. and G. West (2010), 'A unified theory of urban living', *Nature*, **467** (7318), 912–13.

Börjeson, L., M. Höjer, K.H. Dreborg, T. Ekvall and G. Finnveden (2006), 'Scenario types and techniques: towards a user's guide', *Futures*, **38** (7), 723–39.

Chiffi, D. and A.-V. Pietarinen (2017), 'Fundamental uncertainty and values', *Philosophia*, **45** (3), 1027–37.

Chiffi, D., A.-V. Pietarinen and M. Proover (2020), 'Anticipation, abduction and the economy of research: the normative stance', *Futures*, **115** (October), 102471.

Christensen, K.S. (1985), 'Coping with uncertainty in planning', *Journal of the American planning association*, **51** (1), 63–73.

Cozzolino, S. (2019), 'The creative city: reconsidering past and current approaches from the nomocratic perspective', in F. Calabrò, L. Della Spina and C. Bevilacqua (eds), *New Metropolitan Perspectives. Smart Innovation, Systems and Technologies*, Cham: Springer, pp. 606–14.

Delaney, D. (2010), *The Spatial, the Legal and the Pragmatics of World-Making: Nomospheric Investigations*, London: Routledge.

Dequech, D. (2000), 'Fundamental uncertainty and ambiguity', *Eastern Economic Journal*, **26** (1), 41–60.

Dequech, D. (2001), 'Bounded rationality, institutions and uncertainty', *Journal of Economic Issues*, **35** (4), 911–29.

Derbyshire, J. and G. Wright (2014), 'Preparing for the future: development of an "antifragile" methodology that complements scenario planning by omitting causation', *Technological Forecasting and Social Change*, **82** (1), 215–25.

Driesen, D.M. (1997), 'The societal cost of environmental regulation: beyond administrative cost-benefit analysis', *Ecology Law Quarterly*, **24** (3), 545–617.

Driesen, D.M. (2006), 'Is cost-benefit analysis neutral', *University of Colorado Law Review*, **77** (2), 335–404.

Giezen, M. (2013), 'Adaptive and strategic capacity: navigating megaprojects through uncertainty and complexity', *Environment and Planning B*, **40** (4), 723–41.

Goulter, I.C., H.G. Wenzel Jr and L.D. Hopkins (1983), 'Watershed land-use planning under uncertainty', *Environment and Planning A*, **15** (7), 987–92.

Haddawy, P. (1994), *Representing Plans under Uncertainty: A Logic of Time, Chance, and Action*, Berlin: Springer.

Hajer, M.A., R. Hoppe and B. Jennings (1993), *The Argumentative Turn in Policy Analysis and Planning*, Durham, NC: Duke University Press.

Hansson, S.O. (2007), 'Hypothetical retrospection', *Ethical Theory and Moral Practice*, **10** (2), 145–57.

Hansson, S.O. (2009), 'From the casino to the jungle', *Synthese*, **168** (3), 423–32.

Hansson, S.O. (2011), 'Coping with the unpredictable effects of future technologies', *Philosophy and Technology*, **24** (2), 137–49.

Harper, D.A. (1996), *Entrepreneurship and the Market Process. An Enquiry into the Growth of Knowledge*, London: Routledge.

Hayek, F.A. (1982), *Law, Legislation and Liberty*, London: Routledge.

Hoekveld, G. and B. Needham (2013), 'Planning practice between ethics and the power game: making and applying an ethical code for planning agencies', *International Journal of Urban and Regional Research*, **37** (5), 1638–53.

Holcombe, R.G. (2013), 'Planning and the invisible hand: allies or adversaries?', *Planning Theory*, **12** (2), 199–210.

Howlett, M., M. Ramesh and X. Wu (2015), 'Understanding the persistence of policy failures: the role of politics, governance and uncertainty', *Public Policy and Administration*, **30** (3–4), 209–20.

Jabareen, Y. (2013), 'Planning the resilient city: concepts and strategies for coping with climate change and environmental risk', *Cities*, **31** (April), 220–29.

Kahneman, D. (2011), *Thinking, Fast and Slow*, New York: Farrar, Straus and Giroux.

Kahneman, D., P. Slovic and A. Tversky (eds) (1982), *Judgment under Uncertainty: Heuristics and Biases*, Cambridge: Cambridge University Press.

Kartez, J.D. and M.K. Lindell (1987), 'Planning for uncertainty: the case of local disaster planning', *Journal of the American Planning Association*, **53** (4), 487–98.

Kasper, W. and M.E. Streit (1998), *Institutional Economics*, Cheltenham, UK and Lyme, NH, USA: Edward Elgar.

Kato, S. and J. Ahern (2008), '"Learning by doing": adaptive planning as a strategy to address uncertainty in planning', *Journal of Environmental Planning and Management*, **51** (4), 543–59.

Keys, P. (1987), 'Planners, uncertainties and methodologies', *Public Policy and Administration*, **2** (3), 23–34.

Kiang, J.E., C. Gazoorian, H. McMillan, G. Coxon, J. Le Coz, I.K. Westerberg, et al. (2018), 'A comparison of methods for streamflow uncertainty estimation', *Water Resources Research*, **54** (10), 7149–76.

Langlois, R.N. (1986), 'Rationality institutions and explanations', in R.N. Langlois (ed.), *Economic as a Process*, Cambridge: Cambridge University Press, pp. 225–55.

Langlois, R.N. (1994), 'Risk and uncertainty', in P.J. Boettke (ed.), *The Elgar Companion to Austrian Economics*, Aldershot, UK and Brookfield, VT, USA: Edward Elgar, pp. 118–22.

Langlois, R.N. (2007), 'The entrepreneurial theory of the firm and the theory of the entrepreneurial firm', *Journal of Management Studies*, **44** (7), 1107–124.

Langlois, R.N. and M.J. Everett (1992), 'Complexity, genuine uncertainty, and the economics of organization', *Human Systems Management*, **11** (2), 67–75.

Martelli, A. (2014), *Models of Scenario Building and Planning: Facing Uncertainty and Complexity*, New York: Palgrave Macmillan.

Mazza, L. (2004), *Piano, progetti, strategie*, Milan: Angeli.

McDaniel, R.R. and D.J. Driebe (2005), 'Uncertainty and surprise: an introduction', in R.R. McDaniel and D.J. Driebe (eds), *Uncertainty and Surprise in Complex Systems: Questions on Working with the Unexpected*, Berlin: Springer, pp. 3–11.

Mohapatra, D.R. (ed.) (2017), *Economic and Financial Analysis of Infrastructure Projects*, New Dehli: Educreation.

Moreau, F. (2004), 'The role of the state in evolutionary economics', *Cambridge Journal of Economics*, **28** (6), 847–74.

Moroni, S. (2007), 'Planning, liberty and the rule of law', *Planning Theory*, **6** (July), 146–63.

Moroni, S. (2010), 'An evolutionary theory of institutions and a dynamic approach to reform', *Planning Theory*, **9** (4), 275–97.

Moroni S. (2011), 'Land-use regulation for the creative city', in D.E. Andersson, C. Mellander and A. Andersson (eds), *Handbook of Creative Cities*, Cheltenham, UK and Northampton, MA, USA: Edward Elgar, pp. 343–64.

Moroni, S. (2015), 'Complexity and the inherent limits of explanation and prediction: urban codes for self-organising cities', *Planning Theory*, **14** (3), 248–67.

Moroni, S. (2020), 'La falsa alternativa tra pianificazione forte e pianificazione debole. Verso orizzonti più radicali', *Scienze Regionali*, **19** (1), 149–56.

Moroni, S. and S. Cozzolino (2019), 'Action and the city: emergence, complexity, planning', *Cities*, **90**, 42–51.

Needham, B., E. Buitelaar and T. Hartmann (2019), *Planning, Law and Economics: The Rules We Make for Using Land*, London: Routledge.

Nyseth, T. (2012), 'Fluid planning: a meaningless concept or a rational response to uncertainty in urban planning?', in J. Burian (ed.), *Advances in Spatial Planning*, Rijeka, Croatia: InTech.

O'Driscoll, G.P. and M.J. Rizzo (1985), *The Economics of Time and Ignorance*, London: Routledge.

Pearman, A.D. (1985), 'Uncertainty in planning: characterisation, evaluation, and feedback', *Environment and Planning B: Planning and Design*, **12** (3), 313–20.

Portugali, J. (2011), *Complexity, Cognition and the City*, Berlin: Springer.

Portugali, J. (2012a), 'Complexity theories of cities: implications to urban planning', in J. Portugali, H. Meyer and E. Stolk (eds) *Complexity Theories of Cities Have Come of Age*, Berlin: Springer, pp. 221–44.

Portugali, J. (2012b), 'Complexity theories of cities: first, second or third culture of planning?', in G. de Roo, J. Hillier and J. Van Wezemael (eds), *Complexity and Planning*, Farnham: Ashgate, pp. 117–40.

Prigogine, I. (1997), *The End of Certainty: Time, Chaos, and the New Laws of Nature*, New York: Free Press.

Rauws, W. (2017), 'Embracing uncertainty without abandoning planning: exploring an adaptive planning approach for guiding urban transformations', *disP – The Planning Review*, **53** (1), 32–45.

Rauws, W. and G. de Roo (2016), 'Adaptive planning: generating conditions for urban adaptability', *Environment and Planning B*, **43** (6), 1052–74.

Rittel, H.W. and M.M. Webber (1973), 'Dilemmas in a general theory of planning', *Policy Sciences*, **4** (2), 155–69.

Ross, G.M. and J. Portugali (2018), 'Urban regulatory focus: a new concept linking city size to human behaviour', *Royal Society Open Science*, **5** (5), 1–11.

Salet, W., L. Bertolini and M. Giezen (2013), 'Complexity and uncertainty: problem or asset in decision making of mega infrastructure projects?', *International Journal of Urban and Regional Research*, **37** (6), 1984–2000.

Savini, F. (2017), 'Planning, uncertainty and risk: the neoliberal logics of Amsterdam urbanism', *Environment and Planning A*, **49** (4), 857–75.

Sela, R. (2016), 'Global scale predictions of cities in urban and in cognitive planning', in J. Portugali and E. Stolk (eds), *Complexity, Cognition, Urban Planning and Design*, Berlin: Springer, pp. 181–96.

Simon, H.A. (1983), *Reasons in Human Affairs*, Stanford, CA: Stanford University Press.

Simon, H.A. (1996), *The Science of the Artificial*, Cambridge, MA: MIT Press.

Skrimizea, E., H. Haniotou and C. Parra (2019), 'On the "complexity turn" in planning: an adaptive rationale to navigate spaces and times of uncertainty', *Planning Theory*, **18** (1), 122–42.

Slaev, A.D. (2016), 'Types of planning and property rights', *Planning Theory*, **15** (1), 23–41.

Spirandelli, D.J., T.R. Anderson, R. Porro and C.H. Fletcher (2016), 'Improving adaptation planning for future sea-level rise: understanding uncertainty and risks using a probability-based shoreline model', *Journal of Planning Education and Research*, **36** (3), 290–303.

Stults, M. and L. Larsen (2020), 'Tackling uncertainty in US local climate adaptation planning', *Journal of Planning Education and Research*, **40** (4), 416–31.

Tatang, M.A., G. Prinn and G. McRae (1997), 'An efficient method for parametric uncertainty analysis of numerical geophysical models', *Journal of Geophysical Research*, **102** (18), 925–32.

Van der Heijden, K. (1996), *Scenarios: The Art of Strategic Conversation*, Chichester: John Wiley & Sons.
Vanden Houten, A. (2002), 'Prudence in Hobbes's political philosophy', *History of Political Thought*, **23** (2), 288–302.
Wubben, E. (1995), 'Austrian economics and uncertainty: on a non-deterministic but non-haphazard future', in G. Meijer (ed.), *New Perspectives in Austrian Economics*, London: Routledge, pp. 106–45.
Xiang, W.N. and K.C. Clarke (2003), 'The use of scenarios in land-use planning', *Environment and Planning B: Planning and Design*, **30** (6), 885–909.
Zandvoort, M., M.J. Van der Vlist, F. Klijn and A. Van den Brink (2018), 'Navigating amid uncertainty in spatial planning', *Planning Theory*, **17** (1), 96–116.
Zapata, M.A. and N. Kaza (2015), 'Radical uncertainty: scenario planning for futures', *Environment and Planning B: Urban Analytics and City Science*, **42** (4), 754–70.

17. Tailoring nudges to self-organising behavioural patterns in public space
Koen Bandsma, Ward Rauws and Gert de Roo

1. INTRODUCTION

Public spaces are full of behavioural patterns. Well-known examples of these patterns include traffic jams (Kerner 1998), pedestrian flows (Helbing et al. 2001), criminal conduct (Malleson et al. 2014) and elephant paths (De Roo 2016). Behavioural patterns affect the quality and safety of public space and collective well-being of communities, but may also trigger feelings of lack of safety, or criminal activities. This raises the question of how urban planning can preserve desired patterns and reduce or transform undesired patterns.

In theorising how behavioural patterns in public space can be addressed, our starting point is that these patterns are a product of self-organisation (see Jacobs 1961; De Roo 2016; Perrone 2019). Self-organisation is a key element in the complexity theories of cities and includes an emergent process in which uncoordinated interactions between many agents in the city can spontaneously aggregate into (new) urban patterns (Rauws 2016). Translated to the domain of public space, this entails that behavioural patterns arise from the actions and interactions of the many users or agents of these spaces, such as pedestrians, car drivers or tourists. Intervening in the production and reproduction of these patterns through nudging may improve the quality of public space and the well-being in neighbourhoods.

Nudging is a policy instrument that aims to influence the behaviours of agents by exploiting the cognitive biases, heuristics and social norms underlying their decision-making. Nudges guide agents towards a mode of conduct, without prohibitions, significant (financial) incentives or coercion (Thaler and Sunstein 2008). They are a promising addition to the planner's toolbox, as these are flexible interventions that can be designed and implemented quickly, used to address various types of spatial behaviour or targeted towards particular social groups or specific situations (John 2018). Another advantage is that nudges address the subconscious and intuitive decision-making that often underlies the behaviour of agents in public space. Other planning instruments (for example, enforcement and sanctioning) target primarily conscious decision-making and are therefore less effective in changing the subconscious behaviours that are prevalent in public space (Thaler and Sunstein 2008).

However, with a dominant focus on individual behaviour, nudge theory pays less attention to the influence of the interaction dynamics between the users of public space on the effectiveness of nudges. Existing positive and negative feedback between agents (Byrne 1998), shared social norms (Bicchieri 2005), and snowball effects between users of public space (Spencer 2018), all demonstrate that the interaction dynamics enable or constrain the effectiveness of nudges. We argue that linking nudge theory to the self-organisation and social psychology literature can deepen understanding of how these interaction dynamics affect the capacity of nudges in stimulating desired behavioural patterns (see also, Spencer 2018). This, in turn, will allow urban planners to identify which behavioural patterns nudges can be effectively applied and enables the tailoring of nudges to self-organisation processes in public space.

The purpose of this chapter is to explore how a self-organisation perspective on behavioural pattern production and reproduction can inform the design of nudges in addressing these patterns in public space. By combining nudge theory, self-organisation and social psychology, the chapter makes three contributions to the practice of urban planning and design. First, the chapter explains how nudging affects human behaviour via various nudge tools, providing the means to preserve desired and to counter undesired behavioural patterns in public space. Second, it shows that nudges are especially effective for those patterns that are relatively unstable as a consequence of socio-psychological frictions in agents' behaviour and the interaction dynamics during self-organisation processes. Finally, the chapter shows how a self-organisation perspective on behavioural patterns provides the possibility of distinguishing nudge archetypes that assist urban planners in adapting their nudges to fluctuations in the level of stability of patterns over time.

The chapter is structured as follows. Section 2 explains what nudging is and how it addresses behavioural patterns. To identify suitable situations for nudging, five social-psychological factors are distinguished that influence the stability of behavioural patterns (section 3). Section 4 explains how pattern reproduction and transformation in self-organisation occur. In section 5, three nudge archetypes are proposed for guiding self-organisation processes within public space. Since interfering into such processes may be perceived as manipulative, section 6 discusses how governmental planners can use these archetypes in a legitimate way.

2.   HOW NUDGES ADDRESS BEHAVIOURAL PATTERNS

Nudges attempt to alter the individual actions that give rise to collective behavioural patterns. Underlying these individual behaviours are a range of cognitive mechanisms that influence how humans act. These mechanisms include many cognitive biases (for example, loss aversion, status-quo bias and optimism bias), heuristics (that is, rules of thumb, such as anchoring) and social norms (for example, agents do what others approve) (Thaler and Sunstein 2008), which indicates the habitual and subconscious nature of many behaviours in public space. These habitual and intuitive behaviours cause individuals to tend to respond in a similar and predictable manner to events, objects and the actions of other agents (Ariely and Jones 2008), which allows behavioural patterns to emerge and reproduce (Portugali 2011). This predictability also allows these underlying cognitive mechanisms to be exploited through nudging (Thaler and Sunstein 2008).

Nudges are policy instruments that influence subconscious decision-making in two ways. First, nudges exploit these cognitive biases, heuristics and norms to subconsciously steer agents towards a particular behaviour. For instance, a nudge can be road markings painted in such a manner that they create the impression that agents drive faster than they actually do, triggering an intuitive response to reduce their driving speed (Thaler and Sunstein 2008). Secondly, nudges can try to reduce the influence of cognitive biases, heuristics and social norms, and stimulate agents to make conscious decisions.

An example of this type of nudging are traffic signs that inform car drivers about their driving speed, providing a form of feedback to stimulate self-reflection (Toy et al. 2014).

Affecting Subconscious Behaviour: Nudge Tools and Nudge Designers

Before explaining how nudges affect patterning, we discuss several nudge tools that are used in altering behaviour, and who applies these tools in nudge-interventions. Both are important steps, as this discussion provides a better understanding of how nudges operate in practice. Even more importantly, the tools serve as ingredients for the nudge archetypes that are proposed in section 5.

Nudges alter behaviour by using one or multiple nudge tools. Four categories of nudge tools can be distinguished: information tools, environmental design tools, defaults and norm tools (see Table 17.1). Information tools influence the way information is presented to affect the decision-making of agents. Environmental tools affect the amount of physical or cognitive effort that is required to conduct a behaviour or they make an action option more salient in public space. Defaults are standard choices that agents automatically follow, unless they explicitly opt out from them. Finally, norm tools communicate what agents should (or should not) do or what most group members do (Lehner et al. 2016). Combining multiple of these tools within a single nudge-intervention allows urban planners to exploit several cognitive mechanisms simultaneously, which increases the likelihood that the intervention is effective.

Table 17.1   Nudge tools for promoting behaviour change

Nudge categories	Nudge tools	Description
Information tools	Simplifying information	Making information more straightforward to understand
	Framing information	Deliberately phrasing information so that it leads to a particular decision
	Providing feedback	Providing direct and personalised information about a decision made
	Implementing prompted choice option	Forcing agents to actively make a decision, without prescribing what they should decide
Environmental design tools	Influencing salience	Structuring how choices are ordered in time and space to their influence saliency
	Influencing effort	Influencing the amount of effort needed to conduct a behaviour
Defaults		Standard choices leading to an outcome, unless agents explicitly opt out
Norm tools	Communicating social norm	Prompting information about what most others approve/disapprove of
	Communicating descriptive norm	Prompting information about what most others do or did

Source: Based on Lehner et al. (2016).

In this chapter, the focus lies upon the use of these tools by governmental planners. However, urban planners are not the sole users of nudges; businesses and semi-private companies also apply nudging to address particular behavioural patterns. For instance, the public transport companies of London, Portland and Amsterdam play classical and ambient music in underground and railway stations to reduce vandalism (Thompson 2017).[1] In addition, local collectives and individual citizens use nudging, such as a group of citizens turning their street into a living-room to reduce car traffic by placing chairs, carpets and other furniture onto the street (Webb 2018). Nevertheless, the focus lies in this chapter upon governmental planners, as they are a central actor in implementing nudges in public spaces and control (or are meant to control) the use of nudging in these spaces by other agents.

How Nudges Affect Patterning

By altering the behaviour of agents, nudges address the collective behavioural patterns that emerge out of these individual behaviours. Behavioural patterns refer to a collective order in the behaviour of (a group of) agents (Portugali 2011). Multiple of these behavioural patterns often exist simultaneously within a public space. Agents ascribe value to these patterns, qualifying them as desired (for example, an anti-littering pattern) or as undesired (for example, littering pattern). The nudge tools offer, in turn, urban planners opportunities to strengthen and weaken these patterns (see Figure 17.1).

Nudges can stimulate the reproduction of desired patterns. They can encourage agents to conduct or maintain performing the behaviour that strengthens the desired pattern (Heylighen 2013). For instance, painting green footsteps on the sidewalk towards a litter bin helps to prevent people from throwing their litter onto the street (Jespersen 2012). Thus, stimulating pattern reproduction through nudging is a policy strategy to prevent deviations of desired patterns and to increase their stability.

Nudges can also try to transform an undesired pattern into a desired one. They can encourage agents to change their current behaviour, which weakens the undesired pattern. When sufficient agents also change their behaviour, this may lead to the development of a new and, hopefully, desired pattern. For instance, signs with pictures of

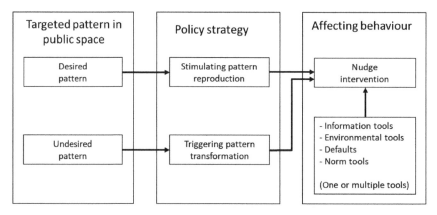

Figure 17.1   Policy strategies to address desired and undesired patterns through nudging

'watching eyes' can trigger feelings of being supervised and subsequently lead to a reduction in bicycle theft (Nettle et al. 2012). Thus, nudging can also be applied by urban planners as a reactionary response to weaken or transform undesired patterns.

However, designing a nudge that promotes desired behavioural patterns and transforms undesired patterns is not straightforward. Questions that may be raised include: can every undesired behavioural pattern in public space be transformed into a desired behavioural one by nudging? Which nudge tool is most likely to promote behaviour change? How can knowledge of the self-organised nature of behavioural patterns improve the design of nudges? In the following sections, these questions are answered. The answers will differentiate several nudge archetypes, with each of them applying particular nudge tools on how behaviour change is promoted among agents to address particular patterns. The next section starts by answering the question of which behavioural patterns can be addressed through nudging.

3. THE STABILITY OF PATTERNS: WHEN TO USE NUDGING

Behavioural patterns differ in their level of stability, referring to how easy or difficult it is to trigger their transformation. Some behavioural patterns are stable (for example, social segregation patterns), while others are relatively unstable and transform easily, such as pedestrian flows or anti-littering patterns. Nudges are most suitable for transforming behavioural patterns that are relatively unstable, as some degree of friction, ignorance or ambivalence among agents regarding the current pattern is needed for a nudge to be effective (Meder et al. 2018).

Based on literature on social norm production (Bicchieri 2005; Cialdini et al. 1991; Sunstein 2019), at least five factors can be distilled that influence the level of stability of behavioural patterns: types of agents, pluralistic ignorance, false consensus, cultural heterogeneity and stigmergy. We discuss for each factor how it influences the stability of behavioural patterns and to what extent these factors enable or constrain the use of nudging.

Types of Agents

The first factor concerns the types of agents that can be identified within a social system. Based on Bichieri (2005), we distinguish pattern breakers, pattern defenders and conditional conformers. Pattern breakers will purposefully ignore the socially desired pattern, even when most agents adhere to it. They may ignore the pattern for various reasons: it may, for instance, divert from their moral convictions and they actively seek to change it (Sunstein 2019), or agents deviate from it owing to a lack of attention or the influence of a cognitive bias or heuristic. Independent of the reason, pattern breakers are the instigators of pattern transformations. The second group, the pattern defenders, conforms to the desired pattern, even when other agents ignore it (see also, Cialdini et al. 1991). These agents have internalised the desired pattern and feel a moral obligation to reproduce it. The third group, the conditional conformers, includes the majority of agents and, reproduces a pattern when they see others following it. Similarly, they also transgress a pattern when others deviate from it. Thus, the stability of patterns depends on whether the pattern defenders or pattern breakers are able to influence the behaviour of the conditional conformers.

The effectiveness of nudges differs among these types of agents. Nudging may prevent that pattern breakers deviate from a desired pattern owing to subconscious cognitive mechanisms, such as a cognitive bias, heuristic or lack of attention. However, nudging is unlikely to be effective for agents who deliberately decide to deviate from the desired pattern (Baldwin 2014). Alternatively, the pattern defenders do not need a nudge, as they will reproduce the desired pattern as the result of a personally felt moral conviction to abide with this pattern (Bicchieri 2005). The third group, the conditional conformers, is most receptive to nudging, as their behaviour is often the result of subconsciously copying the actions of others (Baldwin 2014). Thus, nudges could best be targeted towards the pattern breakers and the conditional conformers.

Pluralistic Ignorance

Pluralistic ignorance entails that an agent incorrectly assumes that others would like him or her to conform to a particular (socially undesirable) pattern, and in return suppresses his or her feelings, beliefs or preferences (Sunstein 2019). To illustrate, some members of a particular local gang may privately disapprove of conducting anti-social behaviour, but nevertheless conduct these activities as they, incorrectly, believe other gang members approve of this behaviour (Wood 2014). It leads to the reproduction of a pattern, without agents feeling a moral conviction[2] to conform to this pattern (Perkins 2014).

Pluralistic ignorance lowers the stability of both desired and undesired behavioural patterns. It makes the patterns easier to transform, as there is already some hidden friction among agents regarding its existence. Once it becomes evident that other agents do not want him or her to follow the pattern, an agent is likely to change his or her behaviour and weaken the behavioural pattern (Perkins 2014).

Pluralistic ignorance reduces the effectiveness of most nudge tools, but the norm nudge tool can effectively help to tackle pluralistic ignorance (Mols et al. 2015). Pluralistic ignorance reduces the effectiveness of most nudges, as the perceived social pressure to conform to the undesired pattern may override the nudge that discourages this pattern and stimulates alternative behaviour (Reijula et al. 2018). Psychological experiments however indicate a notable exception: norm nudges have in several experiments proven to counter pluralistic ignorance by informing agents about the support (or lack thereof) for undesired patterns or how many agents follow the desired pattern (Mols et al. 2015).

False Consensus

False consensus refers to a situation in which some agents incorrectly assume that others share their discontent with a behavioural pattern and therefore they deviate from this pattern. For instance, an agent may overestimate the support within a gang to conduct anti-social behaviour. This increases the likelihood that he or she will conduct this behaviour, which may subsequently induce other gang members to conduct anti-social behaviour as well (Young and Weerman 2013). These deviations may thus be copied by other agents and spread across the system, eventually leading to the collapse of a pattern (Perkins 2014). False consensus therefore increases the instability of both undesired and desired patterns, as it triggers those agents who are affected by the false consensus effect to deviate from and weaken the pattern.

False consensus is the opposite of pluralistic ignorance: it causes a minority to attempt to transform a pattern without the support of most agents, while pluralistic ignorance makes most agents reproduce a pattern without intrinsically supporting it (Mols et al. 2015). When combined, pluralistic ignorance and false consensus can easily result in the destabilisation of a (desired or undesired) pattern, as the majority of agents will not prevent a pattern transformation that is initiated by the minority (Sunstein 2019).

Most nudge tools (except norm nudge tools – Table 17.1) are unlikely to prevent the pattern deviations of agents affected by the false consensus effect. These agents strongly believe that others share their discontent and nudges are unlikely to correct this misperception (Sunstein 2019). Norm nudges are once again a notable exception: informing agents affected by false consensus that they are a minority and that others do not share their views can help to overcome the false consensus effect (Mols et al. 2015).

Cultural Heterogeneity

Agents in public space can have different cultural backgrounds and may belong to various cultural groups (for example, a youth gang, elderly, religious minority, or tourists from other countries). The cultural background of an agent influences whether he or she perceives a particular behavioural pattern as desirable or undesirable (Selinger and Whyte 2010). In public spaces that are visited by agents with heterogeneous cultural backgrounds, it is more likely that some agents will have difficulty with a specific pattern and therefore they may deviate from it (Selinger and Whyte 2010).

Cultural heterogeneity among agents may increase the instability of behavioural patterns. For undesired patterns, mobilising those agents who already perceive a pattern as undesirable, encouraging them to deviate from it, weakens this pattern. Conversely, when desired patterns are perceived by some agents as undesired, the stability of these patterns is weakened and they may transform more easily.

In general, nudges are less effective when agents have different cultural backgrounds. The reason for this is that cultural heterogeneity increases the likelihood that agents interpret the messages or symbols a nudge communicates in different ways, and are therefore less coherent in how they adjust their behaviour (Meder et al. 2018; Reijula et al. 2018). Therefore, nudges may best be targeted towards those agents who share a common cultural background, as they can be linked to the specific norms, values and symbols of this group of agents to increase the likelihood of behaviour change.

Stigmergy

Stigmergy (Marsh and Onof 2008) refers to the indirect interactions between agents that occur by leaving behind traces or markers in public space, such as vandalised street furniture or graffiti. These traces function as indicators of how other agents acted, which indicates what may be efficient, safe or effective behaviour (Bicchieri 2005). This may, in turn, trigger agents to copy the actions that they perceive others were performing (Marsh and Onof 2008). For instance, the presence of trash in a street (that is, stigmergetic traces) has proven to increase the likelihood that other agents will litter as well (Rangoni and Jager 2017). These traces therefore notify agents of existing behavioural patterns and how widely this pattern is supported among other agents (Ploderer et al. 2014).

Stigmergetic traces can both increase and lower the stability of behavioural patterns. An undesired pattern is more stable when these traces indicate that many agents conform to it. However, the stability of undesired patterns is lowered when these traces disappear or are consciously removed, as this makes the dominance of the undesired pattern less visible in public space. In a similar manner, there will be stigmergetic traces that can increase or reduce the stability of desired patterns.

The presence of stigmergetic traces related to an undesired pattern may lower the effectiveness of nudging (Stibe and Cugelman, 2016). In particular, the use of the descriptive norm tool (that is, informing agents regarding what others do; Table 17.1) can be counterproductive when these traces are present. Descriptive norm nudges stimulating the reproduction of a desired pattern are less effective when many stigmergetic traces indicate that (several) agents conform to the undesired pattern (Bolton et al. 2020). For instance, an anti-littering nudge informing agents that others do not litter in a street may stimulate littering instead of preventing it, when it is implemented in public spaces with a great deal of litter (that is, undesired stigmergetic traces) present (Stibe and Cugelman 2016). Thus, some caution is necessary when nudges are implemented in public spaces containing many stigmergetic traces related to undesired behavioural patterns.

The Feasibility of Nudging in Affecting Patterning

The five factors help to assess the level of stability of behavioural patterns in public space (see Figure 17.2). This allows urban planners to identify which behavioural patterns are suitable for nudging and in which instances it is probably ineffective and other instruments are probably more successful.

However, the five factors are not equally informative in understanding the stability of behavioural patterns. Some factors (for example, pluralistic ignorance, false consensus and cultural heterogeneity) concern the interplay between a behavioural pattern in public space and the social norms that agents have learned (Bicchieri 2005). These factors only influence the level of stability of a pattern to the extent a social norm underlies a behavioural pattern. To illustrate, there is often not a socially sanctioned norm that requires agents to follow a pedestrian stream within public space, which means that factors such as pluralistic ignorance or false consensus are unlikely to affect the stability of these patterns. However, traces indicating which route other agents took, may increase the stability of pedestrian flows (De Roo 2016). Thus, the extent to which a social norm underlies a behavioural pattern is important in determining which factors affect the stability of a behavioural pattern.

Not only may the set of factors affecting the stability of a pattern differ, but the factors also already tacitly indicate that the level of stability fluctuates over time. To illustrate, the deviations of pattern breakers lower the stability of an undesired pattern, but their stability is only seriously reduced when the conditional conformers change their behaviour in response to the deviations of these breakers. Another example is the combination of the pluralistic ignorance and the false consensus effects: the small number of deviations from a desired pattern by agents affected by the false consensus effect may grow

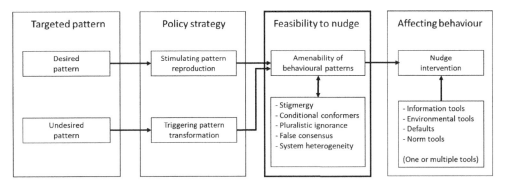

Figure 17.2   Assessing the suitability of nudging for interfering in behavioural patterning processes

in strength when agents suffering from pluralistic ignorance start to deviate from this pattern. These examples indicate that a factor may have a more dominant influence on the stability of a pattern at one time, while its influence can be lower at another time. Owing to variations in the influence of these factors, the stability of behavioural patterns fluctuates over time.

To understand these fluctuations, this contribution adopts a self-organisation perspective (for example, De Roo 2016; Rauws et al. 2016). Investigating how the level of stability of patterns fluctuates during pattern reproduction and transformation processes can help planners to understand changes in the feasibility of nudging over time and to tailor nudges to these fluctuations. Therefore, the next section unpacks patterning as a process of self-organisation.

4.   SELF-ORGANISATION: THE REPRODUCTION AND TRANSFORMATION OF PATTERNS

The self-organisation literature can help to understand how variations in the level of pattern stability occur during pattern transformation and reproduction processes. Self-organisation entails a spontaneous cooperative and competitive process between different agents that can bring about a spatial, temporal or functional order on macroscopic scales (Haken 1980). This section explores how self-organisation provides understanding of processes of pattern transformation and reproduction.

Pattern Transformation: From Undesired to Desired Patterns and Back

Self-organisation helps to explain how the level of stability of a pattern fluctuates during processes of pattern transformation and emergence. The work of De Roo (2016, 2018) helps us to understand how self-organised behavioural patterns emerge or transform through four subsequent phases. To illustrate these phases, the transformation from a clean to a littered public space is used as an example (based on Rangoni and Jager 2017).

Self-organisation starts with a symmetry break (phase 1): a mismatch in the existing configuration of the system that creates an initial, incremental process of change (Rauws et al. 2016). An example of a symmetry break is a pattern breaker who litters in an otherwise tidy public space. This type of break is the result of a change in the actions of one or multiple agents or an external disturbance (Rauws et al. 2016). A symmetry break is easily triggered when patterns are already relatively unstable, possibly owing to (one of) the five factors (discussed in section 3).

The process enters phase 2 when some agents respond to the break and start to deviate from the commonly accepted pattern. With the increasing number of deviations, the instability of the pattern grows. These deviations build up to a critical point, after which the conditional conformers start to abandon the existing pattern (De Roo 2018). For instance, the pattern that most agents throw their litter in the bin is now abandoned. In the case of littering, this critical point is low: already a few pieces of trash can stop most agents (except the pattern defenders) from throwing their litter in the bin (Bicchieri 2005).

After the critical point is passed, the third phase is entered. In this phase, most agents adjust their behaviour, but they have a range of options of how to behave owing to absence of a dominant pattern. For instance, agents throw their litter next to the bin or onto the street, while others may collect the pieces of litter from this street. The instability of the pattern is now at its highest, as most agents have abandoned it and can behave according to their own preferences (Sunstein 2019). Owing to stigmergetic traces, the design of the public space or interactions with other agents, the range of behavioural options eventually converges to a point at which a critical mass of agents aligns their actions and conduct similar behaviour.

This brings about the fourth and final phase, in which a new behavioural pattern has emerged that has gained some stability. Referring to the example, it implies that littering has become a persistent and undesired pattern in public space. The emerged pattern is reproduced by enough agents to assure some persistence (Portugali 2011), at least until a new symmetry break occurs. The implementation of a nudge may trigger such a break. In conclusion, these four phases indicate that both the level of stability and the influence of the factors fluctuates over time and across these phases.

Pattern Reproduction: Preserving Desired Patterns

Next to pattern transformation, the adhered self-organisation also explains the reproduction of behavioural patterns in public space. Once the behaviours of agents have converged into a relatively stable pattern (phase 4: establishment of a dominant order), its existence depends upon a sufficient number of agents reproducing this pattern.

Pattern reproduction occurs in the view of Haken (1980) through enslavement. Enslavement entails that an established behavioural pattern induces agents to reproduce it (Haken 1980; Portugali 2011). It can be considered a form of feedback that affects the behaviour of agents, making them likely to reproduce this pattern (Partanen 2015). Agents are sensitive to this feedback, as following the crowd may reduce the likelihood of being socially sanctioned or indicate what is considered an efficient, safe or effective way to act (Bicchieri 2005).

A requirement for enslavement is that the attention of agents is focused on those stimuli in public space that correspond with the dominant pattern (Portugali 2011). Such stimuli can, for instance, include other agents reproducing a particular pattern, an implemented nudge or stigmergetic traces that are present. When these stimuli draw the attention of agents, these agents are likely to subconsciously follow the corresponding pattern (Bicchieri 2005). Thus, drawing the attention of agents towards those stimuli that correspond with the desired pattern through nudging is essential in promoting the enslavement of agents to a specific pattern.

In this section, the process of self-organisation has been unpacked to understand why and how the level of stability of behavioural patterns fluctuates over time. The next section explores how this understanding can advance nudge design.

5. THREE ARCHETYPES OF NUDGES

Based on the phases of self-organisation, we propose three nudge archetypes. These archetypes link the design of a nudge to a particular level of pattern stability to provide two advantages. First, these archetypes apply a different behaviour change logic in affecting the behaviours of agents. This behaviour change logic refers to a generic rule of how behaviour change can best be promoted with regard to a specific level of pattern stability. Moreover, these archetypes help urban planners to select which specific nudge tools can trigger behaviour change.

For each archetype, its aim and its connection with a particular phase of the self-organisation process are discussed. Trigger nudges are the first archetype and aim to start the transformation of an undesired pattern into a desired one by triggering a symmetry break and spreading the impact of this break through the system. A second type, named coordination nudges, tries to coordinate agents to allow a desired pattern to emerge, in case there is no dominant pattern in public space. Finally, stability nudges stimulate the reproduction of a desired, yet relatively unstable pattern. Next, the three archetypes are explored in more detail.

Trigger Nudges

Trigger nudges try to start the transformation of an unstable (undesired) pattern into a new and more desired pattern. These nudges are therefore orientated towards the first and second phases of self-organisation: they lower the threshold for agents to deviate from the undesired pattern. This increases the likelihood that symmetry breaks occur (phase 1) with the intention to push the agents further towards criticality (phase 2). Trigger nudges are especially effective when the undesired pattern is already relatively unstable owing to the influence of the five factors (Mols et al. 2015).

The self-organisation perspective helps to deduce the behaviour change logic that trigger nudges apply in promoting behaviour change. These nudges discourage the behaviour that reproduces the undesired pattern, but they do not explicitly recommend or guide agents towards a specific action option that agents should perform in the view of the urban planner. An example of a trigger nudge is shared space, that is, public spaces in which the barriers between different traffic modalities are removed (Colander and Kuper 2016). Shared spaces raise the amount of information the brain needs to process, which prompts agents to drive more carefully and lower their driving speed. Shared spaces make the undesired behaviour (for example, speeding) more difficult to perform, but do not recommend a particular action to drivers or proscribe which route they should take (Colander and Kuper 2016).

The self-organisation perspective is also informative in the selection which nudge tools can be applied by this archetype. Trigger nudges can incorporate most of the nudge tools (see Table 17.1) to prevent the undesired behaviour without explicitly guiding agents towards a particular action option. Two exceptions can be mentioned: trigger nudges are unlikely to employ the tools 'defaults' and 'framing': defaults explicitly favour a behavioural option unless agents opt out, and framing refers to the deliberate rephrasing of information so that agents make a particular decision. Trigger nudges cannot apply these tools, as the tools explicitly guide agents towards a behavioural option.

Coordination Nudges

The purpose of coordination nudges is to stimulate the realisation of a new pattern in the event that the former one has largely been abandoned. Establishing a desired pattern can sometimes take time, especially when agents remain acting in an uncoordinated manner. This may occur, for instance, when the communication between different agents is distorted (Sunstein 2019). This uncoordinated situation may lead to selfish behaviour and conflicts among agents, and raises the likelihood that an undesired pattern emerges (Sunstein 2019). The implementation of a coordination nudge helps to converge these different actions towards the realisation of a new, hopefully desired, pattern (Heylighen et al. 2013). Therefore, these nudges are linked to the third phase of self-organisation.

Also for coordination nudges, the phases within a self-organisation process help to deduct the behaviour change logic that this archetype employs to stimulate the emergence of a new and desired pattern. Such nudges try to prevent selfish and unco-ordinated behaviour and align agents' actions towards the realisation of a pattern by providing direct and personalised feedback about agent's behaviour or by communicating what other agents did or could have done (Heylighen 2011; Heylighen et al. 2013). Interactive traffic signs informing car drivers of their driving speed and whether it is in line with the speed limit are an example of personalised feedback (Toy et al. 2014). Informing agents about the behaviour of others can be done either directly or indirectly. For instance, nudges can directly communicate how many car drivers earned a small marginal financial bonus for the local community by sticking to the speed limit (SOM 2017) or encourage agents to leave stigmergetic traces behind that indirectly communicate which mode of conduct they performed (Heylighen 2011). Aligning agents by providing direct and personalised feedback, and informing them what others do or approve of, can converge the range of action options towards the most dominant action.

Based on Heylighen (2011) and Heylighen et al. (2013), at least two tools from Table 17.1 can stimulate the coordination among agents. The feedback tool can be used to personally inform agents in respect of their behaviour, while the norm nudge tool can inform agents in respect of what others (could) have done or is appropriate behaviour in this public space (Lehner et al. 2016). Thus, coordination nudges try to encourage agents to conduct similar behaviour, which allows a desired pattern to emerge.

Stability Nudges

Stability nudges stimulate the reproduction of a desired yet unstable behavioural pattern. As we have argued, an emerged and desired pattern may be relatively unstable and transform easily, for instance, owing to the five factors. These nudges relate to the fourth phase of self-organisation as they try to increase the level of stability of an already emerged pattern.

Considering nudges as interferences in the self-organisation process, their logic in encouraging behaviour change can be clarified: stability nudges are stimuli within public spaces that try to notify agents about the existence of a desired pattern. When the attention of agents is subsequently focused upon this nudge, the pattern corresponding to the nudge is likely to enslave agents. From this, it follows that these nudges need to be as salient and explicit as possible within public space (Noggle 2018), since this increases the likelihood that the nudge triggers an enslavement effect.

Linking nudging to self-organisation also helps us to understand which nudge tools can be used to increase the saliency of beneficial patterns. Stability nudges employ the following nudge tools: norms (Bicchieri and Dimant 2019), feedback, simplification and framing (Thaler and Sunstein 2008), effort (Lehner et al. 2016) and salience (Noggle 2018). For instance, Kort et al. (2008) and Jespersen (2012) show how nudges that increase the saliency of litter bins (such as placing a mirror above a litter bin) prevent littering. When these nudges are implemented in tidy public spaces, they reproduce the tidiness pattern and can be considered stability nudges.

Concluding Remarks

Table 17.2 summarises the key characteristics of the nudge archetypes that we have proposed. By linking nudging to (the four phases of) self-organisation, the logic these archetypes use to alter behaviour can be understood and suitable nudge tools identified. Thus, Table 17.2 shows how the design of nudges can be tailored to the fluctuating level of stability of behavioural patterns along the phases of self-organisation processes.

Tailoring nudges to a particular phase in the self-organisation process does not exclude the option of combining multiple archetypes in one nudge-intervention. The argument is that the nudge-intervention may, for different groups of agents (for example, youth gang, tourists, a cultural minority), overlap as regards the behavioural patterns it tries to address. For instance, playing classical music in train stations prevents rowdy youths from hanging around and promotes behaviour change among this sub-group, and may therefore be considered a trigger nudge (Thompson 2017). Meanwhile, this same nudge-intervention can simultaneously be a stability nudge for other agents, preventing them from conducting the discouraged behaviour. These combined effects emphasise the importance of identifying which group of agents the nudge should target.

While the proposed archetypes may improve the design of nudges, the use of these archetypes needs obviously to be legitimised by urban planners (Schmidt 2017). Therefore, the next section addresses how manipulative nudges can be avoided and the interests of agents safeguarded.

Table 17.2   Three proposed nudge archetypes and their main characteristics

	Trigger nudges	Coordinating nudge	Stability nudges
Phase	Phase 1: triggering a symmetry break Phase 2: reaching a critical point	Phase 3: coordinating agents' actions	Phase 4: an emerged pattern
Aim	Triggering a symmetry break and spreading the impact of this break to reach criticality	Coordinating the diverse range of actions towards the realisation of a (desired) pattern	Preventing pattern transformations
When?	Undesired pattern	In case of frictions or conflicts between agents or an desired pattern is likely to emerge	Desired pattern
Behaviour change logic	Making the undesired behaviour less attractive	Stimulating the convergence of agents' actions towards a particular behaviour	Reminding agents what the desired mode of conduct is
Nudge tools?	Most nudge tools can be used, except defaults and framing	Providing feedback, social norm nudges	Social norm nudges, framing, saliency, effort

6.   MANIPULATING SELF-ORGANISATION, MANIPULATIVE NUDGES?

While this contribution is supportive of the use of these nudge archetypes, their implementation, similar to all spatial interventions, needs to be carefully legitimised by planners. Thaler and Sunstein (2008) argue that the use of nudging is generally legitimate, as they promote desired behaviours and behavioural patterns that improve the well-being of agents or the local community. However, as the factor cultural heterogeneity (section 3) already tacitly indicated, what is considered desirable behaviour and a desired pattern may differ among agents and between spaces (Hausman and Welch 2010).

Urban planners are likely to use nudging to encourage those behaviours and behavioural patterns they perceive to be desirable and important. Consequently, the nudge designs of urban planners are influenced by their ideologies, cognitive limitations, assumptions and social norms (Majoor and Schwartz 2015). As nudging provides urban planners with subconscious influence over the actions of agents, it makes their behaviours instrumental in realising the policy goals of planners often without their consent, support or, even, awareness. For this reason, nudging is considered by some scholars to be manipulative (Goodwin 2012).

Several remedies can be brought forward to prevent the manipulative usage of nudging. The five factors discussed (in section 3) indicate that the archetypes need to reflect somehow the norms and values of agents in order to be effective (Sunstein 2019). Therefore, many nudges support a mode of conduct (for example, safe traffic and less crime) that is widely found important by most agents, also when they have different cultural backgrounds. When this is not so, and nudges promote a behaviour that deviates from the core norms and values of the majority of agents, nudges are more likely to be ignored. Hence, there is little space for using these archetypes in a way that they infringe upon the core beliefs, preferences or values of agents (Sunstein 2019).

Another way to prevent manipulation is to improve democratic control over nudging. This enables agents to influence the use of nudging by urban governments through democratic elections or other forms of citizen participation (Schmidt 2017). This democratic control can take various forms, such as co-designing nudges in a cooperation between urban planners (John 2018) and locals, or formal approval of the city council for implementing a nudge or the start of a nudge programme (Schmidt 2017).

Finally, the transparency of nudges may be increased by disclosing why a nudge is implemented and how it seeks to change agents' behaviour. This enables agents to make an informed decision as to whether they follow the guidance from a nudge or explicitly opt out of it (Thaler and Sunstein 2008). When these different strategies are applied, there is no reason to perceive nudges as more problematic than other policy instruments in urban planning.

7.   CONCLUSION

This chapter provides a theoretical exploration of how a self-organisation perspective on the production and reproduction of behavioural patterns can advance the design of nudges in public space. As a policy instrument that exploits a range of cognitive biases, heuristics and social norms to stimulate behaviour change, nudges can address spatial behaviours that harm or benefit the quality of public space and the collective well-being in neighbourhoods. However, by focusing individual behaviours and their underlying cognitive mechanisms, the value of nudging in addressing the behavioural patterns these individual actions collectively generate remains largely unknown.

To explore the value of nudging in addressing these patterns, this chapter investigates how nudge designs can be adapted to fluctuations in the levels of stability of behavioural patterns. Assessing this level of stability is key, as it determines how easy or difficult it is for urban planners to transform a pattern and thus helps to establish whether nudging is a potentially effective instrument in affecting this pattern. This chapter demonstrates how the level of stability changes during a self-organised patterning process and is fuelled by a range of social-psychology frictions within the behaviour of agents. Combining these insights from nudge theory, self-organisation and social psychology enables urban planners to identify which behavioural patterns are sufficiently unstable at a particular moment in time to be effectively addressed by nudges.

In adapting nudge designs to fluctuations in the level of pattern stability, three nudge archetypes are proposed. Trigger nudges attempt to start the transformation of an undesired pattern by creating the conditions in which a symmetry break is likely to occur, without directing agents towards a particular direction. Coordination nudges try to align the individual actions towards the realisation of a desired pattern by providing personal feedback or informing agents about what others do or could have done. Finally, stability nudges try to stimulate the reproduction of desired patterns by drawing agents' attention towards it to enslave them. While these archetypes require further empirical testing in field experiments in public space, they show how the stability of a respective pattern can be used to tailor the use and design of nudges to the interaction dynamics within public space.

As illustrated by these archetypes, combining scientific knowledge in respect of human behaviour and self-organisation can directly improve the understanding of the dynamic interactions within public space and why undesired patterns may emerge or be sustained. Even more importantly, it can aid the design of planning interventions by adapting their design to the interplay of cognitive mechanisms determining the behaviour of agents and interaction dynamics within cities.

NOTES

1. Nudges differ, however, from marketing efforts by private businesses or social sanctioning between neighbours. They aim to benefit the collective well-being or the well-being of those subjected to them (and not a private agent) and occur by modifications in the choice architecture.
2. As discussed during the explanation of the former factor, when agents feel a strong moral obligation to conduct a particular behaviour, they do not need to be nudged to conduct it. A strong obligation almost ensures that agents will conduct the desired mode of conduct.

REFERENCES

Ariely, D. and S. Jones (2008), *Predictably Irrational*, New York: Harper Audio.
Baldwin, R. (2014), 'From regulation to behaviour change: giving nudge the third degree', *Modern Law Review*, **77** (6), 831–57.
Bicchieri, C. (2005), *The Grammar of Society: The Nature and Dynamics of Social Norms*, New York: Cambridge University Press.
Bicchieri, C. and E. Dimant (2019), 'Nudging with care: the risks and benefits of social information', *Public Choice*, July, 1–22.
Bolton, G., E. Dimant and U. Schmidt (2020), 'When a nudge backfires: combining (im)plausible deniability with social and economic incentives to promote pro-social behavioral change', doi:10.2139/ssrn.3294375.
Byrne, D. (1998), *Complexity Theory and the Social Sciences*, London: Routledge.
Cialdini, R.B., C.A. Kallgren and R.R. Reno (1991), 'A focus theory of normative conduct: a theoretical refinement and reevaluation of the role of norms in human behavior', in M.P. Zanna (ed.), *Advances in Experimental Social Psychology*, San Diego, CA: Academic Press, pp. 201–34.
Colander, D. and R. Kupers (2016), *Complexity and the Art of Public Policy: Solving Society's Problems from the Bottom Up*, Princeton, NJ: Princeton University Press.
De Roo, G. (2016), 'Self-organization and spatial planning', in G.de Roo and L. Boelens (eds), *Spatial Planning in a Complex Unpredictable World of Change – Towards a Proactive Co-evolutionary Type of Planning with the Eurodelta*, Assen: InPlanning, pp. 54–96.
De Roo, G. (2018), 'Ordering principles in a dynamic world of change – on social complexity, transformation and the conditions for balancing purposeful interventions and spontaneous change', *Progress in Planning*, **125** (10), 1–32.
Goodwin, T. (2012), 'Why we should reject "nudge"', *Politics*, **32** (2), 85–92.
Hausman, D.M. and B. Welch (2010), 'Debate: to nudge or not to nudge', *Journal of Political Philosophy*, **18** (1), 123–36.
Haken, H. (1980), 'Synergetics: are cooperative phenomena governed by universal principles?', *Die Naturwissenschaften*, **67** (3), 121–8.
Helbing, D., P. Molnár, I.J. Farkas and K. Bolay (2001), 'Self-organizing pedestrian movement', *Environment and Planning B: Planning and Design*, **28** (3), 361–83.
Heylighen, F. (2011), 'Self-organization of complex, intelligent systems: an action ontology for transdisciplinary integration', *Integral Review*, **134** (6), 1–39.
Heylighen, F. (2013), 'Self-organization in communicating groups: the emergence of coordination, shared references and collective intelligence', in À. Massip-Bonet and A. Bastardas-Boada (eds), *Complexity*

Perspectives on Language, Communication and Society. Understanding Complex Systems, Berlin: Springer, pp. 117–49.

Heylighen, F., I. Kostov and K. Kiemen (2013), 'Mobilization systems: technologies for motivating and coordinating human action', in M.A. Peters, T. Besley and D. Araya (eds), *The New Development Paradigm: Education, Knowledge Economy and Digital Futures*, New York: Routledge, pp. 115–44.

Jacobs, J. (1961), *The Death and Life of Great American Cities*, New York: Random House.

Jespersen, S.M. (2012), 'Green nudge: nudging into the litter bin', accessed 11 December 2019 at http://www.inudgeyou.com/green-nudge-nudging-litter-into-the-bin.

John, P. (2018), *How Far to Nudge? Assessing Behavioural Public Policy*, Cheltenham, UK and Northampton, MA, USA: Edward Elgar.

Kerner, B.S. (1998), 'Experimental features of self-organization in traffic flow', *Physical Review Letters*, **81** (17), 3797–800.

Kort, Y.A. de, L.T. McCalley and C.J. Midden (2008), 'Persuasive trash cans: activation of littering norms by design', *Environment and Behavior*, **40** (6), 870–91.

Lehner, M., O. Mont and E. Heiskanen (2016), 'Nudging – a promising tool for sustainable consumption behaviour?', *Journal of Cleaner Production*, **134** (10), 166–77.

Majoor, S. and K. Schwartz (2015), 'Instruments of urban governance', in J. Gupta, K. Pfeffer, H. Verrest and M. Ros-Tonen (eds), *Geographies of Urban Governance*, Cham: Springer, pp. 109–26.

Malleson, N., L. See, A. Evans and A. Heppenstall (2014), 'Optimising an agent-based model to explore the behaviour of simulated burglars', in V. Dabbaghian and V.K. Mago (eds), *Theories and Simulations of Complex Social Systems*, Berlin: Springer, pp. 179–204.

Marsh, L. and C. Onof (2008), 'Stigmergic epistemology, stigmergic cognition', *Cognitive Systems Research*, **9** (1–2), 136–49.

Meder, B., N. Fleischhut and M. Osman (2018), 'Beyond the confines of choice architecture: a critical analysis', *Journal of Economic Psychology*, **68**, 36–44.

Mols, F., S.A. Haslam, J. Jetten and N.K. Steffens (2015), 'Why a nudge is not enough: a social identity critique of governance by stealth', *European Journal of Political Research*, **54** (1), 81–98.

Nettle, D., K. Nott and M. Bateson (2012), '"Cycle thieves, we are watching you": impact of a simple signage intervention against bicycle theft', *PLoS ONE*, **7** (12), e51738.

Noggle, R. (2018), 'Manipulation, salience, and nudges', *Bioethics*, **32** (3), 164–70.

Partanen, J. (2015), 'Indicators for self-organization potential in urban context', *Environment and Planning B: Planning and Design*, **42** (5), 951–71.

Perkins, H.W. (2014), 'Misperception is reality: the "Reign of Error" about peer risk behaviour norms among youth and young adults', in M. Xenitidou and B. Edmonds (eds), *The Complexity of Social Norms*, Cham: Springer, pp. 11–36.

Perrone, C. (2019), '"Downtown is for people": the street-level approach in Jane Jacobs' legacy and its resonance in the planning debate within the complexity theory of cities', *Cities*, **91** (8), 10–16.

Ploderer, B., W. Reitberger, H. Oinas-Kukkonen and J. Gemert-Pijnen (2014), 'Social interaction and reflection for behaviour change', *Pers Ubiquit Comput*, **18** (7), 1667–76.

Portugali, J. (2011), *Complexity, Cognition and the City*, Berlin: Springer Science & Business Media.

Rangoni, R. and W. Jager (2017), 'Social dynamics of littering and adaptive cleaning strategies explored using agent-based modelling', *Journal of Artificial Societies and Social Simulation*, **20** (2), doi:10.18564/jasss.3269.

Rauws, W. (2016), 'Civic initiatives in urban development: self-governance versus self-organisation in planning practice', *Town Planning Review*, **87** (3), 339–61.

Rauws, W., G. de Roo and S. Zhang (2016), 'Self-organisation and spatial planning: an editorial introduction', *Town Planning Review*, **87** (3), 241–51.

Reijula, S., J. Kuorikoski, T. Ehrig, K. Katsikopoulos and S. Sunder (2018), 'Nudge, boost, or design? Limitations of behaviorally informed policy under social interaction', *Journal of Behavioral Economics for Policy*, **2** (1), 99–105.

Schmidt, A.T. (2017), 'The power to nudge', *American Political Science Review*, **111** (2), 404–17.

Selinger, E. and K.P. Whyte (2010), 'Competence and trust in choice architecture', *Knowledge, Technology & Policy*, **23** (3–4), 461–82.

Smart Online Marketing (SOM) (2017), 'Nudge: kleine verandering met GROTE gevolgen', accessed 23 December 2019 at https://smart-online-marketing.nl/nudging/nudge/.

Spencer, N. (2018), 'Complexity as an opportunity and challenge for behavioural public policy', *Behavioural Public Policy*, **2** (2), 227–34.

Stibe, A. and B. Cugelman (2016), 'Persuasive backfiring: when behavior change interventions trigger unintended negative outcomes', in A. Meschtscherjakov, B. De Ruyter, V. Fuchsberger, M. Murer and M. Tscheligi (eds), *International Conference on Persuasive Technology*, Cham: Springer, pp. 65–77.

Sunstein, C.R. (2019), *How Change Happens*, Cambridge, MA: MIT Press.

Thaler, R. and C. Sunstein (2008), *Nudge: Improving Decisions about Health, Wealth, and Happiness*, New Haven, CT: Yale University Press.
Thompson, M. (2017), 'To soothe or remove? Affect, revanchism and the weaponized use of classical music', *Communication and the Public*, **2** (4), 272–83.
Toy, S., A. Tapp, C. Musselwhite and A. Davis (2014), 'Can social marketing make 20 mph the new norm?', *Journal of Transport & Health*, **1** (3), 165–73.
Webb, D. (2018), 'Tactical urbanism: delineating a critical praxis', *Planning Theory & Practice*, **19** (1), 58–73.
Wood, J.L. (2014), 'Understanding gang membership: the significance of group processes', *Group Processes & Intergroup Relations*, **17** (6), 710–29.
Young, J.T. and F.M. Weerman (2013), 'Delinquency as a consequence of misperception: overestimation of friends' delinquent behavior and mechanisms of social influence', *Social Problems*, **60** (3), 334–56.

18. Evolutionary games in cities and urban planning

Sara Encarnação, Fernando P. Santos, Francisco C. Santos, Margarida Pereira, Jorge M. Pacheco and Juval Portugali

1. INTRODUCTION

Cities are prime examples of complex adaptive systems (Portugali 2000; Batty 2008; Batty and Marshall 2012; Portugali et al. 2012). They emerge as the (un)intended coordination among many actors and as a by-product of, among others, social relations of control, domination and power. More than inorganic agglomerations of concrete, cities can be seen as spatial forms of social production (Lefebvre 1991). As a stage for interactions between self-regarding beings – potentially with antagonistic drives – cities are (also) subject to the pasture dilemmas so clearly put by Garret Hardin in his 'The tragedy of the commons' (Hardin 1968) where, in the absence of externally or self-enforced rules, individuals may threaten the sustainability of the common good. Resource depletion, crime, overpopulation, environmental degradation, inequality and social conflict are henceforth examples of negative externalities that can undermine the sustainability of cities in general. Cities also create a complex ecosystem, where citizens' work, knowledge, cooperation or ideas interact in a non-trivial way leading to returns that benefit everyone (Bettencourt et al. 2010). These dynamics may be potentiated by the use and integration of large-scale datasets that cities effortlessly aggregate, creating a new type of common good. Understanding how to cope with these challenges while taking advantage of the extraordinary capacity of humans to cooperate can positively affect the living standards of a considerable fraction of humanity: The percentage of world population living in urban areas surpassed the 50 per cent mark in 2018 (55 per cent) and is expected to reach 68 per cent by 2050 (United Nations 2018).

In this context, planning can be employed both to avert cities' difficulties and to sustain collective good. Planning may be understood as an attempt to shape the future by current acts and practices (Wildavsky 1973). How and when to plan are, however, timeless questions without lasting answers. Modern planning was initially understood as a top-down, centrally driven process where the State intervened to secure the common good (Friedmann 1987; Taylor 1998), in line with the prescription of Garret Hardin. This rational comprehensive planning approach assumed that, by means of science, it could be possible to predict the future (for example, future demand for housing and roads) and to plan accordingly. Its basic tools were the master plan, the development plan and zoning. This planning model ended up in failure: the future proved to be unpredictable, master and development plans were never implemented as intended, while zoning entailed the 'death' of cities (Jacobs 1961).

The limitations of a rational view of planning are further revealed by several unsuccessful stories (Taylor 1998) and because planning has, meanwhile, changed from a two-sector setting – between public institutions and private bodies – to a three-sector arena – comprising public, private and civil actors.

The limitations of top-down planning brought to light governance alternatives set up in a bottom-up fashion, whose success was demonstrated by (Ostrom 1990). This realization called for alternative strategies that could also promote a bottom-up, self-organized governance. Two interrelated alternatives emerged: communicative or collaborative planning (Innes 1995; Healey 1996) and, more recently, the complexity approach. Communicative planning, which was directly inspired by Habermas's (1984) theory of communicative action, replaced prediction with urban vision by means of the participation of the third sector (for example, non-governmental organizations and local communities) in planning committees. In the complexity approach, there are two views about the role of planning: (1) planning as intervention, in an otherwise self-organized city and (2) planning as participation (where each urban agent is a planner at a particular scale). In this last view, planning as an integral part of the system it intervenes in is also subject to dynamics of adaptation and self-organization, thus requiring a change from prediction-based planning to rules-based planning (Portugali 2011).

These renewed approaches are not alien to problems associated with rationally bounded agents (Forester 1982), conventionally viewed as myopic and inherently suboptimal decision-makers. Bottom-up approaches may (also) lead to lock-in states that prevent the realization of social good originating in coordination failures. In this instance, actors interact strategically following individual preferences that include, for example, incentives, sanctions, coercion, bargaining and competition, but also different power positions, conflicts between local and global interests of the actors involved, and the weakening of the state. This complex setting calls not for rivalry between top-down and bottom-up approaches, but for the realization of their nested nature. In addition to this strategic reasoning, if we regard individuals as influenced and influencing agents embedded in large communities, it becomes essential for the planning endeavour to understand and, if possible, predict, control and adapt to the long-term dynamics of strategies employed. Thus, game theory, viewed as a planning tool, should not only be applied in a static way, but also motivate dynamic analysis of how city actors' decisions unfold over time, turning evolutionary game theory (EGT) into a relevant candidate to address this type of problems (Encarnação et al. 2018).

As we exemplify in this chapter, EGT enables the study of the strategic dynamics resulting from diverse decision-makers (players), strategies and interaction rules. Adopting available strategies in space and time leads to a dynamic process, whereby individuals influence and are influenced by others. Evolutionary game theory focus on the properties and characteristics of the population as this co-influence dynamics unfolds in time. After providing more details on classical game theory and EGT (section 2), we highlight the potential role of EGT in planning (section 3). We then focus on the particular case of dynamics between different types of city players – representing various sectors of society. To this end, we exemplify the application of EGT concepts (section 4), following the analysis proposed in a recent set of studies (Encarnação et al. 2016a, 2016b; Santos et al. 2016). We focus on the dynamics of strategy adoption and long-term behaviour of individuals from public, private and civil sectors, providing the existence of different mechanisms (for example, taxes, subsidies, electoral pressure and civil activism) at work within and between sectors. We end the chapter by discussing the results obtained, framing them in a wider planning perspective and elaborating on future research avenues that may rely on EGT to guide urban planning (section 5).

2. A BRIEF INTRODUCTION TO (EVOLUTIONARY) GAME THEORY

Planning may be conceived as an attempt to shape the future through present acts (Wildavsky 1973). This endeavour requires anticipation of the effect of different policies, in order to select (today) the acts that most likely materialize the planners' intentions (tomorrow). Linking acts and consequences across time is challenging, to the same extent that predicting is difficult – especially the future, as in the famous quote attributed to Niels Bohr. Planning often ignores that actions induce population adaptations, which in turn change the environment conditions from where the planning project departed, rendering them inexact and, by *force majeure* suboptimal. Planning should be approached with just-in-time strategies, allowing incorporating the natural features related to planning of a complex adaptive system (Portugali 2000; Alfasi and Portugali 2004; Levin 2006; Miller and Page 2009; Lo 2017). This endeavour requires improved conceptual and predictive tools. The object being planned (from land to transportation systems or markets), and whose dynamics should be comprehended and predicted, may differ in size, temporal scale, predictability and control. The conceptual tools employed must be adapted accordingly. Planning may require understanding how infrastructures respond to temperature variability, resorting to chemistry and material sciences; planning may require anticipating the weather or shoreline dynamics for the coming decades, demanding meteorology; planning may require calculating the net return of old and current investments, relying on finance; and planning may benefit from upcoming health and sanitation insights, or knowledge about new transportation and communication means. Planning calls for a myriad of disciplines but, at a fundamental level, planning requires comprehending, predicting – or at least reason about – the responses of decision-makers to environment, social, economic and political challenges. In these scenarios, it is fundamental to understand dynamics of cooperation, conflict and coordination among city actors.

The discipline of planning evolved to reflect how coordination between individuals is understood (planning theory) and dealt with (planning practice). The very idea of coordination in planning has evolved consistently with societal changes. Reff et al. (2011) review the evolution of the coordination concept in public governance through the lens of public administration, organization and planning theories. Common to all three theories is the definition of coordination as collective action that results from the successive adjustment of actions by different actors. This notion implies that actions, and thus decision-making, are conditioned by the way others act. These interdependences introduce new levels of uncertainty to the urban game that planning tries to control, but of which it is also a part of. Considering strategic reasoning in planning is thereby central, in a way that is very similar to that embodied in the realm of game theory (GT).

Game theory is a sub-field of applied mathematics that gained momentum after the seminal work of John von Neumann and Oskar Morgenstern, with the publication of *Theory of Games and Economic Behavior* in the 1940s (von Neumann and

Morgenstern 1947) – despite some initial definitions of GT being attributed to Émile Borel (von Neumann and Morgenstern 1947; Fréchet 1953). Game theory can be understood as the science of rational decision-making in the context of strategic interactions (Osborne 2003). By rational decision-making is meant that individuals will behave following a set of well-defined preferences (for example, Alice prefers spending time in a park rather than commuting). Strategic interactions refer to situations in which the outcomes' value depend on the decisions made by the players involved (for example, the enjoyment of Alice in the park depends on how many people also use it). In an urban context, it is evident already that GT can serve the planner (for example, guiding how to structure traffic to prevent jams), the citizen (for example, informing Alice which route to take in order to maximize leisure time at the park), the analyst (for example, explaining why only some routes get congested) and the fortune-tellers (for example, predicting which route is most likely to be selected by rational agents). Even if predictions cannot be accurately made, GT provides, at the very least, a way to (1) formalize the essence of the strategic interaction, serving as a potential filter to help one disregarding irrelevant details, (2) abstract the challenges associated with particular interactions and identify principles that apply to a range of problems (identifying old solutions to new conundrums), and (3) communicate in a straightforward fashion how modifying our behaviour may affect social welfare. Several interaction paradigms are well studied and allow us to identify common behaviour patterns and solutions at ease. In two-player, two-strategy situations, interactions of interest often configure social dilemmas with the ingredients of a prisoner's dilemma, snowdrift dilemma or stag-hunt dilemma (Macy and Flache 2002), whose payoff table is summarized in Table 18.1.

In all those situations, individuals decide to use one of two possible strategies: say, cooperate or defect. The socially desirable outcome is achieved if individuals simultaneously decide to cooperate ($R > P$). However, incentivizing cooperation is not easy: In a prisoner's dilemma, individuals are always better off by defecting, regardless the strategy selected by their peers: both the temptation to cheat ($T > R$) and the fear of being cheated upon ($P > S$) are present. In a snowdrift dilemma, if an individual cooperates and

Table 18.1   Payoff table of two-person two-strategy social dilemmas

		Column player	
		C	D
Row player	C	R;R	S;T
	D	T;S	P;P

Note: Individuals can adopt one of two actions, cooperate (C) or defect (D). Each table entry reports the gains for the row player (first quantity) and column player (second quantity), for each possible combination of strategies. The peculiar relationship between the quantities obtained by the row player and column player reflect that the game is symmetric, that is, both players get the same payoff whenever confronted with equivalent situations. If both individuals cooperate, they both receive reward (R). When a cooperator plays with a defector, the first receives S (sucker's payoff) while the latter receives T (temptation). If both individuals defect, both receive punishment (P). A prisoner's dilemma results from the condition $S < P < R < T$, a snowdrift from $P < S < R < T$ and a stag-hunt from $S < P < T < R$.

Source: Skyrms (2014).

another defects, then no one has interest in modifying their strategy (T > R but S > P): the temptation to cheat may incentivize high levels of defection, and too much cheating becomes detrimental. In a stag-hunt dilemma (P > S but R > T) there is only fear and no temptation: individuals have a risky option that maximizes their payoff (to cooperate or, according to the game metaphor, aiming to hunt a stag), yet to defect is the safer option (defect, that is, going for the hare); thus fear may prevent cooperation (Macy and Flache 2002). In city interactions, taking good care of a building façade or individual garden suggests a stag-hunt dilemma: the value of keeping everything tidy is contingent on the decision of each neighbour, so that if everyone puts effort into cleaning their property (or if no one does) then there is no incentive to deviate from that status quo. The possibility of sharing the commuting with a neighbour giving him or her a ride (or sharing a Wi-Fi account) may introduce a prisoner's dilemma, where a social benefit can be created at the expense of the cooperator. Finally, the dilemma of removing the snowdrift blocking a common road introduces (unsurprisingly) a snowdrift dilemma.

Despite the multiple advantages of GT, two main criticisms are typically made of classical game theoretical analysis: first, GT provides a toolkit for a static study of interactions. That is, by resorting to solution concepts of classical GT, we may learn which strategies configure an equilibrium; it remains difficult to reason about how particular strategies might come to be played – and the ensuing dynamics. Second, GT relies on extremely strong rationality assumptions, by supposing that individuals know the actions that they themselves and their rivals can employ, together with the costs or gains associated with these actions. In reality, people may lack that information, and often individuals resort to simple heuristics to adapt their behaviour instead of exactly computing the expected returns associated with each combination of actions. Individuals may imitate each other (Lieberman and Asaba 2006; Rendell et al. 2010) or change their actions through trial and error (Erev and Roth 1998), learning with their own experience.

In biology, a new toolkit was eventually proposed: evolutionary game theory (Lewontin 1961; Smith and Price 1973; Smith 1982). Initially, the goal of EGT was grasping mathematically how particular behaviours evolve through natural selection in animal species; for example, conflict (Smith and Price 1973) or cooperation (Trivers 1971). Soon after, social scientists started applying EGT to circumventing the drawbacks of classical GT, listed above (Weibull 1997). All previous paradigmatic dilemmas introduced (prisoner's, snowdrift and stag-hunt dilemmas) can be understood from the standpoint of a dynamical, population perspective (Santos et al. 2006). Regarding urban planning, the biological inspiration to address strategic dynamics seems particularly appropriate: We may conceive cities as concrete jungles, in which individuals from many different sectors (as species) interact embedded in ecologies that constantly adapt over time. This multi-sector interaction paradigm is elucidated in section 4.

In addition to introducing a dynamical perspective and relaxing the rationality assumptions, EGT helps to refine important equilibrium notions of classical GT. While in GT we are often interested in identifying Nash equilibria, that is, situations from which no part is interested in deviating, unilaterally (Nash 1950a) – in Table 18.1, both individuals choosing D would be a pure Nash equilibrium if S < P – with EGT it is of corresponding interest to determine evolutionary stable strategies (ESS), that is, strategies in a population that cannot be invaded by any other mutant strategy (Smith and Price 1973). Again resorting to Table 18.1, a strategy D would be an ESS if P > S or, if P = S, then T > R (Nowak 2006). This means that a mutant strategy (C) must either perform worse against the incumbent (D) or, if performing equally well, perform worse against C than D against C. Moreover, EGT allows the easy determination of population equilibria, that is, population configurations at which point no configuration changes will occur (in the absence of mutations) and, importantly, determines the nature of these equilibria. The analogy with mixed Nash equilibria is evident, although here both the determination of the equilibria as well as their nature need not invoke any additional probabilistic assumptions. Unlike static game theory, EGT not only allows us to identify the possible equilibria, but also to understand to what extent these equilibria are attainable, depending on where we are in the configuration space (that is, the fraction of individuals adopting different strategies). As well as adding concepts such as stability to (mixed and pure) Nash equilibria, EGT enables us to use the well-developed analytic machinery of differential equations, since the process of strategic adoption becomes a dynamical system described by the well-known replicator equation (Taylor and Jonker 1978). These tools can be handy for comprehending dynamics associated with city planning (Santos et al. 2016; Encarnação et al. 2016a, 2016b).

The role of EGT in planning can be foreseen if we regard individuals as influenced and influencing agents embedded in large communities, such that it becomes useful to understand, and thus predict, in the simplest scenarios, the long-term dynamics of strategies' adoption. By using concepts from EGT, we can characterize collective behaviours that emerge from individuals' decisions (Schelling 1978), such as the decision to live in a city or neighbourhood, as traits that spread and eventually endure in space and time owing to some perceived advantage over other places in which to live. Evolutionary game dynamics can account for different types of players, representing various sectors of society. For that, we employ multi-population (Weibull 1997) or asymmetric models (Samuelson and Zhang 1992; McAvoy and Hauert 2015). In urban games, we consider the interaction of players from multiple sectors, such as the civil, private and public sectors. The integration of a multi-sector framework, where interdependencies between and within sectors are allowed, may provide new insights on the intricate nature of cities' dynamics. With these stylized models, we can account for the role of incentive mechanisms between sectors and peer-influence dynamics (for example, imitation and social learning) within sectors. Similar to how fitness drives evolution in genetic evolution, we can assume that strategy adoption depends on perceived success: individuals may compare how they perform relative to their peers, which may lead them to adopt a different behaviour. Relative success associated with a given behaviour will lead to its proliferation in a population of city actors, in a similar way to how variants with a relative advantage will reproduce more and, as a result, outcompete other variants in biological populations.

Altogether, adopting an evolutionary game theoretical perspective over planning can be advantageous for three reasons. (1) It allows reasoning mathematically about different aspects of conflict or cooperation that a particular policy (or plan) may introduce, both within and between city sectors. (2) EGT permits reasoning about the lock-in states that different sectors may fall into, whose stability analysis may provide a justification for observed coordination failures or allow testing solutions that circumvent such states (the models reviewed will shed light on how coordination between sectors can be tamed to achieve socially desirable outcomes). Finally, (3) EGT allows us to explicitly consider the frequency-dependent nature of planning. We assume that strategy reproduction is frequency dependent, that is, contingent on how each actor and sector is performing at a given moment in time, and how represented they are in the entire city population.

3. EVOLUTIONARY GAME DYNAMICS IN CITY PLANNING: FROM LAND USE TO ILLEGAL SETTLEMENTS

Social dilemmas are characterized by two main properties: (1) individuals have a greater benefit by adopting non-cooperative strategies, and (2) all individuals would be better off if they all had cooperated (Dawes 1980). In its simplest interpretation these two properties reflect conflicts between individual and collective interests – the type of situations in which planning finds a large part of its theoretical and practice reasoning. How society uses and organizes space (a common and finite resource), is one evident example of a social dilemma that urban planning faces, with land classification and zoning schemes constituting the archetypal planning instruments for its regulation. These regulate the use of land by defining rights and restrictions on property rights. They are discretionary instruments available to, for example, municipalities that aim to manage urban growth and protect the territory as a common good. Also, space functions as a driver for development and growth and, pragmatically, as an important funding source for municipalities from which dynamics of competition can, and do, emerge. Thus, one of the basic questions in urban planning is to know how much space should be allocated to, let us say, urbanization and construction. There is no definitive answer to this question and a great deal depends on policy and political agendas, themselves mutable in space and time. Each municipality will look to its own territory and define via a master plan, typically a ten-year development strategy. However, municipalities do not exist in isolation; they are part of a wider, interrelated territory. A best option for one municipality can have detrimental impacts in an adjacent or nearby municipality.

   To illustrate this complex dynamics, we can rewrite Table 18.1 as a game between two municipalities – our players. When designing their master plan, each municipality can adopt one of two strategies: Constrain or Maintain the urban growth model. Let us assume that the total combined capacity to build is four (arbitrary units). When players align their strategy they equally share this construction capacity, and hence receive equal payoffs. When both adopt strategy Maintain, each will get a payoff of two. By contrast, when both adopt the Constrain strategy they not only share the investments, but also receive, arguably, an extra payoff point for increased sustainability levels – each receiving a payoff of three. This payoff advantage is informed by the transformation of policies and planning agencies worldwide as a result of new scientific and technical knowledge, together with new ways and demands of living, sustainability, governance and quality of life (Montgomery 2013; Sennett 2018). Finally, when strategies do not align, the municipality that does not constrain growth will receive in full the payoff available (in this instance, four) while the other municipality receives zero (Table 18.2).

   Payoff Table 18.2 follows a (symmetric) prisoner's dilemma (PD) structure characterized by the inequalities $T > R > P > S$. The best option for each municipality is to independently choose Maintain, leading to the equilibrium Maintain/Maintain. Once again, the dilemma arises because, despite Maintain being the best move, if both municipalities adopt this strategy, it will bring a lower return than mutual adoption of

Table 18.2   Payoff table for two municipalities

| | | Municipality B | | |
		Constrain		Maintain
Municipality A	Constrain	3;3	→	0;4
		↓		↓
	Maintain	4;0	→	**2;2**

Note: Municipalities can adopt one of two strategies: Constrain or Maintain urban growth model.
The table reports the gains for both players, for each possible combination of strategies. Arrows indicate
the preferences of municipalities (vertical for municipality A and horizontal for municipality B). Bold is the
equilibrium of the game.

Source: Rasmusen (1994).

Constrain measures. Moreover, if the Maintain equilibrium co-occurs with fragmented
and dispersed growth, evidence shows that costs of infrastructure and facilities or loss
of natural resources can become significant (Carvalho 2013). However, the (immediate)
future is often too distant and not easily discounted (Frederick et al. 2002; Levin 2012),
especially when decisions are framed in election cycles. We could also argue that following assumptions in PD-like games, both municipalities would not communicate with
one another, thus increasing the perceived risk in constraining growth; that is, neither
municipality would have any incentive to change from Maintain when Constrain is open
to free-riders.

This game, though simple, can alert us to the importance of understanding strategic
decision-making in real planning situations. Overall, it is a convenient starting point –
trading specific details for generality and abstraction power – from which more complex
models aiming at specific contexts could be built. For instance, we can envisage scenarios
where an external entity, such as the central administration, would apply sanctions,
which would reduce the payoffs of strategy Maintain to zero. In many countries, non-
compliance with centrally designed guidance can have severe consequences, for example,
non-approval of master plans, suspension of licensing mechanisms or, in European
countries, impediment of application for European funds, being just a few examples.
In that case, the equilibrium of the game would change to the alignment of the strategy
Constrain.[1] Examples abound in which the unwillingness, inability or failure to actively
intervene promote undesired outcomes, such as growth of dispersed and fragmented
peripheries and cities (Carranca and Castro 2011), which in turn contributed to the loss
of natural and agricultural areas (Encarnação et al. 2012), increased costs for municipalities with infrastructures (Carvalho 2013), and social amenities and facilities (Pereira
2004).

Planning games can also occur at both vertical and horizontal levels. Scale matters and
levels are interdependent. Also, EGT benefits from a long tradition of analysing conflicts
at different, interrelated scales in ecological contexts (Levin et al. 2012). As an example,
the above-mentioned top-down solution, however successful in many cases, can give
rise to other or similar social dilemmas at the scale of cities, communities and individuals. Importantly, planning becomes part of the game, as in general complex adaptive

systems – a player whose strategic decisions affect, but are also contingent to, those of other players in society. For example, as master plans are approved and come into force, property owners' rights will be differently affected by means of an artificial limit created by zoning schemes that aim to protect the territory as a sustainable collective good. In this regard, the discretionary effect of planning itself creates a social dilemma, since by its own action it alters land rents and corresponding added value. This, in turn, will change the behavioural response of property owners. Therefore, planning should account for this uneven distribution of individual rights, and develop mechanisms for equitable solutions and compensation systems (Carvalho 2012) or put into practice land readjustment schemes (Hong 2007). The dilemma can then become a bargaining game, where there is the potential to achieve mutual benefits but where players depart from divergent interests (Nash 1950b; Binmore 1990). Models of this type can help understand how players could reach an agreement and how benefits would be distributed. Different models of bargaining can be used and adapted to the problem and conditions at hand, possibly taking into consideration the players' utility functions, information, risk aversion, time preferences, costs, and so on (Binmore et al. 1986).

Failure to acknowledge that planning is an integral part of the (evolutionary) dynamics of cities, and that its role surpasses that of regulation to enter the realm of a market player (Adams and Tiesdell 2010), can create unbalance situations in the future. Again, (evolutionary) game theory can help to reason about this type of problems. For example, by adopting a first-mover role, forming coalitions or designing different schemes for risk distribution, planning enters the evolutionary game of cities as an economically active player (Lord and O'Brien 2017). However, since planners are part of this complex adaptive system where uncertainty is paramount, unexpected results can emerge. Trust and confidence that planning creates in investors, as a first mover, can lead, in time, to risk aversion and to a reduced initiative of private investors, or it can expose planning agencies to greater financial risks when economic and financial contexts change quickly (Lord and O'Brien 2017). The role of first mover can also be fundamental in situations where the risk of investment is high, as in economically depressed urban areas where only public support to private initiatives can trigger the necessary initial change (Weiler 2016). Triggers of this type may also induce collective self-organization through imitation of successful private investors that act as first-movers. After reaching some threshold of imitators, many cities and communities witness large transformations, as it happens with gentrification or short-term rental dynamics. This type of effect portray the frequency dependence of strategies in a population of players. In some instances, the more people in a population adopt a given strategy, the more people will tend to choose this same strategy. Ultimately, the structure of the game at stake will influence the detailed frequency dependence observed.

From a theoretical perspective, these situations often translate into equilibria that are not social optimal (Camerer 2003). This may occur when changing the status quo implies the need for action that is costly (for example, by adopting greener vehicles or public transportation) (Encarnação et al. 2018). Coordination failures can also result from unbalanced socio-economic dynamics, and availability of affordable housing is just one of these examples. In this regard, let us use a Portuguese example, characterized by a combination of multi-sector and multilevel (top-down and bottom-up) interventions and conflicts and of difficult resolution for more than 40 years of planning interventions.

Illegal settlements[2] in Portugal grew considerably during the 1960 and 1970s, owing to multiple factors, including, for example, migration towards major cities and lack of affordable housing (Salgueiro 1977; Williams 1981). These settlements located primarily at the peripheries of cities, where control from authorities was easier to avoid and where land prices and construction costs were significantly lower (Salgueiro 1977). At first, this was a win-win situation for all actors involved. Sellers could initially buy rural land at cheap prices, divide it illegally and sell it at higher prices; buyers could own a piece of land and construct their own home, a scenario impossible to achieve otherwise; and the state could ignore the persistent housing shortage problem for which it had no financial capacity to respond. Perceived advantages of acquiring and building in these areas (most of them rural and not equipped for urban growth) gathered the support of a growing number of people. By the 1980s and 1990s (and even today), there was a high demand for illegal settlements, also as second homes (especially in areas located near the sea). In time, statistics on the number of people living in these areas brought to light the magnitude of the problems: non-existent basic infrastructures (water and sewer networks), green spaces and transportation, an absence of legal ownership of property and construction, and so on. The initial advantages for buyers and the state started to dwindle.

During the past 40 years, several solutions have been implemented by the central administration (Silva and Farrall 2016), creating different games with different players and mostly resorting to punishment through, for example, fines or demolitions. However, the cost of implementing punishment hindered some solutions and the lack of financial capacity hindered others. In 1995, new legislation required municipalities to integrate these areas into the municipal urban area and transferred most responsibilities to owners and their commissions of conjoint administration (responsible for receiving quotas from owners and the management of the legalization process). The consequences were not what were expected: 15 years later only 30 per cent of those areas covered by the law were successful (Ramos 2002; Raposo 2010). Legalization processes became hostage to circumstances particular to each community (for example, lack of financial resources, occupations in environmentally sensitive areas and in areas of risk). These processes were also vulnerable to free-riders owing to divergent and hidden interests among players (from the resident owner to the renter owner, both with very different local interests) (Pereira and Ramalhete 2017). Added to a lack of important mechanisms, such as mutually agreed coercion measures (Ostrom 1990), it comes as no surprise that the law was largely ineffective. Notwithstanding, the legal principle of reaching legalization through solutions that are more proximate to the population is in line with evidences showing that local bottom-up institutions can increase cooperation, when compared with global institutions (Ostrom 1990; Vasconcelos et al. 2013). The creation of a Commissions of Conjoint Administration (CCA) in each community, although theoretically positive, was flawed in practice, perhaps by not accounting for dynamics of strategic decisions between groups of people, avoiding free-riding escalation or by recognizing the importance of sanctioning measures internal to the group, and self-governance (Vasconcelos et al. 2013). Perhaps the legislation should revise how CCAs work, namely, by adapting self-sanctioning schemes. When uncertainty of results pile up in time (for example, owing to the presence of free-riders that block the process for years), evidence shows that cooperation levels tend to drop, as in other problems of collective action (Vasconcelos et al. 2015). In this regard, the design of local institutions or other mechanisms, such as public participation and collaborative planning, should take into account factors necessary to achieve higher levels of cooperation. Elinor Ostrom summarizes these as: information on past actions, small groups, face-to-face communication, costs of arriving at agreements, symmetrical interests and resources and development of shared norms – all based on paramount mechanisms such as trust, reputation and reciprocity (Ostrom et al. 1999). Planning problems such as those faced by CCAs and their communities can be understood as games with repeated encounters, where players can have information on the previous decisions of others. In these scenarios, social norms, past reputations and (indirect) reciprocity can strongly influence the dynamics of the game, but require an understanding of the complexity underlining these dynamics (Santos et al. 2017, 2018).

Evolutionary dynamics in city planning have always been the result of interdependencies between and among the multiple actors involved. However, urban planning has been slow to acknowledge and act accordingly. As theory and practice increasingly incorporate new forms of participatory and collaborative planning, the number of players from different sectors of society augments the complexity of (and the possibilities associated with) decision-making. It becomes paramount to find ways to study and comprehend how the decision of one affects the decision of others. In the next section, we review such a framework based on EGT.

4.   A FRAMEWORK FOR SELF-ORGANIZING DYNAMICS IN MULTI-SECTOR SCENARIOS

In this section we show, first, how EGT changes when introducing different types of players, representing various sectors of society. Importantly, and in line with what was stated before, the planners (represented by the public sector) are part of the game. The set of mathematical and computational methods at hand to deal with these effects is wide, and some guidance may ease their application (Encarnação et al. 2016a; Santos et al. 2016). From an EGT perspective, the dynamics of the game unfold through the way strategies reproduce in populations of players. The players' success (when adopting a given strategy or behaviour) is measured by computing their average gains obtained in several different interactions with other players adopting different behaviours. Similar to the role of fitness in biological populations evolving through natural selection, here relative success will convey the capacity of behaviours and policies to reproduce in a population of city actors. Success, and thus strategy reproduction, is frequency dependent, that is, contingent on (1) how each actor and sector is performing at a given moment in time and (2) how represented they are in the total city population. The resulting dynamics and eventual equilibria can be adjusted – or in the context of the previous discussion, planned – and framed as a three-sector game (Figure 18.1, top panel).

If we assume a game between three populations (one for each sector of society), where each agent can adopt one of two strategies, we first need to define an interaction table that returns a payoff for every interaction possibility. These returns may include incentives, subsidies or taxes, applied between and within different societal sectors; may consider other parameters that enable additional policy instruments; and may also include less obvious effects, such as positive synergies, boycott or punishment (Henrich

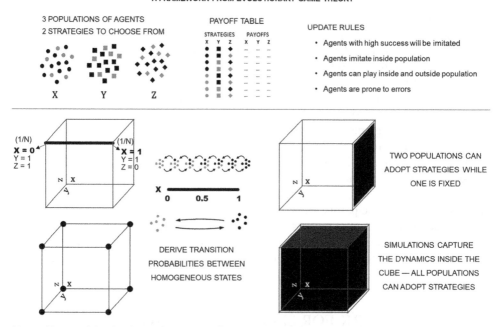

Note: Top panel: in planning settings, X can, for example, correspond to the public sector, Y to the private and Z to the civil. Bottom panel: the cube's, vertices (associated with homogeneous states, where all individuals of each population adopt the same strategy), edges (linking transitions between homogeneous states in which only individuals from one population change strategy), faces (mixing more strategies from more populations) and interior (mixing all possible strategies) all provide information on the dynamics of the game (see text for more details).

Figure 18.1   A general approach to a multi-sector evolutionary game: top panel – three-player, two-strategy game with the corresponding payoff table and game rules; bottom panel – cube representing the phase space of the population dynamics

and Boyd 2001; Sigmund et al. 2001; Stolle et al. 2005; Balabanis 2013) between sectors. The behaviour of agents will be updated following schemes of social learning principles that translate into dynamics in which more successful strategies will be more often imitated in each population (Traulsen et al. 2006; Sigmund 2010). Furthermore, agents can interact with individuals of their own, as well as with individuals of other populations (sectors); for example, when an individual in the public sector subsidizes individuals in the private or civil sector. Finally, individuals are prone to make errors. This last rule means that imitation will occur with a given probability (myopic individuals) whose degree can be adjusted via a single parameter: the higher its value, the less myopic individuals become.

It is important to note that this approach provides several advantages of interpretation, because the strategy phase space of this problem is represented by the cube representing the phase space of the population dynamics, and supported by other plotting schemes (Figure 18.1, bottom panel).[3] As stated in the note to Figure 18.1, vertices are associated with homogeneous states, that is, three-population configurations where all individuals of each population adopt the same strategy. Edges, in turn, link homogeneous states in which only individuals from one population change strategy, while the other two populations remain in their homogenous states (that is, fully adopting one or other strategy). Thus, by analysing the dynamics emerging along these edges (Imhof et al. 2005; Fudenberg and Imhof 2006; Vasconcelos et al. 2017) we provide the means to intuitively comprehend some simple features of the dynamics of cities encompassing multiple sector interactions, employing a language that facilitates a useful multidisciplinary dialogue. We can start by calculating the conditions that, on each edge, determine the most likely direction of evolution. Indeed, when each individual member adopts a different strategy, a transition occurs from one point in the cube to another, with a probability that we know how to compute (assuming a given payoff table). It is thus possible to map all the individual transition probabilities (that is, small steps along the edge, in this example) into a global transition probability between two vertices connected by one edge, which conveys how likely it is for a whole sector to transit from one strategy to the other. These global probabilities also depend on additional factors, such as the number of individuals belonging to each sector. Once individual and global probabilities are computed, one may define a (reduced) Markov chain, where states correspond to vertices and transitions to evolutionary transitions proceeding along the edges. By studying the stationary distribution associated with this stochastic Markov chain process, we may understand how likely it is for the whole population to stabilize in different configurations (in respect of strategies adopted in each sector). We are thus able to quantify the long-term outcome of the dynamics intuited by the edge conditions mentioned previously.[4] Information about the edges will also enable us to acquire the behaviour on the faces of the cube, where only one population has fixed strategies and the members of the two remaining populations can adopt an arbitrary combination of strategies. Finally, the interior of the cube depicts the rich dynamics emerging from the entire game played by the three sectors. By setting a given set of initial conditions about the fraction of adopters in each population, it is possible, numerically, to study the most likely evolution of strategy adoption when individuals from all sectors can simultaneously change their behaviour.

As an example, let us resort to a simplified version of the model developed to study the transition to more greener policies and behaviours (Encarnação et al. 2016a, 2016b), detailed in the supplementary material of that paper. As a first step we need to define a payoff table that describes the payoffs accruing to each sector, in each combination of strategies (Figure 18.2, top left).

In the table in panel A in Figure 18.2, we make use of widely used mechanisms in public policy, such as sanctions and subsidies. The state (public sector) has the capacity to grant subsidies (s), at a cost to itself, to both the private and civil sector (for simplicity, we gave to both sectors an equal share, but other parameters can be included to play with different shares). Sanctions can assume different forms. The state can apply fines (φ)[5] to private defectors, reducing their benefit (b) and this will enter as a positive payoff on the public sector side. The civil sector may punish (P) public defectors (for example, in election votes or acceptance rates) or boycott (P_b) private defectors. Although both types of punishment are costly, it is reasonable to assume that these costs will diminish as more players in the civil sector adopt the cooperation strategy (thus the factor

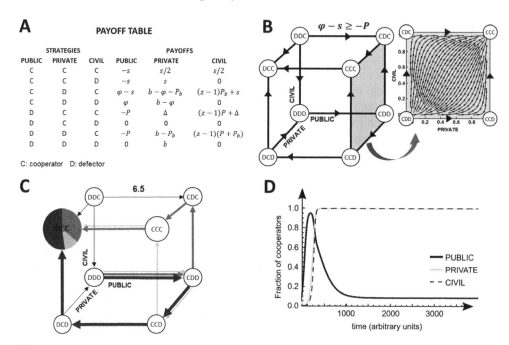

Notes:
(A) Payoff table describing the game (see text for parameters' description; the 24 entries of the table can be written in terms of six independent parameters). (B) Evolutionary dynamics along the edges of the cube and on the face of the cube (right) where the public sector is in full cooperation homogeneous configuration (shaded face in the cube). (C) Stationary distribution of the reduced Markov process, identifying where the system spends most of the time, the most probable paths and the transition probability (relative to neutral probability) of the edge DDC→CDC. (D) Trajectories form the inside of the cube shown here in respect of the time evolution for each population. See text for more details.
Model parameters: $s = 0.19$; $\varphi = 0.0.66$; $P = 0.18$; $P_b = 0.16$; $b = 0.2$; $\Delta = 0.19$.

Figure 18.2   Simplified model for three sectors (public, private and civil) and two strategies (cooperate, C, and defection, D) game

$(1 - z)$ in the payoff matrix). Finally, a synergistic effect between the private and the civil sectors is introduced (Δ) when both meet a public defector. Note that this game always provides for an interaction between three participants simultaneously, one from each population.

From the description of this simplified model it is evident that when the state (as the public sector) is included in the game as a player, it is possible to follow the impact of different measures on all players, including the state (Santos et al. 2016). This information can be crucial when we need to understand how, for example, financial limited capacities of a government can affect, in the long run, the outcome of a policy. Alternatively, it enables us to reason about the effectiveness of some financial effort of public finances. In Figure 18.2, panel B, arrows represent the direction of the dynamics along the edges of the cube. For each edge, we can calculate the relationship between parameters that indicates the most likely direction to take place in the corresponding edge. In the example, the system will transition from state DDC to state CDC with high probability when $\varphi - s \geq P$. By also considering within-population interactions, other edges present more complex transition probabilities (for example, CDC to CDD). To complement this, we can also calculate the most probable path trajectory between the edges of the cube in order to reach the stable state in DCC (Figure 18.2, panel C). This analysis, relying on the stationary distribution of the reduced Markov process, provides a simple but powerful intuition of the full dynamics, which can always be obtained by following the time-dependence of the configurations in each population, as shown in Figure 18.2, panel D. Moreover, the stochastic nature of the Markov process dictates that, whenever two populations' configuration always obtains the same relative payoff, then there is no favourable direction of evolution, which is the social planning equivalent to neutral drift in genetics. The value of the neutral drift is trivial to calculate analytically, and is often used as the reference value for the transition probabilities along the edges; thus, the value of 6.5 of edge DDC → CDC means that the transition is 6.5 stronger than neutral drift. For the interior of the cube, where all eight possible combinations of strategies of the three populations may coexist, numerical simulations provide information about the time dependence of the configuration of each population, departing from a set of initial conditions (Figure 18.2, panel D). In the example given, and starting from 10 per cent of cooperators in each population, it is evident that cooperation in the private and civil sectors only starts when the public sector reaches its peak of cooperation. More interestingly, the model also predicts that, for these parameter values, the private and civil sectors will sustain high values of cooperation irrespective of whether the public sector remains cooperative or not. Furthermore, stationary distributions such as those shown in Figure 18.2, panel D, enable us to explore quickly the parameter space and develop an intuition of the most likely dynamics of such a complex adaptive system.

The framework presented in this section summarizes three studies that accounted for the quantitative and qualitative changes of analysing games where the role of a regulator agent is explicitly modelled as a player, as it often occurs in relationships between the state, business and society (Santos et al. 2016). More specifically, a similar approach was applied to develop an evolutionary game theoretical analysis of the possible occurrence of paradigm shifts in society (Encarnação et al. 2016a, 2016b) and of the viability of the adoption of electric vehicles (Encarnação et al. 2018). In all studies, the structure of the interaction framework remained unchanged; only the game table needed to be adapted to the specificities of each problem. In each study, the scenarios accounted for instruments such as taxes (for example, green taxes applied to different types of vehicles), subsidies to support a change in status quo, given by the public sector, but also synergies between sectors and punishment. Synergies showed that costs in one sector can be alleviated by positive dependencies with another sector, as, for example, when financial costs with subsidies in the public sector are compensated by a high approval rate from civil society. Punishment could take different forms and be adopted by different sectors. For example, punishment from the civil sector can be applied to the public sector through election votes and to the private sector through boycotts. However, this type of punishment is costly, in the same way as subsidies can be costly to the public sector and curtail its use, and sometimes can give rise to second-order free-rider problems. How to solve such problems requires future developments and new applications, such as those presented in the following, final, section.

5.   FINAL REMARKS

In this chapter we started by developing a brief introduction to (evolutionary) game theory, followed by how it can shed some light on the evolutionary dynamics of cities and city planning, using several examples. It became apparent that understanding strategic decision-making, between and among agents, can positively contribute not only to planning theory but also to its practice. New forms of governance imply new roles for all agents involved, but also new forms of thinking and acting in cities. The complexity emerging from these new interactions calls for news ways to reason about them. In this regard, we presented in section 4 a framework of EGT that enables the analysis of games with three populations and two strategies. This framework can be adapted to a multitude of problems and domains. As application examples, we mentioned how this approach can be tuned to provide insights on (1) paradigm shifts towards the adoption of green products (Encarnação et al. 2016a, 2016b) and, more specifically, (2) the adoption of electric vehicles in a society dominated by combustion engines (Encarnação et al. 2018). In both domains, we show how the public sector is crucial in initiating the shift, and determine explicitly under which conditions the civil sector – reflecting the emergent reality of civil society organizations playing an active role in modern societies – may influence the decision-making processes accruing to other sectors (that is, public and private). Conceptually, however, we define different payoff tables that implement particular scenarios in each case.

Other authors use similar approaches for different applications, for example, to study incentive mechanisms to promote the transition from traditional tourism to more sustainable tourism, through an evolutionary game model that assumes players as tourists, enterprises and the local government (He et al. 2018). Authors identify key factors such as brand benefit for enterprises and green preferences of tourists. Support from local government towards brand benefit is needed especially when green preferences on the tourists' side is low, otherwise, local government intervention can be relaxed. In another study, authors treat the provision of healthcare services and patient satisfaction as an evolutionary game between public providers, private providers and patients (Alalawi et al. 2019). By resorting to the technical framework developed in Encarnação, et al. (2016a, 2016b) the authors model the evolution of cooperation between the players and measure the cost of healthcare provision. Their findings show the role patients can have by introducing punishment and reputation of healthcare providers.

To study the effect of government policies on the diffusion of electric vehicles, Li et al., apply an evolutionary approach to the underlying complex network linking the government, manufactures and consumers (Li et al. 2019). Their study analyses the impact and effectiveness of different policies in China for promoting the adoption of electric vehicles. The manufacturers' payoff in the game will be influenced by the industries' social network and this allows for surpassing the common assumption in EGT studies of using well-mixed populations. As the authors acknowledge, in reality, social systems are closely influenced by the network structure that interconnects them (Li et al. 2019) – an observation that applies to systems beyond government–manufacturer–consumer networks (Pinheiro et al. 2014), and which is often noted as an enabler of cooperation in general (Santos and Pacheco 2005; Santos et al. 2008). In this regard, the authors show that (1) the network scale of the automobile manufacturers has an important impact on the success of the diffusion process, (2) subsidies to the supply side have a higher positive effect that those on the demand side, and (3) to achieve full diffusion of electric vehicles a set of different policies and instruments is needed. More recently, Zhu et al (2020) also applied a similar approach to that introduced here, to study the strategic dynamics of individuals (belonging to the regulators and private sectors) participating in retail electricity market in China.

Ours and these more recent examples show how many instances in planning can be analysed through (evolutionary) GT as depicted in this chapter. The sheer activity and role of the decision to plan should thus be modelled beyond that of regulation and taking into account the actors it acts upon (Knaap et al. 1998). Others applied GT to study conflict between protected areas and urban expansion. They include in their model not only the conflicts between government and land developers (two-player game) but also ecological compensation mechanisms when designing zoning schemes for protected areas (Lin and Li 2016). The model was able to increase by 10 per cent the average benefit of ecological and economic benefits (Lin and Li 2016). However, planning games can also exist inside the governmental planning system and between different planning institutions, as described in one of the first works on GT and planning to study the process of town expansion in England (Batty 1977), showing how power positions and bargaining power can interfere in the process of negotiation and formation of coalitions. When the number and diversity of players in the planning stage increases, the complexity of the overall dynamics can also increase. In these types of settings, new tools become crucial not only to develop theory in planning, but also to develop new methods of planning practice. New participatory and collaborative approaches can only gain from the development of new approaches, of which GT is an integral part (Gomes et al. 2018).

Future work should accommodate other questions and challenges that planning faces. The aforementioned synergies can be difficult to interpret and model owing to the challenges imposed on quantifying and comparing them to other more directly measurable parameters. Another issue lies in integrating heterogeneous populations into models of urban planning. In this, the growing worldwide pressure of global financial players on cities is paramount. They are external players with no connection to the city or place of investment and, more often than not, the investments target is external and not the internal population that is left on the margin in the absence of interventions by players that multi-sector (evolutionary) game theoretical models can help design. Asymmetries in city games are also seen in planning issues that incorporate not only institutions from different levels (for example, central and local administration), but also institutions with different policy agendas and views (for example, political parties). Recognizing and understanding how strategic behaviour and decision-making influences evolutionary trends and dynamics of city and planning games proves paramount for future developments of planning theory, but most of all for a better adaptive and flexible planning practice.

NOTES

1. In reality, competition will continue, for example, through floor area ratios or other market dynamics, but for simplicity we do not explore that further here.

2. Illegal settlements here refer to those cases where the division, selling and buying of land for future construction did not conform to legal procedures, namely, through a municipal licence. In many instances, especially at the beginning of the phenomena, buyers were led to believe they were buying a piece of land in their own right, when instead they were just buying a quota part of a bigger land (usually not urban and without any basic infrastructure). After selling all available sites, the seller's role terminated and the process would start elsewhere.
3. We should note that different types of games define different strategy phase spaces, and thus different visualization settings. For example, the cube representation of Figure 18.1 is appropriate for a 3-population, 2-strategy (3×2) type of games. By contrast, a triangle (2-dimensional simplex) would be required for 1×3 and a pyramid (3-dimensional simplex) for 1×4 type of games. That is, the number of populations and strategies of the problem at hand determine the geometric properties of the object in use.
4. Note that this reduced Markov-chain technique greatly simplifies the overall evolutionary game theoretical analysis. As noted in Vasconcelos et al. (2017), simple extensions of the simplest formulation allow for an accurate treatment, when in instances where the dynamics along the edges entail stable coexistence states.
5. A more realistic scenario would be to include green taxes, as in the original model (Encarnação et al. 2016a, 2016b).

REFERENCES

Adams, D. and S. Tiesdell (2010), 'Planners as market actors: rethinking state–market relations in land and property', *Planning Theory & Practice*, **11** (2), 187–207, doi:10.1080/14649351003759631.

Alalawi, Z., H.T. Anh, Y. Zeng and A. Elragig (2019), 'Pathways to good healthcare services and patient satisfaction: an evolutionary game theoretical approach', doi:10.13140/RG.2.2.30657.10086.

Alfasi, N. and J. Portugali (2004), 'Planning just-in-time versus planning just-in-case', *Cities*, **21** (1), 29–39, doi:10.1016/j.cities.2003.10.007.

Balabanis, G. (2013), 'Surrogate boycotts against multinational corporations: consumers' choice of boycott targets', *British Journal of Management*, **24** (4), 515–31, doi:10.1111/j.1467-8551.2012.00822.x.

Batty, M. (2008), 'Cities as complex systems: scaling, interactions, networks, dynamics and urban morphologies', in R. Meyers (ed.), *Encyclopedia of Complexity and Systems Science*, New York: Springer, accessed 28 May 2021 at https://doi.org/10.1007/978-0-387-30440-3_69.

Batty, M. and S. Marshall (2012), 'The origins of complexity theory in cities and planning', in J. Portugali, H. Meyer, E. Stolk and E. Tan (eds), *Complexity Theories of Cities Have Come of Age*, Berlin and Heidelberg: Springer, pp. 21–45.

Batty, S.E. (1977), 'Game-theoretic approaches to urban planning and design', *Environment and Planning B: Planning and Design*, **4** (2), 211–39, doi:10.1068/b040211.

Bettencourt, L.M.A., J. Lobo, D. Strumsky and G.B. West (2010), 'Urban scaling and its deviations: revealing the structure of wealth, innovation and crime across cities', *PLoS ONE*, **5** (11), e13541, doi:10.1371/journal.pone.0013541.

Binmore, K. (1990), *The Economics of Bargaining*, P. Dasgupta (ed.), Oxford: Blackwell.

Binmore, K., A. Rubinstein and A. Wolinsky (1986), 'The Nash bargaining solution in economic modelling', *RAND Journal of Economics*, **17** (2), 179–88.

Camerer, C.F (2003), *Behavioral Game Theory: Experiments in Strategic Interaction*, Princeton, NJ: Princeton University Press.

Carranca, M.A. and N. Castro (2011), 'Dinâmica Dos Perímetros Urbanos Nos PDM Revistos Após a Publicação Do PNPOT. Fase 1: Análise', Technical Document 9/2011. DGOTDU, Lisbon, accessed 3 March 2020 at http://www.dgterritorio.pt/static/repository/2013-12/2013-12-04145402_54ab20bb-0b19-4b78-b3b7-038c54e07421$$8DFEBCB8-39BF-4D6B-9005-B78E0D8DC9F4$$2E32EF24-BA61-4B73-B2E4-B23373C91482$$File$$pt$$1.pdf.

Carvalho, J. (2012), 'Renda fundiária, ordenamento e perequação', *A: International Conference Virtual City and Territory, 8° Congreso Internacional Ciudad y Territorio Virtual, Río de Janeiro, 10, 11 y 12 Octubre*, Rio de Janeiro: Universidade Federal do Rio de Janeiro (UFRJ), doi:10.5821/ctv.7889.

Carvalho, J. (2013), *Ocupação Dispersa, Custos e Benefícios à Escala Local*, Lisbon: DGT.

Dawes, R.M. (1980), 'Social dilemmas', *Annual Review of Psychology*, **31** (1), 169–93, doi:10.1146/annurev.ps.31.020180.001125.

Encarnação, S., M. Gaudiano, F.C. Santos, J.A. Tenedório and J.M. Pacheco (2012), 'Fractal cartography of urban areas', *Scientific Reports*, **2** (1), 1–5, doi:10.1038/srep00527.

Encarnação, S., F.P. Santos, F.C. Santos, V. Blass, J.M. Pacheco and J. Portugali (2016a), 'Paradigm shifts and the interplay between state, business and civil sectors', *Royal Society Open Science*, **3** (12), 160753, doi:10.1098/rsos.160753.

Encarnação, S., F.P. Santos, F.C. Santos, V. Blass, J.M. Pacheco and J. Portugali (2016b), 'Supplementary material from "Paradigm shifts and the interplay between state, business and civil sectors"', accessed 19 May 2021 at https://royalsocietypublishing.org/doi/suppl/10.1098/rsos.160753.

Encarnação, S., F.P. Santos, F.C. Santos, V. Blass, J.M. Pacheco and J. Portugali (2018), 'Paths to the adoption of electric vehicles: an evolutionary game theoretical approach', *Transportation Research Part B: Methodological*, **113** (July), 24–33, doi:10.1016/j.trb.2018.05.002.

Erev, I. and A.E. Roth (1998), 'Predicting how people play games: reinforcement learning in experimental games with unique, mixed strategy equilibria', *American Economic Review*, **88** (4), 848–81.

Forester, J. (1982), 'Planning in the face of power', *Journal of the American Planning Association*, **48** (1), 67–80, doi:10.1080/01944368208976167.

Fréchet, M. (1953), 'Commentary on the three notes of Emile Borel', *Econometrica*, **21** (1), 118–24, doi:10.2307/1906949.

Frederick, S., G. Loewenstein and T. O'Donoghue (2002), 'Time discounting and time preference: a critical review', *Journal of Economic Literature*, **40** (2), 351–401, doi:10.1257/002205102320161311.

Friedmann, J. (1987), *Planning in the Public Domain: From Knowledge to Action*, Princeton, NJ: Princeton University Press.

Fudenberg, D. and L.A. Imhof (2006), 'Imitation processes with small mutations', *Journal of Economic Theory*, **131** (1), 251–62, doi:10.1016/j.jet.2005.04.006.

Gomes, S.L., L.M. Hermans and W.A.H. Thissen (2018), 'Extending community operational research to address institutional aspects of societal problems: experiences from peri-urban Bangladesh', *European Journal of Operational Research*, **268** (3), 904–17, doi:10.1016/j.ejor.2017.11.007.

Habermas, J. (1984), *The Theory of Communicative Action*, Boston, MA: Beacon Press.

Hardin, G. (1968), 'The tragedy of the commons', *Science*, **162** (3859), 1243–48, doi:10.1126/science.162.3859.1243.

He, P., Y. He and F. Xu (2018), 'Evolutionary analysis of sustainable tourism', *Annals of Tourism Research*, **69** (March), 76–89, doi:10.1016/j.annals.2018.02.002.

Healey, P. (1996), 'The communicative turn in planning theory and its implications for spatial strategy formations', *Environment and Planning B: Planning and Design*, **23** (2), 217–34, doi:10.1068/b230217.

Henrich, J. and R. Boyd (2001), 'Why people punish defectors: weak conformist transmission can stabilize costly enforcement of norms in cooperative dilemmas', *Journal of Theoretical Biology*, **208** (1), 79–89, doi:10.1006/jtbi.2000.2202.

Hong, Y.-H. (2007), 'Assembling land for urban development', in Y.-H. Yu and B. Needham (eds), *Analyzing Land Readjustment: Economics, Law, and Collective Action*, Cambridge, MA: Lincoln Institute of Land Policy, pp. 3–34.

Imhof, L.A., D. Fudenberg and M.A. Nowak (2005), 'Evolutionary cycles of cooperation and defection', *Proceedings of the National Academy of Sciences of the United States of America*, **102** (31), 10797–800, doi:10.1073/pnas.0502589102.

Innes, J.E. (1995), 'Planning theory's emerging paradigm: communicative action and interactive practice', *Journal of Planning Education and Research*, **14** (3), 183–9, doi:10.1177/0739456X9501400307.

Jacobs, J. (1961), *The Death and Life of Great American Cities*, New York: Random House.

Knaap, G.J., D. Lewis, P. Hopkins and K.P. Donaghy (1998), 'Do plans matter? A game-theoretic model for examining the logic and effects of land use planning', *Journal of Planning Education and Research*, **18** (1), 25–34, doi:10.1177/0739456X9801800103.

Lefebvre, H. (1991), *The Production of Space*, Cambridge, MA: Basil Blackwell.

Levin, S. (2012), 'The trouble of discounting tomorrow', *Solutions*, **3** (4), 20–24.

Levin, S.A (2006), 'Learning to live in a global commons: socioeconomic challenges for a sustainable environment', *Ecological Research*, **21** (3), 328–33, doi:10.1007/s11284-006-0162-1.

Levin, S.A., S.R. Carpenter, H.C.J. Godfray, A.P. Kinzig, M. Loreau, J.B. Losos, et al. (eds) (2012), *The Princeton Guide to Ecology*, Princeton, NJ: Princeton University Press.

Lewontin, R.C. (1961), 'Evolution and the theory of games', *Journal of Theoretical Biology*, **1** (3), 382–403.

Li, J., J. Jiao and Y. Tang (2019), 'An Evolutionary analysis on the effect of government policies on electric vehicle diffusion in complex network', *Energy Policy*, **129** (June), 1–12, doi:10.1016/j.enpol.2019.01.070.

Lieberman, M.B and S. Asaba (2006), 'Why do firms imitate each other?' *Academy of Management Review*, **31** (2), 366–85.

Lin, J. and X. Li (2016), 'Conflict resolution in the zoning of eco-protected areas in fast-growing regions based on game theory', *Journal of Environmental Management*, **170** (April), 177–85, doi:10.1016/j.jenvman.2015.11.036.

Lo, A.W. (2017), *Adaptive Markets: Financial Evolution at the Speed of Thought*, Princeton, NJ and Oxford: Princeton University Press.

Lord, A. and P. O'Brien (2017), 'What price planning? Reimagining planning as "Market maker"', *Planning Theory & Practice*, **18** (2), 217–32, doi:10.1080/14649357.2017.1286369.

Macy, M.W. and A. Flache (2002), 'Learning dynamics in social dilemmas', *Proceedings of the National Academy of Sciences*, **99** (supp. 3), 7229–36, doi:10.1073/pnas.092080099.

McAvoy, A. and C. Hauert (2015), 'Asymmetric evolutionary games', *PLoS Computational Biology*, **11** (8), 1–26, doi:10.1371/journal.pcbi.1004349.

Miller, J.H. and S.E. Page (2009), *Complex Adaptive Systems: An Introduction to Computational Models of Social Life*, Princeton, NJ: Princeton University Press.

Montgomery, C. (2013), *Happy City: Transforming Our Lives Through Urban Design*, London: Penguin.

Nash, J.F (1950a), 'Equilibrium points in N-person games', *Proceedings of the National Academy of Sciences*, **36** (1), 48–9.

Nash, J.F. (1950b), 'The bargaining problem', *Econometrica*, **18** (2), 155–62, doi:10.2307/1907266.

Nowak, M.A. (2006), *Evolutionary Dynamics: Exploring the Equations of Life*, Cambridge, MA: Harvard University Press.

Osborne, M.J. (2003), *An Introduction to Game Theory*, New York: Oxford University Press.

Ostrom, E. (1990), *Governing the Commons: The Evolution of Institutions for Collective Action*, Cambridge and New York: Cambridge University Press.

Ostrom, E., J. Burger, C.B. Field, R.B. Norgaard and D. Policansky (1999), 'Revisiting the commons: local lessons, global challenges', *Science*, **284** (278), 278–82, doi:10.1126/science.284.5412.278.

Pereira, M. (2004), 'As Metamorfoses Da Cidade Dispersa', *GeoInova*, **10** (14), 129–42.

Pereira, M. and F. Ramalhete (2017), 'Planeamento e Conflitos Territoriais: Uma Leitura Na Ótica Da (in)Justiça Espacial', *Finisterra – Revista Portuguesa de Geografia*, **104** (April), 7–24, doi:10.18055/Finis6972.

Pinheiro, F.L., M.D. Santos, F.C. Santos and J.M. Pacheco (2014), 'Origin of peer influence in social networks', *Physical Review Letters*, **112** (9), 098702, doi:10.1103/PhysRevLett.112.098702.

Portugali, J. (2000), *Self-Organization and the City*, Berlin and Heidelberg: Springer.

Portugali, J. (2011), 'A self-planned city', in J. Portugali, *Complexity, Cognition and the City*, pp. 299–311. Berlin and Heidelberg: Springer, pp. 299–311.

Portugali, J., H. Meyer, E. Stolk and E. Tan (eds) (2012), *Complexity Theories of Cities Have Come of Age*, Berlin and Heidelberg: Springer.

Ramos, V. (2002), 'Áreas Urbanas de Génese Ilegal: Sentido Para o Caos', *RevCEDOUA* **5** (9), 157–65.

Raposo, I. (ed.) (2010), *Reconversão de Territórios de Génese Ilegal – Actas Do Workshop I*, Lisbon: Faculdade de Arquitectura, Universidade Técnica de Lisboa, accessed 21 May 2021 at http://www.gestual.fa.utl.pt/pro jetos-de-investigacao/bairros-de-genese-ilegal/reconversao-de-territorios-de-genese-ilegal-lDKIFLDgqM.

Rasmusen, E. (ed.) (1994), *Games and Information*, 2nd edn, Cambridge, MA: Wiley.

Reff, A.P., K. Sehested and E. Sørensen (2011), 'Emerging theoretical understanding of pluricentric coordination in public governance', *American Review of Public Administration*, **41** (4), 375–94, doi:10.1177/0275074010378159.

Rendell, L., R. Boyd, D. Cownden, M. Enquist, K. Eriksson, M.W. Feldman, et al. (2010), 'Why copy others? Insights from the social learning strategies tournament', *Science*, **328** (5975), 208–13.

Salgueiro, T.B. (1977), 'Bairros Clandestinos Na Periferia de Lisboa', *Finisterra*, **12** (23), 28–55, doi:10.18055/Finis2281.

Samuelson, L. and J. Zhang (1992), 'Evolutionary Stability in asymmetric games', *Journal of Economic Theory*, **57** (2), 363–91.

Santos, F.C. and J.M. Pacheco (2005), 'Scale-free networks provide a unifying framework for the emergence of cooperation', *Physical Review Letters*, **95** (9), 098104, doi:10.1103/PhysRevLett.95.098104.

Santos, F.C., J.M. Pacheco and T. Lenaerts (2006), 'Evolutionary dynamics of social dilemmas in structured heterogeneous populations', *Proceedings of the National Academy of Sciences*, **103** (9), 3490–94.

Santos, F.C., M.D. Santos and J.M. Pacheco (2008), 'Social diversity promotes the emergence of cooperation in public goods games', *Nature*, **454** (7201), 213–16, doi:10.1038/nature06940.

Santos, F.P., F.C. Santos and J.M. Pacheco (2018), 'Social norm complexity and past reputations in the evolution of cooperation', *Nature*, **555** (7695), 242–5, doi:10.1038/nature25763.

Santos, F.P., J.M. Pacheco, A. Paiva and F.C. Santos (2017), 'Structural power and the evolution of collective fairness in social networks', *PLoS ONE*, **12** (4), e0175687, doi:10.1371/journal.pone.0175687.

Santos, F.P., S. Encarnação, F.C. Santos, J. Portugali and J.M. Pacheco (2016), 'An evolutionary game theoretic approach to multi-sector coordination and self-organization', *Entropy*, **18** (4), 1–15, doi:10.3390/e18040152.

Schelling, T.C. (1978), *Micromotives and Macrobehavior*, New York: W.W. Norton.

Sennett, R. (2018), *Building and Dwelling: Ethics for the City*, London: Penguin.

Sigmund, K. (2010), *The Calculus of Selfishness*, Princeton, NJ: Princeton University Press.

Sigmund, K., C. Hauert and M.A. Nowak (2001), 'Reward and punishment', *Proceedings of the National Academy of Sciences*, **98** (19), 10757–62, doi:10.1073/pnas.161155698.

Silva, P. and H. Farrall (2016), 'From informal to formal: what can be learned from reviewing 50 years of

Portuguese models, policies and politics', in S. Attia, S. Shabka, Z. Shafik and A. Ibrahim (eds), *Dynamics and Resilience of Informal Areas: International Perspectives*, Cham: Springer International, pp. 25–42.

Skyrms, B. (2014), *Social Dynamics*, Oxford: Oxford University Press.

Smith, J.M. (1982), *Evolution and the Theory of Games*, Cambridge: Cambridge University Press.

Smith, J.M. and G.R. Price (1973), 'The logic of animal conflict', *Nature*, **246** (5427), 15–18.

Stolle, D., M. Hooghe and M. Micheletti (2005), 'Politics in the supermarket: political consumerism as a form of political participation', *International Political Science Review*, **26** (3), 245–69, doi:10.1177/0192512105053784.

Taylor, N. (1998), *Urban Planning Theory since 1945*, London and Thousand Oaks, CA: Sage.

Taylor, P.D. and L.B. Jonker (1978), 'Evolutionary stable strategies and game dynamics', *Mathematical Biosciences*, **40** (1–2), 145–56.

Traulsen, A., M.A. Nowak and J.M. Pacheco (2006), 'Stochastic dynamics of invasion and fixation', *Physical Review E*, **74** (1), 011909, doi:10.1103/PhysRevE.74.011909.

Trivers, R.L. (1971), 'The Evolution of reciprocal altruism', *Quarterly Review of Biology*, **46** (1), 35–57.

United Nations (2018), 'World urbanization prospects: the 2018 revision – key facts', United Nations, accessed 21 May 2021 at https://population.un.org/wup/Publications/Files/WUP2018-KeyFacts.pdf.

Vasconcelos, V.V., F.C. Santos and J.M. Pacheco (2013), 'A bottom-up institutional approach to cooperative governance of risky commons', *Nature Climate Change*, **3** (9), 797–801, doi:10.1038/nclimate1927.

Vasconcelos, V.V., F.C. Santos and J.M. Pacheco (2015), 'Cooperation dynamics of polycentric climate governance', *Mathematical Models and Methods in Applied Sciences* **25** (13), 2503–17. doi:10.1142/S0218202515400163.

Vasconcelos, V.V., F.P. Santos, F.C. Santos and J.M. Pacheco (2017), 'Stochastic dynamics through hierarchically embedded Markov chains', *Physical Review Letters*, **118** (5), 058301, doi:10.1103/PhysRevLett.118.058301.

von Neumann, J. and O. Morgenstern (1947), *Theory of Games and Economic Behavior*, Princeton, NJ: Princeton University Press.

Weibull, J.W. (1997), *Evolutionary Game Theory*, Cambridge, MA: MIT Press.

Weiler, S. (2016), 'Pioneers and settlers in lo-do Denver: private risk and public benefits in urban redevelopment', *Urban Studies*, **37** (1), 167–79, doi:10.1080/0042098002348.

Wildavsky, A. (1973), 'If planning is everything, maybe it's nothing', *Policy Sciences*, **4** (2), 127–53. doi:10.1007/BF01405729.

Williams, A. (1981), 'Portugal's illegal housing', *Planning Outlook*, **23** (3), 110–14, doi:10.1080/00320718108711624.

Zhu, C., R. Fan and J. Lin (2020), 'The impact of renewable portfolio standard on retail electricity market: a system dynamics model of tripartite evolutionary game', *Energy Policy*, **136** (January), 111072, doi:10.1016/j.enpol.2019.111072.

19. *Homo faber*, *Homo ludens* and the city: a SIRNIA view on urban planning and design
Juval Portugali

1. INTRODUCTION

Homo faber – Latin for 'Man the maker' – generally refers to humans' ability to control their life, fate and environment by making, that is, producing, artifacts. Since its origin in third-century AD Rome it has received several interpretations; the interpretation used here is that of Henri Bergeson (1911 [1998]) in his book *Creative Evolution*:

> If we could rid ourselves of all pride, if, to define our species, we kept strictly to what the historic and the prehistoric periods show us to be the constant characteristic of man and of intelligence, we should say not *Homo sapiens, but Homo faber. In short, intelligence, considered in what seems to be its original feature, is the faculty of manufacturing artificial objects, especially tools to make tools, and of indefinitely varying the manufacture.* (Bergeson 1911 [1998], p. 139, emphasis added)

For Bergeson the production of, and interaction with, artifacts is the elementary property of humans – prior to the intelligence of *Homo sapiens*. The centrality of artifacts in human nature, as suggested by Bergeson, is provocative in light of the antagonism between nature and artifact that typifies the sciences. In his *The Sciences of the Artificial*, Herbert Simon (1969 [1999]) observes that 'the term "artificial" has a pejorative air about it'. We do not want artifacts in our data or results. Also, in the preface to the 1999 edition of that book, he writes: 'The contingency of artificial phenomena has always created doubts as to whether they fall properly within the compass of science'.

Homo ludens, that is, the view that game and play are basic elements of life, have attracted many writers ranging from the pre-Socratic Heraclitus to Plato, Aristotle, and, in our age, to Kant, to Wittgenstein's 'language game' (see section 8 in this chapter), to the mathematical game theory and its extension to evolutionary game theory (EGT), the so-named serious gaming, through to Conoway's game of life, and more. However, the most prominent voice regarding game and play was no doubt Johan Huizinga (1938) in his book *Homo Ludens: A Study of the Play-Element of Culture*. The first section in his Foreword to the book links the notions of *Homo sapiens*, *Homo faber* and his *Homo ludens*:

> A HAPPIER age than ours once made bold to call our species by the name of *Homo Sapiens*. In the course of time we have come to realize that we are not so reasonable after all as the Eighteenth Century, with its worship of reason and its naive optimism, thought us; hence modern fashion inclines to designate our species as *Homo Faber*: Man the Maker. But though *faber* may not be quite so dubious as *sapiens* it is, as a name specific of the human being, even less appropriate, seeing that many animals too are makers. There is a third function, however, applicable to both human and animal life, and just as important as reasoning and making namely, playing. It seems to me that next to *Homo Faber*, and perhaps on the same level as *Homo Sapiens*, Homo Ludens, Man the Player, deserves a place in our nomenclature.

While Bergeson contradicts *Homo sapiens* to his *Homo faber* – 'say not homo sapiens but homo faber', Huizinga contrasts his *Homo ludens* with the 'quite so dubious' *Homo faber*; the view put forward in this chapter is that the three *Homos* do not negate, but instead complement each other as aspects of human nature, and that the complementarity between the three *Homos* is central to urban dynamics in general and to the role of urban planning and design in that dynamics in particular. Regarding planning and design, it is further shown in the chapter, that these complementary relations between the three *homos* follow, first, from the role of artifacts and play in the emergence of human agency, that is, 'the feeling of controlling an external event through one's own action' (see section 2 in this chapter). Secondly, from one of the basic cognitive capabilities of humans – chronesthesia or mental time travel (MTT), that is, the ability to travel in time back to the past and forward to the future. Thirdly, from our theoretical notions of synergetic inter-representation networks (SIRN), information adaptation (IA), and their conjunction SIRNIA.

The discussion in this chapter commences with the notion of agency which is suggested to be the implicit cognitive potential for humans' capability for planning and design (section 2). The chapter then introduces chronesthesia, that is, humans' cognitive tendency for MTT as the explication and materialization of the implicit potential for planning and design (section 3). This innate tendency of humans to plan and design have not escaped the cognitive science and, as shown in section 4, long before MTT was identified, the 'Homo planner' became a domain of study under the title of cognitive planning. The property of agency, its explication in the form of MTT, and humans' cognitive planning capabilities come into being by means of a conjunction between two processes developed in the past: (1) SIRN referring to the ongoing interaction between urban agents and their environment in terms of a synergetic play between internal and external representations, and (2) IA that complements SIRN by elaborating on the way the mind/brain processes information. Section 5 is a short reminder of SIRN, IA and their conjunction SIRNIA. Section 6 further elaborates SIRNIA by focusing on its third sub-model, which refers to urban dynamics and is studied by means of the city game that has also become a tool for collective urban design. The implication from the above is that cognitive and institutional planning thus interact; but how? Section 7 introduces two approaches: one based on EGT and the other on an attempt to develop a self-planned city. Based on the above and on an analogy to Wittgenstein's notion of language game, section 8 interprets urban dynamics and the role of planning in it, in respect of a city game, that is, a play between *Homo ludens* and *Homo faber*.

2.   AGENCY

The common view in complexity theories of cities (CTC) is that cities emerge from the bottom up, out of the interaction between their parts – the urban agents. However, what is an urban agent? What is an agent? What is agency in the first place?

Agency refers to the feeling, awareness and ability of controlling an external event through our own action. As suggested by Kelso (2016), it arises at a very early stage of infants' development by means of self-organized play between a baby and an object in the environment. Kelso's suggestion is an interpretation of a seminal experiment

(A)   Uncoupled   Coupled   Uncoupled
       (0–5 min)   (5–20 min)   (20–27 min)

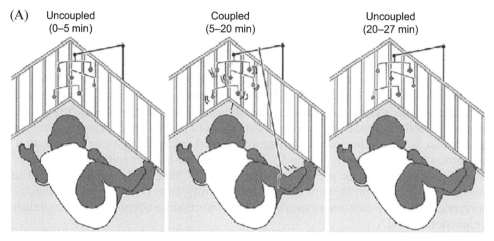

Figure 19.1   The baby–mobile experiment: (A), the three phases of the MCR paradigm

conducted by the late Carolyn Rovee-Collier (1942–2014) and her associates (Rovee and Rovee 1969) regarding the phenomenon termed mobile conjugate reinforcement (MCR), as illustrated in Figure 19.1.

In a typical MCR experiment (Figure 19.1) a ribbon is attached from a 3-month-old infant's foot to a mobile suspended overhead. As illustrated in Figure 19.1 (left-hand side), at the beginning the baby and mobile are uncoupled. The mobile is still and the baby exhibits spontaneous kicking. At around t = 5 (Figure 19.1, middle), the baby realizes that by kicking, it can make the mobile move, resulting in that the baby and the mobile are coupled and the baby's kick rate and the amplitude of the mobile movement rapidly increase up to a steady state. Moreover, the phase relationship between the baby's leg movement and the motion of the mobile increases, characteristic of a resonant coupled state. At t = 20, the baby and the mobile are again uncoupled; the kick rate decays back to a baseline level. Using the concepts, methods and tools of coordination dynamics, Kelso and Fuchs (2016) presented a theoretical model which reproduces these experimental results and predicts a number of additional features that can be experimentally tested. According to Kelso (2016):

> the birth of agency is due to a eureka-like, pattern-forming phase transition in which the infant suddenly realizes it can make things happen in the world. The main mechanism involves positive feedback: when the baby's initially spontaneous movements cause the world to change, their perceived consequences have a sudden and sustained amplifying effect on the baby's further actions. The baby discovers itself as a causal agent.

There are four interesting aspects to this: the general one is that agency arises out of interaction with objects in the environment. In principle, instead of a toy (the mobile in Figure 19.1) there could have been a branch of a tree, and agency would still emerge. The toy indicates that someone – an agent – planned and designed this artifact using his or her agency capacity in order to construct an artifact that, according to Bergeson (1911 [1998], p. 139, original emphasis), a particular human agent was using his or her '*faculty of manufacturing artificial objects, especially tools to make tools*'. A third aspect is that we are dealing with a free, spontaneous, purposeless, self-organized, game or a play between the baby and the artifact – a play/game that still, despite being free, spontaneous, purposeless and self-organized, creates one of the most important properties of human life, action and behavior. The fourth aspect is that in this MCR experiment the artifact mobile is an integral part of the cognitive process that gives rise to agency; the implication is that artifacts, the products of humans' planning, design and production, are an integral part of cognition – an aspect further elaborated by Portugali in Chapter 1 of this volume.

The notion of agency enters the city through two doors: the first door is the agency–structure debate in social theory orientated urban studies – in particular in structuralists' and Marxists' perspective on cities (for example, Giddens 1984). In these studies, the focus of interest is on the interplay between the individual (free?) agent and the social structure, when the city is the external representation of these relationships. The second door is in the context of CTC, and in two interrelated ways: the most prominent is via agent-based (AB) urban simulation models; the second is in discussions about the relationships between the parts of a complex system and its whole. Here the notion of agency exists only implicitly in the view that cities emerge out of the interaction between their parts (apparently the urban agents) from the bottom up.

I add that the emergence of agency as in the above scenario, that is, the emergence of feeling, awareness and ability, of controlling an external event through our own action, is the cognitive origin of planning and design as one of the basic cognitive capabilities of humans. However, the emergence of agency creates the potential for planning and design; this potential is materializing in the emergence of the cognitive capability for MTT – chronesthesia.

3. CHRONESTHESIA

Chronesthesia, or MTT, refers to a spatial type of memory that enables humans to remember not only past or present events, as usual, but also future events. That is, events that have not yet happened, and might never happen. Chronesthesia is associated with three cognitive research domains: first, prospective memory, exploring humans' ability to remember to perform an intended or planned action (Haken and Portugali 2005; McDaniel and Einstein 2007); second, cognitive processes that support episodic simulation of future events (Schachter et al. 2008); third, and directly related to the present context, cognitive planning, which studies the cognitive ability of humans to think ahead to the future and to act accordingly in the present (Miller et al. 1960; Das et al. 1996; Morris and Ward 2005; Portugali 2011, ch. 13).

Originally hypothesized by Endel Tulving (1983) in respect of episodic memory, MTT is supported by more recent neurological studies indicating that specific regions in the brain were activated differently when the subjects thought about the past and future compared with the present. Notably, brain activity was very similar for thinking about all the non-present times (the imagined past, real past, and imagined future) (Nyberg et al. 2010). These processes comprise what has been termed 'the prospective brain' that employs past experiences and memories to anticipate future events (Schacter et al. 2007, 2008).

Studies show that the brain's default mode of operation is mind wandering or stimulus-independent thought (Raichle et al. 2001; Buckner et al. 2008) and that humans spend about half of their waking hours 'thinking about what is not going on around them, contemplating events that happened in the past, might happen in the future, or will never happen at all' (Killingsworth and Gilbert 2010, p. 932). In light of the latter findings, Portugali (2020) has suggested that the planning and design of artifacts are direct manifestations of humans' chronesthetic memory. Humans are, in this respect, planners and designers by nature. Furthermore, not only do humans have the ability to mentally travel in time, and are thus capable of MTT and of planning and design, but they cannot avoid mentally travelling in time and thus cannot avoid planning and designing; in the context of cities, urban agents are planners and designers by nature and therefore cannot avoid planning and/or designing.[1] This innate tendency of humans to plan and design has not escaped the cognitive science and, long before MTT was identified, the 'Homo planner' became a domain of study under the title of cognitive planning. Not all human action and behavior is planned or designed, the implication being that we need to distinguish between planned behaviors and unplanned behaviors – a distinction that will have to await subsequent studies.

4.   COGNITIVE PLANNING, DESIGN AND BEHAVIOR

Cognitive planning as a research domain accompanies the cognitive sciences from their origin (Miller et al. 1960). It explores the cognitive ability of humans to think ahead to the future and to act accordingly (Portugali 2011, ch. 13). While there is a debate about the claim that planning is a property that separates humans from the rest of animals, there is no doubt that planning is specifically characteristic of humans. In their *Plans and the Structure of Behavior*, Miller et al. (1960) suggest seeing a plan as analogous to a computer program, and planning as a hierarchical problem-solving operation that guides action. At a later stage, a distinction was made between opportunistic planning, referring to cases where the person/planner responds to opportunities as they come (Hayes-Roth and Hayes-Roth 1979), versus global and hierarchical planning (Friedman and Scholnick 1987; Das et al. 1996; Ormerod 2005). More recently Davies (2005) further added a distinction between well-defined planning where the required information is available at the start of the planning process versus ill-defined planning which commences with only part of the required information (Ormerod 2005). Ill-defined decision and planning situations are associated, on the one hand, with Simon's (1957) bounded rationality and, on the other, with Tversky and Kahneman's set of decision heuristics that people tend to employ in situations of high uncertainty in decision making and planning (Tversky and Kahneman 1974, 1981; Kahneman 2003).

As noted in a previous study (Portugali 2016), it is common to associate the various cognitive capabilities with distinct forms of behavior. For example, the ability of animals and humans to construct cognitive maps (Tolman 1948) is termed cognitive mapping (Downs and Steas 1973, 1977), while their related ability to find their way informs wayfinding behavior (Golledge 1999). Related to both is exploratory behavior, referring to the animal (and human) tendency to start a process of exploration when introduced to a new environment (Eilam and Golani 1989; Drai et al. 2001). Similarly, it has been shown that the various cognitive planning capabilities of humans entail two distinct forms of behavior: planning behavior (Portugali 2011) and design behavior (Portugali 2016).

The notions of planning behavior and design behavior lead to a new view of the city, its dynamics and the urban landscape: first, every urban agent is a planner at a particular scale, and as already shown (Portugali 2011, 2020), in many cases the planned/designed action of a single urban agent might be more influential than the planned/designed action of a city planning team (compare Chapter 6 in this volume). Secondly, when observing a city, urban agents perceive not only the existing urban landscape of visible building, streets, parks and so on, but also expected buildings and other urban elements, that is, they see an urban landscape composed of urban entities that have been planned or designed but do not yet exist and might never be realized. As a consequence, agents' behavior and action in cities is determined not only by responses to the present city, but by uncertain plans that have not yet materialized, that is, by what they and other agents expect, plan or intend to do. At first sight, this might sound bizarre, but note that agents' behavior in the stock markets, for example, is very similar to this perception of the planned/designed city in that it is largely dominated by expectations about uncertain future events – expectations that affect our immediate future whether they come to pass or not.

From the notion of cognitive planning and design it follows that there are two forms of planning and design associated with the dynamics of cities (Portugali 2020): cognitive planning and design as a basic cognitive capability of humans and thus of each individual urban agent, and professional or institutional planning and design, referring to governmental attempts to regulate the dynamic of cities by means of planning and design. As recently suggested (Portugali 2020) the two are interrelated, interwoven with each other in a type of circular causality via the processes of SIRNIA, which is introduced next.

5.   A SIRNIA VIEW ON URBAN PLANNING AND DESIGN

The notions of SIRN, IA and their conjunction SIRNIA, have gradually developed since 1996 (Portugali 1996; Haken and Portugali 1996, 2021); first, SIRN and its sub-models were developed, then more recently, IA (Haken and Portugali 2015) and the conjunction SIRNIA (Haken and Portugali 2019, 2021; Portugali 2020; Chapters 1 and 6 in this volume). In parallel, links between SIRN and urban planning and design were developed (Portugali 2000, 2011; Stolk and Portugali 2012; Tan and Portugali 2012; Portugali and Stolk 2014; Portugali 2020). Based on the latter studies, in this section I briefly elaborate on the planning and design dimension of the SIRNIA conjunction as illustrated graphically in Figure 19.2. I describe first the SIRN component of SIRNIA, then its IA component and, finally, SIRNIA's three sub-models – the intrapersonal, the interpersonal and the collective, which is also a planning and design city game.

The SIRN Component

The SIRN component of SIRNIA refers to an urban agent as a cognitive planner or designer that is subject to two flows of information (Figure 19.2): on the one hand,

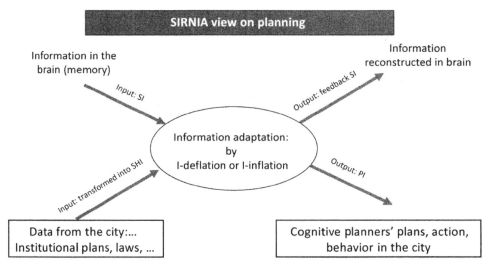

Figure 19.2 *SIRNIA view on the play between cognitive planning and professional-institutional planning*

externally represented information that comes from the city and includes, in addition to the city's morphological artifacts (buildings, roads, parks, and so on), the products of institutional planning in the form of plans and planning policies; on the other, internally represented information constructed in the cognitive planner's mind/brain. The interaction between these two flows of information, gives rise to external representations in the form of the agent's planned action and behavior in the city, and internally represented information in the form of feedback to the agent's mind/brain.

The Information Adaptation Component

The IA component of SIRNIA (Figure 19.2) complements the SIRN process by referring to the interaction between the externally represented information that comes from the city and includes city plans, regulations and laws made by the city's professional planners, and the internally represented information constructed in the urban agent's memory. By means of the processes of information inflation or information deflation (compare Chapter 6 in this volume), this interaction gives rise to a quantitative Shannon information (SHI) referring to the quantitative information conveyed by the city, pragmatic information (PI) in the form of the plans, action and behavior the agent takes in the city, and semantic information (SI) that feeds back to the agent's memory.

The Three SIRNIA Sub-Models

In order to refer to real case studies, three SIRN sub-models (Figure 19.3) were derived from the basic SIRN model: The intrapersonal (Figure 19.3, top), referring to a solitary agent, for example, a planner/designer at work; the interpersonal-sequential (Figure 19.3, middle), that refers to a sequential dynamics of several agents, such as the space–time diffusion of a particular planning solution (for example, New York's lofts); and the interpersonal collective (Figure 19.3, bottom) that models the simultaneous interaction among many agents. At a small scale, the third sub-model might refer to a planning team engaged in a planning process (Portugali and Alfasi 2008), or to what is described below as 'collective design'; at a larger scale this third SIRN sub-model is also a model of urban dynamics (Portugali 2011).

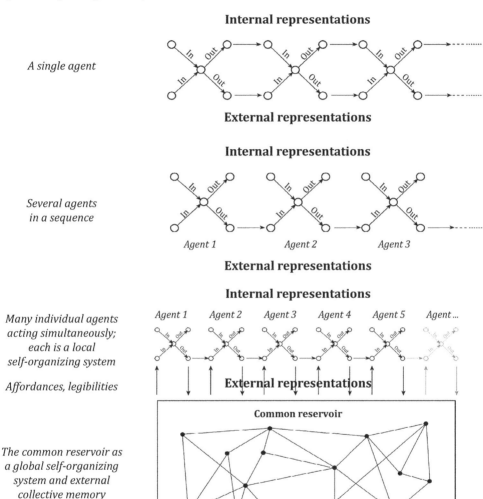

Note: In this sub-model, information and interaction between the urban agents are mediated by the common reservoir (for example, a city).

Figure 19.3   *The three SIRN sub-models: top, the intrapersonal; middle, the interpersonal-sequential; bottom, the interpersonal collective*

A typical example of a complex system is language. To this can be added that a conversation is a typical example of the SIRNIA process. This conversation can take the form of intrapersonal communication (Schlinger 2009), interpersonal communication and collective social communication. Similarly to language, a city is also a typical example of a complex system, while the SIRNIA processes of planning and design are forms of urban conversations.

The Intrapersonal SIRNIA Design Model

Consider a designer at work using sketching; for example, an architect or an urban planner. The designer's starting point is a specific idea internally constructed in the designer's mind as an internal representation. The designer then externalizes this idea by drawing it on sketch paper as an external representation. The drawn sketch triggers a new idea, or problem, or solution in the designer's mind, which he or she then externalizes as a second sketch, and so the process continues as a play between internal and external representations until the designer is satisfied with the outcome. An example is the sequence of design sketches by architect Santiago Calatrava in Figure 19.4.

The intrapersonal SIRNIA process is a form of conversation, and the use of sketches by designers has been likened by Schön (1983) to a conversation. As emphasized by several studies, a major advantage of sketches is that they are not accurate and thus convey a high level of information in the previously noted information adaptation component

Source: Tzonis (2004).

Figure 19.4   Series of sketches from Calatrava's notebook

of the SIRNIA process (for the definition of information, compare Chapter 6 in this volume). More recently Tversky and coworkers (reviewed in Tversky and Suwa 2009) have presented a series of studies on the various properties of sketches, their advantages compared with other media, the way they are used and can be interpreted, and being thinking devices. 'Early sketches', write Tversky and Suwa (2009, p. 82), 'typically capture very general aspects of a design, using a limited range of domain-specific visual elements. As design progresses, sketches become more articulated.'

The Interpersonal–Sequential SIRNIA Design Model

The prototypical process of the interpersonal–sequential-design sub-model is described as follows (see Figure 19.5, left-hand panel): it starts with a certain design object (design 1) that already exists in the world. Designer 1 looks at design 1 and internalizes its form in his or her memory and then, based on this internalized representation, produces design 2 as an external representation, and so on.

Note, first, that designs 1 and 2 in Figure 19.5 are mediated by designer 1's mind (body), designs 2 and 3 are mediated by designer 2's mind (body), and so on. Secondly, note that owing to each pair in the sequence being mediated by a designer's mind (body), there is always the possibility of a copying mistake, that is, for a cultural mutation (Cavalli-Sforza and Feldman 1981). Thirdly, we have here a play between internal and external representations.

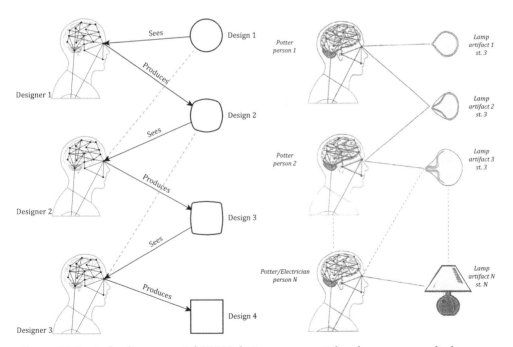

Figure 19.5   *Left: the sequential SIRN design process; right: the process applied to the morphological evolution of (oil) lamps from the middle of the second millennium BC to date*

This sequential SIRNIA process leads to a gradual change in the morphology of artifacts – a property at the core of the practice of relative chronology in archeology, that is, using the form of pottery for dating. This method, first introduced by Sir Flinders Petrie (1853–1942), is also termed sequential dating or seriation. The right-hand side of Figure 19.5 shows the morphological evolution of oil lamps that first appeared in the Middle East during the second millennium BC. For a recent case study of this process at an urban scale, consider 'the butterfly effect of Tel Aviv balconies' (Chapter 6 in this volume, s. 3.4.2).

6.   THE CITY GAMES

Third is the interpersonal–simultaneous SIRNIA sub-model. In order to illustrate its dynamics, Portugali (1996) devised a set of experiments termed city games (Figure 19.6). A city game can be seen as a group dynamics involving 20–70 participants whose aim is to build a city on the floor, representing the site for a new city. Each player is given a 1:100 mock-up of a building and, on his or her turn, is asked to place it in the virtual city on the floor, in what he or she considers to be the best location for that building. In a typical game, the players observe the city as it develops, and in the process also learn the spontaneously emerging order on the ground. It is typical in such games that, after a few initial iterations, an observable urban order emerges. The participants internalize this emerging order and tend to locate their buildings in line with it. In most city games conducted so far, the only rule of the game was that when placing their buildings the participants were not allowed to block other buildings' entrances.

The city games in Figure 19.6 exhibit the main properties of the SIRNIA process: a sequential interplay between internal and external representations, the emergence of a collective complex city as an artifact, and a typical synergetic process of self-organization. The city game is just an illustration of the dynamics of cities as complex self-organizing systems.

Tan and Portugali (2012) have further elaborated the city game, transforming it into an urban design tool. Initiated and organized by Ekim Tan as part of her PhD research, this design city game was played in the context of a real urban project (http://www.theresponsivecity.org/), the plan to add 350 homes to the new town of Almere Haven, in the Netherlands. The game was played on a two-dimensional map of Sportpark de Wierden, Almere, when the players (15 graduate students) simulated the future residents

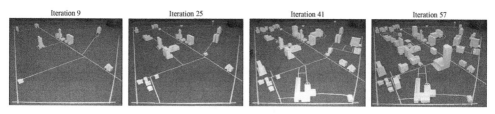

Figure 19.6   *A city game with the rule that 'each building must be connected to the city's road network', that is, a player can locate a new building either along an existing road, or must add an access road to the new building*

of Almere. In a three-hour experimental game the participants played 13 rounds, placing mock-ups based on their resident profiles.

As in previous city games, the players took location decisions sequentially. However, here we have added an additional rule that 'in a case of conflict, existing buildings will have priority over the new intended ones'. Figure 19.7 shows several snapshots from the game as it developed, while Figure 19.8 shows the outcome. The game was interesting in several respects.

First, while it started with the two simple rules, specified above, other rules came into being as emerging properties during the game; among them rules of development, network and form. Secondly, as can be seen in Figure 19.8, the resultant urban landscape is highly (self-) organized, rich and articulated. Thirdly, and in association with the above, despite there being no single mind behind the evolving urban form, no one in the game was concerned about the final urban form of the evolving area, so the outcome is rather creative.

The design city game sheds light, first, on collective design, which is an emerging field in the domain of design thinking (as is evident from the new journal *CoDesign*). Secondly, it shed light on the level of scale in the design process.

Source: Tan and Portugali (2012).

Figure 19.7   *Several snapshots from the design city game as it developed in the area of Sportpark de Wierden, Almere Haven, the Netherlands*

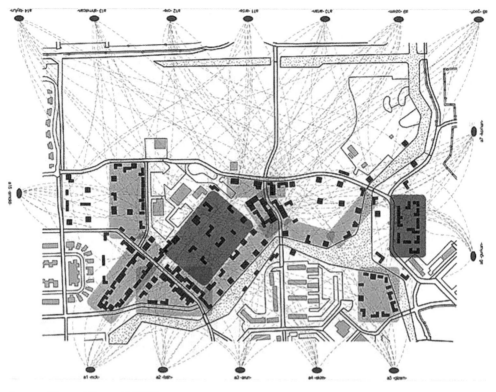

Source: Tan and Portugali (2012).

Figure 19.8   The outcome from the design city game in Figure 19.7

7.   INSTITUTIONAL URBAN GAMES

Cognitive and institutional planning thus interact; but how? Traditional planning systems – rational comprehensive planning – were built on the separation between the planners and the planned (the non-planners) and did not recognize the planning potentials and capabilities of urban agents. A similar view is shared by most new complexity theory approaches to planning that consider planning as an intervention in an otherwise complex self-organized city. The view suggested here is that institutional planning is not an intervention but participation in an urban game between agents/ players, some of which are cognitive planners and some institutional planners. This view is akin to collaborative (or communicative) planning that perceives planning in terms of governance – as a discourse between the public sector (for example, government) with its professional planners, the private sector with its planners, and civil society composed of non-governmental organizations (NGOs) that employ their own professional planners (Healey 1997, 2007; Innes and Booher 1999). Two questions arise: how to conceptualize and study the interaction between sectors, and can there be a planning system that accommodates cognitive and professional planners and the play between them?

A *Homo ludens* answer to the first question comes from Encarnação et al.'s study 'Evolutionary games in cities and urban planning' (Chapter 18 in this volume), that suggests an EGT approach to urban planning. For the details of this approach, the reader is advised to read Chapter 18 of this book. In the current context it is important to emphasize two novel aspects of Encarnação et al.'s chapter that can contribute to our understanding of cities and their planning: First, similarly to classical game theory (and to games in general), EGT involves strategic thinking, namely, when taking decisions, urban agents take into consideration, in addition to their aims, their evaluation of how other players are expected to behave and act. Secondly, and this is the novel property of EGT, the chapter treats each of the three sectors (public, private and civil) as a population and their interactions as a play between three populations. Thus, similarly to a city's citizens, some of which behave/act in one way while some in another, so also are the population of a government (for example, the professional urban planners and other decision makers) and of the various NGOs of the civil sector. An example is the lockdown decision in the COVID-19 pandemic: in each of the three sectors we could observe a variety of views regarding the necessity and efficiency of lockdown, and consequently several forms of behavior and action.

A *Homo faber* answer to the second question comes from the notion of SPCity – 'A self-planned city' (Portugali 2011, ch. 16 and further bibliography). Collaborative planning is based on an extended version of the traditional top-down planning system that now also includes NGOs as representatives of the third sector and civil society. Individual urban agents as cognitive planners have no room or role in this system. The SPCity is a planning system in which cognitive and professional planners are treated as equals. It suggests a three-layered planning system composed of three planning authorities (Figure 19.9): The legislative authority whose aim is to determine and/or redefine planning laws – similar to the legislative authority of a democratic nation-state. The executive authority, the aim of which is twofold: first, to supply information to the many planners (cognitive or institutional) that operate in parallel in the city; and,

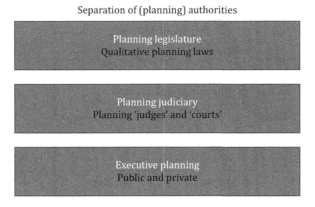

Separation of (planning) authorities

Planning legislature
Qualitative planning laws

Planning judiciary
Planning 'judges' and 'courts'

Executive planning
Public and private

Source: Portugali (2011, fig. 16.1).

Figure 19.9 The three-layer system of SPCity: the legislative, the judiciary and the executive

second, to prepare plans but only to those domains that are essential to the operation of the city, but that the other planning agents cannot or do not plan (for example, public goods, such as the city's transportation system, its schools' network or urban system of open spaces). In between there is the planning judiciary system which is the most innovative component of this system: first, since the planning laws of our self-planned city are derived not from short- and long-term plans made for the city, but instead from general planning rules (codes) made for the city; and, secondly, since the decisions to approve or reject new projects in the city are taken not by planning committees, but rather by planning courts.

The key mechanism of SPCity is the process of planning hermeneutics, which enables dynamics and change and thus makes SPCity an adaptive complex system, as illustrated in Figure 19.10. Imagine two planners: an individual cognitive planner aiming to renew the façade of his or her house and, a public institutional planner, for example, representing the city's planning department. In Figure 19.10 the two planners, the private and the public, have to go through the same process. Each has to submit the proposal to the planning 'court' and to convince the planning 'judge' that it can or should be approved. If the planning court decides that the proposal is in line with the current planning rules the result is a regular approval. If not, it is being rejected. Both cases strengthen the current planning and thus keep the system in its current steady state. If, however, the court decides on an innovative interpretation of the planning law, then we are dealing with a planning precedent, which from now onwards becomes the planning rule that will apply to all future planning applications. As in regular judiciary systems, this type of hermeneutic process enables an ongoing play between steady state and phase transition.

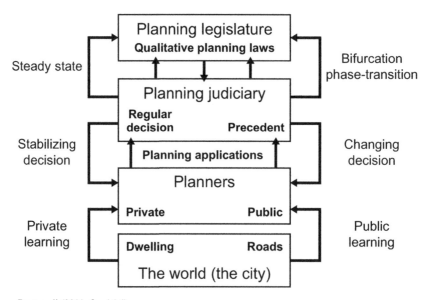

Source: Portugali (2011, fig. 16.4).

Figure 19.10   Planning hermeneutics

8. URBAN DYNAMICS AS A PLAY BETWEEN *HOMO LUDENS* AND *HOMO FABER*

One of the intriguing aspects of cities concerns the question, 'What is a city?' Initially, the answer is trivial. We are living in the age of cities; more than half of the world's population lives in cities, and yet the various attempts to define the category 'city' failed the Popperian test of falsification; whenever a definition was suggested it was possible to find a falsifying black swan. This was the case with Gordon Childe's (1950) ten-point definition in his seminal 'The urban revolution' and with subsequent attempts, until interest in this issue faded away (Portugali 2000, 2011). The issue has re-appeared in connection with the subject of urban scaling/allometry, since the (big) data upon which scaling studies are based might be affected by the way cities are defined. Once again, attempts failed the Popperian test (Haken and Portugali 2021, ch. 12). The question is, why? The answer is to be found in the discussion on categories in cognitive science.

The classical view in philosophy and cognitive science was that categories are nomothetic, implying that the category city, for instance, must refer to a set of entities that share some necessary and sufficient properties that differentiate the members of the category 'city' from non-members (in categories such as 'villages', or 'farms', for example). This view on categories was challenged by Wittgenstein's (1953) notion of 'family resemblance' as elaborated by him in paragraph 66 of his *Philosophical Investigations*. In that paragraph, Wittgenstein uses the example of the category 'game' in order to demonstrate that the members of the category 'game', as well as the members of many other categories, do not share common properties and, by implication, do not form categories by virtue of some necessary and sufficient conditions. 'Games' still make a category, however, by forming a family resemblance network. Looking at the various proceedings that we call 'games', writes Wittgenstein (1953, para. 66),

> You will not see something that is common to all, but similarities, relationships and a whole series of them at that . . . Look for example at board-games, with their multifarious relationships. Now pass to card games; here you find many correspondences with the first group, but many common features drop out . . . when we pass next to ball games. . . . And the result of this examination is . . . a complicated network of similarities overlapping and criss-crossing: sometimes overall similarities, sometimes similarities of detail.

As I showed elsewhere (Portugali 2000, 2011) the same applies to cities; yet my purpose is not to discuss the category city per se, but the dynamic of cities, and in this I follow Wittgenstein, whose aim in the above example was not the category game per se, but a set of processes that are central to his work that he termed 'language games'. 'We can also think of the whole process of using words', he writes,

> as one of those games by means of which children learn their native language. I will call these games 'language-games' . . . Think of much of the use of words in games like ring-a-ring-a-roses. I shall also call the whole, consisting of language and the actions into which it is woven, the 'language-game'. (Wittgenstein, 1953, para. 7)

In order to explain 'what is common to all these activities [termed language games], and what makes them into language or parts of language', he gives the example of the category 'games' as a family resemblance category. In his words:

Instead of producing something common to all that we call language, I am saying that these phenomena have no one thing in common which makes us use the same word for all, – but that they are related to one another in many different ways. And it is because of this relationship, or these relationships, that we call them all 'language'. I will try to explain this. (Wittgenstein, 1953, para. 65)

Then comes paragraph 66, quoted above: 'Consider for example the proceedings that we call "games"', and so on.

My suggestion is that the same applies to cities and city games – to rephrase Wittgenstein's paragraph 7:

We can also think of the whole urban process (of planning, designing, producing and using artifacts) as one of those games by means of which children learn to manipulate artifacts (toys) and to build sand castles. I will call these games 'city-games' . . . Think of much of the use of artifacts in children games . . . I shall also call the whole, consisting of city and the actions into which it is woven, the 'city-game'.

This link between language and cities was already made by Wittgenstein (1953, para. 18):

ask yourself whether our language is complete; – whether it was so before the symbolism of chemistry and the notation of the infinitesimal calculus were incorporated in it; for these are, so to speak, suburbs of our language. (And how many houses or streets does it take before a town begins to be a town?) Our language can be seen as an ancient city: a maze of little streets and squares, of old and new houses, and of houses with additions from various periods; and this surrounded by a multitude of new boroughs with straight regular streets and uniform houses.

There are three important issues here. First, note once again the first part of Wittgenstein's sentence (emphases added):

ask yourself whether our language is *complete*; – whether it was so before the symbolism of chemistry and the notation of the infinitesimal calculus were incorporated in it; for these are, so to speak, suburbs of our language. (And how many houses or streets does it take before a town begins to be a town?)

Wittgenstein thus suggests that, similarly to towns and cities, our language is never completed; always incomplete. What I emphasize here is that incompleteness is a basic property of a complex system – a corollary of the property of being in a far from equilibrium condition, and never at rest.

Language is never completed, our towns and cities are never completed, and neither are the various city plans and designs that take place in a city, made as they are by cognitive and professional planners and designers. Rittel and Webber (1973) have termed this property of incompleteness in urban planning and design a wicked problem; which is the reason why Rittel and Webber's 1973 paper is considered to be one of the forerunners of the complexity of cities. However, note that the incompleteness of urban plans and designs is a 'problem' and 'wicked' only if we expect cities to be simple, mechanistic closed systems and urban planning and design an aspect of social engineering. Cities, as this handbook suggests, are complex systems, and therefore open and non-mechanistic, and so are the urban planning and design activities that take place by urban agents in their capacity as cognitive or professional planners and designers. From this perspective there is nothing wicked or problematic in urban planning and design.

Secondly, similarly to cities, languages are complex systems, which is one justification why I am treating, for example, 'words' – the building blocks of a language – as similar to the artifacts that form the (literal) building blocks of a city (for example, houses and roads). The common view in CTC is that cities come into being out of the interaction between their parts – the urban agents. To this, 'Synergetic cities' adds that once they come into being, cities enslave the behavior of urban agents that, by obeying, support the city and so on in circular causality (compare Chapter 6 in this volume). The basic paradigmatic case study of synergetics was the laser paradigm (compare Chapter 6 in this volume). However, a common and more intuitive way to convey this circular process was from the start language. In Haken's (1983, p. 353) words:

> Using the terminology of synergetics, languages are the order parameters slaving the subsystems which are the human beings. A language changes only little over the duration of the life of an individual. After his birth an individual learns a language, i.e., he is slaved by it, and for his lifetime contributes to the survival of the language. A number of facts about languages such as competition, fluctuations (change of meaning of words, etc.) can now be investigated in the frame established by synergetics.

In synergetics, language is an example for a complex system; in the domain of cities there have been suggestions – notably by Alexander and Hillier – that cities are languages with syntax semantics, pragmatics and all the rest (compare Chapters 11 and 12 in this volume). This view is further supported by the IA component of SIRNIA, according to which, the city conveys to its urban agents – cognitive and professional planners and designers – SHI, SI and PI, based on which they plan, design and act in the city, thus producing artifacts that conveys SHI, SI, PI, and so on, in circular causality.

The second justification for treating the building blocks of a language (for example, words), as similar to the building blocks of a city (for example, houses and roads), commences from Chomsky's (1986) distinction between I-(internal) and E-(external) languages. According to Chomsky, unlike his innate internal 'I-language' that according to him enables 'statements about something real and definite, about actual states of the mind/brain and their components', external 'E-languages are mere artifacts [and therefore appear] to play no role in the theory of language' (Chomsky 1986, pp. 26–27). As elaborated previously (Portugali 2000, 2011) and as implied by the above discussion on agency, while E-languages are indeed artifacts, they are an integral part of cognition. Also, as the notions of SIRN, IA and their conjunction SIRNIA indicate, cities too are artifacts and, similarly to E-languages, they too are an integral part of cognition. More specifically, a city is a hybrid complex system composed of artifacts that are simple systems and human urban agents, each of which is a complex system that by means of their innate planning and design capabilities produce the urban artifacts and so on. My personal view is that the same applies to languages – they are composed of artifacts (for example, words, and the rules of their relationships, for example, grammar) and human agents that by means of their innate linguistic capabilities speak and reproduce the artifacts E-languages and so on. However, further elaboration is beyond the scope of this chapter.

While the city game is the *Homo ludens* representation and manifestation of urban dynamics, its outcome is the *Homo faber* manifestation of it. That is, as recently noted (Haken and Portugali 2021, ch. 12), urban dynamics is a production process, that is, the planning, design and production of artifacts of all kinds. Some are the direct outcome of explicit planning, design and production, for example, city plans and designs, buildings, parks and roads, while others emerge out of the interaction between urban agents with their plans, designs and action, for example, sociocultural entities/products such as socio-economic or cultural areas (neighborhoods), and more.

Urban dynamics as a production process leads us directly to the SIRNIA dynamics discussed previously. The various urban artifacts produced in the city (for example, buildings and roads), cannot interact among themselves, but they convey data from which urban agents extract SI and PI with their entailed SHI; then, on the basis of, or in response to, the extracted information, urban agents behave and act in the city. To the information extracted from the built-up components of cities, we should add the products of the institutional urban planning and design which are par-excellence information-production entities – informing the urban agents, about the current state (action possibilities) of the city, about their city's urban vision, the plans for the future, the city's possible future structure, and so on. We have termed this SIRNIA process the city's information production.

This information production process can be seen as, or gives rise to, the city's order parameter that affords a particular urban routine in all aspects of city life, ranging from commuting routinized patterns, to a steady production of residential, commercial, cultural and other goods and services.

9.   CONCLUDING NOTES

Cities (as noted in Chapter 1 of this volume), are hybrid complex systems, composed of artifacts that are simple systems, and human urban agents, each of which is a complex adaptive system. It is the human urban agents that by means of their interaction among themselves and with the artificial components of the city, that make cities complex systems. By means of its capacity as a *Homo faber*, each urban agent is engaged in the planning, design and production of the artifacts of which the city is composed, while by means of its *Homo ludens* capacity, each urban agent is engaged in the city's SIRNIA game that extracts information from the urban artifacts and by means of this information reproduces and produces the urban artifacts and so on in a circular causal urban dynamic.

NOTE

1. Not all human action and behavior is planned, and we thus need to distinguish between planned behaviors and unplanned behaviors.

REFERENCES

Bergeson, H. (1911), *Creative Evolution*, 1998 trans. A. Mitchell, New York: Dover.
Buckner, R.L., J.R. Andrews-Hanna and D.L. Schacter (2008), 'The brain's default network: anatomy, function, and relevance to disease', *Annals of the New York Academy of Sciences*, **1124** (March), 1–38.
Cavalli-Sforza, L.L. and M.W. Feldman (1981), *Cultural Transmission and Evolution: A Quantitative Approach*, Princeton, NJ: Princeton University Press.
Childe, G.V. (1950), 'The urban revolution', *Town Planning Review*, **21** (1), 3–17.

Das, J.P., B.C. Kar and R.K. Parrila (1996), *Cognitive Planning: The Psychological Basis of Intelligent Behavior*, New Delhi: Sage.

Davies, S.P. (2005), 'Planning and problem solving in well-defined domains', in R. Morris and G. Ward (eds), *The Cognitive Psychology of Planning*, Hove: Psychology Press, pp. 35–51.

Downs, R.M. and D. Stea (1973), *Image and Environment: Cognitive Mapping and Spatial Behavior*, Chicago, IL: Aldine Press.

Downs, R.M. and D. Stea (1977), *Maps in Minds: Reflections on Cognitive Mapping*, New York: Harper & Row.

Drai, D., W.N. Kafka, Y. Benjamini, G. Elmer and I. Golani (2001), 'Rats and mice share common ethologically relevant parameters of exploratory behavior', *Behavioural Brain Research*, **125** (1–2), 133–40.

Eilam, D. and I. Golani (1989), 'Home base behavior of rats (Rattus norvegicus), exploring a novel environment', *Behavioural Brain Research*, **34** (3), 199–211.

Friedman, S.L. and E.K. Scholnick (1987), *Blueprints for Thinking: The Role of Planning in Cognitive Development*, Cambridge: Cambridge University Press.

Giddens, A. (1984), *The Constitution of Society*, Cambridge: Polity Press.

Golledge, R.G. (ed.) (1999), *Wayfinding Behavior: Cognitive Mapping and other Spatial Processes*, Baltimore, MD: Johns Hopkins University Press.

Haken, H. (1983), *Advanced Synergetics*, Berlin, Heidelberg and New York: Springer.

Haken, H. and J. Portugali (1996), 'Synergetics, inter-representation networks and cognitive maps', in J. Portugali (ed.), *The Construction of Cognitive Maps*, Dordrecht: Kluwer Academic, pp. 45–67.

Haken, H. and J. Portugali (2005), 'A synergetic interpretation of cue-dependent prospective memory', *Cognitive Processing*, **6** (2), 87–97.

Haken, H. and J. Portugali (2015). *Information Adaptation: The Interplay between Shannon and Semantic Information in Cognition*, Berlin and Heidelberg: Springer.

Haken, H. and J. Portugali (2019), 'A synergetic perspective on urban scaling, urban regulatory focus and their interrelations', *Royal Society Open Science*, **6**, art. 191087, doi:10.1098/rsos.191087.

Haken, H. and J. Portugali (2021), *Synergetic Cities: Information, Steady State and Phase Transition. Implications to Urban Scaling, Smart Cities and Planning*, Cham: Springer.

Hayes-Roth, B. and F. Hayes-Roth (1979), 'A cognitive model of planning', *Cognitive Science*, **3** (October), 275–310.

Healey, P. (1997), *Collaborative Planning: Making Frameworks in Fragmented Societies*, London: Macmillan.

Healey, P. (2007), *Urban Complexity and Spatial Strategy: Towards a Relational Planning of Our Times*, London: Routledge.

Huizinga, J. (1949), *Homo Ludens: A Study of the Play-Element of Culture*, London, Henley-on-Thames and Boston, MA: Routledge & Kegan Paul.

Innes, J.E. and D.E. Booher (1999), 'Consensus building and complex adaptive systems: a framework for evaluating collaborative planning', *Journal of the American Planning Association*, **65** (4), 412–22.

Kahneman, D. (2003), 'Maps of bounded rationality: psychology for behavioral economics', *American Economic Review*, **93** (5), 1449–75.

Kelso, S.J.A. (2016), 'On the self-organizing origins of agency', *Trends in Cognitive Sciences*, **20** (11), 490–99.

Kelso, S.J.A. and A. Fuchs (2016), 'The coordination dynamics of mobile conjugate reinforcement', *Biological Cybernetics*, **110** (1), 41–53, doi:10.1007/s00422-015-0676-0.

Killingsworth, M.A. and D.T. Gilbert (2010), 'A wandering mind is an unhappy mind', *Science*, **330** (6006), 932.

McDaniel, M.A. and G.O. Einstein (2007), *Prospective Memory: An Overview and Synthesis of an Emerging Field*, London: Sage.

Miller, G.A., E.H. Galanter and K.H. Pribram (1960), *Plans and the Structure of Behavior*, New York: Holt Rinehart & Winston.

Morris, R. and G. Ward (eds) (2005), *The Cognitive Psychology of Planning*, Hove: Psychology Press.

Nyberg, L., R. Habib, S.A.N. Kim, B. Levine and E. Tulving (2010), 'Consciousness of subjective time in the brain', *Proceedings of the National Academy of Sciences*, **107** (51), 22356–9.

Ormerod, T.C. (2005), 'Planning and ill-defined problems', in R. Morris and G. Ward (eds), *The Cognitive Psychology of Planning*, Hove: Psychology Press, pp. 53–70.

Portugali, J. (1996), 'Inter-representation networks and cognitive maps', in J. Portugali (ed.), *The Construction of Cognitive Maps*, Dordrecht: Kluwer Academic, pp. 11–43.

Portugali, J. (2000), *Self-Organization and the City*, Berlin, Heidelberg and New York: Springer.

Portugali, J. (2011), *Complexity, Cognition and the City*, Berlin, Heidelberg and New York: Springer.

Portugali, J. (2016), 'What makes cities complex?', in J. Portugali and E. Stolk (eds), *Complexity, Cognition, Urban Planning and Design*, Berlin, Heidelberg and New York: Springer.

Portugali, J. (2020), 'Information adaptation as the link between cognitive planning and professional planning', in G. de Roo, C. Yamu and C. Zuidema (eds), *Handbook on Planning and Complexity*, Cheltenham, UK and Northampton, MA, USA: Edward Elgar, pp. 203–19.

Portugali, J. and N. Alfasi (2008), 'An approach to planning discourse analysis', *Urban Studies*, **45** (2), 251–72.
Portugali, J. and E. Stolk (2014), 'A SIRN view on design thinking – an urban design perspective', *Environment and Planning B: Planning and Design*, **41** (5), 829–46.
Raichle, M.E., A.M. MacLeod, A.Z. Snyder, W.J. Powers, D.A. Gusnard and G.L. Shulman (2001), 'A default mode of brain function', *Proceedings of the National Academy of Sciences*, **98** (2), 676–82.
Rittel, H.W.J. and M.M. Webber (1973), 'Dilemmas in a general theory of planning', *Policy Sciences*, **4** (June), 155–69.
Rovee, C.K. and D.T. Rovee (1969), 'Conjugate reinforcement of infant exploratory behavior', *Journal of Experimental Child Psychology*, **8** (1), 33–9.
Schacter, D.L., D.R. Addis and R.L. Buckner (2007), 'Remembering the past to imagine the future: the prospective brain', *Nature Reviews Neuroscience*, **3** (September), 657–61.
Schacter, D.L., D.R. Addis and R.L. Buckner (2008), 'Episodic simulation of future events: concepts, data, and applications', *Annals of the New York Academy of Sciences*, **1124** (March), 39–60.
Schlinger, H.D. (2009), 'Some clarifications on the role of inner speech in consciousness', *Consciousness and Cognition*, **18** (2), 530–31.
Schön, D.A. (1983), *The Reflective Practitioner: How Professionals Think in Action*, New York: Basic Books.
Simon, H.A. (1957), 'A behavioral model of rational choice', in H.A. Simon (ed.), *Models of Man, Social and Rational: Mathematical Essays on Rational Human Behavior in a Social Setting*, New York: Wiley.
Simon, H.A. (1957), *Models of Man: Social and Rational*, Cambridge, MA: MIT Press.
Simon, H.A. (1969), *The Sciences of the Artificial*, repr. 1996, Cambridge, MA: MIT Press.
Stolk, E.H. and J. Portugali (2012), 'A SIRN view on urban design – the case of Almere Hout', in J. Portugali, E. Tan, V.J. Meyer, E.H. Stolk (eds), *Complexity Theories of Cities Have Come of Age*, Berlin and Heidelberg: Springer, pp. 391–412.
Tan, E. and J. Portugali (2012), 'The responsive city design game', in J. Portugali, E. Tan, V.J. Meyer, E.H. Stolk (eds), *Complexity Theories of Cities Have Come of Age*, Berlin and Heidelberg: Springer, pp. 369–90.
Tolman, E. (1948), 'Cognitive maps in rats and men', *Psychological Review*, **56** (4), 189–208.
Tulving, E. (1983), *Elements of Episodic Memory*, Oxford: Clarendon Press.
Tversky, A. and D. Kahneman (1974), 'Judgment under uncertainty: heuristics and biases', *Science*, **185** (September), 1124–31.
Tversky, A. and D. Kahneman (1981), 'The framing of decision and psychology of choice', *Science*, **211** (January), 453–58.
Tversky, B. and M. Suwa (2009), 'Thinking with sketches', in A. Markman (ed.), *Tools for Innovation*, Oxford: Oxford University Press, pp. 75–84.
Tzonis, A. (2004), *Santiago Calatrava: The Complete Works*, New York: Rizzoli.
Wittgenstein, L. (1953), *Philosophical Investigations*, trans. G.E.M. Anscombe, Oxford: Blackwell.

Epilogue: cities and complexity in the time of COVID-19

Hermann Haken, Juval Portugali, Michael Batty, Stephen Marshall, Nick Green, Peter M. Allen, Pierre Frankhauser, Carlos Gershenson, Alan Penn, Vincent Verbavatz, Marc Barthelemy, Daniele Chiffi, Stefano Moroni, Koen Bandsma, Ward Rauws and Gert de Roo

The various contributions to this handbook were written during the period of COVID-19 – a pandemic that came into being and evolved as a typical complex system exhibiting properties such as abrupt change, non-linearity, unpredictability and uncertainty. Furthermore, cities and urban life had, and have, important effects on the space–time diffusion of the pandemic, its ups and downs and other properties. In light of this and in coordination with Edward Elgar Publishing, each of the contributors was asked (if they were willing and had time) to write a short statement about the pandemic from their chapter topic's viewpoint, as well as from their personal perspective and experience. The various statements form the content of this epilogue for our *Handbook on Cities and Complexity*.

A SYNERGETIC CITY PERSPECTIVE ON THE COVID-19 PANDEMIC

Hermann Haken and Juval Portugali

COVID-19 as an Order Parameter

The COVID-19 pandemic came into being and evolved as a typical complex system, exhibiting many of the components of complex systems, including abrupt change, non-linearity, unpredictability, and uncertainty. From the perspective of the synergetic approach to complex systems (Haken 1977), and of our new book *Synergetic Cities* (Haken and Portugali 2021), COVID-19 has become an order parameter (OP). The notion OP is the basic conceptual and mathematical construct of the synergetic approach. Order parameters emerge spontaneously, by means of self-organization, out of the interaction between the parts of the system – the urban agents in respect of cities. However, once a city OP comes into being, it describes and prescribes – enslaves in the parlance of synergetics – the behavior of urban agents. By obeying (that is, by their collective behavior), the agents reproduce and keep the OP and urban structure alive, and so on in circular causality (Figure 20.1).

A typical property of a self-organizing system including COVID-19 is the absence of direct control of the individual parts/agents, which requires indirect control instead.

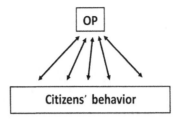

Note: By means of their behavior, the citizens give rise to the OP that, once it emerges, enslaves the behavior of the citizens.

Figure 20.1   A schematic representation of the circularly causal relationships between citizens' behavior and OPs, such as language or a city

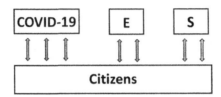

Figure 20.2   Via the citizens' behavior, COVID-19 evolved from a single OP into a dynamics of three OPs

For example, the virus cannot be killed by medication, but its multiplication can be prevented by the appropriate behavior of the citizens.

The emergence of COVID-19 as an OP entailed a conflict between the innate human tendency to come together and the dictate of the pandemic to stay apart. As a consequence of the tension between these two conflictual tendencies, COVID-19 evolved from a single OP that concerns citizens' health, into a conflictual dynamics between three OPs (Figure 20.2): COVID-19 that requires staying apart and keeping social distance, versus economy (E) and social life (S) that require the exact opposite – interaction and cooperation, collective happenings, coming together and maintaining social closeness.

This conflict entails a strange, and unfortunate, role of the city. On the one hand, it is the location/institution where most of the people become sick or even die because of this disease, where expensive hospital treatments are needed, where numerous people become jobless over shorter or longer periods because of lockdown and so on. On the other hand, city authorities, generally, have no legal or financial means for countermeasures of any kind.

As the study of complex systems indicates, a dynamics between three OPs might lead to several parameter-dependent scenarios: (1) a steady state which in the COVID-19 example is likely to be highly unstable; (2) oscillations, a scenario analogous to the Lotka–Voltera predator–prey cycle (Lotka 1920; Voltera 1931); and (3) chaos, which might take several forms, such as Lorenz chaos (1963a, 1963b), Rössler chaos (1976), Shilnikov chaos (1965) and, possibly, other types. All share the property of the butterfly effect, entailing unpredictability and uncontrollability, unless some parameters are changed by drastic measures, which is a delicate task owing to the interdependencies among the three OPs.

In our *Synergetic Cities* (Haken and Portugali 2021) we study in detail the role of information, steady state, phase transition and fluctuations in the dynamics of cities. We show that as complex systems, cities are subject to ongoing random fluctuations of various types. When a fluctuation occurs during a stable steady state, the system is resilient to its effect and enslaves it. However, when the system is in an unstable state, and thus vulnerable, a minor fluctuation can give rise to grand outcomes. An example is the fluctuation that took place at the end of 2019 when a single person was infected with a virus from an animal at a single location – (probably) at the now world-famous Huanan seafood market of Wuhan, China. Within a few months, the virus underwent a space–time diffusion process and turned from a minor local fluctuation into a global OP of world society, describing and prescribing the life and behavior of millions of people around the world. At the early stage of the process, there was no awareness of the (latent) instability and vulnerability of the global system of cities.

Latent Instability

In retrospect and owing to the pandemic, we now know that the global system of cities was in a latent unstable and vulnerable state, ripe for an event such as COVID-19 to erupt. Global society was more highly urbanized and geographically connected than ever before in human history. Smart high ground and air connectivity enabled the fast spread of the virus from city to city all over the world, while urbanization, with high population densities, made it easy for the virus to spread from one person to the other within cities.

Both urbanization and smart connectivity have always been perceived as advantages that make global society and its cities economically, socially and culturally resilient. There were signs that this was not the case: the 2008 economic crisis was a hint that high connectivity has its drawbacks; and the 2011 Fukushima Daiichi nuclear disaster in Japan exposed the vulnerability of a highly dense urbanized society. Yet these lessons were not generalized to other domains. The negative aspects of globalization, urbanism and connectivity were largely overlooked. Generally, what was overlooked was that each system has its weaknesses; that the very properties that make a system resilient in one domain, say, against economic fluctuations, might make it vulnerable to another type of fluctuation. The implication is that a system's resilience is context or fluctuation dependent.

Therefore, a key question may be: what can a society – not a sole city – do to be prepared to meet these global unpredictable events? A possible answer is to maintain an army of scientists/specialists in many fields who can help society react efficiently. We are currently witnessing such a situation with the development of a vaccine against the COVID-19 virus. Simultaneously, there seems to be a lack of socio-economic political concepts/initiatives which aim at extinction (or even mitigation) of COVID-19.

Manifest Instabilities

When a fluctuation occurs during a stable steady state, the system is resilient and enslaves it, but when the system is in an unstable state, and thus vulnerable, a minor fluctuation can give rise to grand outcomes. The COVID-19 event started as a fluctuation when societies and cities were in the midst of three interrelated instabilities: the crises of governance, urbanism and democracy.

Governance

The notion of governance came to the fore in recent decades as a consequence of privatization, urbanization and globalization processes that, in their turn, entailed the weakening of the nation state, specifically its welfare services, the emergence of the third sector (civil society) as a dominant player, and the transformation of urban dynamics and planning from a two-sector game (public and private) to a three-sector game (public, private and civil society). It can already be observed that democratic societies were caught by surprise as regards COVID-19: on the one hand, owing to deteriorating welfare services, many national governments seem ill prepared to deal with the virus; on the other, local governments and civil society organizations (NGOs) have no means and authority to deal with the pandemic and thus have only a partial role in overcoming it.

Urbanism

We have heard time and again in past decades that society is becoming urban, that for the first time in human history more than 50 percent of the human population lives in cities, and so on. This is true, yet it creates the wrong impression that, by becoming more urban, world society is also becoming more uniform, that the old town–country antagonism (Marx and Engels, in *The German Ideology*) has gone, as we all experience the same global urban reality. Yet this is not so. The old town–country antagonism was replaced by a new spatial antagonism, this time between society in the big global/world cities (described by Richard Florida as 'the creative class') that form the hubs of the borderless global society and economy, versus society in the local peripheral towns and cities confined by, and dependent on, national boundaries and governments (Figure 20.3).

Democracy

The spatial antagonism of urbanism is an external representation of the crisis of democracy that takes the form of a spectrum of positions. At one end of the spectrum is 'non-liberal democracy' while at the other is 'non-democratic liberalism'. The crisis takes different forms in different countries: for example, Brexit, Trump's presidency and the *Mouvement des gilets jaunes* (yellow vests). Some, such as Yascha Mounk (2018) see this tension as *The People vs. Democracy*, some such as Steven Levitsky and Daniel Ziblatt (2018) claim that we are witnessing *How Democracies Die*, while Christophe Guilluy (2014), in his *La France périphérique*, suggests we view this tension as the center versus the periphery. More recently, in *Freedom: An Unruly History*, Annelien de Dijn (2020) responds to Mounk's *People vs. Democracy* claim by saying that it is 'a specter raised by privileged elites afraid to lose their position. If history teaches anything at all, it's that individual rights and liberties are far more likely to be threatened by elite rule than by popular government'. Democracy, which for half a century since the mid-twentieth century, was marked by stability owing to a delicate balance and complementary relationship between liberalism and the rule of the demos, is currently in a state of instability and strong fluctuations.

When a system is in an unstable state, a minor fluctuation can give rise to grand outcomes. COVID-19, started as a fluctuation and became an OP. What would be its effect on the crises of governance, urbanism and democracy? Will it strengthen the

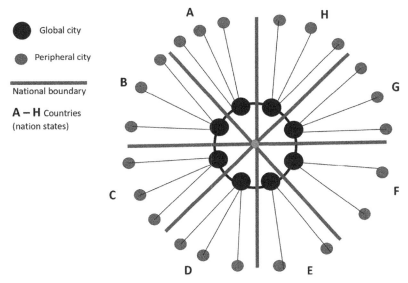

Figure 20.3   *The new global–local urban antagonism: directly connected global cities (with their creative classes) forming a global net irrespective of national boundaries, versus peripheral cities and towns that are weakly connected to the global nets, confined by, and dependent on, national boundaries and governments*

countryside – the side of the national(ist) demos – or that of global liberal urban society? Will it lead to oscillations, or steady state, or to chaos? Will there be a bifurcation, and a new reality will emerge?

'To tell you the truth, though, I still haven't made up my mind . . .' (Thomas More, *Utopia*)

COMPLEXITY, PREDICTION, AND COVID-19

Michael Batty

One of the central premises of complex systems (which Batty emphasizes in his chapter in this volume) is that their future is unknowable. It is impossible to predict in any absolute sense. The structure of these systems can never be defined with perfect certainty as they are always evolving. Moreover their evolution is invariably driven from the bottom up at the level of individual system elements and, although there may be many scales of action, the uncertainty of this evolution across all scales and aggregations of individuals is generic to everything that we define as a complex system. Systems such as cities increase in complexity as they evolve, and our theories about their form and function are always lagging behind. This means that our understanding of them can never be complete. We have to take a different view from that which has dominated the physical and social sciences hitherto, for we can no longer assume that the systems we need to understand and change can ever be predictable.

When complexity theory first emerged as the systems approach was found wanting and when the model of a typical system changed from being machine-like, dominated by negative feedback, to more like an organism whose behaviors were akin to genetic recombinations, some of the first demonstrations were with respect to deterministic chaos. Systems that appeared well defined but manifesting sufficiently intricate positive feedbacks, began to be thought of in relation to disequilibrium and unpredictability. Mathematicians, such as Edward Lorenz, Robert May, Mitchell Feigenbaum and Benoit Mandelbrot, provided many demonstrations of this unpredictability through non-linear dynamics, catastrophes, discontinuities of all kinds, fractal recursions, and far-from equilibrium states that never settled down. The notion of very small changes, almost imperceptible but always different, leading to much bigger changes and what appear to be well-defined deterministic processes admitting many different outcomes that are never reproducible, have become central to the notion of complexity. Moreover as complex systems evolve all the time owing to changes that cannot be anticipated as it is impossible to pin everything in the world down and observe it, unpredictability is their hallmark.

Take the emergence of COVID-19. In trying to figure out where it emerged, there is great uncertainty. Currently it appears to have jumped from animal to man and has been associated with a wildlife market in the Chinese city of Wuhan, near the main railway station in Hankow where a cluster of very early cases were identified. However, this is not certain. Even if it did emerge there, then it is pure chance from a human perspective that it occurred anyway. It is so rare an event that most of us, other than those who specialize in such histories, were taken by surprise. Before the end of 2019, had you asked a representative sample of the world's population for the probability that the world would be stopped in its tracks two months later by a virus, most would have said this would be unlikely. Once the event had occurred, then its diffusion and growth from epidemic to pandemic was never certain either, and our reactions to it were largely based on a conservatism that stopped us from judging its severity, and even the search for a vaccine could not be assured. We still do not know whether we will find a workable drug that will shield our immune systems from COVID-19, and we also have little idea of the long-term damage that this virus is doing to different age groups, ethnicities and those with other health ailments. There is still remarkable uncertainty in all of these matters.

Even though we cannot and never will be able to predict the emergence of these viruses, we do have good models for enabling us to predict their course. The Susceptible, Exposed, Infectious, Recovered (SEIR) model, first suggested nearly 100 years ago by Kermack and McKendrick (1927), provides remarkably robust trajectories of the way most epidemics behave. Exponential growth following those who are susceptible and then exposed, those that then become infected, followed by their recovery, reaches a point where enough of the population become immune – the herd effect – to quell the epidemic. Then, as the epidemic declines, the rate of transmission falls rapidly to the point where the virus is squeezed out of the system. This model can be fitted to generate all types of exponential and capacitated exponential growth, such as the logistic, but the biggest problem in using these models to predict the course of any particular pandemic is fitting what is a remarkably simple model to data which is always uncertain. In the UK, for example, many of these models have been fitted but, since the growth rate of the pandemic is incredibly sensitive to the time series over which is it fitted, dramatically different predictions can and have been generated. For example, initial predictions in February 2020 in the UK suggested that there would be

500 000 deaths, soon after revised downward to about 50 000, and then, as the second wave began in the late summer of 2020, it was forecast there might be 1000 deaths a day which has now been revised upwards to 4000. All of this is based on a selected set of data points from the existing time series which are used in calculating the growth rate. We will never know until the pandemic works itself out what the most appropriate set of data points are and, therefore, we can only develop a robust analysis in hindsight. In brief, we never know what the initial conditions are until the set of events has passed, just as we will never know the impact of our own interventions until the epidemic is over.

Not only was the emergence of the pandemic entirely unpredictable, so has been its trajectory. Add to this the impact on cities and the responses to the general fear in the population which has led to a dramatic collapse in public transport – bus and rail – and a dramatic increase in the use of personal transport – the car, then predicting these responses is problematic. An increase in walking and a massive increase in working from home, as well as increased demands for living in low-density environments were all but unthinkable before the pandemic. Up until March 2020, for the previous 30 or so years, cities had been slowly concentrating resources in their centers and becoming more compact, with a gradual move away from the private car in many western cities at least. Many of these changes are now being reinforced in strange and convoluted ways by our need to social distance from one another, and it is unlikely that all of these trends will be reversed when the pandemic ends, as it surely will. How it ends is equally unpredictable because one possibility is that COVID-19, like influenza, becomes endemic in the population and we drift to a new normal where there is much greater focus on public health, on using information technology to work from home, and on a long-term decline in public transport.

All this demonstrates that the future structure of human systems, in general, and city systems, in particular, are impossible to predict, that we must live with this unpredictability, and that this casts our models in a very different light from earlier times when we assumed that a great deal of the future was knowable. The new perspective that complexity brings to cities is that models should be used to inform the debate, and to condition a dialogue between all those involved, empowered and mandated to think about the future. Complexity theory defines the scope and limits to such thinking, and at the same time provides us with rational instruments for exploring different futures and speculating on how best to use science to identify possible designs and plans. Although we cannot predict the future, we have the power to invent it, at least in principle if not in practice (Batty 2018). The conundrum of complexity theory, however, is that although we can invent the future, we cannot predict what we can invent. The great power of this theory is to enable us to see our way through the great entangled web of ideas, and the emergence of this virus provides a clear demonstration of complexity in action.

MAJOR TRANSITIONS IN THE STORY OF URBAN COMPLEXITY

Stephen Marshall and Nick Green

One thing that the study of complexity teaches us is that history is not a simple linear track of progress. Instead, there can be perturbations, disruptions, divergences, setbacks, regressions, sidetracks and dead ends. The COVID-19 pandemic in some ways shook up 2020, stopped it in its tracks or put it on hold, but, in others, business continued as usual or adapted to new methods. At the time of writing, it is not clear to what extent we will return to anything like normal life as it was before the pandemic; most likely, we will resume something that has a familiar ring of normality but there could be some things lost that do not resume, meanwhile new practices will have been simulated or be evolving.

The course of history has always been messy, and it is only in the broad sweep of a historical perspective that the past can be seen as anything like a simple progression. The setbacks and changes in course were always there, but we tend to overlook them in the telling of what we hope to be a rapidly comprehensible narrative sweep. To take just one example, the drop in population in many European cities at the time of medieval plagues would be a clear exception to the notion of ever-burgeoning urbanism. At the same time, looking back in detail to the vivid specifics of life during the times of plague can conjure up a sense of the enduring patterns of human nature and behavior (Schama 2020).

The potential change in society wrought by COVID-19 reminds us that history is open-ended and without a fixed arrow of direction or foreseeable destination. This is a lesson already learned from biological evolution, since evolutionary progress for some species could mean leaving the sea to adapt to the land, then heading back to adapt to the sea, or growing then losing body hair, over evolutionary timescales. We see roughly analogous reversals, too, in technological innovation and evolution, whereby electric cars, eclipsed for most of the twentieth century, are now making a comeback, and urban tramways have seen a renaissance in cities where they had once been ripped up. Similarly, the apparently relentless centralization of broadcast media through most of the twentieth century was ultimately shattered into a cacophony of social media sound-bites by the advent of the Internet.

As we face the future, in the urban sphere, the swing towards densification that characterized much of the last 30 years may swing back to a desire for more open-plan layouts and green space. The growth and resurgence of public transport has suddenly declined as commuter trains run at a fraction of their capacity, and it is not yet clear if the flight to home-working suburbs will become a more permanent settling down. Meanwhile, as the daytime population of commuter suburbs and villages fills out, there could yet be a blossoming of local communities and walk-in facilities in once depopulated village and suburban centers.

Since we are living through it, these perturbations loom large, close up and all around us, and we may be temporarily disorientated. With hindsight, we can recognize previous periods of accelerated change – akin to punctuated equilibrium – that in the long perspective of history could look more like background fluctuations, but which can also be seen, with hindsight, as crystallizations of permanent change. In the long sweep of history, COVID-19 may perhaps be seen as simply an accelerant of changes that might have happened anyway – the pandemic impelling us to leap more precipitately to adopt new technologies and business models, while ushering the premature demise of exhausted formats and old ways of working.

Then again, suppose COVID-19 turns out not be the perturbation we think it is. Will habits really change significantly? Trains run empty, buses too. Cycling, which in spring

2020 had been prophesied a renaissance, was by the autumn as neglected as public transport, as people took to their cars, fearful of infection on a crowded tram or train. Perhaps the shift to online meetings and teaching will reach its limits, as people reach theirs, and begin to realize that even the most comfortable home can become a prison if we never leave it. Society itself, and the cities it inhabits, is remarkably persistent in how it functions, though details change. The devastating influenza pandemic of 1918 is overshadowed by the war that preceded it. What to us may seem to be a major perturbation, may, to the historian of 2120, look like nothing of the sort; not the tear we think it is, but merely one of myriad creases in history's fabric.

COMMENTS ON THE COVID PANDEMIC

Peter M. Allen

What should we learn from the COVID-19 pandemic? In particular, in the context of this handbook concerning the evolution and changes in the urban system, it has shown us that we should not be surprised by a surprising occurrence. This pandemic will lead to changes in the patterns of locations of businesses and shops, and on the flows of people and traffic that characterize our towns and cities. The changed origins and destinations will affect the pattern of communications and traffic flows, which will, in turn, affect the patterns of origins and destinations. Habits and patterns will shift, and these shifts will change the prices and costs of the different patterns of growth and decline.

What does it take to build systems that can adapt and respond to new issues and threats? The answer is resilience, and resilience involves the coexistence of different ways of doing things, and different patterns of diversity of desires and needs. Resilience has always been a key factor in evolutionary processes. However, in human systems, such as towns and cities where the economy is largely competitive, ideas such as profit maximization and cost minimization tend to diminish resilience. It is therefore important to maintain a balance between efficiency, costs and responsiveness, and possible adaptation. Evolutionary success and resilience are both about micro-diversity and multiplicity of pathways. If we accept that 99.9 percent of species have become extinct, then we must see that natural evolution explores viabilities in a complex way, and that over-specialization is a constant danger.

Our societies have an interesting conundrum at their heart: to find a balance between top-down and bottom-up power, in forging a successful and fair society, if that is our collective aim. Some believe that market-based decision making leads (miraculously perhaps and conveniently for them) to the common good, while others think that unfettered and unplanned development leads to a great outcome for a few, a bad outcome for the majority and a terrible outcome for some. Which approach leads to the greater public good? Are commercially based, market-driven decisions best for society, or can an institution set up by local, regional or national government better define what is in the common good? The idea that market-driven decisions are best for society is simply a belief that Adam Smith had, but which also supposes that the players involved uphold Christian beliefs and morals, and that the economy does not reduce to a small number of very large players. The alternative idea that the state can best decide what should be done is based on the idea that instead of leaving things to chance actions and interventions, it is better to have a plan. This plan might be to improve living conditions for the poor, or could be to build an even bigger palace for the Great Leader!

However, if centralized decision making and planning lead to static systems that tend not to be naturally adaptable, then so too does a free-market system where the players in the system may evolve to one of maximal profits and minimum costs for a few massive players. In the past anti-monopoly laws ensured some limits to the dominance of winning companies, but now anti-monopoly laws seem be ignored. Perhaps the growth of novel sectors, such as those that inhabit the digital world, left law makers behind. So, both centralized and market systems can stifle diversity and creativity and lead to system fragility where there is not enough natural resilience. Then, when some new, unexpected danger emerges, they do not have the internal richness to respond. Probably the succession of dominant civilizations that we have seen through history is explained by such ideas. In the longer term, resilience is what matters.

In many ways this constitutes one of the main political and philosophical questions that drive and divide us: should we embrace a bottom-up or a top-down system? A totally top-down system, whether run by a (possibly well-meaning) left-wing government or by an appalling despot, appears to make evolution and innovation very difficult. Instead of a permanent flow of diverse novel innovations and ideas from multiple (free) minds and, as a consequence, a regime that tries out all sorts of things, the top-down regime has a narrow focus and lots of opportunities for uniformity. The bottom-up market system may initially try out all sorts things that no single mind or committee can imagine, but profits tend to reinforce success, and cost reduction and economies of scale may combine to give a fierce, rapacious and boring outcome for people and society. Systems, whether centralized or market driven, are prey to feedback processes of self-reinforcement of personal and monetary power, and Adam Smith, understandably, had not really thought about this.

Any model or representation will necessarily become inadequate eventually. This is because the agents and processes not only change in their relationships with each other, but also change internally as they grow older, and as experience, ideas, new issues (for example, climate change) new concerns and desires change behaviors and responses. Therefore, all interpretive frameworks and models will eventually need revision because of this internal evolution.

This does not render modelling pointless, since only the comparison between a model and reality enables us to see that divergence is occurring and, therefore, that something in reality has changed. Without models or interpretive frameworks, we are blind. So modelling, comparing results with reality and reinventing and reimagining will be constantly necessary. Modelling can help our attempts to decide which is the best plan to adopt, but what we must guard against is assuming that any current calculations and models will work for ever. Where possible, we need to be ready to revise our plans and models when we can discern divergence between them and reality, or when conditions that underpinned them have changed.

Every decision and choice is really an experiment that we carry out and which tests whether our beliefs are still at all correct. When our experiences seem to agree with our beliefs, then we tend to reinforce our interpretive framework, but when experience does not meet our expectations, we are forced to modify our previous beliefs and get closer to understanding reality. However, there is no scientific or correct way to modify previous beliefs. That is, our beliefs, models and values are just part of the ongoing complex evolutionary processes of the world, and of our attempts to learn. They are not so much true as just part of the system. These ideas show that we need to imagine and simulate possible responses and policies to events such as COVID-19 and other social or economic changes that have not yet occurred. Our world and our lives are not heading towards some perfect ultimate solution. Life will always possess multiple possible pathways into the future – some good and some bad. What matters is the resilience and diversity within systems that can respond in new ways to surprise events and dangers. This requires creative, diverse people able to explore possible futures using the type of creative learning models that we have briefly described in Chapter 5 in this volume. This requires a multiplicity of views and ideas, and a broad exploration of possibilities, instead of a harsh focus on any one pathway. We need diverse scientists and disciplines, entrepreneurs, innovators and activists, as well as imaginative and daring investors, if we are to have a resilient system with resilient people and institutions.

COMMENTS ON THE ACTUAL CRISIS OF COVID, FRACTALS AND PLANNING

Pierre Frankhauser

The situation we have lived in now for many months, and which still continues without our knowing how it will evolve, is very disturbing and has a fundamental impact on society. Until now, the diverse measures taken did not enable the eradication of the pandemic. Hence, in France, a new confinement for at least four weeks with similar restrictions to those during the first confinement was set up. This time, economic activities are to continue, but many social and leisure activities are prohibited. On the one hand, people live in fear; on the other, the important restrictions in social contacts and social controls that have been set up to ensure the rules are respected, are experienced increasingly badly.

From the viewpoint of complex system theory, and particularly from synergetic, we may interpret what happens as a fundamental destabilization of a system, with unpredictable reactions and outcomes. We are still living in an unstable transition period that affects everyday life, since forecasting, even on a short time period, seems difficult or impossible. The event has changed the lifestyle of individuals, making them part of the mobile society, and restricting freedom of movement for citizens. Moreover, it badly affected economic activities, as well as leisure activities and associated economics. Socially, home confinement touched, and will again touch, even worse than before, large families living in small flats in social housing. Generally, densely populated areas were most concerned by the pandemic, but also by social tensions owing to crowding. Social contacts are reduced or stopped within a very short time; they exist only by virtual contacts provided mainly by new information and communication technology (NICTs). This may lead us to several reflections about future planning and social impacts.

First, it seems questionable that densifying housing at all costs on a large scale is a good solution. Instead of over-densifying, we should ask if concepts, as presented in my

Chapter 8 in this volume, articulating denser and less dense zones, are better suited to the future. In France, promotors confirmed that the demand for individual houses in low-density zones increased since the crisis. One of the most important impacts was the boost of teleworking, and we can expect teleworking to be more generally used in future. This could be viewed as a positive effect on energy consumption and pollution, and reducing commuting, but recent studies show that the impact on car use remains limited. On the one hand, this may be because in suburban areas everyday needs cannot be satisfied in the vicinity of the housing areas; on the other, commuting is often overestimated in relation to trips for shopping or leisure activities. If people are working more on a local scale, the good accessibility to shopping and basic leisure equipment becomes crucial, and corresponds to the concept discussed in my chapter. However, working is not only the act of producing, but also refers to social contacts. In the context of work, this could also encourage the development of teleworking centers in order to avoid isolation, but let us remember that pure teleworking is not recommended, since exchanges between colleagues is important not only for efficiency but also for social contact, and thus the well-being of personnel.

Social contact is a basic human need. Psychologically, isolation increases the risk of depression on the individual level but also becomes dangerous on the societal level. Hence, restricting people over a long period of time seems questionable. The social impact can turn out to be serious, too, as regards public health, even if less measurable than a pandemic. This leads to more fundamental reflections about the increasing obligation to use NICTs for all types of proceedings, which risks increasing isolation and a lack of social interaction. Indeed, conserving human contacts in services seems important.

Globalization has increased long-distance trips for professional reasons, but also for leisure activities, what is one of the reasons for the recent crisis. Hence emerging diseases no longer remain local. Transparency and rapidly adapted restrictions seem the only way of avoiding pandemics in the future. We are then confronted by the economic effects of globalization. The crisis made evident that particular goods, for example, those relating to public health, should be produced on a more local scale, thereby avoiding dependence on other countries and the competition between them. This brings us back to the hierarchy of needs. Particular goods should be produced according to their importance on a local, regional, national or, for example, European level, which seems reasonable from the viewpoint of sustainable development.

As regards travel mode, the situation generates ambiguous impacts. Reducing long-distance trips is certainly ruinous for the aviation industry and airlines, but ecologically it is beneficial. However, on a local scale, public transportation suffers from the popularity of used vehicles. Aiming to reduce density in vehicles would necessitate increasing public transport, and its density on the networks, which reduces the ecological advantage compared with individual car use and mainly requires high investments in infrastructure. Another negative impact was the recommendation to avoiding car-pooling. These effects are clearly counter-productive in respect of climate change and sustainable development. However, on a local scale, bicycle use benefited greatly from the crisis. In many city centers, dedicated cycling lanes were rapidly put in place and cycle use increased spontaneously. This is a good evolution from the environmental perspective, and for public health.

Another impact was the increase in shopping on the Internet. This again is an ambiguous effect. It favors multinational enterprises at the expense of local shops and accelerates their decline. City centers, and commercial areas generally, are less frequented, and this contributes again to reducing the opportunities for social contact. We could argue that home delivery services reduce individual car use, but it generates more transport which in most organizations are badly managed; local logistic centers should be developed to avoid a large number of delivery vans circulating half empty.

Let us now turn to some political aspects of the crisis. We can see that the pandemic situation was best controlled where authorities reacted early, where hospitals were sufficiently well equipped and tests were possible from the beginning of the pandemic. Even if production on a local, regional or national level were to be better developed, there is a risk that we will be confronted by a comparable crisis in the future, owing to climate change and urbanization and the recent evolution confirms this risk. We must be aware that the virus will continue to mutate and there is a risk that new ones will appear. In order to avoid such situations as much as possible coherence and preventive measures seem essential; however, without deviating towards authoritarianism. Hence, reducing the number of hospital beds for rentability reasons is no longer acceptable as well as renouncing more local basic health services.

We may conclude that using the discussed hierarchical organization of service offer and goods production according to human need may help to reduce the risks of these harmful situations we live with, even if does not prevent them. This concept avoids crowding in monocentric megalopolises. It refers to smart cities and to subsidiarity, where local units benefit from relative autonomy, while linked to superior centers. This requires insuring good accessibility to amenities according to their importance. Moreover, the decline of public services in particular, but not only, in public health must be stopped. I am very worried about some recent restrictions which reinforce authoritarianism and may introduce new types of stigmatization. Hence, in France from now on only people who have been vaccinated or tested recently will have access to many amenities as well as long-distance trains. Moreover, the nursing staff must be vaccinated. This divides the population and risks generating severe social tensions.

Personal Experiences

In France, home confinement in March was put in place just after I lost my wife to a serious illness, and it was not easy to live through. I was isolated over this period, and mourning became difficult even though I used the period to answer letters I received and I had telephone contacts. I had compassion for all those who had not had the opportunity of being with their loved ones until the very end.

What was, and is still, difficult for me to accept is the incoherence of some measures, for example, the prohibition of walking in rural forest areas during the March confinement, whereas shopping in supermarkets was allowed, which was more or less well managed. Applying the same rules to densely populated areas or highly frequented sites as to sparsely populated rural areas did not seem very useful. Several measures remain incoherent and badly managed, and have not turned out to be really efficient, which is alarming for the future.

CYBERNETIC POST-PANDEMIC CITIES

Carlos Gershenson

The COVID-19 pandemic has mainly affected urban areas, since a high population density favors transmissibility. Cities have been impacted drastically in the wake of the coronavirus: healthcare systems overburdened, activities restricted, economies shocked, behaviors modified and uncertainty surged.

All of these unexpected changes could have been better managed if cities were more cybernetic, that is, had real-time information to detect situations early, algorithms to assist decisions and agents to act in the best possible way. We were forced to adapt but, in most instances, we were ill prepared, and so adaptation was difficult and suboptimal.

Will we learn from the experience, and invest more in urban cybernetic systems? It is evident that there will be similar crises in the future, so it makes sense to try to be prepared beforehand. Still, many cities struggle with solving their daily challenges, procrastinating long-term planning and interventions.

Nevertheless, the pandemic has offered a reset opportunity. For example, until recently, many cities were investing in shifting mobility from cars to public transport, but now public transport can be a disease transmission hotspot (especially if face masks are not used). Several cities implemented temporary bicycle lanes, and many people shifted to cycling for their commute, as it is safer and in many cases faster and cheaper than public transport. Some cities have already made these temporary bicycle lanes permanent. Thus, the public health crisis could do more to favor non-motorized mobility than years of activism have.

Another adaptation forced upon us was remote working (for sectors where this is viable). Some people were already doing it, but there was still strong resistance. People working from home reduce urban mobility demand, time, money and stress spent commuting, and potentially increase the effectiveness of working hours. However, not every home has appropriate spaces for home office and home schooling for all household members at the same time. Also, casual physical interaction seems to promote creativity, bonding and better social relationships. Thus, the question is: how far will we return to how things were before the pandemic?

Ideally, we will be flexible about it. Some people will need to commute as before, others will be better continuing with a home office, while perhaps the majority will benefit from a hybrid: some days attending work in person (to do things that require physical contact), some days working remotely (to take advantage of its benefits). The precise balance probably will be dynamic, another reason for building adaptive systems that follow the cybernetic model.

The pandemic is probably worsening other urban problems, such as inequality. Whether we will take the opportunity to improve urban systems during and after the pandemic is more a matter of politics: we have the science and technology to do it.

EPILOGUE

Alan Penn

I started writing this chapter sitting in the laboratory at University College London (UCL) surrounded by Bill Hillier's library of books. Little did I know then that I would spend the rest of the year working from home. I have spent most of that time, as chief scientific adviser to the UK Ministry of Housing, Communities and Local Government and as a member of the UK Government's Scientific Advisory Group for Emergencies (SAGE), on the response to the pandemic. There is no doubt that this has shaped my thinking. At the most practical level, lockdown gave me the excuse for a project, to read Marx and Pareto, and aside from that, various do-it-yourself jobs around the house, and to watch the full HBO box set of *Game of Thrones*. At a more fundamental level it has allowed me to observe the effect of crisis and epidemic on the way that government works, and in particular on the way that science fits into this. This seems to me to be central to the issue of human progress which has long been a personal interest but became the guiding motivation for my Chapter 12 in this volume.

The dense urban settlements that I suggest were a sparking point for a surge in human progress, must have provided, at the same time that they created the conditions for an early economy, the density of contact needed to support epidemics of contagious disease. I suspect that the response may have involved the development of organized religion, medical practice and the apparatus of the early state. Viewed this way, the evolutionary influence of epidemics and war may ultimately have been to stimulate both the development of science and state building.

It is no coincidence that in developing the argument for the chapter, I turned to Pareto's distinction between logical and non-logical reasons for deciding how to act. I am left in no doubt following experience of recent years – of Brexit, Trump and others, and the debate surrounding each – that winning both hearts and minds are key to the function of government and politics in the modern state. They are also key to managing a pandemic, itself a task that falls to the machinery of government.

The SAGE group has three main sub-groups, one on virology, one on epidemiology and one on human behavior. There are others, but these three have been the drivers of policy in the UK. Ultimately, the hope is that understanding the virus will help us treat the disease and reduce mortality of those infected, and then produce an effective vaccine. However, we know that this takes time, and during that time we need to understand as much as possible about what to expect so that we can prepare and build capacity in our hospitals to treat the ill.

The epidemiologists develop models that chart the spread of the disease through the community. These models are rational but built on assumptions that come from data, and these data are inevitably imperfect at the outset. The early models made use of data from previous epidemics of respiratory influenza virus, before building in data from the current SARS-CoV-2 virus epidemic in other countries, and eventually data of our own. Every virus is different in how and who it affects, how it transmits and its time course. Every country is different in its geography, its culture and social connectivity, as well as in its healthcare systems, government and approach to management of an epidemic. They also differ in capacity to test for infection and in the way that they count mortality, making the data variable and the job of modelling an imperfect one. This means that rationality in epidemiological modelling is inevitably bounded.

Epidemics are defined by exponential growth. Until effective treatments or vaccinations have been developed, all we can do is try to reduce transmission. Transmission from person to person for a respiratory illness is by people coughing out droplets and aerosols containing the virus, and others either breathing these in directly or possibly touching surfaces where the droplets have landed and transferring the infection to mucosa in the mouth, nose or eyes. This means that to reduce transmission we must change human behavior: wearing face coverings, washing hands and so called 'social distancing'. Also, as far as possible, we need to reduce the chances of people being in the same space at the same time – to reduce connectivity in society. All these measures can be fed into the parameters of the epidemiological model to see what effect they might have on the 'r' – the reproduction rate. This is where the behavioral science group comes in, to help determine how best to implement policies designed to change behavior, how best to communicate these and what level of compliance might reasonably be expected. As we know from Pareto (1916 [1935]), human behavior is driven in part by rational decision making, and in part by sheer instinct and emotion. If we fail to recognize this, our interventions may not work or they may even backfire.

For the government, however, there is a conundrum. Connectivity in society is a driver of both the epidemic and the economy. In order to stop transmission, we have effectively to shut down a major part of the economy. This in itself carries long-term consequences for every walk of life; for jobs, innovation, culture, sport, health, education and the rest. The pain falls unequally on society, with the poorer suffering most as these tend to be most dependent on face-to-face services for employment. This then is the realm of politics. The most difficult decisions in society are those for which there is no single rational way of arriving at an answer. This life or that one? The infection or the economy? This is the role of government and the primary rationale for building the apparatus of state; to make difficult and contested decisions on behalf of society where no single option is obvious. In this situation politicians will listen to the rational evidence supplied by scientists and economists but, ultimately, they will make decisions based on their gut instinct for political survival.

In the modern western state, government depends for legitimacy on a democratic mandate and its record of good government. In order to achieve the democratic mandate at the ballot box, politicians set out their views and principles – their ideology – alongside a set of more prosaic manifesto pledges. What counts in the election is ideology, and this is a matter of instinct and belief for the voter. Reputation for good government is decided on track record, after the fact. Management of the pandemic will be seen as defining good government in every nation.

I argue that the rational and the non-rational are also key to science. This may strike you as odd. Surely science is eminently rational; was not this the basis of Pareto's (1916 [1935]) thesis? Here I refer to Thomas Kuhn (1962), who observed that the history of scientific thought shows us that scientists as a species often behave in ways far removed from Karl Popper's (1969) objective ideal. Scientists seek to defend their theories against new theory, and all too often this becomes a matter of emotional attachment to something that they have invested in heavily instead of a purely objective analysis of evidence. What Kuhn demonstrated was that science is a social product, and that scientific debate, as with any other area of debate in society, is driven to a large degree by emotion. Arguments are heated, scientific positions become ideological and personal identity becomes bound up with which side of the argument you join. These issues serve to polarize opinion.

This seems to be a paradox. If non-rational thinking plays such an important role in the progress of science, how can we consider science to be objective? It was one of Bill Hillier's working principles that a paradox indicates a questionable assumption in the underlying paradigm, and so paradoxes offer fertile territory for Kuhnian paradigm shifts. In this case the underlying assumption is that rational and non-rational thought are somehow in opposition to one another. Advances in psychology and neuroscience since Pareto's time suggest instead that gut instinct and emotion are integral aspects of the way rationality itself has developed and operates. Sigmund Freud's *The Interpretation of Dreams* (1899) pointed the way, but it fell to more recent neuroscience to provide an explanation.

Briefly, the thinking is that instinct and emotion were very early behavioral traits and sit deep in the brain. When rational thought evolved it did not emerge separately from or replace, but was built out of, these structures. There are several theories about how this might work. Seymour Epstein (1994) proposes a direct incentive to act, induced by positive or negative feelings. For him the experiential and analytic systems run in parallel. Antonio Damasio (2006) proposes the somatic marker hypothesis. 'Somatic' since it is related to gut feelings which are bodily. Imagine the sinking feeling you get when you realize that you have just been subject to a con trick, or the feeling of embarrassment when you make a social faux pas. These gut feelings are instinctual early brain warnings and they serve to train our neural networks in a rational processing system of what to avoid. Sometimes we wake in the night sweating to think of how stupid we have been. This presumably is when consolidation or reconsolidation is taking place and the somatic marker is involved. There are equivalent positive feedback feelings, of ecstasy or exultation that serve the opposite purpose, of reinforcing the networks.

Here we have an argument that, instead of considering rational and non-rational traits as being in opposition, both form an integral part of decision making. Perceptions of risk are important in delivering behavior change in the face of a pandemic. For example, epidemiologist Geoffrey Rose defined the prevention paradox that faces many public health interventions (Rose 1981). We call on many people at low risk of a disease to change their behavior in order to protect a smaller number of people at high risk. It turns out that this creates tension, especially when behavioral interventions are not zero cost but have negative effects for the individual and the economy. Paul Slovic (1999; Slovic et al. 2004) reviews the evidence for the way people consider risk. He defines 'risk as analysis', 'risk as feelings' and, when these two come into conflict, 'risk as politics'. This last is where the tension between managing the infection and maintaining the economy become political.

Contrast the effectiveness of authoritarian China, the origin of the epidemic, with 4800 fatalities out of a population of 1.4 billion, and libertarian USA, with its sophisticated disease control system as well as forewarning of the epidemic, which had 240 000 fatalities out of a population of 330 million by November 2020. The scientific understanding of the virus and epidemiology is equal in both nations. I suspect that it is the difference in ideology between the two that accounts for these different outcomes. In China the individual is subsumed to the collective, in the USA the reverse. Against these ideological backgrounds the two governments were free to make different choices. In seeking to protect the economy, Donald Trump chose to let the epidemic run its course. The result has been an 8 percent reduction in the US gross domestic product (GDP) and a recession projected to last several years. China chose to quash the epidemic rapidly. The result has been that China has, after just nine months, almost recovered its pre-COVID GDP.

I suggest that there are currently just two fundamentally different ideologies at play in the world: the first holds that human progress is based on survival of the fittest and competition. This carries the Spartan implication that those who are less fit do not deserve to survive. It also justifies prioritizing the individual over the collective. If there is an elite, that is because they are fitter. If the least fit fail to thrive, that is the will of nature. The second, alternative, ideology holds that human progress is due to our ability to collaborate, empathize and be altruistic. This places Geoffrey Rose's paradox at the center. It argues that the many may need to reduce their social contacts in order to reduce the transmission rate of the virus and so protect a small number of the vulnerable.

So, a question remains. Why do these two ideologies coexist? If one were right and the other wrong, surely the latter would eventually wither and die out? One answer could be that both ideologies are of value, perhaps at different times or in different contexts. These seem to me however, to offer yet another example of the two-way 'each produces the other' processes that we might describe as a dialectic at work in the social realm. I suggest an alternative. Instead of seeing these as two separate processes, working in relative isolation, or one replacing the other in a Paretian cycle of elites, or a Hegelian cycle of thesis, antithesis and synthesis, I prefer a different conception. The close coupling of competitive and collaborative ideologies, each intimately related to and driving the other, may provide the source of the apparent direction of advance in science, of state building and, ultimately, human progress.

Under this conception the force that powers progress and development is the continual tension between competitive and collaborative ideologies. It is this that defines in-group and out-group structures, and by keeping these in a state of dynamic tension, maximizes both conservation of valuable traits and innovation. Perhaps it is this that keeps social forms far from equilibrium and provides an impetus to progress.

EPILOGUE: POST-COVID CITIES

Vincent Verbavatz and Marc Barthelemy

The pandemic that spread throughout the whole world from the beginning of 2020 will certainly have important socio-economic impacts in the future. In particular, it forced us to reconsider our mobility, our way of working and even how we live in cities (Batty 2020). Although it is difficult at this stage to make some predictions, we can make a few observations.

In the short term, we observe that car traffic is back to normal in most cities and even, in some instances – for example, in some French cities – above normal,[1] while public transport levels are still very low.[2] In the longer term, it is uncertain if we will go back to normal public transport levels or if we could assist with permanent changes for the following reasons. First, many workers stopped taking public transport and now drive to their offices owing to the fear of becoming infected by the virus (moreover, we have to expect higher unemployment rates which will also impact commuting patterns). Second, some workers worked from home. With the lockdown, we got to know better remote working and its advantages, but also its risks, such as social isolation. This experience made it possible for companies to assess the pros and cons of remote working. Third, we also observed substitute modes, such as walking or cycling, which could constitute a serious trend, especially if work is undertaken to improve infrastructures and the safety of these transport modes.

If our relation to work changes, it will have a huge impact on the spatial organization of cities. Mobility patterns are governed by the spatial distribution of jobs and housing demand. This simple observation shows that many of the keys for future cities are in the hands of politicians and of companies. Remote working and differentiated working hours, will be important aspects that will modify mobility patterns in cities. More dramatically, we might assist the delocalization of some activities to new communities far from city centers, either in remote suburbs or in rural areas. We can even wonder if cities will disappear. After all, it is generally believed that cities result from the need for a spatial concentration of jobs and, if this concentration is no longer necessary, we might conclude that there is no reason for cities to exist any longer. However, cities should not be considered from a purely economic aspect, as in particular the need for social interactions seems to be an important reason for cities to continue to exist.

It is interesting to note that the impact of this virus is accelerating existing trends that are aligned with changes needed to mitigate the effects of global warming: most of these new behaviors go together, reducing levels of congestion, making better use of public transport and making better spatial organization of activities and housing. It is also evident that these observations will not apply to every city in the world. It is very likely that, in emerging countries, urbanization will follow its increasing trend. In western countries, where the urbanization rate is already very high, it is not that simple.

We could argue that there will not be any post-COVID cities (Couclelis 2020), and that most of the observations, such as the impact of remote working or moving to rural or peri-urban areas, were already made some time ago. Remote working has been tried in the past – for example, it has been the subject of discussion for more than 20 years in France – without a great success, although an increasing share of workers adopt it. We can argue that the technology is now better than it was even five or ten years ago and, probably more importantly, we understand that 100 percent remote working is not a good thing. However, working remotely even only part-time might have a huge effect on the organization of cities, and we cannot exclude that this is an important trend enhanced by the current virus crisis. A possible delocalization of activities into peri-urban or more rural areas is difficult to predict, and this problem has been the subject of many debates among scholars. There is more than one barrier to overcome when moving out of a city center; a convergence of interest of various actors – territories, companies and individuals – might explain why we this has not yet happened on a large scale. Pollution and quality of life became central subjects, and the increasing demand for a better life might trigger to a new level this movement towards the countryside.

Humanity and cities have survived other pandemics, and it is tempting to think that nothing will change. However, this is not only a post-COVID world, it is also a global-warming world, with many ecological problems as well as social and economic inequalities. Most of the future will depend on economic considerations, and business and political decisions. Mobility and economy are coupled to each other, and their probable reorganization makes it very difficult to predict what will happen for these complex systems that are cities.

COVID-19: CITIES, RISKS AND UNCERTAINTIES

Daniele Chiffi and Stefano Moroni

The COVID-19 pandemic is a highly complex and uncertain phenomenon. Although many pandemics in the history of humankind have shown some known recurrent features (frequent attribution of pandemic origin to Asia; westward spread to Europe, directional spread within Europe and acceleration of global spread; and presentations of different waves) (Morens and Taubenberger 2011), the severe uncertainty associated with the COVID-19 pandemic and our failure to understand the determinants of present and past pandemics keeps us from important information that could help us to prevent and control modern pandemics in general. The spatial diffusion of the COVID-19 pandemic is particularly affected by (wild) urbanization; this context is highly significant owing to the disease's respiratory transmission mechanism enhanced by people's proximity to one another. Further, marginalized and vulnerable groups living in urban areas are disproportionately affected by COVID-19 and its related impacts (Sharifi and Khavarian-Garmsir 2020).

Following the classical distinction among forms of uncertainty between types of quantifiable (probabilistic) risk and types of severe uncertainty that may resist a (probabilistic) quantification (Knight 1921), in our contribution to this handbook (Chapter 16, 'Complexity and uncertainty: implications for urban planning') we have investigated the uncertain and complex structure of cities, and the need to differentiate approaches to urban planning based on the type of uncertainty. Even if the distinction between risk and severe uncertainty cannot always be clearly delineated, under conditions of risk, we can compute the probability of future events and their consequences. In contrast, under conditions of severe uncertainty, this calculation is not always possible, as we might face forms of uncertainty that may be unquantifiable because we do not know the statistical distribution of the events or we even ignore them (Chiffi and Chiodo 2021; Hansson 2021). Moreover, under conditions of severe uncertainty, all the potential events we wish to evaluate may not be easily listable in those unexpected situations and novel scenarios may occur.

This interplay between conditions of risk and severe uncertainty has also been acknowledged in connection with the outbreak of the COVID-19 pandemic (Hofmann 2020); test accuracy (sensitivity, specificity and predictive values) of the various tests in different contexts, the effects and side-effects of new promising treatments, and the prevalence of the disease are evidently connected with conditions of risk. Further, viral spreading, treatment outcomes, levels of immunity, effectiveness of intensive-care treatments, and so on occur under conditions of severe uncertainty. Hence, both the COVID-19 pandemic and contemporary cities are complex systems that require planning policies targeted toward conditions of risk and conditions of severe uncertainty. Unfortunately, the interaction of these two complex systems may pose socio-spatial and environmental challenges that are difficult to rectify. This is because of the spatial unlimitedness of the current interaction between highly uncertain systems (Hansson 2011), such as cities, paired with the novel problems the pandemic poses; this combination should invite us to be particularly alert to the unknown. While probabilistic trends, urban statistics, and so on are useful for understanding the impact of the pandemic on cities, urban planning strategies cannot solely rely on them; instead, they must be open to critically managing several different types of severe forms of uncertainty. That is, not only factual uncertainty regarding the available evidence but also normative uncertainty regarding the goals of specific planning programs should be considered when trying to approach extremely difficult urban problems during this pandemic. In the presence of normative uncertainty, a simple appeal to an adaptive perspective in planning may easily fail, as we do not know toward which goal we want to reorientate our actions and policies. We need to think outside the box: (1) imagining new forms of scenario-building and planning, (2) avoiding the over-regulation of specific situations and (3) implementing clear and value-based considerations in planning activities.

Indeed, in our chapter, we critically discussed particular methodological, pragmatic and procedural strategies to deal with the unknown in planning decisions from the perspective of public decision-makers. These can be applied to the urban dimension of the current COVID-19 pandemic.

COVID-19 AND BEHAVIORAL INTERVENTIONS: THE BENEFITS OF A COMPLEXITY PERSPECTIVE

Koen Bandsma, Ward Rauws and Gert de Roo

If COVID-19 indicates one thing without doubt, it is that centrally imposed legislation and lockdown strategies are insufficient for large, disruptive events that turn into enduring crises. While legislation and lockdown strategies are certainly necessary, their effectiveness in mitigating COVID-19 largely depends on how these interventions are received by individuals and other stakeholders. This is perhaps most visible in the behaviors of individuals in urban public spaces, such as that people visibly distance themselves from others, disinfect their hands or wear a face mask. Visible preventive behavior stimulates others to conduct these behaviors as well, while simultaneously allowing for the emergence of new social norms (for example, it is appropriate to wear a face mask) that help to tackle COVID-19.

Considering the need to establish new social norms, it is not surprising that urban authorities adopt behavior change interventions (Ijzerman et al. 2020). For example, nudges are used in public space to remind people to keep their distance, and mass-media campaigns for stimulating people to wear face masks are started. These interventions typically exploit particular cognitive biases or tap into the social nature of humans to promote preventive behavior. While behavioral interventions are widely applied against COVID-19 (Ijzerman et al. 2020), the question arises: what happens when these interventions leave the design desk of policymakers and are implemented in the chaotic and overwhelming complexity of public space?

This reflection discusses how the effectiveness of behavior interventions, such as nudging, boosting and mass-media campaigns, is affected by the complexities within urban public spaces. We argue that first of all the complexity sciences can foster a holistic perspective on the use of behavioral interventions, in which the effectiveness of interventions is enabled and constrained by the interactions within and between different social systems. Second, the complexity sciences stimulate the development of a dynamic perspective that helps to understand how the effectiveness of interventions fluctuates over time and, thus, contributes to the development of more effective behavioral interventions.

Complex Adaptive Systems: A Holistic Perspective

A complexity lens emphasizes the open and dynamic nature of urban areas. Cities are considered complex adaptive systems (CAS). These systems are open and adapt to internal or external interferences, while simultaneously being robust and able to cope with these interferences (De Roo 2018). This CAS perspective is evident in relation to COVID-19: while the pandemic has a significant impact on the structure and functioning of cities, and radically affects its subsystems and individuals, cities simultaneously remain in existence and functioning.

When portraying cities as CAS, it becomes obvious that the effectiveness of behavior change interventions in enabling or constraining the emergence of particular social norms is affected by interacting subsystems and individuals. For instance, the effectiveness of nudges in stimulating the emergence of social-distancing norms is influenced by the degree to which schools, shopping centers and communities adopt this norm and support it over other norms (e.g., if it is appropriate to shake hands). The CAS perspective also emphasizes that social norms are inherently dynamic.

A Dynamic Perspective: Fluctuations in Norms and Interactions

The development of COVID-19 fluctuates over time and space, as do the social norms that social systems uphold in reducing infections. In contrast, the studies on which behavioral interventions for fighting COVID-19 are based, typically assume that motives of people and the nature of their interactions are static (John et al. 2009). A CAS perspective helps to develop a dynamic understanding of how these ingredients of behavioral change feed the emergence of social norms.

To illustrate, during the start of the COVID-19 pandemic, the issue was highly salient for many individuals. Initially, there was a great deal of willingness among individuals to alter their behavior and conform to the newly emerged social norms. However, this level of awareness decreased when the number of infected cases went down, many prohibitions were lifted and hospitals were no longer almost overwhelmed by COVID-19 patients (for example, in Germany, RIVM 2020). Consequently, the willingness to adhere to the new norms decreased gradually, allowing COVID-19 to return in many countries.

It is in understanding these social-norm dynamics that the value of the complexity sciences becomes evident, as they offer an understanding of how, out of individual actions, new social norms emerge (Chapter 17 in this volume). Offering conceptual tools such as self-organization and system transformation, the incorporation of complexity thinking in behavioral research can advance the understanding and identification of social norm evolutions, as well as the enabling and constraining factors triggering these evolutions (for example, Muldoon et al. 2014).

Equally important, a dynamic perspective helps to design more effective interventions (Chapter 17 in this volume). It teaches us, first, that the inherent dynamics within and between the social systems that are a part of cities require constant monitoring and revision of behavioral policies. Moreover, the complexity sciences can help to identify at which opportune moments interventions may be implemented to prevent the transformation of preventive social norms, as well as to identify when to implement interventions to develop such norms. This would be an important contribution in countering volatile, but enduring pandemics, such as COVID-19.

CONCLUSION

Applying behavioral interventions in public policy has become a common approach to mitigating COVID-19. This short reflection advocates for a complexity lens in the use of such interventions to advance the emergence of social norms out of individual action and social interactions. Taking these dynamics seriously means that expectations about the effectiveness of behavioral interventions should be tempered, but also that more intelligent interventions are possible when making use of the knowledge on dynamics in social systems that complexity thinking provides.

NOTES

1. 'Keeping Waze updated during the COVID-19 outbreak', accessed 20 May 2021 at www.waze.com.
2. 'Citymapper Mobility Index: % of city moving compared to usual', accessed 20 May 2021 at www.citymapper.com.

REFERENCES

Batty, M. (2018), *Inventing Future Cities*, Cambridge, MA: MIT Press.
Batty M. (2020), 'The coronavirus crisis: what will the post-pandemic city look like?', *Environment and Planning B: Urban Analytics and City Science*, **47** (4), 547–52, doi:10.1177/2399808320926912.
Chiffi, D. and S. Chiodo (2021), 'Risk and uncertainty: foundational issues', in A. Balducci, D. Chiffi and F. Curci (eds), *Risk and Resilience: Socio-Spatial and Environmental Challenges*, Cham: Springer, pp. 1–13.
Couclelis, H. (2020), 'There will be no post-COVID city', *Environment and Planning B*, **47** (7), 1121–3.
Damasio, A. (2006), *Descartes' Error: Emotion, Reason and the Human Brain*, New York: Avon.
De Dijn, A. (2020) *Freedom: An Unruly History*, Cambridge, MA: Harvard University Press.
De Roo, G. (2018), 'Ordering principles in a dynamic world of change – on social complexity, transformation and the conditions for balancing purposeful interventions and spontaneous change', *Progress in Planning*, **125** (10), 1–32.
Epstein, S. (1994), 'Integration of the cognitive and psychodynamic unconscious', *American Psychologist*, **49** (8), 709–24.
Florida, R. (2002), *The Rise of the Creative Class: And How It's Transforming Work, Leisure, Community and Everyday Life*, New York: Basic Books.
Freud, S. (1899), *Die Traumdeutung* (*The Interpretation of Dreams*), Leipzig and Vienna: Franz Deuticke.
Guilluy, C. (2014), *La France périphérique. Comment on a sacrifié les classes populaires*, Paris: Flammarion.
Haken, H. (1977), *Synergetics – An Introduction*, Berlin, Heidelberg and New York: Springer.
Haken, H. and J. Portugali (2021), *Synergetic Cities: Information, Steady State and Phase Transition. Implications to Urban Scaling, Smart Cities and Planning*, Heidelberg, Berlin and New York: Springer.
Hansson, S.O. (2011), 'Coping with the unpredictable effects of future technologies', *Philosophy & Technology*, **24** (2), 137–49.

Hansson, S.O. (2021), 'Can uncertainty be quantified?', *Perspectives on Science* (forthcoming).

Hofmann, B. (2020), 'The first casualty of an epidemic is evidence', *Journal of Evaluation in Clinical Practice*, **26** (5), 1344–6.

Ijzerman, H., N.A. Lewis, A.K. Przybylski, N. Weinstein, L. DeBruine, S.J. Ritchie, et al. (2020), 'Use caution when applying behavioural science to policy', *Nature Human Behaviour*, **4** (11), 1092–4.

John, P., G. Smith and G. Stoker (2009), 'Nudge nudge, think think: two strategies for changing civic behaviour', *Political Quarterly*, **80** (3), 361–70.

Kermack, W.O. and A.G. McKendrick (1927), 'A contribution to the mathematical theory of epidemics', *Proceedings of the Royal Society A*, **115** (772), 700–721.

Knight, F.H. (1921), *Risk, Uncertainty, and Profit*, Boston, MA: Hart, Schaffner & Marx; Houghton Mifflin.

Kuhn, T. (1962), *The Structure of Scientific Revolutions*, Chicago, IL: University of Chicago Press.

Levitsky, S. and D. Ziblatt (2018), *How Democracies Die*, New York: Broadway Books.

Lorenz, E.N. (1963a), 'Deterministic nonperiodic flow', *Journal of Atmospheric Science*, **20** (2), 130–41.

Lorenz, E.N. (1963b), 'The mechanics of vacillation', *Journal of Atmospheric Science*, **20** (5), 448–65.

Lotka, A.J. (1920), 'Analytical note on certain rhythmic relations in organic systems', *Proceedings of the National Academy of Sciences of the United States of America*, **6** (7), 410–15.

Marx, K. and F. Engels, *The German Ideology*, accessed 28 May 2021 at https://www.marxists.org/archive/marx/works/1845/german-ideology/.

Morens, D.M. and J.K. Taubenberger (2011), 'Pandemic influenza: certain uncertainties', *Reviews in Medical Virology*, **21** (5), 262–84.

Mounk, Y. (2018), *The People vs Democracy: Why Our Freedom Is in Danger and How to Save It*, Cambridge, MA: Harvard University Press.

Muldoon, R., C. Lisciandra, C. Bicchieri, S. Hartmann and J. Sprenger (2014), 'On the emergence of descriptive norms', *Politics, Philosophy & Economics*, **13** (1), 3–22.

Pareto, V. (1916), *Trattato Di Sociologia Generale*, English 1935, A. Livingstone (ed.), *The Mind and Society*, 4 vols, London: Cape.

Popper, K. (1969), *Conjectures and Refutations: The Growth of Scientific Knowledge*, London: Routledge & Kegan Paul.

RIVM (National Institute for Public Health and the Environment Ministry of Health, Welfare and Sport) (2020), *Waarom wel of niet naleven van de gedragsregels?* accessed 10 November 2020 at https://www.rivm.nl/gedragsonderzoek/maatregelen-welbevinden/verklaringen-gedrag/.

Rose, G. (1981), 'Strategy of prevention: lessons from cardiovascular disease', *British Medical Journal*, **282** (6279), 1847–51.

Rössler, O.E. (1976), 'An equation for continuous chaos', *Physics Letters A*, **57** (5), 397–8.

Schama, S. (2020), 'Plague time: Simon Schama on what history tells us', *Financial Times*, 10 April, accessed 19 November 2020 at https://www.ft.com/content/279dee4a-740b-11ea-95fe-fcd274e920ca.

Sharifi, A. and A.R. Khavarian-Garmsir (2020), 'The COVID-19 pandemic: impacts on cities and major lessons for urban planning, design, and management', *Science of the Total Environment*, **749** (December), art. 142391.

Shilnikov, L.P. (1965), 'A case for the existence of a denumerable set of periodic motions', *Soviet Mathematic Doklady*, **6**, 163–6.

Slovic, P. (1999), 'Trust, emotion, sex, politics and science: surveying the risk assessment battlefield', *Risk Analysis*, **19** (4), 689–701.

Slovic, P., M.L. Finucane, E. Peters and D.G. MacGregor (2004), 'Risk as analysis and risk as feelings: some thoughts about affect, reason, risk and rationality, *Risk Analysis*, **24** (2), 311–22.

Volterra, V. (1931), *Leçons sur la théorie mathématique de la Lutte pour la vie (Lessons on the Mathematical Theory of Struggle for Life)*, Paris: Gauthier-Villars.

Index

Printed and bound by CPI Group (UK) Ltd, Croydon, CR0 4YY

16/04/2025

14658494-0002